MATURITY
IN
HIGH SCHOOL TEACHING

PRENTICE-HALL INTERNATIONAL, INC., *London*
PRENTICE-HALL OF AUSTRALIA, PTY., LTD., *Sydney*
PRENTICE-HALL OF CANADA, LTD., *Toronto*
PRENTICE-HALL FRANCE, S.A.R.L., *Paris*
PRENTICE-HALL OF JAPAN, INC., *Tokyo*
PRENTICE-HALL DE MEXICO, S.A., *Mexico City*

MATURITY
IN
HIGH SCHOOL TEACHING

Gail M. Inlow, Ph.D.
Professor of Education
Northwestern University

PRENTICE-HALL, INC.
Englewood Cliffs, New Jersey

Current printing (last digit):
15   14   13   12   11   10   9   8   7   6

© , 1963, by
PRENTICE-HALL, INC.
Englewood Cliffs, New Jersey

Library of Congress
Catalog Card No.: 63–9026

Printed in the United States of America
56620–C

DEDICATED TO

My wife, Joanne, who was a constant source of
assistance and support throughout.

Mrs. Joan Smutny, whose contributions were most
helpful. She provided the unit plan on the short
story and much of the section on the language
laboratory. She also served as my personal editorial advisor.

PREFACE

This book has been designed for use both as a text-book and as a resource book. As a textbook, it is suited for college courses in general methods of im-struction and principles of secondary education. As a resource book, it should be a useful reference to the student teacher, the in-service teacher, and the school administrator.

Throughout, teaching is treated as a subtle proc-ess whereby the classroom instructor establishes a learning environment for pupils. In this climate, the teacher, pupils, and curriculum mutually interact to the end of optimum pupil growth. The emphasis is on the teacher, not primarily as an imparter of knowl-edge, but more fundamentally as a leader and a social engineer. In such a role, the maturity of the instruc-tional leader becomes focal. To the extent that the teacher is sufficiently mature, he is more able to relate with fidelity to himself, his pupils, and the behavior of both.

Teaching is consistently described as being just as complex as young people and the world of learn-ing are complex. So conceived, teaching involves the totality of the pupil and an extensive but selected body of curriculum content. Learning is considered as organismic, oriented in the many ramifications of behavior, past and present, outside as well as inside the school, and attitudinal as well as cognitive.

We bring to the textbook a humanistic convic-tion that the true values of life reside in individual realization and consequent well-being. We even pos-tulate that unless this point of view is more universally practiced in our culture, the Occident as currently known will soon be no more, sacrificed, as it will be, on the altar of selfish materialism and irrational competition. Teachers, therefore, have a mandate not only to impart cognitive substance, but also to help students develop a discerning value system based on human dignity and worth.

A selected few of the individuals who influenced this book directly or indirectly are as follows: Joan Smutny, who, without the pressures of many personal and professional demands, would have been a co-author; Joanne Inlow, my wife, whose patience and unstinting help assisted me over many obstacles; Muriel and Dr. Raymond Olson, my sister and brother-in-law, respectively, for whom social action is a way of life; Lorraine Rinehardt, a respected colleague and friend, who contributed many helpful ideas when the manuscript was taking shape; and Dr. Jean D. Grambs of the University of Maryland, a reviewer whose insightful comments were of great value in the manuscript's final revision.

In addition, we recognize with gratitude the willingness of publishers and individuals to permit the use of selected quotations and other written materials; and the assistance rendered by numerous personnel of Prentice-Hall, Inc., a publishing concern that regularly takes the extra step of professional courtesy.

G. M. I.

CONTENTS

18

19

CHAPTER 1

THE TEACHER'S VITAL ROLE IN SECONDARY EDUCATION

Secondary education from its inception has evolved developmentally, usually mirroring in great part a local and a national image while, at the same time, hastening needed change. As a public institution designed for service, education can never get too far out of step with the culture it serves without soon being called to task and forced back into reasonable conformity. Neither, however, can it ever be an exact mirror of society without perpetuating a *status quo*. Education's position is, thus, mildly inconsistent: it must adhere basically to cherished tenets and attitudes but also provide leadership. To the extent that society at any given time has a fundamental unity of purpose and beliefs, these two functions operate in harmony; but when serious divisions develop, the direction of education becomes correspondingly blurred.

When first conceived in the Latin Grammar School of Boston in 1635, secondary education in America had a clear-cut mandate: to teach the basic skills of communication, prepare selected young people for the professions, and immerse all possible in the sanctioned religious traditions. These goals were in tune with the demands of the market place, the system of differential class values in the world of work, and the code of the Puritans. Greek, Latin, philosophy, and the *Bible,* long the respected essentials of education, had positions of unquestioned eminence. The first two enabled the scholar to reach beyond the limited scope of literature in the vernacular. The latter two reached into the province of Protestant orthodoxy with the avowed purpose of getting students ready for the after life. Whatever the exact nature of the secondary curriculum in colonial times, it was an extension of cultural expectations and demands. Thus, differences regarding what the Latin Grammar School should teach were almost nonexistent because of the unanimity of public opinion.

With the growth of the middle class in the eighteenth century, secondary education broadened its scope as a result of social demands. Under the leadership of Benjamin Franklin, the evolving Academy began to minister to the needs of the economically unfavored without neglecting the continuing needs of the aristocratic and professional groups. Throughout this and subsequent periods of change in the secondary school, the classical languages made many concessions to the Romance languages and English; philosophy, in great part, gave way to the sciences; religious instruction was converted to a process of indirection; and the practical and fine arts achieved greater importance.

In the second half of the nineteenth century, secondary education came to be recognized as a basic public function; and in the twentieth century, it has become a social institution for all the children who might profit from it. The outstanding exceptions to this rule of "education for all the children" today are the ill, the mentally retarded, the delinquent, and those who voluntarily drop out at the legally permissible age. The growing conviction that secondary education should be for the vast majority of the country's adolescents has not been easy to make operative, however. When the Latin Grammar School served a select population and the academy only a slightly less select group, homogeneity of purpose and design were simple to achieve. Now the high school has to serve a population with a wide diversity in abilities, needs, interests, and aspirations that has worked against the outcome of homogeneity.

Today, at both elementary and secondary levels, education is probing for the hard core of national expectancies and, understandably, is experiencing some frustration. Here are a few issues that are mildly or bitterly divisive, depending on the locale and the personalities affected by them:

1. Should the schools be engineered into "crash programs" of science and mathematics that are supposed to increase the chance of national and individual survival; or should the schools continue a balanced program of the humanities, social sciences, natural sciences, arts, and physical education? The first alternative is a manifest expediency of the times; the second alternative, a long-term plan for psychological as well as physical survival.

2. If physical survival is the keynote, should more time and energy

be expended on the gifted, or should comparable attention be paid to all, regardless of ability?

3. Should the curriculum be made more strict and challenging, and, if so, in what way?

4. Should the tenets of mental health become an inseparable part of the stream of education, or should they merely be permitted to remain in the shallows subject to call?

On these issues we offer the opinion that the nation as a whole desires an emphasis on the sciences but not at the expense of the other equally important curriculum components; that it wants all individuals to be accorded equal respect and opportunity to grow, regardless of ability; that it wishes the curriculum not to be made either easier or more difficult, but to be fitted to the individual; and that it embraces the desirability of mental-health practices in the schools.

Probably the most controversial of these assumptions is that relating to mental health, which has not, as yet, completely established itself. Enlisted in active support of the mental-health point of view are a century of organized theory, more than half a century of experience by therapists, and allegiance by a well-informed representation of the general population. Enlisted against it is a militant group whose verbal protests are often eloquent. Acceptance of mental-health principles in elementary education is almost universal; in the high school, less uniform but substantial. Against this background of attraction-and-repulsion by society and even by some educators, secondary education appears to be progressing toward a firmer compact with mental-hygiene proponents and practices in the conviction that the cause is right and in the belief that society's support of it is increasing.

On this growing relationship between education and mental health, we build our case for teaching method. The main proposal is that children and youth can best develop when education conceives growth broadly as being mental, emotional, social, physical, and ethical in character. A corollary of this concept is that the highest good in life is man's optimum growth in all these areas, and that such growth is a requisite to maturity. Accordingly, secondary education is obligated to provide a curriculum that in its scope includes many dimensions and a teaching method that is sensitive to the over-all personality needs as well as the knowledge needs of each student. From this vantage point, then, the humanities, natural sciences, social sciences, physical education, and arts serve the over-arching purpose of education, which is the complete growth of the individual.

In such a framework, bigotry in a classroom gives a teacher as much concern as intellectual incompetence. Personality deficiencies in students demand as much attention as retardation in the skills of reading and writing. And at the level of the greater social scene, inequities arising from such practices as colonialism and international power alliances are judged to have not only military and political, but moral, implications. Education, as we thus conceive it, places all personalities and events on a high plane of cause-and-effect relationships, motives, attitudes, and other aspects of personal and social as well as intellectual dynamics. And students, in the process of their probings and deliberations, are accordingly helped to direct the complex interpretations of individuals and events at themselves as basic to emotional growth and self-understanding. Such a point of view rescues education from the incompleteness of the purely substantive by giving it a value emphasis.

In this transformation of learning from the sterility of the unimaginative to the richness of values the teacher is the pivot. And a premise underlying it is that adolescents can be guided along the road to mental health only by an adult authority figure who himself has made adequate progress along that road. It is inherent in the premise that the teacher will be not only intellectually competent and well informed but also emotionally mature. A bright and knowledgeable teacher who has too many unsolved emotional problems can make the learning process for students frustrating, uneconomical, and one-sided. In contrast, another teacher who has faced and solved the more demanding problems of self and who has constantly extended his developing horizons can convert learning from formless tedium to artistry. If mental health is essential to each pupil and the totality of education, it clearly cannot be achieved, even approximately, unless teachers have risen to meet many of its exacting demands.

GOALS OF MATURITY

What, then, are some personality outcomes to which candidates and in-service teachers should be aspiring? A number of these will be developed briefly, with no intent to simplify the maturing process—which, at best, culminates a lifetime of effort. They are not cure-alls, but are designed to stimulate the reader to think about himself—about himself as a person on the threshold of a people-oriented world, where what an individual basically is, as a human personality, underlies everything that he does.

The self-image should be satisfactory

A primary essential for the classroom teacher is that he be able to accept himself, through the possession of a self-image that is moderately satisfying. His self-acceptance under no circumstances is to be confused with egotism or any other form of narcissism. In fact, the teacher is expected to regard his personality assets matter-of-factly. Our proposition is basically this: that teachers face themselves realistically, identifying and modifying those shortcomings that are amenable to change, and accepting others that are not. This admittedly is a sobering demand; yet it will spur the motivated as well as channel the indifferent into other interest fields.

The instructional leader with adequate self-insight and an acceptable self-image is able to relate realistically to situations and individuals; the one with less insight is able to relate only inappropriately, at best. The following situations might be expected to lead to the suggested outcomes, depending on the degree of self-understanding and acceptance the teacher has achieved.

Situation A: An adolescent flippantly comments aloud in the classroom: "Those who can, do; and those who can't, teach." This would constitute a mild or serious threat to the insecure instructor, who, unable to recognize or tolerate his insecurity, might lash back in compensation for the personality invasion. To a somewhat more secure instructor, however, who had faced and accepted his limitations, the flippancy would probably be dealt with in some appropriate way outside the framework of a clash of personalities and the felt need of the teacher to retaliate. In the latter instance, the episode would be steered away from the person of the teacher to its proper context of adolescent immaturity. Punishment might be meted out in some form, but reason, not the emotions, would make the selection. A frontal acceptance by the teacher of his strengths and weaknesses would thus serve to forewarn him against the possible consequences of his actions.

Situation B: A gifted student corrects a teacher of average ability on an error of fact, and adds insult to injury by documenting the corrections with irrefutable evidence. To the degree that the instructor has accepted his own average ability as a personality trait that he can live with comfortably he is able to tolerate this act of ego deflation, and perhaps even capitalize on it in some way. However, to the extent that he is unable to accept the limitation because of an inadequate self-image, he will be tempted to degrade the affronting student. In this turn of events, he would be bending his own emotions back on the other individual.

To the charge that teachers and teacher candidates are being asked to peer into their unconscious minds, we plead guilty. The process is advocated, however, in the framework of relativity, recognized as potentially extensive for some, greatly limited for others, but possible for all. The degree of insight will always be dependent upon factors of the individual person and his environment. Our point of view is simply this: that, although teachers are far from being masters of their personality structures, they can make changes in important life patterns through self-analysis and resulting self-understanding. These will lead ultimately to self-acceptance and change.

After all, what is education but a means to self-growth and the associated change in personality structure? What is introspection but a means of peering into motivations and circumstances en route to better understanding? And what is therapy but self-analysis encouraged by a counselor? In the latter connection, Karen Horney, the late Neo-Freudian psycho-analyst, devoted a book-length treatment to the plausibility of man's analyzing himself apart from the services of another.[1] She contended that man can come to terms with his inner motivations and modify himself and his behavior as a result.

A major responsibility of any teacher, then, is to peer through the shadows of his unconscious on the way to uncovering his beliefs and at-titudes, the reasons for them, and finally, his "self." The veil may be difficult to lift, and the images that appear in view may be uncom-plimentary, but the process of self-discovery will make life's relationships more authentic and therefore richer. Reality operates upon the person only when he can get in tune with it. Self-understanding is always emerging, never complete; and to achieve the greatest benefits of such insight, teachers need to pursue the mental-health goal of achieving the optimum in all areas of development. In this way, one component will serve as a check and bal-ance on another, such as the physical on the social, or the ethical on the mental.

So oriented, a teacher candidate faces himself as a total personality and accepts what he sees. If he ranks low in class but has done his best, he accepts the outcome with a minimum of regret and recrimination. But by the same logic, if he ranks high in the arena of performance, he removes from the outcome any aura of prestige. Such factors as what society ex-pects, his relative standing, and ego-building values are made secondary to his having measured up to an optimum level of expectancy.

A mental-health approach to growth and understanding, we submit, is not just an answer to the many problems of teacher education; more broadly conceived, it should aid in solving many of the vexing problems of the world. Whenever on the international scene a large number of indi-viduals will begin to work for and reach their high potential in the many growth areas, a rational approach to problems will begin to win over irrational tendencies. It will do away with a continuing overemphasis on the material and the cognitive. Both are important, but so, too, are the ethical and the social. When people begin to understand and apply the many inner resources of human nature, too long neglected in the face of ego-centered values, benefits of undreamed magnitude will be possible.

A teacher should enjoy social relationships

Once the teacher has come to grips with himself, he will be better able to relate to his associates at all levels: to students, faculty colleagues, administrators, and parents. In fact, this relating is a built-in requirement

---

[1] Karen Horney, *Self Analysis* (New York: W. W. Norton and Company, 1942).

of his profession, since it is oriented in a world of people. So oriented, it has tremendous appeal for those who manifestly enjoy the company of others. But, by the same logic, no profession can be more depressing or unsatisfying for an individual who is apprehensive of, or who shuns the company of, his many classroom and greater-school associates.

The danger of this point of view is that it can become distorted in interpretation. Already such value rejoinders as the following have probably occurred to many: Must teachers always be other-directed? Need they be Babbitts? What's wrong with introversion? Our reply is that teachers need only effect a reasonable balance between extroversion and introversion to be happy and productive in their work. We associate too much "outgoingness" with a shallow level of contemplation; yet too little of it in teaching may place the instructional leader too far from the learners.

Since human relationships are vital to the teacher, it behooves the candidate just a step away from the classroom to take an inventory of his social skills and tendencies. If at college he has related in a satisfactory way to fellow students, if in the community he relates well to acquaintances and friends, and if in the home he relates harmoniously to family members, we can predict with fair accuracy that his relationships in the school milieu will probably be satisfactory. When reflection, however, reveals that his social image falls short of desired standards, the candidate should realize that he can change this image for the better. Like many other personal characteristics, gregariousness needs to be nurtured and developed. Practice is needed no less in the social skills than in the motor or academic skills, where time and effort properly applied pay dividends. With a people-centered profession awaiting him, it thus becomes his duty, as a means of fulfillment, to seek the company of others and so secure an opportunity to carve out his needed social role. He does not methodically and mechanically set about making social contacts—although he might even do this on occasions—but neither does he treat lightly those that normally come his way.

The teacher candidate who is unable to make satisfactory adjustment to associates should not regard the shortcoming as a minor one. Rather, he should look on it as a danger signal which, if ignored, might lead to unhappiness in his contemplated profession. Teaching makes rigid demands in both scholarship and social integration; but excessive development in one never compensates for serious deficiency in the other.

Reasonable fulfillment is essential

Parallel with insight and satisfying human relationships is the need for the teacher to be a reasonably fulfilled person in all of the essential areas of living. When this basic requirement is not realized, wholeness becomes elusive. The essentiality of the physical requirements of food, clothing, shelter, and good health is uncontested. Unless all are consistently attained in adequate amounts, the deprived individual becomes one-sided or, at times, almost primitive in his reactions to persons and events. And if the physical essentials are so important for social existence, the psychological are certainly not less so. Each individual's need for moral and ethical standards to live by, and for leisure-time interests as well as human associations, is fundamental.

When the teacher achieves an adequate level of satisfaction in the many phases of the life process, he can see classroom problems in clearer perspective. Being himself intellectually fulfilled, he pursues the development of a similar outcome in student associates more realistically. Unlike his less secure fellow worker, who strives for excellence in himself and students in part for the trappings of prestige that accompany it, he regards the outcome as completely desirable in its own right. Recognizing differences in abilities, he is satisfied with varying levels of intellectual accomplishment.

Being emotionally fulfilled (relatively speaking), a teacher can better relate himself to the emotional needs of students. Having received sufficient satisfaction in this one area of life, he can relate to others from a frame of reference that is not ego-centered and thus distorted. A bonus, in this regard, is that his routines can be invaded without undue upset. Being socially fulfilled, he can live at peace with himself when he is temporarily denied the satisfactions of social relationships. The emphasis here is on a balanced life—although not a superficial one. It is on the need for teachers to be sufficiently fulfilled in all the important growth areas so that they will view events with authentic fidelity. This goal is admittedly an ideal; but, like all ideals, it should propel some individuals toward it and direct others away from enfeebling one-sidedness.

From provincialism to an extended base

The process of psychological growth begins at birth and progresses through ever-advancing levels of interpretation and insight. Sensation comes first, then narrow perception, and ultimately breadth of value appraisal. Stated differently, growth clusters first around self, then around a selected few, next around an expanding world, and finally—at the level, once more, of the ideal—around a cosmic universe. Regardless of the exact manner of the progression, the principle of outward extension is fundamental, with growth most significant when projected from one to many and from the specific to the general. The teacher candidate can well follow this principle of outward extension as he prepares for his professional role.

At a lower rung of this hierarchical structure is the classroom leader, who having lived narrowly—and thus been denied the richer opportunities for growth—tends to evaluate behavior and events in an equally narrow frame of reference. His intellectual insights are rarely broader than those developed by the culture of four years of baccalaureate training. His experiences are usually just as limited as his intellectual growth, and his attitudes are equally circumscribed. He may be the victim of a too closely-knit family environment which has kept him infantile, or he may be the product of a local community which has likewise curtailed his growth.

Whatever the reason, this type of narrowness inevitably is transferred to the classroom, with a resulting adverse effect on learners and learning. Not having extended their own horizons, such teachers make it difficult for adolescents to extend theirs. These teachers are the ones who are usually satisfied with the single textbook, for in its simplicity they find security. They freely generalize from the specific instance. Under their influence, literature tends to lose affinity with the eternal, the arts are converted to a series of acts to perform instead of being treated as a means of emotional fulfillment, and true understandings are lost in the securing of knowledge for its own sake. Such individuals may be regarded by society as adjusted, but in the classroom they cannot be so regarded because of their constricting influences upon students.

In contrast to the previously described individual is the expanding teacher whose horizons are ever extending outward from the confining narrowness of self, a family, and a community into a broadening world of knowledge, understandings, and values. This outward projection demands enlargement of the teacher's frame of living reference by ever-increasing concentric circles leading to contact with the human race. Short of this ideal, an increasing tolerance of other people, their ideas, and their attitudes will be an indicator of growth.

A change will inevitably take place in the teacher's value system when he reaches out more extensively, because breadth educates and experience emancipates—at least, to a degree. Within the limits of this broader psychological setting, the children of those who are manually employed will be as highly regarded as the offspring of the more affluent professional people. The slow learner will be as well accepted as the gifted. "Old Country" influences will no longer be looked upon with disfavor. The broader evaluative horizon will lead to a more mature attitude toward all people—even including their differences. Furthermore, gross inequalities of living standards will disturb such a teacher just as much when existing in India as when found in North America. Corruption in government will assume the same importance whether it occurs in Nationalist China or in Cuba. War will be no less heinous because casualties are light on "our" side and heavy on "theirs." Values will become more universal and more vital when applied to all, not just to some, of the people. In the process of the extension of values, children, youth or adults, wherever they are found, will assume a deserved eminence. Figure 1 capsules man's progression toward this level of maturity.

Power with, *not power over*

While any individual is maturing away from a more circumscribed to
a more expanded life structure, he will note an associated progression from
the practice of power *over* to a relationship of power *with* others. A symptom developmentally appropriate for the child, youth, or immature adult
is the need to dominate, to stand out in a group or organization as a figure
of great importance, to be first or best—in brief, to have eminence over
others. The tyrannical authority figure, the headline seeker, and the compulsively driving valedictorian are recognized examples of this behaviorial
symptom. So, too, are teachers or administrators who conceive of their
roles, consciously or unconsciously, as means of becoming unchallenged
power personalities—kings on academic thrones.

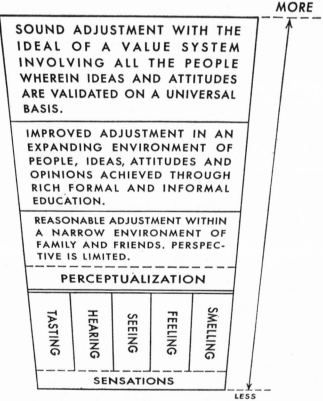

Figure 1   From Less to Greater Maturity

Alfred Adler, the first disciple to break with Freud, built an entire
psychology around this power, or superiority, complex, as he called it.[2] He

[2] Alfred Adler, *The Practice and Theory of Individual Psychology,* trans. by
P. Radin (New York: Harcourt, Brace & World, Inc., 1929), pp. 1–15.

hypothesized that every human being wants superiority over others, and, failing to attain it in sufficient degree, will compensate for the lack in some way: by tyrannizing over the weak, by feigning inadequacy to get attention from the strong, or by withdrawing from the scene of conflict. The developmentally emergent individual, however, sensitized to this need, will seek to supply his want in acceptable ways. He will refrain from exploiting, will do his best but not at the expense of associates, and will give recognition to, as well as receive recognition from, others.

The classroom instructional leader, almost above all others, is expected by society to resist the seduction of the power-over lure and to channel his need for dominance into situations where satisfactions come from cooperative endeavor. This orientation is a social one, aligning a teacher with his student or adult associates. In the relationship with students, the teacher, without abdicating his legal responsibilities, drops all pretenses of sham and artificiality, communicating to students in the process that he exists solely to work with them individually or as a group and to enable them to work more profitably and comfortably with one another. The emphasis is on "us," not "me"; on what "we can do together," not on what "I as a teacher in charge of the class can do to get you to work harder or behave better."

This positive teacher-pupil orientation tends also to transfer to student-student relationships, dulling the impact of unwholesome rivalries which divide groups and harm personalities. In no sense does, or should, the "power-with" concept encourage less individual initiative or performance or lead to exclusively social outcomes devoid of personality uniqueness. Instead, it casts individualism in a different light and leads to a sharing of strength without a compensating loss to the person, to a desire to perform to the optimum but not to surpass another, to a willingness to learn from others without harm to the self-ego. The "power-with" concept is developmentally sound, because it projects personality, in great part, toward others—a definite indication of growth progress. It stands in dramatic contrast to the "power-over" pattern which has long been the standard bearer of the self-dissatisfied and unsure teacher who stands as a roadblock to sound classroom relationships. And it avoids the even worse consequence of this aggressive approach: the encouragement of those who bear the brunt of the power impulse to bide their time until they, too, can be in a position of authority dominance. In the process, the gentler emotions are invariably suppressed while the power-over anarchy perpetuates itself.

Teacher actions should respect personality

As the maturing teacher develops a more satisfying self-image, extends his contacts into an expanding world of people, and successfully compensates for unfulfilled superiority desires, he develops a keener insight into people and values. This humanistic orientation elevates personality to a high plane where, along with other cherished qualities, it will be shielded from unjust attack. Just as the teacher needs an adequate self-image, so do students and other associates with whom the teacher works. Thus, although it behooves the instructional leader in his many day-to-day and long-term contacts to take appropriate action when rules are being violated and the personality of another is being injured, he must not be an instrument of injury.

This means that teachers need to focus their attention on problems through the eyes of a person objective and detached, not through a disarrangement of ego-distortions and personal biases. So oriented, the teacher is able to relate to negative situations without doing major damage to the individuals involved. A similar point of view is brought out by A. H. Maslow, a well-known practicing psychologist and author, who describes the "self actualizing person as one who is problem-centered, not ego-centered."[3] This type of individual can relate to the crux of a problem situation without being affected by his prejudices for or against the characters involved in the interplay of forces. He attends to the problem in such a way that personality is not degraded. His goal is always to support, not to destroy, human relations, regardless of the circumstances.

By way of illustration, we interpolate the following episode:

Paul, a trailer-camp youngster of Slavic origin, moves into the high-school community and enrolls. Having shifted for himself much of his life, he is somewhat careless in appearance, not too clean, and ruggedly independent. As a result of having had to fight many battles alone, he is aggressive toward other males in the class and even occasionally insolent to the teacher. One day, when asked by the teacher to stop talking to the boy in the next seat, he retorts: "I'll stop when I get ready."

The reader is asked to evaluate the following teacher reactions in terms of their probable effect on the personality of the adolescent. Each option involves a verbal retort and an after-school follow-up.

1. "You are insolent and a trouble maker, Paul. There seems to be something nasty in you that delights in hurting others. You will see me at 3:30 in this room, and I insist that you be here! We shall get to the bottom of this!"
2. "You seem to need a lesson in manners, Paul, particularly regarding your attitude toward adults. I hope that your show of belligerence doesn't reflect a deliberate desire to offend. I wish to see you here at 3:30 today."
3. "Your remark, Paul, is out of line with acceptable standards of the classroom and school, as well as my own. Please see me after school so that we can discuss other ways of meeting problem situations. I shall expect you at 3:30 or shortly thereafter."

In option 1, the teacher makes no effort to disguise his negativism. Paul is addressed sharply, the act is generalized out of context, and a flat

---

[3] A. H. Maslow, *Motivation and Personality* (New York: Harper & Row, 1954), p. 12.

order is given for Paul to report at 3:30. The harm to personality goes unquestioned because the student is portrayed as a sadistic personality whose pleasures come from hurting others. In option 2, the tone is softened but personalized negativism still dominates. Option 3 alone is supportive of personality by directing attention at the act while protecting the dignity of the actor. Devoid of sentimentality, it conveys the impression that limits have been set which cannot be ignored lightly. But the act itself is rescued from color terms and wrongly applied generalizations that harm personality while not alleviating the situation.

Any teacher, even under ideal circumstances, is destined to be irritated by episodes and events that are outside the pale of defensible social behavior. The extremely ill-mannered adolescent, the excitable colleague, and the unreasonable parent will challenge the poise of any teacher. However, professionalism will be his to the extent that he can manipulate the situation objectively without degrading the personality of the offender. In contrast, when he succumbs to the immaturity of name-calling, generalizing falsely, and other examples of emotionalism, he lowers himself to the level of the erring individual whom he is properly expected to help.

Internalization or mature appraisal of values?

In progressing toward a higher level of development, a teacher needs to evaluate with increasing thoroughness the opinions, ideas, and attitudes that he claims to possess. Are they theoretically sound? Can they be defended in practice? Are they more suitable in certain situations than in others? In essence, are they the outgrowth of careful deliberation or are they primarily the reflection of family or community influences?

In infancy and childhood, the immature human organism by necessity absorbs the values of his immediate environment. He may, for example, parrot the dogmatism of a strong-willed father; he may reflect the attitude biases of a mother; and he may generally "internalize" the values of the local culture. And when he "internalizes," thought and reason defer to custom and to maintaining conditions as they are.

As childhood gives way to adolescence and the latter to adulthood, the process of passive internalization normally begins to be replaced by thoughtful analysis. The more mature individual increasingly demands the right to think for himself. As he reasons more independently, he begins to question the validity of many of his previously maintained points of view. In the process of questioning, sacred cows often fall and are smashed, and under scrutiny cherished dogma may fade away.

In his search for truth, the teacher candidate must select his standards of truth carefully. If he operates on presumptions from an absolute philosophical or religious orientation, he has the security that only sanctioned dogma can bring, but he thereby accepts too much of life without question.

The issue then becomes, What in life is to be questioned and what is to be accepted without question?

Outside the province of religion and philosophy, an analysis of the influences that help to formulate one's beliefs and attitudes should prove beneficial. Several such influences will be found in the popular communications media: the newspaper, the radio, and television. The teacher, even more than the typical citizen, needs to evaluate with care the points of view that flow from these. Certainly a questioning mind is essential as he makes his analyses. If employed, it will lead him to reject conclusions drawn from evidence that is limited or not genuine and the absolute finality that characterizes propaganda. In the process of questioning, he will train himself to consider how competent the individuals who represent the aforementioned media are: whether they are trustworthy, well informed, and relatively free of biases. And he will test what he hears against a broad base of knowledge gained from many sources. In this way, he will resist the tempting luxury of internalization—the tendency to believe without the support of an adequate foundation.

Ideally, then, the maturing student of life's values has a mission to glean truth from the most authentic sources available to him at each developmental level of growth. To the child, truth is synonymous with family opinions and attitudes. To the adolescent, truth emanates from a number of sources, among which the family holds a place of dominance. To the reasonably mature teacher, truth exists primarily when scholarly judgment, tested practice, and careful contemplation support a statement or proposition. At this level of development, internalization can no longer be a primary life process. In fact, when employed too frequently, it falls into the category of arrested development—development fixated at a too early age.

Leaving the abstract for the concrete, the reader is asked to respond to the following four questions and then to justify his responses:

1. Why do I favor the political party of my choice?
2. Why do I subscribe to the religion of my choice
3. If I had the option of sitting on a bus next to a German, Russian, Negro, Italian, Swede, or Greek, which one would I select? Why would I prefer not to sit next to the one or more of those listed?
4. Do I consider some of the following occupations to be less respectable or prestigious than the others: lawyer, school-teacher, bank teller, ten-cent-store clerk, housemaid, physician, postman?

In answering these questions, if the reader discovers that such influences as family beliefs and customs, social expectancy, and illogical biases enter into his responses, he can quite properly suspect internalization as the culprit. He should be almost as suspicious when he is unable to state why he answered as he did. Many of life's influences are subtle, and the unconscious mind is a powerful motivator; thus, not knowing why one believes as one does may be revealing of the tenaciousness of internalization.

Mature responses to the above four stimulators might well be somewhat as follows:

1. I am currently a Republican because I believe in less rather than more centralized government. Furthermore, I prefer the Republican figures who are in key leadership positions to their counterparts of the opposing party.

2. I am a Congregationalist because I favor a religion with an unrigid creed or a religion that permits me to work out my own creed with a mimimum of outside pressure. Also, I feel that church government and property should be in the hands of the local congregation.

3. At the theoretical level, I would have no preference regarding the race of the person sitting next to me on the bus. However, to be completely honest, I must admit to unsupportable prejudices against Italians and Germans.

4. In terms of my basic values, I regard all of the occupations listed as equally respectable. However, because I live in a society that assesses occupational worth artificially, I confess to a preference for the physician, schoolteacher, and lawyer, in that order. Yet this listing of preferences arouses guilt, because I realize that other-directedness, in great part, has shaped my values.

These excerpts move in the direction of responses based on analytical questioning and soul searching. To the extent that unconscious motivation has been controlled, so that integrity of response is possible, the replies satisfy defensible criteria. They meet the standards of critical objectivity, so necessary for the teacher, whose primary function is to guide others critically.

Man should be himself in all situations

The last growth concept to be discussed in this chapter is naturalness. The reader might envision himself in each of the following situations: at dinner for the first time in the home of the local mayor or chief administrator of the town in which he lives; at lunch with a close friend in the local college snack shop; in the home of the minister, rabbi, or priest who administers to his religious needs; in the office of a college professor; on the athletic field. In what way would his actions and personality differ from situation to situation? Of even more importance, why would they differ?

That he would be more formal in certain situations and less in others could be taken for granted. His behavior would differ from place to place in terms, for example, of the types of stories he would tell; in terms of his greeting of the host, hostess or athletic leader; in terms of his dress; and in terms of his speech habits. He would play a different role in each place, but the choice of role and his reason for making it would be the factors by which maturity would, in part, be assessed. If his role-playing were dictated by reasonable social expectancy, maturity would be the guiding influence. If, however, it were governed by desires for ego-building, ulterior motives would be the guiding influence.

The correct and wholesome approach is for the teacher to be basically himself within the framework of reasonable social demands. A preferable order of priority is the *teacher-person* first and then the *teacher-educator,* not the reverse. The natural, unpretentious classroom leader who engages in a minimum of role-playing just for the sake of making an impression is the one who will "wear" the best with students and adult associates. He will be the predictable and consistent individual in most situations, changing only to meet the reasonable demands of social expectation. In contrast, the teacher who in varying situations is sweet and petulant, submissive and domineering, permissive and exacting, leaves associates just as confused as his own personality is uncertain. It is hard to resist the trite advice, "Be yourself." The teacher who adheres to it, however, will thereby project to associates at all levels a kind of intellectual honesty that is bound to be respected and admired.

THE MATURING TEACHER

The teacher needed in the almost countless classrooms throughout the country is the individual who initially brings a pattern of reasonable adjustment to the college or university. During the period of collegiate training, he progresses satisfactorily toward the mental-health goal of optimum development broadly conceived. He does not reject a considerable amount of intensive specialization, but constructs a firm foundation on which specialization can be successfully developed and nurtured.

By necessity, the teacher's early life is dominated by family influences. Then a local neighborhood and the immediate community join with the family as determiners of attitudes and behavior. Subsequently his horizons extend, as far as opportunities will permit, into an ever-broadening frame of reference. As his understanding of ideas, people, and events increases, his values become more universally oriented.

However, the process of maturing is a function of each person: there are not fixed dimensions for all. Because of a richer genetic or environmental heritage, one teacher will move further along the route than another who is less favorably endowed. But each, regardless of his endowment, is expected to be a dynamically growing person. Maturity in teachers and teaching is accordingly conceived, not as an absolute outcome, but as an emerging process.

Supporting our demand for greater developmental growth in teachers is social expectancy as interpreted by law. Legally the teacher is one who acts as "the reasonable man" should act. He is the "legal parent," the "agent of the state" to whom are entrusted the community's children. And he is expected to be worthy of the trust. Unlike the blood parent, who often can be guilty of excesses without incurring undue legal or social disfavor, the academic parent is commissioned by law to satisfy high standards both of parenthood and of his profession.

When, short of unattainable perfection, these standards are more nearly realized, teachers will exemplify more completely the characteristics that are the desired outcomes of education: for example, careful scholarship, emotional adjustment, ethical relationships, good citizenship, and social competency. Since maturity breeds maturity, secondary school pupils should be under the sponsorship of mature personalities. Teaching is both what the teacher basically is as well as what he says and does.

But to achieve his high potential, the teacher must have a burning desire for change, he must be convinced that change is possible, and he must possess the attributes of physical and mental health required to effect the desired transformation. Desire as a conspicuous motivator of growth usually appears in the wake of dissatisfaction with self. In contrast, the teacher who is content with present conditions is an elusive candidate for self-help. Accordingly, our emergent teacher is envisioned as one who, avoiding complacency, questions the adequacy of himself and his values while pressing toward positive goals. He finds life dynamic, and he falls in step. His desire for growth must be accompanied by a conviction that change is possible.

Arrayed against such a conviction are the predeterminists and certain environmentalists who believe that basic personality change after childhood is difficult if not actually impossible of attainment. The former conceive man as the more or less helpless end-product of a foreordained set of determinants. Man merely plays out his destiny without being able to alter it. The second group may be blanketed by the familiar saying, "Give me the child until he is six and I will make him what he will be for life." While there may be limited support for the aphorism, aligned against it are education and the mental-health disciplines which avowedly exist for the sole purpose of effecting change—even in basic personality. A compromise is for any emerging person to recognize the fixed limits of growth, to understand the peculiar significance of childhood influences, but to press for change within this framework of reality.

Education thus operates to enrich the environment of the learner at every level so that a vital transformation in him can take place. The better the physical and mental health of the learner, the greater the possible extent of transformation; yet with high motivation, even major disabilities will not always be serious handicaps.

A necessary condition for insight and resultant personality integration is a broad general education. Without assuring the open mind, it often provides the key to it. Teacher candidates cannot afford to neglect general education while en route to a professional degree or certificate. If dissatisfaction with self is a prerequisite of growth, one way to achieve it is for students to become intelligently steeped in knowledge about the past and present, to study many cultures and to learn about many people. Unless the process humbles the student and makes him receptive to more knowledge, either the quality of the liberal education or the adequacy of the student should be questioned.

Although general education is usually associated with formalized course work at either the high school or the college level, self-directed efforts outside this framework should not be ignored. Included in this category is the education that the college student secures after graduation. The effective teacher candidate should regard himself as forever the student of knowledge. The greater the breadth of his knowledge, the more effective will be his ability to relate affairs of the classroom to a satisfactory background of value concepts.

A comprehensive general education is potentially an agent that frees and liberates. It raises tolerance levels and broadens understandings. It enhances artistic appreciation. It encourages humility by creating standards which reveal the artificial and arrogant for what they are. Its goal is the increase of knowledge, comprehension, and sensitivity to the end of a more refined system of life values. Its practical goal for the teacher is the application of insights to adolescents and the learning situation.

Maturing students will take their general education just as seriously as they do their professional training. The emancipating forces should be permitted to operate extensively in the personal and professional lives of pre-service and in-service teachers. General education conceived in this way is an indispensable associate of the maturing process.

Under the stabilizing influence of general education studies, environmental horizons will be confidently projected to a world of more people and places. Altruism will almost inevitably become a primary motivator of life, demanding that the evolving person extend his social world broadly. And the geographical world will increase proportionately as he travels, physically or by armchair, more widely to study new places and cultures. Understandably, few teachers can afford the luxury of world travel, but each can extend his "social and place" horizons to the limits permitted by circumstances.

On this structure of dynamic personal growth, we rest our case for teaching method. Method will be effective only to the extent that the structure is stable.

SUMMARY

The maturing process is developmental for adults as well as for children and should be assessed throughout life. When the process slows or is halted, causes to be suspected might well be the limitations of heredity or the environment, the seductive effects of the unconscious mind, a power drive that is improperly controlled, the distortions which result from lack of fulfillment, social horizons that are too limited, an ego rather than a problem emphasis, a regression to internalization, or ill-conceived role-playing.

The maturing teacher is one who brings a reasonable level of adjustment to the teacher-education institution, secures a solid foundation of general education, and extends his world horizons broadly. Teaching method is thus projected as an extension of the maturing teacher.

REFERENCES

Abrahamsen, David, *The Road to Emotional Maturity*. Englewood Cliffs, N.J.: Prentice-Hall, Inc., 1958.

Bonney, Merl E., *Mental Health in Education*. Boston: Allyn and Bacon, Inc., 1960.

Fromm, Erich, *The Sane Society*. New York: Holt, Rinehart and Winston, 1955.

Horney, Karen, *Our Inner Conflicts*. New York: W. W. Norton and Co., 1945.

————, *Self Analysis*. New York: W. W. Norton and Co., 1942.

Inlow, Gail M., "Adjustment for What," *The Journal of Educational Sociology,* Feb., 1957.

Jourard, Sidney, *Personal Adjustment*. New York: The Macmillan Company, 1958.

Jung, Carl, "God, The Devil, and The Human Soul," *Atlantic Monthly,* Vol. 200, Nov., 1957, pp. 57–63.

Maslow, A. H., *Motivation and Personality*. New York: Harper & Row, 1954.

Merry, Frieda Kiefer, and Ralph V. Merry, *The First Two Decades of Life* (2nd ed.). New York: Harper & Row, 1958.

Overstreet, Harry, and Bonaro Overstreet, *The Mind Alive*. New York: W. W. Norton and Co., 1954.

Redl, Fritz, and Wm. W. Wattenberg, *Mental Hygiene in Teaching*. New York: Harcourt, Brace & World, Inc., 1959.

Stevenson, George S., and Henry Milt (M.D.), *Master Your Tensions and Enjoy Living Again*. Englewood Cliffs, N.J.: Prentice-Hall, Inc., 1959.

THE
MANY-SIDED ROLE
OF THE
TEACHER

Assuming the presence of the emergent teacher described in Chapter 1, what role would he be expected to play in the typical high school? The responses to this question by the "man in the street" and the teacher himself would undoubtedly differ.

The layman conceivably would oversimplify the teacher's role by confining teaching to the formalized practices of the classroom itself. The teacher's only task, he might say, is to make children learn: by making assignments, asking questions, encouraging "right" answers, chiding the unprepared, and reassigning work that has been done badly. This is the too commonly accepted stereotype of teaching, although in part, it is justified. In fact, Eggleston's Hoosier School Master of the 1860's could apply for a position in a few secondary schools today—and be hired.

The teacher himself, when asked to describe his teaching position, would enumerate the duties in the plural, not the singular. Included in his response would be such descriptive role titles as group-discussion leader, planner, tutor, evaluator, club sponsor, counselor, disciplinarian, classroom manager, parent interviewer, part-time administrator, and trouble shooter. He would view his position as diversified and complex, involving parents as well as children, extra-classroom as well as classroom functions, and the intangibles as well as the tangibles of learning.

The average daily teaching load reveals the futility of trying to reduce teaching to a single-patterned entity. It typically involves five classes totaling 125 to 150 students, two to three subject-matter preparations, a service assignment of some kind during one period (hall duty, cafeteria supervision, study hall, and so forth), and administrative responsibilities after school hours. The latter include, among others, extracurricular activities, faculty meetings, departmental meetings, faculty committee meetings, and parental interviews. This rich variety the dedicated teacher accepts with good grace, but it leaves him only mildly tolerant of the commonly accepted image of teaching as narrowly dimensional.

The teacher's academic responsibilities do not end when he leaves the school environs. The dual requirements of preparing for the next day and also evaluating the work of that morning or afternoon are ever his. If he teaches science, he may have experiments, projects, or workbooks to grade; if mathematics, he has the inescapable exercises and problems to check; if English, a seemingly endless number of themes, term papers, and book reviews to examine; if a foreign language, he has translations and exercises to grade. The academic responsibilities are almost infinite, and the myth of the six-hour day or the five-day week vanishes in their presence.

Education is not exclusively a pedagogical process. It has expanded to include the development in youth of wholesome attitudes, proper channeling of youthful emotions, and growth on the part of the young in social living as well as in academic scholarship. Like most other aspects of the curriculum, this greater demand reflects changes in societal expectancies that have occurred during the past half-century. As people have gained new insights into mental health, they have insisted that this awareness be evidenced in the classroom. On perceiving more clearly how differences in children relate to teaching, they have insisted on a corresponding improvement in educational practice. As industrialization has re-patterned daily living, citizens have expected teachers to help pupils meet the new technological demands. Education, it is to be recalled, both mirrors society and also leads it.

While gaining these new responsibilities, the teacher has lost few of the old. Even though he still must be significantly dedicated to scholarship, he is expected to assume the broader role.

As the teacher candidate stands on the threshold of his new profession, greater realism will be his if he views it in proper perspective. Uncomplicated it will not be. Routine it will not be. Serene it will not regularly be. Rather, it will be active, challenging, and consistently rewarding.

THE TEACHER AS ACADEMICIAN

Of the many functions that a teacher performs, none is more important than or so indispensable as the academic. Whatever their philosophical leanings, from reactionary to radical, educators agree that cognitive learnings are essential to the evolving human organism. Neither education nor life itself can exist independent of knowledge and intellectual understandings. The so-called "great debate" is not over the issue of intellectuality versus non-intellectuality in schools. It is between the advocates of intellectualism as almost the sole constituent of a curriculum and those who envision intellectual learning as a major but not an exclusive constituent.

By accepted definition, then, the secondary school teacher, besides his other duties, must be an academic leader. In this framework, his function is to help adolescents acquire significant knowledge about the past and present that will serve them as a tool of comprehension. Knowledge as a discrete, unrelated entity has limited justification. First of all, learning theorists are only on the threshold of discovering the more subtle mysteries of transfer. Second, assuming that knowledge and facts have worth regardless of whether they are applied to anything useful, the pyramiding mountains of historical and current information are a challenge to appropriate and accurate selection. Herbert Spencer's conundrum of a century ago, "What knowledge is of most worth?"[1] is still unanswered.

Yet, through the years, certain curriculum components have enjoyed the support of the majority of the people. The skills of reading, writing, listening, speaking, and computing have been accepted without question. The teaching of the basic traditions and events of the Occidental (less of the Oriental) culture has been justified consistently as a means of perpetuating the best of the past. And education being primarily a local function, high schools have defended as important aspects of a curriculum selected content that has local application: for example, the study of agriculture in a rural community, industrial arts and business education in communities where many adolescents terminate their education with high school, and driver's training in urban communities.

These justifications for education usually operate in a framework wherein adolescents are encouraged to explore broadly, to specialize with moderation in a few areas of interest, and to meet the requirements of their immediate environments.

In the past half-century, without rejecting time-honored content, educators have increasingly demanded that students be encouraged—even required—to make evaluative judgments of events, concepts, and other cultural constituents. As a result, such curriculum terms as *problem solv-*

---

[1] Herbert Spencer, *Education: Intellectual, Moral, Physical* (New York: Appleton-Century-Crofts, Inc., 1896).

ing, critical thinking, and *the questioning mind* have become commonplace. Motivated by this newer stress, many adolescents are literally turning beliefs, attitudes, and opinions inside out in an honest effort to discover a basic value system. Supporting this trend, Elmer Davis in his best seller of 1954, *But We Were Born Free*,[2] identifies the right of open skepticism as the most eloquent reason why the West must be saved from destruction. This right, as well as obligation, encourages youth to evaluate *what is* to the end of deciding *what should be*. The emphasis is on qualitative analysis more than on memory and perpetuation.

THE TEACHER AS GUIDANCE WORKER

Not antagonistic to the teacher's role as academician is his role as a guidance worker. In the latter, without denying the importance of knowledge, he attempts to work with the "whole pupil." From his mental-hygiene position, he helps pupils develop high emotional tolerances, social skills, ethical values, and physical attributes. Attention is invited to the following episode as illustrative.

Lynn Berman, a fifteen-year-old sophomore, is a popular girl in high school. Her friends, both male and female, are numerous. As a student, she rarely receives a grade lower than B. In school activities, she is a leader: class officer, member of the glee club, and representative to the student council.

Toward the end of the sophomore year, following a period of open scandal attended by adverse newspaper publicity, her parents are divorced. Lynn develops acne at this time, probably associated, at least, in part, with the emotional problem in the home. With her lowered self image, both psychological and physical, she withdraws from most of her former school friends, resigns from the school-activity positions, and loses herself in academic work. With this newly-found dedication, she studies at home from twenty to thirty hours per week and is first in her class at the end of the year.

How would the guidance-minded teacher react to Lynn's metamorphosis? Although certainly not displeased with her academic accomplishment, he would evaluate it against a comprehensive profit-and-loss balance sheet of many values. Concerned over Lynn's withdrawal from social life, he would want to have the seriousness of the emotional impact of the parents' divorce upon her assessed.

Whereas an academic extremist might consider the improvement in Lynn's achievement as the most significant of the many changes in this student, his guidance-minded co-worker would be less inclined to regard it as an unmixed blessing. Rather, he would withhold judgment until the academic gain could be measured against the total personality structure. Only then would he decide whether to protect the gain while attempting to

[2] Elmer Davis, *But We Were Born Free* (Indianapolis: Bobbs-Merrill Company, Inc., 1954), pp. 175–176.

repair the losses or to sacrifice, if necessary, some of the academic progress in an effort to reverse the adverse emotional and social symptoms.

The teacher-guidance worker thus plays his role against a broad projection of values. Conscious of the dangers of developmental distortion, he takes a stand against one-sidedness, as displayed, for example, by the athletic coach who makes academic accomplishment a difficult commodity, by the senior-play sponsor who may forget that a secondary school is not Broadway, or the rigid disciplinarian who may have forgotten that adolescence is a combination of both growth and regression.

In this guidance role of many parts, what are some of the more specialized functions that the teacher performs?

Observing students

As an interested analyst of adolescent growth, the teacher must be a careful observer of the many extensions of adolescent behavior. A teacher of world history, for example, should be a reputable scholar in his specialized field and sufficiently acquainted with teaching method to make world history a dynamic learning experience for pupils. But solidifying these two requirements should be a concern for the welfare of youth which, without detracting from the demands of world history, rises above them.

As a responsible legal parent-figure, the qualified teacher of any secondary school subject takes an interest in students as individuals and observes their reactions carefully. When noting aggressiveness, without reacting to it in kind he attempts to discover possible causes as a requirement preliminary to a cure. When observing apathy, he analyzes himself, the curriculum, and the students themselves as suspected inducers. Upon discovering the introvert, he provides him with subtle opportunities for extrovert expression. He helps the tense to relax, the hypercritical to be less judgmental, and the self-effacer to gain confidence.

Redl and Wattenberg testify to the significance of observation in the following:

The differences among children and the differences in the way they do things which are apparently similar are important indicators. The expressions on faces, differences in habitual postures, and the manner of talking, all provide clues. Many an adult has learned to chuckle at the famous remark, "It wasn't what she said, it was the way that she said it." There is even greater wisdom in watching how children act. It is not so much what they do, but the way in which they do it that can speak volumes to anyone who pays close attention. A very dramatic illustration is supplied by the film Balloons, produced by the Department of Child Study at Vassar College. In the film two boys are seen hitting balloons. One strikes them with tense gestures; after the blows, his fists remain partially clenched. The second boy hits with smooth, confident motions, after which his hands and arms fall relaxed. The differences in behavior are interpreted to mean that the first boy is bottling up strong destructive impulses, which he also feels are very naughty; the second boy has no such conflict.[3]

The best teacher-observer has an abiding interest in young people and enough background in the behavioral sciences to interpret what he sees with reasonable accuracy. These attributes, combined with enough proficiency in his content field to free him from an over-dependence on lesson notes, enable him to satisfy the demands of knowledge learning while he studies the reactions of students to the total learning situation.

Using information contained in guidance records

A controlled method of observation is that employed by the teacher who studies the personal and academic records of class members. A controversial issue among teachers, in this regard, is whether they should have in their possession such information as reading scores, intelligence quotients, and written anecdotes on personality manifestations. Many teachers profess a desire to begin a classroom relationship with students "unprejudiced" by prior information. Others wish to know as much as possible about students before and after the act of exposure to them.

Since most high schools possess personnel records which contain meaningful information, we feel that the truly qualified teacher, who is desirous of knowing as much as he can about students, should use this information to heighten growth. Nor should he be any more prejudiced as a result of exposure to negative information than a physician would be about a history of social disease, a clinical psychologist about emotional disturbance, or a marriage counselor about the matrimonial difficulties of a client.

A ninth-grade teacher, for example, should work more effectively with John Jones if prior knowledge indicates that John's reading score is at the sixth-grade level, his I.Q. is 110 on the Binet and 95 on the Otis, and his record in seventh grade was characterized by many behavioral disorders, including a case of petty thievery and aggressive bodily contact on several occasions with other boys his age. This information, rather than prejudicing a teacher, should guide him in his many relationships with the boy. As a result of it, reading would be assigned at the sixth- or seventh-grade, not the ninth-grade, level; enrollment in a remedial class might be effected; and John would be studied in an attempt to discover why he is belligerent with his male classmates. To the professional teacher, such information should be liberating, not prejudicial.

[3] Fritz Redl and William W. Wattenberg, *Mental Hygiene in Teaching* (New York: Harcourt, Brace & World, Inc., 1959), pp. 36–37. Reprinted by permission.

Administering and interpreting tests and inventories

Unlike other types of observation which are more or less common to all teachers, controlled observation through standardized tests and inventories varies in practice among school systems. In the schools that can afford a competent staff of specialized guidance workers, a common practice is for one or more of such workers to assume responsibility for almost all phases of a standardized testing program. For instance, when academic aptitude tests are given, centralized specialists assume all, or almost all, responsibilities for the giving, timing, collecting, and interpreting of the testing instruments. At the end of the process, an interpretive profile may or may not be sent to the teacher.

In the smaller schools, and these are in the vast majority, the teacher administers and interprets standardized tests and inventories for the simple reason that no one else is available to do the job. And over a long period of time, when the teacher has greater responsibility for testing, the gains may be greater for all concerned. When the teacher becomes involved in the testing process, he quite naturally takes a greater interest in it than when the process remains outside his province. And with such involvement, he tends to weave the results into the larger framework of classroom evaluation.

However, in the smaller schools where necessity dictates, and the larger schools where a philosophy engulfs teachers into a standardized testing program, the responsibility placed on classroom teachers is considerable. Such a practice either presupposes a prior knowledge of testing instruments, for example: the California Test of Mental Maturity, the Otis Self Administering Test, the Kuder Interest Inventory, the Stanford Achievement Test Battery, and the Iowa Silent Reading Test, to name just a few. Or it assumes that a teacher or administrator who has specialized in the field of testing will exercise leadership in an in-service program to help other teachers become better qualified to give and interpret the tests and inventories that are used.

Regardless of school practices, the teacher prospect should have some prior knowledge of testing procedures or should be willing to learn the necessary facts of testing while on the job. Prior knowledge on the teacher's part serves two purposes: he will escape at least one of the fears of the unknown that many students have in anticipation of the first position; and, positively speaking, he will make a greater immediate contribution to the students and to himself when he becomes a teacher.

Interviewing students and parents

Along with the guidance responsibilities of observing, utilizing records, and testing are those related to working with students and parents in a one-to-one relationship. Every teacher in the course of a day is not only a group leader but a counselor of individuals—most frequently of pupils; occasionally, of parents. It is in the personalized relationship with pupils that the teacher often finds his most immediate satisfactions and his greatest challenge to insight. Through this medium he is able to share ideas, consider values, understand behavior, and motivate progress based on the newly discovered insights.

The teacher's major responsibility is to try to see a situation through the eyes of the younger individual—to tune in, as it were, to the different psychological wave length and to study the evolving scene with empathy. For the young teacher, this role will be difficult to play because of a developmentally normal preoccupation with self. Escaping from parents, home, and a superimposed code of living is no easy task, but the subsequent readjustment will inevitably lead to an increasing relatedness to others. Despite possible obstacles to success, the young teacher, like his older counterpart, is a counselor *in fact,* and part of the role involves the interviewing of pupils and parents. Accordingly, it behooves him to anticipate the intimate give-and-take of this close relationship. Friendliness, tact, sincerity, and naturalness are requisite. Furthermore, a willingness to listen as well as to talk is basic to the interviewer who desires to see situations through the psychological eyes of another. And, as Williamson points out, "the attitudes, facial expressions, inflections, gestures and verbal expressions of the counselor determine in large part the reactions of the student."[4]

The interview is a person-to-person situation usually involving the following essentials: achieving rapport, receiving information, providing information, reconciling differences, and agreeing on a plan of action. This listing, however, may differ in order and in relative importance depending upon circumstances.

Whatever the basic purpose of the interview—to inform, to correct, to receive information, or to synthesize ideas—the teacher must ever be on guard against a tendency to dominate. By definition, the interview is two-sided, and when the teacher is too heavy-handed, the purpose of the process is defeated. If his goal is other than to "lay down the law," he needs to keep the channels of communication open at both ends.

Particularly in a counseling situation with parents must the teacher recognize the interview medium as a two-way channel. Without stereotyping teacher-parent consultations, it is safe to say that most of them are designed to include an exchange of attitudes, feelings, and points of view. However, when the teacher is unable to control a tendency to dominate, he may, at the termination of the so-called exchange, find that he has obtained too few of the ideas and opinions of the parent. But when his attitude is permissive, he invariably will increase the flow of information.

The following interviews should illustrate vividly the necessity for a

[4] E. G. Williamson, *Counseling Adolescents* (New York: McGraw-Hill Book Company, Inc., 1950), p. 138.

two-sided relationship. Mr. Allen has asked Bob Vick's father for an interview, which by mutual arrangement takes place in Mr. Allen's home-room at 4:00 P.M. on the designated day. The issue is the failing grades of Bob, Mr. Vick's son.

Situation A: "Good afternoon, Mr. Vick. I'm glad that you were able to make it here today because I must discuss Bob's grades with you. Won't you sit down?"

"What is the story on the grades, Mr. Allen? Bob has never been the best student in the world, but neither has he ever received grades that were very low. In fact, in Vandalia where he attended high school for two years, he had, I believe, only one D."

"Well, I'll be specific, Mr. Vick, about what is happening here. For the first six-weeks marking period this fall Bob received two D's and two F's. Furthermore, since he is eighteen and a senior, if he continues to make grades at such a low level, it could jeopardize his graduation."

"Take it easy, Mr. Allen. Do I hear you right—do you say that Bob may not graduate next June after all our planning and hoping? That's inhuman!"

"I didn't mean it that finally, only that it was a possibility." Etc.

Situation B: "I'm glad to see you, Mr. Vick; won't you be seated? From your remarks over the phone the other day, your getting away from the Buick Sales Company at this time must be quite an accomplishment. It was con-siderate of you to change your schedule around for me."

"Thanks, Mr. Allen. Maybe I was just trying to impress you with my importance. Seriously, however, this is one of our busy times, and making our quota of sales keeps us all from doing important things on the outside."

"Have you been with the agency long?"

"I shall complete my tenth year this December. I started in the shop, then later moved into sales. With the market as it is today, I often wonder if I shouldn't be back in the shop—although not really, I guess. This way I have more to complain about."

"I think I notice a resemblance between you and Bob, Mr. Vick, to the credit of both of you. We enjoy Bob very much. He has many friends and worthwhile interests in the school."

"Well, Mrs. Vick and I are proud of him and aren't planning on giving him out for adoption. But what's the story on Bob's grades? He has never been a genius, but has been getting by fairly well. I didn't relish those two D's and F's."

"To be frank, I have no set 'story' to tell, Mr. Vick. My only purpose in asking to visit with you was to see if, by a comparing of notes, we can help Bob pull his grades up next time." Etc.

Even though the episodes have been abbreviated, it is obvious that the parent, Mr. Vick, was rushed along at a too rapid pace in the first instance. The topic of Bob's grades was introduced immediately, with the father thrown off balance as a result. He quite understandably took the defensive, escaping into Bob's record at a previous school. Then came the threat to the boy's graduation—an issue which probably should not have been introduced at all. It forced the teacher into a modification which helped to cloud more than to clarify. All in all, this was an instance of negative substance being brought into play without regard to timing, rapport, and context.

In Situation B, Mr. Allen treated Mr. Vick first as a respected acquaintance before touching on an emotional subject. The school representative, as may be noted, removed barriers by conversationally meeting the parent on his home grounds—the job at the Buick agency. In this way, good will was secured by Mr. Allen before the delicate subject of the grades was introduced. Furthermore, Bob as a person was brought into the conversation via the remark about the resemblance between father and son. At that point, the parent took the initiative in facing the conceivably unpleasant topic of the interview.

With the outsider invariably on the defensive in a school situation, the teacher-counselor should first meet the visiting parent on pleasantly neutral grounds. Once having achieved rapport, he can then introduce the serious business of the interview. But the exchange should continue on a considerate give-and-take basis throughout. The teacher cannot ever afford to overpower. As a professionally trained person, he is responsible for conducting the interview in a professional way, even when a parent refuses to cooperate. More often than not, a teacher's sincere interest, poise, and fairness will ameliorate problems that otherwise might lead to acrimony.

The vocational role of the teacher

More delimited than the other guidance functions already discussed is that of a teacher's helping adolescents prepare for their future vocational roles. Since the end of the first decade of this century, secondary schools have increasingly recognized their vocational-guidance responsibilities; in fact, guidance had its origin in the vocational movement. However, because of the magnitude of this area of guidance, schools have had to establish limits. Those with vocational specialists obviously offer more extensive services in this area than do those without them. And yet even the specialists are baffled by the implications of a *Dictionary of Occupational Titles* that, in its last edition, listed approximately 56,000 job titles. What, then, is the plight of the unspecialized classroom teacher in this regard?

Although not a vocational specialist, the teacher of any subject has the following minimum vocational responsibilities: to support consistently the view that all vocations are honorable and equally respectable; to refer individuals who are searching for detailed occupational information to a more specialized guidance source; and, whenever possible, to justify the existence of a course in terms of vocational as well as other legitimate outcomes.

The first of these responsibilities involves almost an ethical commitment by the teacher to upset the attitudes of society about job respectability. The acid test is not the job or position that is filled, but whether the individual is in an occupational outlet that challenges the best in him. If mental health demands the optimum of personal development, job placement should utilize man's optimum talents. The test of quality, thus, is not prestige, but the proper matching of ability and job demands. When these conform within reason, the lathe operator or die caster is every bit as respectable as the vice president in industry or the physician in private practice. But admittedly, a teacher with middle-class values faces the necessity of hurdling his biases before being able to embrace this new set of attitudes.

The responsibility for referral demands a sensitivity to the vocational needs of pupils, an understanding of one's limits of specialized competency, and, finally, the canalizing of problems to the proper sources of help. In large high schools, the latter might be found in a central guidance office; in the smaller schools, the sources might exist only in a limited way in local business and industry or a library. In such an event, the vocational program would be obviously circumscribed.

The third responsibility of the classroom teacher for vocational guidance is one of justifying the existence of the courses which he teaches in terms of possible vocational outcomes. Whenever a positive and somewhat direct relationship may be shown to exist between a secondary school subject and an occupation, the subject receives a motivational lift. For instance, the teacher of Spanish, French, German or Russian is remiss in not relating the individual language to such possible sequels as the import-export business, the diplomatic service, or teaching. In like manner, mathematics should be related to market analysis, accounting, or actuarial prediction; the physical sciences, to pharmaceutical laboratory research, or chemical, electrical, or mechanical engineering; and English to journalism, secretarial work, creative writing, or editing. Without reducing at all their general-education value, teachers should recognize subjects that lead to vocational outcomes and should capitalize on this further means of curriculum enrichment.

The educational advisement role

Paralleling the vocational is the educational function of the teacher in the guidance of pupils. This function is two-pronged, pointing both toward higher education and toward the secondary program itself. While helping the student get ready for his educational future, this guidance function should never be made distinctive from the more immediate educational present.

College and university to some students are what the post-high school world of work is to others. Both are too complex to be the responsibility of other than a guidance specialist. However, in those schools without organized guidance programs, the classroom teacher can well serve as an educational resource person in his major field. In this capacity, he can advise students regarding the quality programs that exist at the baccalaureate and graduate levels in colleges and universities throughout the country. But in the process he will have to resist the common tendency to sell his Alma Mater to all listeners.

The teacher's second educational responsibility is as an academic adviser in the high school. In this role, he should know in general about, and be able to describe intelligently, the basic content of the 12 or 13 departmental areas that are included in the curriculum. Failing this standard, he should be able, at least, to prescribe selected courses that lead to the acquiring of credits for general education, majors, minors, and graduation.

Regrettably, the new teacher in many high schools finds it difficult to acquire the knowledge needed to become an effective educational adviser. In schools with specialized guidance workers, the problem is of limited significance; but in the majority of schools where the counseling responsibility is not set apart from teaching, it assumes great importance. Some schools make available to the new teacher a handbook which serves as an introductory guide to the educational program. Other schools provide almost no help.

Ideally an orientation program should begin at the time of hiring and continue as an in-service program. A major purpose would be to ready the teacher to counsel pupils wisely through the maze of courses in the academic, fine arts, and practical arts fields. A second purpose would be to make him better informed about the activity program and the various services of guidance, health, and the library. With such knowledge of the high school—its program and community expectation—the teacher inescapably would become a better counselor. Because the teacher cannot abdicate the role of educational adviser, he needs to get ready for its challenges despite the frequent inaccessibility of information.

THE ADMINISTRATIVE ROLE

Not only does a teacher work with students academically in a classroom situation and play the many parts required of the teacher-guidance worker, but usually he also is a vital factor in the administration of the school.

The type of role that he may play depends on the philosophy of administration practiced by the local school board, superintendent, or principal. On one extreme is the autocracy which can emerge from any line organization. If a school administrator believes that he is the "head of the school" and acts accordingly, the administrative duties of the teacher will be chiefly routine ones, such as requisitioning supplies and keeping attendance records.

The second approach to organization is the democratic one in which the administrator conceives of his primary functions as serving, not dictating to, his co-workers, stimulating them to more articulate accomplishment in the achievement of common purposes, inviting and receiving suggestions and even criticism without affront, and organizing the school program in such a way that the many functions of administration can most successfully operate.

The advantages of the democratic approach are numerous. Participants will respond, communicate, and share because they are involved in the process of decision-making. They will have a feeling of genuine belongingness because of their closer identification with, and a resulting greater allegiance to, the school system. Furthermore, an exchange of the ideas of the many will almost regularly make for better administrative decisions than will an unshared point of view of one person, no matter how capable he may be. A third advantage of the democratic approach is that the people who work together in an administrative capacity usually develop leadership characteristics as a by-product of the process, thereby becoming more effective contributors to the program as a whole.

Yet the democratic approach is not without limitations. One is that participants restricted in outlook and experience may fail to realize the inappropriateness or inadequacy of some of their proposed contributions. Another limitation is that debate may be substituted for, or unnecessarily delay, action. Illustrative is a faculty that discusses issues excessively, to the end of postponing needed change. For instance, a change of textbooks may be delayed or the extent of student leadership go undetermined because a faculty is unable to reach a consensus.

Few school administrations are ever completely democratic, and few completely autocratic. Even the usually autocratic superintendent occasionally asks teachers for advice. And the democratic principal, on occasions, when speed is of the essence, will make a unilateral commitment and ask his co-workers to "go along." The key to democracy in a school is for an administrator rarely, if ever, to announce a policy without previously consulting with those who are to be affected by it; likewise, never to make policy without listening to those who are as expert as or more expert in the field than he. With schools becoming more and more complex as the problems of society multiply, school administrators who have vision will be those who think in terms of "we," not "I." With such administrators, we hope the readers will have an opportunity to work in their first as well as in subsequent teaching positions.

Methods of working democratically

Teachers perform the duties which are inherent in democratic administration in a number of ways, but the most common is the committee method—effective in most instances, abused in a few. An Illinois suburban high school in 1956 had 41 standing committees, an obvious abuse of the method. It is inconceivable to the author that the mission of any high school could be cut up 41 ways. A more common practice is for only a few standing committees to be in existence at any one time, with selected committees for special cases appointed from time to time as supplements. Committee membership, although not glamorous, still should be regarded by the teacher as a valuable organizational medium and therefore to be actively supported.

The prospective teacher can plan on being a member of one or more administrative committees most of his teaching lifetime. If he is in a school system where democratic administration is practiced, his role will be active: either to help make policy and recommend it to the faculty, or serve in an advisory capacity to the administrator. In anticipation, the prospective teacher should conceive his committee role properly, accepting the committee appointment willingly and working discerningly at it. Tact, moderation, sincerity, tolerance, and perceptiveness—desired qualities of mature group participation of any kind—are particularly essential to effective committee participation. We urge students to refine these attributes as they get closer to their first teaching commitment.

Other opportunities for teachers to work together democratically exist in faculty meetings, pre-school workshops and in-service conferences. Whatever the method, the degree of democratic participation is in large part determined by the background and philosophy of both the administrator and the faculty. The attitude of the teacher should never be that administration is only for the principal and the superintendent, but rather, that it is a function to be shared by informed personnel whatever their job titles.

Areas in which democratic administration is exercised

The range of school activities where democratic administration can be employed is almost as extensive as the school program itself. The most common focal point is the curriculum, which, to a greater or lesser degree, is the unique province of the teaching faculties of most schools. Normally a curriculum committee exists with a continuing assignment of studying the program for possible deletions, additions, and changes in approach. The committee usually operates on broad matters of curriculum policy, with the respective departments assuming the more specific responsibilities for change.

Guidance is another focal point, with a guidance committee common in many schools. Teacher members serve in liaison capacity with the faculty. One of their most important roles in most large schools is to keep the centralized guidance program from becoming too detached from the classroom. Being teachers themselves, they press for a program to fit the needs of students as seen through the eyes of classroom teachers.

Other focuses of democratic administration are frequently in the areas of salary, welfare, health, library, building construction, and teacher unions, to name only a few.

Record-keeping

This section on the administrative responsibilities of the teacher should not be terminated without a brief look at the record-keeping function of the teacher. Although not extensive, it is a taskmaster which demands obedience. The more important forms or records with which the teacher is involved are these:

(1) *Daily attendance record.* In all states, a record of school attendance is required by legal dictum. When pupils enroll in the high school for the first time, a record is made of their names, ages, names of parents and siblings, schools previously attended, and other related information. Thereafter the school is required to maintain a daily record of the pupils' attendance and to submit it periodically to the state department of public instruction. State aid, if any, is normally computed against this record.

Although the school administrator is directly responsible for the attendance register itself, the teacher is required to take the roll every class period and to report absences to the school attendance office so that the register may be kept up to date. Procedurally, he may have a pupil assume the task for him, but he remains responsible for its being performed accurately.

(2) *Inventory of supplies and equipment.* At any time, a teacher is required to know the status of supplies and equipment that are under his control. A running inventory is normally maintained of such materials of instruction as texts and reference books, and of such items of equipment as microscopes, typewriters, shop apparatus, and maps. Although special equipment for the teacher of most subjects is limited, it is extensive for the teachers of science, art, physical education, home economics, industrial arts, agriculture, music, and shop courses. Inventory for these teachers often runs into thousands of dollars and thus is an important budget item at any time. Although teachers are not usually held financially liable for an occasional loss or theft of any item, they are expected to keep close tab on equipment and supplies that are issued them. In the event of gross carelessness, however, they may be held financially accountable for losses.

(3) *Estimates of equipment and materials needed for the new year.* In a well-run school system, teachers are expected to submit to the central administration or a department head a list of the supplies and items of equipment that will be required for the following year. Although in some schools this responsibility is assumed by the principal unilaterally, it is

normally a shared one. If an accurate estimate of needs is to be made, two requisites are a knowledge of the curriculum by the teacher, and fair dealing by both the teacher and the administrator. When the latter requisite is disregarded, the teacher's formula for planning is often to ask for twice as much as is needed because the principal always divides the request by two. Mutual confidence eliminates the need for such conniving.

(4) *Requisitions.* Teachers should never buy anything directly on the open market unless authorized. Rather, they are expected to requisition supplies on standard forms, thereby making financial accounting an organized function. The bane of the administrator's existence is the teacher who buys a curriculum item from a local source and then tries to collect, after making the purchase. At that time, the self-control of the typical principal is somewhat taxed and not infrequently the teacher has to pay for such purchases from his own pocket.

(5) *Reports to parents.* The function of marking cannot be escaped by the teacher. It is a part of the job that he inherits when he becomes a teacher and that he lives with to the day of retirement. This is one of the most difficult problems for the new teacher, who lacks the academic perspective which many of his older colleagues possess to a greater degree. In Chapter 14, the issue of marks and marking will be covered more fully.

(6) *Reports to principal.* In addition to the above records, periodical reports to the principal are required in all school systems. They may consist, for instance, of special reports on absences, reasons for drop-outs, number of failures, anticipated failures with projected reasons, property damaged, supplies lost or stolen, and repairs needed. These reports differ from school to school but exist in some way in every school.

THE CO-CURRICULAR ROLE

In addition to his academic, guidance, and administrative duties, the teacher also may perform many co-curricular functions. Increasingly, high schools are hiring teachers who can do more than teach young people in a classroom, important though this function is. The "extra" duties with adolescents that a prospective teacher can perform are of significance when the candidate is being considered for a position; in fact, they are often pivotal.

Schools need teachers who can exercise leadership in the diversified co-curricular (the term *co-curricular* is synonymous with *extracurricular*) program that exists in almost all secondary schools: (1) club activities related to the curriculum—creative writing, debate, extemporaneous speaking, dramatics, science, nature study, aeronautics, politics, choral music, orchestra, marching band; (2) vocational-type clubs—Junior Achievement, Future Teachers of America, Future Nurses, Future Farmers, Future Homemakers; (3) honor organizations—academic, athletic, special activity; (4) athletics—major sports, golf, tennis, wrestling, tumbling, trampoline; (5) hobby activities—camera, hiking, chess, bridge; (6) student-government activities.

The above listing, detailed though it is, is only a cross-sectional sample of the co-curricular activities and organizations that are in existence throughout the country. The multiplicity of these activities is the source of the multiple need of leaders who, for the most part, are the teachers hired to do more than instruct in mathematics or printing or chemistry. With co-curricular organizations the legal responsibility of the school, they should, with rare exception, have the leadership of people who have legal status in the school and who are well qualified for their roles.

Unusual is the teacher who does not sponsor a co-curricular activity on the average of at least every other year. Therefore, the prospective teacher should take an inventory of his personal attributes to discover where he can most comfortably fit into an anticipated program. Nor when he later assumes the duties can he afford to take them lightly. Faithful attendance, earnestness of purpose, motivation of student interest, and comfortable relationships with other faculty members involved are all integral aspects of the sponsor's responsibility.

Working with high school students in co-curricular activities involves a different type of relationship from that which usually typifies a class. Informality invariably is the keynote, with sponsors and students exchanging ideas more freely in a give-and-take manner. In contrast, an activity is almost always unproductive when it is led by a teacher who, because of his greater age and experience, feels that he alone should exercise leadership. Students on their way to independence are prone to withdraw from the dictatorial leadership of advisors. They sincerely desire wise counsel, they crave encouragement, they will even accept a dictum with good spirit, provided it is reasonable; but fundamentally they seek as much independence as they can handle and sometimes more. Wise, therefore, is the teacher who works with, not over, them; who provides them with as much freedom as they are ready to assume in any given situation.

PARTICIPATION IN PROFESSIONAL ORGANIZATONS

Participation by teachers in professional organizations is supportive of their roles as academicians, guidance workers, sharers of administrative duties, and sponsors of co-curricular activities. Such organizations are designed to make both the individual teacher and the collective body of teachers more effective, and only to the extent that they accomplish this mission are they successful. What are some of the more important organizations in which teachers have memberships? Also, what are the apparent benefits of belonging?

Professional organizations

Membership in selected professional organizations is possible at three educational levels: high school, college, and in-service. The high school pupil who develops an early interest in teaching can contribute to, and get a feedback from, The Future Teachers of America. In an F.T.A. secondary school club, he has the opportunity to explore the extent of his interest in what might later become a life's vocation. By reading, discussing, listening to interesting speakers, and visiting classrooms, he gets a pre-vocational insight into teaching as a profession and into himself as a candidate for it.

At the college level, he can pursue his interest further by joining one of the many F.T.A. chapters that exist in the various institutions of higher learning throughout the country. Denied this opportunity, he can become a student member of the professional association which exercises leadership in his major field. For instance, in the year 1951–1952, 6,210 students from 281 institutions belonged to the Music Educators National Congress. Their dues were $1.50 annually, which entitled them to receive the scholarly publication of the association and attend regional meetings as nonvoting members.[5] Similar opportunities are open to students with majors other than music.

At the in-service level, active participation of teachers in many professional organizations is possible, with the real problem being one of discovering those that provide the greatest benefits. Rising above all other educational groups is the National Education Association. Founded in 1857, its membership now totals well over half a million. Its purposes are many, including: research, publication, defense of teachers against unfair administrative practices, upholding high standards of selection and performance, and coordination with the work of various governmental agencies. Membership in the N.E.A. should be a goal of every teacher candidate. Through its many departments, divisions, and commissions he should find satisfactory ways of improving himself professionally: by reading its publications, participating in local group projects, attending regional meetings, and supporting in other ways an organization that has made an invaluable contribution to teaching. It is difficult to describe this greatest of all educational organizations without superlatives.

At the state and local levels are teacher associations, some of which are extensions of the N.E.A. and others not. The Association for Supervision and Curriculum Development, an N.E.A. affiliate, has national, state,

---

[5] T. M. Stinnett, *The Teacher and Professional Organizations* (Washington, D.C.: National Commission on Teacher Education and Standards, The National Education Association, 1956), p. 40.

and local components. Also, each state has a counterpart of the N.E.A. at the state level: for example, the Iowa Education Association or the Kentucky Education Association. The primary group at the local level is usually the city or county teachers' association which has in-service growth as its major purpose. This and other purposes are listed by Stinnett and associates as follows:

1. To provide teachers with a medium for the study of their own problems.
2. To provide a means for the exchange of ideas among teachers.
3. To develop common aims and staff morale.
4. To provide a medium by which teachers are enabled to participate in the formation of policies for the local school system.
5. To provide opportunities for self-development and the exercise of initiative and leadership.
6. To provide a means for the improvement of the professional, economic, social, and civic status of teachers.
7. To help improve classroom procedures.
8. To promote cooperation for the improvement of the community and school.
9. To stimulate professional enthusiasm, initiative, and spirit.
10. To provide a local organization to support and influence state and national programs.
11. To foster a spirit of fellowship among members thru social and recreational activities.
12. To help in the orientation of the beginning teacher.[6]

More specific than the organizations which cut across the various levels of teaching are those which provide leadership in the individual subject-matter areas. Selected ones are as follows:

1. American Association for Health, Physical Education and Recreation, Washington, D.C.
2. American Federation of Modern Language Teachers Associations, Ann Arbor, Mich.
3. American Home Economics Association, Washington, D.C.
4. American Industrial Arts Association, Washington, D.C.
5. American Vocational Association, Washington, D.C.
6. Music Educators National Conference, Washington, D.C.
7. National Art Education Association, Washington, D.C.
8. National Association of Journalism Directors of Secondary Schools, Washington, D.C.
9. National Business Education Association, Washington, D.C.
10. National Business Teachers Association, Bloomington, Ind.
11. National Council for the Social Studies, Washington, D.C.
12. National Council of Teachers of English, Champaign, Ill.
13. National Council of Teachers of Mathematics, Washington, D.C.
14. National Science Teachers Association, Washington, D.C.
15. Speech Association of America, Washington, D.C.

These specialized associations have annual or semiannual meetings; publish a journal, usually monthly, containing descriptions of curriculum

[6] *Ibid.,* p. 65. Reprinted by permission.

innovations and current practices; and, in general, exercise a leadership function over those teachers who share a common teaching field.

Another organization that merits comment because of the sizable number of teachers that it affects is the American Federation of Teachers, formulated in 1916 as an affiliate of the American Federation of Labor. Its membership today is around 50,000. Its official organ is *The American Teacher*. Like any union, its mission is to protect members from exploitation by the various levels of management and to raise working standards. Unlike other unions, it cannot call a strike of its members.

The A.F.T. is growing in stature largely because the collective body of teachers has been too disorganized, fearful, or indifferent to set its own house in order. As long as the one million teachers and administrators continue either to exist without a professional organization similar to A.M.A. in the medical profession, or without enough self-discipline to fight abuses and excesses without the aid of such a body, unionism will continue to prosper. The issue is not the desirability of unions in general; it is rather the desirability of unions within the ranks of a service group which approximates the status of a profession. Consensus among leading educators is that teachers should shed their timidity and work more militantly for improvement directly within their own ranks. However, that the A.F.T. has improved the status of teaching in many school systems is not open to argument.

The benefits of professional memberships

Although having alluded several times to the benefits accruing to teachers who belong to one or more professional organizations, we now wish to face the advantages directly. The primary bonus is the involvement of teachers in problems and issues of common interest and concern. The individual who remains outside the arena of organizational activity invariably achieves less growth than his counterpart who assumes some direct responsibility for the affairs of teaching. The latter brings to the collective group an attitude of, "There is professional work to be done, and I can contribute to the cause." Like the maturing person described in Chapter 1, he is willing and eager to unfold his horizons outward. In the group process, when he and his colleagues face up realistically to the shortcomings both within themselves and in the larger organization of teachers, they are well on their way to correcting the uncovered defects.

Even if an occasional teacher as a single individual profits less than he desires from organizational activities, he should continue to participate collectively for the greater effectiveness of the total educational body. If too many teachers had "gone it alone" during the past century, classes might still be held in the little red schoolhouse, Greek and Latin might still dominate the curriculum, and the National Educational Association might still be an infant. The concern of the teacher, at least in part, should be, "Which of my talents can I give to the profession to make it better?" The more each teacher gives, the higher will be the standards of professional selection, the effectiveness of the incumbents, and the quality of the student product!

In omission of such other benefits as defense of teachers against unjust attacks, coordination with governmental agencies, and teacher welfare in general, we move to the professional journals of the various associations. These, as previously stated, are the printed organs which usually accompany membership in the general or special-interest groups. One of them, *The Science Teacher,* will be analyzed briefly for the sake of illustration.

This journal is the spokesman of The National Science Teachers Association, a department of the N.E.A., founded in 1895. A regular membership costing $6.00 yearly entitles one to receive *The Science Teacher* monthly. It is directed at teachers of grades 7 through 12 and includes articles in the fields of general science, health education, biology, physics, physical science, and non-academic biology.

The October, 1961, issue (Vol. 28, No. 6) contains the following sections of interest to science teachers:

1. A series of articles with selected titles such as "Microrelief on the Sea Floor," "Teaching Genetics with Flannelgraphs," "Study of High School Physics Achievement," and "Atomic Arrangement in Solids."
2. Extensive advertising of books and science paraphernalia of various kinds: microscopes, decanters, models, projectors, weather instruments, and films.
3. A description of recent activities of the Association.
4. Book reviews of texts and general references.
5. Briefs on science teaching materials and methods.
6. Recommendations for professional reading.

Like the journals of the other subject-matter fields, *The Science Teacher* helps the interested teacher keep up to date in the area of his specialty. The worth of such a medium is inestimable. The periodicals of the various professional associations, even when unsupported by other benefits, are probably justification enough in themselves for the continued existence of the organizations which they represent.

Of significance is the prevalence of teachers who belong to one or more professional associations without being active. This lethargy may emanate from the individual himself or from an over-zealous administrator who high-pressures teachers to join, thereby dulling or destroying the spontaneous interest of teachers and the virility of the organization.

While suggesting that teacher candidates resist unethical attempts at coercion, we urge them to become affiliated with those professional societies that will facilitate their growth. The lowest denominator of membership probably should be in the National Education Association and the association which serves their special-interest needs.

THE TEACHER CITIZEN

Implicit throughout this discussion of the many functions of the teacher has been the tacit realization that, regardless of the true nature of his professional responsibilities, the teacher also is a private citizen. In his professional role, he is expected to be the composite of such characteristics as scholarliness, diplomacy, empathy, morality, philanthropy, and dedication. Ideal though this composite may be, it is not unrepresentative of society's aspirations for teachers. With such a weight of professional expectancy hanging tightly over him, can he ever be just plain John Q. Citizen: a husband, father, lodge member, part-time politician, social reformer, or, maybe, agnostic? Just how much can he be a citizen unencumbered by middle-class stereotyping?

Is his predicament similar to that of the rabbi, priest, or minister, who is expected to play a part almost wherever he is? Or does he have the greater freedom of a businessman to live his office life in one way and his home life, after work hours, in another?

The ethics of the teaching profession

A partial answer to the above questions may be supplied by the teaching profession itself. While lacking a sanctioned code of ethics, the profession has adopted informally the code prepared by the National Education Association, excerpts of which follow.[7]

CODE OF ETHICS for the TEACHING PROFESSION

WE, THE MEMBERS of the National Education Association of the United States, hold these truth to be self-evident—

—that the primary purpose of education in the United States is to develop citizens who will safeguard, strengthen, and improve the democracy obtained through a representative government;

—that the achievement of effective democracy in all aspects of American life and the maintenance of our national ideals depend upon making acceptable educational opportunities available to all;

—that the quality of education reflects the ideals, motives, preparation, and conduct of the members of the teaching profession;

—that whoever chooses teaching as a career assumes the obligation to conduct himself in accordance with the ideals of the profession.

As a guide for the teaching profession, the members of the National Education Association have adopted this code of professional ethics. Since all

[7] The National Education Association, "Code of Ethics for the Teaching Profession," *N.E.A. Handbook* (Washington, D.C.: 1957–1958), pp. 62–64. Reprinted by permission.

teachers should be members of a united profession, the basic principles herein enumerated apply to all persons engaged in the professional aspects of education—elementary, secondary, and collegiate.

First Principle: The primary obligation of the teaching profession is to guide children, youth, and adults in the pursuit of knowledge and skills, to prepare them in the ways of democracy, and to help them to become happy, useful, self-supporting citizens. The ultimate strength of the nation lies in the social responsibility, economic competence, and moral strength in the individual American.

.   .   .

Second Principle: The members of the teaching profession share with parents the task of shaping each student's purposes and acts toward socially acceptable ends. The effectiveness of many methods of teaching is dependent upon cooperative relationships with the home.

.   .   .

Third Principle: The teaching profession occupies a position of public trust involving not only the individual teacher's personal conduct, but also the interaction of the school and the community. Education is most effective when these many relationships operate in a friendly, cooperative, and constructive manner.

In fulfilling the obligations of this third principle the teacher will—

1. Adhere to any reasonable pattern of behavior accepted by the community for professional persons.

2. Perform the duties of citizenship, and participate in community activities with due consideration for his obligations to his students, his family, and himself.

3. Discuss controversial issues from an objective point of view, thereby keeping his class free from partisan opinions.

4. Recognize that the public schools belong to the people of the community, encourage lay participation in shaping the purposes of the school, and strive to keep the public informed of the educational program which is being provided.

5. Respect the community in which he is employed and be loyal to the school system, community, state and nation.

6. Work to improve education in the community and to strengthen the community's moral, spiritual, and intellectual life.

.   .   .

Fifth Principle: The teaching profession is distinguished from many other occupations by the uniqueness and quality of the professional relationships among all teachers. Community support and respect are influenced by the standards of teachers and their attitudes toward teaching and other teachers.

The above selections, although directed primarily at teacher behavior in the school milieu, contain a few specific allusions to the teacher as a citizen. The preamble to the *PRINCIPLES* states in forthright terms that the teacher "assumes the obligation to conduct himself in accordance with the ideals of the profession." The *Third Principle* is just as unequivocal in its insistence that the teacher "Adhere to any reasonable pattern of behavior accepted by the community for professional persons." The significance of these passages is their obvious reference to teachers as members of a profession with an associated obligation to wear their professional robes with dignity. The code assigns to teachers the same responsibilities to conform to reasonable social norms as society assigns to physicians, lawyers, dentists, and clergymen.

Legal demands on teachers

Supporting the Code, which admittedly is only a diffused influence, is statutory law. In this regard, almost every state has made some sort of statutory declaration on the expected conduct of teachers. For example, Alabama lists "immorality or immoral conduct" as justifiable causes of dismissal. California similarly lists "unprofessional conduct, immorality or immoral conduct, conviction of any crime involving moral turpitude." In like manner, Valusia County, Florida, considers as reason for dismissal "habitual use of alcohol"; Louisiana, "dishonesty"; Massachusetts, "conduct unbecoming a teacher"; and Missouri and Montana, "violation of laws."[8]

The unresolved issue in the several laws cited is the degree of offending necessary to result in dismissal. For instance, in Missouri, how many laws have to be violated? Is speeding for the first time sufficient? In any of the 24 states which consider immorality a just cause for not extending tenure, just what constitutes immorality? None defines the term. And in the few statutes that regard intemperance as grounds for suspicion, would a state of intoxication in the confines of one's home fall within the confines of the law?

The sheer vagueness of legal wording may indicate a liberalizing of society's attitude toward teacher deportment. In most instances, this unwillingness or inability to define limits results in an emphasis on excesses of negative behavior, not on occasional violations.

Another positive feature of educational legislation during the past several decades is its insistence that teachers not be dismissed for political, religious, or marital reasons. The law, in reality, takes a stand almost identical with that of the profession itself: it demands that the teacher take his service responsibilities seriously and that his private life not be permitted to act as an obstacle. The relation of law to the teacher in the school environs will be discussed in the next chapter.

The influences of a local community

Although influenced in varying degrees by professional codes and statutory legislation, the teacher invariably must define his teacher-citizen role in the context of the mores and expectations of a local community. The process usually involves a modest compromise between his values and

[8] Research Division, National Education Association, *Research Monograph 1959–M3* (Washington, D.C.: 1959), pp. 37–39.

those of the locale. The reconciliation of differences by necessity must be within a fairly narrow range of variance, because neither party to the contractual relationship should be expected to concede significant values. Too much concession leads to ultimate disenchantment by either the school system or the teacher.

It is important, then, that a prospective teacher investigate a community before signing a contract to teach there. The greatest freedom of action is usually provided by the suburban school system in which such practices as social drinking and the defense of sometimes even radical points of view are accepted with little or no question. Almost as much freedom is permitted in the large-city position, although for a different reason; in this situation, the teacher usually lives far enough from the school to have a private life set apart from the job. The small towns and rural areas are probably the most restrictive of teacher freedom, but even these are more liberal than formerly, when such actions as card-playing, non-church attendance, and smoking by female teachers were catalogued as social evils.

Fortunately for society as a whole and for teachers specifically, the extremely conservative demands upon public servants are mostly throwbacks to the past. As recently as 1928, however, male teachers in Kansas City were forbidden to smoke, and even more recently, gambling in the rural South was tantamount to asking for dismissal. Other social practices and mores accepted almost universally today, according to Beale, were tabooed a quarter-century ago: for example, divorce, marriage, late hours, not participating in worthwhile community causes, weekends away from the town, not teaching Sunday School, dancing, campaigning for a political party, and trying to organize a teachers' union.[9]

With few exceptions, the teacher-citizen has broad latitude in determining the private-social role that he will play outside school hours. Our personal fear is not so much that teachers will be denied the privilege of participating in the many activities that citizens in general accept as their birthright, as that, because of minor pressures, they will hesitate to assume the mature roles of effective citizenship. If an unprincipled ward-heeler is permitted to influence others with his political opinions, can a well-informed teacher in his private life be denied the same right?

The issue of social action has become controversial in today's world. Extreme religious elements are willing to rest their case on the hereafter, washing their hands of responsibility for the here and now. More liberally oriented groups of socially conscious individuals are dedicated to putting their philosophy to work to help solve some of the problems of this world: poverty, disease, corruption in politics, colonialism, and war.

Social action is also an issue to be faced by teachers. Individuals who

[9] Howard K. Beale, *Are American Teachers Free?* (New York: Charles Scribner's Sons, 1936), pp. 381–397.

are responsible for bad government, the exploitation of minorities, free enterprise which knows no limits, the myth of ultra-nationalism at the sacrifice of other values, and intimidation of those who wish to fight corruption are anxious that the schoolteacher and the social worker who have their eyes on today's problems do nothing which might upset the *status quo*. In opposition, we suggest that the teacher never permit himself to be so hemmed in by a local code of behavior that he becomes powerless to play a citizenship role vigorously and courageously. Teachers must do more than lecture to students on controversial subjects if some of the critical world issues are to be resolved.

Regarding teacher independence, of importance is the growing tendency of courts to support teachers in their progress toward freedom. Tenure has helped to place the burden of proof on the plaintiff when the behavior of a teacher is in question. But, regardless of social and legal forces that bolster a teacher and enhance his prestige, the candidate who has received a job offer should investigate thoroughly the social and professional expectancies of the school and community. If significant change is required of either party to the prospective contract, one or both should reconsider.

The professional teacher of today should be permitted, within reasonable limits, to live a normal life. It should be his decision whether he goes to church or not, smokes off the school grounds, participates in a political rally, or suns in appropriate attire in his backyard. Still highly controversial is the advisability of a teacher's tutoring for pay a student whom he has in his class or of working nights in the local liquor store. Legitimate grounds for dismissal are considered universally to be frequent inebriation in public, sexual immorality, and other behavior that is far removed from an accepted societal code. For the most part, however, proof, not hearsay, is demanded of accusers; and when in doubt, courts tend to rule in favor of the teacher, not the accuser.

A WORD TO THE TEACHER CANDIDATE

Whether the teacher candidate who has read this chapter agrees with the manner in which the position of teacher has been divided is relatively immaterial. It *is* important that he regard the teacher's role as complex.

In this day of heavy demand for and short supply of teachers, at least a few candidates seem to regard teaching as a relatively undemanding process that lasts from 8:30 A.M. to 3:30 P.M. five days per week, forty weeks per year. The Christmas holidays and spring and summer vacations further encourage the escape to unreality. Candidates should envision teaching as it actually is. It rarely ends when the eighth-period bell rings, for the work that is started in school is more often than not continued in the home.

Individuals who are preparing for teaching therefore should make a realistic job appraisal before they accept a position. If willing to do classroom teaching and perform the many other jobs that are inherent in the total teaching role, they have an excellent chance to succeed. But if the guidance role, administrative duties, co-curricular activities, and organizational obligations are "for other teachers" but not for the job applicant, he might well reconsider his choice of career. Teaching, not routine and undemanding, is more often taxing but satisfying.

SUMMARY

The position of teacher has been described in this chapter as many-sided. The most obvious side, and the only one seen by many observers, is that which places the teacher in classroom contact with pupils. The other roles of the teacher, with which the casual observer is unacquainted, are those which relate to guidance, school administration, the co-curriculum, professional teacher organizations, ethics, and good citizenship.

The twofold and often conflicting roles of teacher and ordinary citizen were discussed at some length. The point of view expressed was that the two roles are merging more and more into one, and that the social narrowness of school boards and society itself is gradually, even rapidly, disappearing.

REFERENCES

Anderson, Vernon E., Paul R. Grim, and Wm. T. Gruhn, *Principles and Practices of Secondary Education.* New York: The Ronald Press Co., Inc., 1951. (Chapters 19–20)

Alexander, Wm. M., and Paul Halverson, *Effective Teaching in Secondary Schools.* New York: Holt, Rinehart and Winston, 1956. (Chapter 16)

Beale, Howard K., *Are American Teachers Free?* New York: Charles Scribner's Sons, 1936.

Bent, Rudyart K., and Henry H. Kronenberg, *Principles of Secondary Education.* New York: McGraw-Hill Book Co., 1955. (Chapter 17)

Brown, Edwin J., and Arthur T. Phelps, *Managing the Classroom.* New York: The Ronald Press Co., Inc., 1961.

Grambs, Jean D., Wm. J. Iverson, and Franklin K. Patterson, *Modern Methods in Secondary Education.* New York: Holt, Rinehart and Winston (rev. ed.), 1958. (Chapter 22)

Hansen, Kenneth, *High School Teaching*. Englewood Cliffs, N.J.: Prentice-Hall, Inc., 1957. (Chapter 14)

Macomber, Freeman G., *Teaching in the Secondary School*. New York: McGraw-Hill Book Co., 1952. (Chapter 14)

National Education Association, *National Education Association Handbook for Local, State, and National Associations*. Washington, D.C.: N.E.A., 1952.

National Education Association, *Report of the Professional Ethics Commission*. Washington, D.C.: N.E.A., 1957–1958.

Risk, Thomas M., *Principles and Practices of Teaching in Secondary Schools*. New York: American Book Co. (3rd ed.), 1958. (Chapter 3)

Spears, Harold, *The High School for Today*. New York: American Book Co., 1950. (Chapters 13 and 15)

Stinnett, T. M., *The Teacher and Professional Organizations*. Washington, D.C.: Hugh Birch–Horace Mann Fund (N.E.A.), 1953.

Thut, I. N., and J. Raymond Gerberich, *Foundations of Method for Secondary Schools*. New York: McGraw-Hill Book Co., 1949. (Chapter 20)

METHOD
AND
ITS
SETTING

The subject of method, to this point, has been approached indirectly: first through the individuality of the teacher, then through the many functions that constitute his role. Regarding the former, emphasis has been placed on the teacher's personality, which in childhood initially centers around the self and progressively bends outward into an expanding horizon of people-centered values. In other words, secondary education needs teachers of breadth. They should be intellectual but not one-sided intellectualists; interested in others but not at the sacrifice of themselves as individuals; integrated personalities but not at the expense of specialized trait development. The necessity of such breadth has its origin in the growing preoccupation of secondary education with the totality of the student. Inversely stated, with the program of the school becoming many-sided, the one-sidedness in teachers is a luxury that cannot be justified.

Assuming a school system with teachers who satisfy the professional expectations mentioned, how much freedom will they have in selecting method? Conversely, what forces and influences within the school and community environment will be operating as restraints? To oversimplify, teachers as a collective body have a greater range of choice than the typical candidate would suspect but a narrower range than the rugged teacher individualist might consider desirable. As public servants operating within professional-legal bounds, teachers are obligated to conform to the reasonable expectancies of society, but the restrictions are far from stifling.

Before we discuss the specific forces that limit teacher freedom, however, a few definitions are in order. These will be followed by an introductory statement on teaching method.

A CONTEXT FOR METHOD

Pedagogical terms are subject to a variety of interpretations. We therefore propose a few operating definitions.

Teaching is any organized activity related to planning, initiating, sustaining, and/or evaluating a learning environment.

Method (in the singular) is the composite or combination of means whereby a learning situation is initiated or sustained.

Methods (in the plural) are the various individual means whereby a learning situation is initiated or sustained. These run the gamut from the formal lecture to informal homework, from individual teacher performance to committee activity in a group, from strictly assigned work to the student's freely selected activities.

Learning is the modification of behavior resulting from the dynamic interaction of the individual and his environment. The goal of all learning is change in the person.

Subject matter is a body of organized content consisting of the basic skills of learning, information about the past and present, attitudes toward such information, the esthetics, physical development, and the creative extension of all of these. Its purpose is the insight of students into themselves and the universe. As students acquire these skills, information, and development, truth emerges as a value; distortion, bias, and unwarranted prejudice are revealed as blockages to truth.

Inherent in these definitions is the recognition that teaching involves many stages of planning as well as the more obvious activities of the classroom; that method is designed to economize the process of learning; and that learning itself is directed at change. These are a far cry from teaching conceived as an activity whereby one who knows more imparts his greater knowledge to one who knows less; and from learning conceived primarily as the absorbing by a student of the teacher's ideas and attitudes.

In actuality, a triangular relationship exists among the learner, teaching method, and subject-matter content. The learner undeniably is the focal point of the three; in fact, he is the only *raison d'être* of the other two. Content serves by liberating and providing insight; and method, by making learning more economical and thorough. The individual outside of a formal educational setting could achieve most curriculum outcomes, but the process would be shamefully wasteful of time and energy.

Probably a better term than *teaching method* is *learning method,* which properly places more emphasis on the consumer and his achievement, and less on the overt efforts of the teacher. The latter, then, in addition to being a transmitter of knowledge and a perpetuator of a heritage, is a learning engineer who works with, not over, students. He establishes the broad boundaries for educational involvement, tailors method to both the pupils and the educational design, and then guides the process as it unfolds.

The teacher may be likened to parents who desire their child to increase his reading speed and comprehension. While making frontal assaults on the problem by planned-help sessions, they supplement such formal efforts by less direct methods. Through travel, the parents make abstract symbols come alive for the child; through discussions, they encourage him to listen and speak more fluently; through exposure to a home library of eye-catching and meaningful reading materials, they heighten his motivation. In the long run, the subtle approaches conceivably accomplish as much as, or more than, the planned methods.

The instructional leader involved in the educational enterprise has almost innumerable choices of method from which to select: the lecture, discussion, group reading in class, silent reading in or out of class, panels, committees, symposiums, recitations, homework activity, research, written projects, laboratory experiments, individual oral reports, films, recordings, and many more. To augment and amplify the specific media, he can utilize the library, replete with reference materials; course syllabi and curriculum guides from other high schools; the surrounding community as a source of guest speakers and field-trip possibilities; and professional organizations.

The teacher's major responsibility is the selection of those media that have the greatest likelihood of success. As a teacher-engineer, he experiments in and evaluates the effectiveness of the many avenues of learning at his disposal. His criterion is always the growth of adolescents, whose abilities, interests, and aspirations vary widely.

The engineering comparison is capsuled quite well by Bernice Baxter, whose remarks, although directed at elementary teachers, are equally applicable to high school practitioners.

It is evident that to-day's education requires the teacher to be the informed, well-integrated, and far-seeing adult member of a children's community. It is no longer enough that the teacher be the possessor of knowledge. To-day's teacher must be a "social-engineer" capable of setting up a provocative environment for children's learning, charting the course of each individual child through the ever-changing social relationships in which he is involved and assisting each pupil to grow in his understanding of himself and of others. American education prescribes further that the teacher be responsible for teaching children to respect the personalities of others and for teaching them to work and play co-operatively with others under restrictions and privileges established and maintained by majority will.

The challenge to education and to teachers as outlined is one of great magnitude. The general preparation for such teaching requirements should be broad. The teacher needs a liberal education and should be both a student of the world's culture and a student of the sciences, particularly of those sciences which afford insight into human behavior and growth. Teaching requires scholarship, mental ability, and genuine delight in the pursuit of knowledge, but above all else, teaching demands a human being who is capable of establishing rapport with children and who personally is worthy to be an influencing factor in the environment in which children are growing and to which they are reacting.[1]

Teaching is never simple or predictable. Its certainties are change, spontaneity, and, at times, emergency. But the position of the teacher becomes more challenging as a result of the many-directional cross fire. If this picture of the job of teacher is not in harmony with the stereotype, our experience leads to a defense of the portrayal. In brief, the adolescent in the secondary school should be absorbed by a stimulating curriculum which, with the aid of effective teaching method, helps him acquire desirable skills, meaningful knowledge, esthetic appreciations, and defensible attitudes. These should then lead to better self-understanding, to higher life values, and consequently to changes in behavior which conform to the newly acquired insights.

FACTORS THAT INFLUENCE METHOD

Against this orientation, we return to the question: To what extent will teachers have freedom in their choice of method? Although far from being hemmed in by restrictions, they will be delimited mildly or much by the factors identified and discussed in the remainder of the chapter.

The goals of learning

A major determinant not only of curriculum content but of teaching method is the goals of secondary education, which are conceived in varying dimensions and implemented in different ways throughout the country. That the high school as a unit, or even educators themselves, have not formulated and rallied around a precise set of objectives should not be surprising to the thinking reader. The reasons for this difference among objectives are basically twofold.

First of all, although education legally is a function of each state, operationally it is under the day-to-day control of each local community.

---

[1] Bernice Baxter, *Teacher-Pupil Relationships* (New York: The Macmillan Company, 1941), pp. 7–8. Reprinted by permission.

And with communities disagreeing often dramatically in their expectations and demands, educational goals are bound to run a wide gamut of difference. Despite the superstructure of control at the state level, extensive latitude is permitted at the local level.

A second reason for the dissimilarity of goals is that education, like the nation as a whole, does not conceive universal purposes and values in the same way. If a major goal of education is to perpetuate what the United States is and what it has been, education then needs be directed at those methods which will lead to an acceptance of the existing conditions, but not necessarily to critical evaluation. But if a primary purpose is change in society, a passive knowing about the past and present is only preliminary to the more arduous process of appraisal and then change.

Similarly, if education's almost exclusive concern is with the cognitive, the secondary school should deal only lightly, if at all, with emotional growth, social development, and the development of attitudes. These latter needs might be supportive of such a goal but never primary. On the other hand, if secondary education conceives its purpose in the mental-health framework, method must be directed at the emotional, physical, social, and ethical as well as the cognitive.

The two following situations are presented by way of illustration. Miss Roberts, a teacher of literature, is a classical scholar in the philosophical idealist traditions. She believes that the great minds and great ideas of the Occidental World are the straight and narrow road to education. Counseling, the practical arts, and the co-curriculum she refers to as "frills." Her choice of method is relatively uncomplicated: all adolescents are assigned certain classics to be read, she conducts discussion-drill sessions on the content, examines, and then moves on to another classic. Such conditions as the poor reading habits of a few, the limited range of comprehension among many, with the resulting frustrations, and excessive homework might give her some concern but not enough to redirect her from the preconceived goal.

In contrast, Mr. Sellers believes that secondary education exists to prepare young people to live, not just to think and to know. He is concerned over such facts as: that 55 per cent of all hospital beds are occupied by neurotic and psychotic patients; that the majority of individuals in business and industry who lose their jobs do so because of personality deficiencies; and that integrity among nations and national leaders is not universally regarded as a virtue. These and other social, ethical, and emotional phenomena give him pause when he relates them to his classroom. They lead him to get better acquainted with individual pupils as a first step in determining what curriculum content might best serve their needs. They lead to such other outcomes as encouraging pupils to share responsibilities so that they will learn to integrate better with others; reducing the load occasionally for the student whose tolerance level is temporarily low; assigning work that will challenge each child but not over- or under-challenge any; and maintaining an awareness of moral as well as intellectual growth.

Since the goals of learning are indistinct in the general-welfare clause of the Constitution, since they are more administratively than functionally conceived at the state level, and since they are usually prescribed only broadly at the local level, it is a responsibility of the individual teacher to formulate his own specific objectives of education. Although working within an area of some prescription, his operational radius will nevertheless be considerable. And the goals, when developed, will serve as invaluable radar guides for method.

School policy

Not unrelated to, but more specific than, objectives as an influence on teaching method is school policy. School policy, being forged from the broad goals, thus bears their stamp, but is usually more specific. An objective might be the achievement of independence by pupils, whereas the associated policy might include an adolescent-oriented student council for the employment of independence. Specific instances of the close relationship between school policy and method are contained in the following examples. In each, a school policy (S.P.) is identified, followed by some possible implications for method. (I.M.)

1. S.P. Examinations are to achieve honor status when individual teachers believe that students in specified classrooms are ready for such freedom.
   I.M. To help determine when examinations should be placed on an honor basis, the teacher conceivably would extend freedom slowly at first and then progressively faster as students give evidences of maturing emotionally and ethically. To accelerate the process, he would engage in some of the following methods or activities: have the adolescents discuss the proposed action, facing the problem of ethical and moral values; give them increasing opportunities to engage in student-led activities, such as committee projects, school drives, and determination of classroom policy; leave the room on occasions and then discuss how well they accepted the projected responsibility for their actions; and work toward consensus whenever possible. The important constituent here is that teachers would have to employ methods specifically designed to harmonize with the announced policy.

2. S.P. Teachers of slow-learning homogeneous classes can give grades no higher than an occasional C; more often, only D's and F's.
   I.M. The grading system would have to be explained and then de-emphasized lest morale degenerate. More than ever, teachers would need to breathe interest into the curriculum so that its vitality would motivate students despite the grading policy. Learning would also need the reinforcement of close teacher-student relationships, soliciting for purposes of increased growth the support of social relations.

3. S.P. Report cards are to be sent home monthly instead of the usual time of every six weeks.
   I.M. Teachers would probably give more written work and examinations to provide an objective-looking defense for the more frequently given grade symbols.

4. S.P. Teachers must be out of the building by 3:45 so that the janitors can "lock up."
   I.M. Counseling, help sessions, and retention of students after school hours for guidance and academic purposes are methods that would be denied the teacher.

5. S.P. Final-examination grades must be turned in to the "front office" 24 hours after the day of the examination.
   I.M. Teachers would be inclined to give objective instead of essay-type examinations.

6. S.P. The administration frowns on teachers who send students to the principal for disciplinary infractions.
   I.M. Teachers would be inclined to study students more closely in the classroom, analyze clinical data about them in the guidance office, have more personal interviews with pupils and parents, and heighten the interest of the curriculum as a preventive measure.

7. S.P. Silence in the classroom is insisted on as a sound basis for learning.
   I.M. Heated give-and-take discussions, preparation for committee work, and other types of group activity would be tabooed methods. The resulting tension might eventuate in an occasional emotional explosion when the teacher leaves the room.

Method, far from being isolated from school policy, must join hands with it in conformance with a predetermined set of objectives. When the two are discordant, objectives are sabotaged or the teacher lives behind a façade; neither is a wanted outcome. It is necessary, then, that a teacher investigate school policy before accepting a position, and that a school system hire teachers only when acquainted with them as personal and professional individuals.

Leaving specific policy dictums for more broadly conceived policy influences, the question is raised regarding the impact of a curriculum guide on method. In the typical city, such a guide or syllabus is prepared by a committee consisting usually of several teachers in the specific field of interest, a principal, and a curriculum specialist. In the smaller systems, a department will often prepare its own guide.

Regardless of how the document comes into being, to what extent does it serve as a dictator of method? Although student candidates regularly seem to fear its impress on their future, on-the-job teachers, in the experience of the author, report that its influence on method is minimal; that on curriculum content, it is considerable but not excessive. For the most part, the syllabus establishes what will be covered in a semester or year, but rarely settles how such coverage will be made.

For instance, the typical guide in biology contains a proposal that the cardio-vascular system of the human being be included as part of the course content. It usually provides additional detail about what organic and functional aspects of the cardio-vascular system are to be covered: for example, the heart with its many parts, the blood vessels, the ducts, and the blood itself, along with their many life-giving and life-sustaining purposes. But rarely is the guide so prescriptive as to instruct a teacher to spend a specific amount of time on the unit, and almost never does it suggest, much less insist, that specific methods be employed in the teaching of the cardio-vascular system. It might recommend that the Denoyer-Geppert or some other model of the human heart be utilized, but such a suggestion would be more a helpful recommendation than a mandate.

Instead of fearing the possible adverse impact of a curriculum guide on method, the teacher candidate more logically should be apprehensive when such a teaching support is nonexistent. Its intent and effect are almost uniformly positive, and it tends to provide systematic structure without unduly circumscribing the creative teacher. Occasionally a written curriculum guide may have a claustrophobic effect on the users; more routinely, it will be a foundation for effective instruction.

The pupils

Along with educational goals and school policy as controlling factors of method are the pupils themselves. Although later chapters will embrace more comprehensively the topics of individual differences and motivation, it is pertinent at this point to recognize that the response of adolescents to teaching method is a function of their total personalities. The maturation levels, the unique interests, the abilities, and the home backgrounds that accompany youth to school unmistakably influence the methods that a teacher selects to guide their growth.

Degrees of maturation vary from almost the infantile emotional behavior exhibited by a few to the near-adult behavior of the many, from painful reticence to social competence, from physical latency to near-maturity, and from mental retardation to precociousness. The teacher attuned to these differences selects methods which conform. When working with the emotionally immature, he employs many different methods in response to such cues as the growing restlessness of individuals or the group, obvious irritability, or withdrawal. When working with the emotionally mature, he can employ a single method for a longer period without loss of interest. When associated with a socially advanced class, he can utilize more effectively such methods as committees, panels, round tables, and give-and-take discussions.

The interests of pupils likewise interact with method. And in this regard, the interlocking relationship between interest and effort is a phenomenon that cannot be ignored without some sacrifice of learning's potential. Whether the adolescent brings interest to, or is helped to discover it in, the learning situation, the classroom instructor is indeed insensitive who fails to capitalize on this component.

Nor does his approach have to be particularly subtle. In a geometry class where athletes predominate, two-dimensional space configurations can be profitably related to the local football field, a big-league baseball stadium, or the school's outdoor track. In a social studies class in a rural community, such topics as subsidies, soil conservation, supply and demand, and earned income can be made more vital by at least an initial focus on their local application. Or in a physics class of whatever location, such topics as heat, electricity, and pressure can be integrated into the immediate environment.

Particularly in the field of counseling are the immediate interests of students an important pathway to rapport. Adolescents are often apprehensive in the initial stages of an interview, but they can be put at ease with passing references to their personal interests or activities, for instance, a 4-H contribution at the county fair, a vocal performance at a musicale, a key basket in an intramural game, or a favorite author.

And if instructional practices are, in part, an outgrowth of student interests, they are likewise a function of student abilities. This relationship will be touched on only lightly here, however, in deference to its more detailed development later in Chapters 10 and 11. Fundamentally, the problem is one of the slow learner versus the fast learner. Of common knowledge to teachers is the fact that slow-learning students respond to instructional situations differently—not in a completely different but in a somewhat different manner—from their brighter counterparts, with the result that teaching method must of necessity reflect the differential responses. The slow learner, more often than not, is relatively non-verbal, short in attention span, and more disinterested in school than the more gifted student.

With the slow learner responding only with great effort, if at all, to a typical curriculum geared to the verbal level of the average and bright, the teacher must in some way provide learning experiences that are within reach of the slow. This outcome may be achieved in several ways: by changing the substance of learning content, by slowing the pace of instruction conducted at the verbal level, or by reinforcing abstract learning richly with the concrete.

The content of the curriculum can be changed for the slow student in two ways. As one method, it can be channeled from the academic subjects of English, social studies, science, mathematics, and foreign languages to the manual or esthetic subjects in the content areas of the industrial arts, shop, business education, music, and art programs. Without rejecting this alternative in all instances, we object to it as a universal solution because the absence of academic interests and abilities does not necessarily reflect countering manipulative and esthetic interests and abilities. As a second method, within the framework of the academic program itself, changes can be made so that the slow learner is provided with more appropriate learning materials, is taught at a more moderate pace, and is introduced to more concrete methods of understanding the abstract.

This second alternative we underwrite. Within its framework, learning tasks must be at different qualitative levels—not just be fewer in number. Thus, the slow learner, instead of being made to read fewer pages of Faulkner, should read a literary work more at his level of comprehension. And even when the literary substitution has been made, the length of assignments and the pace of learning should be reduced. And, finally, the more abstract the content, the more it should be reinforced by concrete experiences.

The beginning teacher often has difficulty in bringing learning to a basis of concretion, particularly if he teaches the academic subjects. It is easy for him to understand how the teacher of the industrial arts, fine arts, and home economics or shop programs can make learning functional, but it is not easy for him to envision a similar resultant in the fields of the academic subjects. Fundamentally, learning in the concrete is a figurative as well as literal term, and therefore it is capable of application to the academic as well as the non-academic subjects. In reality, it is synonymous with bringing learning to the most basic level. In a shop program, this level might be the detailed examination of an electric motor, the making of a wood cabinet, or the operation of an electric saw. Through the several senses of seeing, feeling, and hearing, the student would make contact with reality.

In the academic subjects, the counterparts to multi-dimensional concretions would be the verbal examples and illustrations employed by a teacher or students to endow concepts, ideas, or attitudes with richer meaning. For example, the term "psychological self" is a vague concept to many college students, but when associated with such near-synonyms as the *psyche, ego,* or *spirit,* it takes on greater meaning. Then when further identified with that part of the self that "wants to be omniscient," "expects to be successful," "dislikes one's figure," "fears adults," or "dreads meeting strangers," its vividness is increased. Next, when the concept is related to individuals, real or fictional, who conceive and project their psychological selves in a unique way, it moves a step closer to reality. Finally, when the process of understanding leads to an actual analysis by students of themselves and others, then only will learning have arrived at a level of true insight.

The bright student is as deserving as the slow student of specialized method. If bored when required to remain unduly long in the area of the basic skills or elementary learning concepts, he needs course content that will be geared to his level and teaching method which likewise harmonizes. His is the type of personality that demands challenge, that insists on the right to question and even contradict accepted dogma, and that thrives on creativity. Over-arching all of his other qualities is a hunger for the abstract. For instance, the accelerated adolescent would respond to the sophistication of a *Don Quixote,* perceiving both its philosophical and its satirical import; in contrast to the slower learner, who would probably see little beyond the level of the overt humor of windmills, a faithful squire, a bony nag, and the "appealing" Dulcinea. The bright student would welcome the opportunity to move into such "greats" of literature as Goethe, Machiavelli, Dostoevski, Tolstoi, Balzac, and Ibsen. Such excursions would provide him with a much-needed stimulus for analysis and creativity.

The home background of pupils

When relating method to maturational levels, interest, and abilities, the teacher should realize their close kinship to the home and family environments of the students. In educational circles today, the trite statement is heard increasingly that the child never comes to school alone; that he brings his parents and a myriad of past experiences with him. And indeed he does! In infancy, he starts the process of internalizing the emotions, attitudes, habits, and ideas of family members, with the process continuing unabated until maturity slows it down or terminates it. These influences which accompany the adolescent to the high school must be reckoned with when method is being weighed. For purposes of this discussion, because of its magnitude, only selected facets of this area will be commented on, and then only briefly.

In this regard, one of the major deterrents to learning is the adverse attitude toward it which many students absorb from the home and community. First- or second-generation immigrants and the lower socioeconomic classes of whatever racial or ethnic origin seem to gravitate toward attitudinal extremes about education: it is often considered either as a certain passage to success or as a luxury that children should not have if it was previously denied to parents.

When education lacks prestige in the home, creating an interest in it in the school becomes a difficult—sometimes even an insurmountable—task for the teacher. In suburban high schools, a reasonable expectancy is that education will have respected status, and that time spent on homework, the earning of high grades, and careful preparation for examinations will be regarded as rather normal routine. This outcome is in partial, or even vivid, contrast to that typical of many large-city schools, where students who are serious about their education are suspect by their classmates. This state of affairs invariably is a reflection of adverse home or community attitudes. And of importance to the teacher is a recognition that his role becomes more demanding as such opposition grows in significance.

Unhappily, the teacher is thus placed in the position of having to work against, instead of through, the values of the family. The final outcome may plausibly be far from satisfying to the teacher or the cause of education. Not infrequently, however, the teacher is able to break through the environmental blockage in two ways: by being an admired identification figure, and by making subject content and method so stimulating that students exchange old antagonisms for allegiances to a new set of values— grudgingly at first, then with increasing positivism. Method in this frame of reference accordingly must be attuned to interest and motivation.

Almost paralleling the problem of interest of students in a curriculum is the amount of freedom that a teacher can proffer them in classroom affairs. The key to amount is found in the home as well as the school. The student who is dominated at home may overcompensate in the school. The one who is unbridled at home may first tend to project his neurotic-like behavior into the classroom, but will usually conform, within reason, when confronted with firm limits. In any event, even though freedom of action by an adolescent on his way to independence is a cherished goal, it should never be separated from readiness. A starving man, if uncontrolled, will be voracious about food as a counteraction to previous deprivation. Accordingly, he will need the assistance of an authority figure until able emotionally to relate food intake to health needs. In recognition of similar factors, a teacher cannot rush students into uncontrolled choices. He should be sensitive to the familial heritage and weave it into the mosaic of method. Those methods which place adolescents "on their own" must await readiness, but teachers receptive to cues should not delay the rewards of freedom.

If freedom in the classroom has a correlate in the home, it has a special reciprocal relationship to the dominant male parent in the ranks of certain ethnic groups. In a number of such minorities, the male parent is "Lord of the Manor" and thus the only voice of real authority in the household. The female parent, although loved by the children for her helpfulness and goodness, has to grasp for the respect that comes to the father naturally. As her surrogate, the female teacher might well have to "demand" the students' respect, particularly of boys, if she can get it in no other way. Faced with this ethnic phenomenon, she would be wise to keep the reins taut at the beginning of the year, easing them after she becomes an established authority figure. This sequence is more acceptable than having to coerce, once infractions have gotten out of hand.

Another home conditioner of teaching method is the factor of socio-economic status. That social stratification exists and that it can disease the values of people was recognized long before *Elmtown's Youth* appeared. To the discerning teacher, deprivation of a pupil in any area of living, be it social or economic, is a danger signal; and when it ignites, he should look for, and usually will find, one of the two behavioral extremes predicted by Alfred Adler in such circumstances: aggression or withdrawal. A recognition of either by the teacher will have a direct effect on the method he employs in working with pupils.

Aggression he should contain within acceptable limits while initially dealing with the symptoms; after that, he should attempt to penetrate into causality. He approaches repression more sensitively, recognizing it as a more subtle and complex escape from a problem. In the event of either manifestation, he is still faced with the necessity of neutralizing the effect of social and economic inequities. This he attempts to accomplish by engineering members of the various class groups into positions of proximity, thereby encouraging them to think and work together. The result of this interaction not infrequently terminates in better understanding, then in greater tolerance, and finally in altruistic attitudes.

In a heterogeneous socioeconomic classroom situation, the teacher should distribute among the various subgroups leadership opportunities lest they gravitate, as they customarily do, toward the more favored classes. In this way, adolescents are removed temporarily from their in-groups and given the greater overview of the larger mixed group. Artificial barriers might becomes less permanent as a result. Contiguity, shared responsibilities, and shared leadership are powerful allies against bias, prejudice, and gross inequality.

Miscellaneous home factors supplement those already discussed: that is, parental and adolescent attitudes toward the school, freedom as a correlate of readiness, and socioeconomic differences. Other diverse influences on method may be operative: for example, illiteracy of parents, provincialism of ideas, strictures of religious dogma, siblings of genius proportions, old-country family habits, bilingual speech, and nonconventional dress. These and other home conditioners crop up, often unexpectedly, to dictate a change in method. Judicious is the teacher who refuses to ignore them!

Past educational experience of pupils

The secondary-school student brings an educational as well as a familial heritage to each classroom. Experiences in the previous high school or elementary grades, or both, are instrumental in formulating the personalities that young people bring to later educational levels, and these, too, influence method.

Illustrative is the freshman-level home economics instructor who employs the individual or small-group method extensively. In a unit in textiles, for instance, she customarily would have individuals working on specialized projects at their desks. A few might have to share a common garment design or pattern from time to time, bringing them into close proximity with one another. To the extent that these students had been under rigid controls during all or part of the eight previous grades, close supervision to prevent manifest disorder might be required. But to the extent that they had lived with and adjusted to freedom, a minimum of supervision could be anticipated.

In like manner, caution has had to be exercised by school systems contemplating the adoption of a core program. Fundamental to it is not only curriculum amalgamation of subject matter but also extensive student leadership. Requisite to success in core programs are teachers and students who can accept their new roles and play them creditably. These specifications invariably are more readily met by junior and senior high schools which draw from favored elementary systems. The latter customarily funnel into the school of higher rank young people who have worked closely in student councils, adhered to Roberts' Rules of Order in their homerooms, operated as classroom officers, and in many other ways become sensitized to the obligations of organizational processes.

Not unlike the analogy of core, field trips, library research, assembly programs, athletic performances, and dramatic exhibitions achieve more satisfying outcomes when preceded by supporting educational experiences and activities. What transpired in the kindergarten and grades one through eight unmistakably has a marked influence on the success of learning methods that are employed in grades nine through twelve. Continuity makes for a greater readiness and sophistication of student response.

The importance of teacher beliefs about learning

Another force, and a powerful one, which exerts its influence on method is the teacher's attitudes about learning. Although in later chapters this topic will be amplified in different settings, the present context demands at least a capsule treatment. Attention will be directed more at the basic assumptions that a teacher makes about learning than at formal learning theory itself. Within these limits, the secondary school instructional leader consciously or unconsciously has to make decisions on the following issues or questions.

Should students be provided first with a foundational body of facts, from which at some later period they can develop understandings and make applications, or should the three elements move in concert at each level? In support of the former point of view, at least a militant minority in education today would insist that the ground level of skills and knowledge be made secure before students are encouraged to question seriously and apply what they have learned. A teacher with this belief would select teaching method designed to build this sizable foundation. Assigned readings, lectures, recitations, examinations, and reviews would be appropriate up to the point of critical questioning.

The teacher with a contrasting orientation would alternate between helping students to acquire facts and encouraging them to be skeptical of their newly found acquisitions. The probing tactics would occur, not as a finale to months or years of educational experiences, but as an almost day-to-day feature of the learning process. For instance, if he were conversing about the period of the colonists' wars with the American Indians, his interest in the historical facts of the situation would be matched by a concern over the ethics of America's pre-empting the land from the Indians, the primitive emotions that the wars precipitated in the combatants, and the current plight of the Indian. Such a unit could well terminate with a treatment of the question: In what way are the United States and other parts of the world usurping the rights of other nations, races, or individuals today?

This alternating sequence of content and query might lead in a social studies class to such methods as: (1) the reading of newspapers and periodicals for current information to supplement ideas contained in a textbook; (2) open discussions—with few holds barred—on the right of a dominant group to subdue a weaker one; (3) the study by students of sociological conditions in their communities; and perhaps (4) the examination of how attitudes are formed. The results would be more than factually cognitive because of the teacher's underlying philosophical attitude about what learning is of most value.

A second basic question involves the limited versus the multiple approach to learning. Is the process sufficiently, or even reasonably, adequate when a single textbook is employed? Or are several texts and additional supplementary references required? An affirmative response to the first question might provide students with only a single point of view, whereas the same type of response to the second would leave them with multisided opinions. The first would confine students to the classroom and would encourage a more passive acceptance of ideas, whereas the second would expand their learning horizons and encourage an agnostic posture until learning content could be refuted or substantiated.

A third question is basically this: To what extent are the outcomes of learning dependent on the active participation of the learners? And a related question is: To what extent can a high school student learn only by listening? The answer to the latter is that he can learn from the narrowness of the lecture, but the outcomes will often be limited, for they will always be a variable of the lecturer's finesse and the listener's brightness, verbal ability, and interest. The answer to the former is that learning is a direct correlate of the active involvement of the learner. Thus, the teacher can never leave the student detached from the dynamics of the instructional situation without endangering the desired outcomes of learning. The more active the participation, the more productive the results.

A fourth and final issue to be treated briefly within this context revolves around the despairing question asked by teachers throughout the ages: How can I teach them when they don't want to learn? Resisting the glib answer of "You can't," we propose the following tenets:

1. First of all, teaching must be conceived as more than the filling of little pitchers, as described satirically in Dickens's *Hard Times*.

2. From a broader perceptual base, it involves surrounding students with richness and variety so that they will have the necessary stimuli for learning, once they get the urge. These stimuli should include teacher re-

ceptiveness and permissiveness, interesting learning materials, group activities to enhance learning, the establishment and enforcement of reasonable limits, and tolerance of imperfections.

3. Learning must be regarded as flowing at an uneven pace—sometimes fast, sometimes slowly, sometimes not at all.

4. When the teacher has exhausted his immediate resources, he maintains control while pursuing further alternatives.

5. If, despite his best efforts throughout a semester or year, he has failed his mission, he stops short of suicidal tendencies in recognition of the facts that pupils are complicated, that learning is relative, and that teaching often has delayed results.

6. Learning, in the last analysis, has to take place inside the student.

The subject which is taught

Another factor which prevents the crystallization of method is the course variety in any curriculum. A few individuals in teacher education imply that method is of general rather than specific essence, and that it can be applied in somewhat the same way in all subject matter areas. This point of view is incompatible with empirical evidence, which contrariwise conceives method as almost a direct function of the subject matter specialty.

The topic of teacher-pupil planning is illustrative in this respect. Some observers profess to believe that almost all teachers can employ it as a learning device, regardless of subject. Yet how can a teacher of an abstract subject like geometry or physics engage pupils in the planning of content with which, before the act of exposure, they are unfamiliar? Teacher-pupil planning is feasible only in those areas where students can call on prior knowledge and understandings: for example, core, civics, and biology.

Also oversimplified is the recommendation that all teachers use the laboratory method of teaching. Yet is this method practical in equal degree for the teachers of science, French, woodworking, and world history? And in the controversial method of drill, contrary to the complaint of the critics who feel "modern educators" have done away with it, we doubt seriously if any educator even in his more progressive moments would want drill to disappear from the academic scene. In fact, all would fight vigorously for its retention. However, competent educators of whatever orientation would agree that drill is a function of both a specific teaching situation and a specific subject. Routine drill unquestionably is more functional for the skill subjects of mathematics, grammar, and woodworking than for problems of democracy or physical science. But even in the last two, it has a place.

If method is a function of the subject being taught, it is likewise related to the learning situation within a subject. The teacher, in introducing a new principle in physics, justifiably would use a method different from one to be employed when demonstrating an application of the principle. And if drill serves the needs of grammar, it would certainly be incongruent in a creative writing project. When properly conceived, method becomes the servant of the curriculum situation of the moment.

Space and room arrangement

More mundane than the abilities of pupils being taught and the type of subject matter being covered, but of considerable influence on method none the less, are space and room arrangement. Almost legion are the conscientious teachers whose attainment of defensible goals of education is denied by the lack of adequate facilities. The desire to administer to the individual needs of students has occurred more frequently than its fulfillment because of a shortage of classroom space. Individualized or group instruction is much easier to accomplish when conflicting elements do not compete for space within the confines of a single room.

Guidance textbooks quite properly advise teachers to hold individual conferences with pupils, but the conducting of such conferences at a front desk with twenty-nine other students demanding attention can lead to only partially successful outcomes. The private-interview technique which relies for success on rapport, a frank interchange of ideas, and uninhibited displays of emotion can only approximate its objectives when the atmosphere is not conducive to therapeutic results.

Teachers in old, outdated school buildings are particularly victimized by the deficiency of facilities. One teacher may yearn for a learning situation wherein a circular chair arrangement seems to be almost a necessity, only to realize that the chairs and desks are fixed. Another envisions a classroom library which might break the barriers between adolescents and books, but can find no place to encase the needed volumes. A teacher of algebra may desire to send an entire class to the blackboard, but may have to compromise when but six students can be accommodated at the blackboards at one time. Often a teacher of science has no option except to work in a crowded laboratory which, by necessity, is forced to serve as an all-purpose room for lectures, demonstrations, and experimentation. If he lectures, he has trouble maintaining contact with the boys in the rear rows of the long, narrow room. If he demonstrates, he almost has to distribute binoculars to these same pupils to draw them into the learning situation.

Method is uniquely a function of space and room arrangement. Notwithstanding the fact that excellent teachers can teach effectively in a one-room schoolhouse, and many actually have done so, these hypothetically superior teachers surely would have been even more competent performers if their choice of method had not been restricted by factors of space. Adverse physical factors cannot destroy good teaching, but they can certainly make it more difficult of accomplishment.

The personality of the teacher

From the physical aspects of the classroom we make an abrupt detour to another partner of method, namely, the personality of the teacher. Teaching techniques and procedures cannot ever become coldly detached from the individuality of the instructional leader himself. Method is not this stereotyped! Rather, it is the lengthened shadow of a person who rejects what does not harmonize and incorporates what will synthesize with him as a person.

The criteria for judging a teacher's personality are such factors as voice quality and projection; inclination toward introversion or extroversion; need for agreement or tolerance for disagreement; ability to play only a few or many personal-professional roles; security when in, or not in, a dominant position; and the need to concentrate on one classroom activity at a time or a willingness to allow students to engage in several. Against these and other personal characteristics, the teacher candidate can properly evaluate himself.

The lecturer with a small voice and defective diction should quite properly seek other ways to help young people learn. The extrovert, high-pressure teacher would do well to shun core methods, which rely on a recessive instructor role. The mechanically inept should think twice before making extensive use of audio-visual equipment. And the restless, driving personality will chafe or fail completely when engaged in the process of group decision-making.

The obvious moral is that, to be successful, a teacher must adopt methods that will permit him essentially to be himself. Moderate adaptation to new methods is expected, but wholesale change is not only ill-advised but impossible. Rather than become ineffective—and even occasionally ludicrous—by wearing procedural apparel that fits badly, the candidate should tailor his method over the foundation garment of naturalness.

Legal provisions

A final consideration, and one of oft-concealed importance, is the impact of school law on the teacher and his classroom practices. Basic to this discussion is the Latinism *in loco parentis,* which identifies the teacher as the legal parent who during the school day takes the place of the blood parent. And the legal substitute is expected by law to act not as befits a mediocre blood parent, but rather as a knowledgeable, perceptive, empathetic father or mother.

The evaluative criterion for judging the teacher's actions resides in another legal term, *the reasonable man*—that mythical figure who inhabits the courtrooms of the country. When a juryman or judge is in doubt about what decision to render, law admonishes him to make judgment according to how "the reasonable man" would have reacted to a similar set of circumstances. With the fusion of the two technical terms, the teacher is thus portrayed legally as standing in place of parent and acting always in a reasonably mature way.

The two types of man-made law with which educational personnel come in contact are statutory and common. The former is the organized body of legislative enactments which relate to the schools of the state; and almost, without exception, they appear in each instance as *The School Code*. This document invariably addresses itself more to the mechanics of getting schools into being and their over-all operation than it does to teaching method. Statutory edicts routinely define the responsibilities and rights of the various school functionaries, make provisions for school elections and referendums, set policy on finance, establish the length of the school year, and in other ways give structure to the state's educational enterprise.

But they also make some inroads into teaching method by prescribing responsibilities for the teacher, such as roll-taking and care of property, and by specifying items to be included in a curriculum. In this latter regard, the Code of Illinois, for example, demands that schools make coverage of the evils of alcohol, the obligations of citizens to vote, the proper display of the flag, and the merits of kindness, honesty, justice, and moral courage. Just as precisely in the field of method, it states that textbooks when adopted must be used for five years. This provision protects the taxpayer but restricts the freedom of a teaching staff, particularly members of a new regime, who are thus forced to use the texts which have been selected by a former regime. The teacher of biology is forthrightly told that:

> No pupil shall be required to . . . participate in instruction on diseases if a parent or guardian files written objection thereto on constitutional grounds, and refusal to take or participate in such instruction on such grounds shall not be reason for suspension or expulsion of such pupil. Nothing in this act shall prohibit instruction in sanitation and hygiene. . . . [Also that]
>
> No experiment upon any living animal for the purpose of demonstration in any study shall be made in any public school. No animal provided by, or killed in the presence of, any pupil of a public school shall be used for dissection in such school, and in no case shall dogs or cats be killed for such purposes. Dissection of dead animals, or parts thereof, shall be confined to the classroom and shall not be practiced in the presence of any pupil not engaged in the study to be illustrated thereby.[2]

From the above-mentioned examples, it may be inferred that a teacher should become more than superficially familiar with the school code. Although we have no desire to send teachers into the classroom with a code under one arm and a textbook under the other, a minimum

[2] N. E. Hutson and R. F. Deffenbaugh, *The School Code of Illinois, Circular Series A No. 98,* 1955 pp. 249–250.

requirement is that they be acquainted with the major statutory provisions which are designed to govern their actions.

The second type of judicial enactments which often affect the teacher appears in the common law of the land, the substantive content of which emanates from civil and criminal court cases. Whereas statutory law usually broadly governs the actions of the teacher, common law makes intimate contact both with him and with his methods. The law and the person usually come together in tort cases, where a plaintiff parent questions the right of a defendant teacher to act in a designated way. Before entering the classroom, the teacher should become familiar with society's legal stand on the following controversial issues.

(1) *Religion*. How, if at all, to provide for religious instruction during the school day has been a chronic and, at times, an acute issue during the first half of the present century. The question of the constitutionality of released time on school property for religious instruction came to court in 1948 in Champaign, Illinois, in the case of McCollum vs. Board of Education of School District No. 71. Mrs. Vashti McCollum, the plaintiff, contended that religious services on school property violated the principle of the separation of church and state and basically constituted a denial of educational rights to all children, particularly to those whose religious interests were nonexistent or not represented by any of the denominational services held in the school. The court decided in her favor and thereby made illegal formal religious instruction of a denominational nature conducted on school property. Justice Black gave the Court's majority opinion in his statement: "For the First Amendment rests upon the premise that both religion and government can best work to achieve their lofty aims if each is left free from the other within its respective sphere."

The practice of released time off school property for occasional religious instruction in the church of a pupil's choice was declared legal in 1952 in the case of Zorach vs. Clausen, New York. Still to be determined, however, is the amount of time away from a school that legal authority is willing to justify. It would hardly permit all-day religious instruction, with no secular education included, regardless of the sacred religious rights of an individual.

Bible reading is normally permitted for ceremonial or "mood" occasions, provided pupils are not tested on what is read. Most states that permit Bible reading insist that it be without interpretation or comment. Sixteen states have authorized the reading of the Bible. Four states, Illinois, Louisiana, South Dakota, and Wisconsin, have ruled that it is sectarian.

In September, 1959, in the case of Schempp vs. School District of Abington, a United States Circuit Court of Appeals decided that Pennsylvania's law requiring daily Bible reading and recitation of the Lord's Prayer violated both the First and Fourteenth Amendments. The court stated that such a practice "amounts to religious instruction or a promotion of religious education" and that Bible reading that is compelled "prohibits the free exercise of religion."

Teachers have a right to teach "about" religion in the context of history, for example, the Catholic Church in the Middle Ages, Martin Luther's secession in the sixteenth century, Puritanism in the colonial period, and other historically relevant religious events or movements. Also, they have a right, even an obligation, to implant curriculum experiences in an ethical and moral foundation. But they must stay remote from denominationalism. Even the Christ Story and related pictorial displays in public schools at Christmas time are illegal, despite practices to the contrary. Schools which break the law at Christmas usually "get by" because "would-be" objectors accept the displays and rituals more as social than as religious portrayals.

(2) *Corporal punishment of pupils.* Possessed of just as much potential volatility as the religious issue is corporal punishment, and the teacher should thus be aware of its legal status. Unless a state or local board of education forbids its employment, corporal punishment falls within the parental rights of a teacher. When the practice is forbidden, however, the teacher should know that even the less dramatic bodily contacts are regarded legally as corporal punishment: for instance, the squeeze of a student's arm, a tap on the hand with a ruler, or a slight shove. In fact, legal assault does not require any bodily contact whatsoever—just a convincing gesture of intent to harm.

Since value judgments regarding corporal punishment will be made in a later treatment of discipline, it is sufficient to say at this time that the judicious teacher thinks before he makes any type of contact with the body of a child. The key to the issue is manifest intent, whether friendly or threatening. If the latter, he needs one or more of the following defenses: the approval of state law or local authorities, action in harmony with the aggravation, self-protection, or the protection of others. Short of one or more of these defenses, he is usually legally, if not morally, culpable.

(3) *Group penalties.* Another legally involved classroom practice is the group penalty assessed to all for the fault of one or only a few. When thirty pupils are detained because an unidentified student has been guilty of a misdemeanor, the teacher surprisingly could be made to face a civil suit brought by a parent on the grounds of "false imprisonment." The theory behind the suit would be that society, except in emergency situations, forbids the punishment of innocent victims. And when a teacher keeps an entire class after school with only a modicum of justification, he improperly denies freedom to the innocent. Again, our emphasis at this time is only on the legality, not the social advisability, of this and other practices.

Before retaining a group after school, the teacher should assess whether the purpose is defensible and broadly applicable to all, and whether the period of retention will jeopardize the safety of the child on his way home from school. Only then can he feel professionally and legally secure.

(4) *Courtesy dismissals.* Before a teacher dismisses a pupil from the classroom for professed emergency reasons, he should first get approval from the principal. If in a school where responsibility for such an action has been delegated, the teacher is obligated legally to ascertain that the request for dismissal is valid, that is, sanctioned by a parent or legal guardian for a legitimate purpose. A court case is not unlikely when an unauthorized person is given temporary custody of a child because of the blameworthy actions of the teacher in an unwarranted dismissal. And the primary danger of kidnapping cannot be ignored.

(5) *Predictable hazard areas.* The curriculum areas most laden with danger to pupils and liability for the teacher or school are the laboratory, shop, and physical-education programs. In each, the danger of injury is great unless adequate preventive measures are employed. Thus, such equipment as poisonous acids and trampolines and such potentially dangerous practices as experiments with electricity and football scrimmaging must be associated with adequate supervision. When in doubt about the precautions needed, the teacher should ask: What would be expected of the "reasonable man"?

In football particularly are the dangers great and the legal stakes high. In the case of Welch vs. Dunsmuir High School, California, 1958, the grim story is revealed of an injured player being removed from the field by eight boys. The injured youngster, paralyzed after his removal, received from the school damages in the amount of $206,804 as a result of not having received proper medical care on the field.[3]

The teacher is reasonably expected to instruct adolescents before permitting them to use dangerous equipment or to engage in dangerous activities, keep lethal equipment locked when not in use, and supervise students when danger is an ingredient of any situation.

Even though the school system is more often held liable for injuries and injustices than is the teacher himself, the latter should remember that in any state, gross negligence and unreasonableness place the teacher potentially in legal jeopardy. Thus, he should shun the appearance of negligence, carelessness, and poor judgment. Such actions as sending pupils into crowded areas for personal services, asking them to lift heavy objects, retaining them until safety precautions have been removed, failure to warn of dangers, permitting hazing, and ignoring potential hazards—these and others make the teacher or the school liable, depending on the specifics of state law.

For professional as well as personal reasons, the teacher candidate is admonished to think carefully about his future role of legal parent, remembering that the "reasonable man" will be an extra member of each

[3] National Education Association, Research Division, *The Pupil's Day in Court: Review of 1958* (Washington, D.C.: N.E.A., 1959), p. 32.

of his classes. The school cannot collect state aid for the additional member, but he is none the less present as a mythical standard. The mature teacher, in his march toward professionalism, will be expected to play the role of legal parent with distinction and wisdom.

SUMMARY

This chapter treats of method in the expansive setting of the home, school, and community. Teaching method is defined as the establishing of a climate wherein young people are helped to learn. The teacher is presented more as an engineer of learning situations than one who operates aggressively, and almost exclusively, as an imparter of knowledge.

The central motif of the chapter is that method does not and cannot exist as a discrete entity. Rather, it is a direct function of such factors as educational purpose, school policy, the characteristics of pupils, home backgrounds, past educational experiences, teacher beliefs about learning, subject matter, the teacher as a person, and school law.

REFERENCES

Baxter, Bernice, *Teacher-Pupil Relationships*. New York: The Macmillan Company, 1941.

Coyle, Grace Longivell, *Group Work With American Youth*. New York: Harper & Row, 1948.

Edwards, Newton, *The Courts And The Public Schools*. Chicago: University of Chicago Press, 1955.

Garber, Lee O., *Handbook of School Law*. New London, Conn.: A. C. Croft, 1954.

————, *Yearbook of School Law*. Danville, Ill.: Interstate Printers and Publishers. (Yearbooks)

Haiman, Franklyn, *Group Leadership and Democratic Action*. Boston: Houghton Mifflin Company, 1951.

Hollingshead, August de Belmont, *Elmtown's Youth, The Impact of Social Classes on Adolescents*. New York: John Wiley and Sons, 1949.

Hunter, Floyd, *Community Power Structure*. Chapel Hill: University of North Carolina Press, 1953.

Remmlein, Madaline Kinter, *The Law of Local Public School Administration*. New York: McGraw-Hill Book Company, Inc., 1953.

Ross, Murray G., and Charles F. Hendry, *New Understandings of Leadership*. New York: Association Press, 1957.

CHAPTER 4

PLANNING
AND
RESOURCES
FOR PLANNING

A well-conducted class is invariably a proscenium behind the scenes of which are concealed the extent and quality of planning that took place earlier. To the uninformed observer, things may seem to "break right" for a given teacher on a given day; but to the instructional leader himself, things rarely "break right" unless painstaking preparation has preceded the opening of the class period.

Planning should start early in the life of a teacher and can never end. The first organized impact of the necessity for planning is felt when the student becomes a candidate for the educational profession. Its demands continue throughout the period of college enrollment, and the student's response must meet the test of cumulative adequacy prior to an acceptance of the first position. At this juncture, the individual who has planned wisely is ready and able to face the demands of his new role.

In the critical pre-service period of self-analysis, the maturing candidate is prone to look specifically and objectively at himself as a person, at the dimensions of his competency in his teaching major and minor, and at his ability to relate to youth. And when at least moderately satisfied with the image, he will undoubtedly identify preliminary planning as a significant causal factor. Such a student, having set his sights early enough on certain well-defined and worthwhile goals, will inherit the rich benefits of gratifying achievement.

The same candidate who reaped the harvest of planning as a college student will tend to transfer its advantages to the classroom. Distasteful of futility and disorganization, and attracted to economy of effort, he will regard planning as the most economical means of consummating academic goals. So viewed, learning will be conceived well in advance of its classroom implementation, and then will be adjusted to the demands of the immediate present.

This chapter will cover the reasons for planning, the academic areas where planning should take place, a frame of reference for planning, selected materials of instruction, excesses to be avoided, and the pros and cons of teacher-pupil planning.

WHY PLAN?

Fundamental to the theme of this chapter is the question: Why should a teacher plan? Selected answers, with brief remarks added to appropriate items, follow.

1. Planning is requisite to organization and direction. Rare indeed is the individual who in teaching "plays as well by ear" as by "reading the notes."

2. Planning is an insurance policy against forgetting and against improper emphasis.

3. Planning endows teachers with that assurance and confidence that only familiarity with a subject can bring. The guarantors of successful conduct of a learning situation are an anticipation of outcomes, research built around the outcomes, and careful structure.

4. Teacher assurance breeds pupil confidence both in the learning process and in the learning authority figure. Aimless rambling and schemelessness, on the other hand, lead to a loss of teacher respect by students.

5. Planning underwrites correct long-term sequence. Without it, sequence is halting, at best: some important ideas are omitted and others are the victims of uneven emphasis.

6. Planning clarifies thought. A teacher who organizes and schematizes prior to the act of teaching is more likely to refine concepts, ideas, and attitudes and clothe them with an enrichment of meaning.

7. Planning by teachers sets a pattern that will encourage a like habit in students. Teaching thus operates by example as well as by verbal precept.

8. In general, the process of planning invests learning with dignity. Change of behavior on the part of students is of the essence, and nothing

short of the best content and the best methods should suffice. And since teachers are fallible, the learning atmosphere should reflect the extra precautions of careful preparation.

AREAS OF INDIVIDUAL TEACHER PLANNING

Only an occasional individual will contest the need for a type of structure that only forethought can provide, and we thus call attention to those academic areas with which such forethought should be involved. Simply stated, prior planning should take place in any part of the curriculum that is regarded as important, and at any time that quality of performance and economy of effort are significant factors. Specifically, the insightful teacher charts the goals that he thinks the curriculum should cultivate, designs content to get the goals achieved, selects method to convert the content into vitalized learning, and arranges the mechanical features of the classroom to assure optimum results.

With educational objectives in the nature of a foundation to all organized learning, they logically should be the focal point of emphasis for planned classroom activities. When carefully thought through and expressed, they establish clear purpose and direction that a knowledge of the desired learning alone can provide. Yet, despite the apparent obviousness of the directional value of objectives, many teachers regard them but lightly. One reason may be the teachers' own indifference, but another equally plausible reason may well be the ineffectiveness of educational literature in conveying proper meanings for such descriptive words as *aims, goals, purposes,* and *objectives.* Practically speaking, these are terms designed to force a teacher to contemplate the desired outcomes of learning. Rejecting semantic artificiality, the teacher in planning a learning activity should simply ask: What do I want this activity to accomplish? The proper answer to this question would then constitute the goals of the specific learning segment. Throughout this treatment, the terms *aims, goals, purposes,* and *objectives* will be employed interchangeably, all identifying the intended direction that learning is to take.

The organizing effect of goals may be observed, for example, when a teacher of biology plans a unit on genetics. In addition to the more evident objectives that he would routinely conceptualize might be the goal for students to understand that "man is never completely master of his fate." With this desired outcome established early, it would inevitably condition the future shape of the unit. Supplemental to the coverage of such substantive terms as *chromosomes* and *genes,* of such concepts as acquired and inherited characteristics, and such individuals as Darwin, Lamarck, and Mendel would be the directional emphasis on man as an inheritor of biological and psychological limitations. The unit thus slanted by a predetermined purpose would logically lead into such issues as free will, psychic and divine determinism, nature-nurture, and fate. Without the pre-established goal, these outcomes would be possible but not necessarily assured.

While planning is essential to goal determination and subject-matter content, it is no less vital to method. Method, never a discrete academic entity, is always an outgrowth of purpose and curriculum substance. As the *how,* it follows on the heels of the *where* and the *what.* Thus, our teacher of biology, after formulating the specific goal and identifying the body of content that might best support it, would give thought to the teaching methods that should highlight the learning experience. The methods also would be planned well in advance of their classroom implementation, so that they would be more applicable.

Finally, as the emerging learning scene approached, the discerning teacher would make the classroom mechanically ready for the unfolding of the learning process. Stated simply, he would attend to all those preliminaries of learning usually categorized under the academic term "classroom management." Teacher involvement in this area would include planning for such more or less important tasks as:

1. Regulating heating, lighting, and ventilation.
2. Seating pupils according to a prior plan.
3. Arranging chairs, if not attached to the floor.
4. Passing and collecting materials of instruction in the most expeditious manner.
5. Making certain that all necessary learning materials and equipment, for example: microscopes, slide films, reference sources, and handouts were intact and ready.

These and other mechanical features of the classroom situation, although not always stimulating features of learning, are none the less important. They are similar to the significance placed by playwrights on stage properties. The latter do not make the play, but they can certainly heighten or reduce its effect. And if important, they need be planned in advance, whether in a classroom or on the stage.

The results of planning for classroom management are rewarding. Fulfillment is realized when a pupil efficiently takes the roll and unobtrusively places the attendance slip in a predetermined slot, when examination papers are distributed in a matter of seconds, when aisle monitors collect papers with a minimum of confusion, and when adolescents play their roles in a fire drill maturely. These and other practices are brought about by advance planning.

To accomplish these and similar positive outcomes, the teacher, prior to the beginning of any class, must arrange to have materials of instruction on hand organized in such a way that learning will eventuate naturally. If reference books are to be used, they need to be available in sufficient quantity. If a film is to be shown, it should be previewed and the projector checked just before showing time to assure uninterrupted operation. The prudent science teacher, for instance, well in advance of class time takes inventory of chemicals, slides, or other materials of instruction to guarantee an adequate supply. The teacher of core, when not assigned one specific classroom for the entire school day, arrives at a class a few minutes early to see that chairs are arranged in a desired order. And the art teacher not infrequently spends after-school time getting the classroom and materials ready for the next day.

In contrast, how unprofessional and embarrassing for a teacher to search futilely for a handout that was left at home, to effervesce over "just the right illustration" in a book that was "accidentally mislaid," or to pull down the map of Europe in the midst of a unit on the Far East. Scarcely less excusable is the bulletin board that is months out of date, wall displays that are no longer applicable, and blackboard work that relates to a previous rather than a current learning situation. These are consequences of a teacher's failure to make provision ahead of time for the mechanical requirements of learning. Every teacher admittedly falls into the occasional error of neglect, but those instructional leaders are in demand who have only passing associations with chance and its whimsies.

Of comfort to the teacher candidate is the fact that smoothly run classes are almost uniformly the product of student as well as teacher effort. Granted that careful teacher planning behind the scenes is fundamental, the externals of effective management usually focus on students with whom a secure teacher has shared responsibility.

Selected administrative functions that the teacher can delegate without loss of efficiency are roll-taking, dissemination of materials, care of equipment, regulation of heating and lighting, issuance of books from and their return to a classroom or school library, policing the classroom, maintaining bulletin boards, and cleaning blackboards. Delegating responsibility to adolescents for these and similar tasks has a number of advantages. First, when students are permitted to share the duties of the classroom, they develop more interest in its activities. Second, the tasks are customarily performed with greater efficiency when shared by many than when performed by only one. Third, when the routine jobs are proceduralized, the teacher has more time for the professional ones. Whenever directly involved in taking attendance, passing out materials, and performing other classroom tediums, the teacher is thereby diverted from more important curriculum concerns and the personal problems of students. How much better is it that a teacher use his valuable talents where they will have the most telling effect.

When delegating tasks to students, the teacher should never sell short the importance of careful selection and training. Selection should strike a balance between what will be valuable for the individual student and what will be in the best interests of all. Conferring on slow learners leadership opportunities is to be encouraged, provided the other students are not penalized as a result. Affording the extrovert an energy outlet is also laudable when not harmful to others. It is vital, however, that the welfare of the total group never be relegated to the background.

Also, once a selection has been made, students should be instructed in how to perform their newly assigned tasks. The training period is usually of brief duration, but is no less important because of its brevity. Rather than engaging in a "telling" situation, the sensitive teacher both solicits ideas from the involved adolescents and offers personal opinions and preferences. The effect is twofold: students know more about what is expected of them, and they take their duties more seriously because the teacher has dignified their roles.

However, there are several routines which are the exclusive responsibility of the teacher: fire drills and seating are the principal ones. The first is his because of the seriousness of purpose of the routine. Thus, the teacher is well advised to proceduralize fire drills even when the school administration is a bit lax. Overtraining in this significant area is vastly preferable to the underselling of its importance.

The determination of a seating arrangement is also the teacher's responsibility, because of its relationship to the goals of education as he conceives them. If the teacher is interested in adolescents' enlarging their circle of friends, he seats them randomly to bring strangers into contact. If interested in making the classroom informal and casual, he permits cliques to perpetuate themselves—at least until they disturb others. But if desirous of learning names as rapidly as possible, he may insist on alphabetical placement at first, providing the opportunity for change once he has gotten acquainted with all individuals in his classes. The latter practice usually results in few shifts of seating after the initial period.

THE REFERENCE FRAMES
OF PLANNING

Assuming that all effective teachers make an early determination of educational objectives, course content, learning method, and classroom procedures, each teacher will conceive them in a frame of reference that differs from situation to situation yet has common features throughout. Planning, wherever employed, is always a function of time, the teacher's background, the constituency of the class, and the facilities and materials of instruction.

The factor of time is consistently a conditioner of the teacher's efforts to shape learning for the future. When engaged in long-term planning, he places emphasis primarily on large subject-matter areas, extensive chronological time blocks, and key personalities. A four-year English curriculum in the field of composition might well be conceptualized by such expressions as "a graduated progression from the one-paragraph theme to a term paper of ten pages," or "from the simple sentence, the student will proceed to themes of several pages wherein he demonstrates an ability to use the complex and compound sentence with effect." The long-term scheme for the teacher of United States history might well consist only of those broad guidelines provided by such subject-matter divisions as the pre-colonial period, the founding of the colonies, and the constitutional period. The longer the period of projected teacher planning, the more general it is likely to be.

Equally valid is the assertion that short-term planning is likely to be characterized by considerable detail relating both to content and to method. Specific dates, particularized events, and the fractionated elements of larger wholes vie for attention. In the same manner, method assumes greater distinctiveness when the time block is smaller.

The background of the teacher, transcending all other factors, fore-shadows the extent and quality of planning that should take place. Each teacher candidate is unique in the knowledge, understandings, and attitudes that he brings to both the major and the minor subject-matter fields. Generally speaking, to the degree that his dowry is limited, he must plan in greater detail; to the degree that it is ample, he will need less bolstering —but he will never graduate to a point where the need is completely non-existent.

However, as indicated in Chapter 3, regardless of the background and competencies of any teacher, he can never be moored other than to the realities of the classroom. Thus, his planning will always need to take into account the curriculum expectations of the particular school system and the personalities and interests of the pupils which it serves.

The existence of a curriculum syllabus is always somewhat prescriptive and therefore a factor to which planning must relate. The English curriculum guide that prescribes the group reading of *A Tale of Two Cities* and "one other novel of the teacher's choice" confronts the teacher with the need to accept in good grace the recommended novel of Dickens, next to select a second literary work, and finally to convert both to a learning situation. The guide that only broadly demands coverage of a specified Spanish grammar in the first-year course is a mandate to the teacher to work out the planned details independently.

And if a syllabus is circumscribing, the pupils are even more so. Selected determinants that always compel attention are the ability range, specialized talent, age, motivation, emotional maturity, and previous school background. For the bright, as has been noted, learning should rise to the abstract and be endued with intensity; for the slow, making the abstract concrete must characterize the teacher's efforts, with extensity the key.

Regarding the factor of specialized talent, a teacher of music, for example, would have to plan a curriculum for the vocally and instrumentally talented while not neglecting their interested but less favored fellow pupils. Of necessity, such planning would include opportunities for the gifted to perform individually, or in ensemble, at their competency levels. Whether or not they appeared before public gatherings or at local and state contests would be coincidental to the more important outcome of their having worked up to capacity. In the same manner, the less gifted would have to be given comparable opportunities to perform at their levels of competency.

Planning as a function of age would dictate, for instance, more variety and concreteness for the younger than the older students; as a function of motivation, it would require greater stimulation for the less interested than for those with greater interest; as a function of emotional growth, more freedom for the mature than for the less mature; and as a function of previous school experiences, a need to build on the existing foundation of accumulated school experiences. In all situations, planning should be conceived in the context of the student with provisions made for observed and anticipated similarities or diversities.

PLANNING AND SELECTED
MATERIALS OF INSTRUCTION

Assuming an instructor convinced of the merits of planning, and willing to adapt it to the appropriate elements of a local situation, what materials of instruction could he call on for support? First of all, his baccalaureate days would have supplied him with a foundation on which future growth could later take place, but it should never be regarded exclusively as the superstructure. The teacher's further growth should likewise be formed from the insights that he develops "in service." In broad terms, these divide into three categories: those which apply directly to his fields of curriculum specialization—the major and the minor; those related to adolescents; and those of a professional nature shared in common by all teachers of whatever discipline.

Planning in the fields of the major and minor will receive signal assistance from the appropriate professional journals. From Chapter 2 the reader will recall the contributions made by *The Science Teacher*. This and comparable publications of the other subject fields contain provocative articles, review the newer books of note, identify and describe audio-visual innovations, inform the teacher of instructional methods being employed elsewhere with success, editorialize on significant issues, and contain digests of professional conferences. These journals are "planning musts" for the teacher desirous of keeping abreast. Selected ones in the various disciplines are as follows:

Professional Journals

Art

Art Education
California Art Journal

Business Education

American Business Education
Business Education World
Business Teacher
Journal of Business Education
National Association of Business
  Teachers

English

English
English Journal
Educational Theatre Journal

Foreign Languages

Modern Language Association of
  America
Modern Language Forum
Modern Language Journal

Home Economics

Journal of Home Economics

Industrial Arts

Industrial Arts and Vocational
  Education
Industrial Arts Teacher

Mathematics

Arithmetic Teacher
Mathematics Teacher
School Science and Mathematics

Music

Educational Music Magazine
Music Educators Journal

Physical Education

American Association for Health,
  Physical Education and Recrea-
  tion Journal
Journal of Physical Education

Science

Science Education
Science and Mathematics
The Science Teacher

Social Studies

Educational Sociology
Institute of Social Studies Bulletin
Journal of Social Studies
Social Education

Speech

Central States Speech Journal
Quarterly Journal of Speech
Speech Teacher
Debaters Digest

Two other valuable sources of information for planning in the specialized secondary fields are the National Education Association and the United States Department of Health, Education, and Welfare, Office of Education. The respective addresses to which requests for materials can be mailed are:

(N.E.A.) 1201 Sixteenth Street, N.W., Washington 6, D.C.
(U.S. Dept. of Health, Education, and Welfare) Superintendent of Documents, U.S. Govt. Printing Office, Washington 25, D.C.

Teachers should get on the mailing lists of both agencies.

In the vital area of the audio-visual, important film and filmstrip sources are as follows:

Films and Filmstrip Sources

Educational Film Guide. H. W. Wilson Co. This will be in practically all school libraries. It is the most inclusive listing of films available.

Filmstrip Guide. H. W. Wilson Co. The statement above is also applicable here.

Society for Visual Education. 1345 Diversey, Chicago, Ill. This is one of the largest producers of filmstrips.

Sources of Educational Films, Filmstrips, and Slides. National Education Association, 1201 Sixteenth Street, N.W., Washington, D.C. This is published periodically, and the latest issue should regularly be consulted.

U.S. Government Films. Superintendent of Documents, Government Printing Office, Washington, D.C. This is always stimulating and up to date. The range is broad.

In the areas of adolescent growth, guidance, and sociology, a number of monthly, quarterly, or yearly publications are recommended to the teacher who has a more than casual interest in the young people with whom he is associated. The list proceeds more or less progressively from the less difficult to the more difficult and technical.

Scientific and Technical Periodicals

1. *Child Study,* 132 East 74th St., New York 21, N.Y.
2. *Child Welfare,* 345 East 46th St., New York 17, N.Y.
3. *Crime and Delinquency,* 1790 Broadway, New York 19, N.Y.
4. *The Personnel and Guidance Journal,* 1605 New Hampshire Ave., N.W., Washington 9, D.C.
5. *The Journal of Intergroup Relations,* 426 West 58th St., New York 19, N.Y.
6. *The Journal of Negro Education,* Howard University, Washington, D.C.
7. *The Journal of Negro History,* 1538 Ninth St., N.W., Washington, D.C.
8. *Mental Hygiene,* 49 Sheridan Ave., Albany 10, N.Y.
9. *Daedalus, Journal of the American Academy of Arts and Sciences,* 280 Newton St., Boston, Mass.
10. *Sociology and Social Research,* University of Southern California, Los Angeles, Calif.
11. *Yearbook, National Society for the Study of Education,* University of Chicago, 5835 Kimbark, Chicago 37, Ill. (Some apply here; some do not.)
12. *Group Psychotherapy,* 259 Wolcott Ave., Beacon, N.Y.
13. *Journal of Counseling Psychology,* 135 South Locust, Dubuque, Iowa.
14. *Child Development,* Yellow Springs, Ohio.
15. *American Psychologist,* 1333 Sixteenth St., Washington 6, D.C.
16. *Journal of Conflict Resolution,* 820 E. Washington St., Ann Arbor, Mich.
17. *American Journal of Orthopsychiatry,* 1790 Broadway, New York 19, N.Y.
18. *Journal of Abnormal and Social Psychology,* 1333 Sixteenth St., Washington 6, D.C.

These all deal in some way with children, youth, and older individuals as dynamic organisms trying to relate to others in their environments. The first eleven, with an occasional exception, are within the comprehension range of almost all teachers; the last seven, although more technical, contain many articles and points of view that are meaningful to both the classroom instructor and the technician. We strongly urge teacher candidates to scan a number of the listed publications to the end of ultimately subscribing for one or more that have the greatest appeal. Because any secondary curriculum is only as effective as the adjustment of the child to it, the sensitive teacher can never de-emphasize the personal equation in the classroom. As a guidance worker, then, he needs to enlist the stimulation of publications which place a primary emphasis on the student as a person. This second concern complements although it never replaces the emphasis on the cognitive.

Selections from a third category of resources are presented because of their message to educators of all orientations. The listing should be basic to the kind of planning that requires the use of extensive educational information.

Basic References and Guides

Biography Guide, H. W. Wilson Co. This quarterly publication provides biographical excerpts which have recently appeared in other periodicals.

Book Review Digest, H. W. Wilson Co. This is a monthly publication which gives brief reviews of new books.

Course outlines and syllabi from other school systems. These are in most school libraries; if not, they can be procured by writing directly to the individual schools. If the teacher is near a teachers college or university, he can secure them there.

Educators Index to Free Materials. Educators Progress Service, Randolph, Wisconsin. This is an invaluable source of diversified materials of all kinds, and is free of charge.

Free and Inexpensive Learning Materials. One is published by the George Peabody College; another, by the Federal Government. These also are valuable indices of information.

National Education Association Journal. N.E.A., Washington, D.C. This is published monthly by the National Educational Association and contains information about current legislation, issues, and innovations in education. It is an important general reference.

Readers Guide to Periodical Literature. H. W. Wilson Co., New York. This is a semi-monthly publication by topic and name index which lists articles that have appeared in the better-known periodicals.

Human Resources

The teacher, other teachers, school administrators, pupils, and carefully selected specialists from the local community.

Environmental Resources

The school itself, with its many opportunities for learning—library, departmental facilities, and perhaps a curriculum laboratory.

Local community resources: governmental, social, and artistic.

Larger community resources: museums, theatres, public institutions, and governmental agencies.

The foregoing resources have meaningful implications for teacher planning, although a frontal approach to most of them apart from a functional context is not recommended. However, when consulted in connection with an educational problem that needs researching, they are invaluable. Their judicious employment, in fact, can often make the difference between scholarliness and superficiality. The teacher's repertoire of resources should always be extensive; his search for new and enriching information, continuous.

Once resources have been discovered and digested, efficiency and economy require their organization and perpetuation. Ideally, the procedures for the teacher in this regard should be little different from those employed by a college student or researcher at any level. Minimum essentials are the recording of data—quotations, titles, names, teaching methods, or resource listings—on cards or sheets of paper. In all instances, for the sake of future reference, the source of the information should be recorded along with pagination. Then after notes have been taken, they should be organized according to a plan: by topic, period, or idea, or in some other logical way to facilitate future reference. Their subsequent resting place, when not in immediate use, should be one of a series of folders, a file box, or a filing cabinet. Organizational activity which at the moment may seem to reflect perfectionism may pay lavish dividends in the long run. In contrast, the student or teacher who relies too heavily on capricious fortune is likely later to spend untold hours attempting to recapture an idea that would have been just as close as a filing cabinet, provided he had recorded it at the time of first contact. Planning today is an investment in tomorrow's outcomes.

EXCESSES IN PLANNING TO
BE AVOIDED

Breaking through the aura with which we have surrounded planning, we warn against some obvious pitfalls in the process. The first is the allure of narrowness. The temptation is always great for any individual in search of organization to limit it to the confines of a single point of view, slanted references, or resources close at hand. The relaxing comfort of such circumscription resists change that has in its wake hard work, long hours, and the disturbance of new ideas.

Illustrative of this truth was a class led by a student-teacher, which the author observed recently. The student, with approval from the teacher of a unified-studies class, had developed a unit on communism. Courageous indeed was his noble venture, but less commendable the outcome. Instead of highlighting both the substantive and the emotionalized aspects of the topic, he strictured it into an identification and a discussion of the arguments that adolescents should use in combatting communism. Lost in the process was the basic philosophy of communism and its principles; in fact, free enterprise and competition made the real topic an almost forgotten issue. The student thus reflected the limitations of undue narrowness and one-sidedness in pre-planning.

Combatting narrowness is no less difficult than resisting the temptation to put every minute particle of a plan into operation, once it has been finalized. After creating a design for learning, teachers, like the proverbial clergyman, often seem compelled to "preach their sermon," regardless of a change in circumstances. As will be noted in the treatment of lesson designing, a plan is only as applicable as the demands of the moment make it. In a proper educational setting, planning must ever be regarded as a guide, but must never be permitted to crystallize.

In such a setting, the dangers of both over-planning and under-planning are to be avoided. The former is not uncommon in the insecure individual who, with less than sufficient confidence in himself, lives out a desire for perfectionism by doing too much. In his striving for security, he tends always to extend his activity just a little further than anyone else. He is the veritable master of resources. His is the file cabinet laden with note cards and other systematized data. Not unlikely, also, he is the teacher who will make adolescents and faculty colleagues cringe from the impact of his compulsive efforts.

At the other pole is the happy-go-lucky person who acts as if tomorrow will never come; indeed, the drudgery of anticipation is not for him. He is tardiness-prone. He begins to think about the next class when the opening bell tolls, and only after conveying his uncertainty to students does the accident of circumstances sometimes rise in his behalf. Things may get accomplished, but more often as a product of the sheer nature of psychic energy which steers positively when not detoured.

Somewhere in between these overdrawn extremes is the teacher who plans enough but not too much. He realizes that successful outcomes on any given day had their birth in the past. Thus, as he reaches into resources for the stimulants of learning, his academic eye is on the future. To him planning, although not always enticing, escapes drudgery because of the rewards that it brings. Education he considers so vital as to merit the best in design and organization.

TEACHER-STUDENT PLANNING

Up to this point, the teacher's contribution to planning has been treated more as an individualized than as a shared activity. However, like almost any other educational practice, it can become a cooperative venture between a teacher and pupils. When conceived in both contexts, leadership is observed to flow sometimes from the teacher directly, but at other times from teacher and pupils working in concert. The latter synthesis of effort is designated by the academic term "developmental planning," descriptive of a learning situation wherein all members of a class engage in the process of planning. The focus might be on a topic outline, a field trip, a choice of learning method, classroom decorum, selection of a class play, or a research project. Or it could be on the criteria for evaluating an opera in a music class, the formulation of goals in a health class, or care of property in an art class.

In all of these instances, the underlying premise is that the junior

partners in the enterprise know at least enough about the issue at hand
to share ideas and opinions about it. When, in contrast, the blind are
asked to guide those with vision, progress becomes a misnomer. It is necessary then that the teacher be sensitive to those curriculum opportunities
which lend themselves to a judicious employment of developmental effort.
Obviously, a class in chemistry where students are groping for understanding is not a case in point. But in a study of supply and demand, or
the right of eighteen-year-olds to vote, the class members could logically
be expected to bring enough understanding to the scene of planning to
contribute to, and grow in the process of designing, learning's outcomes.
Whether the activity would be for a day, a month, or even a semester, as
in a core class, is incidental to the process itself.

A teacher and students in a large suburban school were recently observed planning a unit on "The Newspaper." Their mutual deliberations
extended over a wide expanse of topics: Which newspapers did the class
members and their parents read? How can newspapers be evaluated?
What are the particular biases of selected papers: *The Chicago Tribune,
The Washington Post, The Indianapolis Star?* What interests are covered
in most newspapers, for example, sports, editorials, women's fashions, the
stock market, and so forth? After pooling their shared and individualized
knowledge and opinions for a period slightly exceeding two days, they
emerged with a design of content and proposed activities for a future time
block. And even if the several days devoted to planning were at the expense of other learning endeavor, who can deny that the gains in motivation, the values of problem solving, and the social compensations did not
outweigh the time "lost"?

The essentials of developmental planning are basically as follows:

1. The teacher must be secure enough to confine informality to work-
able dimensions. Mild confusion is inherent in the group process, but it
must be controlled.

2. The class members should have had past educational relationships
with individuals who permitted them to enjoy some benefits of freedom.
A background of authoritarianism does not serve this criterion well.

3. The class members should have worked together for at least a
brief period before extensive group planning is encouraged. A class first
must "jell" socially if it is to perform to a reasonable optimum.

4. The occasional "bad actors" who seem to plague at least a few
classes may necessitate directive methods by the teacher, if group pressures
have proved unsuccessful.

5. The progression should be from the planning of less important to
more important curriculum tasks. An early delegation of responsibilities
for roll-taking, decorum, and materials of instruction is possible. Planning
a unit, however, should come later.

6. The objectives of the developmental process should be identified
and discussed openly.

7. The obligations placed on students by the process should also receive careful emphasis.

8. Finally, limits should be defined and understood. Since a teacher can never delegate legal or professional responsibility, he should make crystal-clear the frame of reference in which the group process has to operate.

The teacher's role in shared planning is a sensitive one, changing, as readiness permits, from more to less directiveness. Although the instructional leader never becomes just one of the pupils, as he gets closer to them he plays his part more subtly. In essence, he becomes the social engineer and guide that we discussed earlier. A major task for him is to effect a climate of seriousness, mutual respect, and interest in learning so that group thinking can be effective. He directs the attention of the group at themselves, pointing up their need for self and group analysis. The need is for a group climate in which the members can initiate and sustain purposeful activity.

As the group achieves greater structure, the teacher then moves more into the role of resource person: stimulating, occasionally suggesting, answering when required, but rarely dictating. The sequence is not necessarily in neat arrangement from directive teacher, to engineer, to resource person, because the group process ebbs and flows unevenly, often moving ahead, sometimes regressing.

When the teacher plays his role with subtlety, he permits the group to assume as much independence as it can, and as rapidly as it can, even though some mistakes are made in the process. The leader who withdraws delegated authority upon a minimum of provocation would do better not to delegate at all. Nothing is more destructive to the group process than a front of democratic leadership.

As the teacher recedes gradually from overt leadership, pupils of necessity must become commensurately more active. Expressed similarly, with the teacher delegating more of his responsibilities, pupils must compensate for the loss of adult leadership by filling the created vacuum. Requisite to a proper balance, however, are readiness and timing. Not all adolescents are ready in the same way to participate in the dynamics of group relationships; in fact, young people unattuned to the complexities of group association often tend to become impatient with the tedium of the democratic process, turning consistently to the teacher for packaged answers. And a teacher impatient for quick outcomes may be inclined to provide such answers prematurely. What is needed is a teacher with receptiveness to cues coupled with a keen understanding of the characteristics of group activity. It is customarily painstaking and slow, the results are not immediately discernible, and it is demanding of thought and patience, but the long-term rewards are usually worth the effort.

The new teacher, however, should move gradually into the process. Before a too considerable involvement, he should become proficient in subject matter, have confidence in himself, and be more than passingly comfortable with adolescents. Until these outcomes are achieved, he should steer the course slowly. It is preferable to postpone action rather than to achieve only mediocre success or precipitate failure.

SUMMARY

Planning as conceived by the author is fundamental to effective teaching. The time spent in getting ready for a future outcome leads to future dividends. The process should begin as early as possible in the period of candidacy and never terminate. It differs in kind and amount, however, depending on such factors as purpose, curriculum expectations, pupil characteristics, and teacher attributes.

Its reasons for being are to give direction, insure against forgetting, provide confidence, underwrite sequence, clarify thought, and set a worthwhile example for youth.

The teacher plans in the areas of objectives, content, personnel, classroom management, and method. And he plans both alone and with students. A major goal is for him to delegate as much responsibility to adolescents as he can without abdicating legally or professionally. In this connection, he should consider the group process as a means of reaching decisions and as an instrument of growth for students. However, it was insisted upon that the very important preliminaries of the process should never be ignored.

REFERENCES

Alexander, William M., and Paul M. Halverson, *Effective Teaching in Secondary Schools*. New York: Holt, Rinehart and Winston, 1956. (Chapter 8)

Association for Supervision and Curriculum Development, *Creating a Good Environment for Learning, Yearbook*. Washington, D.C.: N.E.A. (Chapters 4 and 5)

Bossing, Nelson L., *Teaching in Secondary Schools*. Boston: Houghton Mifflin Company (3rd ed.), 1952. (Chapter 3)

Burton, William H., *The Guidance of Learning Activities*. New York: Appleton-Century-Crofts, Inc. (2nd ed.), 1952. (Chapters 12–14)

Macomber, Freeman G., *Teaching in the Modern Secondary School*. New York: McGraw-Hill Book Co., Inc., 1952. (Chapters 4 and 5)

Miel, Alice, and associates, *Cooperative Procedures in Learning*. Teachers College, Columbia University: Bureau of Publications, 1952.

Mills, Hubert H., and Harl R. Douglass, *Teaching in High School*. New York: The Ronald Press Company, 1957. (Chapter 10)

Schorling, Raleigh, *Student Teaching*. New York: McGraw-Hill Book Co., Inc., 1949. (Chapter 6)

UNIT
AND
DAILY
PLANNING

We have already established the postulate that, because planning is a foundation to all meritorious endeavor, the individual who desires to be productive must ready himself. When a person ignores the preliminaries, he becomes a victim of ensuing events which his lassitude and procrastination have helped to create. When attentive to the preliminaries, however, he becomes an organized instrument for the designing and shaping of life's tasks and situations.

Significant in the world of social endeavor is education, unique in its potential for changing existing conditions of human affairs. Its agents are the one million classroom teachers possessed of almost awesome power. With the stakes high, they can ill afford the luxury of purposelessness in any of education's important processes. On the contrary, their commission is a built-in orientation toward the future, with a commitment to plan for what is to come. The way will always be indefinite so long as the future is indefinite, but mature planning will remove at least some of the vagueness.

In Chapter 4 we presented a rationale for planning in a generalized frame of reference. In the current chapter, we deal more specifically with teaching operations, relating planning to both its daily and longer periods of implementation.

Priority over either daily or unit planning, however, must be given to the curriculum overview. Ideally, this should extend from the early elementary grades to the time of high school graduation and even beyond. Unfortunately, the backward look is usually myopic because of the vagaries of local school organization and the halting efforts of some administrators. In regard to the first deterrent, high school districts in many states are frequently independent of the feeder elementary schools. In this situation, it is not unusual for a secondary school to draw its personnel from as many as 12 to 14 independent elementary school systems.

With the curriculum diversity resulting from such decentralization, even a high school with an enlightened administration finds it completely impossible to build on a common base, because there is none. In fact, there might be as many bases as there are elementary districts. Faced with such a situation, the high school, through its background of past experience, a sound testing program, and improved efforts at articulation, discovers a compromise starting point and then projects into the three-, four-, or six-year future, depending on the local school organization.

Ideally, this projection should be formalized in a curriculum guide or syllabus designed to give scope and reasonable uniformity to the program. In schools which fall short of this ideal (and they constitute a majority) the teacher himself frequently has to create a long-term design that extends through the final year. In this way, he provides for himself range and context that are denied him by other administrative arrangements.

Regardless of how over-all curriculum structure comes into being, some semblance of a plan is a requisite for the purpose of overview. An exploratory industrial arts course in the ninth grade divided equally among woods, metals, printing, mechanical drawing, heavy shop, and electricity may be ill conceived if designed in isolation from a similar eighth-grade course. Likewise, a tenth-grade course in physical education which stresses only those major sports which might have been overstressed previously can scarcely be justified by logic or common sense. In similar fashion, the teacher of a course in algebra needs to know the coverage of the prerequisite course. The need for sequence in the foreign languages is just as obvious.

For reasons beyond his control, it may be impossible for a teacher to consummate articulation between schools, but he cannot escape the censor when he fails to relate those elements of a curriculum for which he is responsible to the larger whole. It is wise, then, for him to start with the cumulative *Gestalt* and then work forward. Into this setting we shall bring a defense for the unit method of teaching.

THE UNIT OF LEARNING

Leaving, operationally, the long-term curriculum pattern, the teacher must next look for ways of dividing the pattern into meaningful parts. These parts must be defensible individually while at the same time fitting into a unified whole. One such means of subdividing the curriculum is the unit method, which, while making positive contributions to education, has probably given rise to more disagreement on meaning than any other term in the field. There are a number of reasons for the confusion. First of all, educators at the elementary and secondary levels interpret the unit concept differently. The former make it a focal point of the entire curriculum about which all subjects revolve. For instance, the fifth-grade teacher engaged in a unit on frontier living would use it as a point of emphasis for arithmetic, creative writing, history, science, art, and music. The high school teacher of social studies, if he adopted the same topic and built a unit around it, would take a more restrictive view, confining his activities primarily to the one major teaching field.

Adding to the confusion is the tendency of at least a few educational writers to attribute almost magic-like importance to the unit method. Without under-evaluating its significance, we consider this method primarily as an extension and reorganization of learning approaches that the academic world has long known about and employed. However, its lack of originality in no way belittles the extent of its contribution.

A clarification of nomenclature early in the discussion should prove helpful. We shall use the following terms interchangeably: *unit of learning, unit of teaching, unit plan,* and *unit plan of teaching.* Of these, the term *unit of learning* we regard as the most descriptive.

What is a unit of learning?

A unit of learning is a comprehensive series of meaningful learning experiences built around a central theme or idea and organized in such a way as to result in appropriate behavioral changes in pupils. This definition, although providing a structure for the unit concept in broad terms, is admittedly too abstract at this point to convey clarity of meaning. Thus, we shall move immediately to the more specific, presenting first two unit plans, then following with a discussion of the sub-parts and the various concepts which undergird them.

The first unit to be considered is: "How Free—Yesterday, Today, Tomorrow?" It will have the format of a two-column analysis with the *what* (content) being paralleled by the *how* (method). It is intended for use in a twelfth-grade class in problems of democracy.

UNIT PLAN NO. 1

Unit topic: How Free—Yesterday, Today, Tomorrow?

Orientation to students: (To be mimeographed and distributed to them)

This unit probably will extend over a period of nine to ten weeks. We have studied in our text, reference books, and other sources the topics of the early germs of democracy, an ideal comes alive, the rise of the common man, nineteenth-century democracy, and twentieth-century problems. The course will probably terminate with this unit, since only eleven more weeks remain. A week or two at the end may be saved, however, for some last-minute things.

Readings have been selected which are broad in scope and varied in difficulty. I shall arrange a session wherein books and pupils can be paired off, that is, for those of you who wish this kind of help. If you run into books on the subject, not listed in the bibliography, that seem interesting, please see me about them. Maybe we can arrange a few substitutions. I want all of you to read at least two books. The fast readers should sign out the longer ones or read more than two.

In addition, I suggest that each of you do a short term paper on one of the basic freedoms, or discuss a substitute project with me. Later on, I'll hand out some instructions to you on this project. Let's confine it to around 1,000 words, or less, except for you "expert" writers who should not feel limited to 1,000 words. But don't bore both of us with filler.

Throughout the unit I shall be available in class, and occasionally after school or in a free period, for a personal interview with anyone who is struggling and in need of help. However, please don't come to me until you have worked conscientiously at solving your own problem. Maturity, remember, should lead whenever possible to independent problem-solving.

Get ready for an examination at the end of the unit. If we decide on one before, you will receive ample warning.

Objectives—General: (Also to be mimeographed and distributed)

1. Develop an understanding of the freedom we know in the United States and the demands placed on everyone by freedom.
2. Develop an increased capacity to meet the challenges usually associated with freedom.

Objectives—Specific:

1. Knowledge: Understand the
   a. Historical development of freedom,
   b. Obstacles to freedom,
   c. Role that citizens must play in a free society,
   d. Relativity of freedom.

2. Attitudes: Develop
   a. An increased devotion to freedom and its obligations,
   b. A greater tolerance of minorities and minority opinions,
   c. A greater appreciation of reading materials,
   d. A more positive attitude toward classmates and the classroom learning situation.

3. Skills: Develop
   a. A feel for the real as contrasted with the artificial in the application of freedom,
   b. Greater skill in classroom living,

c. Vocabulary proficiency,
d. Ability to do some independent research,
e. Greater writing skill.

Unit outline:

Content Outline	Methods and Techniques (suggested)
I. Historical Background	Teacher will introduce the unit and lead a discussion on the topics listed in I A, 1–10.
A. Events leading to Bill of Rights	
1. English jury system in 800's	List points 1–10 on board and discuss.
2. Common law in England	On the second or third day, pass out the book list.
3. Magna Charta	
a. Separation of church and state	Ask for a few volunteers to lead future classroom discussions. See them after class to plan further.
b. Origin of parliament	
c. Embryo of habeas corpus	
4. Mayflower compact	
5. Colonial affirmations of freedom	
6. Taxation without representation	
7. Colonies move toward unity as England becomes tyrannical	
8. First and Second Continental Congresses	
9. Articles of Confederation	
10. Ordinance of 1787	
B. Constitution and Bill of Rights	Show filmstrip: "Bill of Rights" (from Pictorial Events, 597 5th Ave., N.Y.) (about 40 minutes, including discussion).
1. Constitutional Convention of 1787	
a. State versus federal rights	Take 20 or 25 minutes to discuss the term paper on one of the basic freedoms.
b. Leaders	
c. Slavery	
2. The Constitution, 1789	
3. Bill of Rights	Cover B 1–6 by discussion, but ask two pupils previously designated to "take over" for half a period or longer.
a. Reasons for amendments	
b. Areas dealt with: religion, speech, meeting, press, arms, quartering of soldiers, searches, jury trial, life, liberty, property, rights of accused, those reserved to states, others.	Play record, "No Man Is An Island" (Paine and Patrick Henry) (Am. Book Co.) (8 mins.).
4. The 13th, 14th, and 15th Amendments	Volunteers for a bulletin-board committee will be solicited. They will assume responsibility for posting clippings pertinent to topics under discussion.
a. Slavery	

    b. Due process
    c. Rights—race, color
  5. The 19th Amendment—
    women's vote
  6. Other amendments and
    their implications for free-
    dom

II. Freedom in This Century

  A. 1900–1914
    1. Speech
    2. Press
    3. Religion
    4. Assembly
    5. Petition
    6. Before the law
    7. Suffrage
    8. Personal liberties
    9. Federal government's at-
      titude
    10. Minorities
    11. Free enterprise
  B. During First World War—
    (same eleven as in IIA)
  C. During the "Prosperity
    Decade"
    (same eleven)
  D. During the "Depression
    Decade"
    (same eleven)
  E. During Second World War—
    (same eleven)
  F. From 1945 to present—
    (same eleven)

Make a pupil responsible for at least half a period of discussion on each of the eleven topics.

Lead a discussion on the material not covered by the pupils.

Spend a day in class working with the group on the term paper.

Let them read in class or sign out books during a class. Help them in their choices.

Ask class to keep a list of the best television programs on freedom and have the list mimeographed.

Play record: Roosevelt's Jan. 11, 1944, message to Congress: "The Economic Bill of Rights" (Linguaphone Institution) (11 mins.).

III. Factors That Limit Freedom

  A. Citizens' refusal to perform
    duties
  B. Opposing groups don't follow
    democratic means
  C. War
  D. National emergency
  E. Subversive activities
  F. Propaganda
  G. Uninformed public
  H. Irresponsible communications
    media
  I. Pressure groups

Have the class form into buzz sessions to discuss each of these. Then ask for brief reports to the class.

The teacher will fill in the omitted material.

Ask about school propaganda, if any.

Relate all topics to the present as much as possible: television irresponsibility, biases of periodicals and newspapers, lethargic public, and so forth.

Give a period of class time for an introductory book review or two.

Ask all to keep vocabulary lists in notebooks.

IV. Formal Groups Defend Civil Liberties
   A. Congressional—Dies, La Follette, Velde, McCarthy, McClellan committees, etc.
   B. Civil liberties unit in Dept. of Justice
   C. Civil liberties unit of The American Bar Association
   D. American Civil Liberties Union
   E. N.A.A.C.P.
   F. Others

Ask class to read about and bring clippings, notes, and so forth, to class.
Ask class to evaluate the sources of information.

V. Freedom and Its Responsibilities
   A. Relativity concept
   B. Positive versus negative aspects
   C. Rights versus privileges
   D. My freedom must be honored by others

Teacher leads a discussion of these issues.
Hand out a list of technical words the class members should be familiar with.

VI. The Young Adult and Freedom
   A. Leadership responsibilities
   B. Self-control
   C. Being informed—if possible
   D. Common individual and group courtesies
   E. Others

Structure a socio-drama involving a racial situation.
Then do some role switching.
Next continue with the discussion.
Give quiz on selected technical expressions, e.g., *propaganda, editorializing, slanting.*

VII. Are more safeguards to freedom needed? If not, in what ways does society need to improve?

Use the buzz-session technique again.
Emphasize that improvement must come from within.
Relate discussion to operative value systems.

VIII. Evaluation

Class participation.
Book review by pupils, written in class.
Term paper.
Vocabulary notebooks.
Quiz on technical expressions.
Ask class to respond to two or three comprehensive essay questions on selected areas of the unit.
Class growth in citizenship as determined by observation.
Independence demonstrated throughout the unit.

Resources—Pupil

Basic Text
   Miers, Earl S., and Allan Nevins, *The American Story* (Great Neck, N.Y.: Channel Press, 1956).

General Readings—Non-Fiction

1. Allen, F. L.: *Only Yesterday,* Harper & Row.
2. Beard, Mary R.: *A Short History of the American Labor Movement,* The Macmillan Co.
3. Buckmaster, Henrietta: *Let My People Go,* Harper & Row.
4. Hendrick, B. F.: *The Age of Big Business,* Chronicles of America Series, Yale University Press.
5. (*and many more*).

Biography

1. Andrews, M. R. S.: *His Soul Goes Marching On,* Charles Scribner's Sons (Theodore Roosevelt).
2. Gosnell, H. F.: *Champion Campaigner: Franklin D. Roosevelt,* The Macmillan Co.
3. Sandburg, Carl: *Abe Lincoln Grows Up,* Harcourt, Brace & World, Inc.
4. (*and many more*).

Fiction

1. Steinbeck, John: *Grapes of Wrath,* The Viking Press.
2. (*and many more*).

Pamphlets

Those from B'nai Brith, Institute on Propaganda, Public Affairs Committee, National Conference of Christians and Jews, and so forth, will be listed.

Resources—Teacher

In addition to the above, all films and other materials needed will be listed for future resource reference by the teacher.

A second unit is "The Modern American Short Story—What Is It Like, and How Can It Be Interpreted?"[1] Before proceeding with the unit, a few explanatory comments are in order. It is for an English class at the junior level whose abilities are basically average and above average. This unit is usually taught early in the school year because the short story motivates easily and evokes ready identification with pupils' reading tastes and interests.

UNIT PLAN NO. 2

Unit topic: The Modern American Short Story: What Is It Like, and How Can It Be Interpreted?

Orientation to students: All of us have read a short story. It is actually the most-liked and best-known of all literary types. Short stories appear in books and current periodicals, many in such current magazines as *McCall's, Saturday Evening Post, Harper's,* and *Atlantic Monthly.* The story is primarily American in development and, with its brevity, intensity, and quick climax, appeals to millions.

[1] This unit plan was prepared by Mrs. Joan Smutny, former teacher of English at the New Trier Township High School and currently in charge of the "Cherub" program at Northwestern University. We express our thanks.

In the next five weeks of the unit, we'll answer these questions: What is the modern American short story like? What are some of its basic features and characteristics? Is there more to understanding a short story than just reading it for plot or to discover the villain's identity? You will be asked to read and interpret five of the short stories from your anthology and/or paperbound text. Two or three stories will be assigned and discussed per week, with one or two days' class discussion on each in order for us to penetrate more deeply into the core of a story. Analyzing and interpreting the short story will become a natural part of our class discussion.

In addition to the daily reading and discussion, I'd like you to choose a modern American writer and read three or four of his stories to broaden your perspective of the way he writes and what he writes about—his characters, pictures of society, values, and views of life. The total list of authors you may choose from includes Lardner, Thurber, Steinbeck, Hemingway, Faulkner, Aiken, Cather, and Benét. During the next week I'll confer with you about the authors and stories you might enjoy reading and interpreting. A paper of about 500 to 750 words, in which you analyze and compare these stories, will be requested at the beginning of the fourth week of the unit. The theme's content, format, organization, and adequacy of coverage will be detailed later.

Class members with identical choice of author will discuss the author and his stories in individual groups and then share insights with the entire group. Also, a few students will have an opportunity to lead discussions on short stories that the group reads. Our library has some excellent collections with stories by all the authors listed, and, as the librarian knows about our project, feel free to ask for her help in finding materials.

We shall have time to read in class one story from the *Saturday Evening Post, McCall's, Atlantic Monthly,* or *Harper's* in order to obtain an introductory view of a lesser-known contemporary writer.

At the end of the unit, an essay exam will be given on much of the material; no surprise quizzes, however! You may expect an examination at the end of the unit on the technical vocabulary of the short story. (See appended list.) My free periods for conferences include before and after school, second and fourth, in the English Office.

Objectives—General:

1. To stimulate an understanding of the development of the modern American short story.
2. To encourage the class to read and interpret stories more analytically; to achieve a heightened enjoyment and increased response to the short story in literature—what it is and does for the individual reader.

Objectives—Specific:

1. Knowledge: Understand the
   a. Short story as a literary type,
   b. Variety of content and treatment by the individual author, e.g., Thurber compared to Faulkner; Steinbeck compared to Aiken.
2. Attitudes: Develop increased
   a. Sensitivity to the short story,
   b. Empathy for literature—sense of identification with characters and their problems,
   c. Enjoyment of the dynamics of discussion and group processes,
   d. Empathy for members of the class through smaller discussion groups and reports to class.

3. Skills: Develop greater
   a. Ability to interpret and evaluate the short story by means of class discussion as well as individual work,
   b. Skill to work independently in reading, organizing, and writing term papers,
   c. Skill in participating in, as well as leading, group discussions,
   d. Vocabulary growth.

Unit outline:

The Modern American Short Story
(from 1900 to the present)

I. Introduction.

  A. What a short story is.
   [Teacher will introduce the modern American short story, discuss reasons for its popularity, ask about stories students have read and their personal responses to them. Hand out orientation and objectives mimeographed.]

  B. Brief historical background.
   [Teacher will discuss briefly the development of the short story up to 1900 and then show the filmstrip, "The Modern American Short Story." (Society for Visual Education, 1961) (40 minutes, including discussion)]

  C. The elements of a short story: action, characterization, setting, climax, point of view.

  D. Interpretation of the short story: ability to
   1. Understand various purposes of author: to entertain, inform, pose a problem, describe a situation or aspect of society.
   2. Analyze points of view from which story is told: first or third person, subjective or objective.
   3. Penetrate emotions, feelings, and attitudes of characters.
   4. Analyze story's action and point of climax.
   5. Comprehend author's view toward any or all of these topics: man, society, life, good and bad.
   6. Appraise story's inclusion of universality of idea, theme, emotions, as well as individuality of content and style.
   [Teacher will initiate discussion of these points, show how they can be applied to a story, and support the explanation visually with filmstrip, "Interpretation and Evaluation of the Short Story." (Society for Visual Education, 1961) (40 minutes including discussion)]

II. Three Basic Types of the Modern American Short Story.

  A. Realistic—author endeavors to portray life as it actually is, not should be.

  B. Psychological—author focuses on the emotions and attitudes of the characters, analyzing their motives and behavior.

  C. Satirical—author uses mockery or ridicule to criticize an idea, person, situation, or condition.

III. Three Types Illustrated.

  A. Realistic.
   1. John Steinbeck—"Flight."

      2. Ernest Hemingway—"Old Man at the Bridge."
      [Teacher will assign these stories for the class to read, discuss, and interpret. Concept of realism to be applied to both stories.]
  B. Psychological.
      1. William Faulkner—"Two Soldiers."
      2. Conrad Aiken—"Silent Snow, Secret Snow."
      [Teacher will discuss role of the psychological in writing and its influence on the 20th century. Assign class to read Faulkner and Aiken for group discussion. Concept of symbolism will be introduced—its appearance in the arts and literature, and inclusion in Aiken's story.]
  C. Satirical.
      1. James Thurber—"The Secret Life of Walter Mitty."
      [Teacher will introduce concept of satire; ask students to bring in examples of satire from newspapers, magazines, and literature for group discussion. Teacher will select student to lead class discussion on Thurber's story.]

IV. Short Stories in Periodicals.

  A. *The Saturday Evening Post.*
  B. *McCall's.*
  C. *Atlantic Monthly.*
  D. *Harper's.*

      [Teacher will request students to bring in magazines, will assign each a story to be read in class, later to be discussed in groups led by class members. Applying skills of interpretation as well as recognition of the type of story will be an integral aspect of these discussions.]

Student activity sheet:

1. Students will read for class discussions five short stories from the anthology and paperbound text: "Flight" by Steinbeck, "Old Man at the Bridge" by Hemingway, "Two Soldiers" by Faulkner, "Silent Snow, Secret Snow" by Aiken, and "The Secret Life of Walter Mitty" by Thurber.

2. Students will read one story from one of the following magazines: *Saturday Evening Post, McCall's, Atlantic Monthly,* and *Harper's.*

3. Students will read outside of class three or four stories by one of the following authors: Steinbeck, Hemingway, Thurber, Lardner, Aiken, Cather, and Benét. These will serve as a basis for the theme referred to in No. 4. (Refer to bibliography at end of unit for titles of anthologies and paperbacks in which stories may be found.)

4. All students will write a 500- to 750-word paper interpreting and comparing three or four stories by one of the above-mentioned writers. Students will evaluate their own papers before turning them in.

5. Students who have read stories by the same author will meet in small groups to analyze and compare their common ideas.

6. Next, each group will report back to the class, sharing results of the smaller group discussions with the entire class.

7. All students will be asked to evaluate the effectiveness of each student-led discussion.

8. Each student will be expected to appraise his own growth as an individual and member of the group, criteria to be decided developmentally.
9. The entire group will take an essay exam on the short stories read and discussed; only comprehensive questions will be asked.

Technical vocabulary of the short story:

characterization and character
   development
conflict
setting
point of view—subjective or
   objective
single effect
theme
style
realistic

psychological
satirical
universality
individuality
symbolism
local color
colloquialism
interpretation
evaluation

New words in the short story:

1. "Flight" by Steinbeck

aphido
metate
manzanita
clefts

dulces
keen
chaparral
meridian

abalones
cress
shale

2. "Old Man at the Bridge" by Hemingway

kilometer
Ebro

fascists
Barcelona

3. "Two Soldiers" by Faulkner

"the consolidated"
case history
"britching strap"

vetch, "Law"
"Yoknapatawpha County"

4. "Silent Snow, Secret Snow" by Aiken

carnelian
terrestrial
temperate zone
obliterated
abstracted quality
disingenuous
desiccated
externality
delta
congealed

perfunctorily
mortared
grotesque
parody
dalliance
prestidigitation
imminent
sibilance
alien
exulting

5. "The Secret Life of Walter Mitty" by Thurber

rakishly
carborundum
referendum
inscrutable
coreopsis

initiative
derisive
anesthetizer
tousled

Student resource sheet:

Basic Texts

Gehlmann, John, and Mary Rives Bowman, *Adventures in American Literature*, 1958. (Anthology)

Great American Short Stories. Edited by Stegner and Stegner, 1958. (Paperback)

Supplemental References (Anthology and Paperback)

Canby, H. S., and Bailey, K.: *The Book of the Short Story*, 1948.

Cerf, Bennett: *Modern American Short Stories*, 1945.

Day, A. Grove, and William F. Bauer: *The Greatest American Short Stories*, 1953.

Havighurst, W.: *Masters of the Short Story*, 1955.

Jessup, Alexander: *Representative Modern Short Stories*, 1944.

Kielty, B. A.: *A Treasury of Short Stories*, 1947.

O. Henry Memorial Award: *First Prize Stories, 1915–1954, from the O. Henry Memorial Awards*, 1954.

Schramm, Wilbur: *Great Short Stories*, 1950.

Stein, Phillip Van Doren: *The Pocketbook of Modern American Short Stories*, 1954.

Warren, Robert Penn, and Albert Erskine: *Short Story Masterpieces*, 1956.

Here are some specific points to note about the two units of learning. First of all, they were apparently inspired by the desire of the teachers to organize materials around a topic—not the materials of a textbook, but of their own choosing. Second, they provided the teachers with the opportunity to include a variety of learning methods: some teacher-centered, some pupil-centered. Third, they did not follow preconceived, set patterns, but rather they grew out of teacher organization.

Some of the elements contained in the units are as follows: (1) a brief transition from preceding subject-matter content, (2) class orientation to the unit and objectives, (3) suggested assignments with a certain amount of pupil choice, (4) subject-matter content to be covered, (5) teaching methods highlighted by variety: lecture, discussion, film, filmstrip, recordings, buzz sessions, pupil teaching, laboratory work in class, bulletin board activity, research, reading, and so forth, (6) a listing of pupil and teacher resources, and (7) methods of evaluating.

Important to remember, however, is the fact that the unit plan, not in itself possessed of magic, is no more or less effective than the teacher who develops and employs it. When rigidly prescriptive, it fails at least one of the criteria. When little more than an outline guide for the lecture, it is not considered by the author as a unit of learning at all. It is fundamental for the unit of learning to meet the standards of unity, reasonable comprehensiveness, methods variety with some student choice, and imaginativeness. Other attributes fall into place when these are present.

The reader should realize, however, that the term *unit plan,* or any of its synonyms, is conceived somewhat differently by different theorists and practitioners.

The several types of units

Educational literature is literally replete with distinctions between and among types of units without, in our opinion, the existence, at times, of any important basic differences. For example, readings uncover such terms as the Morrison unit, the unit of adaption, the subject-matter unit, and the experience unit—to name just a few. The last two, in particular, are contrasted frequently. The "subject-matter" unit is referred to as a unit that allegedly contains only "barren" content and makes little or no provision for pupils' participation. The so-called "experience" unit is correspondingly described as one that reaches to the core of true learning and that culminates in active pupil experience. Whatever the label, a unit must contain subject matter; and any unit that is effective must culminate in meaningful experiences for pupils. Thus, an artificial separation into set types may well confuse more than clarify.

Basically, we feel comfortable about distinguishing between units only on the criterion of how they come into being, that is; were they teacher-prepared or were they developmentally conceived? If the former, as exemplified by Plans Nos. I and II presented previously, the teacher does most of the planning behind the scenes and presents the pupils with a more or less completed whole. However, even within this framework, the creative teacher is willing, even anxious, to accept suggestions from students after they have become dynamically involved. The second, or developmental type, is one created by pupils and teacher working together. But the teacher is by no means thereby relieved of the task of preparing; rather, he prepares so as to become an informed resource individual who, in such a role, can help pupils better to achieve well-formulated goals and then to implement these goals with intelligent action.

Purposes served by units of learning

Up to this point, the topic of unit teaching has been pursued through the medium of the two unit plans themselves and selected generalizations about them. In this last part of the treatment, we propose to reinforce the foregoing by a more detailed discussion of the specific features of a unit plan. Each has been introduced by an italicized statement.

The first topic to be treated in such manner is the purposes served by the unit of learning. Just why has the academic world become so interested in the unit as a teaching device, and what are its unique contributions?

The unit encourages organization into larger wholes. The simple fact that units extend beyond a one-day period encourages teachers to organize learning into larger blocks, effecting clearer perspective as a result. Unitary wholeness is certainly a factor to be cherished. That the upsurge of interest in unit learning coincided roughly with the development of gestalt psychology was not coincidental. Both are concerned with wholeness of vision, emphasizing that the totality of an event or situation is greater than the sum of its parts.

The teacher and pupils who would use the unit plan "How Free— Yesterday, Today, Tomorrow?" should emerge with a greater feeling of wholeness and a perspective on freedom than if they had encountered the concept several dozen times in a year's course in United States History. Even though the same over-all coverage might have been made through the additive method, the result would not have been the same. The concept of freedom might well have been lost in, or dulled by, the period approach to history. The illustrated unit, in contrast, is lifted from the context of other historical variables and made to stand out in sharp relief as an entity of unique importance.

The unit stimulates teacher activity. Anyone who brings a unit of learning into being is propelled thereby into an active role, and any act of creation is accompanied by labor. The unit plan is not an exception. The teacher of the unit, of necessity, must personally plan the specific content materials that will be covered and detail the selected activities in which students will be encouraged to engage. And ideally he should, whenever practicable, consult students for their suggestions on both content and method. Following the planning phase, the teacher next has to activate the unit and keep it moving in a desirable direction. His is a dynamically creative role but also, again, an engineering role.

The teacher of the unit stands in contrast to the teacher who methodically pursues a textbook sequence; the latter loses much of his academic identity in the too-slavish following of the ideas of another. This individual has little need for the greater intricacies of planning, because, not being a creator, he can follow the line of simplicity.

The unit should precipitate a greater variety of materials and methods. When the teacher is responsible first for the conception and then for the development of a concept or schema, he is prone to invest more of himself in the project's success. A usual dividend of this greater personal involvement is enrichment of the materials of learning emanating from both conventional and less conventional approaches. For example, he may draw into use a previously unused reference in the school library, a community agency eager to assist, or a new employment of student resources. Such variety is a natural by-product of the creative act which removes teaching from the base of the routine and commonplace.

Some not uncommon classroom transformations to be expected from use of the unit might be a change from the single text to many texts, from teacher planning to developmental planning, from large-group to small-group or individual learning, and from extensity to intensity of content emphasis. These results do not automatically accompany the unit of learning, but they become more realistically possible as a result of its application.

Some essential characteristics of the unit

Although previously treated in descriptive terms, the specific characteristics of a unit will be outlined here with brief comments, to serve as a check-list or guide for the teacher who is preparing a unit of his own.

The unit must be unified and delimited. Redundant though this statement may be, the meaning is of significance. A unit needs balance and wholeness, and its theme must emerge from and move toward unity. This outcome can be best achieved when the purposes of the plan are defined clearly, when the content is envisioned as teachable, and when the plan is reasonably circumscribed in time. A unit captioned "United States History" is conceivable as a topic of a unit plan, but it fails the test of teachability and time circumscription. A number of smaller units with more cohesiveness are preferable to a larger one which gets lost in its own size.

It should fit into context. The unit should never lose its identity as a part of a greater whole. The progression is always from organized curriculum experiences of the past to related experiences of the future. Without this contextual tie-in, the danger is ever present that learning will be fragmented and left to exist in isolation.

It should motivate. With its greater variety of method, with the freedom it allows to students, and with its unity, the unit method is richly endowed with motivational power. But the teacher of wisdom, taking nothing for granted, devotes as much time as needed, at the beginning of the unit, to selling its importance to students. As with any long-range design, an early oversight or failure can adversely affect the anticipated outcomes of the project. Therefore, intelligence demands the employment of almost all legitimate means, short of melodramatic ones, to get the unit moving interestingly in the right direction.

It should provide methods variety. This feature is listed here only for the sake of completeness. It was covered in the previous section.

It should be reasonably comprehensive. Having previously cautioned against the overwhelming effects of a sweepingly broad topic, such as "United States History," we now warn against the other extreme: the topic of too limited dimensions. *The Masque of the Red Death* might lend itself logically to unit teaching, but it would fit better into a larger unit on the short story or on the combined works of Poe. Even more circumscribed would be such topics as "The First Personal Pronoun," "The Battle of Shiloh," or "The Indefinite Article in Latin." The unit demands comprehensiveness, and minutiae often must concede to breadth and interrelationships.

It should reflect the purposes of learners as well as of teachers. Whether the unit is developmentally or teacher conceived, provision should be made for pupil purposes and interests. The breadth of subject matter covered and the variety of methods employed should facilitate the meeting of the needs of differing individuals. Choice of activities by the pupils, whenever practical, is recommended.

It should lead to problem-solving activities. Whenever practicable, the effective unit should confront students with problem situations that lead to decision-making. In a unit on Poe, such a situation might arise from the commission: "Of the six short stories of Poe that you have read, select the one which you consider best; then defend your stand." Or, in a unit in arithmetic: "Now that you know how to divide fractions, investigate the underlying reasons for inversion and multiplication." These active processes of learning are always preferable, when the context permits.

It should never lose direction. Our reason for insisting on objectives as being vital to the unit plan, as previously indicated, is that they provide direction. They have radar-like properties which keep the unit on course. At the end of the project, teachers should regularly reread the objectives as a check on the unit's validity: Did it arrive at its destination, and in the proper way?

It should provide for evaluation. If an initial task of the unit is purpose, a final task is an evaluation of how well the purpose has been served. The answer to the question several lines above would entail evaluation, not necessarily by testing alone but by the most appropriate and effective means available.

It should provide resource lists. Whenever a teacher or students can gain from a separate listing of unit resources, the list should be provided. The teacher gains in the sense that such a list perpetuates names, titles, and other information that he may need at a later date. The student gains by being provided with tools that he can immediately employ: a bibliography, a list of activities to perform, or instructions to follow.

Method and content should be integrated. The presentation of content (the what) always needs to be accompanied by an immediate consideration of method (the how). A unit outline of content followed several pages later by suggestions on method denies to these two elements an otherwise functional relationship. In Unit I, a two-column analysis was employed; in Unit II, an alternating content-methods sequence. Integration, not an exclusive feature of content and method, is, in fact, a desirable component of all parts of a unit plan. Only through integration is unity possible.

A few dangers and weaknesses of the unit of learning

Like any procedure, the unit plan has fallibility, and an early recognition of the sensitive areas should make for a more intelligent utilization.

It demands much of the teacher. The unit method is not suited to the teacher who likes the comforts of a short week. On the contrary, the unit is so demanding of effort that usually only the more dedicated teachers are willing to organize and implement learning this way. Another look at the sample units will reveal that, despite some weaknesses, they were not developed in a few hours. But when employed functionally, the resulting increase in teacher originality, with the consequent extension of pupil response, would serve in great part to compensate for the additional expenditure of time.

Its usage should be spaced by the inexperienced teacher. Because of the tyranny of its demands, the unit approach should be used sparingly by the first-year teacher. The teacher will do better to walk before trying to run. Until the inexperienced person gets his feet solidly on the ground, he should set limits to his use of the method. Insecurity and relative unfamiliarity with youth and the high school curriculum do not compose a fertile ground for well conceived learning units.

Units should rarely be borrowed from others. Although Teacher A may be nice enough to exchange units with Teacher B, and vice versa, neither one may be getting a bargain. For the unit to be effective, it should be the reflection of a teacher's unique personality. If creativity and originality are its keynotes, it is then futile for the teacher to attempt to realize them through another's efforts.

Units get out of date. Planning would be relaxing if units could be accumulated over a long period of time and did not require modification as the occasion warranted. Like textbooks and other written materials, however, units, too, become outdated. Therefore, some revision is almost regularly needed before they can be used for repeat performances.

Units may affect time sequence adversely. In the use of units, the teacher cannot permit the factors of time to be ignored or confused. Chronology is needed in almost every organized situation, the classroom not excepted. If units fail to meet the goal of chronology, additional means will have to supply it. Fortunately, however, most good textbooks provide for this need.

A last word on the topic

The unit, as we have conceived it, is an escape from the built-in sequence of a textbook and from the depressant of superimposed content with directed implications for method. More than any of its other attributes, the unit returns the robes of professionalism to the teacher, commissioning him to tap his own creativity. It demands that the teacher, by extending his research and reorganizing his ideas, bring something new into being. Admittedly, he will not create daily or weekly; but, when the spirit moves, the unit method will become a vehicle on which individualism can ride. It is preferable for the teacher to bring imagination to the classroom than for him to opiate students with "tired" subject matter that is never really changed but is only dusted off.

THE DAILY LESSON PLAN

Within the comprehensive scope of a school curriculum which reaches from the early elementary grades to the final grade of high school, the individual teacher, with or without a formalized curriculum guide, needs to chart a yearly course. Within this setting he decides which parts of the year's work, if any, should be converted into units of learning. Irrespective of this decision, he regularly has to prepare for the demands of any given day or class. A unit plan may extend from a minimum of several days' duration to one of weeks or months, depending on the content; whereas the daily plan is only for the following or some other single school day of the future.

The lesson plan, even though for only a delimited period, is no less necessary. For any school that has remained in operation, tomorrow has always come, and with it the inevitability of program requirements along with teacher-preparation for them. Regardless of the specific nature of a class's activities—a discussion, a field trip, a supervised study period, lecture or even an election of officers in a home room—all must be predesigned in some way.

The sheer act of getting ready for a specific class by reducing an anticipated plan to writing is a step in the direction of assuring definiteness and orderliness. The design might be in almost word-for-word detail (on rare occasions), in the form of a short or lengthy outline, or occasionally in just a few informal notes jotted down. Regardless of form, the lesson plan can go far in contributing structure to the learning situation.

Does the effective plan necessarily have to be in written form? Or will memory suffice? This issue has been debated at length almost from the time of the first formal school. Although experience gives license to short cuts, the human frailties of most teachers dictate the need of a written prop. To these individuals, an insurance policy against forgetting and resultant disorganization is worth all the time spent in reducing planning to writing. A close analogy exists between planning for a public address and for teaching. In each instance, memory alone may suffice, but with its capriciousness, the danger that it might fade out at the wrong time with embarrassing consequences is always present. In either instance, whether for a speech or for a teaching experience, a written plan of some kind is a useful mechanical aid.

In addition to the advantages mentioned, a lesson plan serves two other purposes: first, it perpetuates in skeleton form what has transpired; second, it meets a requirement of many school systems that teachers, in anticipation of possible illness, plan learning activities from a day to a week in advance and always have written plans available for a substitute teacher. Even though these administrative reasons are less important than the professional ones mentioned, they provide additional support for a before-the-fact articulation of ideas.

Whatever the specific purpose of a plan, appropriate length should be a major consideration. At the one extreme is the perfunctory notation or two which might bail a teacher out of a few difficulties but which would provide only a minimum of organization. At the other pole is the perfectionist's plan with so much structure that any teacher could get lost in it. The ideal obviously is a balance: the plan needs to be long enough to guide the instructional leader to his predetermined goals without being so lengthy as to stifle spontaneity along the way. As a minimum, it should provide an overview of the curriculum's focus for that day, should jog the teacher with enough symbols to insure organization, and should be in a format that will permit easy referral with only a glance or brief fixation.

Notwithstanding the merits of lesson planning, the plan itself should never become an inviolable determiner of the curriculum. In this connection, in the early 1950's, General MacArthur was returning from Japan to deliver what later turned out to be his "Old Soldiers Never Die" speech. At the time, the author was university supervisor of several student teachers, one of whom had been placed in a world history class in a near-by suburban school. The MacArthur story was actually making history, electrifying old and young alike. One stop in his trek from the Orient to the Nation's Capital was in a suburb of a large midwestern city, on which occasion the local multitudes turned out to greet and be greeted at a distance by the international personality. For days the censored general was the center of news and discussion wherever one turned.

In the midst of the saga, the supervisor visited the classroom in which the student teacher mentioned had been placed, arriving on a day when the students were almost demanding that the unit on the Russo-Japanese War of the early twentieth century concede to a discussion of the MacArthur story. The classroom teacher's response was a strongly worded "turndown," informing the students that a lesson plan had been prepared on the Russo-Japanese War, and that the plan was going to be followed to the letter. Granted that a case could be built to support the teacher's decision, a certain element of rigidity characterized it. Although plans should customarily be followed, they should never be extended to tyranny. The teacher in question may have become the servant of the plan rather than its master.

Lesson plans as aids to the individual teacher should fit his specific needs, being usually longer for the beginner and shorter for the experienced. It is important that they be in the teacher's own style of English usage, while being also understandable to the possible substitute. No combination of statements can cover all situations for all teachers. It is enough to say that each teacher needs to feel his way in daily planning until he satisfies himself in the light of the minimum standards of a school and his own high professional ones.

The basic elements of a daily lesson plan are: a topic, goals, curriculum content, and method, with time estimates included. In addition, depending on circumstances, the plan may include transitions, an assignment, proposed methods of evaluation, and a summary. However, we state with some obviousness that no set format will suffice for all classroom occasions. With a curriculum varying so widely, from the informality of a core class to the formality of a lecture situation, and from group drill to individual research, uniformity is a naïve expectancy. Thus the two specific examples of daily plans which follow we identify as illustrative only.

The first of the following plans is one with minimum structure—much too little, probably, for the formalist—but reasonably adequate for the flexible, experienced practitioner.

DAILY LESSON PLAN I

Date: October 1, 19___ *Class:* Seventh-Grade Mathematics

Goals: To acquaint pupils with the symbolic language of the circle graph, as an economical means of conveying mathematical concepts.

Classroom activities: The first half of the hour period will be spent with the teacher introducing the topic verbally, then projecting an example of a circle graph on the blackboard.

Next, the assignment will be given: Construct a circle graph around either of the topics: (1) How I Spent Yesterday, or (2) Where My Money Goes.

During the last part of the period, the students will begin the assignment at their desks, assisted by the teacher.

This is a rather specific description of a projection of one day's activities. It presents the motif of the learning situation, establishes direction, suggests methods to be employed, and sets time limits. We admit that a seasoned performer would go into many classes with even a briefer plan than this.

A second example, built around a study of the ballad, is somewhat more detailed than the first.

LESSON PLAN II

Date: Sept. 14, 19___ *Subject:* 9th Grade English *Topic:* Stories in Song

Objectives: Introduce the ballad content and origin in a musical setting as a key to people and cultures.
Develop appreciation for it as a literary form.

Outline of Content	*Methods To Be Used*
1. What is a ballad?	Get ideas from pupils; after a few minutes, give them a definition.
A romantic or sentimental song. A song that tells a story— emphasize: simplicity repetition refrain, etc.	Then ask them to illustrate with modern ballads. Pass out mimeographed sheets of "Floyd Collins" and "Oh Susanna."
(15 mins.)	
2. Gleaning the story from a ballad. (10 mins.)	Play from record of Bellafonte—2 ballads.
3. Conduct a brief discussion of the types of people who would sing ballads; who sang them long ago. (10 mins.)	Call on those who have been saying little of late.
4. What are their favorite ballads? (5 mins.)	Have each one write a favorite ballad title on a piece of paper and then tally totals. See which ballad is most popular.

Assignment: The early Renaissance ballads in the anthology, pp. 79–85. Have the class get ready to relate the content to the terms used today: *simplicity, repetition, refrain, story.* Start on the assignment toward the end of the hour and help at desks.

This section we terminate on the theme that, regardless of outside suggestions concerning daily planning, the teacher himself must create his own plan, conceived in an ongoing situation. Personalities, purposes, and subjects differ too widely for stereotyping to be condoned—much less encouraged. Four practices, however, are definitely to be condemned: too little or no planning, slipshod planning, too much planning, and a foolish consistency in planning. Outside of this framework of error, we recommend wide latitude, with enlightened teacher individualism determining what is correct for a given situation at a given time.

SUMMARY

The focal emphasis of the present chapter has been planning, first in broad and later in daily perspective. Ideally, the process should begin with an overview reaching from kindergarten through high school, to be followed by a yearly projection, then reduced to a unit size, and finally ending with planning for each day's activities.

Two specific unit plans were introduced, one on the freedoms, and the other, on the short story. The contrasting styles were a two-column content-and-methods analysis, as opposed to an alternating content-methods presentation. Regardless of style, the unit of learning was defended for the unique opportunity it affords teachers to create rather than to follow too closely the contributions of another.

After a detailing of the pros and cons of unit planning, two lesson plans were presented, one on the circle graph, and another on the ballad.

The chapter ended on the note that planning, within approved perspective, must be the function of each teacher in the light of all situation variables.

REFERENCES

Alexander, William M., and Paul M. Halverson, *Effective Teaching in Secondary Schools*. New York: Holt, Rinehart and Winston, 1956. (Chapter 8)

Alberty, Harold, *Reorganizing the High School Curriculum*. New York: The Macmillan Company (rev. ed.), 1953.

Alcorn, Marvin D., Richard A. Houseman, and Jim R. Schunert, *Better Teaching in Secondary Schools*. New York: Holt, Rinehart and Winston, 1954. (Chapters 3 and 4)

Bossing, Nelson L., *Teaching in Secondary Schools*. Boston: Houghton Mifflin Company (3rd ed.), 1952. (Chapter 3)

Burton, William H., *The Guidance of Learning Activities*. New York: Appleton-Century-Crofts, Inc. (2nd ed.), 1952. (Chapters 12–14)

Macomber, Freeman G., *Teaching in the Modern Secondary School*. New York: McGraw-Hill Book Co., Inc., 1952. (Chapters 4 and 5)

Peel, J. C., "The Ubiquitous Unit," *Phi Delta Kappan*. December 1955, pp. 119–121.

Rivlin, Harry N., *Teaching Adolescents in Secondary Schools*. New York: Appleton-Century-Crofts, Inc., 1961. (Chapter 5)

Strickland, Ruth G., *How to Build a Unit of Work,* Bulletin No. 5. Washington, D.C.: U.S. Office of Education, Federal Security Agency, 1946.

FOUR
NEW EXPERIMENTAL
TEACHING
METHODS

Planning, when other than perfunctory, demands a prior determination of what methods of instruction will be employed to accomplish the goals of any given curriculum. And the range of methods for selection is broadening in many public and private school systems to accommodate some recent arrivals upon the methods scene. With new processes being rarities in any phase of a culture, the growth of the late-comers to education in the past decade has been little short of astonishing. Centers of attention in this chapter will be four of the most important of these new methods: teaching by television, team teaching, teaching machines, and the language laboratory. All but the second are technologically oriented, and even this one has leanings in that direction.

TEACHING BY TELEVISION

With the coming of commercial television in 1946, progress in communication was accelerated in an unforgettable way. Only the telephone, telegraph, and radio could come close to matching its impact. Its influence on the amusement habits of people was immediate; on education, not long delayed. Even at its inception, little imagination was required to envision the tremendous power that it could wield over the minds of men. Accordingly, education began almost immediately to solicit its good services.

The story of the ultimate marriage is an intriguing one, and the written coverage voluminous—so voluminous that this textbook's purpose can be best served by a reporting of only broad trends. We desire, however, to give special recognition to the following stimulating treatments:

1. Dunham, Franklin, Ronald Lowdermilk, and Gertrude Broderick, *Television in Education*. Washington, D.C.: United States Department of Health, Education, and Welfare, Office of Education, 1957.
2. Ford Foundation, *Teaching by Television*. New York: The Ford Foundation, 1961.
3. Lewis, Philip, *Educational Television Guidebook*. New York: McGraw-Hill Book Company, Inc., 1961.
4. Midwest Program on Airbourne Television Instruction (Mary Howard, ed.), *Television in Education*. New York: McGraw-Hill Book Company, Inc., 1961.
5. Stoddard, Alexander J., *Schools for Tomorrow*. New York: The Ford Foundation, 1957.
6. Tarbet, Donald G., *Television and Our Schools*. New York: The Ronald Press Company, 1961.

The union of television and education received fulfillment at three points of contact: through commercial outlets, a relationship more frustrating than satisfying; through educational channels, an experience compensatory for the earlier frustrations; and through closed-circuit media, likewise rewarding.

Of the three approaches, open-circuit television is the instrumentality with the greatest educational potential, but when employed primarily to serve commercial interests, the greater social values can be only approximated. Yet within this framework of avowed materialism, the television industry, denied excesses by governmental controls, has known moments of culture. Programmers of vision have recognized that the tastes of the few, as well as the appetites of the many, must be satisfied if the medium is to be for all the people. Thus, as a reflection not only of enlightened self-interest but selected consumer desires as well, the industry has brought to the people Shakespearean drama, symphonies, the poetry of Frost and Sandburg, the Lanza legend, and even an occasional novelette of Conrad. Admittedly, however, these reversals of form are too rare for open-circuit television to make other than an incidental contribution to formal education. Even when a sequence with commendable learning possibilities is offered, the school is often plagued with the problem of scheduling. The early evening or week-end program can be accommodated, with effort. The late night period is impractical, and the daytime program may cut across class-period limits.

Recognizing, without unduly condemning, commercial television's limitations, education next began to investigate the possibilities of securing a number of channels which it could directly control. If this venture should prove successful, instructional programs of a high order could be conceived and projected with only the legitimate objectives of education governing. The competitive influences of commercial sponsors and programs would be minimized.

This new effort was crowned with success in 1952 when the Federal Communications Commission set aside 242 channels for the exclusive use of education. Within a short period, the initial allocation was increased by fourteen to 256; and by 1961, was increased by eleven more to a total of 267. The pioneering stations extended from WHYY-TV in Philadelphia to KCTS-TV in Seattle; and from KTCA in Minneapolis and St. Paul to WBIQ in Birmingham. The Midwest was represented, for instance, by WTTW of Chicago and KETC of St. Louis.[1]

The old communications form thus newly directed soon found expression in telecourses both for and without college credit, in live experiences of educational significance—such as Albert Schweitzer's philanthropic activities, in worthwhile hobby programs, in more legitimate drama, in displays of famous works of art, in more stark realism—such as contained in Dreiser and Wright—and in household-interest tips of significance. The telecourses themselves have been, and still are, in almost every curriculum area, from guidance to the classically academic, to the fine and applied arts.

The colleges and universities which have pioneered in offering and accrediting such courses are increasing in number each year. In the mid-fifties, according to Dunham and his associates, approximately twenty such institutions were experimenting in this area.[2] At the present moment, the total is many times that number and is still increasing at a rapid pace.

The gains made possible by this specialized educational offshoot of the older medium have been considerable, but progress has not been without attendant problems. These reside primarily in the arduousness of the television process itself: the need for and the tediousness connected with licensing; difficulties in determining appropriate areas of coverage; the almost insurmountable cost of the technical personnel needed in the mechanical process of programming; the finding of performers who can meet both the technical and the educational demands of their assigned roles; and the difficulties in discovering and relating to the levels of the fluctuating audiences.

Television's third entente with education occurred with the first closed-circuit experiment in 1955. The two communication forms have become more intimately associated with the passage of time. The earliest pioneer of stature was the Washington County School System of Hagerstown, Maryland, which in 1956 embarked on its closed-circuit venture

[1] Franklin Dunham, Ronald Lowdermilk, and Gertrude Broderick, *Television in Education.* (Washington, D.C.: U.S. Department of Health, Education and Welfare, 1957), pp. 97–98.
[2] *Ibid.,* pp. 9–10.

which by 1961 involved almost 17,000 students daily. Following in the wake of this experiment, between 30 and 40 other school systems moved into the field of closed-circuit television during the next several years. Most of these systems were located in suburban and large-city areas. Some of these were single-building school systems with the new medium employed in only the one building. Others were multi-building systems with the medium piped to selected institutional outlets or to all of them. Wherever television was introduced, the respective staffs embarked on a project of curriculum analysis in preparation for the advent of the anticipated newcomer.

Closed-circuit television basically is a means whereby a school system or other institution can create and project a program of its choosing to an audience within the reach of its coaxial cables. The three necessary elements are: facilities where programming can take place, a cable system which will carry the program to the audience, and receptor equipment. Ideally, all the facilities, along with a master antenna system, should be built into a school system at the time of construction. Such foresight is a significant money saver. Without it, installation costs rise appreciably.

The personnel needed are of four types: (1) television performers, usually designated as Master Teachers, who are "on camera" when a program is being projected; (2) teacher monitors or proctors, who, in the respective receiving rooms, keep order, collect and distribute materials and equipment, answer questions, evaluate, and record progress; (3) pupils, for whom the whole process is conceived and who must know their expected roles; and finally, (4) engineering personnel, who advise on mechanical matters, maintain equipment, and make needed repairs.

The operation begins at the level of planning, wherein one or more teachers create a design for subsequent projection. Planning flows into the programming phase, wherein a Master Teacher performs either on tape or "live." Following this performance, other professional individuals associated with the Master Teacher usually work with their smaller, class-sized groups, interpreting, implementing, reiterating, and possibly reviewing. The last phase is evaluative, occurring sometimes in the large group, at other times in the small group.

The curriculum avenues of closed-circuit television are almost as numerous as the respective areas of the curriculum, differing, however, from school to school and from system to system. As reported in the Ford Foundation's *Teaching by Television,* the Hagerstown experiment extended into all six grades of the secondary school and was employed to provide instructional opportunities in the following curriculum areas: conversational French, core, English, general science, mathematics, music, physics, practical arts, and United States history.[3] As many as seven subjects were taught via television at the seventh-grade level, but only three at the ninth- and tenth-grade levels.

[3] Ford Foundation, *Teaching by Television* (New York, 1961), p. 47.

The advantages attributed to the medium of instructional television are extensive, consistently including several or all of the following:

1. Instructional television capitalizes on the specialized competencies of teachers by employing those with greater ability and talent as television performers. In this way, a larger pupil audience receives the qualitative best of a teaching staff.

2. Through the same process, it encourages the less capable teachers to improve through the observation of their colleagues.

3. It permits, through team teaching, the rotation of teachers before the television screen, thereby securing the best from each performer.

4. It encourages more careful preparation by program personnel, in recognition of the greater demands placed on them by the larger audience, including fellow teachers.

5. It encourages a qualitative assessment of the curriculum, as teacher teams debate and decide on curriculum problems which relate to television.

6. It results in better curriculum organization because of a higher quality of planning.

7. It encourages students to accept more responsibility by denying them the opportunity of immediate questioning.

8. It is less costly than educational television.

The limitations of, and some problems inherent in, the medium are these:

1. It is primarily a lecture-demonstration method relying almost exclusively on telling, explaining, and showing.

2. It sells short the intangibles of educational outcome such as attitudes and social-citizenship skills. These attainments are relegated to a status secondary in importance to the knowledge learnings.

3. It places the teacher "on camera" in a de-personalized relationship with students.

4. It can attend only inadequately to the individual differences and specialized needs of students.

5. It is injurious to the morale of those teachers who have little or no opportunity to perform on the screen.

6. It demands more cooperative endeavor among teachers—often a difficult commodity to come by.

7. It forces on teacher education a new dimension in teaching—television performance. Until the profession is readied for the new responsibility, quality performers will be at too great a premium.

8. It may be more costly for these reasons:
   a. A lighter load is imperative for the teacher performer.
   b. No saving of other personnel is possible if small classrooms are employed as receiving stations and teachers have to man them.
   c. Installation and maintenance of equipment constitute a substantial financial item.

Reported evaluations, up to the present limited in number, and suspect by some of considerable bias, indicate that when achievement examinations are the criterion of evaluation, pupils who are engaged in the process of closed-circuit television education do as well as their control counterparts.[4] However, cautious reservation regarding the findings is in order. Any new experiment tends to bring out the best in the participants. Furthermore, the number and time limits of the experimental projects are as yet too restricted to be statistically significant. Also, evaluations have invariably been made by foundations or school systems that have underwritten the experiments in the first place—a research situation scarcely conducive to objectivity.

Just as objectionable as premature optimism, however, is unsupported skepticism. Thus, the author recommends a kind of agnosticism during this experimental period in which teacher candidates, as practical individuals, should look forward to possible participation in some phase of television education. A too-early taking of sides should be replaced by a sensible planning for a conceivable outcome.

At least, we can say that the educational value of television is no longer in doubt, and, as with other audio-visual methods of the past, its potential will continue to be studied; its employment will increase, perhaps at an almost too rapid pace; and its true merits will always be a product of the specific situation of the moment. When employed as part of an ensemble, its services will be commendatory; when overused or when implemented at the improper place or time, its value will be lessened.

Certainly, educational television will be the servant of, but will not replace, teachers any more than films have replaced them. It will modify but will not radically change the curriculum. Its effect will invariably be more to enrich what already exists than to bring into being a new dimension. The real job of the future, in our opinion, will be not to determine whether television as an educational medium is here to stay, but to discover how it can best serve. In the meantime, candidates should anticipate a possible future role involving the new medium.

In the final analysis, the curriculum significance of educational television probably will depend on the success of educators in satisfactorily answering the following questions:

1. Which areas of learning respond best to a telling-listening-showing situation? When these are more clearly determined, television will then be used with greater confidence.

2. Which important outcomes of learning cannot be accomplished by telling, listening, and showing? Can independence, altruism, citizenship, research skills, emotional control, effective speaking habits, analytical thought, or problem solving be achieved through these means—and, if so, to what degree?

4 Arthur D. Morse, *Schools of Tomorrow Today* (Garden City: Doubleday and Co., Inc., 1960), pp. 87–88.

3. When telling, listening, and showing are effective learning media, what is the proper balance in any curriculum area between the impersonal, large audience and the more personal, small-group approach?

4. How can teachers not in the prestigious on-camera category be made to feel professional? Might they not in the future create a turnover problem of serious proportions?

5. Can non-certified teachers or teacher helpers be employed effectively—and specifically in what way—as monitors or proctors?

6. Will television teaching be as effective when the glamor wears off as it seems to be at present?

7. And last, is evaluative research adequate when based primarily on achievement testing?

Because these questions reach to the roots of organized education, they will never be answered, except in part. But while better answers are being sought, experiments in television education should continue. In the interim, however, in deference to the limited information available, greater modesty should typify announced results. The medium should be permitted to operate in a healthful climate of scientific objectivity, remote from the emotionalized biases which surround it in many schools.

TEAM TEACHING

An intimate curriculum affiliate of closed-circuit television is team teaching, which may operate without the aid of the electronic paraphernalia. Both utilize the alternating large-group, small-group technique, but team teaching usually employs a "live" performer in a large-sized classroom when the greater student audience is receiving instruction.

Actually, team teaching is not new to education. For decades, elementary schools have employed it in varying ways when deviating from the structure of the self-contained classroom. The visiting art specialist and the classroom teacher, for instance, constitute a team. At the high school level, however, the approach is more of an innovation, serving as one of several experimental answers to those who regard secondary education as almost sealed against change.

In the past three to five years, having received impetus from "The Commission on the Experimental Study of the Utilization of the Staff in the Secondary School"—a Ford Foundation protégé, born in 1956—a number of schools have embarked on experiments in team teaching. Selected examples from various parts of the country are the schools of Jefferson County, Colorado; the Wahlquist Junior High School of Weber County, Utah; the San Diego schools in California; the Newton High School in Massachusetts; and the Evanston Township High School in Illinois. More schools, in fact, are testing the merits of team teaching than closed-circuit television, because the cost is less.

The two best sources of information on the subject of team teaching are the January Bulletins of the National Association of Secondary School Principals for the years 1958–1962 and the publication by Trump and Baynham, *Guide to Better Schools, Focus on Change.*[5] The former report the initiation, progress, and evaluation of experiments in selected school systems. The latter projects the American Secondary School into a somewhat imaginative school world of tomorrow wherein teachers, schedules, curricula, and buildings more nearly conform to educational theory and the liberal practices of a few existing schools.

Just what is team teaching? Fundamentally, it is an arrangement of method wherein several teachers—usually three or four—work together in a cooperative pupil-learning effort. Identifying features of the composite of all team-teaching projects would be essentially as follows:

1. Two, three, or four classes (usually the latter) of an identical subject, at the same grade level, which meet at the same time of day, would form a team block. For example, four classes of freshman civics at a large high school could be scheduled into a block during the third period.

2. The respective teachers of the four classes would constitute the teaching team.

3. In a number of instances, a secretarial clerk also would be a team member, as is the case in Jefferson County, Colorado; or a non-certified paper grader might be a member of the team, as in Evanston Township High School, Illinois.

4. Leadership would reside in a so-called Master Teacher, or the leadership function would be cooperatively shared. If the former, the Master Teacher would customarily have more staff seniority, have more teaching experience, and be more skilled in group dynamics.

5. At times, the four classes would combine into a large-class group; at other times, they would retain their discreteness.

6. When they were combined, a room capable of seating from 100 to 150 students would be needed. This might be a large classroom or a special-purpose room; less ideally, it might be an auditorium or cafeteria.

7. Also, when the classes are combined, the large-group teacher would customarily be the individual who, in the light of the curriculum content to be covered and the personality characteristics deemed essential, would have been identified as the best qualified. Such assets as specialized knowledge, voice projection, organizational ability, skill in using visual supplements, and poise before a large audience would have been regarded as significant.

8. When the students are divided, each of the four teachers would utilize class time to pursue the curriculum interest of the moment, possessing as much flexibility in choice of method as most high school teachers have routinely.

[5] J. Lloyd Trump and Dorsey Baynham, *Guide to Better Schools, Focus on Change* (Chicago: Rand, McNally & Co., 1961).

To illustrate the features of team teaching in the previous list, the reader's attention is invited to two approaches which were made in the academic year 1959–1960 in a Midwest high school. In the field of junior English, four teachers cooperatively shared responsibility for the year's work. In the area of literature, three of the teachers had specialties in the drama, novel, and poetry, respectively. Accordingly, responsibility for the large-group assemblies in each of these areas was made the province of the appropriate specialist. The fourth teacher was best prepared in composition and research, which thus became his large-group focus. The curriculum was planned monthly along broad lines and weekly in greater detail. Although the method of consensus was their goal in decision-making, they often had to settle for majority vote. When an even split occurred, a substitute proposal was then introduced.

In the small class-sized groups, each teacher contracted to follow up on the large-group presentation but reserved the right to employ his own methods. In addition, each asked for and was granted the right to have not less than a fifth and as much as a third, if needed, of the year's total class time to pursue curriculum projects of his own selection. The participants went on record at the end of the year as in favor of continuing the experiment.

In another department—in the field of the social studies—a second team-teaching approach was employed at the same time. The basic difference between the two situations was in the posture of leadership. In the latter, one of the four teachers was designated from the start as team leader. He was put in charge of the team and directed its efforts throughout. This teacher could be described as an individual of esteem in the high school, scholarly, a capable speaker, and basically well liked. He performed considerably more often before the combined class members than did his colleagues. Regarded as only moderately successful, the experiment terminated at the end of the year. Purportedly, low staff morale and too much domination by the one individual was the reason—this despite the fact that he ranked high in the social and professional skills. A needed ingredient of team teaching may thus be the basic right of sharing in decision-making. However, a sample of one is admittedly inadequate for generalization.

A third pattern is followed in a number of schools: two teachers with the same students in alternating periods occasionally combine to form a team. For example, Teacher A has 25 students in world history in period 1; Teacher B has the same students in freshman literature in period 2. Each has the other's students during the alternate period. By agreement, at times, they combine their two classes to engage in a project of mutual interest.

Regardless of the exact organization, the size of the group determines the kind of teaching which eventuates. Pertinent to the large assembly of students is content that demands uniformity of coverage. Being essentially the lecture method, large-group teaching lends itself to the presentation of introductory material, the explaining and clarifying of terms and concepts, and the conveying of specialized, hard-to-get information. Unlike the straight lecture, it purportedly is most successful when accompanied freely by demonstrations which draw heavily on visual aids. Evaluation is another one of its strengths.

Apropos of method most suitable for the small group is Trump's excellent summary statement:

> In these classes, teachers will weigh pupils' reactions to lesson content and will assess pupils' knowledge. They will also observe pupils' ability to handle data and solve problems and, highly important, how they react to one another. Instructors will guide and stimulate students' thinking, directing discussion along useful, fruitful lines; they will serve as consultants and advisors.
>
> Small-group classes will combine four purposes:
>
> Provide opportunities for teachers to measure individual students' growth and development and to try a variety of teaching techniques which will be suited to the students' needs.
>
> Offer the therapy of the group process, whereby students are induced to examine previously held concepts and ideas and to alter rigid, sometimes mistaken, approaches to issues and people. Students will learn, in other words, how to become better group members.
>
> Permit all of the students to discover the significance of the subject matter involved and to discuss its potential uses, rather than just to receive it passively and return it in tests, as happens too often in today's classrooms.
>
> Provide students with opportunities to know their teacher, on a personal, individual basis.[6]

Regardless of organization, team teaching makes definite demands.

1. Teachers must be able to work together cooperatively in determining what curriculum content will be included, what emphasis it will receive, whether it will be presented by all the teachers or by one, who will be made responsible for large-group assignments, how much time each will have to pursue individual goals, whether pupils will take the same or different examinations, and when and how often the team will meet for planning purposes.

2. The teacher who is designated to meet with the combined group of pupils must possess the attributes which will make for successful large-group teaching.

3. A room large enough to accommodate the combined group of pupils must be in existence and available, or closed-circuit television must be available in lieu thereof.

4. The goal of team teaching should be enrichment and more effective teaching, not the saving of teacher time.

The advantages of team teaching are essentially those following:

1. Teachers are able to utilize their professional strengths more effectively.

[6] Trump and Baynham, *op. cit.*, pp. 24–25.

2. Pupils accordingly are exposed to better teaching.

3. When responsible for the combined classes of pupils, teachers usually prepare more carefully.

4. Enrichment materials, particularly visual, seem to meet higher standards.

5. Teachers have fewer preparations.

6. Teachers stay "on their toes" more and engage in a higher level of professional reading and research.

7. They are more frequently relieved of routines by non-certified personnel.

8. Students are made to assume more responsibility for their own learning.

And, as in any point-counter-point situation, the disadvantages offset some or many of the advantages:

1. The lecture approach to pupils in a class of 100 or more is by necessity impersonalized.

2. The shy, more introverted pupil responds less favorably than the extrovert.

3. Teacher coordination of effort is difficult.

4. Teachers spend a disproportionate amount of time in preparation for the large-group presentation.

5. Evaluation is probably less accurate because of the inherent impersonalization.

6. The existence of a Master-Teacher often affects teacher morale unfavorably.

7. Frequently teachers who are effective with small classes are not so effective with large ones, in which event they may be accorded second-class citizenship.

8. The teacher who regularly teaches in content areas where he is strongest tends to maintain the *status quo* of development.

9. Team teaching is only for the large school where three or four parallel sections in any one period exist.

10. Thus, it is more effective for the "constant" subjects where more pupils are enrolled than for the "electives" where fewer pupils are enrolled.

11. It is more successful in the area of cognitive learnings than in the emotional intangibles of attitude, social growth, and personality development.

12. Classrooms to seat 100 to 150 are rarely available, or desirable, unless planned for before a building is constructed.

13. When clerks or teacher aids are used to grade papers or perform other professional tasks, the student is often the sufferer.

The greater frequency of the listed limitations is no indication of a negative attitude toward team teaching on the part of the author. On the contrary, it is regarded as another excellent frontier of experimentation. The fact that it features the physical presence of the performer earns it a higher rating than closed-circuit television. The latter, however, excels in the flexibility that teletapes provide and in its greater breadth of coverage. Both, however, are potential media for the better utilization of current methods of teaching rather than contributors of new methods. Their true place in secondary education is locked in the future.

The mandate of the new devices to the teacher candidate is definite, but should not prove threatening. More speech training is an obvious preparative. The development of a flair for the dramatic is another. Poise in front of a sizable audience is a third. Others are the ability to work comfortably with colleagues, a careful command of the English language, tolerance for the unexpected, and a capacity for uneven hours of work.

With the two media rocking the security of secondary education today, students need to become accustomed to the existence of these factors and to get ready to meet them before the first actual contact. Taking these into account along with the many other teaching prerequisites in an organized sequence is better than after-the-fact attempts to adapt to them.

TEACHING MACHINES AND
PROGRAMMED LEARNING

Lurking uncertainly on the fringes of elementary and secondary education for approximately thirty-five years, and now making an occasional inroad, are teaching machines, the third methods innovation to be discussed in this chapter. As early as 1926, Sidney Pressey, at Ohio State University, conceptualized and brought into being the first of these mechanical devices. This contrivance and later devices of this pioneer dealt primarily with testing: first confronting a testee with stimulus items, then providing him with response alternatives, and finally rewarding him when he chose correctly or withholding reward when he was unsuccessful.

Pressey's breakthrough in the 1920's foreshadowed the mechanical things to come. The subsequent decades, in fact, were characterized by a rash of experimentation with teaching appliances. With the heightened activity came a transfer of honors from the innovator to the contemporary heir, B. F. Skinner. Two more names deserve comment before we pursue the topic at hand: A. A. Lumsdaine and Robert Glaser, who co-authored a collection of articles on mechanical instruction, *Teaching Machines and Programmed Learning,* which is basic for anyone who desires to extend the limits of his specialized knowledge.

Educators are responding to teaching machines in varying ways. Some endow selected devices with seemingly human-like properties and expect them almost independently to solve the many problems of skills learning; others look to them for a casual contribution at best. The author rejects both extreme views; he regards the better self-instructional devices as supplements to the teacher which, when employed with discernment, can add enrichment to the learning process.

Teaching machines are of varying kinds, sizes, and complexity. The pioneering machines of Pressey operate on the principle of recognition. With Pressey's Punchboard type, the student is confronted with a multiple-choice situation and asked to respond to the correct answer by punching the appropriate hole. If the pencil makes the appropriate penetration, the selection is declared accurate. The Disk machine developed by Professor Skinner emphasizes recall more than recognition. It contains two slots in the top of an otherwise unobstructed surface. The student reads the question in the left-hand slot and then writes the answer on a paper tape on the right. When he raises the lever, the right answer is projected, permitting him to determine the accuracy of his response. It is of interest to mention at this point that Skinner reduces material to small units so that the student can be rewarded frequently with the knowledge of his correct answers. He also supports the practice of making the student write out his answer rather than letting him select a multiple-choice alternative.

Others of the programmed devices are: the Subject-Matter Trainer of Besnard, Briggs, and Walker; the Stolurow-Porter Sight Vocabulary Machine; the Skinner Arithmetic Machine; and the Rothkopf Polymath. These are just a few of the many. The programmed approach via the printed word has been developed with considerable success by Stolurow, Bergum, Homme, Glaser, and Crowder, among others.[7] This method projects a student into a prepared script which leads him step by step to the end of a learning sequence, although not without regressive detours in instances of error. In Crowder's scrambled-book innovation, the student, upon completing a given response to a verbal stimulus, is directed to a designated page which either introduces the next level of stimulus material or explains the mistake he made in the preceding step. Through the repetitive process of reading, responding, and then progressing (or maybe regressing for further instruction), the student moves directionally through the various steps of a learning sequence.

In physical appearance, most teaching machines are relatively uncomplicated. Normally they are no larger than an average typewriter and simple in design and operation. The student operates the machine as he would an adding machine or a typewriter.

With the foregoing as a background to programmed learning, we move next to the basic essentials of machine teaching:

1. A body of subject matter content is first conceptualized as appropriate for employment by the available machine. Such content is usually

---

[7] Lawrence M. Stolurow, *Teaching by Machine* (Washington, D.C.: U.S. Department of Health, Education, and Welfare, 1961), pp. 37–38.

limited to facts or other specific curriculum elements which involve right-or-wrong answers.

2. Next, the generalized content is sequentially detailed into a program, consisting usually of stimulus items graduated in order of difficulty and complexity. The creator of a program needs to know both the school's curriculum and the world of teaching machines. Any single item of a program is called a *frame*.

3. The program when inserted into the teaching machine is presented to the student frame by frame.

4. Assuming student cooperation, the frame stimulates thought, which leads to a selection of what the student believes to be a correct answer.

5. By pressing a button, punching a punch board, turning a crank, or manually writing an answer, the student makes known his response.

6. When the response is correct, the student is so informed, usually by the sequential appearance of the next frame.

7. When the response is incorrect, the process is repeated until success rewards the act. The student then proceeds to the next frame.

In support of the process are several important aspects of learning theory. First and foremost, the student performs at his unique level of readiness. Instead of a teacher's assuming that the whole class is ready in exactly the same degree, the student himself is the judge of his readiness. Continuous incorrect responses would indicate to one student the need of a program or frame geared to a lower level. Successively correct responses would reflect to another student his readiness or over-readiness.

A second defense of the procedure on the grounds of learning theory rests in the act of reinforcement. The machine relays to the individual an immediate signal of rightness or wrongness, which, if the former, constitutes a psychological reward, thereby reinforcing the act of learning. The key to the process is the immediacy of the reinforcing act. This result, along with the overlearning resulting from the interspersed repetition of a stimulus, underwrites the case for transfer.

A third defense rests on the greater possibilities available for spaced learning when the machine is employed than when a class is teacher-controlled. With the machine, the student can leave and return to the exact spot in a program where he left off. When he returns, the circumstances will be relatively unchanged: by the simple pressing of a button, he can start where he originally stopped. A teacher cannot guarantee such synchronization.

Despite the support that can be mustered for teaching machines, a strong case can be made for the opposition, based mainly on the limited research available to defend the employment of machines in organized education. To date, the machines have been essentially an inhabitant of psychological laboratories dealing too little with the learning substance of elementary and secondary education. Yet they are more than upon the threshold of the latter, having actually entered a number of classrooms, mostly suburban, throughout the country. The extent of their influence is limited, however, by an understandable dilemma. Conscious of community opinion, most school systems insist on a high quality of product before buying. And by this very insistence, they deny to researchers the human laboratories needed for the assaying of quality.

When purchased by the occasional school, teaching machines are usually employed in a curriculum of factual content and skills. These components are basic to the more sophisticated levels of learning, however, and the narrower base of employment should not be considered as depreciating their value. When they perform their intended tasks well, machines ideally should release the teacher for more professional duties.

The greatest obstacle to the success of machine teaching or other programmed learning is found in the difficulties of programming. Sequences must be worked out carefully, step by step, with intervals at just the right distances. Dealing only with issues of right or wrong—never with matters in between—the programs must follow a careful progression toward the final right answer. A serious error of estimate along the way jeopardizes the outcome. Unfortunately, at the moment, specialists who know the curriculum usually do not know the machines. Therefore, the burden of programming has fallen heavily on the shoulders of fringe educational organizations which are at too great a distance psychologically from the classroom.

Another issue is the cost of a total machine program adequate to meet the high standards of a school. The less expensive machines usually lack some of the mechanical features essential to program projection and attendant learning reinforcement. The more expensive, and therefore more efficient, machines, when procured in sufficient quantity to achieve their mission become, at times, a prohibitive budget item. Unfortunately, mass production, as a basic means of cost reduction, awaits a long period of experimentation, which, as we have said, the schools are rendering difficult by their hesitancy to try out the electronic devices. In the process of experimentation, the impact of novelty ever needs to be taken into account. An initial reaction of enthusiasm by students may well fade into apathy when the newness of the mechanical gadgets wears dim.

A final issue revolves around the actual need for a teaching machine once a written script has been adequately prepared. In this regard, assuming a script like the following, modified from Crowder,[8] how much would a machine add to the learning situation?

Instructions: In the following are algebraic problems which you are to solve.

[8] Norman A. Crowder, "Automatic Tutoring by Intrinsic Programming," in *Teaching Machines and Programmed Learning,* ed. by A. A. Lumsdaine and Robert Glaser (Washington, D.C.: National Education Association, 1960), pp. 289–290.

In each instance, after you have reached a solution, compare your answer with that provided at the end of the chapter. When the two differ, attack the problem a second time. When the two agree, proceed to the next problem and repeat the process.

Problem 1. An already learned division rule is that

$$\frac{x^a}{x^b} = x^{(a-b)} \text{ Therefore,}$$

$$\frac{x^2}{x^2} = x^{(2-2)} = x^{(\quad)}. \text{ (See page \_\_\_ for answer.) Thus, since}$$

Problem 2. $\dfrac{x^2}{x^2} = 1$ and $\dfrac{x^2}{x^2} = x^0$

$$x^0 = \_\_\_ \text{ (See page \_\_\_ for answer.)}$$

From the foregoing, the generalization emerges that any positive number with an exponent of zero equals one.

With this kind of sequence, the question arises as to whether a machine is actually needed. After all, aren't most machine programs really just sequential developments of a logical order of verbal or mathematical events which are just as meaningful on a printed page as when projected by a machine? And if so, is the machine really necessary? The response of the proponents of the electronic devices would be that it is necessary because of the reinforcing value of the correct answer when communicated immediately to the student by the machine. Yet this value conceivably might be overrated, or, at least, an expensive value when the cost of the machine is considered.

This and other issues regarding teaching machines can be resolved only when future research provides adequate answers. Some individuals like Simon Ramo[9] envision the school of the future operated by push buttons, with pupil registration, films, and even most teacher activities geared to gadgets that will keep the pupil alert, ready to make responses when asked, and informed of progress. More conservatively, we envision a vital place for teaching machines in the schools of 1963 or 1973, but their employment, we predict, will never be a controlling learning influence. As long as education is social and emotional as well as cognitive, dedicated to attitudes as well as ideas, and aspiring to problem-solving dimensions as well as devoted to mundane things and places, teaching machines will reach fulfillment, if at all, only in the skills and factual content areas.

THE LANGUAGE LABORATORY

An important and rapidly growing aural-oral approach to learning, the language laboratory, is the fourth of the

[9] Simon Ramo, "A New Technique of Education," *op. cit.,* pp. 367–381.

newer experimental teaching methods to be discussed in this chapter. Although it has some limitations, the language laboratory is regarded by most informed observers as a highly effective instrumentality for the oral teaching of languages. The increasing popularity of this relatively new technique may be seen from a recent report by the United States Office of Education indicating that in 1960 there were more than one thousand such laboratories in operation throughout the country. A further finding was that the increase in their number has been considerably greater than the corresponding increase in foreign-language enrollments.

The benefits of the laboratory are noteworthy. First, it guarantees that oral expression will have native-like fidelity. Second, it incorporates students actively into the learning process. And finally, by the injection of novelty, it removes much of the tedium from repetitious drill. However, for the process to achieve these benefits, the mechanical features of the laboratory must be manipulated with consummate skill by the teacher leader. Only in this way can the drill exercises reach their optimum effectiveness.

The laboratory is a classroom with a number of individual booths, or other type of pupil stations, each of which contains a microphone, a set of earphones, and circuit control. The respective stations are connected by a network of audio wiring to an electronic monitoring console which is controlled by the teacher. The latter is equipped with a switchboard and tapes or disks, by means of which the teacher can send one program, or a combination of programs, to any or all of the pupil stalls. The communication system also permits the teacher to listen to, or conduct a two-way conversation with, any student, thus enabling him to monitor and assist individual students without disturbing others.

The language laboratory is of two operational types: the broadcast and the library.[10] The broadcast type, although most suited to large-group activity, can be readily adapted to small-group instruction by the simultaneous utilization of several different tapes or disks. When employed in such a manner, it performs essentially the same function as does ability grouping. However, it is not primarily designed for extensive individualized instruction. Because its cost is less, its refinements are also less. The so-called library type, in contrast, possesses the flexibility needed to individualize instruction for a large number of students. Thus, whenever a school can afford the added features of the library type, the individualized needs of students may be somewhat better served as a result. However, for schools not so fortunate, the broadcast type should prove adequate for most instructional purposes in the field of a language. With either type, a learning situation is possible wherein, for example, a group of honor-level students might be responding to a drama of Molière, an average group enjoying a vicarious experience with a middle-class Madrid family at a fiesta, and a skills group drilling on syntax.

[10] Edward M. Stack, *The Language Laboratory and Modern Language Teaching* (New York: Oxford University Press, 1960), pp. 48–51.

The *library* type of language laboratory can be used to greater advantage at the college level, where students work more as individuals and at their own speeds. It is characterized by the following features: a tape recorder in each booth, students listening to the same or different sound tracks, students recording their own oral responses to content stimuli, and the backtracking of tapes to encourage reinforcement by providing a second attempt at difficult material. The advantage of this system is that the student may go over a drill exercise again and again at his own speed until overlearning is achieved. In contrast, the broadcast type does not permit such extensive opportunities for reinforcement; in fact, repetition is usually possible only when the entire lesson is repeated. Whatever type of laboratory equipment is selected, a high school must remember that the ensuing curriculum value depends primarily on the effectiveness of the drill material transmitted. Many excellent tapes are currently available commercially for use in language courses. Disk recordings which present drills based on specified textbooks are also available in quantity; and some book companies, in certain instances, offer master tapes without charge to schools which adopt their texts.

The many advantages of the language laboratory, of whatever type, may be listed roughly as follows:

1. The language laboratory lends itself efficiently and conveniently to the oral-aural method of instruction whereby a language spoken with native fidelity can be listened to by students.

2. It likewise permits students to emulate native speech and then listen to a playback of their taped or disked performances. Such a process is conducive to improved speech habits in the foreign tongue.

3. It enables a teacher to communicate various levels of content to different groups of students in the light of their language readiness.

4. Teachers are enabled to monitor any single student without distracting other members of the class.

5. Teachers are enabled to work in a unique way with selected subgroups of students, at any propitious time, without distracting other subgroups or individuals.

6. Students are kept more active during any given classroom period than when in a more conventional classroom setting. The latter forces them into a relatively passive role except when they are reciting. In the laboratory, they are active performers most of the time.

7. Distractions are minimized because of the earphone reception and the resulting close relationship that it effects with the monitor panel.

8. Students can hear well wherever seated.

In addition to these advantages, the library-type language laboratory possesses the following additional features:

1. Each student can work at his own pace and respond to curriculum content geared to his own unique ability and needs.

2. The mechanical tutor never tires of repeating. Thus, language content can be played, listened to, re-played, and emulated as long as the individual student desires to pursue the process.

3. Progress of the student of limited ability is not retarded by embarrassment over his shortcomings. This is in contrast to the sensitivity of slow-learning students in a conventional class, and their resulting retardation, when their limitations are displayed before others.

The following disadvantages of the language laboratory should also be recognized:

1. The language laboratory is a somewhat costly teaching device which not all schools can afford.

2. The laboratory may add to the teacher's workload, because extensive preparation or careful selection goes into making laboratory drills attractive and effective.

3. The laboratory is a fairly elaborate electronic medium, demanding of teachers considerable mechanical as well as curriculum "know-how."

The general consensus of educators is that the language laboratory holds excellent promise of facilitating the growth of foreign languages in high schools. Those individuals who have used the laboratory consistently support the finding that students become more proficient in less time. We feel the need to emphasize, however, the fact that a laboratory is only as effective as the material it transmits and the proficiency of teachers and students who engage its services. If second-rate tapes are used, if teachers are poorly prepared, or if students are not properly oriented and supervised, the value of this costly instrumentality can be greatly reduced. All in all, however, it is one of the better teaching devices to be developed in recent years; but its ultimate usefulness will depend on the extent of its projection into the many secondary schools throughout the country. Mass production and employment are needed to reduce its cost and thus make it more accessible to all systems.

A FINAL WORD

These four experimental methods of instruction have been selected for presentation because, of all the experimental methods being tried out in the many school systems of the country, they probably show the greatest promise of making a significant contribution to education. Like other liberal innovations, however, they are the recipients of attacks or abuse from the conservative elements who desire to maintain the *status quo*. Counteracting such conservatism is the coterie of ultra-enthusiasts who predict almost revolutionary success for the experimental methods. Skinner is a case in point in regard to teaching machines, and selected Ford Foundation personnel in regard to airborne or closed-circuit television.

Regardless of the ultimate success of the various new methods being employed throughout the country, the significant factor is education's growing willingness to experiment even in face of attacks by many reactionaries. Such pioneering, with the imaginative effort going into it, should lead to more bold, new ventures in the future and to changes in curriculum programming. But the need for teachers will not diminish, even if the experiments are vastly more successful than most have been to date, for the intangibles of growth can never be taught by mechanical means, and mechanical instruments can never be operated professionally by other such instruments. The axis of education's enterprise will continue to be the sensitive, knowledgeable, mature teacher.

SUMMARY

Four experimental approaches to education have been presented in the current chapter: television, team teaching, teaching machines, and the language laboratory. Television progressed from open, to educational, to closed-circuit, with the last having the greatest academic impact. The second innovational method, team teaching, was identified as accomplishing essentially the same outcomes as closed-circuit television. The major difference is that teachers usually perform directly in front of an audience. Both conveniently feature the master performer, large-group instruction, the verbal method supplemented by demonstration, shared personnel effort, audience detachment, and a preoccupation with knowledge learnings. Both also permit decentralized small-group teaching in between the larger-group sessions. The two methods were described as having significant possibilities for future growth and success.

Teaching machines were next discussed, with the following observations being made: (1) to date, their employment in public and private schools is limited; (2) they are best geared to the skills and the more mechanical processes of a curriculum; (3) programming for them has been inadequate up to the present, with only a mild hope for dramatic change in the future; (4) their ultimate success is uncertain in view of the limited research available on which a prediction might be based.

The final experimental method discussed was the language laboratory. With its actual and potential contribution already observable, the method was described with optimism. Its most commendatory features were identified as the ease with which it lends itself to a small-group or individualized teaching, its guarantee of accurate pronunciation and enunciation, and the diminished boredom in drill work through the injection of novelty.

All four were portrayed as supplements to teachers, none as replacements.

REFERENCES

American Council on Education, *Teaching by Closed-Circuit Television.* Washington, D.C.: 1956.

Cram, David, *Explaining "Teaching Machines" and Programming.* San Francisco: Fearon Publishers, 1960.

Dunham, Franklin, Ronald Lowdermilk, and Gertrude Broderick, *Television in Education.* Washington, D.C.: United States Department of Health, Education, and Welfare, Office of Education, 1957.

Educational Policies Commission, *Mass Communication and Education.* Washington, D.C.: National Education Association, 1958.

Ford Foundation, *Teaching by Television.* New York: 1961.

————, *Television in Education.* New York: 1961.

Fry, Edward B., Glenn L. Bryan, and Joseph W. Rigney, "Teaching Machines, an Annotated Bibliography," *Audio Visual Communication Review.* Vol. 8, No. 2, 1960.

Johnson, Marjorie C., and Catharine C. Seerley, *Foreign Language Laboratories in Schools and Colleges.* Washington, D.C.: United States Department of Health, Education and Welfare, Circular 524, 1959.

Lewis, Philip, *Educational Television Guidebook.* New York: McGraw-Hill Book Co., Inc., 1961.

Lumsdaine, Edward, and Robert Glaser, *Teaching Machines and Programmed Learning.* Washington, D.C.: National Education Association, 1960.

Midwest Program on Airborne Television Instruction, Mary H. Smith, ed., *Using Television in the Classroom.* New York: McGraw-Hill Book Co., Inc., 1961.

National Association of Secondary School Principals, *Bulletin.* Jan., 1958, 1959, 1960, 1961, 1962.

Schramm, Wilbur (ed.), National Educational Television and Radio Center, *Television in Education.* Urbana: University of Illinois Press, 1960.

Stack, Edward M., *The Language Laboratory and Modern Language Teaching.* New York: Oxford University Press, 1960.

Stoddard, Alexander, *Schools for Tomorrow, an Educator's Blueprint for the Advancement of Education.* New York: The Ford Foundation, 1957.

Stolurow, L. M., *Teaching by Machine* (Cooperative Research Monograph No. 6). Washington, D.C.: United States Office of Education, 1961.

Tarbet, Donald G., *Television and Our Schools.* New York: The Ronald Press Company, 1961.

Trump, J. Lloyd, and Dorsey Baynham, *Guide to Better Schools, Focus on Change.* Chicago: Rand, McNally & Co., 1961.

SELECTED METHODS
OF
INSTRUCTION:
PRIMARILY ORAL

Some years ago, the author served as the college supervisor of a student teacher who had been placed with a teacher of slow learners in the field of English. Some of the pupils had low I.Q.'s; others were maladjusted as the result of a wide variety of underlying causes: early childhood physical disorders, disturbed parents, and an inability for assorted reasons to cope with their environments. A few had been victimized by the failure of elementary school teachers to help them develop the skills and study habits needed for high school work. The teacher of these high school freshmen was a well-meaning but inadequate person who expressed and regularly reflected the attitude that not much could be done with slow learners "like these." The best he could expect, he said, was to keep them reasonably quiet, protect other classes from undue disturbance caused by them, and hope that a few, from time to time, might learn a little. Consistently, his approach to grammar was to introduce a skill or concept briefly by the oral method, ask for questions (only to be met by sullen or blank looks), and then tell the pupils to do drill exercises in their workbooks for the remainder of the period.

131

That the results were appalling is an understatement, as evidenced by the unconventional and erratic behavior of the students: some spent entire class periods with heads on the desks; a few walked around the room aimlessly and unapologetically; others cyclically defied or cowed before the teacher; and all showed sufficient signs of nervousness to convince any moderately alert teacher that the group needed to be handled in a specialized way. Unfortunately, the assigned teacher either missed the blatantly obvious cues—scarcely a likelihood—or deliberately ignored them because of an inability to cope with their implications for teaching method.

Two years later, the author had the opportunity to see the same class in action with another teacher of English. While making allowances for the two additional years of maturity and the many experiences that contributed to it, he was amazed at the differences in the group. The random movement was minimal, nail-biting had almost disappeared, most pupils were alert and attentive, all seemed to enjoy the class, and the majority were courteous to one another. An observer, unless knowing of their previous backgrounds, would have considered them "normal" children.

The almost phenomenal change encouraged the author to visit the class frequently that year, and these are a few positive characteristics of the learning situation that he observed:

1. The teacher genuinely liked the group and let them know in many subtle and overt ways that he believed in them.

2. The class was started promptly with vigor and was businesslike throughout.

3. The teacher used a great diversity of teaching methods: flash cards for vocabulary building, notebooks where word lists and grammatical blunders were recorded, a constant relating of classroom activities to the immediate happenings in the lives of the pupils, much pupil participation in the affairs of the classroom, extensive discussion, the challenging of pupils by other pupils over points of view expressed, frequent use of the blackboard, a proper balance of abstraction and the concrete, and, in general, teaching method that was both effective and extensive.

How much the growth which had taken place in the class was attributable to the increased maturation of the pupils during the interim period, and how much specifically to the well-integrated personality of the assigned teacher, will never be known. However, much credit for the better integration of the students could not be isolated from the mature teaching methods which were being employed.

From this actual example and many others like it, as observed and reported by a convincing array of qualified authorities, we feel comfortable in the generalization that carefully designed teaching method can do wonders in making learning vital. But its success depends on an intelligent orientation to educational purpose, the dynamics of the pupils, and the curriculum content of the moment. Only in such perspective can method, thus properly clothed with relevance and meaning, make its most valid contribution.

The previous chapter introduced the reader to the more innovational types of teaching method. The present chapter intends to engage him in a consideration of the more conventional and time-tested oral (or primarily oral) approaches to learning. The subsequent chapter will then introduce him to the primarily non-oral methods, or, at least, to those methods that do not depend basically on the oral. The first of the so-called oral methods to be considered here is the lecture.

THE LECTURE

One topic in education that is subject to acrimonious dispute in certain circles is the lecture method of teaching in the secondary school. Participants in this controversy readily agree that its employment in the early grades must be sparing, if at all; that in the middle and junior-high grades, it is permissible if judiciously implemented. But concerning its use in the secondary school, the issue sharpens. In one camp are the university and college-oriented faculty members, supported by a number of high school teachers who, having lived off the benefits of the lecture, recommend its extensive usage in the high school. In opposition are professional educators and a sizable group of high school practitioners who advocate caution in the use of the medium. We personally feel that the issue has been attacked too frequently on an "all or nothing at all" basis, with the combatants thereby forced into artificially extreme positions. Reconciliation will eventuate only when the two camps direct their efforts at discovering what outcomes the lecture best accomplishes, with what age or other-type groups it can be most advantageously employed, and how frequently it should be used.

A common reason for misunderstanding is the failure of individuals to define the term *lecture* in such a manner that all understand it in the same way. For purposes of this treatment, the *formal lecture* (also called the *lecture*) is regarded as "a verbal presentation of subject matter content, formally organized and unsupported by other learning media, extending over a protracted period of time." Although the time factor is relative, we arbitrarily assume that a formal lecture worthy of the title should cover a period of not less than fifteen to twenty minutes.

By thus circumscribing this one learning medium, other verbal situations admittedly are in need of explanatory labels to prevent misunderstanding. Accordingly, the term *informal lecture* will be employed to describe such verbal situations as a teacher's orienting students to a new topic, giving instructions, reporting an incidental event, or summarizing. The informal lecture, furthermore, tolerates, or even encourages, student interruption and may be associated with visual media. The medium of *discussion,* as will be observed later, is a planned give-and-take exchange between or among individuals, with all having a right to be heard.

The formal lecture

The best-known of the verbal teaching methods, the formal lecture, has an honorable tradition. Reaching as far into history as the classical period, its greatest fulfillment occurred during the medieval days, when a book was a rare item. The formal lecture, in effect, thus was a substitute for the printed word, which was at premium. The popularity of the formal lecture has been little diminished by time; in fact, it is still so dear to the hearts of universities that its perpetuity seems assured. One of the highest compliments from a student about a professor is the statement: "He is a good lecturer."

Small wonder, then, that students exposed to the oral-aural influence of the university tend to transport the formal lecture to the high school. Learning theory would explain its almost inevitable transmission by such Thorndikean terms as *contiguity, frequency,* and *intensity.* But the same learning theory would probe more deeply into the validity of the transfer by questioning whether the two learning environments are sufficiently similar for the medium to work equally well in both. On the answer to this question, a case for the formal lecture in high school can well be built or destroyed.

Under what circumstances, then, might the formal lecture be employed with effect in a secondary school classroom? An unavoidable reply is that it should be employed only when the purposes of the learning situation can thus be best served. In other words, whenever the designed goals of the curriculum can be most effectively and economically accomplished by the employment of the formal lecture, it should have the spotlight.

Within this criterion is the situation where the classroom instructor has information not accessible to students, or information that is difficult for them to procure. This he can make available to them by the economical method of "formal telling." Nor in the process need he be apologetic, regardless of some extremists to the contrary. A teacher with four or more years of collegiate training and the many less formal experiences that accompany greater maturity should not sell short this birthright by withholding appropriate parts from students. Neither should the widely traveled classroom leader hesitate to lecture to students on his global observations if the content fits the curriculum moment and the group can respond actively.

Another legitimate use of the formal lecture is for purposes of reinforcement. Learning has been established in this text and elsewhere as a multi-sensory phenomenon, heightened whenever the several senses can be enlisted in aid of the one. Accordingly, any teacher is justified in reinforcing the written word with oral methods, one of which might well be the formal lecture. With some students being good readers but poor listeners, and others with these attributes reversed, the several-sensory approach would have merit. Without at all recommending a frequently employed, monotonous "student read–teacher lecture" routine, we are suggesting, however, that such a sequence is defensible on occasions if in harmony with learning's goals.

The formal lecture, furthermore, has justification when serving as a change of pace. Any single teaching method—be it discussion, textbook reading, committee activity, the lecture, or drill—has a narcotic effect when drawn on too consistently. But when infrequent in appearance, any single method, like a relative from out of town, is welcomed with sincere warmth and cordiality. When becoming "The Man Who Stayed for Dinner," however, the early enthusiasm might wear a trifle thin. And yet, even as a change of pace, the lecture is not proper for certain groups, as will be noted later.

A fourth vindication of the lecture is economy. In instances where time is short, many sources or extensive material needs to be synthesized, and universal coverage by all students is indicated, the lecture could well be the only method by which to get the mission accomplished with dispatch. It is characterized by a unique ability to reach far and wide for information, which, when organized and compressed into capsule form, can be made available to others in an economical way.

The lecture is a function of the learning climate and can be successful only when the learning conditions are receptive. Thus, the assumption that the lecture in a high school program can be justified presupposes the existence of certain operational variables which need to be assessed with care before the learning environment is declared favorable. The more important of these variables will be listed subsequently, with comments after each. The components relate to the listeners, the lecturer, and the lecture itself, in that order.

1. First of all, the listening audience of adolescents must be verbal enough to respond to the method of "telling." With the lecture by definition grounded in symbolism, it can communicate only to individuals who employ the language used by the speaker. These are almost universally the more capable students, to whom the abstract appeals. Brightness is significantly correlated with size of vocabulary, meanings which figures of speech convey, and a minimum of dependence on overlearning methods. The lecture's high potential for compressing ideas, canalizing concepts, and synthesizing points of view is thus realized only with those adolescents who are verbally adept and, usually, possessed of high I.Q.'s. However, even with them, it should be regarded as *only one,* not *the,* method of instruction.

2. For the slow and many average learners, the formal lecture, except

as an incidental procedure, is wasteful and destructive to morale. The proposition is just as simple as this: If adolescents are not verbal—and the slower learners usually are not—they cannot respond to the concentrated medium of the formal lecture. When, however, circumstances are such that students become forced participants, the lecture will not be a total loss if delivered slowly, with frequent emphases, and with the simplest of vocabulary usage. But, preferably, other oral media, such as the discussion or informal lecture, should be substituted.

3. Apropos of the students, once more, is their need of prior instruction in listening and note-taking if the lecture is to achieve its optimum benefit. Regarding the former, the formal lecture fulfills its purpose best when the way has been carefully prepared. At the start of using the formal presentation, the teacher would do well to interrupt himself periodically with such class questions as: "Charles, what do you think is the main idea discussed so far?" Or "Pat, will you please paraphrase the two points that I just presented?" This solicitation of student response would tend to discourage complacency by making the entire class accountable for the lecture's content. Also, the teacher would be wise at the beginning to interpolate in the lecture requests for definitions of specialized words, identification of places and significant personalities, and explanations of meanings conveyed by figures of speech. In this way, a class is paced into, and therefore not overwhelmed by, the lecture method.

In addition, instruction in the art of note-taking is mandatory. It must include, for example, the need for the student: to devise language short cuts, for example, *w/o* for *without,* or the Gregg symbol ⌐ for *the;* to listen for the main idea; to record only the important parts of the lecture; and to listen while also writing. When such instruction is followed by a short "lecture-note-taking session," with the notes later corrected and returned to the pupils, the result will invariably be more attentive listening in the future.

4. The lecturer himself needs to be a composite of high-quality personal and professional attributes. Like any other performer, it is desirable that he have audience appeal, projecting warmth, friendliness, and competence. A voice that meets more than minimum standards of pitch, resonance, and projection is also a goal of high priority. And of equal importance, use of the English language can rarely be merely adequate but needs to aspire instead to a high level of competence in syntax, word selection, enunciation, pronunciation, and the employment of meaningful figures. Although this portrayal admittedly is a bit idealized, unless a teacher can measure up reasonably well to the standards listed, he should be reluctant to assume the pose of lecturer.

5. Regarding the lecture itself, unless prepared with care, it may become more an off-the-cuff verbal presentation, unnecessarily replete with repetition, *non sequiturs,* and misplaced emphases. Conscientious planning, in contrast, leads to meaningful organization and, consequently,

greater clarity of presentation. Another feature of high value is interest— the quality that makes the inert come alive, that imbues the commonplace with a modicum of drama, and that transcends a commonplace style. The lecture, thus, is quite properly conceived as a medium that increases vitality, not somnolence.

6. A further requirement is pacing, that is, the relating of delivery to the content of the lecture and the type of activity expected of note-taking class members. Introductory information, for instance, thrives on a rapid cadence of words; the basic substance of a lecture begs for a moderation of tempo; and the content that "makes or breaks" is lost unless rescued by deliberateness. Backtracking over salient ideas often is the makeweight of success. A lecturer, engaged in something vastly more complex than planned talking, is like a vocal soloist, who is discordant when oblivious to the music's nuances, and who takes liberties with the emotions when sensitively interpreting the musical script. In like manner, the delivery of the learning performer must harmonize with the substance of the learning content.

One primary difference exists, however, between the vocalist and the lecturer. The former is obligated to interpret the script as the composer intended it, making only minor changes in the light of the wishes of the audience. The latter, in contrast, is obligated to place the audience first, making whatever changes are necessary in both the script and the manner of presentation to enhance audience appeal. In learning, subject matter is useless if not geared to the human equation.

Whatever the case for the formal lecture, it has its definite limitations. These are enumerated, and elaborated as required, in the following.

1. Being verbal, the formal lecture many times forces the lecturer to "downgrade" expression so as to meet the learner at his level. This is not only difficult but may well make what would otherwise be interesting prosaic.

2. Being directed at a class-size or larger group, it makes little provision for meeting the differing needs of individuals.

3. It is a one-way teaching operation, directed at adolescents without allowing them to interrogate or seek other means of clarification in return.

4. It is narrowly cognitive in orientation, making minimum contribution, at best, to the learning intangibles of personality, citizenship, attitude formation, and social living.

5. By excessively emphasizing memory outcomes, it relegates research, problem-solving, and reflective thinking to positions of secondary importance.

6. It may have a similar effect on reading skills.

7. Finally, its efficacy is so dependent on the verbal skills of the teacher that it falls by its own weight when these are lacking or deficient.

In summary, the formal lecture is a function of time, place, learning context, and the teacher. As a medium for institutions of higher learning, it passes muster because the more capable individuals are in attendance. In such situations, the learning performer, like the soloist, can, by giving his best, almost always reach the listeners. In secondary schools, with their more heterogeneous populations, however, the lecture is a teaching method that must be employed with care. Rarely should it be permitted to dominate an entire class period, being more effective when employed for briefer intervals of fifteen to twenty minutes' duration. If learning is most productive when multi-sensory and varied, the lecture should be just one method in an ensemble. A teacher can never go wrong, however, if he makes the lecture await arrival of the educational situation that it will best serve.

The informal lecture

A more suitable method for the high school than the formal lecture by itself is the approach whereby the verbal, usually assisted by the visual, is employed with audience participation encouraged. One example of the latter is the so-called *lecture-demonstration,* long a feature of science classroom procedures. It is comprised of a teacher's introductory remarks followed by a demonstration to the accompaniment of explanatory comments. At any time, students have the right and privilege of raising questions and of requesting clarification.

Another informal departure from the lecture, although still verbal, occurs when a teacher introduces a new topic, a complex concept that needs explaining, or a unit of learning that is in the offing. In each instance, the oral may be supplemented, as needed, by a written handout, a film slide, or a model; and, once more, audience participation is a goal that is encouraged, not repressed. The same principles apply to the summarizing of material that has been learned.

The more relaxed verbal methods are similar to the lecture but, escaping its formalism, are thereby more suited to the high school learning situation. Their greatest contribution is a recognition of the adolescent as a moderately restless specimen who should not (or cannot) be coerced into a listening posture for too long a time or in too many situations. The verbal-oral, as one learning avenue, is irreplacable in the repertoire of methods. But it must be tailored to the specific demands of a learning environment.

THE DISCUSSION

A step—in fact, a giant stride—away from the teacher-dominated lecture is the discussion, where the learning lens is on the class group as the primary object and on the teacher basically as an instrumentality for the cognitive, social, and attitude growth of the group members. Whenever employed, it is a living admission that learning can have vitality when a teacher guides as well as directs. As a dynamic technique that stimulates pupils to engage actively in the growth process, discussion is the stock in trade of teachers at any of the twelve or thirteen grade levels of education. Evading a definition that would contribute little, we direct attention to the type of learning context that is conducive to this teaching method.

Criteria for usage

Although there is throughout the nation's schools a gravitation toward the discussion method, certain elements are needed to bring out the best results from the use of this method. First of all, a discussion that aspires to satisfactory fulfillment must be focused on a problem or issue that is common to all potential participants. The teacher properly deserves reproach who expects students to share what they do not even possess. It is evident, then, that certain educational contexts lend themselves to the discussion technique whereas others do not. The contexts that meet the criterion of common knowledge are those, for instance, which follow an assignment, that emanate from a controversial issue of common interest, or that arise from a shared school problem. Thus, a well-designed and fruitful discussion can only proceed from the known.

A second requisite of the discussion method is that the subject matter with which it is concerned be of such a nature that clarification will take place when a group faces it verbally. Capable of meeting this criterion are such topics, issues, or questions as: "Adolescent delinquency, its cause and effects," "Should the United Nations admit Red China to its membership?" or a more mundane one, "Why do we need to study percentages?" Each of these and the several others they bring to the mind of the reader would, more often than not, be better understood when subjected to the analytical process of the discussion method.

A third criterion of the applicability of the discussion method is whether many individuals in a class group, not just a few select ones, will participate. The teacher tête-à-tête with a single pupil definitely evades the criterion, as does the discussion which elicits only a sprinkling of participation. Ideally, an issue should stimulate an entire class into verbal activity.

Fourth, a topic that is to be grist for the mill of discussion must, at least at the beginning, be controversial or several-sided. For instance, the topic, "Is style adversely affected by the split infinitive?" is controversial and accordingly meets the criterion; whereas a resolution of the question, "Is one's life span increased by good eating habits?" would be too one-sided to meet the criterion of eligibility. Also excluded is the question designed to elicit a "yes" or "no" or only a very limited group response.

Desired outcomes of the discussion

Since any teaching method is defensible only in terms of outcome, attention is next addressed to the results that can be reasonably expected from the discussion method. These will now be listed, once more with brief annotations.

1. The discussion confronts students with controversial or disputable content that makes them take sides, defend their points of view, and then live with the consequences. Since life is rarely black and white only, getting students ready for the intervening shades is one of the purposes of the high school. The maturing process, as was emphasized in Chapter 1, is away from internalization (more a danger of the lecture) and toward thought-provoking choices (more a product of the discussion).

2. It makes students more responsible for their own learning and, therefore, more active, thus meeting the criterion of learning as involvement.

3. It encourages them to express themselves with clarity in the area of oral communication, still the most widely used medium. Although the content of the discussion must not be lost to a perfectionistic preoccupation with speech habits, neither can the latter be neglected without the teacher's deserving criticism.

4. It provides a focus wherein adolescents, despite mild or even sharp differences of opinion, can be taught to respect others even though rejecting their points of view. This harks back to the first chapter.

Qualities needed by the discussion leader

A discussion that satisfies the criteria previously enumerated and elaborated, and that moves directionally toward the four outcomes listed can still miss its mark unless it is guided by a skilled and knowledgeable leader. This individual is a composite of many roles and needs to be blessed with certain personality attributes in order to play them with effect.

The many parts that the discussion leader plays relate to the process of initiating activity, sustaining it in an effective manner, and establishing cloture. More specifically, the leader:

1. Establishes an emotional climate where adolescents have the comfort and security prerequisite to individualism without being extended license. In this regard, the teacher must extend the privileges of allowable freedom while conveying subtly the fact that limits have been established.

2. Introduces issues in such a way that the group is eager to "take hold." The colorless "What do you think about the minority problem of

the Negro?" should give ground to the greater vigor of "Minorities have helped make the world what it is. Under what conditions might they make even greater contributions in the future? And what are society's obligations (and yours) to bring these conditions into being?" If the latter is too slanted to emerge multi-sided, a more realistic approach might be taken, as in the following: "We live in a world of minority groups. What should be society's (and our) role toward them in the future, and their role toward each other and us?"

3. Becomes a pilot once a group engages a problem and becomes involved. He steers the discussion positively and progressively; moves it in the direction of some students and away from others; backtracks to pick up loose ends or to highlight inconsistencies; clarifies; and, in general, assures goal orientation.

4. Plays the role of human-relations engineer by encouraging as near universal participation as possible, keeping all alert even when not actively engaged, and blunting the otherwise penetrating barbs of the more outspoken.

5. Finally, synthesizes and brings about consensus, or identifies areas of difference.

With the discussion process being so demanding of the more outstanding human and professional virtues, the ability of anyone to measure up may properly be questioned. However, a compromise with the ideal will obviously once more suffice. And yet, at least a minimum of such personal attributes as the following is required: self-assurance, poise, respect for others, tolerance of controversy even when heated, sense of humor, self-abasement when demanded by the circumstances, orderliness in the face of diversity, and objectivity. These help keep a discussion moving; and, as may be noted, they are the components which enhance the group process even, if necessary, at the loss of some of the leader's ego. The heavy hand has no place in the discussion; rather, deftness and finesse are the welcome attributes here. The purpose of the leader is to *draw out,* and to *draw out of* the group—not to pour into it his own finalized opinions.

A sample discussion

Ending this section on a specific note, we submit the following as somewhat illustrative of the dynamics of the discussion, admitting that only when the reader observes the actual attack by adolescents upon a "live" issue will he be able to discover the deeper subtleties of the method. The topic is the one, previously touched on, pertaining to minority groups. The discussion will be cut short after having served its intended purpose.

Teacher: Yesterday, as you will recall, we agreed to discuss the problem of minorities. Because this topic is sensitive in our community—in fact, it is sensitive almost everywhere in the world—I strongly urge you to be objective

in your comments. State your beliefs but refrain from emotionalism. Also remember that all of us have ideas; so don't dominate—at least, not too much.

Let me re-state the issue: *"We live in a world of minority groups. What
should be society's (and our) role toward them and theirs toward society
(and us)?"* Ray, I see that you want to pounce on it first.

Ray: Our Constitution and American way are based on all having equal
rights; so we have no choice but to accept them as equals.

Mary: But aren't you forgetting, Ray, that theory and practice are often
miles apart? What our Constitution says and what we do—well, they certainly
aren't close.

Marie: Let's face it: I don't care how much we talk here; Little Rock
isn't going to treat all people alike.

Teacher: These are very interesting and mature comments, but let's not
forget that the topic emphasizes what we *should* do; not what is done, although
maybe we shall have to consider both later.

Bob: When we talk about what we should do, we need standards. Plato
believed in slaves and we don't. But what we really believe in is hard to say.

Ron: Maybe we can't catalog our standards definitely, but we do believe
that people are awfully important, although we don't always act as if we do.

Teacher: Jeff, you have been trying to break in. Do you want to pursue
the people-centered value further or inject a new idea?

Jeff: I don't know what Ron means by this people business, but I do know
that religion of all varieties has something to say about human relationships.

.   .   .

Teacher: For almost a period we have faced the minority issue. It is a
controversial one, as your differing opinions have demonstrated. Now let me
summarize what I think we subscribed to and differed about. Correct me later
if I'm wrong.

1. Theoretically, all people are equally deserving of respect.

2. Practically, many people, mostly because of environment, not inner
cruelty, fail to practice what they believe.

3. Our obligation as educated people is to put theory to work whenever
we can.

4. But we differed today on ways and means of converting theory to action. Some felt that even at the risk of losing long-term goals, we should practice what we preach. Others, a majority probably, felt that the time and the
place should be determiners of how we act toward minorities.

This discussion excerpt was illustrative of the following elements:

A. An issue that lends itself readily to discussion.

B. The value of a proper emotional climate.

C. A discussion led deftly.

D. Extensive participation by the group.

E. The emphasis on *we* and *you*.

F. The need to bring a discussion back to the track.

G. The need to invite an interested member into the inner sanctum
   when group enthusiasm keeps him outside.

H. The balance given by summary and final closure.

The discussion admittedly is not always so logically oriented and
openly accepted; but, even when only moderately successful, it justifies

frequent employment in the light of what it contributes to learning. However, careful planning and subtle implementation can do wonders in advancing its effectiveness. More often when the discussion is unsuccessful, the teacher and the content are more in error than the discussion method itself. The latter has survived more than one assault and is still very much with us; also, we do not predict its early demise.

THE QUESTION-ANSWER METHOD

Inherent in, yet distinctive from, the informal lecture and discussion is the so-called question-answer teaching method, which, because of its long tradition, warrants separate treatment. Its roots reach into the traditional past when education was conducted almost universally on a read-recite-review-evaluate basis. In this setting, after assignments had been made in the single textbook, the drill master spent a major part of the school day assuring himself that his wards had done their work well. Denied such assurance, punishment or more work, or both, were the result.

Not uncommon to the classroom of the past was the schoolmaster behind his desk, textbook open, asking questions directly from it and recording grades as the students searched their memories for as near word-for-word answers as they could produce. This use of the question-answer technique was geared to the read-recite approach, and based its utility on the importance of immediate recall.

Although a number of classrooms of many secondary schools today would make an observer wonder if fifty years had actually become history, the question-answer technique in today's typical school is less a separate method and more a part of the informal lecture, discussion, or other daily give-and-take between teacher and pupils. Still employed to determine retention, its base has broadened to include the stimulation of analytical thought on issues of significance. Whatever the purpose of the questioning procedure, the teacher should adhere to certain well-defined and approved practices; for instance, he should:

1. Word his questions carefully so that ambiguity will not block effective communication. Both the teacher who fumbles for the right word or phrase, and the pupil who is thereby made to grope for proper interpretation are harmed by the wastefulness and vagueness of the process. In contrast, questions wisely selected and carefully phrased can contribute substantially to learning's potential.

2. Normally ask questions of the entire class, not just of one individual. In this way, all class members are made to feel responsible for learning's demands. The one-to-one relationship between teacher and pupil, by excluding other pupils from the focus of learning, may cause some to recede completely from further participation or involvement.

3. Make questions evocative. The yes-no question should be used sparingly; the probing, analytical question, more frequently. Entirely different responses are aroused by the two following questions: (1) "Should we pursue with continued vigor our efforts to land man on the moon?" (2) "What issues are involved in our program to land man on the moon? Identify and then discuss each from the vantage point of its social, moral, political, and military implications." The first would elicit a flat yes-or-no response. The second might even overstimulate.

4. Refrain from harassing those students who do not or cannot give the correct responses to questions. Teacher-nagging inevitably breeds antagonism, not only in the single student being "third-degreed," but in the entire class as well. And yet the game of intellectual combat is difficult for many teachers to avoid. Like Socrates, they become experts at interrogating a victim into a verbal position and then delight in the verbal counterassault. In such situations, they may well win the battle of intellect but lose the cause of rapport.

5. Avoid wording questions bookishly. The learning situation moves a pace backward when the teacher with open text drones out an uninspiring, book-centered question and then insists on a stereotyped answer. The printed word should almost regularly be paraphrased to increase its naturalness and make it more context-centered.

The teacher candidate, with justification, can make the question-answer technique a valuable member of his repertory of methods. In uncovering the known, it is conceivably overrated. But in probing into the deeper recesses of concepts, issues, and meanings, it is of great value. As a tool of analysis, it needs no other reason for being.

COMMITTEE ACTIVITY

The verbal methods considered to date, namely: the lecture, discussion, and question-answer, are either completely or in great part teacher-centered, making vigorous leadership demands on the instructional figure. The three methods to be treated next—the committee, the panel, and the symposium—channel the leadership function toward the students. They are commonly referred to as *socialized* methods, thereby indicating not that the cognitive is a missing ingredient, but rather that it shares the learning sphere with the social component. In each of the three, the teacher generally plays a subtle engineering role behind the scenes, and only seldom a frontally aggressive one.

The first of the socialized approaches to be analyzed is the student committee, with the many functions that it serves. One of the manifestations of this approach is the standing committee, with its long-term responsibility for such activities as maintaining bulletin boards, managing materials of instruction, and attending to housekeeping details. Another manifestation is the impromptu committee, which is formed on the spur of the moment, for instance, a small-group buzz session. A third form is the academic committee, whose members, because of common interests and goals, work together on shared projects. It is this latter type of committee that will be the central focus of this section.

The academic committee is formed when the goals of a curriculum can best be fulfilled by the efforts of students working together in a common venture. The use of the academic committee is based on the assumption that students learn not only when under the direct influence of the instructor, but also when, through mutual effort, they move toward a collective learning outcome: for example, when they work on a group report to be prepared and presented to the class, on a shared research project, or for some other learning resultant of united effort. The justifications offered for such group activity is that students become more motivated when given more responsibility, that they learn the art of give-and-take when working closely with others, and that they often penetrate more deeply into knowledge when obliged to meet their own standards as well as a teacher's.

However, despite a temporary delegation of functions, the teacher can never abdicate responsibility for any of a committee's actions. He alone must bear the brunt of either a legal or a professional attack. Thus it is his obligation to assure efficiency by selecting members wisely, by setting limits as guides to student interaction, by taking necessary steps when controls seem to be breaking down, by insisting on a high level of academic performance as a final outgrowth of committee functioning. With class time a valuable commodity, he cannot tolerate lackadaisical performance during the period of organizing, of planning, or of reporting. Accordingly, as in any other group activity, the teacher as an authority figure, while delegating to the limit of reasonableness, must stand ever ready to "move in" when quality is breaking down.

One of the many issues inherent in the committee system is the method of formulating memberships. Should students follow their interests, or should they be channeled into activities which serve their needs? When their own interests predominate, adolescents, with eyes more on the present than the future, may tend to elect already familiar outlets: the artist consistently volunteers for the art committee, and the verbally adept, just as consistently for the performance role—this despite the fact that both might profit more by electing an area of weakness rather than their area of strength. However, when the needs approach is too rigidly employed, learning suffers equally from being too adult-dominated and too future-oriented. The compromise occurs when, over a period of a semester or a year, both interests and needs have opportunities to govern.

Another issue that every teacher who employs the committee system has to face is the proper frequency of its employment. Certainly the "committee-happy" teacher who organizes almost every classroom endeavor around this one method is guilty of excess, but not more so than his fellow teacher who acts as if learning can never take place unless he has a dominant hand in it. The final determiners must be the learning situation, the teacher's philosophy, and what is best for students at a given time.

While far from solving the major problems of education, the committee method of teaching when in the proper setting has learning potential of vital significance. Quite possibly it has become an overused academic instrumentality in many classrooms, primarily as an antidote to stifling traditionalism. Such excess we do not condone, regardless of circumstances. However, the teacher who is sensitive to the dynamics of learning possibilities will often gravitate to it, but in the process he will be aware of the need for "quality control" of it as a means of enhancing its effectiveness.

The following sequence is rather typical of the committee process; in this illustration, it is built around the topic, "The Physiology of the Emotions" in a biology class. The topic itself may be seen to extend beyond the substance of a textbook, thereby enabling a group of four or five adolescents to "bite" into the core of research. The progression would probably be somewhat as follows:

1. In a long-term unit on the nervous system, the physiological base of the emotions would emerge as one of a number of subjects to be attacked at some depth.

2. Student volunteers for various committee memberships would be solicited by the teacher. From those volunteering for the topic at hand, in view of its sophistication, the more capable pupils would be selected for participation.

3. The five selected volunteers, along with other focal groups, would be given several periods of class time initially to organize themselves and to plan ways and means of researching the problem.

4. Sooner or later, with the teacher acting as consultant on room space, bibliographical references, method, and task assignments, the group would move into a period of library investigation.

5. Subsequently, they would meet again to pool their combined insights, deciding, in the process, what further information was needed.

6. Once the research had been completed, the next steps would involve organization of the data and methods of presenting them to the class, orally or in written form, to produce the best learning effect.

7. Finally, if an oral presentation had been decided upon, the committee would have part of a class period or an entire period to present its findings on such sub-parts of the topic as the autonomic, central, and peripheral nervous systems, the hypothalamus as a focal emotional center, and other related physiological phenomena.

It would be incumbent upon a teacher in such a situation to provide class or after-school time for committee deliberations; to consult with the group when it needed rescue from an impasse; to make space available—

if such existed—for small-group work; to motivate the students to work up to high standards; and, finally, to help them, as required, in selecting methods for presenting their hard-earned knowledge.

The entire procedure, far from being incidental, would challenge the best in teacher and pupils alike if favorable outcomes were to be forthcoming. And the greater the preliminary investment of effort, the less likely any "sacrifice" of the class at the time of consummation. The value of committee activities for the committee members themselves goes almost unchallenged; but the value for a class as a whole when a committee is reporting is inseparably related to the quality of planning and organization that pupils and teachers invest in the many sequential phases of the process.

THE ROUND TABLE

A second socialized method of instruction is the round table. Like the academic committee, the round table involves the inception of an idea or project, a period of development, and the act of reporting to the larger group. Basically, it is a method whereby usually three, four, or more students share their ideas informally with a class. One of the members customarily serves as chairman, assumes responsibility for initiating the discussion of selected topics, sustains the discussion by eliciting responses from his colleagues, and then gives it a conclusion through summary.

Like any other method, however, the round table cannot be permitted the luxury of careless planning. The apparent spontaneity exhibited by the more adept round table or panel (a synonymous term as used herein) members normally belies the effort expended in the period of preparation. Lacking such prefacing, the panel can easily degenerate into a formless exchange of ideas or shallowly conceived concepts.

In its extensive employment in both industry and secondary education, the round table serves several praiseworthy purposes. A primary contribution is that it draws a number of individuals into the learning act, thereby making them feel more responsible for the outcome of learning. A second contribution is that it changes the pace of an educational environment that may have become stuffy from an excessive employment of the lecture or public speech as a teaching method. When formality has reigned too long, the panel eases tension. Two other outcomes which relate particularly to the classroom are, first, the round table's emphasis on effective speech habits; second, the emotional growth in students associated with verbal exchanges which often are mildly, and occasionally very, controversial. To accept another individual while differing, often violently, with his point of view is a step toward the widely cherished goal of altruism—the mark of a truly mature individual.

The round table is employed in two organizational ways. In one, the spotlight is concentrated on the panel group itself, with the audience playing a secondary listening role. In the other, after the panel has introduced and opened a topic for airing, the non-panel members are invited at almost any point in the presentation to question or ask for clarification. The latter organizational approach tends to increase interest by making the audience co-participators, and for this reason we prefer it. The danger, however, is that, unless a reasonably skilled individual is leader of the round table, the audience may steal the play from the panel group, or at least dislocate the pre-planned time schedule.

Once more it should be noted that the teacher's role is not lessened by the temporary delegation of authority to the student members of the panel. His familiarity with content is as requisite as if he were directly involved in the performance. The only real difference is that his preparation must be appropriate to his anticipated role of resource person, a role that makes peremptory demands for breadth, flexibility, and security when anticipating the unforeseen. Such preparation is less definitive, and therefore more taxing, than when directed at the greater tangibility of the predictable. Paralleling these more challenging aspects of the learning process, however, are the necessary procedural ones: working side by side with panel members as they evaluate one another's ideas, softening personality clashes while arbitrating differences, giving support to the diffident, and sometimes rescuing a round-table presentation that has lost itself in illogic or irrelevance.

THE SYMPOSIUM

Related to, and yet distinct from, the round table is the symposium. The symposium is characterized by the formality of its structure. Whereas the round table or panel specializes in give-and-take exchanges among and between its members, the symposium is designed for presentation of the several sides of a given topic or issue. For instance, the topic: "Is Free Enterprise Becoming Passé?" might subdivide into the following distinctive tangents:

1. Free enterprise is as vibrant today as it ever was.
2. Free enterprise is not dying, but, like all political components, is being modified.
3. Free enterprise is losing its significance as social legislation exacts a serious toll from its independence.
4. Free enterprise exists in name only.

Each of these represents a point of view shared by many political economists and other serious-minded citizen-thinkers. And to the degree that the total issue of free enterprise could be made more understandable by a defense of the four logical subdivisions, the symposium would have served its purpose well.

The first demand of the symposium is the careful selection of subject matter—a task of no mean proportions, because not many topics lend themselves conveniently to a logical division. A second demand is the separating of the topic into such divisions, making certain that the sub-parts are distinctive yet graduated away from one polarity toward another. A third requirement is the selection of individuals who, as in a debate, will adopt a point of view and defend it vigorously as if it were really their own. Only through such role-playing do the shadings of an issue emerge with clarity. When the defense is half-hearted or manifestly insincere, the technique loses its effect. Finally, the listening audience—a high school class or a business group, as the case may be—must be brought into the act of participation. This last requirement customarily occurs through the directing of questions by the audience at one or more of the speakers apropos of a point made, the consistency of the slanting, or the over-all logic of the presentation.

Like the panel, this method has a number of benefits. It can be used to advantage as a departure from teacher domination, as a means of ventilating an issue of significance at the moment, as a departure from the adolescent's proneness to regard issues as black or white, and as a means of eliciting class enthusiasm. Its occasional employment is normally associated with strong student interest. Over-use, however, tends to nullify the needed dramatic effect which is characteristic of its more sparing employment.

The three social methods treated in this section, and others not discussed, such as the buzz session, socialized recitation, and role-playing, are more pertinent to certain curriculum areas than to others. They obviously have little contribution to make to the skill subjects of mathematics and grammar, or to any academic situations where new substantive content is being introduced; but in such areas as speech, literature, social studies, and science, in which ideas or concepts can be made more vivid by socialized planning and presentation, these methods fill a definite need.

THE VISITING SPEAKER

The last verbal method to be considered is one with a different dimension from those previously covered: we refer to the visiting speaker who appears in the classroom from time to time as a resource person from outside the school environment. This redirection of method usually reflects a sensitivity by the teacher to the broad scope of learning opportunities that exist in the community proper. These opportunities are almost legion in most large-city and suburban areas, where service agencies, public facilities, technological developments, and human resources literally abound. And the invited speaker does not have to be of tycoon proportions, even though the occasional "name" individual is often willing to volunteer his presence for educational purposes. More often than not, the visitor is a service-minded citizen who, although not of renown, has a specialized message to bring. He might be a parent recently returned from a far-off land, a local scientist of some note, a public servant, an educator from a near-by college, or a businessman with a challenging idea. To the extent that such philanthropic-minded people can enrich a curriculum, their guest participation, within reason, is to be encouraged.

However, careful forethought should characterize the process from the time the germ of the idea is first conceived until the period of consummation after the guest speaker arrives. Without this test of precaution, the method is fraught with negative possibilities. It is not uncommon for a teacher to find himself red-faced with embarrassment when he asks into the classroom guests, unknown to him but "acknowledged leaders," who not only come unprepared but go off on tangents or present obvious biases: for example, the "vote-getter" who ignores the previously arranged topic and takes up the cause of party politicking; the silver-tongued orator "by reputation" who throws speech habits back a semester or two; and the actor of "Hollywood proportions" who acts as if drama is yet to be created —these and others like them are ample reasons for caution in planning for the visitor.

To prevent such disasters, the teacher should not invite resource persons to a school unless he knows from first-hand experience what quality of performance he may expect of them. He should even hesitate to take the recommendations of friends and colleagues. He alone will know the exact context of the learning situation, and the responsibility for the success or failure of the venture is always exclusively his. Not only should a teacher have seen or heard a resource person perform before he extends an invitation, but he should have a prior planning conference with the anticipated guest. This device provides a medium whereby the visitor can learn the purpose of his anticipated visit, be informed of the level of the pupils in the class, and be helped to see how the presentation can be integrated with other facets of the curriculum. Some speakers have a tendency to talk down to high school students, with resulting loss of motivation. Others communicate at a too-high level of sophistication. Regardless who the person may be, a teacher who learns first-hand whatever he can about a speaker prior to issuing an invitation, and then shares with the speaker all pertinent information about a group, invests in the probable success of the undertaking.

On the other side, the pupils also should be informed of the background of the visitor—his particular perspective, the reasons for the appearance, and his position in the community. The type of response that will be expected of them should likewise be communicated to them. Intelligent orientation can discount the possibility of discourteous or rude behavior. The visiting speaker can make a vital contribution provided careful teacher-pupil planning underwrites the effort.

SUMMARY

In Chapter 7, seven verbal methods of instruction have been covered in some detail. Three of them are rooted deeply in education's past and present: the lecture, the discussion, and the question-answer technique. The formal lecture was identified as having only a modest, certainly not a dominant, position in the secondary school classroom. The informal lecture, discussion, and question-answer approaches were treated as more pertinent.

Three methods more innovational in nature were next considered: the committee, the round table, and the symposium. These, along with such other approaches as the buzz session and role-playing, were categorized as socialized methods of teaching, adding the component of the social to the cognitive. In all of them, despite the delegation of considerable responsibility to adolescents, the teacher was described as never being able to delegate the right for students to plan carelessly or to perform lackadaisically.

Finally, the potentially considerable contribution to learning from the visiting speaker was discussed, with the need for planning once more emphasized.

REFERENCES

Bossing, Nelson, *Teaching in Secondary Schools*. Boston: Houghton Mifflin Co. (3rd ed.), 1952. (Chapter 4)

Burton, William H., *The Guidance of Learning Activities*. New York: Appleton-Century-Crofts, Inc. (2nd ed.), 1952. (Chapters 16–18)

Faunce, Roland C., and Morrel J. Clute, *Teaching and Learning in the Junior High School*. Belmont, California: Wadsworth Publishing Company, 1961.

Giles, Harry H., *The Integrated Classroom*. New York: Basic Books, Inc., 1959.

Grambs, Jean D., William J. Iverson, and Franklin K. Patterson, *Modern Methods in Secondary Education*. New York: Holt, Rinehart and Winston (rev. ed.), 1958. (Chapters 10 and 11)

Kettelcamp, Gilbert C., *Teaching Adolescents*. Boston: D. C. Heath and Co., 1954. (Chapters 6 and 7)

Macomber, Freeman G., *Teaching in the Modern Secondary School*. New York: McGraw-Hill Book Co., Inc., 1952 (Chapter 8)

Rivlin, Harry, *Teaching Adolescents in Secondary Schools.* New York: Appleton-Century Crofts, Inc., 1961 (Chapters 3–5)

Van Til, William, Gordon Vors, and John Lounsbury, *Modern Education for the Junior High School Years.* Indianapolis: Bobbs-Merrill Company, 1961.

SELECTED METHODS
OF
INSTRUCTION:
PRIMARILY NON-ORAL

Since the human organism is possessed of at least five known senses: hearing, seeing, tasting, smelling, and touching—not to mention the possible existence of the so-called *extrasensory* phenomena—education is dilatory when it relies too heavily on any one sense to the neglect of others that might act as primary or reinforcing learning agents. For centuries, the oral-aural method was pre-eminent in classrooms all over the world. Then, with the invention of the printing press, the visual vied for, and soon achieved, important status. The senses other than hearing and seeing have usually played their learning roles only in specialized or supportive ways.

In the previous chapter, a number of oral-teaching media were developed in some detail. In the present chapter, those methods which are not exclusively associated with the oral will be the center of interest. For instance, drill has been included in the latter category because it can be pursued in the written as well as the oral medium. Essentially the same may be said of homework. The first so-called non-oral teaching method to receive attention in this chapter is a multi-faceted and complex one, "problem-solving."

PROBLEM-SOLVING

During the approximately two millennia that philosophy was the uncontested queen of the sciences, namely, from Socrates to a few centuries ago, empiricism and scientific inquiry rarely fought more than an infrequent rear-guard action against the then-superior tenets of deduction. However, when the cumulative discoveries of such eminent natural scientists as Bacon, Galileo, Spencer, and Darwin became so overwhelming that complete refutation was impossible, an old approach to knowledge, the scientific method, was reborn and crowned with respectability. The term "old" is a proper description, because Aristotle and others of the ancients employed the method extensively, although not exclusively.

With the rebirth of scientific inquiry, it is our contention, philosophy in no way lost significance. The current minority vogue of analytical positivism, whose leading exponent is Bertrand Russell, we question on the grounds that neutrality is too weak a stand to take on selected vital issues that cannot be scientifically proved. Agnosticism, when carried too far, discourages active interest in, and the adopting of tentative positions on, such matters as God, religion, and other value intangibles. In contrast, we are convinced that the scientific way not only can coexist with but actually serves to reinforce the method of philosophy—only its dimensions are different.

With the advent of science in the world of knowledge, the new terms, the *scientific method, reflective thinking,* and *problem-solving,* came into being. For purposes of the present brief treatment, they will be regarded as interchangeable. All of them mutually represent an inductive way of analyzing knowledge and even life itself. They are descriptive of the probing mind, the practice of withholding generalizations until most or all of the evidence is in, and the courageous willingness of the scholar to analyze even the sacrosanct without fear. Although problem-solving is a particular heritage of the brilliant mind, it is also within the reach of the learner of more limited abilities. Like maturity, which people achieve at varying levels, the problem-solving approach to knowledge may be engaged in by all, in varying degrees.

Essentially, the method of the problem-solver consists of the following sequence of steps:

1. A problem, issue, or question requiring an answer or solution is identified.
2. Data about the problem are collected.
3. The data are organized and analyzed.
4. A tentative solution to the problem is hypothesized.
5. The hypothesis is tried out.

6. The hypothesis is supported or rejected.

7. If supported, the problem is solved. If not supported, the problem in its initial or modified state is re-attacked.

Contrary to popular opinion, the scientific method of relating to life does not confine itself to absolute facts in themselves. If it did, its contribution would be narrowly limited, because most of what man claims to know is clearly inferential—and therefore non-factual. Even the historian would readily admit to subjectivity. In this connection, for a rainy-day project, the reader might compare the respective accounts of the American Revolution as presented by an English, a French, and an American historian. Or he might compare the War Between the States narrative as seen through the eyes first of a Southerner and then of a Yankee. Or, even more definitively, he might expose himself to the unmitigated positivism of a high school English grammar with respect to split infinitives and possessive pronouns which "must" modify gerunds, and then read the alternatives proposed by such scholars of the English language as Robert Pooley and Albert Marckwardt. At the end of such a project, he would be more skeptical of the excesses of categorical positivism.

Interestingly, the discovery of these contradictions might all be revealed as products of problem-solving techniques. Researchers are exposed to disparate as well as identical evidence, and all sooner or later reach a point of having to decide between, or among, alternatives. Then, even though the approach previously taken may have been very sound, their subjective judgment, based on the uniqueness of their personalities and experiences, governs. Even with differing final judgments, however, none of the investigators could be unduly criticized, provided that he gathered data, evaluated them, and then drew conclusions based on a rich accumulation of evidence. The perfectionist researcher who waits until "all the evidence is in" usually dies in the middle of his project, not being endowed with eternity.

Problem-solving, in the classroom or elsewhere, although at times a separate method of investigation, is also basically a means of approaching life's tangibles and intangibles with the questioning mind and the discoverer's verve. In this sense, it can be a feature of most methods of instruction. When a lecturer gathers and then presents a respectable body of evidence on a given issue, postulating or asking a class to postulate intelligently from it, he is loyal to the scientific traditions. The teacher-discussion leader is also loyal when guiding a group into the hard core of a controversial issue, leading them, in the process, to discover and weigh evidence, to reject falsity, and to arrive at consensus or a scholarly difference of opinion. The teacher-counselor who, regarding this method as inherent in the counseling process, rejects the ease of giving advice for the sounder and more productive approach of placing the final onus of decision-making on the counselee, also pays allegiance to the scientific method. The teacher-therapist helps by uncovering data and identifying alternatives, but the counselee alone is left with the agonizing task of deciding. Undramatic examples of problem-solving occur any time that alternatives demand selection or rejection. The Wellingtons make this point clear in their quotation from Frost's "The Road Not Taken." The Frostian character looks back to an early fork in life's road and quietly reminisces about the long-term influence of that choice.[1] He had solved a problem and was living with its consequences.

Problem-solving is, however, more than just a state of mind; it is a process that demands frequent fulfillment in an action situation. To make opportunities for decision-making available to students in the school environment, the teacher needs to structure the curriculum, and the administrator the co-curriculum, around this desired outcome. The teacher of algebra, for instance, when treating the concept of negative numbers, must press for learning that extends beyond minus signs and mechanical formulas. His ultimate goal is to involve the student in a problem situation wherein the mechanics of the concept will be understood and then applied functionally and understandingly. As a further example, the teacher of physics should make the scientific method of inquiry a goal which looms just as important as, if not more important than, the content of electrodynamics. And even the teacher of an aesthetic subject like art should resist the lure of forcing appreciation down the throats of students and help them instead to assess works of art according to criteria which they themselves help to develop.

As a further example, let the reader identify himself with an eighth-grade unified-studies class where the teacher and pupils are examining the relationship of religion to the presidential election of 1960. The problem-solving approach would demand the gathering of extensive data, including the Al Smith story of 1928; an analysis of recent changes in attitudes toward minority religious groups; and a consideration of the more recent climate of religious opinion of the moment. Pupils would be asked then to organize their findings, to raise sensible questions about them, and through such reflective thought to arrive independently, or as a group, at a defensible point of view. This analytical approach would be in harmony with the traditions of problem-solving.

When students are encouraged to question and then to implement their conclusions with action, they will, of course, make mistakes. But even the mistakes, when they are sequels to reflective thought, are educational. We prefer the analytical mind, even though sacred cows may topple, to the passive stultification of unquestioning acceptance.

---

[1] C. Burleigh and Jean Wellington, *Teaching for Critical Thinking* (New York: McGraw-Hill Book Co., Inc., 1960), p. 27.

THE TEXTBOOK

From the lofty heights of problem-solving we descend abruptly to the earthy level of the textbook, the bugbear of professional educators these many years. As mentioned earlier in the chapter, the oral-aural medium had a long reign of supremacy in organized education prior to the invention of the printing press. With printing, however, the written word challenged the supremacy of the oral. The first challenge came from the older classics, most of which had lain dormant in the various monasteries of Europe or Asia for decades or centuries. The next threat came from the more current publications, which were regarded as useful but too provincial to give serious competition to the classics.

The greatest written threat of all, however, was the school textbook, which in America has been characterized by phenomenal growth during the nineteenth and twentieth centuries. First came the primers, then the readers, and finally textbooks for all subjects of the curriculum. For a century and a half, educational personnel have alternately praised and castigated the textbook, with the practitioners generally more favorably disposed and the theorists less so.

The values of the textbook

To partially resolve the textbook controversy, we propose to subject to brief analysis first the values, then the limitations, of this important academic instrument.

Probably the textbook's most positive feature is the structure that it affords a curriculum. Courses that under the leadership of an inexperienced and incompetent teacher might otherwise have little or no organization at all are assured of at least a minimum, if textbooks of quality are adopted. And the extent of their quality is dependent on three factors: (1) the artistry of the individuals who serve as authors, (2) the editorial competency and ethics of book publishers, (3) and the abilities of teachers to select the best available books. The first and third factors are more or less under the control of organized education, and thus are subject to positive manipulation. The second is basically commercial—a few university presses to the contrary—and therefore only indirectly controllable by educators. With marketability the prime criterion of excellence, some outstanding manuscripts remain unpublished whereas other mediocre ones reach the careless consumer. The competition of free enterprise merely increases, without guaranteeing, quality.

In assessing the worth of a textbook, the following factors should be taken into consideration.

1. *Is the textbook current?* The date of copyright should always be checked to make sure that the book is fairly recent. Remember that any publication reflects the climate of the period.

2. *What are the author's credentials?* Is he recognized in his field? Has he had practical experiences to support the theory he presents? Does he give evidence of being informed and scholarly? Can he write effectively and interestingly? Do his biases stand out as reasonable and consistent within an understandable frame of reference? Does he evidence a scholar's familiarity with points of view other than his own?

   3. *Does the content meet acceptable standards?*
      A. Does it fit into the purposes, subject matter, and procedural dimensions of the course for which it is being considered?
      B. Is it sufficiently comprehensive?
      C. Is it geared to the level of the class for which it is being considered?
      D. Does it reflect the newer innovations of the day?
      E. Is it factually accurate?
      F. Does it follow a defensible sequence of ideas, concepts, or points of view?
      G. Does it properly develop the complex and significant areas of coverage in more detail than the less complex and less significant areas?
      H. Is it devoid of "filler" substance?
      I. Does it properly elicit reflective thought?

   4. *Does the style meet acceptable standards?*
      A. Are the intended meanings conveyed lucidly?
      B. Is the expression interesting?
      C. Are ideas and concepts expressed economically?
      D. Is the vocabulary at the level of the intended consumer?
      E. Are technical and difficult concepts developed with understanding and care?
      F. Is the plan of headings adequate?

   5. *Does the textbook meet esthetic standards?*
      A. Does the cover have eye appeal?
      B. Is the paper quality adequate and pleasing?
      C. Is the type attractive and easy to read?
      D. Is the book of satisfactory shape and size?
      E. Does the format have appeal?

   6. *Does the textbook document sources sufficiently without becoming encyclopedic?*

   7. *Does the textbook meet accepted mechanical standards in regard to the preface, table of contents, glossary (if needed), and index?*

The teacher should employ the above list, or one similar to it, when engaged in the selection of a text. When adoptions are made from inadequate criteria, the too-frequent result is student protest or mild rebellion and teacher regret. And the mistake cannot be rectified readily in those states which establish by law a minimum period of textbook tenure.

A second distinctive feature of the technique under discussion is that it is a time-saver for the teacher. A textbook, besides making for structure that might otherwise not exist, conserves the valuable time of a busy teacher. If the new college graduate, with a major, for instance, in social studies, arrived in his seventh-grade classroom with no textbook available, the problems he would face in the teaching of United States and world history concepts, national governmental concerns, and local civic issues would be frustrating, to say the least. Over a period of time, admittedly, he could effect curriculum organization by synthesizing appropriate library materials, college notes, and contributions from other teachers, but what a tragic waste! Teaching is vastly more efficient and economical of effort when the textbook serves as a useful prop, thereby freeing the teacher for the more professional obligations of his position.

In addition to the two advantages already discussed, the textbook also provides a common meeting ground for students. Notwithstanding the fact that adolescents, because of their differences in abilities, backgrounds of experience, and potentials may not react in the same way to the textbook's stimuli, the teacher can nonetheless be assured that all will have had equal access to a unifying source. This shared source lends itself conveniently to group reading, the single assignment, the intensive coverage of a significant idea or passage, and transition to other activities. As an organizing and unifying device, the textbook has unquestioned merit.

Limitations of the textbook

Despite its positive features, however, the medium under discussion is not an unadulterated blessing, although its limitations admittedly are more often the result of mis-employment by a teacher than of restrictions in the medium itself. A primary limitation is the single point of view that it too frequently presents. For instance, the old *McGuffey Reader* was just as broad or narrow in viewpoint or selection of material as was McGuffey himself. If he believed that Longfellow was a better philosopher and poet than Emerson, more of Longfellow got into the *Reader*. In like manner, modern texts are prone to represent the slanted opinions, ideas, and interpretations of an author or co-authors. A fundamentalist who writes on William Jennings Bryan's attitude toward evolution and the Scopes trial is bound to color the situation differently than would a modern scientist. And even the writer who prides himself on presenting all points of view on a controversial topic may be deluding himself, because objectivity is the attainment of only the very mature. In reality, since no writer can evade a minimum of editorializing, the teacher who uses exclusively the one-textbook approach narrows the frame of learning reference, thereby closing the door, at least in part, on the treasured process of critical thinking.

Such constriction has a deleterious effect on students at all levels, but particularly on the more capable, who become frustrated when denied the intellectual enrichment that accompanies selected variety. In the category of the single text is included the anthology which unduly capsules. Its products are considerably more fruitful when supplemented by paperbacks and the complete works of an occasional author.

A second drawback of the textbook is its easy seduction of a teacher into a sequence of ideas, concepts, or drill procedures which are all of another's choosing. Some or even much of the structure of any textbook may well be related to the curriculum context of the classroom moment. But the lure for a teacher to follow this structure, even though unrelated, is hard to resist. When the teacher resists the easy lure, as a professional individual must, he then must provide direction apart from the content of the textbook. Such interpolations, even though time-consuming, rescue learning from the purely mechanical and make the textbook a more defensible instructional medium.

A third shortcoming is one which relates to the limited verbal abilities of certain pupils. A self-evident comment is that, if pupils are to learn from a textbook, they must be verbal enough to read it with understanding. And yet, reading is a skill that students inevitably possess in uneven quantities. One sophomore in an English class not inconceivably will read at a rate of 125 words per minute, in contrast to another who will read at a rate from three to four times that number. With such a range to be realistically expected, a teacher cannot assume that all pupils will respond in the same way to a common textbook assignment. And even more important than the student's response as measured in words per minute is the degree of comprehension reflected by the response. Some students will read and interpret the material with real sophistication; others will find that the meaning is obscured by their linguistic deficiencies.

A final shortcoming to be anticipated is the ease with which a too-close adherence to a single text can stifle teacher-initiative. In contrast to the unit of learning which leads toward new horizons and aspires to a high level of thought, the more delimiting method restricts individualism and creativity. The teacher who follows the path of ease resists with difficulty, or not at all, a paginated approach to content, the often inappropriate questions at the end of a chapter, and the temptation of the read-recite-review-examine sequence. The textbook, like the proverbial Rock of Gibraltar, is a bulwark for the overly dependent teacher, but what a price for security when it is permitted to dominate!

How a textbook can be used to best advantage

From the background of advantages and disadvantages of the textbook emerges the need for a description of the academic setting in which the method can be used with most success. Like any other acceptable medium of instruction, it can be effective when employed with acumen. What, then, are some of the more effective ways?

In learning areas that deal with social and humanistic concepts, such as civics, history, and literature, multi-text use is preferable to the use of a single text. The former provides greater opportunity for differences and shadings of opinion to become manifest to the students, thereby detouring, at least temporarily, the search for an absolute. Whenever possible, multiple textbooks should be selected on the basis of their differences. Textbooks in social studies, for instance, should present contrasts in analysis; those in literature, variations in content; those in art, differences both in selection and in point of view. In any field, textbooks at varying levels of reading difficulty should be chosen. The resultant variety can go far toward meeting the respective needs of students. The demand for a multi-text approach is less impelling in the subject areas of the skills, for instance, in mathematics, grammar, and speech; but even in these, the second or third point of view is often necessary.

Regardless of whether one, or more than one, textbook is employed, the curriculum should be enriched by supplementary library readings. Textbooks normally provide extensity; supplementary readings, intensity. In physics, for example, a pupil who seeks a greater understanding of kinetic energy than the textbook can offer should be encouraged to delve into specialized references. In biology, the students referred to in Chapter 7 who, as a committee, elected the intricate study of the emotions and their physiological correlates would require the assistance of specialized references. Not only in science but in all subject areas, both depth and breadth of comprehension are inherent educational goals. The textbook as a single method fails by its very nature the first of these purposes.

When used alone or in conjunction with other references, the textbook should rarely be pursued sequentially from the beginning to the end. This procedure assumes, among other things, that the author's order of events is automatically that of the teacher, that all of the book's ideas are relevant to the school's curriculum, and that the students are psychologically ready for the predetermined progression. None of these assumptions is tenable. However, all are probably more tenable for the skill subjects, which are dependent on a strictly graduated sequence, than for the subjects which deal with philosophical ideas and concepts.

In brief, the text should be an organizing influence but not the only one; it should stimulate but not be the only stimulus; in general, it should contribute to without being the exclusive means of learning. As a guide, effective teachers should support it wholeheartedly; when permitted to become an academic tyrant, it must be relegated to its proper place in the classroom pattern as just one of many educational devices.

THE ASSIGNMENT

Related to the textbook, but not its exclusive property, as traditionalism has made it out to be, is the assignment of future academic work to be done. This responsibility may receive less attention from the teacher candidate than it deserves, but the in-service leader rarely gives it only brief time. Although somewhat overlapping the topic of homework, which is next to be considered, the assignment is important enough in the classroom panorama to justify special treatment. As will be defended subsequently, the assignment should be (1) made as early as possible, (2) explained as clearly as possible, and (3) differentiated as much as possible.

Regarding the first of the three, whenever feasible, the assignment should be made well in advance of the time that work is due. This statement assumes a curriculum that has been designed in sufficiently large blocks to make this outcome achievable. The advantages are greater flexibility of study habits and the increased growth potential associated with more student independence in planning his work schedule. Yet despite these benefits, most teachers cling to the short-term view. A 1961–1962 study of 30 high schools, engaged in jointly by the author and associates at the Evanston Township High School, indicated that 80 per cent of the instructional leaders of the schools studied employed exclusively or primarily the daily-assignment technique.

And if long-term assignments are beneficial, a careful explanation and clarification of them by the teacher are no less so. When the teacher disregards the merits of orienting students to assigned projects—by failing to present the reasons for the projects, by failing to explain anticipated outcomes, or by failing to help students to get started—he tends to defeat the destined purposes of the assigned work.

A third requisite of the assignment is that it be fitted to student needs and interests. This goal is not attainable in all classroom situations, particularly when projects common to the entire class are being planned; but to the extent that work can be related to the individual, it becomes proportionately more meaningful. The unit plan achieves this objective by providing a certain amount of student choice of activities. Other instances of its employment occur when a teacher deliberately breaks the assignment down three or four ways to conform to small-group differences, or when he sets a minimum requirement for all and strongly urges the more capable and more strongly motivated to move beyond the minimum base.

With a wide range of abilities, reading speeds, interests, and aptitudes operative in any class, even a so-called homogeneous one, a differentiated assignment is often a mandate. Differentiation does not need to be blatantly obvious. A teacher of algebra, for example, can make a minimum assignment for all with the suggestion that pupils who find the going rather easy move ahead to problems of a more complex nature. He resists the temptation to assign more of the same-level problems, however. He might good-naturedly remark, "I know pretty well who is having more trouble and who less; so act accordingly." Admittedly, the motivated pupils will do the "extra" work and the laggards will not; but, when rapport exists, adolescents have a way of demonstrating gratifying enthusiasm and effort. The differentiated assignment is consistent with the expectancy that students should be encouraged to work to the level of their innate capacities.

STUDY ACTIVITIES AND HOMEWORK

A sequel to the assignment, whether short or long-range, is the work associated with getting it accomplished. This is performed in three settings: in the classroom proper through the method of supervised study, in a free study period, or at home. Regardless of the place or manner of performance, the academic world is divided on the fundamental questions of, How much? How often? and By what means? It is rare for even an individual school system to answer these questions coherently—much less for the greater educational enterprise to agree on universal standards. This lack of uniformity is not surprising in view of the decentralization of American public and private education, with its resulting correlates of curriculum diversity and differing teacher practices.

Since anything resembling uniform standards in this area is nonexistent, we shall present, in their place, a few central tendencies of the homework study referred to in the previous section. The 30 high schools, being primarily suburban, were slanted toward a college-bound pupil population: the range was from a low of 25 per cent of seniors who attended college to a high of 94 per cent, with a mean average of 70 per cent. Accordingly, the reported practices must not be regarded as typical of large-city, small-town, or rurally located secondary schools, which, despite considerable overlap, would differ somewhat from the described standards. Invariably the phenomenon of a high percentage of college-preparatory students is accompanied by a greater school and community expectancy for homework performance.

Statistics on some of the more mechanical features of the 30 programs are as follows:

1. The median average length of period was 55 minutes.
2. The median average number of school periods was 6.
3. The median average number of study periods per pupil, per day, was 1.
4. Ten per cent of the students were enrolled in 3 subjects with homework involved, 75 per cent in 4, and 15 per cent in 5.
5. Only 6 of the 30 schools had stated written policies on homework.
6. The amount of homework time spent per pupil, per course, per day was 44 minutes, which, when paired with items 3 and 4 above, indicates that the average student spent just short of three hours of out-of-classroom time per day on assignments: approximately 2 hours at home and 55 minutes in school.

7. Regarding the assignment, 23 of the schools reported giving it exclusively or primarily on a daily basis; only 6, on a long-term basis.

8. Regarding outside help on homework assignments by family or friends, 10 were negative toward the practice, 8 were positive, 2 ambivalent, and 10 did not reply.

9. Fifteen schools stated that the brighter students should spend more time on homework; 3, that the slower should spend more time; and 12, that all should spend the same amount of time.

Regardless of the statistics, interesting and meaningful though they are, selected principles which emerged from the study eclipsed them in importance. The most recurrent was that homework which reaches optimum significance needs to be carefully planned to harmonize with curriculum goals and needs to be almost painstakingly explained in order to prevent wasted or uneconomical effort by students. The superintendent of the Chapel Hill High School of North Carolina, Joseph M. Johnson, has made this point with the greatest of clarity: "What I am trying to say here is that homework is a necessity. However, it should not be 'the be all and the end all here.' It must be intelligently planned and programmed. It must have a real learning purpose. It must not be just work for work's sake."[2] Johnson's aversion to busy work was verbally shared by most of the respondents.

Discordant with this point of view are a number of teacher practices that permeate many classrooms. One is the punitive assignment—that academic Sword of Damocles used to threaten students with extra homework for being bad actors. The punitive 500-word theme, the ten more algebra problems, or the two pages copied from the textbook—all of these do harm, and none does much good, if any. The net result too often is a resentment for the teacher and a dislike of the school curriculum—neither an exactly happy outcome. A second practice almost as indefensible is the assignment made to keep idle minds from breeding mischief. Both conflict with the truism that unless homework has relevance, it should not be given.

A second principle that echoed throughout the thirty-school study, and is confirmed by educational theory, is that homework should contribute to the nourished academic goal of independence. Alexander Anderson, of the Washington-Lee High School, Arlington, Virginia, underwrites this concept in the statement:

All students should be encouraged to do additional work outside of class. The purpose should be a deeper, richer understanding of the material. All academic work especially should encourage this independent supplementary type of work. College preparatory students must engage in much reading and investigation beyond the classroom. They should acquire the library habit; be able to con-

---

[2] Joseph M. Johnson, in reply to a questionnaire dispatched by the Evanston Township High School, March, 1962.

centrate in study not alone to do assignments, but to really broaden their education.

. . . Homework may take many forms including long term assignments, major projects, review work, as well as daily assignments.

. . . It is also correct that in our advanced programs the objective is study in depth, not just covering more material. However, it is also obvious that work that tends to be on the college level demands more from students, and they demand more of themselves. These students approach the ideal of "independent study."[3]

Other supportive concepts commented on by the respondents and endorsed by the author are that homework:

1. Should be required of all.
2. Should be individualized whenever possible. In this regard, Walter Heischmann, Superintendent of the Upper Arlington High School, Columbus, Ohio, writes that

Blanket homework assignments for all students have little value. Homework assignments should be individualized and be a continuation of classroom work. This is difficult for most teachers to do since it requires additional work and they have had very little preparation for it in their four years or more of college training.[4]

3. Should accent quality more than quantity.
4. Should never be assigned on a "Let's get tough basis." Apropos of this, Mr. Knute Larson, of the Cranston East High School, Rhode Island, decries the current practice of trying to "beat the Russians to the moon" by assigning "more of the same."[5]

5. Leads to outcomes that are significantly correlated with teacher quality.

From the foregoing, homework emerges as a vital part of a school's program, challenging the best in teachers to make it meaningful. It serves as an antidote to teacher domination by enabling adolescents to develop independent study habits removed from formal academic influences. Regarding the controversial issue of parent help, we align with the minority in the study who expressed themselves in favor, provided parents not unduly delay progress of their children toward independence. Regarding the amount of homework, although any arbitrary total is indefensible, we regard the mean average of two hours as reasonable. However, the goal of every teacher should be the motivation of students away from time limits toward the more professional goal of optimum growth.

We conclude this topic by reproducing parts of a policy statement on homework adopted in 1957 by the Lower Merion Public Schools, of Ardmore, Pennsylvania, which is highly pertinent:

[3] Alexander A. Anderson—part of the same survey as in footnote 2 *supra*.
[4] Walter B. Heischmann—part of the same survey as in footnote 2 *supra*.
[5] Knute Larson—part of the same survey as in footnote 2 *supra*.

Role of the Teacher in Homework Assignments
The teacher should:
Make certain that the assignment has *real meaning* for the *pupil.*

Make the purpose of the assignment *clear.*

Give the kind of *instructions* that will enable the students to proceed independently.

Supervise the beginning of any assignment that depends upon thorough understanding by the pupil of methods of study needed to complete it.

Provide help in developing *good study skills.*

Know the individual differences in the class so that the needs of the pupils can be met successfully when they use *their abilities effectively.*

Ascertain the availability of needed materials.

Be aware of other demands on the pupil's time.

Use time-required guides considered appropriate for the grade.

Allow adequate time for the *appraisal* of completed assignments.

Role of the Pupil in Homework Assignments
The pupil should:
Make certain he understands the requirements of the assignment as to its *purpose,* the *time when due,* and the *method of preparation and presentation* to be followed. An assignment booklet kept by the pupil and available for checking by the teacher or parent at any time is a helpful reminder.

Assume willingly responsibility for completion of *individual assignments.*

Accept the assignment as one means of furthering his educational growth.

Utilize fully study helps and available materials.

Use study time properly and efficiently in school and at home.

Carry out his part of any assignments *involving* the *cooperation* of one or more of his classmates.[6]

SUPERVISED STUDY

More than a casual relationship exists between study at home and study at school, with the essential difference being the presence of the teacher in the latter as an ameliorating influence. For several decades, the primary justification of educators for the hour-, or near-hour-, length period has been the greater opportunity thus provided for adolescents to study under the guiding influence of the instructional leader. The longer class period permits the teacher to pursue a facet of the curriculum in a somewhat formal way during the first part of the period, but such an approach should not consistently be taken at the sacrifice of the last 15 to 20 minutes of supervised study activity. On occasion, regardless of the length of a period, certain teachers devote the entire time to student study.

[6] Elwood L. Prestwood, *et al., Homework in the Lower Merion Public Schools,* September 1957.

Such practices are to be recommended for a number of reasons. In the first place, students frequently need classroom orientation to a homework assignment, which only the teacher can provide. If it is a long-term assignment, an entire period, or even longer, might well be allocated for the orientation. If the curriculum component is of smaller proportions, obviously less time would be needed.

But more than utilizing class time merely for the explaining of an assignment, supervised study enables a teacher to assess the work habits of students, including their powers of concentration, interest in the course material, and other personality mannerisms of varying dimensions. Through this more personalized organizational approach, he can more nearly approximate the educational ideal of accepting the individual where he is and working with him there. The slow student can be helped over obstacles, the fast learner encouraged, the unsure given confidence, and the idler motivated. With supervised study a function of time and place, while we refrain from specialized recommendations, we urge teachers not to overlook its many advantages.

DRILL

One of the most controversial members of the constellation of teaching methodology is drill. Long associated with the mechanical-like schoolmaster of Puritan days, who demanded repetitive responses in exchange for escape from the lash, the time-honored method is currently undergoing scrutiny in educational circles. The radicals are burying it verbally as too outmoded to be tolerated. The liberals urge judicious employment of it. The conservatives engage its services without apology. And the reactionaries nostalgically await its victorious return. Our position is closest to that of the liberals who, although aware of the danger of excess, advocate the employment of drill when in harmony with learning theory.

With respect to this relationship, our plea is that drill be inextricably interwoven with meaning and relevance. To be of value to the student, it must have meaning. Thus, for a teenager who doesn't know what a subordinate clause is, the monotonous intoning of: "A nonrestrictive clause must be separated by commas" could lead to nothing but time wasted. But after discovering the real meaning of grammatical subordination, and the associated necessity of separating the mildly irrelevant from the relevant, the adolescent's underlining of nonrestrictive clauses in the page of a textbook might well be productive. The comments made previously about busy work and punitive assignments are equally applicable here, because, as with them, drill must not be allowed to become mechanical.

A second requirement for drill procedures is that they be given variety. This dimension, by providing a multi-sided approach to learning, is more likely to enhance interest in it. The informed teacher thus seeks ways to divert drill from a monotonous single track of whatever kind, be it a workbook, blackboard exercises, homework, or desk study. Instead, the result ideally is a configuration of these and other drill methods designed to contribute greater diversity to learning and greater resulting motivation to the student.

A third requisite for drill is an early re-integration of drill materials with the broader life context from which they were originally dissociated. Learning theory would include this under a study of transfer. The sequence is customarily as follows: a new process unfamiliar to students is introduced in context; it is next isolated from the natural learning situation for reinforcement purposes; when mastered, it is finally returned to its natural setting. For example, a seventh-grade class engaged in a study of percentages is artificially made to perform exercises apart from an ongoing life situation. When left apart, although some bright students would effect transfer, many of the less gifted would not. It is incumbent upon the teacher, then, to remove the drill concepts from the workbook or blackboard; to reinsert them in their natural places in the world of business, finance, home budgeting, or perhaps church tithing. Although classrooms will always be a step removed from reality, the closer their relationship with it, the more vital learning will be. A close application of drill concepts to a "real world" thus becomes paramount.

A fourth principle of drill as a teaching method is that it should be used only in those instances where greatest student benefit will accrue. These almost universally occur in the skill subjects of mathematics, music, grammar, and foreign languages, and in the motor subjects of physical education, shop, business education, and the industrial arts. And these subjects, we wish to make clear, are only partially of a drill nature, containing conceptual learnings in addition. In those subjects, or parts of subjects, which are inherently conceptual, however, drill should be used sparingly, if at all. For instance, in a study of democracy in a United States history class, of ethics in a comparative religions class, or of evolution in a biology class, more important than verbal definitions of these concepts is their being understood by students. For content, then, that responds to mechanical repetitiveness, drill is relevant; for content which deals with the conceptualized intangibles, it may be mildly or often totally irrelevant.

A fifth truism regarding drill is that it increases in effectiveness to the extent that adolescents are kept informed of their progress. Research supports this convincingly. For instance, students who practice to improve their speed of reading improve more rapidly when aware of gains than do their control counterparts who are not aware of gains. In fact, in almost any learning area, the individual who is enabled to read his thermometer of progress is motivated to improve more. Sensitive to this phenomenon, teachers may require students to evaluate their own progress by having them maintain in an English class a notebook of spelling errors; in a foreign language class, a listing of syntactical errors; or in a mathematics class, a record of arithmetical mistakes in the four basic processes. Performance so revealed would prove diagnostic to the teacher as well as informative to the student.

A final comment is that drill, to be of most benefit, should be conceived in the unique needs of students and thus be related to their specific strengths and limitations. Group drill has a definite function when new processes are being introduced, but in its wake should follow drill procedures more narrowly related to the needs of the individual student.

REVIEW

Review, like drill, to be defensible, must also be grounded in sound learning theory, meeting the demands of such criteria as immediacy, relevance, variety, intent, and integration. With the primary purpose of review being reinforcement, to the extent that it succeeds in making for long- as well as short-term retention, it can be justified. Its greatest support in this regard comes from research on the importance of frequency and spacing as reinforcing learning agents. Pertinent to the former, Thorndike made a research defense of the common-sense principle that, up to the point of diminishing returns, learning possibilities are intensified by the frequent application of stimulus elements. In this connection, review can be regarded as such an element. Apropos of spaced learning, the case for review is its appearance at periodic intervals following the original learning situation, thereby making for reinforcement or even occasional overlearning.

On these sound psychological grounds, review can be readily defended, but the specific nature of its employment is always related to the function of the learning context at any given time. If complex and intricate: a law of physics, an abstract social studies concept, or a difficult syntax in German, review should be recurrent, at frequent intervals over a fairly long period of time. Such persistent repetition, spaced intelligently, makes for increased retention. When the content is less complex: for example, a new word, a simple fact of history, or a fairly obvious concept in science, the review needs to be less habitual and encompassing. A daily summing up might even suffice.

Review is generally conceived not only as a reinforcing but as a synthesizing procedure. It can take place at the beginning of a day's lesson as a tie-in with the previous day's work, at the end of a class period to sum up the day's coverage, or at the end of a unit as a unifying agent. It can even be interpolated in the middle of a unit. Whenever loose academic ends need to be joined, or whenever complex learning concepts need reinforcement, review becomes timely.

While reaping the benefits of review, the teacher should avoid identical routines within the framework of the read-recite-review sequence. Like any other method component, review needs the refreshment of surprise and variety, neither of which is provided by repetitive patterns. If a teacher for several days reviews homework by means of an oral discussion, he would do well to effect a change to perhaps a short quiz or student-led question-answer period. Or if the blackboard is used too routinely as a method of review, the teacher could profitably substitute desk work, a balopticon projection of review materials, or a buzz session.

THE WORKBOOK

Incidentally alluded to a number of times to date is the workbook, the favorite whipping boy of many educators. In support of the technique are its practical usefulness as a drill procedure and the greater richness of examples that it can provide through the careful forethought of a curriculum specialist. Arrayed against its use are arguments regarding its detachment from the curriculum main stream, its tendency to assume independence, the ease with which it lends itself to busy work, and its frequent failure to transfer to lifelike situations.

The extreme animosity that the workbook has generated undoubtedly has been due to the excesses connected with its employment. Like any drill medium, the technique under discussion must be an integrated part of a planned learning context and be approached with meaning, interest, and variety. When so employed, unfamiliar concepts or educational processes are first approached in the abstract; then the concretions of the workbook are turned to as supporting agents; finally, the reinforced insights are reincorporated into the broader learning context. To insure these outcomes, however, the teacher needs to study first the learning context carefully and then the content of a workbook to ascertain whether the two are in harmony. If they are, he must next insure against the selection of an overabundance of workbook examples—an error that would justify the accusation of "busy work." Once the examples have been identified by the teacher and pursued by the students, the teacher's next obligation is to desert the workbook detour for the greater learning context. When the workbook is so utilized, the teacher needs no defense against possible criticism.

However, when a teacher permits the technique to be the basic, not the supporting, learning medium; when he uses it as an excuse for paper grading or other escapes from classroom obligations; and when he selects it or uses parts of it without a thoughtful analysis of curriculum purposes, the teacher deserves the opprobrium that will be heaped on him by critics of the method—or the abuses of the method.

THE FIELD TRIP

The last so-called non-oral teaching method to be discussed in this chapter is the field trip. As indicated in the last chapter, the visiting speaker enables the school to bring a community resource to the school; the field trip, in contrast, takes the school to the community. Both, however, reflect the need of any school system to increase its base of operations by reaching into the surrounding environment for enrichment. For the field trip to achieve its optimum potential, the classroom teacher should be aware of and adhere to certain time-validated principles, some of which follow:

1. The trip should be conceived in the context of a classroom learning situation. Thus, a visit by students of a civics class to a courtroom is defensible, whereas a comparable visit by a science class could not be equally, if at all, defended. But even in the former, the visit should emanate from the specific curriculum content of the moment—for example, a unit on the judiciary rather than one on the legislative branch.

2. The teacher should make a preliminary reconnaissance visit to ascertain whether the contemplated trip will serve its intended purpose. This "dry run" will enable him to make mental notes of specific experiences that may need highlighting during the period of orientation. The more detailed his information beforehand, the greater will be his effectiveness as a resource person throughout the many stages of the planned project.

3. He next needs to identify and arrange the administrative details: means of transportation, cost, time to be spent en route and at the agency, key people to contact, and the itinerary, if any, to be followed on arrival. And a detail that over-arches all others in significance is the need to secure parental approval in advance of the trip. Allegedly, in some states, the teacher is legally liable if he takes young people on a trip off school grounds without the specific approval of parents. For this reason, most schools provide a form that the teacher sends home with each student wherein the parent is asked to approve the trip and accept legal responsibility for it. The term "allegedly" was used a few lines back to identify the legal ambivalence regarding teacher liability for unauthorized field trips. In this regard, since the length of the school day and the breadth of the curriculum are being more liberally interpreted by the decade, it is quite conceivable that, assuming the exercise of proper precautions by teachers, no liability would exist even if parental permission were denied. However, pending more definite legal word, the signed statement becomes a precautionary step, if nothing more. And the signed statement that waives teacher liability is legally invalid in case of carelessness or negligence by the instructional leader, because a citizen cannot be made so easily to abandon his legal rights.

4. Next, for maximum learning outcomes to occur, the pupils should be prepared for the visit. Preparation is necessary for academic as well as administrative reasons. Academically, pupils should be made conscious of the over-all purpose of the experience, have key situations pre-identified for them, and be informed of selected methods of discovering them. When a meaningful introduction to the trip's advantages has been made, the results are more richly rewarding to both pupils and teachers.

5. Finally, after the trip has been completed, some type of appraisal as a synthesizing influence should take place. Although rejecting as unnecessary the written test as an automatic follow-up procedure, we advocate some means of ascertaining how well the academic excursion has achieved its anticipated outcomes. A trip worth taking demands not only careful planning, but analysis upon completion.

Almost as important as adhering to these five rules is it to avoid common negative practices, one of the most heinous of which is using the field trip as a lame excuse for a teacher and class to evade the rigors of school-work. An escape to the "big city" for purposes other than academic cannot be tolerated. While accepting education's responsibility for the personal and social growth of adolescents, we insist that the field trip not be used for other than justifiable purposes.

A final comment is in order about the field trip, relating to its disruption of the school day. With the 40- to 60-minute class period in vogue, a field trip is not possible for one teacher without an invasion of the academic time of another. Thus, if a trip to a science museum will consume a four-hour time block, some provisions must be made to lessen the possible impact on the teachers of English and Spanish who were incommoded. One method is an administrative one whereby a school sets aside two or three days per year for field trip purposes. This approach we reject because it violates the criterion of curriculum relevancy: no trip should be made unless it fits into an immediate learning context. Rather, we urge that teachers unbend to a point of making occasional concessions to other teachers who wish to broaden education's horizons. Better this professional give-and-take than administrative fiat which distorts learning sequence.

SUMMARY

Covered in order in this chapter were the primarily non-oral methods of instruction: problem-solving, the textbook, the assignment, homework, supervised study, drill, review, the workbook, and community visits.

Highlighted in the chapter were the following concepts:

1. Problem-solving is a way of studying life by the gathering, collating, and evaluating of data which have been directed at predetermined hypotheses. It lifts learning from memory tedium to a level of sophistication. However, it supplements without pre-empting the place of philosophy or religion.

2. The textbook must be employed to support, but never to give unquestioned sequence to, learning. It must serve but not be the "end all."

3. The assignment, like homework, was identified as best when individualized. The long-term assignment was identified as vastly preferable to the daily assignment.

4. The justification for homework was built on the extent of its contribution to student independence and the degree of its individualization. When consistently undifferentiated for the masses, however, its validity should be questioned.

5. Regarding supervised study, the author went on record as being decidedly in its favor, in view of the close pupil-teacher relationships that it provides.

6. Drill and review were defended on the basis of learning theory. Rather than outmoded, they were identified as meaningful when in harmony with contextual demands.

7. The workbook was defended if carefully selected, used sparingly to concretize learning, and laid aside when conceptual learnings assume pre-eminence.

8. The field trip was defended as an effective means of broadening the school's curriculum base. But, again, the importance of curriculum relevancy and planning was emphasized.

REFERENCES

Bossing, Nelson, *Teaching in Secondary Schools*. Boston: Houghton Mifflin Co. (3rd ed.), 1952. (Chapter 4)

Bowker, R. R., Co., *Textbooks in Print: The American Education Catalog*. New York: (published annually).

Burton, William H., *The Guidance of Learning Activities*. New York: Appleton-Century-Crofts, Inc. (2nd ed.), 1952. (Chapters 16–18)

Dewey, John, *How We Think*. Boston: D. C. Heath and Co., 1933.

Faunce, Roland C., and Morrel J. Clute, *Teaching and Learning in the Junior High School*. Belmont, California: Wadsworth Publishing Company, 1961.

Giles, Harry H., *The Integrated Classroom*. New York: Basic Books, Inc., 1959.

Grambs, Jean D., William J. Iverson, and Franklin K. Patterson, *Modern Methods in Secondary Education*. New York: Holt, Rinehart and Winston (rev. ed.), 1958. (Chapters 10 and 11)

Hullfish, H. Gordon, and Phillip G. Smith, *Reflective Thinking: The Method of Education.* New York: Dodd, Mead and Co., 1961.

Kettelcamp, Gilbert C., *Teaching Adolescents.* Boston: D. C. Heath and Co., 1954. (Chapters 6 and 7)

Macomber, Freeman G., *Teaching in the Modern Secondary School.* New York: McGraw-Hill Book Co., Inc., 1952. (Chapter 8)

Rivlin, Harry, *Teaching Adolescents in Secondary Schools.* New York: Appleton-Century Crofts, Inc., 1961. (Chapters 3–5)

Van Til, William, Gordon Vors, and John Lounsbury, *Modern Education for the Junior High School Years.* Indianapolis: Bobbs-Merrill Company, 1961.

Wellington, C. Burleigh, and Jean, *Teaching for Critical Thinking.* New York: McGraw-Hill Book Company, Inc., 1960.

CHAPTER 9

USING
AUDIO-VISUAL AIDS
IN THE
CLASSROOM

As a sequel to Chapter 6, which introduced the reader to three of the more innovational audio-visual methods of instruction, namely: television, teaching machines, and the language laboratory, this chapter's preoccupation will be with the more conventional audio-visual instructional media. Attention will be focused on those which, with few exceptions, are commonplace in the many classrooms at all elementary and secondary grade levels. Yet, despite the casualness with which they are now regarded, at one time they, too, like their more experimental counterparts of today, underwent struggle for acceptance. The new order, whether in education or any other discipline, by its very quality of newness seems to experience opposition from the old before being permitted to relax its defenses.

However, despite education's initial, and often sustained, reluctance to welcome such audio-visual aids as realia, films, and models, just to name three of the many, its hand was finally forced by the plausibility of the case in their behalf. Enlisted in support were too many sound principles of learning to be ignored. Education for years had been in a verbal lock step, with its success almost universally dependent on the power of words, printed and spoken, to bring meaning to students' minds. The underlying assumption was that, if young people could accumulate enough verbal knowledge about the world of names, places, and events remote from as well as close to themselves, the additive effect of such abstract learnings would make for the educated mind. This approach had some, and often even considerable, success, particularly with the gifted, but it fell short of learning's rich potential, which is best realized when a multi-sensory approximation or attainment of realism is effected.

Only in recent years has the academic world, aided by psychologists and semanticists, become convinced that meaning does not exist in the written or oral word in itself. Either is just a symbolic stand-in for its real-life counterpart and, being a symbol, can be interpreted with fidelity only to the extent that an individual can bring insightful experience and accurate understanding to it. These latter are truly realized only when perceptive individuals are in direct contact with real-life situations or things, or when they can approximate these situations and things through contrived experiences made possible by audio-visual means.

Testifying to the inadequacy of words alone is, for example, the city-bred child whose knowledge of farm life comes almost exclusively from the indirect sources of the printed page and parental anecdotes. Such terms as *disking, fertilizing,* and *harvesting,* while a part of his vocabulary, might just as well be in a foreign tongue as far as true understanding is concerned. But give him a summer on a farm, and the words come to life. Then he is able to invest with richness of meaning such rural delights as a wheat field ripe for harvest, the social give-and-take that only a closely knit group can have, and the appealing cacaphony of nature's sounds. The grimmer realities also appear in more faithful perspective: droughts, soil erosion, insect infestations, tedium of work in the fields, and the trauma of early rising.

In the same vein, the tourist is naïvely surprised at the sights that appear along his itinerary, despite prior exposure to them in verbal form. The White House may fall short of his expectation. The mountains may surprise him with their rolling approaches, since he may have expected a series of precipitous cliffs dropping off at right angles. And the celebrity met for the first time may fail to measure up to the symbolic stereotype: the congressman orator who turns out to be a halting conversationalist, the theatrical star who disappoints when not favored by lighting and make-up, or the name ball player who is ill at ease in a drawing room. Words would fail to predict all of these disturbing reactions with fidelity because human experience simply cannot be conveyed to another by such symbolic means.

Fiction's greatest offender in this regard is Dickens's hard-nosed Mr. Gradgrind of *Hard Times,* so enamored of the potency of words that he allowed them to force direct experience into a back seat. To him, the primer's definition of a horse held priority over reality. What he always wanted, he said, was the

. . . "Facts. Facts alone are wanted in life. Plant nothing else, and root out everything else. You can only form the minds of reasoning animals upon Facts: Nothing else will even be of any service to them."

. . .

"Girl number twenty," said Mr. Gradgrind, squarely pointing with his square forefinger, "I don't know that girl. Who is that girl?"
"Sissy Jupe, sir," explained number twenty, blushing, standing up, and curtseying.
. . . "Let me see. What is your father?"
"He belongs to the horse-riding, if you please, sir." . . .
. . . "Give me your definition of a horse."
(Sissy Jupe thrown into the greatest alarm by this demand.)
"Girl number twenty unable to define a horse!" said Mr. Gradgrind . . . "Girl number twenty possessed of no facts, in reference to one of the commonest of animals! Some boy's definition of a horse. Bitzer, yours." . . .
"Quadruped. Graminivorous. Forty teeth, namely twenty-four grinders, four eyeteeth, and twelve incisive. Sheds coat in the spring; in marshy countries sheds hoofs too. Hoofs hard, but requiring to be shod with iron. Age known by marks in mouth." . . .
"Now girl number twenty," said Mr. Gradgrind. "You know what a horse is."

Unhappily, the Mr. Gradgrinds are not exactly extinct in today's classrooms, even though the outward pose may be a more acceptable one. Pedagogues still exist who are satisfied when pupils repeat the proper words even though meaning is vague or nonexistent. The non-acceptance by thoughtful educators, however, of words as other than symbols of reality has led the academic world to seek out learning reinforcements. The first step in this direction is to clarify certain words by the use of other words, through explanations and verbal illustrations. Even more supportive may be such visual media as the map or globe in a history class, the still picture in a literature textbook, the model of the human torso in biology, and the obsidian fragment in general science. These devices and such multi-sensory media as the sound film and television are dedicated to the aim of bringing learning as close as possible to reality.

The progression of teaching method historically has been from the personal oral—as employed, for example, by the ancient Greek peripatetics; to the written—accelerated by the advent of the printing press; to the visual—first through works of art and later through photographic means; and finally through the audio—with the coming of the Gramophone, sound film, and television. Throughout this period of evolution, however, educators of all epochs made pleas for education to encompass reality. Aristotle, the first recognized inductivist, was willing (Plato was less so) to test theory empirically. With the rapid growth of science several millennia later, progress toward the real was dramatically accelerated. More recently, such recognized educational figures as Pestalozzi, Rousseau, and Froebel became so extreme in their defense of the real that they relegated the abstract to a level of near-insignificance.

In the drama of the science movement three centuries ago occurred an event that seemed not too significant at the time but which has taken on increasing import as time has passed: we refer to the publication of Commenius's *Orbis Pictus,* probably the first illustrated textbook. In it were more than a hundred pictures, each a point of departure for some object lesson. The initial modest effect on education of this little book was in sensational contrast to the impact that it subsequently had on the academic world. In reality, it ushered in the visual aids which not long after became commonplace in the classrooms of all lands.

World War II gave special impetus to the development and refinement of audio-visual media, employing them as substitutes for equipment and material in short supply. They were used at training centers early in the war in lieu, for example, of the unavailable Springfield or Garand Rifles, machine gun, tank, pontoon, or half-track. Later, as the effectiveness of these contrived aids in training people "in a hurry" became generally accepted, they were employed to supplement, or at times to replace, instruction at many different levels. The sound film, in particular, became almost as common a commodity in basic training centers as the cadre of teacher-lecturers. In any event, the supply of audio-visual equipment at many training centers early in the war almost equalled the supply of weapons of all kinds. Unbelievable numbers of films, filmstrips, charts, maps, opaque projectors, and other types of related equipment became a routine part of the inventory of most military centers.

During and after the war, industry became so impressed with the results achieved by the armed services in the field of the audio-visual that it adopted many of the better aids. Such well-known business and industrial concerns as Western Electric, International Harvester, the large food chain stores, General Motors, and Inland Steel, to mention just a few, continued to utilize and experiment extensively with audio-visual paraphernalia and the teaching methods associated with them.

Education has, for several reasons, been slower in moving into the field. First of all, caution has demanded that the old not be rejected before the new has been validated. With the sensational postwar expansion of enrollments at the elementary and secondary levels and the resulting increase in educational costs, priorities of expenditure have had to be established and honored. High in initial preferential choice understandably were school buildings, teacher salaries, fixed classroom equipment, and the curriculum essentials. With these necessities assured, schools could direct attention to curriculum supplements such as audio-visual aids.

Schools have responded unevenly to the stimulus of audio-visual materials and equipment. Some have been guilty of excessive enthusiasm and resulting over-utilization; a few have expressed an almost complete disdain for the media. The majority, however, have experimented from moderately to extensively with the many types of aids, evaluating, in the process, their degree of effectiveness. These are the schools which, with supportive knowledge and understanding, are integrating audio-visual education successfully into the total program. And the sequence of their efforts is to be commended: first comes a study of the curriculum to identify purposes; then a conviction that selected multi-sensory media might propel learning toward these goals; next a period of experimentation with the selected media; after this, an evaluation of their efficacy; and only then, implementation.

A DEFINITION

Most audio-visual materials of instruction, such as the film, picture, recording, mock-up, or model, fall so comfortably into category that a general definition would contribute little. However, with a few others, such as the textbook and the visiting speaker, which we might locate on the fringe of this medium, we feel the need of a clarifying definition, and thus we propose the following: *Any instructional materials used to supplement the normal learning process of listening, seeing, reading, and writing are to be regarded as audio-visual aids.* It follows, then that Dickens's novel *Hard Times* is not a visual aid, falling instead into the category of "normal reading"; but a program inserted into a teaching machine that supplements the normal process of reading with pauses, questions, and evaluative procedures is, in contrast, an aid. In like manner, a theorem delineated in a geometry text is not an aid, because it constitutes a normal feature of either the reading or the listening process; but when it is projected on the front wall by means of an overhead projector, the result is a visual aid because of the procedure's departure from routine classroom method. The teacher's oral interpretation of Dylan Thomas's "Fern Hill" can by no stretch of the imagination be regarded as a verbal aid, but when a disk of the same literary piece is played to students, it fits into the category of an audio aid. The emphasis in the definition is on aids as supplements to the normal processes and personages of instruction.

THE VARIOUS AUDIO-VISUAL AIDS

With many well-known and respected authors, like Dale, Dent, Hoban, Sands, Schuller, Wittich, and others, writing long and detailed treatises on the topic to which this text devotes only a chapter, we shall be selective of material and economical of description. Following is a list of audio-visual resources that the author has seen in use in one or more classrooms or existing in the communities that send children to those schools. They range, in descending order of concretion, from reality in Section 1 to distorted reality in Section 7. Section 8 pertains to equipment that is used to provide one of the sensory experiences listed in the previous seven sections.

Audio-visual resources

1. Examples of Reality
   a. In School. Selected illustrations are:
      Animals—(alive or dead) in a biology laboratory
      Automobiles—in an automobile shop
      Clothing—in a home economics class
      Demonstrations—of almost anything in any class
      Food—in a home economics class
      Human models—in an art class
      Mineral specimens—in a physical science class
      Plants—in botany or biology
      Resource persons—in any class
   b. In the Community. Selected examples are:
      Aquariums
      Art museums
      Botanical gardens
      Civic organizations—chambers of commerce, fraternal organizations, and so forth
      Community agencies—settlement houses, hospitals
      Educational agencies—other schools, special and general
      Governmental agencies—courts, city hall
      Industrial concerns and facilities

2. Three-Dimensional Reproductions of Reality. Selected examples are:
   a. Replicas—A life-size reproduction of comparable material, for example, an imitation of a piece of colonial furniture.
   b. Models—A life-size reproduction but with basically different materials —a model of a human torso or human body in a biology class.
   c. Small-Scale Models—Same as 2b, but to scale, for example, a diminutive *Nina* or *Santa María*.
   d. Mock-ups—The over-all object not in scale but a part of it in scale, for example, a smaller-than-life upper torso, but a heart in scale.

3. Pictorial and Audio Reproductions of Reality. Selected examples are:
   a. Film Slides—Sound
   b. Filmstrips—Sound
   c. Movies—Sound
   d. Pageants
   e. Plays
   f. Television Programs or Television Teaching

4. Pictorial Reproductions of Reality. Selected examples are:
   a. Exhibits
   b. Film Slides

    c. Filmstrips
    d. Glass Slides
    e. Pictures
    f. Photographs
    g. Posters
    h. Stereographs (Three-Dimensional Pictures)

5. Pictorial Reproductions in Perspective. Selected examples are:

    a. Charts
    b. Globes
    c. Graphs
    d. Maps

6. Audio Reproductions of Reality. Selected examples are:

    a. Radio Programs
    b. Recordings—Disk, Tape, and Wire
    c. Language Laboratories

7. Distorted Reproductions of Reality. Some examples are:

    a. Caricatures
    b. Cartoons
    c. Puppet Shows

8. Routine School and Classroom Equipment. Selected examples are:

    a. Balopticans
    b. Blackboards
    c. Bulletin Boards
    d. Filmstrip Projectors
    e. Microscopes
    f. Movie Projectors
    g. Opaque Projectors (Projects on screen—pictures or notes)
    h. Overhead Projectors (Projects on screen—pictures or notes)
    i. Screens
    j. Tape Recorders
    k. Tachistoscopes (Mechanical Reading Devices)
    l. Wire Recorders

    The previous listing contains an array of audio-visual media that is extensive—if not somewhat overpowering to the prospective teacher as well as to the teacher in service. However, even more surprising would be the teacher who in a normal lifetime used all of the listed devices. Detailed as the list may appear, it is restricted to the better-known commercial audio-visual devices. Teachers in rural high schools where finances are limited could add to it with little effort, and their contributions would probably be handmade media, about which writers of textbooks have yet to hear. The foregoing list will have served its intended purpose if it is employed principally as a resource aid. The immediate aim is to acquaint the reader with new terms and to orient him to the great variety of audio-visual classroom media available. The broader goal is to provide him with some possible suggestions for future classroom or community implementation.

The almost dramatic psychological difference between the media listed in Sections 1 and 2 is interesting to note. And if this difference between reality and the first step away from it—namely, three-dimensional reproductions—is significant, how much more significant is the tremendous difference between highly abstract verbal symbols and reality.

THE MORE PRACTICAL AIDS
FOR TEACHERS

Of the above-listed aids, opinion unquestionably differs regarding the relative importance of each to the classroom teacher. Therefore, like other teaching methods, their respective relevance and worth need to be assessed within the framework of the curriculum circumstances of the moment. One of the controlling factors is the age and sophistication of the students. The sound film that illustrates a principle or concept already learned verbally might be inestimably valuable for a group of average or below-average ability; but for the gifted, the abstract alone might well suffice and the film serve only to irritate by talking down to the audience. In like manner, a field trip to a local science museum might be a reinforcing medium of real significance for one socio-economic level but a repetitively boring experience for a more favored sociological group.

Another controlling factor is the goals of the learning situation. If a teacher's aim is to introduce, for instance, a grammatical element in graphic fashion so as to lessen the possibility of boredom, the overhead projection of the selected element would serve the designed purpose well. Again, for a class that has just completed a rather "heavy" unit on a designated topic, a teacher might be completely justified in injecting a change of pace, for example: projecting selected caricatures or playing a lightly humorous recording. Although teachers of various orientations will regard educational purpose differently, so long as their choice of audio-visual methods is in harmony with reasonably defensible goals, their actions cannot be severely criticized.

A third and very practical consideration in the choice of supplemental aids is their availability. The film that has to be ordered three weeks in advance of the anticipated date of use is thereby much less serviceable than the filmstrip that can be had for the asking. And the hard-to-get science display that might, but also might not, be available on a given day probably should be passed over for other less spectacular but also meaningful audio-visual materials. Although planning is an educational ingredient that no teacher should be without, when guilty of stealing more than its allotted share of time, it should be directed into channels that are more economical in their demands.

Thus, the most practical aids for teachers are those that best serve the pupils, educational goals, and the criterion of availability. Towering above all others, however, are a select few that are part of the repertoire of the greatest number of classroom teachers. Some, like the blackboard, are downright prosaic; others, like the sound film, possess some glamor. But, regardless of their ability or inability to scintillate, we wish to give selected ones special emphasis in this chapter. For a further acquaintance with the majority that will not be discussed at all herein, we refer the reader to the more specialized texts in the bibliography.

The blackboard

If forced to select a single aid that could be salvaged from a missile attack, the majority of classroom teachers would probably elect the lowly blackboard for survival. Even specialists in audio-visual education, with their greater interest in the more complex and dramatic, might have difficulty undermining the selection, despite the factors that operate against it. Admittedly, the blackboard is often an uninspiring piece of equipment, at times cluttered with trivia or irrelevancies, at other times smudged with chalk dust. Rarely, in fact, does it have esthetic appeal unless utilized deliberately with this outcome in mind.

But though inherently prone to jar on human sensibilities, the blackboard stands at call to give learning needed support and serves a number of specific purposes:

1. First of all, the blackboard injects into the stream of learning the visual component as a replacement for, or a supplement to, its oral counterpart. In either event, it serves as a center of learning, enabling a teacher to direct class attention at a focal point and to rally them around the visual-verbal the way a lecture attempts to do around the oral-verbal. The blackboard can, thus, be used to carry the primary central thread of any appropriate topic, or can be used in support of the oral. In the latter role, it can reinforce learning by the presentation of a graphic illustration, the listing of a key point, the projection of a newly used technical term along with its definition, the emphasis of a title of a pertinent book, or the dramatization of an error in grammar that many students have been making. Its ability to reinforce by providing emphasis is unique in the classroom.

2. Furthermore, like a filmstrip, film slide, or mimeographed handout, the blackboard enables a teacher to prepare materials prior to class time so as to effect their more subtle utilization during the class session itself. Thus, for instance, if the causes for the disintegration of the League of Nations were deemed of sufficient import to be accentuated, the teacher of a class in United States history could list them on the board during his free period, or the afternoon before, cover them with a map, and then expose them to view at the opportune time during the class treatment of the topic.

3. Or, pursuing the topic in 2 above differently, the teacher could

use the blackboard for developmental teaching purposes, leading the students to a progressive identification of the reasons why the League of Nations dissolved, all the while listing them developmentally on the board. This approach would be a natural feature of a good learning situation, involving active student participation and effective teacher leadership.

4. The blackboard further lends itself to individual activity in the routines of classroom learning. The mathematics teacher, for instance, regularly introduces new concepts on the blackboard or has students "go to the board" to copy homework. The industrial arts teacher uses it to diagram projects. Other teachers of drill subjects, for example, grammar or a foreign language, likewise utilize it extensively for individual student performance.

5. Finally, it serves as a place of more or less permanent record on which can be perpetuated designated curriculum elements. One such illustration of this usage is the long-term assignment customarily projected on a predetermined blackboard location until a pertinent unit of work has been completed. So employed, the blackboard stands as a daily reminder to adolescents of future tasks to be performed. A second illustration is the examination questions which frequently find their way to the blackboard, thereby obviating the need of mimeographed or dittoed materials. A third example is the rectangular area of the blackboard set aside by many teachers for the cumulative listing of the new technical words of a course as they sequentially appear in a learning situation. Through this method, the blackboard translates daily the vocabulary that otherwise might block learning's outcomes.

Despite the obvious teaching possibilities inherent in the blackboard, a surprising number of teachers, particularly those new to the profession, either ignore it or sell its good services short. One probable reason is the lack of opportunity during the preparatory college years for students to use, or observe the effective use of, the learning medium. With college professors notoriously oral in their teaching methods, at times almost scorning the non-abstract, an early avoidance of the medium is understandable. A second reason is the glib assumption made by the occasional neophyte that knowledge once verbalized is knowledge thereby learned by the listener or reader. Such naïveté disregards the teacher's own history of learning, which was centered around the many senses, the long-enduring efforts of many teachers to bring about permanent instructional outcomes, and the many other acts of reinforcement.

However, when employing the blackboard as a learning device, the teacher should adhere to certain proven practices. One is to write on the board without standing in front of the written material. The right-handed individual usually stands a pace or two to the left of the spot of projection, thereby enabling class members to follow the unfolding script. When the teacher's non-transparent body intercepts vision, adolescents are encouraged to channel their attention elsewhere. Second, particularly early in a semester, the teacher should refrain from writing on the board for too long a time, lest he lose eye contact with the class for an overly sustained period. If extensive material requires projection, he would do better to write it before school, after school, or in a free period than to risk disorderliness. As will be observed in a later chapter, one of the best preventives of disciplinary infractions is a teacher's visual contact with a class—an opportunity denied the teacher who employs improper blackboard technique. Finally, the teacher candidate should dwell on the obvious: what he writes is intended to be read. The elementary school candidate, especially at the primary level, invariably takes the task of cursory and manuscript writing seriously, knowing that he will be regarded by impressionable beginners as a model. Would that the secondary school aspirant were equally realistic! Within the framework of non-rigid expectation, he should inventory his blackboard writing skills, seeking means of improvement when his performance falls too short of acceptability. Adolescents under his supervision will gain as a result.

Realia

Probably second only to the blackboard in importance to learning, when available, are the so-called *realia,* an educational trade term for the actual or real substance of life. As indicated in the list provided earlier in the chapter, these might be animal life in biology, an automobile in a machine shop, a cooked meal in home economics, a human model in an art class, or a mineral specimen in a physical science class. Realia are the tangible stuff of concrete learning.

The greatest quantitative impact of realia is in the field of science and industrial arts, where real substance conveniently characterizes the curriculum. In a typical biology class, the evolutionary progression involves an early introduction of the real through the microscopic study of a unicellular animal and continues progressively to a culminating study and dissection of a crayfish or frog. A general science class similarly features an analysis of real items and substances—leaves, chemicals, energy-producing processes, earth specimens, and constellations. In the area of the industrial arts, carpentry tools, cabinets, plastic creations, and printed objects are commonplace extensions of reality employed as avenues to more advanced learning.

Although not so prevalent in the academic subject areas, realia are still accessible to the creative teacher. In English, for instance, a best-selling current novel brought in and discussed with a class, a revolving stage observed as part of a community visit by a drama group to a light opera, and a first edition observed by advanced literary enthusiasts through a protective glass—these are ways in which a teacher in an academic area can reach out to encompass reality. The counterpart in a foreign language class might be a native guest speaker robed in provincial costume; in a civics class, the visit to a courtroom or state capital; or, in a geometry class, the surveying of a local plot of ground.

From the foregoing, the generalization emerges that, to the extent that the real in life can be brought to and made a part of the classroom, the more vivid and permanent the learning is likely to be. Slow learners will respond with enthusiasm; and even the gifted, although able to abstract complex meanings from symbols, with rare exception will also respond positively to the supportive value of the concrete.

Three-dimensional reproductions

Lacking the real-life object in most instances, teachers next turn to the three-dimensional substitutes, if available. The *replica,* as one example, is a life-sized reproduction of "the real thing" constructed with comparable material. A chair like the one George Washington sat in, and a Horn Book like the one used in colonial days in lieu of a primer are properly illustrative. A second example is the *model,* a life-sized reproduction but with basically different materials of construction: for instance, a full-sized human torso or human heart made of plastic. A third example is the *small-scale model,* with the dimensional fidelity of the original but constructed to scale. Illustrative are the scale models of an Elizabethan stage in an English class, of an Egyptian pyramid in a world history class, and of an ancient lyre in a music class.

These, along with the mock-up, which features a part of an object in scale, for instance, the human heart, contained in a larger unit not in scale, comprise the three-dimensional reproductions, and all have had considerable impact on elementary and secondary education. As substitutes for reality, they represent education's attempt to propel learning out of the symbolic abstract into a phase of the concrete. Certain subjects, like the natural sciences, have utilized them most extensively, but their relevance has been noteworthy in all curriculum areas. While not insisting that teachers zealously strive for the concrete, neither can we, without blame, do other than recommend that teachers carefully utilize those extensions of reality that are meaningful to the learning context and are readily available.

Films and filmstrips

Further removed from reality than the realia themselves and the three-dimensional representations, but probably as significant educationally, are the contrived media of the film and the filmstrip. About their intrinsic learning value little doubt exists, because of their unique ability to transcend time and space. They can ubiquitously transport the viewer from the Orient to the Occident in a fraction of a second, in complete disdain of the restraints imposed by natural life processes. Nor are they denied access to the known past. The truth is, whatever is or has been known is capable of being reproduced in a sound or filmstrip. Each, possessed with the power to improvise experience and dramatize, thus extends learning's potential.

The filmstrip, as a more practical classroom aid than its heavier academic counterpart, the film, will receive priority of treatment here. Interchangeably referred to as a *slide film, strip film,* and *pictorial,* it actually is a series of picture transparencies on 35mm film projected as a sequence of still pictures. It usually runs from 25 to 40 frames in length, is black and white or colored, may or may not have captions, and may or may not employ recordings as accompaniment.

One of the most obvious advantages over the film is that the filmstrip can be slowed down and even stopped, if necessary, to adapt more comfortably to the learning pattern, in contrast to the sound film, which may ignore the exigencies of the moment and go heedlessly on. The filmstrip is also easily adapted to small-group work and can be conveniently used by pupil groups as a reference source. As an integral element of a unit, the filmstrip is an effective medium at the introductory or concluding stages; in the main body of the unit, unlike the film, it can relate uniquely to the specific learning context of the moment. It also is far less expensive than film, which, because of its greater dimensions, is usually too expensive to buy and thus has to be rented. More frequently written, edited, and revised than the film, the content of the filmstrip also tends to be more up to date and timely.

The practical application of the filmstrip in the various content areas invites attention. For example, a class in eighth- or ninth-grade general science preoccupied with the intriguing concept of space and space travel would undoubtedly respond with enthusiasm to this medium, if properly selected and utilized. The resourceful teacher, aware of its many possibilities, would thus do well, for instance, to have on hand the series, "Space and Space Travel," in which he would have available as material of enrichment the four filmstrips of the John Sternig series entitled: "Leaving the World," "Current Event in Space," "Man in Space," and "Space Travel A.D. 2000."[1]

The teacher described in Chapter 5, who wished to sharpen the edge of student interest with the unit on the short story, could logically have integrated the total learning situation by the showing of one or both of the filmstrips, "Late Nineteenth and Twentieth Century Development" and "The Modern Development of the American Short Story."[2] The unique value of these filmstrips or others of comparable quality, apart from their

[1] John Sternig, *Space and Space Travel.* (Chicago: Society for Visual Education, 1960.)
[2] Joan Smutny, *The Development of the American Short Story.* (Chicago: Society for Visual Education, 1960.)

effect as catalysts, would be their ability to make more graphic, and thus more meaningful, the modern American short story and the associated authors. For instance, the satire of Thurber, the realism of Steinbeck, or the psychological effect of Faulkner and Aiken would be immeasurably heightened by well-selected filmstrip projections.

The sound or silent film also has a legitimate claim of distinctive educative value, although failing the test of comparison with the filmstrip in certain respects. As has been indicated, the film is a rather independent entity in its own right, autonomously constructed around a theme that may have considerable, or, at times, only incidental relevance to the requirements of a given classroom learning situation. Even films designed explicitly for education may be generally without being necessarily directly applicable to all parts of a designated learning context. The sound film is like a textbook. Both are constructed with a generalized set of educational circumstances in mind, and neither can nor should be expected to integrate intimately, at all times, with every detail of a school curriculum.

And yet, even though a teacher must accept a film as a whole in spite of possible irrelevancies, the medium has too many assets to be regarded as other than a highly valuable aid. First of all, it possesses telling dramatic power, and its ability to arouse the emotions is almost unexcelled. A second outstanding feature of the film is its skill in effecting sequence. The filmstrip moves rather heavily from picture to picture, whereas the sound film accomplishes sequential movement with grace and sublety. The over-all pattern is, thus, one of greater unity than is evidenced by the filmstrip. If a teacher ideally could construct sound films to integrate directly with his own personalized learning context, the medium would have almost no parallel.

In the past decade, Harvey White, Professor of Physics at the University of California, took one of the most sensational steps to date in the employment of the sound film as an educational aid. He designed a set of films, approximately 160 in number and of 30 minutes' duration each, to take the place of the customary course in physics that is offered by the larger high schools but which, because of the unavailability of a qualified teacher in the subject area of physics, or the limited size of the class, is not offered by a number of small high schools. He hypothesized that the films, even though projected by a non-specialized teacher, would be a reasonably adequate substitute for the more conventional course in physics. This instance of a film partially replacing a teacher is too recent to be evaluated with anything resembling scientific accuracy, although its employment in the sparsely populated sections of Utah and the South has been considerable. By and large, as attested to by the research reports contained in the January editions of *The Bulletin of the National Association of Secondary School Principals* for 1959, 1960, 1961, and 1962, the White Films have been at least moderately successful. However, we are far from supporting the thesis that any mechanical process of whatever quality can take the place of a teacher.

Like other audio-visual aids, the filmstrip and the film should be treated as welcome parts of the ever-increasing methods constellation. Like other teaching devices, they must be allied closely to the needs of pupils and the particulars of the curriculum environment. Their major purpose is not diversion and amusement, although these goals may be legitimate on occasions. Rather, the aids are intended to supplement the efforts of a knowledgeable teacher, helping him to do more effectively what he would have done in a different way if filmstrips or films had not been available. When allowed to exist and to operate independently, their value is doubtful; but when made servants to an instructional leader who employs them at the right time and place, they bring greater clarity and a breath of freshness to the classroom.

Recordings

An aid that has captured the exclusively audio field almost to the degree that the sound film has captured the combined audio-visual field is the voice or instrumental recording on a disk, tape, or wire. This verbal supplement has come into its own in the past fifteen or twenty years, making the deepest imprint in the fields of speech, music, English, social studies, and the foreign languages. The musical value of the recording has been recognized for more than half a century, bringing into the home such outstanding individual voices as Harry Lauder's, Richard Crooks's, and Mario Lanza's; and instrumental arrangements encompassing both the corrupt vogue of the moment and the best symphonies.

More recently, the recording has become a part of the academic storehouse of teaching methods, realizing its educational while not losing its popular potential. In the area of the foreign languages, we have already commented at some length on the contribution of the disk or tape to the language laboratory—particularly its bringing to the student listener language spoken with native fidelity. In the field of English, the recording is also blessed with the ability to bring the power of the audio to the visual. Thus, students resisting or unable to attune to the alternating beauty and horror of Poe may begin to realize the inherently attendant emotions when listening to Basil Rathbone's interpretations. Students who have difficulty appreciating Shakespeare's drama or Sandburg's poetry may have their interest kindled by listening to renditions by, for instance, Charles Laughton and Sandburg himself.

In the field of the social studies, the faculty of the recording to capture and perpetuate a social or political mood or event of the moment is unmatched except by the event itself. Thus, the hysterical fulminations of a Hitler, the fireside assurances of a Roosevelt, and the bulldog defiance of a Churchill have been made a more realistic part of history through the recording. Even when not reproducing the actual event itself, the tape, wire, or disk can approximate it through faithful imitations. In this regard, the late Senator McCarthy will undoubtedly be repeatedly resurrected whenever Reuben Ship derisively brings him and his methods back to life in "The Investigator." This political satire is a scathing denunciation of the demagogue's ruthless disregard of human rights, the Messiah-like image that a little power can create, and the viciousness of the "big" generalization without the right of rebuttal. Less volatile but equally evocative at a subdued level is Edward R. Murrow's "You Are There," a dramatized panorama of events following World War I and reaching into World War II.

As a means of effecting change in speech habits and of commemorating special school affairs, the tape and wire recorder are the most widely employed. Customary routine in a speech class is for all students to "talk into" a tape or wire and then listen to the playback as a method of correcting deficiencies in pronunciation, enunciation, pitch, and voice quality. In making any recording, however, whether of an individual voice or a larger school event, the teacher should be conscious of the competition from surrounding noises. The classroom play cannot be faithfully recorded when the dramatis personae have to vie with a hallway disorder or lunchroom bedlam for vocal first place. The effective recording, in contrast, is made only when discordant sounds have been controlled.

Pictorial reproductions in perspective

Moving from the audio once more to the visual, we take cognizance of the value of such aids as maps, globes, charts, and graphs, which are generally categorized under the heading of reproductions in perspective. Like the blackboard, they have much to offer but tend to be taken for granted. The map and the globe bring the world into the classroom in perspective, without which the physical dimensions and relativity of distances, locations, population densities, and topography would have little meaning to the adolescent. Yet how commonplace it is for even experienced teachers to ignore their good services!

Learning is immeasurably enriched when the map and globe are used to reinforce it. Literature becomes more meaningful when such famous locations as Chaucer's Canterbury, Shakespeare's Stratford, Thoreau's Concord, Chekhov's Taganrog and Moscow, and Faulkner's Oxford, Mississippi, are made graphic. And the social studies assume greater vividness when given the support of place and time location. The Near East, Africa, and Mohave Desert mean little to the average learner unless identified on a map or globe and fitted into a contextual frame of reference. And with the world changing yearly, the symbols *Germany, Poland, Czechoslovakia,* and *Goa* are only as meaningful as their relative relationship to the rest of the world is understood.

Also of great value are tables, charts, and graphs. For instance, the lecturer who gave forth with the following simple statistics probably would reach a few of the very bright who could grasp the heavy abstractions but would lose most of the less gifted by the sheer weight of the condensation:

More than a decade ago, around 1940, only one out of every six or seven went to college. A decade later the ratio was doubled. And two decades later, about two in every five were in attendance.

These data, presented by the lecture method, might confuse. Presented in written form, they would be less confusing. But if removed from the verbal and translated into the graphic, their true meaning would be revealed for almost all. For example, compare the following bar graph with the preceding verbal passage as a means of communicating the same data. The graph should convey the intended message much more clearly.

Young People in College

			Per cent						
10	20	30	40	50	60	70	80	90	100

1940
1950
1960

While admitting that all symbolism need not be reduced to the concrete—an eventuality that would be dulling, particularly where uncomplicated meanings are projected to a gifted audience—we have noted that teachers are more prone to overuse the verbal than the graphic methods. Thus, without advocating a one-sided reversal in the other direction, we suggest that graphs, charts, maps, and tables be employed whenever learning, as a result, can be extricated from obscurity.

PRINCIPLES UNDERLYING THE USE
OF AUDIO-VISUAL AIDS

With this brief background of the audio-visual media with which every teacher in secondary education should be familiar, we shall next identify and develop a few of the more important principles which should govern their use. No limited set of tenets is capable of covering all aids and all operational eventualities; therefore, only the more basic will be treated.

Aids are supplements to learning

Fundamental to audio-visual instruction is the principle that aids are no more and no less than supplements to the normal processes of learning. They may implement a textbook, but they cannot replace it. They may enrich a unit, but they must fit comfortably into its context. They may alter the course of teaching, but they do not replace the teacher—the White Films possibly excepted. Their function is to give vitality to the classroom by fitting properly into the methods ensemble. Thus, learning is enhanced by classroom leaders who enlist them in the cause of improved learning.

Aids are particularly beneficial to the slow

The closer to realia that a teacher can get, the more meaningful the learning situation will become for the slow learner. More often than not, he reads haltingly and slowly, has a limited vocabulary, perhaps listens as carefully as he can but hears less than others, and generally is inept in a world of abstract symbolism. But when he gets closer to the "things" behind the symbols and to the substance of life itself, meaning begins to stand out in relief for him. Therefore, the teacher of slow learners, whether in a so-called homogeneous or heterogeneous class, can successfully use audio-visual media to underscore and dramatize verbalisms. In this way, symbols, ideas, and objects become interrelated psychologically in such a way that learning emerges with more substantial meaning and significance.

Aids are to inform, only incidentally to amuse

If education is to attain the maturity of purpose for which it is designed, all of its parts must be in reasonable harmony. Therefore, the entertainment provided by audio-visual means can scarcely be other than a by-product of the major goals of learning. Consonant with this point of view, then, audio or visual instruction for the sake only of amusement must be rejected. Although education cannot turn its back on interest, which is a recognized motivator of learning, it cannot allow interest for its own sake to dominate a curriculum. The proper function of interest is to serve the cause of learning by contributing to its major purposes.

An illustration of improper emphasis on interest may be drawn from an incident that occurred several years ago when the author was supervising a student teacher in a high school biology class. He "happened in" at the wrong time, when the regular teacher, not the student teacher, was in charge. The day was a "letdown" Monday after the Thanksgiving holidays, which the classroom teacher had spent in the North Woods on a hunting expedition. He opened the class with the announcement, "While on my trip, I took several rolls of colored film. How many of you would like to see them?" The class, being a normal group of teen-agers more in tune with the pleasure than with the reality principle of learning, spontaneously replied in the affirmative. Obviously, the substitute activity would provide them with an escape from seriousness, and most lunged for it as a drowning man would for a lifeline. Not unlikely, the teacher and student teacher, having had a hard weekend, equally welcomed the escape from responsibility. Regardless of the reasons for the projection, the pictures were shown, half the period was thus more or less wasted, and the learning process was the loser. This episode pointedly illustrates the fact that, when audio-visual aids are allowed to corrupt the legitimate purposes of education, they do not belong in a secondary school's setting. If they only amuse, despite the desirability of "happiness," they are ill-chosen as teaching methods.

Pre-planning is important

Just as dependent on prior planning as the other responsibilities of teaching are the audio-visual media. In many instances, in fact, they may be even more dependent, because a teacher is unable to "ad lib" his way out of a defective device the way he could out of an error of fact or of judgment. Even with the blackboard, an instructional leader needs to plan from class to class, making certain that information of a long-term nature is protected, that otherwise distracting data are erased, and that enough blackboard space is available to get the intended curriculum mission accomplished. The teachers of science and industrial arts should be particularly sensitive to the benefits of prior planning. With much of their respective programs centered in individual laboratory work, the realia and other aids must be in sufficient quantity at all times to go around the class.

But more demanding of attention before the act of teaching than any of the other audio-visual aids are the film and the filmstrip. These make their greatest contribution when the teacher proceduralizes his efforts as indicated in the following rules.

1. Unless available in a school film library, the film or filmstrip needs to be ordered from two to three weeks in advance.

2. Upon receipt, or even if already in the film library, the aid should be previewed. This step is not only a precaution against a mechanical defect in the film or projector, but it is also a means of assuring greater curriculum continuity.

3. The projection equipment must also be arranged for in advance to assure availability at the specific time desired. With such equipment at a premium in many schools, carefully scheduled employment is essential.

4. The class should be oriented to the major theme of the method

supplement and to selected of the more specific features. In this way, students become more motivated to participate in the curriculum situation.

5. Regardless of the number of previous exposures to it, the teacher should remain in the room during the showing, understandably to keep order but, even more important, to symbolize thereby the importance that he attaches to the showing.

6. At the end of the showing, a follow-up should take place: a question-answer period, a discussion, or some other appropriate evaluative method. Contrary to many writers on the subject, however, we reject the examination as a routine follow-up measure. When proper rapport and motivation characterize the class and meaningfulness characterizes the aid, something less formal than the examination should usually suffice.

7. Finally, the audio-visual equipment and materials must be returned to their place of origin.

SOURCES OF INFORMATION ON AUDIO-VISUAL MATERIALS

We terminate this chapter with a few comments on the many sources of information available to teachers who are interested in a wider use of the media than the confines of a local school system normally permit. Because of the increased interest in audio-visual materials of instruction during the past quarter-century, private agencies, educational institutions, and public and semi-public agencies have rallied to support the growing movement. Some of these operate for monetary profit; others, for service. Regardless of motive, the organizations have mushroomed so rapidly that, short of chapter-length treatment, justice could not be meted out to all of them. Rather than a lengthy treatment, therefore, we shall identify and allude briefly to selected primary sources of information—both organizations and individuals—which have made the more significant contributions.

The educational institutions most active in the field are the universities. Indiana University, for instance, employs approximately a hundred highly specialized individuals in its audio-visual aids department. Peabody University in Nashville is best recognized for its pioneering in the area of free and inexpensive learning materials (which is also the title of the annual publication). The University of Illinois is likewise very much in the audio-visual business, as are Ohio State, Yale, Kent State, Florida State, and many other universities and colleges, large and small. Most of these have rented libraries as features of their programs.

In addition to the universities, a major educational source of both information and materials is the National Educational Association. Attention is called specifically to its three-volume publication of 1954, prepared in collaboration with Kent State University, entitled *Planning Schools for*

Use of Audio-Visual Instruction. These volumes treat specifically of "Classrooms," "Auditoriums," and "Centers," respectively. Other educational or quasi-educational agencies concerned in a vital way with audio-visual education are the various state departments of education, state libraries, and the American Library Association.

Another tremendous source of information on, and which is also equipped to provide, the audio-visual media themselves is the Federal Government. The American Council on Education, Defense Department, Department of Commerce, Federal Security Agency, and Library of Congress and many others are actively involved. The various components of the government periodically publish bulletins of films, filmstrips, and other aids which may be procured on request.

Private industry is certainly not overshadowed by public institutions in the curriculum area under consideration. Vast numbers of organizations are in business throughout the country serving the educational needs of industry as well as those of education and individuals. They range in size from such large concerns as Rand McNally & Company and Encyclopaedia Britannica to the very small neighborhood stores. Not to be outdone, such non-audio-visual industries or businesses as General Motors, Sears Roebuck, General Electric, and International Harvester develop and promote films for educational and general public welfare.

A final source of valuable information is the textbooks on audio-visual materials. Some that have made extensive contributions to the field are listed in the bibliography at the end of this chapter. Important among the authors are A. J. Cross, Irene Cypher, Edgar Dale, Ellsworth Dent, Charles Hoban, Lester Sands, Charles Schuller, Louis Shores, Sherwin Swartout, R. Murray Thomas, and Walter Wittich. These and other specialists have in the past few years written lengthy textbooks treating of the many aids themselves; their usage in the school environment, particularly the classroom; sources of information about them; and the contributions of the many other specialists in the field.

As a sampling of the more important selected sources of information, media, and equipment, we invite the reader's attention to the following listing. It is designed to provide some further insight within our dedicated framework of brevity.

Films and Filmstrips

A List of Film Sources. Springfield, Illinois: Illinois State Library.

Educational Film Guide. New York: H. W. Wilson Co., 1936 to date.

Educators Guide to Free Films. Randolph, Wisconsin: Educators Progress Service, 1941 to date.

Free and Inexpensive Learning Materials. Nashville, Tennessee: George Peabody College, most current edition.

Sources of Educational Films. 1201 Sixteenth Street, N.W., Washington, D.C.: National Education Association, most current edition.

U.S. Government Films. Washington 25, D.C.: Superintendent of Documents, Government Printing Office.

Filmstrip Guide. New York: H. W. Wilson Co., 1948 to date.

Educators Guide to Free Slidefilms. Randolph, Wisconsin: Educators Progress Service, 1949 to date.

Society for Visual Education. 1345 Diversey, Chicago, Ill. The largest producer of filmstrips.

Sources of Educational Filmstrips and Slides. 1201 Sixteenth Street N.W., Washington, D.C.: National Education Association, most current edition.

Maps and Globes

Webster's Geographical Dictionary (rev. ed.). Springfield, Massachusetts: G. C. Merriam Co., 1955.

Rand McNally Cosmopolitan World Atlas. Chicago: Rand McNally & Co., 1956.

Goode's World Atlas. Chicago: Rand McNally & Co., 1953.

Prentice-Hall World Atlas (J. E. Williams, ed.). Englewood Cliffs, N.J.: Prentice-Hall, Inc., 1958.

Models and Related Media

Central Scientific Co., Chicago, Ill.

Denoyer-Geppert, Chicago, Ill.

Self Teaching Aids, Los Angeles, California.

Pictures

Standard Catalog for Public Libraries. New York: H. W. Wilson Co., most recent edition.

Recordings

Educators Guide to Free Tapes, Scripts, and Transcriptions. Randolph, Wisconsin: Educators Progress Service, 1955 to date.

Myers, Kurtz, *Record Ratings.* New York: Crown Publishers, Inc., 1954.

A FINAL WORD

Since learning is for some adolescents difficult at best, verbal and arithmetical symbols are often beyond their comprehension range. Consequently, whatever a teacher can do to bridge the gap that exists between symbolism and its reality counterparts will culminate in benefits to these individual learners and to education as a whole. One way to bridge the chasm is with audio-visual aids, carefully selected according to the criterion of relevance. The basic learning media are still seeing, listening, reading, and writing engaged in under the supervision of a guiding teacher; but, when they can be made more productive with the support of audio-visual media, the latter should be welcomed as educational partners. Their primary purpose should always be to supplement, not to replace. Education's ever-existing need is for a blend of teaching methods that will play to the shifting nuances of learning's demands.

SUMMARY

Audio-visual aids have been presented in the present chapter as comprising any instructional materials used to supplement the normal processes of seeing, listening, reading, and writing—media which help to transport the child from a world of symbolism to, or closer to, a world of reality.

The aids themselves were listed in descending order from realia to distorted realism as found in cartoons. Because the number of available aids is so enormous as to baffle even the experienced teacher, we suggested that a teacher judiciously select only the more appropriate ones. Next were discussed the aids regarded as the most practical: the blackboard, realia, three-dimensional reproductions, films and filmstrips, recordings, and pictorial reproductions in perspective.

The principles which underlie the use of audio-visual aids were presented as follows: aids are *supplements* to learning, are of particular help to the slow learner, should inform primarily and amuse only incidentally, and should be carefully proceduralized.

Finally, sources for the securing of the media and information about them were discussed, with the reader's attention being called to their wide diversity.

REFERENCES

Brown, James W., Richard B. Lewis, and Fred F. Harderoad, *A-V Instruction Materials and Methods.* New York: McGraw-Hill Book Co., Inc., 1959.

Cross, A. J., Fay and Irene Cypher, *Audio-Visual Education.* New York: Thomas Y. Crowell Company, 1961.

Dale, Edgar, *Audio-Visual Methods in Teaching.* New York: Holt, Rinehart and Winston, 1954.

De Kieffer, Robert, and Lee W. Cochran, *Manual of Audio-Visual Techniques.* Englewood Cliffs, N.J.: Prentice-Hall, Inc., 1955.

Department of Audio-Visual Instruction, Charles Francis Schiller (ed.), *The School Administrator and His Audio-Visual Program,* 19th Yearbook, N.E.A., Washington, D.C.: N.E.A., 1954.

Department of Audio-Visual Instruction, the N.E.A., and Association for Education by Radio-Television, *National Tape Recording Catalog* (2nd ed.), Kent, Ohio: Kent State University, 1957.

Galanter, E. H. (ed.), *Automatic Teaching: The State of the Art.* New York: John Wiley and Sons, 1959.

Kinder, James S., *Audio-Visual Materials and Techniques.* New York: American Book Co., 1959.

McKown, Harry C., and Alvin Roberts, *Audio-Visual Aids to Instruction.* New York: McGraw-Hill Book Co., Inc., 1949.

National Education Association, Department of Audio-Visual Instruction, *Planning Schools for Use of Audio Visual Instruction, No. 3, A-V Instructional Materials Centers.* Washington, D.C.: N.E.A., 3 volumes, 1954.

National Society for the Study of Education, *Audio-Visual Materials of Instruction.* Chicago: University of Chicago Press, 1949.

Sands, Lester B., *Audio-Visual Procedures in Teaching.* New York: The Ronald Press Co., 1956.

Shores, Louis, *Instructional Materials. An Introduction for Teachers.* New York: The Ronald Press Co., 1956.

Thomas, R. Murray, and Sherwin G. Swartout, *Integrated Teaching Materials.* New York: Longmans, Green and Co., 1960.

Weaver, Gilbert G., and Elroy W. Bollinger, *Visual Aids, Their Construction and Use.* New York: D. Van Nostrand Co., Inc., 1951.

Wittich, Walter Arno, and Charles Francis Schuller, *Audio-Visual Materials, Their Nature and Use.* New York: Harper & Row, 1957.

ADOLESCENT
SIMILARITIES
AND
DIFFERENCES

Probably more provocative than any other problem or issue faced up to this point in the treatment of teaching method is the challenge posed to education by the similarities and differences of students. Each young person shares much in common with his peers: social interests, dress, mores, and gradual withdrawal from adults—to name just a few. This act of sharing, far from a passive process, seems to be distinguished by a demanding compulsiveness which drives youth together. The adult, as he moves toward maturing goals, gravitates toward others as an accepted part of the life cycle. The adolescent, in contrast, literally grasps for the companionship of associates of his age as if propelled to do so by an almost irresistible outside force. The "pack," in a sense, serves as a protective insulation pending the time when he will be better able to attack the problems of life more independently.

Despite the seductive lure of the herd, however, the adolescent is motivated by a parallel drive toward individualism. Along with the almost protoplasmic identification with the masses on one hand is the accompanying struggle not to lose his identity on the other. He needs others, but at the same time he builds a protective cover around his uniqueness. Adolescence is that interim period in life when childhood is behind, adulthood is ahead, and ambivalence is the intervening legacy.

This transitional growth period is ushered in with the onset of puberty, typifying the physical readiness of the young human organism to fulfill the sex function. A delay of fulfillment in Occidental cultures is almost universally demanded by psychological or social factors, but the pubescent organism is none the less ready. With the advent of puberty come glandular changes and their associated physical correlates, nature's way of preparing the emergent individual to play life's biological and social role. The homosexual interests of latency, without materially diminishing, now begin to receive competition from heterosexual attractions.

Research is at variance on the exact ages when puberty appears in the sexes. In females, Shuttleworth in a series of studies, beginning in 1937, reported its arrival at the mean age of 12.5 years,[1] this in opposition to the majority of researchers, who report its occurrence at a later time— more often than not, six months to a year later.[2] The first menstrual period is used as the primary criterion by most investigators. Puberty in males, also identified at different ages by the various researchers, usually occurs between the fourteenth and fifteenth birthdays. In general, then, girls reach biological adulthood about a year earlier than boys. However, within either sex the range is great, extending not abnormally from the tenth to the sixteenth year for girls, and from the eleventh to the eighteenth for boys.

With the mean ages of puberty being approximately thirteen and fourteen years, respectively, for the two sexes, the teacher at the junior high grade levels is consistently confronted with extensive physiological variability. Class size and larger school groups are almost always characterized by the factor of natural selection, with puberty operating divisively. This educational segment is humorously described as the only organizational level where children and adults attend school together. In any prepubertal group will be the brash male youngster, slight of build, usually indifferent to dress, with a voice that can't make up its sexual mind. The female counterpart conceivably will be the tomboy type whose modesty is more externally imposed than inwardly felt, and who often can outdo her male companions in extrovert pastimes. When these relatively undeveloped children are placed in close association with their more mature companions who have already begun adolescence, heterogeneity governs. The more mature will have dynamic interests in their sex opposites, will reveal alternating signs of immaturity and maturity, and definitely will have not as much in common with their less developed as with their more developed student friends.

---

[1] F. F. Shuttleworth, "Sexual Maturation and the Physical Growth of Girls Aged Six to Nineteen," *Monograph Soc. Res. Child Development,* Vol. 2, No. 5.

[2] Elizabeth B. Hurlock, *Adolescent Development* (New York: McGraw-Hill Book Co., Inc., 1949), pp. 32–41.

The intent of the present chapter is to deal first with selected characteristics that high school students have in common, then with those characteristics that are at variance. The next chapter, as a sequel, will identify and describe ways and means by which teachers and well-designed curricula can join efforts in ministering to the differences among young people. The treatment of similarities will be deliberately brief in view of the topic's closer allegiance to the substance of educational psychology than of teaching method.

ADOLESCENT SIMILARITIES

The growth stages prior to adolescence, identified broadly by the nontechnical as "infancy" and "childhood" and by the more psychoanalytically oriented as the "oral," "anal," "phallic," "latent," and "pre-pubertal," are all universally characterized by the individual's basic concern for himself. For example, three- and four-year-olds really don't play together; they play alongside of each other. The older child, while not quite this ego-centered, awaits adolescence to awaken within him the deeper social interests that propel him toward altruism. If a major problem of the junior high school teacher is how to deal with age and personality diversification, an inversely corresponding one of the upper secondary school teacher is how to penetrate the cordon of similarity. Four of the more noteworthy features of any body of adolescents is their search for conformity, their discovery of a new world of interests and knowledge, their heterosexual interests, and their rebellion against adults and adult restraints.

The search for conformity

One of the strongest drives of the adolescent is to be like others his age. Behavioral traits and patterns that at a different growth level might be completely rejected are not uncustomarily embraced by an adolescent if others, too, have adopted them. The desire for conformity even at times crowns the bizarre with respectability, particularly in dress. Cases in point during the past several years have been the buckskin shoe, the commonly labelled "buck," which grew in symbolic value as it became increasingly impervious to water or shoe polish. The contemporary replacement is the "sneaker," which too will run its course before long. The wide-bottomed trouser has lost out to the continental slack, and the "Sloppy Jo" look to more conventional grooming. Dress styles and patterns may vary from year to year and from place to place; but, at any given time and place, adults can rest assured that a specific dress vogue will be shared by almost all adolescents. And, except for those parents who keep the reins taut, the modifier "almost" could be removed from the previous generalization.

In more ways than dress do adolescents strive for common status. As a clannish group, they set themselves also in judgment over the other aspects of social behavior of their members, usually ostracizing, or according second-class citizenship, to code violators. Although social standards are a function of any given group, common to all adolescent groups are the forbidding of fellow teenagers to report violations of adult regulations by members of the clan; of the male, to show emotion in public; of either sex, to associate too frequently with younger children or to enjoy other than certain types of music. These are only a few of the many examples that could be cited.

Although for the most part the tenets are harmless, they at times become harmful when allowed to run counter to the more basic of life's values. Of concern to the adult world, for instance, is the adolescent observer of a major infraction of school or public law who is told by the code to say nothing but by his super-ego values to report the offense. Another example of this is the gifted student, expected by his peers to demonstrate, at best, mediocrity in school work but by his own deeper values and those of family to measure up to his high potential. In these situations, it is basic that teachers and parents never abdicate their obligations as mature adults to establish and enforce defensible standards. But neither can they pretend that the conflicting mores of youth are mere figments. In this struggle of the age groups, adult authority figures—including teachers, parents, and public officials—have to draw the line of principle, demanding allegiance, if unable to get it in any other way, but, when principle is not at stake, to allow, and even encourage, adolescents to affiliate and conform to their heart's content.

Of as much concern to the teacher as the deliberate flaunting of adult regulations should be youths' almost callous treatment of the misfits by the majority group. By "misfits" we refer not only to the extremes of physical disabilities, such as the deformed or unattractive, but to the otherwise eligible adolescent who is denied status because of unconventional dress or non-conformist social mannerisms. These latter evidences of non-conformity are more often than not the result of poverty or parental restrictions; thus, the youth who is thereby created an isolate needs the sustaining support of an understanding teacher during this period of rejection by individuals his own age. Because any person's self-image is dependent in great part on the esteem conceded to him by his associates, it is tragic when an adolescent ostracized by his age associates is not afforded some compensating acceptance or affection by the few adults around him, one of whom is the teacher. In an hour of such stress, whether he is physically attractive or repulsive, outwardly indifferent or manifestly hurt, he looks to the teacher for the personality support he needs so much. It is at such times that the teenager must be to the teacher a human being first and a student second.

A new world unfolds

One of the many inconsistencies of adolescence is that the same young person who in certain moments appears willing to sacrifice much of his identity to the larger group, at other times presses for self-discovery in an expanding world of knowledge and understandings. Still preoccupied with himself, although now as an explorer of the unknown more than one fearful for his very existence, he searches for answers to unsolved personal problems and to problems of the greater society. This is the period when the teenager oversimplifies the baffling problems of government, morality, and human relations, blaming adults, in the process, for not having done a better job with life.

In the 1880's, G. Stanley Hall, the pioneer thinker on the problem of adolescence, described it as a growth era of storm and stress, placing more emphasis on the strains that emanate from physical change than on the frustrations that come to an individual forced to live in a world that he knows little about. If adolescence is a stressful period, and this we basically doubt, unless well-meaning but ill-guided adults make it so, the reason is the unconscious recognition by the adolescent of his own limitations. He so easily runs into blind walls wherever he turns that discouragement may be his occasional lot. Fundamentally, however, we regard this period of life as the threshold of adulthood with its attendant demands and challenges mostly pleasant and only occasionally overpowering.

With puberty comes a greater consciousness of a world of people with whom the adolescent has to live and for whom he has a responsibility. This is both a gratifying and a disturbing insight: the former, because of the new vistas thereby opened; the latter, because of his recognized inadequate preparation to meet the new challenges. As commented on at length in Chapter 1, maturity is the process of moving progressively from self and the strictures of a local culture toward an ever-expanding horizon of values, to be discovered, in great part, in a world of people. Adolescence, then, is a foundational growth stage in the greater social progression of the organism toward a developmental goal. It is at this time that an individual identifies with others, not merely to extricate security from them, but just as basically to give of himself consciously in recognition of an obligation to the human race.

Accompanying and reinforcing the new social demands and insights is the school's curriculum, which should not be of anathema proportions to the normal young person. In this connection, we concur with a basic tenet of psychoanalysis, namely, that the psychic energy in man will flow into positive channels if not influenced adversely by environmental conditioners.[3] It is therefore our contention that, with youth eager to learn

---

[3] Ralph R. Greenson, "The Classic Psychoanalytic Approach," *American Handbook of Psychiatry, Part II* (ed. Silvano Ariete). (New York: Basic Books, Inc., 1959), p. 1402.

more about the universe, a curriculum is faulty, the individual is disturbed, or a culture is at odds when adolescents resist knowledge. Because the greater society is a cumbersome instrument for change, the schools should redouble their efforts to effect enlightened curriculum revision to the end of better serving the natural processes of maturation.

While the curriculum is undergoing a never-ending revision, school personnel must be aware that its relationship to the student is like therapy to the mentally or physically ill. Neither will be curative or, on occasions, even mildly beneficial, unless the recipient is predispositioned to respond. In the case of the curriculum, faulty mental health can make for a compulsive resistance to the combined efforts of both teachers and course content. A male adolescent sullenly resentful of all adult authority; a female teenager unoriented to and therefore ashamed and frightened by the menstrual flow; or a young person of either sex continually informed by parents that school is a place to be departed from at the earliest legal time—is confronted with conditions unconducive to the success of otherwise constructive learning content. The responsibility of the school for the mental health of students is twofold: first, to accept it as an end in itself, just as mathematics, English, and social studies are ends; second, to regard emotional adjustment as a means of heightening the student's response to the uncontested curriculum outcomes of greater knowledge, keener understandings, wholesomely changed attitudes, and greater facility in the skills. The head-in-the-sand approach to the mental health problem only intensifies it by making students more resistant to the curriculum and associated authority figures. Consequently, since psychic energy is with little question inherently positive, why not enlist, instead of distorting, its good services?

Heterosexual interests develop

One reason for the adolescent's desire to conform, and also a vital part of his new world of discovery, is the now awakened sexual component. Understanding and identifying with the sex role is a developmental task of no mean proportions, surrounded as it is by inane prudery, crass ignorance, and spurious knowledge. Like George Gardner in his sympathetic treatment of the topic, "Psychiatric Problems of Adolescence," we, too, wonder how the typical young person ever "becomes a reasonably conflict-free adult."[4]

The primary problem which besets high-school-age youth is how to effect a rapprochement between the, at times, almost relentless biological drives and the super-ego values of a self and a culture pertaining to sex. The dating process is nature's and society's answer, with the individual's

[4] George E. Gardner, "Psychiatric Problems of Adolescents," *American Handbook of Psychiatry, op. cit.*, p. 871.

value system determining the extent to which one will emerge more victorious. Although Western civilization is currently vacillating between Victorian suppression or denial and psychiatry's bid for greater sexual freedom, the schools must take a stand, which, in our opinion, should be a compromise between the extremes. In such courses as biology and health, the problem of sex, like any other curriculum element, should be aired frankly and unashamedly. In other courses, such as English, where a possible incestual relationship is encountered in *Hamlet,* or a suspected homosexual relationship in the study of the author himself, frankness once more demands priority. Since sex is a wholesome function, why shouldn't it be faced in a mature way at the knowledge-learning level?

When away from theory and into the practical, the school is obligated to perpetuate society's image of abstinence. Thus, school social affairs need to be chaperoned so that another of the many invitations to license that confront all adolescents is not provided by the school itself. Within the framework of minimum restriction, however, adolescents should be encouraged to associate with members of the opposite sex as part of the natural process of growing up. School activities, with this goal in mind, thus should be deliberately planned, not as rewards for good behavior, but as opportunities for the two sexes to get better acquainted in socially accepted ways. Admitting that parents have the legal right to establish and enforce standards that are often extremely liberal or reactionary, the school needs to conform to the standard of the "reasonable man," discussed in Chapter 3. On the matter of sex, this mythical character would relegate Mrs. Grundy to the oblivion of the past but would not be receptive to an ultra-liberal replacement.

The adolescent rebellion

A fourth and final common meeting ground of youth is in the area of rebellion against parents, and here ambivalence once more operates. In a sense, the word *rebellion* is improperly descriptive in that it implies an autonomy of status, whereas the process more logically should be treated as a symptom of the basic striving for independence. A number of factors combine to create the family conflict: the heretofore omniscient and omnipotent parents have toppled from their thrones, specialized insights of the offspring are pitted against parental standards, the expanding adolescent has that "little learning that is a dangerous thing," and the demands of selfhood cry out for independence, almost regardless of price. To complicate matters further is the sometimes suppressed, sometimes vented, resentment of the young over their dependency on parents for food, clothing, spending money, and psychological succor. Nor is this negativism the peculiar property of parent figures alone; all parent surrogates sooner or later feel its lash—and particularly the teacher.

Parent figures of whatever type must tread understandingly on what John Horrocks describes as this "fertile ground for difficulties in interpersonal relations."[5] As the more mature participants in the inexorable unfolding of youth's rebellion, while regarding it with objectivity and as a natural developmental process, they should curb any excesses of emotion, adhere to important principle, and depersonalize their roles as much as possible. Although not condoning brash impertinence, neither should they be overly offended at the occasional breach.

The most serious danger of an adolescent's rebellion is his possible allegiance to an ill-chosen authority figure selected to replace the parent. What Gardner calls the "devaluation of parents" is developmentally normal, but a compensating alignment with an unsavory substitute or adoption of a set of false values to replace the family's is cause for common concern. And a major problem is that of distinguishing between the sham and the real. Most teenagers on their road to independence many times only pretend to eschew time-honored beliefs and to espouse the cause of fringe values. Rare indeed is the adolescent or young adult who hasn't had his radical moments in such fields as politics, morality, or esthetics. This flexing of the muscles is more amusing than serious. But when true identification with negativism takes place, strong action is demanded. In this event, the parent or teacher must forthrightly insist on adherence to acceptable standards, and must punish severely, if necessary, to achieve it. (Corporal punishment is not included here.) Weakness and vacillation have no place in crises such as these.

ADOLESCENT DIFFERENCES

Against this background of conformity to herd values, a common thirst for knowledge, the development of heterosexual interests, and the drive for independence, we next project a picture of adolescent differences. The division into two classes created by puberty has already been alluded to, but even when this factor has been neutralized by adolescence, extensive differences remain. The external veneer of likeness, in actuality, is more a product of deliberate conformity than real, as will be noted as the present topic is developed.

Sex variations

The first trait difference to receive attention is the sexual, deliberately limited, however, to its influence on the educational interests and successes of secondary school students. Specifically, to what extent can the future teacher expect a differential response to the curriculum caused

[5] John E. Horrocks, "The Adolescent," *Manual of Child Psychology* (ed., Leonard Carmichael) (New York: John Wiley and Sons, 1954), p. 723.

primarily by the genetic sex factor? First of all, what are the sex differences attributable to general maturation?

As was commented on earlier in the chapter, the girl student reaches puberty approximately one year ahead of the boy and is therefore more advanced physically, socially, and psychologically than her male opposite. In the earlier secondary school years particularly, this added maturity makes for a greater seriousness of purpose and perspective. Since femininity is inherently endowed with more recessiveness to begin with, and since girls have at least a year's maturational start on the boys, the former tend to fit more comfortably into the sedentary school situation. In support of this phenomenon, Bernreuter, for instance, in 1933 discovered males to score significantly higher than females on the trait of dominance.[6] H. M. Bell six years later reported essentially the same results, and based on an even more diverse population.

In the province of the academic subjects, sexual differences at times are nil; at other times, statistically significant. Research supports the following general findings, which we have gleaned primarily from Lewis Terman's and Leona Tyler's chapter in the 1954 *Manual of Child Psychology* entitled "Psychological Sex Differences." Girls at the junior and senior high levels tend to excel in the area of the language arts, particularly in the fields of reading, memorization of words, and sensitivity to speech sounds. In achievement, they perform generally at a higher level in the fields of English, foreign languages, penmanship, and clerical activities. Their interests are more recessive, being most pronounced in drawing, modeling, music, drama, folk dancing, reading, and grammar.

In contrast, boys in the area of science evidence the greatest dominance revealed by either sex over the other. When grades, science awards and honors, or achievement test scores are employed as a criterion, the male student is superior to his counterpart of the other sex. In the specialized categories of the spatial as well as the mathematical and mechanical, he also excels. His interests are of the more aggressively outgoing type and less in such fields as reading and the esthetic.

In confirmation of the phenomenon of masculine superiority in the science-mathematics area, and of a somewhat lesser reverse superiority of the feminine in the language arts, we direct the reader's attention to the *Annual Report* of the National Merit Scholarship Corporation for 1960. Of the 1,008 scholarship awards, offered in great part on CEEB test results, 761 were conferred on boys and 247 on girls. This difference can be explained by the greater number of applications received from the males. Of great significance, however, is that on the mathematics section of the test: 81.6 per cent of the boys but only 61.9 per cent of the girls scored between 700 and 800. On the verbal section, 60 per cent of the girls and 55.1 per cent of the boys scored between 700 and 800. And these differ-

---

[6] R. G. Bernreuter, "The Theory and Construction of the Personality Inventory," *J. Soc. Psychol.*, 1933, vol. 4, pp. 387–405.

ences are all the more meaningful when considered in the light of results of most research reports, which show that males and females in general do equally well on academic aptitude tests. Their I.Q.'s may be comparable, but their specialized abilities are not.

Age

Like the sex factor, age operates to widen the gap among students in any secondary school. As a single entity, it is sufficiently important to motivate teacher candidates, prior to accepting their first contracts, to decide between the junior and the senior high school grade levels. The interpersonal relationships, maturity patterns, and curriculum sophistication differ, often considerably, with the ages of the students. At the lowest seventh grade rung are pupils ranging from a few precocious eleven-year-olds to a few retarded fourteen-year-olds, with a mean age of twelve. This age spread in any single grade, because of retardation, continues into the higher grades, although the dropouts at the age of sixteen in most states decreases the chronological heterogeneity.

Generally speaking, the younger pre-pubescents are more dependent on adults, have shorter attention spans, need more curriculum variety, usually demand more learning concretion, and are more pliable. Eighth-grade enrollments include mostly adolescent girls and pre-adolescent boys, with adolescence prevailing in the ninth grade and above. Early adolescents tend to "test" adults as part of their newly developed aspirations for freedom. They are also characterized by physical gracelessness, self-consciousness, behavior to impress their student associates, moodiness, seemingly endless energy, and a need to expend energy. In the last two years of high school are late adolescents or young adults, aged sixteen to eighteen mostly, who are more poised, relaxed, organized, and systematic. However, at each level are the emotionally retarded and accelerated who extend the range of differences.

Contrary to seemingly popular opinion, no one grade level is necessarily easier or harder to teach than any other. In the last analysis, discipline is more a function of a specific group and the personality dynamics of a teacher than of the age of pupils. Nor is greater or lesser teacher ability and background demanded in the higher grades than in the lower ones. More basic than either of these factors is a genuine liking by a teacher for a designated age group and an understanding of their developmental needs, coupled with an adjustment of the curriculum to meet them. The expectation of breathless silence in a seventh-grade class is just as unrealistic as that of genuine sophistication in the twelfth grade.

Regardless of the actual differences between and among students in the six secondary grades, teacher candidates should avoid the loose generalizations that seem to have crystallized, namely: that teaching twelfth grade is more prestigious than teaching seventh; that the teacher of older children does not have to restructure appreciably a college-level curriculum or his working vocabulary; and that younger children "can never be made to sit still and pay attention." Brightness and dullness, sophistication and artlessness, vitality and apathy are more the result of factors other than age. The latter is only one conditioner; yet it is one that might predispose a teacher on purely preferential grounds to select an older or a younger group.

Intelligence

Even more than sex and age differences, the factor of intelligence, practically speaking, looms large on the educational horizon as the one trait that needs most to be contended with when student variability is being considered. However, candor forces the admission that the academic world is more enamored of the factor itself than cognizant of exactly what it is. Since Cattell in the last part of the nineteenth century began his pioneer work on intelligence, many researchers have treated it operationally as a single entity; the Thurstones and others, as a multiple entity; and Spearman, as a base entity, but not exclusive of certain independent variables. Goodenough substantiates these and other findings in her excellent chapter in the *Manual of Child Psychology*.[7]

Attitudes regarding the validity of academic aptitude tests have experienced the same metamorphoses as those about the trait itself. During the 1920's and 1930's, investigators as a group seemed to feel that they were on the right track, with only refinement needed to make intelligence testing a nearly exact process. For the greater part of the subsequent two decades, however, more skepticism permeated the atmosphere. Most recently, investigators like J. W. Getzels, of the University of Chicago, have cast doubts on the ability of the various testing instruments to evaluate such fundamental elements as creativity and depth understandings.[8] Yet even these researchers concede that knowledge of facts and the less penetrating concepts and processes can be evaluated with relative accuracy.

Despite the shadows of doubt that are being cast upon intelligence testing, academic aptitude scores continue to shine brightly in schools as important indicators of ability and ability differences. Supporting this optimism is education's brief history of practical experience with them, which has been at least moderately satisfying. Our personal conviction is that academic aptitude data are a reasonably accurate and economical means of determining approximately who will do well or poorly in school work, but that their ability to predict with precision must await future

[7] Florence E. Goodenough, "The Measurement of Mental Growth in Childhood," *Manual of Child Psychology, op. cit.,* pp. 459–491.
[8] Jacob W. Getzels, *Creativity and Intelligence* (New York: John Wiley and Sons, 1962).

developments. Thus, teachers should look to intelligence test scores for help without relying on them for the final word.

Whatever the accuracy of the instruments may be, the I.Q. results invariably reflect an extensive range of from 70 to 90 points in any designated school. In Table 1 is presented a distribution of intelligence quotients secured from an Illinois town of approximately 25,000 population and 100 miles, or thereabouts, from Chicago. The data are descriptive of a 1955 school population, grades nine through twelve.

TABLE 1

I.Q. Intervals	Number of pupils	Per cent of pupils
160–164.9	2	.4
155–159.9	3	.6
150–154.9	–	–
145–149.9	8	1.6
140–144.9	9	1.8
135–139.9	8	1.6
130–134.9	–	–
125–129.9	10	1.9
120–124.9	51	10.0
115–119.9	45	8.8
110–114.9	61	12.0
105–109.9	70	13.7
100–104.9	80	15.7
95– 99.9	40	7.8
90– 94.9	42	8.2
85– 89.9	40	7.8
80– 84.9	25	4.9
75– 79.9	12	2.4
70– 74.9	4	.8
	N = 510	100.00

In the distribution, the mean I.Q. is 106.2 and the median, 105.8. Of greater significance than central tendencies, however, is the approximately 90-point range of intelligence quotients. Sixteen of the pupils belong in the slow-learning category; five are in the genius class, if the breaking point is 150, or 22 if it is 140. Here is a dramatic picture of the variability that exists in typical high schools in the country. The reader should expect this outcome and get ready to cope with it. The interesting feature of the distribution is its near-representativeness. The mean may be a point or two below the national average for high school students, but it is a close approximation. The data, as may be noted, tail off more at the upper than at the lower ends, a phenomenon that reflects the siphoning influence of special schools for the educable mentally handicapped, ungraded classrooms, and the high rate of dropouts in the ranks of the slow learners.

The second distribution—a more interesting but also a more untypical one—is of intelligence quotients at a suburban township high school of 916 seniors in 1961. Although the range is, surprisingly, a shade less than that of the former sample—by three I.Q. points—the mean average is 113.28 and the median, 113.18, well above the national norms for secondary school students.

TABLE 2

I.Q. Intervals	Number of Pupils	Per cent of pupils
152–156	1	.11
147–151	1	.11
142–146	7	.76
137–141	13	1.42
132–136	36	3.93
127–131	54	5.90
122–126	88	9.61
117–121	139	15.17
112–116	179	19.54
107–111	168	18.34
102–106	110	12.00
97–101	54	5.90
92– 96	34	3.71
87– 91	17	1.96
82– 86	9	.98
77– 81	2	.22
72– 76	2	.22
67– 71	2	.22
	N = 916	100.10

Such diversities in intelligence revealed by both samples should compel teachers and schools to individualize content and teaching method in some way. The consistent employment of large-group teaching, the single assignment, a similar marking system for all, and the one and only textbook run counter to the data that these two samples provide. What to do about the wide range of I.Q. differences in any school population will be a topic of discussion in the next chapter.

Reading

Analogous to intelligence in over-all educational significance is the factor of reading ability, a topic that has pyramided in emphasis during the past half-century. The reason for its ascendancy has been the growing recognition by instructional leaders and teacher educators of the critical role that reading plays in the development of children and youth. Those who, by a happy combination of circumstances, succeed in mastering the art of reading thereby gain access to a world of knowledge, beauty, and insight denied, at least in part, to their less fortunate fellows. The latter may rationalize their inadequacies, but the façade is unconvincing to the informed.

According to Hook, when easy reading material is the criterion, the majority of secondary school students fall into the 250 to 500 words-per-minute category.[9] Such a range could be tolerated comfortably, even though the speed of the fastest would be twice that of the slowest, but the

[9] J. N. Hook, *The Teaching of High School English* (New York: The Ronald Press Co., 1959), p. 75.

typical high school, which accommodates the extremes as well as the more nearly average, has a range of from fewer than 100 words per minute by at least one student to over 600 words for another. To state the problem differently, the National Council of the Teachers of English, in a 1956 publication, states that classes in advance of sixth grade "Commonly present ranges of at least eight school years in ability to read."[10] These differences, like those of the I.Q., are too staggering to bear the added weight of curriculum conformity.

Without borrowing unduly from the next chapter, we wish to postulate a number of tenets about reading that most high schools fundamentally accept:

1. Reading is not a separate component, but rather a function of the contextual content of the moment. Thus, the reading of a novel and the reading of a chapter in a science text are two psychologically distinctive processes.

2. The implication of point one is that every teacher should be conscious of the reading problem and should help students to respond to the unique subject matter of a particular course. Every teacher, then, is a teacher of reading.

3. Reading, more than a mechanical pastime, is a process in perceptualizing and understanding.

4. Reading increases in meaning as a student gains more knowledge, becomes familiar with more numerous and progressively sophisticated concepts, and has richer experiences in life.

5. Reading is correlated significantly with physical, mental, and emotional readiness factors.

6. A greater familiarity with vocabulary leads to improvement in reading.

7. Reading is a function that varies with student goals and purposes.

8. Each student should know that his reading skills can be improved and should be informed of progress as it takes place.

9. Materials of instruction must be at the readiness level of students, or regression in skill and interest will take place.

Once more we have built a case for some degree of individualization in teaching. If I.Q.'s cannot be tolerated passively, neither can reading abilities. Both must be regarded as radar signals to the knowledgeable teacher dictating that a curriculum not be permitted to ignore their vital messages. By definition, then, a curriculum must make contact with a student body—a task that it has trouble doing when it is at a level different from that of the personnel partner.

---

[10] National Council of the Teachers of English, *The English Language Arts in the Secondary School* (New York: Appleton-Century-Crofts, Inc., 1956), p. 162.

The basic needs

Impinging on sex, age, intelligence, and reading differences, yet distinctive from each of them, are the fundamental needs of youth. The degree to which these are fulfilled by life will decide, in large measure, the extent of a student's happiness as well as his totality of growth. Progressing from the level of survival to one of psychological fulfillment, the needs are basically as follows:

1. Sustenance, rest, and shelter, without which the psychological dimensions are muted.

2. Orderliness and system, as an antidote to debilitating fears and apprehension.

3. Respect for selfhood, as basic to any profound respect for others.

4. Acceptance by others, a basic requisite to selfhood, including such affective emotional components as love, friendship, comradeship, and group loyalties.

5. Cognitive understandings and expanding experiences with life, as a means of projecting life outward toward maturity.

6. Finally, an over-all feeling of having measured up to self and life expectancies.

When viewed from the perspective of these fundamental needs, the high school becomes inextricably intermeshed with such outcomes as the physical well-being of students; orderly system to promote progress and seal off fears; self-acceptance; peer acceptance; cognitive learnings, geared to individual levels of response; and the mental-health goal of measuring up to a given potential. These outcomes can be viewed in two ways: as more or less final stages in the educational process which crown cognitive accomplishment—a view not distantly remote from Hutchins' and Adler's, or from that of other philosophical idealists; or as integral goals of day-to-day educational activity. If the latter, the classroom cannot afford to get bogged down exclusively in intellectual learnings apart from a direct concern for the humanistic development of the total individual and the group. If the former, proof must be presumed to exist that intellectual insights by themselves will culminate in emotional adjustment, wholesome self-respect, and social competency. The author's position on this issue is unequivocal. He believes that the curriculum must make a direct attack on the noncognitive as well as the cognitive. A civilization that is suffering so acutely from neurotic and psychotic disorders should not tolerate less.

If receptive of the broader needs approach, a teacher cannot avoid regarding adolescents in their totality just as would a blood parent. And when pressures make the demands of society too oppressive, he can retreat to, but not further than, a minimal level of expectancy which will always demand that he establish a warm climate of acceptance, implement it with an organized program of learning, and refer to other individuals or agencies those students who are not responding to the classroom stimuli.

As alluded to previously, a permissive climate extends learning possibilities for all while acting as a preventive to emotional disturbance. Learning increases when the psychic energy of a student is freed to support his intellectual-learning efforts. In contrast, when an adolescent exhausts his inner resources by rebelling against a teacher or classroom environment, learning suffers to the commensurate degree that the emotions are not channeled in the proper direction. The concept of parsimony witnesses to the fact that a negative expenditure of energy makes for a corresponding reduction of the positive.

Regarding physical health, teachers should become sensitive to symptoms. Norms reveal how the mythical pupil with average health ranks on a scale, but that mythical individual never seems to be enrolled in a given class. In his stead are young people with differences in the operation of the glands, in vitality, in tolerance for work, in response to psychological pressure, in susceptibility to disease, and in over-all general health status. The reasonable expectancy of the teacher, in this regard, is that he be no less than a legal parent who acts with professional wisdom when face to face with problems of health.

When a student is manifestly tired, undernourished, or even ill, the teacher, as a professional parent, must look to other individuals or agencies for help. As a humanitarian, he cannot and will not ignore deprivation. Accordingly, if in a school with an administration that assumes referral responsibilities, he handles the problem by delegating it to another. This is the typical approach. In instances, however, when he personally has to seek assistance for a child outside the school, he contacts such agencies or individuals for help as the church, a welfare organization, the family physician, a social worker, or the local law enforcement officer.

Admittedly, the school cannot satisfy all the needs of all the children. Yet, without a reasonable approach to basic need gratification, the teacher courts learning failure. And it is important for him to realize that needs should be analyzed through the psychological eyes of the adolescent as well as through his own eyes of adulthood. Empathy of a high caliber is required for such two-way vision.

Interests

Another psychological variable, of little concern to education from colonial days until roughly the turn of the present century, is the interests of students. The puritanically oriented academic master cared little about the personal desires of his class group; he was more preoccupied with doing what the Lord wanted him to do than in making the school program more attractive. With a concept of the Deity figuratively sitting on his shoulder whispering ascetic suggestions, what chance did motivation have?

And even when this rigid orientation was modified somewhat in the parochial, and almost completely obliterated in the public, schools, a residue remained in the guise of formal discipline, the now suspect concept that students, regardless of preferences, should be made to perform difficult curriculum tasks, to the end of getting themselves ready to do difficult things in life in general. Thorndike's final research answer to this issue was that transfer between situations occurs only when they are similar. Thus, a teacher's forcing a gifted adolescent to perform rigorous tasks in differential calculus so that he will be more ready for the difficult life of the university is an erroneous or misplaced attempt at motivation. The student might probably be thus made more ready for advanced mathematics courses because of the similarity of the material, but not necessarily equally ready for the remainder of the university's curriculum.

The modern teacher's concern is to make the curriculum not difficult, but meaningful and therefore attainable. One way to accomplish this feat is to play through students' interests, which are many and varied. At the social level, if proper identification is to take place, preferences of students for certain other students are normal and desirable. These preferences should be honored whenever the curriculum is not harmed and a few adolescents not made isolates as a result. At the curriculum level, students also have favorite subjects and favorite areas within subjects. These, too, should be respected when not allowed to dominate. Other personal interests, particularly in the avocational category, are almost too numerous to mention, encompassing the various sports, club activities, social dancing, sedentary games, and many other activities. Finally, the vocational interests crave identification at many points of contact with the teacher and curriculum.

The insightful teacher, recognizing the many diverse predilections of students, regularly seeks to uncover and enlist them in support of learning. First of all, they can be motivational when the teacher capitalizes on them to stir up initial enthusiasm for an idea or concept. Later, they can be used to sustain curriculum action when allowed to direct activity in a channel of student choice.

However, like others who have attacked the issue of interest, the author recommends that it not be permitted to guide exclusively. It should be utilized for purposes of rapport and stimulation but never as the lone motivator. The needs and interests of a greater society, as much as the unrecognized present and future needs and interests of the individual himself, cannot be allowed to go unattended. In this regard, we agree with Kenneth Hansen that effort generates interest just as interest generates effort.[11] Both should be used as points of departure for learning. Either one, when employed skillfully by a capable classroom engineer, can be rewarded with success.

[11] Kenneth Hansen, *High School Teaching* (Englewood Cliffs, N.J.: Prentice-Hall, Inc., 1957), pp. 131–132.

Socioeconomic factors

Under the broad term of the heading of this section, the author has in mind such specifics as the social status of the family in the community, the prestige value of the father's occupation, the family income, the spending allowance of adolescents, the standards of dress, and the many other related values that cause a middle-class, immature culture to rate certain students as more or less desirable than others.

Warner, Hollingshead, and other sociologists have long since expressed their conviction that America is a class society with differences running the gamut from the privileged controlling group down through the ranks successively of professionals and executives; supervisors, white-collar workers, and artisans; the production-line workers and laborers; and last, the migrants, illiterates, and the vocationally unstable. Members of all the five classes, or of all socioeconomic levels determined in a different way from Warner's and Hollingshead's method, will be in most high schools, with the exact ratio a function of the type and location of the community: whether suburban, metropolitan-favored, metropolitan-unfavored, rural, or a combination of several of these.

The mature teacher is one who takes these differences into account but never for purposes of discrimination, as prevailed in Hollingshead's *Elmtown's Youth*.[12] The teacher's goal needs to be a clinical one in deference to the recognition that, since society has segmented itself along artificial lines, he can work more effectively if he knows the criteria of segregation and the resulting attitudes of subgroups and individual members toward one another. He can neither favor nor just civilly tolerate members of any designated class without losing some of his dignity and professionalism. While realizing that unconscious attitudes cannot always be effectively suppressed, we contend that he can, at least, blunt the more pointedly harmful. The goal is for all—the wealthy or needy, well-attired or shoddy, hotel-privileged or trailer-confined, politically favored or totally uninfluential—to be treated with equal decency and concern. Racial, religious, and economic prejudices, having no defensible status in a good school society, must become increasingly the property of only the maladjusted and immature, whose ranks hopefully will thin out by the year.

The slow and the superior

As a final forerunner to the next chapter's emphasis on those curricular patterns designed to give heed to some of the differences identified and discussed in this chapter, we next direct the reader's attention to the slow and the fast learners. Although obviously overlapping the previous

[12] August B. Hollingshead, *Elmtown's Youth, The Impact of Social Classes on Adolescents* (New York: John Wiley and Sons, Inc., 1949), Chap. 8.

treatment of intelligence, the contrast of the slow with the more talented should inject into the earlier discussion an added significance. In what specific or general ways do the two extremes on the factor of intelligence differ? An answer must be dependent, in great part, on exactly who is included in such labelled categories as the "slow" and the "superior" or the "retarded" and the "accelerated." Since the particularized field of special education related to the exceptional child is much too recent to enable anyone to define individuals or groups categorically, we take the relatively conservative approach of Conant, Jewett, and Hull by identifying the upper 15 to 20 per cent of a typical high school population as superior and the same percentages of the lower population as slow-learning. In general, such a criterion would make superiority descriptive of those individuals with I.Q.'s of 120 and above; and slowness, of those with I.Q.'s of 80 to 85 or below. These percentages have to be applied to a normal population, however, to be meaningful. Giftedness, as a further refinement, is usually regarded as extending upward from an I.Q. of 130.

To add confusion to the picture, a growing number of researchers are rebelling more and more against the I.Q. as the essential criterion of giftedness or slowness. Getzels and Jackson in a 1960 bulletin prepared by the University of Chicago, in conjunction with the United States Department of Health, protest vigorously against such a narrow interpretation, pointing out, as previously indicated, that intelligence, as measured by academic aptitude tests, and creativity as measured in other ways, while not exactly discrete, are far from synonymous. Others, like Noar, protest against the exclusion of such dimensions as the social, manipulative, administrative, and esthetic from the family constellation of the superior or retarded.

Although accepting the broader interpretation of Getzels, Davis, Jackson, Noar, and others, the author has deliberately delimited this section to a treatment of those differences that exist between the upper and lower elements of a high school distribution based on I.Q. alone. Allusions to method will be primarily coincidental. First, for a look at the slow. Just what traits characterize them?

1. They are less verbal than the gifted and, therefore, less able to profit from methods that rely predominantly on the oral or written word. When either is employed, a carefully selected level of communication is indicated.

2. Being less verbal, they respond well to the concrete: to realia, to audio-visual materials, and to copious verbal illustrations when language symbolism is employed.

3. Their insights are less penetrating because of less facility with the abstract.

4. By and large, they are more nervous and restless than the more favored. This may be the result of their having been pushed too hard and

too frequently by adult figures—teachers, parents, and others—who have insisted on their being what they cannot be.

5. Being aware of their limitations, they tend to react to pressures or criticism more defensively, or to withdraw from its effects.

6. Discouragement and frustration are more characteristic of them than of the superior.

7. Despite mental limitations, their ability to enjoy emotional and social situations is little affected.

8. Morally, they rate almost as high as their more gifted counterparts, falling short only when refined judgment between rightness and wrongness is demanded. With morality more habit than cognitively conceived, they are little disadvantaged.

9. As a cross-sectional group progresses through the grades, the slow learners fall further and further behind the average and the bright.

10. The slow thus are universally older than the bright.

These ten identifying features must be interpreted in a strictly relative sense. On almost any of the traits except the first two or three, a slow learner could very well score higher than his brighter classmate. Like almost all mass data, they thus must concede frequently to the individual exception. The same generalization applies to the parallel descriptive statements regarding the superior and gifted, selected of which follow.

1. The superior and gifted are more verbal than the slow, and therefore respond with facility to the abstractions of language symbolism. In this regard, they develop an earlier interest in reading.

2. Because of their abstract powers, they see relationships with a greater depth of penetration.

3. For the same reason, they need fewer teacher explanations and instructions; in fact, they often chafe under them.

4. Their emotional and social development, although greater than that of the slow and average, is not proportionately as much greater as their academic accomplishments and potentials.

5. According to Terman, they are somewhat better developed physically—in height, weight, and strength—than their counterparts.

6. Contrary to the popular inference of narrowness, they have diverse interests in such nonacademic outlets as sports, hobbies, and games.

7. They tend to elect the more difficult courses in the curriculum largely as a means of greater stimulation.

8. They crave, and almost demand, curriculum variety.

9. They develop greater independence at an earlier age.

10. Their giftedness belies a tendency to under-achieve that is not proportionately less or greater than a comparable tendency of the contrasted group.

11. They understand themselves better than the typical student does.

12. Their attention spans are more extensive.

13. They have a better sense of humor.

14. They are only slightly less apt mechanically than their counterparts.

15. Finally, they may be slightly more moral, being better able to make greater refinements in judgment.

From the above list and the one preceding it, the inference is inescapable that slow and fast learners have many qualities that range along a wide continuum, but the fact that they differ more in degree than in substance has significance. The range, except for the election of difficult subjects by the talented, is from "less than" to "more than," not from "none" to "all." Important for the reader to remember is that natural selection has eliminated from the high school classrooms all such categories as Mongoloids and the trainable mentally handicapped, and most of the educable mentally handicapped. These latter are usually in ungraded rooms. The less talented who remain may be slow-normal or slightly subnormal, but they are not abnormal adolescents.

This fact cannot be emphasized too much. The ignoring or diluting of its true import leads many instructional leaders, including even some of the more experienced, to treat slow learners like serious academic misfits who really do not belong in secondary education. Rarely does an I.Q. in grades 7 through 12 fall below 70, and usually not below 75 or 80. And these young people after graduation will marry, work for a living in jobs that are necessarily routinized, vote, and participate in other ways as citizens of a local or greater community. These slow learners cannot just be tolerated, for they, too, have talents that need to be discovered and developed. If low in certain abilities, they may be high, or at least higher, in others. With the mental-health goal of education demanding that all youth be helped to measure up to their optimum potential in the fields of the emotional, mental, physical, and social, the teacher is shortsighted and unenlightened who discriminates unfairly against those with limited endowments. Brightness is not to be worshipped and slowness despised. Both must be considered only as points of departure for learning, and in terms of the limits which they establish.

SUMMARY

The theme of the present chapter is the similarities and differences of high school students. Adolescence, as a life phase, received first emphasis, being described as a no-man's-land between childhood and adulthood, with much uncertainty and ambivalence being the teenager's lot. Yet adolescence was not treated as a primarily traumatic period, but more as a threshold of adulthood with its greater attendant demands. Adolescents were identified as meeting on the common grounds of four basic goals: search for conformity, pursuance of new knowledge and understandings of themselves and the world, insights about members of the opposite sex, and escape from adults on the road to independence.

Factors which distinguish among teen-age youth were identified as those emanating from differences of sex, age, intelligence, reading abilities, basic needs, interests, socioeconomic elements, and slowness or fastness in school work. Differences were identified, however, as being more of degree than of substance.

REFERENCES

Abraham, Willard, *Common Sense about Gifted Children.* New York: Harper & Row, 1958.

Blair, Glenn Myers, *Diagnostic and Remedial Teaching.* New York: The Macmillan Company, 1956.

Bryan, J. Ned (Director of Project), *The Identification and Education of the Academically Talented Student in the American Secondary School.* Washington, D.C.: National Education Association, 1958.

Conant, James B., *The American High School Today.* New York: McGraw-Hill Book Company, Inc., 1959.

Garrison, Karl C., *The Psychology of Exceptional Children.* New York: The Ronald Press Company, 1950.

Getzels, Jacob W., and Philip W. Jackson, *Creativity and Intelligence.* New York: John Wiley and Sons, 1962.

Jewett, Arno, J. Dan Hull, and others, "Rapid and Slow Learners in High Schools," U.S. Office of Education Bulletin No. 5. Washington, D.C.: U.S. Government Printing Office, 1954.

Kettelkamp, Gilbert C., *Teaching Adolescents.* Boston: D. C. Heath & Co., 1954.

Kirk, Samuel A., and G. Orville Johnson, *Educating the Retarded Child.* Boston: Houghton Mifflin Co., 1951.

Rothney, John W. M., *The High School Student—A Book of Cases.* New York: Holt, Rinehart and Winston, 1953.

United States Department of Health, Education and Welfare, Office of Education, *The Gifted Student* (Cooperative Research). Washington, D.C. Monograph No. 2, 1960.

Williams, Harold, *The Retarded Child Goes to School.* Washington, D.C.: United States Department of Health, Education and Welfare, Pamphlet No. 123, 1960.

Witty, Paul (ed.), *The Gifted Child.* Boston: D. C. Heath and Co., 1951.

CHAPTER **11**

RESPONDING
TO THE
DIFFERENCES
OF STUDENTS

The enterprise of organized public education is dedicated to a program for all who can gainfully profit from it. It follows logically, then, that the differences among students should be treated as part of an overall challenge to administrators and teachers. The associated commitment to academic professionals is essentially this: accept each student as he is and where he is, expect him to differ from others, regard reasonable differences as normal, encourage and even demand conformance that is defensible, but adapt learning to the student when he cannot adapt to learning.

If the tenets of this commission seem a bit overwhelming in writing, they are no less perplexing when attempts are made to implement them. An escape is for schools and school personnel to gloss over the problem and to blame mass education for requesting the impossible. This position serves only as a palliative, however, leaving the problem still unsolved. A more justifiable approach is for instructional leaders, without expecting the impossible, to face the differences of adolescents as an invitation to action. They may make a number of attempts at adaptation to differences, only to fail; but in the process they also will realize some successes.

Fortunately, the latter are cumulative, with experience leading not only to a more sensitive recognition of differences but to better ways of meeting them. In this regard, an interesting phenomenon of most research studies on problems of beginning teachers is that the neophyte does not consistently list the differences of children as a major concern.[1] At this stage, he may well be more engrossed in warding off or concealing personal and curriculum inadequacies than conscious of the unique problems of young people. Such an hypothesis is consistent with the concept of maturity as a process of moving more and more progressively from self to others. The same research studies just as consistently reveal a delayed concern for pupil differences once the young instructor has completed the second or third year of teaching. Then the dissimilarities of students tend to loom as one of the two or three most important problems that he has to face.

Practical academic considerations are the best rationale for the content of the present chapter and its extension into the vitals of the ongoing learning situation. If children who differ attend high schools, their differences must be reckoned with by teachers who engage them in a suitable program of activities. The history of individual differences in students has been essentially this: first they were ignored because they were not understood; next they were understood but still ignored; now an understanding is accompanied by a commitment. The specific means of attack that are being employed in the various high schools we shall relate initially to the problems of the slow and fast learners described in the preceding chapter. Whether such methods are the peculiar province of a heterogeneous or homogeneous class is immaterial to this introductory phase of the treatment. The administrative avenues themselves will be described and evaluated later.

METHODS TO BE USED WITH THE
SLOW AND TALENTED

It needs to be emphasized once more that the so-called slow-learning adolescent in the secondary school is not a freak merely serving time. Such captions as "moronic" and "stupid" are more and more seen to be inappropriate as the reader realizes that young people with I.Q.'s of 70 to 80 are merely subnormal learners—not necessarily subnormal future citizens, wage earners, or potential spouses. They are basically less verbal, less perceptive in depth, somewhat more ego-involved, and somewhat more emotional than others, but the differences between them and those with average I.Q. often are more in shades than in sharp contrasts.[2]

[1] Robert Porter Milheim, "A Study of the Professional Problems of Teachers Graduated from the School of Education of Miami University from 1946 to 1954" (Doctor's thesis, Northwestern University, 1955), pp. 10–42.
[2] W. B. Featherstone, "The Slow Learner, Who He Is and What He Is Like," in *Teaching the Slow Learner,* ed. by W. B. Featherstone (New York: Bureau of Publications, Columbia University, 1951), p. 5.

Being less verbal, the slow learners need a curriculum that both qualitatively and quantitatively is geared to their unique response levels. "Qualitatively" would dictate, not just less algebra for the slow, but mathematical content which is more appropriately non-algebraic; not shorter free-reading materials at the same level, but qualitatively more pertinent materials; not fewer science concepts of the same difficulty, but concepts specifically geared to the abilities and interests of the students. The amount of content that can be covered will undoubtedly be less, but, more significantly, it must be appropriately selected. And in the process, care must be exercised to exclude from books grade labels that create inferiority feelings in the student. No normal slow-learning student in the ninth grade would react favorably to an anthology with the title "Sixth-Grade Readings in American Literature" on the cover. Such an outcome is unnecessary, with the many graded curriculum materials that are available without grade labels.

A second requirement for the slow is that the pace of learning be reduced to conform to his more restricted speed of comprehension. Instructions should be given with less haste, questions should be asked at a more comfortable pace, and less comprehensive student responses should be expected. And third, the more relaxed classroom procedures should be accompanied by a corresponding selection of methods to reinforce important learnings—for example, more illustrations of abstract concepts, more relating of them to the student's environment, and more spaced review.

A fourth demand, a corollary of the other three, is that learning concreteness be substituted whenever possible for verbal and other symbolic abstractions. The blackboard, if of general significance to all students, is of even more importance to the slow learner. Other audio-visual media, such as realia, models, sound films, and filmstrips, have unique values in the learning environments of the less talented.

A suggestion supplementary to these four is that students in the category under discussion should not be withheld from abstract concepts pending the time that they have mastered an extensive body of supporting skills. For instance, denying a slow-learning English class the pleasures of literature or speaking until they have "learned the parts of speech" cannot be defended except as a means of encouraging dropouts. Skills, to be meaningful, must always be intermingled with, and related to, other learning content. When rigidly set apart as a steppingstone, they become sterile and devoid of relevance or transfer value. To cite an extreme case, it would be better, for instance, for the educable mentally handicapped with an I.Q. of 60 never to have to mouth the grammar rule: "A pronoun takes the place of a person or thing," than by such rote memory to be denied a curriculum that will appeal to him and challenge him.

A sixth proposal for the teacher of the mildly handicapped is that he place considerable emphasis on their emotional and social development.

These young people, it should be remembered, are not going to be recognized in life for their cognitive contributions. Furthermore, they have undoubtedly already felt too much the heavy-handed impact of teachers and other authority figures desirous of having them work above their capacities in the hard core of knowledge and the skills. Thus, since their future roles in life are destined to revolve vocationally around routine, and to be socially somewhat comparable to normal expectation, the need is for a deliberate attempt to help them grow emotionally by social exchanges and group-project endeavors in the classroom. It is not unlikely as these students begin to know social successes, and thus to like themselves better, for the cognitive content that has been periodically set aside to become more meaningful for them.

Other suggestions to the teacher of slow learners are that he change the pace of instruction frequently; that he give it variety; that he praise success liberally; and that he be even more attentive to mental-health practices than would be expected of teachers in other situations. Since these young people are more than normally emotional to begin with, the therapeutic effects of empathy, fairness, calm acceptance, and warmth cannot be exaggerated. Because they literally crave to be accepted and liked for what they are, a teacher's failure to meet this minimum requirement may well be a contributory factor to emotional deterioration.

Above all, the practice of relegating to the industrial arts, business, and shop programs all who cannot respond positively to a classical curriculum must be stopped. When these individuals desire to pursue an academic-type program beyond the bare essentials of three years of English, one or two of social studies, one of mathematics, and one of science, the typical high school offers them little but discouragement. The advanced levels of these subjects, and worse, even the beginning levels of the foreign languages, are closed to them. This practice cannot indefinitely be condoned. If more general, as well as some specialized, education in the academic areas is profitable for the average and the bright, why would it not be equally profitable, at a different level, for the slow?

Schools that are making academic offerings available at all levels seem to be having at least as much success in the venture as those following the more conventional plan. Although admitting the difficulties to small schools inherent in the proposal, those schools with populations of a thousand or more should have a minimum of such problems. Reaching all students (with the academic subjects) in a more encompassing manner is preferable to "sweeping the slow out of the way" but into other curriculum situations for which they usually are no better prepared. In this regard, the inference that low academic ability has its compensation in high mechanical aptitude is tenuous, at best.

A final issue pertinent to the topic of the moment is whether the slow student should be promoted on the basis of accomplishment measured against his ability or his achievement measured against a predetermined standard. If the former, with certain exceptions he will be promoted approximately on schedule and graduated with his class or only a short time thereafter. If the latter, provided the predetermined standard is fairly rigid, he might be as many as four or five years behind his class and ultimately be denied graduation because of age or social or economic pressures. Although this issue is too complex to be resolved categorically, the author leans heavily in the direction of the first alternative. If the purpose of education is optimum growth of all, how can a good society consistently deny a symbolic reward to an adolescent who has done his best? We do not support automatic promotion, but we do urge a charitable nod in the direction of fairness. However, the specific ramifications of each case customarily condition the outcome as much as does a philosophical point of view on the topic in general.

We turn now from the slow learner to the mentally superior and gifted, once more relegating to the background the specific administrative or curriculum structure that might be employed to achieve the outcomes described here. Reflecting what was said in the latter part of the preceding chapter, we restate that the mentally privileged student possesses an I.Q. of over 120 and is more facile at the verbal level, comfortable in the abstract, very penetrating in insights, developmentally mature, quite varied in interests, relatively independent, fairly well acquainted with himself, and possessed of a longer attention span than his associates who are mentally less favored.

The fundamental need of the superior and gifted, not unlike that common to all students, is to measure up to their optimum of ability and potential. But with these, such gratification is more difficult to come by. One reason is the almost casual ease with which they can perform with relatively high success most of the tasks assigned them in the home, the school, and the community. Doing better than others is no great chore, with the genes on their side. And since they live in a culture that intrinsically is more concerned with firstness and lastness than with sheer excellence of performance for its own sake, they soon learn how to excel relatively without doing their best. A second reason for their not infrequent lackadaisical performance is the fear of exile from the group if they appear too different academically. With individualism having peer prestige value only in limited quantities, a part is often sacrificed for group rewards. This mischievous state of affairs is particularly noteworthy in certain large-city schools, less so in rural schools, and much less so in suburban schools.

When motivation is less than it should be, counter measures from the teacher are called for—and in the last analysis, the best antidote is a curriculum that inspires. Although always competing with adolescent conformity, a curriculum pattern that meets the teenager where he is will rout at least the bugaboo of casualness. The supreme demand is for experiences in the educational processes of listening, reading, seeing, and speaking which are attuned to rich variety, extensive range, and invitation to infer-ences and conclusions. These experiences must be accompanied by an almost compelling insistence by the teacher that students perform to their optimum potentials. Such a curriculum would be less concerned with inert subject matter content than with cause-and-effect relationships, critical evaluation, creativeness, and consistency of viewpoint.

Along with the selection and adaptation of a curriculum appropriate for the fast learner, the teacher in some acceptable way should communicate to him the fact of his giftedness along with the obligation that it carries. The message must be conveyed in such a manner, however, that undue ego inflation will be prevented. Assuming this outcome, the student with the added insight into himself will have a better chance of reaching his growth potential.

With the assets of student motivation and a challenging selection of curriculum content, the teacher's next responsibility is to select teaching methods that will serve as reinforcing agents. In general, these learning media can be expected to reside in the abstract for reasonably long periods, to reach into the treasure of independent study quite often, and to involve problem-solving situations almost at will. The key is to challenge the capable student with teaching methods that are geared to his uniqueness. As an active person mentally, he cannot be held down long with methods that prevent him from questioning and assessing.

Against this theoretical background, we next invite the reader's attention to selected practices in meeting differing pupil needs employed by a combination of 795 junior high schools (grades 7–9), senior high schools (10–12), and regular high schools (9–12), as reported by Jewett, Hull, and others in a 1954 survey. From the thirty practices listed for the "Rapid Learners" and the same number for the "Slow Learners" in each of several curriculum fields, we present the five which in each instance were reported most frequently by teachers of English, social studies, science, and industrial arts, respectively.

English

Rapid learners: 1. Encourage extensive reading of good literature outside of class.
                   2. Require mastery of certain minimum essentials in grammar and usage.
                   3. Teach niceties of expression, such as distinctions between *shall* and *will, between* and *among, go slow* and *go slowly, may* and *can, lent* and *loaned.*
                   4. Emphasize reading of modern literature related to student interests and needs.
                   5. Help students to find good substitutes for inferior comic books and magazines.[3]

[3] Arno Jewett, J. Dan Hull, *et al., Teaching Rapid and Slow Learners in High School, Bulletin No. 5* (Washington, D.C.: U.S. Office of Health, Education, and Welfare, 1954), p. 22.

Slow learners: 1. Conduct drills to eliminate current vulgarisms such as "I ain't," "can't hardly," "he don't," etc.
2. Help students to find good substitutes for inferior comic books and magazines.
3. Emphasize reading of modern literature related to student interests and needs.
4. Require mastery of certain minimum essentials in grammar and usage.
5. Assign printed materials with difficulty approximating the individual's reading age.[4]

Social Studies

Rapid learners: 1. Use current events as an important part of class work.
2. Teach pupils to use the layman's reference books: the dictionary, encyclopedia, *World Almanac*.
3. Teach pupils how to register and vote; give experiences in studying party platforms and personal views of candidates.
4. Encourage pupils to engage in conversation in school and at home on current events, politics, government, and news of school and neighborhood.
5. Encourage pupils to use references in a large library.[5]

Slow learners: 1. Use current events as an important part of class work.
2. Teach pupils how to register and vote; give experiences in studying party platforms and personal views of candidates.
3. Encourage pupils to engage in conversation in school and at home on current events, politics, government, and news of school and neighborhood.
4. Teach pupils to use the layman's reference books: the dictionary, encyclopedia, *World Almanac*.
5. Teach basic skills in reading and writing (including map-reading) to build social studies vocabulary and concepts.[6]

Science

Rapid learners: 1. Insist that students report science experiments honestly and accurately.
2. Encourage students to use scientific encyclopedias and references in preparing science reports.
3. Include student activities to stress basic skills, such as reading tables, observing experiments, and spelling common science words.
4. Guide students to note superstitions and other biases that block fair consideration of scientific evidence.
5. Give students experiences in helping with science demonstrations.[7]

Slow learners: 1. Insist that students report science experiments honestly and accurately.

[4] *Ibid.*, p. 26.
[5] *Ibid.*, p. 34.
[6] *Ibid.*, p. 36.
[7] *Ibid.*, p. 50.

2. Guide students to note superstitions and other biases that block fair consideration of scientific evidence.
3. Include student activities to stress basic skills, such as reading tables, observing experiments, and spelling common science words.
4. Help students understand scientific reasons for fire-safety rules, sanitary standards, and/or first-aid practices.
5. Discuss with students the qualities that help a person hold a job in industry.[8]

Industrial Arts

Rapid learners:
1. Encourage students with original, inventive, and creative ideas, interests, and talents to carry out their ideas.
2. Place emphasis upon student projects which develop problem-solving skills and critical thinking.
3. Conduct demonstrations of processes and operations students use in constructing projects.
4. Encourage cooperative pupil-teacher planning of projects and activities.
5. Place emphasis on the development of simple handtool-using skills.[9]

Slow learners:
1. Conduct demonstrations of processes and operations students use in constructing projects.
2. Place emphasis on the development of simple handtool-using skills.
3. Encourage pupils to undertake simple projects which can be completed in short amounts of time.
4. Provide opportunities for intensive repetitive tool-using exercises.
5. Encourage and assist students to develop industrial arts hobby interests through home workshops and other leisure-time activities.[10]

In appraising these reported practices, an observer of the ones relating specifically to English and science would note some duplication between the fast and slow groups. For instance, in English, both are expected to master certain minimum essentials and to read modern literature related to their needs (2 and 4 rapid; 4 and 3 slow). In science, three duplications exist: both are expected to report experiments honestly, stress basic skills, and be chary of superstitions (1, 3, and 4 rapid; 1, 3, and 2 slow). And yet the implication in most such cases is not that identical material will be covered, but that the same goal will be reached in different ways for the two groups—a rather logical outcome. The industrial arts suggestions reveal an honest attempt to individualize not only content but method as well.

In the final assessment of the effectiveness of instruction of the fast and slow, these criteria must be uppermost:

[8] *Ibid.*, p. 54.
[9] *Ibid.*, p. 70.
[10] *Ibid.*, p. 74.

1. Curriculum materials that differ in kind as well as amount between the two categories.

2. Curriculum materials that differ in kind as well as amount within each of the two categories.

3. Methods of instruction that relate to the factors of verbal facility of pupils, the length of their attention spans, their independence, their need of reinforcement of learning, and the many other personality dynamics of the students and the professional dynamics of the situation.

ADMINISTRATIVE APPROACHES
OTHER THAN HOMOGENEOUS
GROUPING

The camera's eye will now be shifted from the generic to the more specific, with attention focused on the attempts made by schools during the past half-century to serve the variegated needs of a heterogeneous population of students and the uncertain expectancies of the greater society. Receiving a disproportionate share of the limelight is the issue of homogeneous grouping, sometimes crowding out in its intensity other administrative practices that have better stood the test of time. These latter will receive initial priority of treatment, followed then by a coverage of homogeneous grouping and finally by a consideration of the many practices characteristic of heterogeneous classes.

Extensive course offerings, electives, and constants

Among the many administrative provisions for pupil differences, none is more sweeping in effect than the variety of course offerings themselves. It was with this factor in mind that Conant made his case for the so-called comprehensive high school. He contended, and quite justifiably, for the most part, that a school population with a vast spread of differences would become academically undernourished if administered to by a program not equally diversified. That his case was slanted toward the talented constitutes more of a personal bias than a refutation of the basic premise itself.

Unfortunately, only the larger junior and regular high schools can afford this needed diversification. The larger junior high school can afford to offer as separate subjects such specific courses as the slide rule, photography, audio-visual aids, and creative writing because size guarantees a large enough class in each to protect the budget. In like manner, the larger senior or regular high schools (grades 10–12 and 9–12, respectively) can support the enrichment, for instance, of three to four years of each of several foreign languages; courses in journalism, dramatics, and speech arts in English; and courses in economics, sociology, and ancient history in the social studies, to name just a few of the hundreds of possibilities in all the curriculum fields. The smaller school, on the other hand, is more narrowly limited to the more traditionally favored academic offerings, being unable to support small, class-sized groups of 1 to 10 or 15 pupils in other often equally desirable fields.

Of the many courses within the province of a school system, a select few fall into the category of constants and the majority, usually, into the category of electives. This two-way division in itself constitutes another concession to the problem of student differences. It says in effect to the student body: The school believes that you have certain common needs and interests; these will be met by our enrolling all of you in general education courses which are called constants. In addition, in deference to your diversity of needs, interests, and aspirations for the future, the school has designed a number of elective courses which are meant to relate to your uniquely individualistic goal patterns.

Throughout the country, the constant requirements are essentially these, with minor variations from school to school:

	Grades 7–8	*Grades 9–12*
English	2 years	3 years (frequently 4 years)
Social studies	2 years	2 years (frequently 1 year)
Science	1 year	1 year (moving toward 2 years)
Mathematics	2 years	1 year (frequently 2 years)
Fine arts	½ year	——
Industrial arts or home economics	½ year	——
Physical education	2 years	4 years

The course listings, it will be noted, are more heavily prescriptive for the junior than for the regular high school, consuming about three-fourths of a student's load in the former and one-half in the latter.

Remaining, then, is room for electives up to approximately one-fourth and one-half of a load, respectively. The greater amount of election in the higher grades is out of respect for the growing individualism of students who stand in the vestibule of a future world of interests, vocations, and civic and social activities which vie for priority. Through exploring all or part of them, and concentrating by election more heavily on some than others, the adolescent becomes more conversant with a self-related cross section of life than he would if the entire program had been determined for him. The electives, then, accord him the freedom (under guidance) to exercise his individual rights, but not in disregard for the common meeting ground of all youth.

The battle between the constants and electives for a more favorable ratio has been going on for more than half a century. When the country is un-threatened by outside or inside calamity, as was the case in the nineteen-twenties and part of the nineteen-thirties, the electives gain; when holocausts lurk, the constants emerge dominant. The country is now moving toward an increase in the hard-core subjects, particularly science and mathematics, on the assumption that a more determined and adequate resistance to communism will be the resultant. The outcome to be feared, however, is that individualism may be lost in the struggle to protect it. The electives, within reason, should be cherished, as a bulwark against the ever-present threat of an excessively centralized dictation of values. But an overemphasis on unfettered election likewise leads to a danger: that license may replace freedom.

The multi-track approach

Another administrative method of fitting the curriculum to human diversity is the so-called "multi-track" approach, which permits a student in selected content areas to earn a unit of credit by completing one of several possible courses. For instance, in freshman mathematics in many schools, the several available tracks are algebra, general mathematics, and business artithmetic; in junior English, they might be dramatics, speech, journalism, and "English Regular." Some high schools permit the more capable pupils to enroll in biology in the freshman year, whereas the less capable have to enroll in general science, postponing biology until the sophomore year. This, too, is a multi-track, or more appropriately, a dual-track approach.

This multi-track plan can accomplish some of the goals of individualizing the curriculum without the trauma involved in homogeneous grouping. Even though the distinction is only a shaded one, the psychological difference between algebra and business arithmetic is usually less than the difference between "mathematics honors" and "mathematics opportunity." Another distinction revolves around the degree of choice permitted a student. In a homogeneous-group situation, student choice is generally nil. Within multi-track alternatives, the student is most often advised strongly but left with the final choice, dependent on his future college or vocational plans. On this issue, we recommend that the right of the pupil to choose be encouraged, but never to the extent of excessive permissiveness.

The benefits of guidance information

A third administrative medium which enables a school to meet the student more purposefully on his grounds is the guidance information on a pupil which is gathered by a school and then made available to any authorized individual or group of individuals who can best use it. This may take the form of an I.Q. score, a psychometric test grade, a case study report, or some other type of guidance information which might bridge the distance of doubt between alternate choices in any one of a number of areas: academic, athletic, emotional, social, or vocational.

The avowed purposes of a counseling program are essentially these:

1. To direct attention to the individual's academic and personality components that cannot be conveniently and thoroughly attended to by the more traditionally conceived curriculum. Selected of these are the mental-health factors, progress that is out of line with ability, course enrollment as related to future plans, delinquency, home influences on a pupil, and other factors dealing with additional variations in behavior.

2. To build up a supply of information on a student that will provide the school with as nearly complete a picture of him and his background as it can get, within the framework of budget limitations.

3. To make this information available to appropriate faculty personnel as the need arises—such personnel, in this instance, being either teachers or specialists.

4. To direct its entire constellation of services to helping youth make intelligent choices and to pursue them to completion.

Within the framework of the above purposes, any time that a guidance department, whether functionally or organizationally conceived, helps the school to understand a student better and thus administer more competently to his needs, it decreases the importance of differences among individuals which are in need of being recognized and exploited positively. The services themselves vary from system to system, ranging from speech correction to physical therapy, from work with the blind to work with the trainable mentally handicapped, from testing the total school population to giving clinical help to one individual. Whatever their nature, they give articulate testimony to a maturing concern of the schools for underprivileged youth. These services are destined to expand as humanitarian values permeate the thinking of a larger part of society.

Summer school attendance

Another attempt of the high school to take action on the diversification of personality patterns presented by all student bodies is the oft-overlooked asset of the summer school. This component has become such an inseparable part of most systems that the fundamental purpose is almost taken for granted. Historically, it was designed to enable the failing student to catch up with his class by permitting him to repeat a subject or to enroll in a comparable one.

More recently, particularly in the suburban areas, summer-school education has emerged preponderantly as a medium of enrichment for the previous academic year's incumbent and of orientation for the following September's incumbent-to-be, and less as a haven for failures. In the first role, it permits the motivated student to embrace new content that otherwise might be denied him, or to intensify in areas that have already proved stimulating. The future enrollee is enabled to achieve a running start in any beginning course in the curriculum—an experience which serves both to alleviate possible fears of the high school and also to enrich. Any of these three purposes that the high school serves reduces the magnitude of the problem of student dissimilarities.

Limiting and increasing the course load

Another common curriculum practice of most high schools is to forbid the slow achievers from carrying more than a fixed quota of courses, while permitting the high achievers to enroll for extra work. Reasonably valid evidence supports the conviction that the slow learner should be limited to a normal course enrollment. Interestingly, a reduction of the enrollment from the standard four to three subjects rarely encourages a higher level of performance. Conceivably the reason for this phenomenon is that learning is more a product of such complex factors as attitude, work habits, and motivation, and therefore the lesser load becomes only a symptomatic approach to cure. On the other hand, the course load should rarely exceed the normal for the slow-learning student lest he be overwhelmed by too large a quantity.

For the bright student, enrollment in a fifth, or occasionally a sixth, course has been moderately effective when measured by evaluated performance. However, it is the author's considered opinion that the mere addition of a course provides no guarantee of gain in over-all accomplishment. As an alternative, greater benefit might result if teachers placed more emphasis on the qualitative possibilities of a so-called normal course load. This shift gives fundamental priority to intensity of curriculum penetration as being a more desirable learning outcome for the bright student than a mere addition of another block of subject matter.

Associated with the practice of permitting added work for the bright is the corresponding practice of forbidding him to graduate early despite his having earned extra credits. This practice recognizes that early graduation may lead to the pupil's academic achievement outdistancing his social readiness for the next step. However, his retention for four years places a heavy responsibility on the high school to offer him a provocative challenge. It is important in this regard that the bright student not be frustrated by unnecessary repetitiveness of course content in any of the four years. The ensuing boredom and its attendant frustrations encourage shoddy academic performance, an unwholesome attitude toward school, and a gravitation toward the co-curriculum more as an escape than as part of a goal-oriented design.

Selected miscellaneous practices

In addition to the methods already identified and discussed, other main administrative thoroughfares or bypaths which serve to meet the differences of young people are the co-curriculum, job-placement services, the work-study program, the bright helping the slow, career conferences, and the performance of administrative duties by students in the classroom or greater school area. Unquestionably, the interest that schools are taking in the problems of individuals and small groups is most encouraging and gratifying. The goals of the future should be a spread of this concern to a greater number of junior and regular or senior high schools; an appeal to more administrators and teachers to develop like sensitivities; and an eliciting of greater interest on the part of lay members of local communities to move in the same directions.

MEETING DIFFERENCES BY HOMOGENEOUS GROUPING

The administrative practices described and evaluated in the last section have propelled the cause of program individuation in a noteworthy way. They had their birth in the cradle of student diversity; their continuing mission has been to meet young people on their own grounds; and their ultimate goal is the greater realization by all students of their vast potentials. The methods themselves, particularly their implementation, can be criticized, but their purpose is above reproach. This same covering generalization applies to homogeneous grouping, which at present is the administrative method most widely employed in the schools to meet pupil differences. Homogeneous grouping must still be regarded as experimental in view of the hesitancy on the part of many schools and communities to accept it unconditionally. Its status in education is fairly solid, even though it is not yet universally accepted.

Grouping as a design for improvement in instruction was conceived around 1900 and implemented in a few schools shortly thereafter.[11] Its growth initially was slow, but the tempo increased after it became more widely known and accepted. Then, between the years 1939 and 1952, according to Jewett and Hull, a considerable decline was experienced,[12] followed next by a noteworthy resurgence in the 1950's. This resurgence has continued until the present. With the impetus given it by Conant, in his 1960 *The American High School,* surrounded as the latter was with prestige status, homogeneous grouping can accurately be described as a

---

[11] Robert H. Anderson, "Organizing Groups for Instruction," in *Individualizing Instruction, Sixty-First Yearbook,* ed. Nelson B. Henry (Chicago: National Society for the Study of Education, 1962), p. 241.
[12] Jewett and Hull, *et al. op. cit.,* p. 54.

healthy, growing organism in today's schools. The junior high schools are a bit less in favor of it; the upper secondary schools, a bit more.

With grouping relatively new to most systems and inseparable from the intangibles of attitude, personality, and the emotions, as well as cognitive implications, research to evaluate its effectiveness—and we understate—is less than convincing. Most investigators who have made the more thoughtful studies on the subject have uncovered so many contradictory findings that such descriptive terms as *consensus* and *majority* are rarely used. Teachers who report on their own classroom research practices tend to be swayed by on-the-spot results and personal biases. Mental hygienists, on the other hand, are prone to regard the issue as single-dimensional, worrying much about emotional traumas in grouping and less about other factors. From the enigmatically contradictory evidence of research and the author's own first-hand experience with grouping, we shall attempt, in the next several pages, to present selected evidence as support for a qualified stand at the end of the section.

The alleged advantages

Since the curriculum practice of grouping is currently being tried out in a vast number of schools containing all or some of grades seven through twelve, it must be bolstered by a supporting body of logical theory. What, then, are some of the alleged advantages of homogeneous grouping reported by this theory? The one frequently projected advantage is that students who are segregated with others of like abilities and aptitudes should logically learn more. In this more cloistered environment, so the theory goes, the bright student is not held down by the average and slow, nor the average by the slow; neither is the slower student driven into academic withdrawal either by a curriculum which is beyond him or by student associates who respond at higher levels. Logical as this argument is—and it may be factual as well as logical—research, to date, is ambivalent in its support. In view of the ambivalence of research findings on the subject, our advice to the scholar or school system that desires scientific evidence is to remain agnostic until a more convincing case has been made for or against it. As of the moment, we can believe or suspect, but we cannot "prove" anything by scientific evidence.

A second purported advantage of grouping is that in it the teacher need not individualize, because he will have a homogeneous group of pupils in any one class. At this point, we hardly need to ask if the following factors make for homogeneity: an I.Q. range of possibly 15 to 20 points, a reading range of one to two grade levels, an achievement spread of more than one marking symbol, and other differences in work habits, motivation, and personality? It seems clear that grouping will result in more homogeneity only. Differences of sufficient magnitude will continue to exist to dictate many small-group methods of teaching within the framework of even a so-called homogeneous group. The extent of individualization may be less, but it will still be needed. Ninth-grade readers in an eleventh-grade class will still have trouble with *The Scarlet Letter,* and eighth-grade readers in a ninth- or tenth-grade class, with Dickens's *Tale of Two Cities.* Grouping may reduce some of the evils of mass education, but many will remain to plague the dedicated teacher.

Another advantage widely reported is that inter-class grouping permits the better utilization of a staff, with each teacher being assigned to the level of pupils with which he can work most comfortably and efficiently. This argument, although once more eminently logical, is at least mildly specious in view of the failure by most colleges and universities to train teacher candidates so categorically. The argument has more merit when a selection is made by the school on the grounds of individual teacher interest and special aptitude. Furthermore, a strong probability exists that teachers qualified to work with the slow are too infrequent to go around.

A fourth defense is that grouping spreads leadership opportunities more widely, permitting the slow or average to lead when with others who are similar to themselves, whereas they are denied this opportunity when forced to compete with the more gifted. This argument has merit and would carry even more weight if it were backed by a high correlation between academic ability and leadership. In this event, "leadership" would need quite careful definition.

A final advantage consistently proffered for grouping is that the mental health of students improves when they are not forced to compete unequally with their more capable associates. The greater uniformity, it is said, increases self-assurance, minimizes frustrations, and establishes a dependable base on which more defensible cognitive learnings can be superimposed. This alleged advantage has enough logic behind it to deserve credibility until research provides counter testimony.

The alleged disadvantages

Theory and practice are both productive of certain possible negative, as well as positive, effects of homogeneous grouping which should give any school system pause before rushing headlong into the unknown. The disadvantage most universally tendered, primarily by theorists, but also by some practitioners, is that the practice is undemocratic. The accusation, however, usually falls short of a definition of democracy and eases over most often into the area of mental health. The case for the prosecution here is that young people, if in the less privileged groups, are deliberately made to feel different from and even inferior to many of their peers. This, so goes the argument, makes for improper attitudes toward self, brightness and dullness, social relationships, and adult values.

Both the latent and manifest dangers to mental health are too obvious to be questioned except by those whose biases blind their vision. This statement is not tantamount, however, to a declaration that such hazards are absolutely necessary or conclusive. The primary perils are that the slow learner, when faced with the administrative evidence of his slowness, will develop feelings of inferiority that may harm more than grouping will help. A comparable, if not an even greater, possibility is that the talented student will become so enamored of his administrative label that psychological injury of a different magnitude may result. Neither outcome could be other than disturbing.

A second built-in danger of grouping is that school personnel might become so preoccupied with the outward appearances of mass uniformity as to be convinced of its actual existence, losing in the process sight of the uniqueness of the individual. This is a real danger, attested to by the greater amount of large-group work done in homogeneous than in heterogeneous classrooms. The thoughtful teacher cannot afford to be lured by this artificial veneer of homogeneity which, if permitted to influence too much, would undermine the highly cherished commodity of individualism.

Another limitation of homogeneous grouping not to be deftly sidestepped is the ease with which it leads to mediocre teaching practices. The term *homogeneous* itself is seductive, carrying a falsely convincing implication of exactness employed in the process of grouping. But the term is at best only an approximation of the realistic state of affairs, and the teacher who accepts the label at its face value may thereby be lured into large-group practices that may not be pertinent to the needs of the class.

A fourth disadvantage often cited is that a slow-learning class quarantined from the more capable student body is, through that act, denied the right of stimulation by the bright; similarly, that any group so isolated is deprived of a cross-sectional point of view. Although it has no bulwark of proof, this tentative conclusion contains sufficient plausibility to warrant further analysis. In theory, logic supports it. In practice, however, the natural selection that takes place in such elective courses as the foreign languages, advanced sciences, and higher mathematics testifies partially against it. However, the only logic that can be mustered in defense of the slow being isolated for slowness only with or without harm accruing to them must be empirical, and, in this event, the conclusion is only as valid as the teacher who reaches it. If the teacher is indifferent to or antagonistic toward slow learners, he would inevitably give a negatively biased report. If favorably disposed, his reactions would have more validity. In general, teachers who are qualified by training and experience to guide the slow are probably more disposed than indisposed toward the favorable outcomes of grouping.

A fifth disadvantage of homogeneous grouping—and this is a very tangible one—relates to the factor of group size and scheduling. For class segregation to take place along any line, at least two class-sized groups in any given subject must exist. Since the median-sized high school has a population between three and four hundred, this minimum specification is not readily met by the average school. A few subjects, like first- and second-year English, United States history, or civics, would serve segregation's purposes, but not the many others, like chemistry, physics, problems of democracy, the foreign languages, and advanced mathematics courses. With little doubt, homogeneous grouping is almost exclusively for the larger school, because only with size does scheduling have a chance to operate successfully.

A final disadvantage, more operational than inherent, is that the status teachers in the majority of school systems gravitate away from the slow- toward the fast-learning groups. This eye-opening practice is subject to several explanations: maybe the fast are much easier to teach by conventional methods; maybe they stimulate more; or maybe prestige is immaturely associated with the bright. Regardless of reason, the department head, with rare exception, teaches the fast groups; the non-administrative experienced teacher, the fast and average; and the new, inexperienced neophyte, the slow. If homogeneous grouping has trod a rocky path, a primary reason may well be the administrative folly connected with such teacher allocation. In all situations, the criterion, in contrast, should be the qualifications of an individual teacher to work with a designated ability group— not years of service, ill-conceived prestige, or convenience.

The criteria for grouping

Once the advantages and disadvantages of homogeneous grouping have been assessed, with the former emerging victorious, the next step is a determination of the basis for grouping. Exactly what criteria and methods of evaluation will be used to separate students into reasonably homogeneous categories? In Jewett and Hull's 1954 survey of 775 schools, the following factors or devices were found to be employed in descending order of frequency: school marks, group intelligence tests, teacher estimates, standardized achievement tests, physical health, counselors' evaluation, vocational plans, and reading habits and interests.

Drawing on these and related selective methods, we propose the following criteria for the school that is definitely committed to grouping practices:

1. An estimate of intelligence as provided by a group academic-aptitude test. Several scores in this regard are much preferred to a single score.

2. An estimate of achievement as provided by past marks and appropriate standardized achievement scores in the specific subject matter area

for which grouping is being contemplated. The subjective bias of the former will be compensated for by the almost cold detachment of the latter. In cases of doubt, teacher opinion will be decisive.

3. An estimate of reading speed and comprehension as determined by standardized testing instruments. This reading component is particularly significant in the fields of English and social studies and only a little less so in science and mathematics.

4. Emotional tolerance for stress as determined by teacher and counselor opinion. This factor is usually important only in the selection of students for "honor-type" groups, where competition is too often feverish and pressures proportionately insidious.

In truncating the listing with the fourth criterion, we admit to an exclusion of such other potentially important factors as social adjustment, work habits, college plans, vocational aspirations, avocational interests, and all-around personality adjustment. The slighting of these is an admitted concession not only to the more heavily weighted factor of ability, but also to the need for criteria that can be determined objectively. The first three numbered factors satisfy both of these specifications, whereas the possibilities appended afterward fail one or both. Although a broad base is always needed for grouping as a means of neutralizing error, its breadth will be affected by whether or not the selected criteria are susceptible to accurate determination and by their direct relationship to the contemplated outcomes of grouping. For instance, work habits may be a factor of consequence, but if evaluating them as a factor is too unscientific, the criterion loses its significance. In like manner, social adjustment, although a vital objective of education, is only partially relevant to a grouping situation conceived primarily in terms of academic ability.

The number of groups to be formed

Assuming a basis of selection comparable to the one just projected, a problem as yet unsolved consists of the number of groups to be formed and the rationale behind their formation. For purposes of illustration, the following data are postulated: a fairly large high school with a freshman enrollment of 510 and an I.Q. spread as indicated in Table 1, Chapter 10. Artificially ignoring the factors of past achievement, reading, and emotional tolerance, and concentrating only on the I.Q. range itself, the reader is asked to decide on the number of groups. Here are a few questions to be answered.

1. Should the top five students of genius proportions, with I.Q.'s above 155, be kept together even though it would be uneconomical to the budget?

2. Should they be included in a class with the 25 students whose I.Q.'s range from 135 to 150, even though a spread of 25 I.Q. points will result?

3. At the bottom of the distribution, should the 16 students with I.Q.'s from 70 to 79 be formed into one class, or should they be interspersed among other classes in which the I.Q.'s extend as high as 89?

4. If the 30 and 16 fastest and slowest students, respectively, are segregated, what should be the lower and upper limits of the groups formed from the remaining population of 464 students whose I.Q.'s range from 80 to 134? If divided in half, the limits would be from 80 to 107, and from 108 to 134; if divided in thirds, from 80 to 97, from 98 to 115, and from 116 to 134, respectively. None of these groups is very homogeneous, even when the I.Q. alone is the determiner.

If indecision governs when just one factor is manipulated, doubt and confusion multiply when others are added to the foundation. The issue in this regard broadly is between greater and less refinement. If the former, the usual resultant is a number of groups, all of which conform to a comparable range regardless of the measuring unit. If less refinement is deemed desirable, the very slow and the very capable learners are often formed into distinctive sections with the remainder of the student body divided by chance factors alone. Not infrequently, in the junior and small high school particularly, the slow only are segregated for special instruction, with the vast remainder of the population sectioned along chance lines. If forced to choose among these approaches, we would prefer the latter two over the first. Our defense would be on mental-health grounds and in recognition of the unreliability of measuring devices and methods. Regarding both, segregating the extremes of a distribution is almost always more defensible than refining within a narrower range; therefore, mental health suffers less when fewer mechanical mistakes are made. Likewise, when a large middle or middle-upper population is left ungrouped along lines of ability, the danger of personality injury is lessened.

Practices to undergird grouping

On the hypothesis that a school system has committed itself to the practice of curriculum segregation, it should conscientiously search for operational practices which, if adhered to, would guarantee it the most likely successes. Which, then, are the more important of these?

By all odds, the most fundamental requisite is a climate free from pettiness and sham. This presupposes the existence of a sizable number of teachers, parents, non-parent community leaders, and pupils mature enough to separate the real from the false, accepting each other for what each basically is, regardless of ability. Short of this ideal, a school can realize at least limited success in ability grouping if it makes a frontal assault on the fallacy of relating quality with brightness and inadequacy with dullness. Such a stand would announce to any who wished to hear that students, regardless of talents, would be accorded equal respect, help, and affection to the end of their measuring up to a built-in potential. Whether this potential were little or great would be significant only to the learning process itself. In this way, grouping, divested of the trappings of the counterfeit, would stand out uncluttered by emotionalism as a means of meeting certain of the differing needs of adolescents.

The arduousness of the road to the above goal, however, cannot be overemphasized, strewn as it is with the blockages of a long history of counter-attitudes and practices. The almost civilization-old philosophy of idealism, with its exclusive worship of mind, does disservice to a cause that, although regarding mind as an essence of real value, refuses to impute goodness or badness when the mental component is possessed in unequal amounts. Nor are such school practices as posting honor grades, electing students to honor societies, and paying undue homage to brightness in other ways conducive to the climate so desperately needed for success in grouping. The key need is for a wholesome atmosphere, if the process of grouping is to achieve to its optimum.

A second requisite is for the program to be introduced with honesty and frankness—qualities which should likewise characterize it throughout its existence. The unsubtle elementary school red birds, blue birds, and white birds are just as much out of place in the higher grade levels as in the lower, even though the labels might be changed. Although not advocating the brutal frankness which such designations as "slow learners" and "fast learners" would connote, we do favor an open and forthright discussion of the deeper implications of the contemplated or existing program. Regarding the captions themselves, an innocuous A-B-C or 1-2-3-4 approach is less laden with mental-health negativism than such color terms as *honors, opportunity, help, college-level,* and *regular.* The real issue is whether a student body and parents should share with the professional school personnel the issues beneath the labels. If they are deemed unready, maybe the school is unready for grouping, because the climate is not propitious.

It has been implied heretofore, but not yet stated, that grouping should always be a function of each subject, not an across-the-board curriculum practice. So conceived, grouping would relate to each student's unique abilities in any given content area. Thus, if the assumption that boys excel in mathematics and girls in language arts is sound, Rick Etnyre might well be placed in a top Algebra 1 section but in a second-from-the bottom English 3 section; whereas Dolores Curtis might, conversely, be in an Algebra 4 but a top English 1 section. Individual students usually respond in different ways to the various curriculum subjects, and homogeneous grouping has to be flexible enough to respond to these major differences within any one person.

Another practice without which success is jeopardized is the relative freedom of movement of students from one level to another. When pupils are assigned to a designated group, they should not be denied the opportunity for reassignment at periodic intervals, provided the facts warrant such action. The first month or six weeks of any semester should be one of watchful observation and appraisal by the teacher to permit an occasional pupil shift from one level to another. Other opportunities for transfer would logically occur at the end of each semester or year, as new data emerged to support such a change.

Error is too much a part of the entire grouping process for school personnel to endow it with even an approximation of infallibility. First and foremost, the instruments employed to measure such factors as intelligence, reading scores, and achievement are far from exact. Another delimiting factor is pupil biases in testing situations, with the emotions influencing the results often disproportionately. A third limitation is the fact that human and machine errors in the processes of administering and scoring tests are too common to encourage perfectionistic expectations. With these and other possible sources of falsity, teachers at almost anytime should be encouraged to communicate to constituted authority any evidences of improper placements. The latter should be equally ready to effect changes which are manifestly justified.

The marking system should be made to harmonize

Equal in importance to the flexibility of student transfers between groups is the marking flexibility needed by a teacher of any single group. In a number of schools, a fixed marking standard is presumptively established for each sectioned category and then superimposed on the instructional leader. For instance, a teacher of a slow group is told that most pupils therein are to be given D's or F's, with only an occasional C permissible for "outstanding" performance. The logic behind this dictum is that the same pupils, if ungrouped, would receive the same lower marks. The logic is understandable, but the ignoring of the psychological factors is more difficult to fathom. The guidance-minded teacher certainly wants more marking flexibility than such a fixed pattern permits.

Our point of view is that a teacher should never be denied the right to relate a mark to the uniqueness of a student. Thus, we favor the practice of allowing teachers the full, or almost the full, range of the grading scale, regardless of the group level. The A or B might be greater rarities in the slow-learning classes, but the granting of such marks would never be denied the teacher. If grades are insisted on in the identification of class rank or honor students, mathematical weightings can always be applied as an equalizer. For instance, a grade of A in a so-called honors class could be multiplied by a factor of 2.0; the same grade in an average group, by 1.5; and in a slow-learners class, by 1.0. In this way, the prestige marking symbols would be a common factor throughout, without other school values being distorted. This practice prevents the discouragement and depression so common in a slow-learning class in which the teacher can rarely give a mark higher than D.

Smaller classes for the slow

A final practice destined to result in a favorable outcome for ability grouping is the placing of a low ceiling on class size for the slow student. His is a category of adolescents who conform less to norms of school behavior, who need more personal attention, and who thus demand more of a teacher's time in preparing materials, guiding, and individualizing instruction. A class size of from 15 to 20 has become a goal of suburban schools systems for these slow learners, in deference to their unique demands. This lesser ratio for the slow than for the more favored is in no sense an attempt to magnify their importance out of proportion to their numbers. Rather, it is designed to equalize teaching loads and to enable instructional leaders to meet at least minimum standards of effectiveness. Large-group methods are only intermittently appropriate for slow learners, and the greater small-group and individual-instructional load which they place on teachers should not go unrecognized by administrators.

A point of view

In concluding this section, we forthrightly admit to a degree of uncertainty regarding ability grouping. Theory seems to be somewhat opposed; practice seems moderately in favor. Our compromise harks back to the importance of climate. If most, or even many, partners in the project can be made to respond maturely to grouping, regarding it only as a means of providing a better curriculum for the various student consumers, it has a respectable place and mission. But, even then, it must be treated as an experiment until more evidence is accumulated and assayed. However, when ability carries too many esoteric overtones, permitting spurious attitudes to rule the intellect, a school system would do well to wait until the teachers, parents, and student body are more ready to face the issue and to live with it comfortably. As of the moment, our conviction is that most communities are not ready. With careful orientation and promotion by a school system, however, the erroneous attitudes of many communities may be converted to an ever-growing readiness for ability grouping.

THE CLASSROOM TEACHER'S ROLE
IN MEETING DIFFERENCES

Notwithstanding the laudable efforts of a school system to provide a solid administrative structure wherein differences can be accommodated and properly engaged, the figure who makes or breaks the entire operation is the classroom teacher. Whether schools have many constants or few, multi- or single-track systems, homogeneous or heterogeneous classroom groups, their success with the problem of pupil differences rests squarely on the competencies and attitudes of the teachers. Grouping in itself makes for no dramatic conversions unless the curriculum content is meaningful and the instructional leader himself able to evoke a sparkle of academic magic by his teaching methods. And this sparkle in a heterogeneous classroom population might well obviate the need of inter-class grouping.

If the teacher is so essential to learning's outcomes, what methods can he elect that will have the greatest likelihood of administering to a wide range of pupil differences? A list of selected approaches that have been tried with good results in many schools will be discussed in the following, with appropriate comments about each as required.

Information is necessary

Adaptation to a psychological variable in any field of human endeavor presupposes a familiarity with the variable, which in the present instance is student differences. Thus, if the latter are to be adapted to, the teacher must know what they are. The problem can be conveniently, but unsatisfactorily, resolved by calling up the defense of a heavy teacher load and the weight of student numbers to "prove" that the problem is unsolvable. This may provide a soporific, but it is not an answer. No teacher admittedly can develop a clinically complete picture of each of his 120 or more students; but neither can any teacher, without censure, fail to utilize selected pertinent information that is readily available about any or all of them.

A minimum requirement of a teacher of one of the academic subjects in a guidance-minded school is a knowledge of the I.Q.'s and reading scores of all students, which should be listed in the grade book. These data could be supplemented by past marks, test achievement scores, and other behavioral information, as the occasion warranted. To the counter argument that the average teacher does not know enough about such data to interpret them properly, we suggest that it is high time he learned. Ignorance of a basic requirement in any profession compounds, without excusing, incompetency.

Classroom grouping

The effective teacher of whatever subject must be supported by a reasonably adequate understanding of the students' abilities and personalities. He next studies the curriculum to determine what parts best lend themselves to large- and small-group endeavor. Current practice, in this connection, is one of the poorest guides, because its weight of emphasis is preponderantly on the side of large-group instruction. Rejecting accepted practices, the knowledgeable teacher takes his cues from his own classroom observations and from those pertinent clinical data that he has available or can procure from a guidance office. From this mosaic background of information, he emerges with an accordion-like plan which will bring the adolescents together for common endeavor and separate them when their needs and interests can best be served in that way.

We shall illustrate with a description of a ninth-grade English class, not grouped by ability, with an I.Q. range of from 85 to 145 and a reading range on easy material from grades 6 through 12. There is a general departmental curriculum which requires for the first semester: the group reading of *A Tale of Two Cities* and *As You Like It;* the free reading of novels and non-fiction on a book-a-month basis; grammar and written expression to support a maximum goal of a three-paragraph theme for some and at least a one-paragraph project for the remainder; and speech competencies to be developed as an outgrowth of the other activities.

In such an academic framework, the teacher, after relating to the known, next turns to the blanks that demand filling in. In the former are the departmental requirements, student I.Q. scores, grade-level placement of the class, and the reading speeds of the students. In the category of the unknown are student interests, personality types, skills of expression and study habits. The first few weeks of the class he devotes to the process of getting acquainted with students and of orienting them to the curriculum. Also, during that time, he probably administers a pre-test on English usage to provide additional background data.

As the semester begins to unfold, the entire class group holds common sessions on such projects as the group readings, discussions of future requirements, supervised study, speech undertakings, and socializing activities. The purpose of these is the democratic sharing of a wide range of ideas and attitudes emanating from just as many sources as the number present at any one time in the classroom. In the many exchanges, the slow at times retard the fast, and the fast occasionally lose the slow; but the teacher, as a trained mediator, with patience and care unblocks communication with a minimum of dislocation to all.

Interspersed with these class-sized projects are small-group and individual performances related more specifically to unique student interests and needs. If, for instance, ten of the total of 30 students "proficiency out" of grammar drill on the pre-tests, they are excused to engage in more meaningful activity when the other 20 are focusing on usage. And some of the latter depart from the group of 20 as they too convince the teacher of their relative proficiency.

In the area of writing, at least a few of the 30 reveal a dire need for the fundamentals of structure, being uncertain about even the basic sentence itself. These the teacher works with as a group and individually, to help them meet at least minimum standards of competency. At the next level are some students who can write one paragraph fairly well, including a topic sentence, a single idea, and transition to the next paragraph; a few who can do a passable job with a three-paragraph theme; and maybe one or two who can respond to the greater sophistication of creative writing. Whatever the specific levels, the teacher's task is to intermingle small-group with large-group activities in such a way that the boring monotony of repetition for the bright, and the frustrations to the dull who can not understand, are held to a minimum.

In the group-reading sessions, the brighter students are asked to react to the subtler nuances of the social or political episodes related by Dickens in *A Tale of Two Cities* or to the more complex components of personality in *As You Like It*. The less favored, each at his own level, is expected in like manner to respond to appropriate ideas and events. In the area of free reading, the student with the I.Q. of 145 is helped to select, if he does not do so on his own accord, monthly reading projects commensurate with his high response potential. The very slow reader with the I.Q. of 85 likewise is expected to rise up to, but never above, his optimum literary stature.

In such a framework do we envision the needs of students being met in either a heterogeneous or a homogeneous classroom by the thoughtful and well-planned efforts of a classroom teacher. Each curriculum area will inevitably confront the teacher with its unique problems of content and teaching methods; but, in spite of such problems, far more possibilities for intra-classroom grouping exist in any subject than have yet been attempted by most teachers. The horizons of the future, thus, hold a great lure for experimentation within any one class, and the teacher should not be diverted unduly into the pursuit of more sensational means of method innovations which cut across class lines.

The differentiated assignment

Related to the attempts at individualization described in the previous section is the so-called *differentiated assignment*. As the caption implies, this is a multi-faceted assignment which asks for varying levels and quantities of student response. Its lowest denominator is usually a task that the slow can perform within the reasonable work demands of the teacher and school system. By the same logic, the average and fast would accomplish the task with greater dispatch. Superimposed on it for the more gifted customarily are one or more additional projects designed to elicit additional effort. Each of these levels is related only to the ability of a pupil to accomplish; none has any bearing on "extra credit for extra work"—a dubious practice, at best.

The multi-assignment, for example, in algebra, might involve a basic eight problems for all, an additional three of more complex nature for the average, and practical areas of application of the problems, in addition to these eleven, for the fast. Or, in the group reading of *A Tale of Two Cities,* the entire class might be assigned a designated eight to ten pages to be read; a second-level aggregate of pupils might be asked to report on excerpts from the life of Dickens; and a top cluster of students might be invited to gather data and report on the historical background of the novel. Such additional work for the more capable can be accomplished either by a demand built into the assignment or by the friendly persuasion of a personable teacher. The less the assignment coerces, the better.

Method variety is essential

Less spectacular than small-group work and the multi-level assignment, but not of less efficacy in its sensitivity to the differences among students, is method variety practiced by the insightful classroom teacher. As we have stated several times previously, learning is multi-sensory, and instructional media that draw on the several senses provide a better guarantee of learning's outcomes than media that are confined to the single sense. And even within any one sensory dimension, diversification increases learning's possibilities. Thus, the informal or even the incidental formal lecture has a distinct contribution to make if it is not permitted to monopolize. But interspersed in the classroom panorama must also be the socialized methods, the use of selected audio-visual media, verbal analyses in juxtaposition to reading, and the fitting of many other methods into a learning sequence as a defensible means of utilizing variety to adjust to student diversity.

Supervised study

Without belaboring a mode of meeting differences developed earlier in Chapter 8, we re-emphasize the values of supervised study in enabling a classroom leader to identify with a student where he is and to help him to grow from that point. This is one of the individualized methods of instruction that escapes most of the shortcomings of mass education. But if this one-to-one relationship is as highly contributory to growth as most authorities impute, the teacher-dominated group activities in the typical classroom must lose some of their rigidity.

The unit plan

Another backward flash reveals the unit of learning as a dedicated medium of injecting some degree of individualization into teaching. From the teacher's standpoint, it encourages him to create something from the diverse professional knowledges and devices of his own background, relating the creation, not to adolescents in general, as does a textbook, but to an identified group of adolescents in a given classroom. From the student's viewpoint, if properly conceived, it provides him with choices of content and learning method that enable him to respond in a specialized way to new educational vistas. The unit plan, while no guarantor of set outcomes, is designed to encourage both teacher and pupil individualism.

The special conference

Like supervised study, the special free-period or after-school conference between a teacher and a student can do wonders in integrating learning with the needs of the individual student. Alexander and Halverson identify the academic uses of the conference as follows:

1. To talk with the pupil about his learning problems and outline procedures which may help him solve these problems
2. To suggest activities, projects, investigations, and other individual undertakings which may be more profitable to the learner than those which he has selected on his own or in small group planning
3. To discuss learning experiences which the pupil has missed for illness or other reasons, and plan steps whereby he may undertake these or related experiences on his own
4. To explain concepts, processes, or information which the pupil has not understood in group work
5. To answer questions the pupil has raised in class that were not appropriate for group discussion, or questions that he has asked the teacher to answer in conference
6. To give specific direction to study procedures, and observe the pupil in use of these procedures
7. To lend a sympathetic ear to the pupil's problems, and give him the security that comes from confidence in one's teacher
8. To go over specific pieces of work and test papers to help the pupil understand his difficulties, and praise him for improvement and achievement
9. To review the pupil's self-evaluation of his learning experiences, and plan next steps in the light of such evaluation

10. To outline a procedure for study of a problem of interest to the pupil and beyond the interests and abilities of other class members
11. To plan learning experiences which will be related to the pupil's unique vocational interests or present work activities
12. To help the pupil plan for special roles he has in the class or school organization[13]

Commendable as the above purposes may be, the factor of time looms as a block to the conference's effectiveness. Its employment can never be separated from such other obligations as scholarly research to maintain professional status, planning, administrative duties, and evaluative procedures. The conscientious teacher personalizes wherever he can, but escapes guilt by setting up limits.

Referral to specialists

Finally, when a classroom teacher has exhausted his own resources, he contemplates the advisability of referral. The precipitating reason might be one of a number of possibilities: a rapid learner but low achiever who cannot be reached by ordinary means; a student two to three grade levels behind his class in reading ability despite many indications of brightness; a withdrawn student who eludes extrovert contacts; or an aggressive male youngster who is trying to grow up much too fast. The only two sound bases for referral, however, are the best interests of the individual adolescent or of the class. The goal must always be positive, shunning such base purposes as a teacher's desire to escape the added burden that individual differences inevitably bring.

Even when referral is deemed necessary on completely positive grounds, the possibilities are rarely as great or the path as smooth as most guidance texts would indicate. In the median-sized school of 300 to 400 students previously alluded to, the only likely referral agents associated with the school proper would be the teaching principal or a very much part-time speech therapist or county social worker who might make his rounds too seldom to be of help in an emergency. Nor would the principal necessarily be any better trained for referral purposes than the teacher. For these reasons, even though the teacher is scarcely ever a trained therapist, because he will have to live with emotional problems, he will do his best, as a "reasonable" legal parent, to alleviate them. Even though no reading specialist, he will have to improvise ways, if necessary, to render reading deficiencies less harmful. And although no vocational expert, he might well become enmeshed in the administering of an occasional Kuder test as well as in interpreting the results.

[13] William M. Alexander and Paul M. Halverson, *Effective Teaching in Secondary Schools* (New York: Holt, Rinehart and Winston, Inc., 1956), pp. 361–362. Reprinted by permission.

A LAST WORD

As inescapable as planning to be done and papers to be graded will be the ever-manifest or concealed differences of pupils with which the school and the teacher will have to contend. At a time when pupil differences were little recognized, the teacher was justified in regimenting and routinizing educational practices with respect to them. But with the insights that exist today regarding the differences of young people, learning cannot be permitted to stay detached from the dynamics of the learner himself. This point of view categorically does away with a fixed curriculum that rigidly resists change regardless of the needs of the student body. Rather, it charges secondary education with recognizing and responding to the differences of adolescents, whether the students are slow- or fast-witted, non-college or college-bound, resistive or pliant, mechanically or academically oriented, from a submarginal social group or the middle class; regardless of such considerations, the curriculum and teachers must meet the uniqueness of students more than halfway. The individual, for brief periods, might understandably be lost in the mass endeavors of a school, but a rescue can never be too long in forthcoming, if education is to accomplish its mission. Since individual differences are here to stay, the teacher candidate thus needs to face them as a reality. Only then will he be ready, or at least partially ready, for their impact.

SUMMARY

The differences among students identified in the preceding chapter were faced in this chapter from the point of view of teaching method. First of all, it was pointed out that slow and rapid learners must be approached differently in the teaching process, with those methods anchored in concretion succeeding better with the former and with methods drawing on the verbal abstract succeeding better with the latter. Other differences were identified in terms of a need for more versus less curriculum quantity, for greater versus less methods variety, and for a slower versus a faster pace of teaching.

The three broad avenues to teaching students of varying abilities, interests, and skills were identified as: (1) the time-tested administrative measures of constants and electives, the multi-track, the effective use of guidance data, the summer school, and course-load restrictions; (2) homogeneous grouping by ability; and (3) teacher practices in the classroom. Homogeneous grouping was treated as an experiment in education whose results are yet to be fully realized and analyzed. A tentative conclusion was that, with the proper emotional atmosphere existing, a positive outcome may be presaged.

However, the most important key to the process of ministering to student differences that was highlighted throughout was the classroom teacher. It was stated that only through his good efforts could the tremendous curriculum task realize successful fulfillment.

REFERENCES

Blair, Glenn Myers, *Diagnostic and Remedial Teaching*. New York: The Macmillan Co., 1956.

Bryan, J. Ned (Director of Project), *The Identification and Education of the Academically Talented Student in the American Secondary School*. Washington, D.C.: National Education Association, 1958.

Conant, James B., *The American High School Today*. New York: McGraw-Hill Book Co., 1959.

De Haan, Robert F., and Robert J. Havighurst, *Education for Gifted Children*. Chicago: University of Chicago Press, 1957.

Garrison, Karl C., *The Psychology of Exceptional Children*. New York: The Ronald Press Co., 1950.

Getzels, Jacob W., and Philip W. Jackson, *Creativity and Intelligence*. New York: John Wiley and Sons, 1962.

Kettelkamp, Gilbert C., *Teaching Adolescents*. Boston: D. C. Heath and Co., 1954.

Kirk, Samuel A., and G. Orville Johnson, *Educating the Retarded Child*. Boston: Houghton Mifflin Co., 1951.

Magnifico, L. X., *Education for the Exceptional Child*. New York: Longmans, Green and Co., 1958.

National Society for the Study of Education, *Individualizing Instruction, Sixty-First Yearbook*. Chicago: University of Chicago Press, 1962.

United States Department of Health, Education, and Welfare, Office of Education. *The Gifted Student*. (Cooperative Research) Washington, D.C.: Monograph No. 2, 1960.

Williams, Harold, *The Retarded Child Goes to School*. Washington, D.C.: U.S. Department of Health, Education, and Welfare, Pamphlet No. 123, 1960.

Witty, Paul (ed.). *The Gifted Child*. Boston: D. C. Heath and Co., 1951.

EVALUATING
GROWTH
OTHER THAN
BY CLASSROOM TESTING

Like the phenomenon of human differences, the process of evaluation is inseparable from living. Whenever one person reacts to another, he is engaging in evaluation. Whether he reacts innocuously —as, for instance, toward another's appearance—or spiritedly, as toward a character trait, is irrelevant; the important point is that appraisal is taking place. The same inexorable life process goes on when a newspaper is being read, a television program is being observed, or a crisis is being experienced. Anyone who reads or listens with even a limited degree of understanding about the currently increasing decline of colonialism is bound to react to it with a point of view. This is evaluation. And the same individual who agonizes over a speech poorly delivered or a careless remark indiscreetly dropped is analyzing a segment of life. He is an evaluator. In simple terms, *evaluation* is the process of making a judgment about a person, object, episode, or situation. It can be of positive or negative import, significant or trifling, prearranged or incidental; but, regardless of type or quality of the judgment, the act itself falls into the category of evaluation.

Since the process is universal, it has particular

significance for the teacher, whose preoccupation daily, and even hourly, is with pupil actions which invite assessment against a value system. To praise or to blame, to sympathize or to remain detached, to fail or to pass—these are only instances of the myriad of demands for decision-making that confront the teacher as he plays his complex role. To add to the burden, because he is scarcely ever possessed of inviolable evidence to back up his judgments, he must lean heavily on subjective observation for support. But, regardless of inaccuracy, practitioners of psychology and education, because of their close involvement with individuals, are committed to evaluating those with whom they come in contact. Nor can they wait for absolutism, as Thorndike and Hagen made clear in their excellent 1961 book-long treatment of measurement.[1]

When practitioners rely on arithmetical specificity as a basis for making their decisions, their method is referred to as *measurement* rather than *evaluation*. A pencil, for instance, is *evaluated* as usable, short, cylindrical, or hard; but it is *measured* as six or seven inches long and a quarter of an inch wide. In the same manner, a test may be evaluated as difficult, possessed of a low ceiling, long, or diagnostic. But when the term "difficult" is translated into the 10 or 12 low scores of those who failed, "low ceiling" into the revelation that 15 of 30 made perfect scores, "long" into units of time, and "diagnostic" into the specific strengths and weaknesses that the test revealed, the greater specifics of measurement are revealed. *Evaluation* is the broader term, including, but not necessarily being limited to, the arithmetical or statistical refinements of measurement. The cherished goal of all evaluative researchers and practitioners is to reduce the phenomena of behavior to units of measurement and computational specifics; but since this goal is only an ideal, subjective assessment becomes an ally. In fact, since most phenomena are not measurable, evaluators are routinely conditioned to rely on the good services of evaluation apart from the greater refinements of measurement.

PURPOSES OF EVALUATION

The typical school is literally permeated with appraisal. Thus, it is reasonable to suppose that a sustaining body of educational and psychological theory exists to give appraisal greater meaning. Such substantiating theory does exist, but its construction is more along common-sense than statistical lines. This is not an indictment. Grounded as it is in the method of careful observation, such theory is no less an effective guide to educational practice. The fundamental question is: Why evaluate? The answers differ in substance and degree, depending on who is giving them—the profession as a whole, the classroom teacher, or the school administrator.

[1] Robert L. Thorndike and Elizabeth P. Hagen, *Measurement and Evaluation in Psychology and Education* (New York: John Wiley and Sons, 1961), p. 7.

Evaluation and the profession as a whole

To the institution of education as a national or state enterprise, evaluation in the schools serves to keep the mammoth undertaking on the right track. Education, wherever it is found, is underwritten by preconceived purposes. If one of these is pupil growth in the skills of reading, listening, writing, computing, and speaking, appraisal is foundational to a determination of the quality of performance rendered by the profession as a whole or any major part thereof. If other objectives are growth of the emotions, social skills, or attitudes, appraisal is no less necessary merely because these qualities are more resistant to evaluative accuracy. In any event, broad national purposes have set the limits for the many local operational units, and society quite logically expects a constant assessment of the quality of conformance at each level. The centralized projection is understandably in terms of general norms and broad deviations therefrom; the decentralized counterpart is always more specific, directed mostly at smaller group and individual performance.

Evaluation and the teacher

Not unlike his institutional counterpart, the classroom teacher also has purposes which demand continuous analysis both as to their "face validity" and their effectiveness in generating defensible pupil behavior. If a curriculum in English sets for all students at the end of their first semester in school a goal of a well-written paragraph, the plausibility of the goal can be discerned only in terms of tangible results, which must emanate from some type of evaluation. And if, in addition to the local institutional objectives, the teacher interpolates one of his own—namely, that all students will use the dictionary with discrimination—he thereby assigns himself an added task of determining to what extent students are responding to the interpolated curriculum addition.

Unlike the larger enterprise of education, however, the classroom teacher, without rejecting the benefits of mass data, must be vitally concerned with the behavioral characteristics of each individual adolescent under his supervision. More important to the teacher than whether *Silas Marner* should be a part of the curriculum (a moot issue) is whether Bob Burton, with an I.Q. of 90, is responding to the stimulus of the book's content. And of as much concern to the teacher of health education as the cognitive readiness of a class of juniors to discuss the topic of sex is their emotional readiness and that of their parents for the exposure.

The instructional leader's job is thus a diagnostic one, leading him from the relative safety of broadly conceived norms and happenings far away to such close-at-hand questions as: How well have my students been doing in the United States history course that I am teaching three times a

day? And, of equal importance: How well are Jeff Timkin and Jack San-
ford doing as of this moment? In the process of answering these and related questions, the teacher is made aware of the strengths and limitations
of the students and the quality of his teaching. Yet, if a shortcoming is
revealed in the learning outcome, he should not automatically assume sole
responsibility for it. The children are under his auspices only two to three
per cent of their waking moments in any one year. Therefore, he should
no more absorb a disproportionate share of the blame for pupils' failures
than he would for their successes. Regardless of the extent of his responsibility, however, he is professionally obligated to assess growth in many
dimensions to the end of analyzing the adolescent, the curriculum, and
himself as a basic step toward improving any or all of them.

Evaluation thus is an inventory-taking process designed to familiarize
those affected with their progress toward formulated goals. The ever-
present hope is that the insights thereby provided will be of such moment
as to arouse activity which will lead ultimately to change. Evaluation that
is followed by inertia smacks of futility and waste; but when it leads to
dynamic action designed to improve, it is defensibly purposeful.

Evaluation and the administrator

To the school administrator, appraisal constitutes a means of analyzing behavior and then converting it into a language of symbols that can
be interpreted meaningfully at any time and perpetuated economically
when no longer immediately useful. Guidance records of pupils are no
more and no less than symbolic pictures of individuals and the events that
have shaped them. And through the medium of carefully designed appraisal, the picture is condensed to a size that can be comprehended and
understood. Into the guidance record go such components as a counselor's
comments, a pupil's final test score, a nurse's explanation of an absence,
or an I.Q. Each of these is a product of evaluation, which, along with
other "still pictures," soon evolves as a filmstrip which makes possible
more accurate diagnosis and determination of subsequent steps.

Also of considerable significance to education is the administrative
use of evaluation as a determiner of the eligibility of pupils for promotion.
If secondary school enrollment conveys more meaning than just bare attendance for four years, some means of formulating and assessing standards for movement from subject to subject and from grade to grade is
basic. Once more, evaluation offers its good services.

UNDERLYING PRINCIPLES

Possessed of a close affinity to the pur-
poses of evaluation are the principles that undergird its employment.

These, of necessity, must lead to more than a stoic acceptance of the process by a teacher. To achieve maximum benefit, evaluation must, on the contrary, be regarded as an interesting and challenging, even though often frustrating, function. Once more we look to common-sense theory for its viewpoints on the subject.

Evaluation is rarely exact

One of theory's most clearly enunciated and certain-toned statements is that evaluation, even at its best, is seldom exact. This is another way of saying that all human beings are fallible, that the products of their minds are thus commensurately inaccurate, and that standards which have exact dimensions are scarce commodities in life. The twelve-inch ruler, although accurate enough to serve routine purposes, fails the test of exactness. And as one descends the scale of inaccuracy to such poorer approximations of accuracy as oral quizzes, written tests, observation, and other subjectively based methods, the human equation always comes up wanting. Particularly in the area of values does fallibility appear.

In the 1930's, education became enamored of the cliché, "Whatever can be taught can be evaluated." This unleavened bit of positivism generated only a minimum of protest when aligned with the tangibles of learning: for instance, number of sentences corrected properly, number of commas improperly employed, or the errors in developing the binomial theorem. But when allowed to hover too long in the intangibles of ethics, morality, classroom social behavior, or creativity, the rumblings of discontent began to multiply. The opposition, although very much in favor of these behavioral intangibles undergoing appraisal in and out of the classroom, rebelled at the implication that accurate assessment was possible.

Values of any kind make assessment approximate, at best, because standards of value determination are elusive and often situational. In the world of symbols, goodness may be easily distinguished from badness, and rightness from wrongness, but in the world of behavior, distinctions usually are not so readily obvious. And even when they are obvious, degrees of difference are difficult to determine. This value issue is illustrated in the following. The elementary school primers of the 1920's contained an anecdote that left many readers groping. It had to do with a young American soldier who, in the face of enemy fire, rushed up a steep hill to put the American flag back into place after its alleged desecration by the enemy forces. The intended moral was that, although the lad lost his life, patriotism conquered. Teacher or student concerned with intrinsic values, however, could judge the outcome in a number of ways:

1. Since an important national symbol must be protected at all costs, the act was not only heroic but was demanded by the circumstances. (chauvinism)

2. Human worth is of supreme essence; therefore, the sacrifice was inexcusable. (humanism)

3. The military conditions men into Pavlovian-like responses; thus, the act was part of a habitual syndrome. (behavioral associationism)

4. The boy was an exhibitionist and "grandstanded," despite the risks, as a method of building his ego. The act was more bravado than bravery. (dynamic theory)

The crux of evaluating an episode such as the above is the non-existence of an inflexible standard of correctness. This type of confrontation in the classroom is not unusual, usually leading the teacher and class into polarities of thoughtful divergence and diffusion. Evaluation always gets more restive when edging toward the value intangibles where issues are shaded and standards blurred. At the other extreme, evaluation is more comfortable in situations where rightness and wrongness stand out more sharply in contrast with each other.

The teacher is a fallible judge

If evaluation is only rarely exact, one reason is the human error that goes into the process. The foot ruler previously mentioned may be 11.99 or 12.01 inches to begin with; but when applied to measure the circumference of a room, the original marginal error of .01 inch becomes cumulatively greater. What even more dramatic evidence of inaccuracy, then, must exist in a situation where the teacher's personality, particularly under aroused emotion, becomes involved in the function of appraisal? Each teacher evaluates in a particular way because of what he has been, is, and wishes to be. He brings personal qualities and attitudes, professional conditioners, and a unique background of experience to each of his value judgments. Yet, despite the fallibility of teachers, they must make judgments day after day about the mental and physical health of pupils, motivation, achievement, and the many other adjustments of pupils to the multi-faceted dynamics of the classroom.

Evaluation is an inseparable curriculum function. Moreover, personality inadequacy operates against its accurate employment. Therefore, the teacher and teacher candidate need to introspect almost constantly to ascertain whether such diluters of reality as rationalization, projection, and internalization are being kept under control. When these personal factors have free play, judgmental distortions as great as a set of standardized test results scored by the wrong key would be entirely possible. Pertinent to this dependency of the mental upon the emotional is A. H. Maslow's comment, paraphrased, that the emotionally blocked person is not only psychologically off center but cognitively wrong. The following examples project this two-way relationship between the emotional and the cognitive into the classroom.

1. Mr. Donat, a teacher of chemistry, is hired by a local high school. His record reflects honors-type performance throughout college, and he personally reports that science was always easy for him. In his first year of teaching, he operates heavy-handedly with the average and below-average students in his classes, impugning their sincerity and questioning their efforts. In this instance, Mr. Donat's cognitive expectations for certain types of students would be just as erroneous as his ability to see reality was obscured by his own ego involvement.

2. Mr. Cansler has manic-depressive moods. When he is "down," pupil behavior never seems to be right; when he is "up," almost nothing in the classroom environment seems to be wrong. Obviously, his intellect is invariably clouded or otherwise victimized by the extremes of his emotions.

3. Mr. McClure is the strictest of religionists, believing that when youth make incorrect behavioral choices, they are sinning against God. Thus, to him "acting up" is "bad," and plagiarism almost a deadly sin. Accordingly, his counseling effectiveness is destroyed to the extent that his narrow emotionalized views block him from an acceptance of the complex causality of behavior.

Just as surely as the lack of scholarship closes the door to curriculum potential, too much emotional distortion in a teacher, particularly when it veers toward neuroticism, has a comparably devastating effect. Learning substance infiltrated through the disruptive emotions assumes disruptive characteristics. But when infiltrated through the wholesomeness of a mentally healthy classroom teacher, the substance loses emotional falsity. Evaluation, to realize its almost limitless possibilities, thus must be engaged in by one who has not only depth of intellectual background but also clarity of emotional vision.

Evaluation should be continuous and comprehensive

Not just a climax at the end of an episode, evaluation at its best is an interrelated part of the total life of a classroom. It makes an appearance as early as the first few moments of teaching, when tentative judgments are being made about the class as a whole. It is next channeled at the two or three individuals who, for differing reasons, always seem to stand out in some specialized way. And it continues to unfold until interwoven into literally every facet of the learning milieu.

The comprehensiveness of evaluation is just as great as the goals of the classroom are extensive. If these include the cognitive, as they certainly do, evaluation is obligated to do likewise. If they incorporate the personal-emotional, personal-physical, and the social, the latter three also must be submitted to the same revealing mirror of appraisal. The process begins when a class begins, extends into all areas of growth, and legitimately ends only when the school semester or year has terminated.

STEPS IN EVALUATION

In addition to the refining influences of purposes and principles, which have just been discussed, evaluation when applied to a practical situation needs the validating support of structure. Procedurally, the process should pursue a sequence which originates with goal formulation, leads to the accumulation of pertinent evidence, is followed by the making of a value judgment, and is capped by a determination of next steps. Examples of this sequence in two distinctive areas of growth should prove helpful.

Area I—the emotional. John Franzen is a sophomore in high school enrolled in Mr. White's geometry class. He has an I.Q. of 112, does average or better work in mathematics, but manifests personality traits that are off the center of normal. In a class of 28 pupils, John presses aggressively to be the first called on when many or few hands are raised, regularly interrupts others without apology, and customarily relates situations to his own life. When John and a peer associate approach an entrance together, John expects the associate to give ground. When engaged in committee work, John insists on being chairman. When receiving grades of C or below, he always questions the accuracy of the teacher's judgment with a typical remark such as: "But why am I always wrong and you always right?"

Relating to this set of circumstances, Mr. White:

1. *Determines the goal.* In this instance, it would be: the better understanding of John's social behavior, to the end of helping him to make it more acceptable to himself and others.

2. *Accumulates evidence.* Mr. White observes John's behavior carefully for a period of several weeks, prepares anecdotes as required, studies appropriate records in the guidance office, and talks to colleagues who formerly had, or currently have, John in class.

3. *Makes a judgment.* From the accumulated information, Mr. White next makes a judgment that most nearly harmonizes with the evidence at hand. It might be any or none of the following: (a) John is rigidly straitjacketed in the home and thus feels the need to compensate by attention-getting mannerisms in the school; (b) he is the center of attention of fatuous parents in the home, doing almost as he pleases, and plays the same role in school; (c) his self-image is so unsatisfactory that it needs constant bolstering; (d) he is suspected of having an oversupply of inner sadism which gives him pleasure when he hurts others; or, and finally, (e) his case is too baffling to warrant other than a finding of "behavior is un-normal for causes unknown."

4. *Decide on next steps.* Depending on Mr. White's inferential judgment, the next steps might run the gamut from giving John more attention to giving him less, from regarding his behavior as not untypically adolescent to regarding it as very abnormal, from counseling with him personally

to working with him in the group, and from treating the case personally to referring it to another.

Area II—achievement. Barbara Walton is a bright low-achiever with an I.Q. of 122 and a C average "across the curriculum board." Miss Rea has her in a junior English class and, becoming increasingly interested in the problem, goes through a comparable sequential process, as did Mr. White. She:

1. *Determines the goal.* It is to look beneath the surface of external events to determine what dynamic causes exist for Barbara's inadequate performance.

2. *Accumulates evidence.* Miss Rea checks the over-all academic record, takes note of Barbara's co-curricular activities, talks to her about the problem, consults Barbara's counselor, and observes the young lady carefully to discover consistencies and inconsistencies in the learning response pattern.

3. *Makes a judgment.* Like Mr. White, Miss Rea reaches a conclusion: it might be that Barbara is disinterested in school because her parents are indifferent about it; she is in too many activities, thus spreading herself too thin; or she has always followed the pleasure principle of doing "just what I feel like doing"—in itself, only another symptom.

4. *Decides on next steps.* The final action might be a verbal insistence on higher standards of performance, retention after school to assure quality work, a talk to parents, the blocking out of a time schedule for Barbara to follow, or a conference ending on the note: "It is your life, Barbara; only you can choose or reject quality."

In both of these situations, the respective teachers in effect have pursued a problem-solving sequence, utilizing in the process their own resources without ignoring the other resources around them. But, most important, their efforts have been made more meaningful through organization. Such a purposeful approach to insight provides completeness and balance that might be lacking when only hit-or-miss procedures are employed.

SPECIFIC METHODS OF EVALUATION

Whatever specific approaches to appraisal are taken, the broader the scope of the data, the better. In this regard, therapists of almost any orientation—the non-directivists occasionally to the contrary—welcome the added assurance that only extensity along with needed intensity can bring. Since the teacher is a therapist in a broadly conceived sense, he is no exception to this general rule. What, then, are the methods of evaluation other than testing (the topic of the next chapter) in which he might engage, or the results of which he might consult, for counseling purposes? Teacher-employed methods will be considered initially, followed by self- and peer-evaluation. Regarding the former, the following list maps the specific avenues of appraisal open to the classroom teacher.

1. Informal observation.
2. Formal observation.
3. Written projects.
4. Oral methods.
5. Academic record.
6. Interview.
7. Health record.

8. Home and family questionnaire.
9. Home visit.
10. Log and diary.
11. Autobiography.
12. Sociometry.
13. Cumulative record.

Informal observation

Ranking first in the list of evaluative devices is informal observation, which with little hesitation we identify as the most comprehensive as well as the most significant. In the teacher's repertoire, none can take its place, for it is the heart of the evaluative process. The discerning teacher who has observed behavior with keenness of vision for a protracted period of time may experience an occasional surprise at the unexpected outcome of written work or of a test result, but more often the written outcomes will serve only to refine his already formulated estimates. The more specific evaluative methods, such as testing, respond to measurement's mandate of quantification, but they rarely lead to dramatic change in the opinion arrived at through insightful observation.

The modifier "informal" describes the psychological viewing engaged in by a careful observer who is interested in the behavior of people. Behavior itself is treated as a reflector of a pattern of inner dynamics which are better understood when thus mirrored outwardly. Certain readers at this point may react tritely: "We aren't psychiatrists; therefore, we shouldn't be expected to read the externally projected signposts." Our reply is from relativity. If teachers are not psychiatrists, they are at least legal parents to whom has been delegated the responsibility to observe children as keenly as do well-educated, insightful blood parents. This duty places the teacher somewhere between the therapist-specialist and the subject matter extremist who rejects almost any accountability for students.

Informal observation is a profitable, though a demanding, part of every effective teacher's relationship with pupils and the total classroom situation. The instructional leader observes in many ways: by insisting on and maintaining eye contact with pupils; by noticing signs of nervousness, such as glandular secretions, speech irregularities, and kinetic mannerisms; by noting and assaying social behavior; by responding to daydreaming and other indicators of inattention; by reacting to student recitations and other types of academic responses; and by determining gradations of tolerance to the ever-fluctuating academic, social, and emotional pressures. These and other dynamic constituents come under the critical eye and appraisal of the student-oriented teacher who is convinced that, the more he knows about the class members, the better he can relate to their differences. Never pretending to be an expert, he begins teaching recognizing his many shortcomings, and then grows toward insight through cumulative experience and study.

Formal observation

The difference between the informal and the formal types of observation is that the latter is more definitively organized into a system of procedures and time coverage. As a planned implementation of the over-all observational technique, it demands a previously identified focal center of emphasis and a time schedule in which the process of formal observation will take place. By way of illustration, we shall assume a hypothetical situation in which June Amyx, long an object of controversy in the school, is to be studied by the many professional individuals who are in frequent contact with her. As part of the collective study, selected teachers are requested to observe her periodically in a systematic way and, at a convenient time afterward, to write their anecdotes for future clinical analysis.

Assume that the following two anecdotes are turned in to the counselor:

ANECDOTAL RECORD I

Date: February 15, 19—   *Place:* Shorthand 1, Room 304

Name of Pupil: June Amyx   *Teacher:* Alice Merry

I watched June for ten minutes this morning, and she was obviously nervous and upset. She almost seemed to be beside herself. When I called on her for a recitation, she was emotional. This was not her good day.

ANECDOTAL RECORD II

Date: February 15, 19—   *Place:* Office Practice, Room 302

Name of Pupil: June Amyx   *Teacher:* Ruth Inman

I observed June closely for the first ten minutes of class this morning. She arrived two minutes early, went first to the back of the room, looked out the window for a few seconds, clenched her fists once, sat down in a rear seat, and then moved to her own seat when the bell rang.

She bit her nails for two or three minutes after class began, then stopped. She crossed her legs back and forth several times in the ten-minute period.

I asked her in the course of the recitation to discuss the importance of keeping official information, in an office, secret. She stuttered during the first few seconds of her answer, flushed perceptibly, but recited accurately.

Late in the class period, when she seemed not to be paying attention, I asked her if she was listening. She replied: "Of course. I always listen."

Both anecdotes are formally presented, proceduralized, and narrowed to time and place. The first, however, is faulty in that it is unspecific, containing too many color words which have no more exact meaning than the individual who uses or interprets them. The second does a rather commendable job of reporting the facts of the case, pinning them down behaviorally in terms of what was done, for how long, and to what degree of intensity. Furthermore, it refrains from evaluating the anecdote, preferring apparently to let that await the gathering of a larger body of evidence.

The anecdotal-record or formal observational technique, because of its recognized clinical value, is used with reported success by a number of disciplines: psychology, medicine, social work, and education. The teacher's dilemma is that his relationships with "clients" is not primarily a one-to-one affair. In fact, with the masses clamoring for attention, he can employ the technique only sparingly, and then usually only as part of a team approach to a problem. When such occasions arise, however, his assignment is clear-cut: plan the time and place of the observation; pay close heed to the specifics of the behavior; record them clearly, shunning vague, emotional words; and delay a conclusion until the data are considerable enough to warrant it.

Written projects

Complementing the method of informal observation is the written work of various kinds that adolescents do in and outside of class. For some students, primarily the less verbal, it may be a chore; for others, it often constitutes a very necessary release for creativity and expression. For the teacher, written work represents a projection of student personality that invests evaluation with tangible substance.

Written work takes on many shapes and forms in the typical secondary school classroom. In the English class, it may be expository, the personal letter, the business letter, fact reporting, précis, descriptive, or creative. In the science class, it may be an experiment which culminates in a written report; in the language class, a translation; in the social studies class, a term paper or newspaper-article review. In any class, it may be a written examination or a homework assignment.

Regardless of type, the written project constitutes an avenue to appraisal that most teachers would sacrifice only after vigorous protest. When completed with a minimum of help from others, it provides teachers with insight into the ability of a student to report the substance of an event or situation, to report it with clarity, and to report it in a style that is linguistically acceptable or unacceptable. In addition, it is often a manifest extension of student personality, thereby serving as a projective technique. Written work of most kinds—and the written examination in particular—makes students organize their thoughts and ideas. This process of organization forces students to identify what they know about an issue, to relate the many sub-parts to the greater whole, and, finally, to present a defensible point of view. This becomes a synthesizing process which brings knowledge to a point of central focus. Thus, through the good services of the well-conceived written project, such outcomes as logical thinking and depth of concept analysis may be assayed. When the student is found wanting, evaluation will have served the legitimate purpose of uncovering a weakness to which the teacher can pay closer attention in the future.

Oral methods

Like written work in or out of the classroom, the many occasions for oral participation by students can also give the observing teacher a better perspective of performance and personality. Its manifestations are numerous: the informal question to which the pupil responds, the more formal recitation, spontaneous interaction within a class discussion, committee activity, and the formal report.

The purposes of teaching methods which revolve around the oral are primarily three in number. The first is the time-honored one of enabling a teacher to assess the quality of a pupil's academic performance: for instance, in a homework project done the night before, in a class discussion on a newly introduced concept, or in a long-term problem-solving project. Such opportunities provide both students and teachers with an index of student growth in terms of what has been learned factually as well as of the maturity of the students' response to it. Historically, oral methods have been prone to relate almost exclusively to knowledge previously covered, with factual repetition the keynote. The more current trend is not away from such knowledge, but more comprehensively toward the additional goals of greater understanding and refinement and the ability of a student to identify and defend a point of view. These are in harmony with the ever-expanding problem-solving tradition.

A second purpose of oral activities is personal-social. The many affairs of the world are conducted on the oral level, and a general-education function of the school is, thus, to help students ready themselves for the associated demands. From this vantage point, the accent in oral activities expands from the exclusively cognitive to the emerging personality of the speaker. In the process, speech situations are envisioned broadly to include the elements of (1) purpose of the communication, (2) content of the communication, (3) speech mechanics, (4) the speaker as a person, and (5) his insight into the listener. These more comprehensive goals point to oral activities in the classroom as a means of readying students for the speech demands of the social and vocational world. So conceived, they revolve around personality dynamics as much as around content and method, with the outcomes of inner control and sensitivity to the listener looming just as importantly as cognitive meaning.

A third significant function of oral work in the classroom is motivation. The rationale behind this purpose is that, if a student is made orally accountable for an assignment, he is thereby stimulated to complete it more satisfactorily. Adolescents, with the exception of the maladjusted, prefer success to failure in the eyes of their peers, and oral performances that measure up to defensible standards generally have prestige significance.

Whatever the motive, the maturing teacher cannot close the academic door upon speaking opportunities for students. Such rejection blocks his insight into the extent of cognitive learnings, personality growth, and interest. All of these are so necessary that none can be permitted to go undernourished.

The academic record

Another technique that contributes significantly to the appraisal overview is the past and current academic record of a student. Although any one part is unduly susceptible to the marking vagaries of an individual teacher at any given time, the totality of the picture usually has considerable fidelity as an indicator of performance quality, interest, and possible future action. Both the trends and the trend deviations in an academic record are revealing. For instance, a consistent pattern of success in mathematics constitutes at least prima facie evidence of ability and interest that might lead to such future vocational outcomes as market analysis, actuarial endeavor, or engineering. And comparable success in the language arts and social sciences might presage such possible outcomes as literary activity, law, or politics.

The trend deviation from a set academic pattern is also informative, being always suspect of either a teacher inconsistency or tangential behavior by the student. Specifically, we have in mind the long-term pattern that suddenly breaks out in distortion: for example, a student with all A's and B's in science from grades seven through eleven receives a D in the twelfth grade. Once the teacher who gave the low grade is exonerated, attention is next focused on the student, with an operational hypothesis being made that some decided change in the adolescent's life process was causal. The process of evaluation accordingly becomes more preoccupied with the reasons for the low grade than with the D by itself.

A sizable number of teachers, both experienced and neophyte, often hesitate to use the academic record as a tool of guidance lest it prejudice their attitudes toward students. A logical explanation for such hesitancy lies in society's almost morbid worship of those who can perform at a high level and a countering aversion for those who cannot. This immaturity in society can be brushed off more lightly than it can when allowed to permeate the emotions of teachers. The latter, as professionally oriented people, are obligated to develop clinical objectivity in appraising academic performance, and to shun infantile color associations in the process.

The interview

As in the preceding chapter, we again refer to the interview, this time as a diagnostic evaluative technique more than as an informal means of ministering to differences. In whatever discipline it is found, it appears in one of three ways: as *structured, developmental,* or *confessional.* The first is formal and one-sided, planned in advance by the interviewer, and involving a telling-listening situation. The developmental type contains only a modicum of structure, fluctuating with the ebb and flow of the dynamic content of the interview and revolving around two individuals with neither functionally dominant. It is common to therapy of most kinds. The confessional is aimed at catharsis, in which the interviewee purges himself before the interviewer. It is with respect to only the developmental type that we shall address these comments.

By its very nature, the interview is endowed with no prearranged structure, and it resists anything resembling a set sequence; yet it possesses definitive elements that are characteristic of it almost whenever employed. The basal steps are customarily these:

1. The interviewer, as required, establishes rapport.
2. The interviewee, if facing a vital concern, makes a number of false passes at the real problem.
3. The interviewee sooner or later identifies the real problem—sometimes early, sometimes not until hours of interview time have elapsed.
4. The problem is analyzed thoroughly by the participants.
5. In the process, the relevant and the spurious are separated.
6. The relevant is directed toward possible problem solutions.
7. The interviewee is helped to reach his own solutions, with the interviewer acting in a capacity of clarifier and supporter.
8. The agreed-upon plan of action is tried out and evaluated.

Upon examination, these steps are observed to resemble those of any problem-solving situation, as indeed they should, permeated as the interview is with problem content. The above eight steps are more accurately descriptive of a therapeutic session than of the typical school interview on educational, vocational, and non-depth personality matters, although their bearing even on the latter three types is more than incidental. In fact, if steps 2 and 3 were combined, the resulting seven would serve as a meaningful guide for almost any type of interview relationship.

Implied, if not actually stated, are these important considerations: (1) the two partners in the exchange must feel comfortable with each other; (2) the responsibility for this outcome is the interviewer's; (3) the latter can guide and clarify, but he cannot dictate; (4) he does not react with surprise or shock to any type of content; and (5) he regards decision-making the interviewee's responsibility. These principles, vital to any interview outside the framework of the structured type, are of greatest merit in that they unblock authoritarian strictures by encouraging freedom of verbal and emotional exchanges.

In the world of the practical, apart from administrative fiat, the principles of the interview have this message for counselors at any level: help students with problems by providing necessary information, by correcting obvious errors of substance, and by generally sharpening up issues, but don't dictate future action. Thus, if school policy does not forbid, an average-level learner who insists on enrolling in chemistry should probably be permitted to do so; or a relatively non-verbal student should be allowed to press toward journalism as a career if he resists the contrary evidence. The over-all goal of independence is, at best, never easy to reach and becomes even more elusive when the privilege of choosing among alternatives is too long or too often delayed by adult authority. It is better that there should be an occasional error of student choice than that he should not have the right to make it.

The health record

Like the academic record, its counterpart in the area of health provides a long-term overview of a student, often beginning as early as kindergarten although more often at the time of junior or regular high school enrollment. Maintained by a part- or full-time school nurse, it includes a record of the school-entrance examination and subsequent entries of significance. Although not of routine importance to the typical classroom teacher, it is a valuable resource when symptoms demand that health be identified or ruled out as a cause of a personal or academic problem. In this event, the teacher plays the role of observer, formal or informal, and consults with the school nurse or physician for an interpretation of his observed and other pertinent findings.

In a Northwestern University Summer School Class in 1961, fifteen secondary school teachers reported the following pathological symptoms observed during the previous three years in their classrooms, with the indicated results:

1. One case of extreme hypertension in an adolescent, with manifestations of irritability, easily triggered emotions, manic-depressive cycles, and restlessness. The ultimate referral diagnosis was *hyper* thyroidism.

2. Another case of a student who was overweight and lethargic, who slept in class with or without provocation, and who appeared emotionally dull. The referral diagnosis was *hypo* thyroidism.

3. A chronically underweight cougher with an ultimate diagnosis of tuberculosis.

4. Three cases of chronic fatigue and resultant under-achieving, with an ultimate diagnosis of mononucleosis.

5. Literally dozens of referrals of colds and suspected influenza cases which occasionally led to pneumonia diagnoses but more often to nothing more serious than a diagnosis of the common cold.

The teacher's responsibility for the physical health of pupils is one of both observation and referral. Once more, his role is that of the reasonable legal parent who is expected by law to practice common-sense rules of behavior. When religion comes into conflict with such rules, he refers the problem to a health specialist or administrator for final decision.

The home questionnaire

Providing information not readily accessible from other data-gathering devices is the home and family questionnaire, completed by a parent or the student himself immediately prior to, or at the time of, his school enrollment. The data thus provided, constituting a part of the student's cumulative record, are available to the teacher who may wish to evaluate pupil behavior against a background of home and family influences.

The questionnaire universally contains items which relate to the following and related areas:

The Family

1. Number and age of siblings.
2. Schooling of siblings.
3. Occupation of father and mother.
4. Education of father and mother.
5. Health of father and mother.
6. Whether home is owned or rented.
7. Language spoken in the home.
8. Publications regularly subscribed to.
9. How previous vacations were spent.
10. Special interests and hobbies of the family.

The Pupil

1. Elementary school attended.
2. Record of illnesses and hospitalizations.
3. Future occupational preferences.
4. Curriculum areas most enjoyed.
5. Favorite sports and other hobbies.
6. Favorite authors.
7. Clubs belonged to.
8. Specialized talents in music, art, drama, and so forth.
9. Work experience.
10. College plans.

Such information as the above contributes perspective to the guidance-oriented teacher who is searching for a better understanding of a student or students. However, the teacher must never forget the legal imperative to keep the knowledge thus gleaned in strict confidence. When this trust is violated in a careless remark made to an unauthorized recipient, it can boomerang to destroy community faith in the teacher and the school.

The home visit

Not unlike the preceding technique, the home visit also is designed to make the relationship between home and school more substantial. But unlike the contrasted medium, which is the epitome of economy, the home visit is only an ideal in many schools because of the time factor. Many teachers who would otherwise avail themselves of its good services are deterred by the time required to make the visits. Reducing the problem to the coldly practical, a typical high school teacher has 150 students enrolled in his classes daily, with 180 school days constituting the school year. Under these circumstances, to make the rounds once, he would have to schedule and complete almost one visit daily—a nearly impossible task. More plausibly, to prevent a duplication of visits by those teaching the same pupil, a homeroom teacher or a comparable individual could visit 30 students yearly, thus enabling a school representative to get into every home once.

The New Trier Township High School of Winnetka, Illinois, as early as the 1920's solved the situation in almost exactly this way by making such visits an automatic responsibility of each freshman advisory chairman (comparable to a homeroom teacher). The procedure was initiated by one of the outstanding superintendents of the nation, Matthew Gaffney, and has continued uninterrupted at this school to the present.

The initial visit is designed to accomplish a number of predetermined purposes: to establish rapport between the advisor and family members; to create a school image characterized as receptive and unformidable; to provide an atmosphere in which questions of immediate concern may be asked and answered; and to elicit support for future exchanges. This first conference, in most instances, inevitably leads to other contacts between the advisor and the family. These may occur personally in the home or at the school, and also over the telephone. Specifically, they may be concerned with academic performance, breaches of discipline, reasons for pupil absence, vocational or college plans, and parent participation in school activities. The effectiveness of this program of New Trier is attested to by the longevity of its successful operation; by the extensive parental support for adequate teacher salaries, building programs, and academic experimentation; and by the favorable responses to it of pupils, faculty, and the administration. Although all schools admittedly are unable to implement an identical program, each in its own way should press for comparable outcomes.

The log and diary

Another clinical technique used occasionally by the teacher, although more often by the counselor, is the log or diary. It is aimed strictly at the individual student, but mostly at the one who is unable to plan work or allot time properly. It is brought into play, for instance, when a student with low grades is vague about his work habits: when he isn't positive about how much time he studies at night or what his time expenditures are for work or avocational outlets. In this event, a counselor might appropriately suggest that the pupil identify a period of a few days to a week that represent a cross section of his current life pattern, and maintain a time log or diary of his activities during that period. A typical day's entries might resemble the following:

Thursday, January 18, 19—

7:00 Got up.
7:20 Had breakfast.
7:45 Watched T.V.
8:00 Left for school.
3:30 Arrived home, changed clothes.
3:40 Went to John's house.
4:25 Arrived home and studied English.
4:45 Watched T.V. until 5:00.
5:00 Studied again, social studies.

5:30 Phoned Martha about Saturday.
5:45 Watched T.V.
6:00 Ate dinner.
7:00 Phoned Jack about doubling Saturday.
7:30 Studied French.
8:15 Jack came over.
10:30 Went to bed.

A time and activity exposé such as the above would convince even a non-technically trained individual that interruptions were more characteristic of the student's day than study, with the latter consuming a maximum of 1 hour and 35 minutes—and, with the many diversionary breaks, probably much less than that. This revealing portrayal would be particularly helpful to the procrastinator or rationalizer who had an overdeveloped propensity for crowding the unpleasant into his unconscious. Of course, the real issue would be whether such a person could be counted on to keep an accurate log. In this regard, the counselor, in preparing the student for the task, would state and reiterate a guidance truism such as the following: "Remember, George (or Jane), the log will be only as helpful to *you* as *you* let it be. If your entries are faithful, you will have a true picture. If you cheat a little or a lot, you will have wasted your time." It will be noted once more that the counselor here places the onus on the student, refraining from use of "I" or "me." The task is identified exclusively as "yours," not "mine." Integrity in maintaining a log or diary is thus a function of motivation; it fails the test of reliability when desire is low.

Autobiography

Not unlike the log as a mirror of self is the autobiography. Both ask for a personal reflection, and both depend for accuracy on the willingness of the individual to reveal himself to others. And what needs to be added is that the accuracy of any self-revelation is never greater than the confidence of a client, be he student or adult, in the therapist counselor, or whatever kind. Thus, if an autobiography is to provide any real insight, the ingredients of intellectual honesty and faith in the teacher or guidance worker must be present in ample quantities.

The autobiography customarily appears in the curriculum in the eighth or ninth grade, when the teacher of English makes it a written assignment. As a theme project, it is probably no worse than many others that might be assigned. But as a projection of personality, it can be only as accurate as the ability of an individual to reveal his inner self is uninhibited by social pressures and unconscious motivations, and as great as his trust in a counselor figure is substantial. Accordingly, the group-assigned autobiography can lay claim to only modest success as a clinical instrument. As one of many insights into human personality, it fits into a panorama well; but for individual diagnosis, it probably falls short of vital significance.

The sociogram

Another clinical technique of unquestioned merit in certain group situations, but of less significance in the secondary school grades, is the *sociogram*. Conceived by Moreno, a Viennese psychiatrist, in the early part of the century, it has been employed extensively by elementary school teachers, only sparingly in the higher grades. Basically, it is a method of quantifying the social reactions of members of a group to one another.

The process of social assessment is normally precipitated by a lead item such as: (1) In our next unit's committee activity, with which three other students in the class would you most like to work? Or, (2) On our field trip tomorrow, please list the three students with whom you would most like to sit on the bus. From the responses to stimuli such as these, the teacher would then read into the situation a pattern of intra-class relationships, with the isolates and popularity figures standing out in the group.

Despite its salient contributions to the group therapist in non-school-oriented environments, we question the validity of the technique in the high school classroom for three primary reasons. First of all, the data which it provides are never more relevant than the relationship of the responses to the lead item. Conceivably, for instance, Jean might enjoy sitting next to Les on the bus but might prefer to associate with others in committee activity. Thus, the social significance of group responses may have only limited applicability. A second reason for our lukewarmness is that the technique is divisive, always pointing up differences among students. A third reason is that the purpose of the process is usually blatantly obvious to adolescents despite a teacher's attempts to camouflage motives. Our over-all feeling is that, since the same results can probably be secured by an astute observation of class members, the technique in the high school is somewhat superfluous, and at times might even be harmful.

The cumulative record

Deliberately reserved for this final position in the kaleidoscope of teacher-evaluative methods is the cumulative record—the most comprehensive of them all. More than a discrete method in itself, it is the collective center of the known data about a student that have been reduced to organized format. In the record are past grades, health information, teacher and counselor comments, significant written projects, the home questionnaire, and such other information as various school personnel have deemed worthy of perpetuating.

In effect, this record is a resource file of fact and opinion that remains mechanically inert and useless until a school staff member gives it life through purposeful utilization. In between, it may serve the cause of centralized research and statistical analyses, but its uselessness dissipates completely only when the record is made to perform functionally. The most commendable instance of functional use of the record is when a classroom teacher or counselor concerned with a student problem reaches into the record physically and psychologically for whatever light it may cast on a given situation. The problem possibilities are almost numberless: low achievement, work at any level that is below capacity, irregular performance, ill health, social retardation, weak motivation, personality dysfunctions, or delinquency. Possessed of a problem, the personnel worker of whatever kind analyzes the record's contents with discrimination, focusing selected parts in the direction of the problem's aspects.

The yearbook of the Association for Supervision and Curriculum Development, 1955, refers to the Cumulative Record as a significant "tool of guidance," as indeed it is. As such a tool, the record possesses the following characteristics:

1. The cumulative record is comprehensive, reaching beyond the narrowness of single personalities, years, episodes, and moods. Furthermore, it combines into a composite picture the areas of the mental, personal-emotional, personal-physical, social, and ethical.

2. If comprehensive in general, it is genetically extensive in particular, projecting along a lengthy time horizon.

3. It is likewise comprehensive as a cross section of a student's life span at any time.

4. It is economical to use in that it provides a condensation of the many aspects of human dynamics.

5. It is accessible, unless denied teachers by mal-oriented guidance personnel.

6. It stands ever on the threshold of causation, begging to be interpreted.

The cumulative record, to be of greatest benefit to all, should be supported by spontaneity as well as by design. By this we mean that the teacher should contribute information to it even when not required to do so by higher authority; and should utilize its contents in between, as well as at the time of, crisis situations. Viewed in this way, the cumulative record demands more of a teacher, but it contributes more to him as a result.

SELF-EVALUATION

The ultimate goal of all evaluation by teachers and counselors is pupil self-evaluation, a power or attribute which is possessed by all individuals in differing amounts. Increasing or waning at an irregular pace, depending on the classroom situation of the moment and the unique state of the individual at any time, it is distinct from the methods previously discussed in that it is not subject to the same degree of teacher control. The process of maturing for any pupil unquestionably is one of getting better acquainted with the world of knowledge, ideas, and attitudes so that, among other outcomes, he can understand himself more clearly. Consequently, a major function of every teacher is to encourage each pupil to evaluate himself realistically at almost every point of contact with the curriculum. Yet the task so freely proposed here can be accomplished only in part. This discussion harks back to Chapter 1, in which self-understanding was presented as a lifetime assignment that is never completed despite the best effort of many intelligent, well-informed, and conscientious people to give it closure. Like the proverbial will-o'-the-wisp, it always eludes.

In this connection, several members of the School of Education of Northwestern University in 1952 (Charlotte Huck, Gail Inlow, Isabel Lewis, Dale Steffen, and Doris Young) embarked on a project of appraising the accuracy of the self-judgments of student teachers about their performances. The sample members were asked to make self-evaluations on such items as knowledge of subject matter in the content fields, skill in leading discussions, establishing rapport with pupils, and other identifiable elements of teacher competency. The self-evaluations were then compared with appraisals of the cooperating teachers and university supervisors. The results were as follows:

1. The student teachers were not very realistic in evaluating themselves.

2. As a group, they were more optimistic in their self-evaluations than were the university supervisors or critic teachers in evaluating them.

3. The critic teachers and university supervisors agreed much more closely in their evaluations of the students than the students did with either group.[2]

[2] Gail M. Inlow, "Evaluating Student-Teaching Experience," *Jour. Ed. Res.,* May 1952, pp. 105–114.

In a subsequent unpublished study, the same colleagues working with a sample of 100 student teachers discovered a significant range of differential ability among various types of students to appraise themselves. The evaluations of those who did unusually well in student teaching invariably correlated more significantly with the ratings of the critic teachers and university supervisors than did the evaluations of the less adequate student teachers. Apparently, with greater competence comes greater accuracy in self-evaluation. Of interest was the phenomenon of overrating by the lower group. These almost consistently gave themselves high marks on all the traits listed, whereas the better students tended to underrate themselves.

Self-evaluation can be of the informal type that everyone engages in many times in his life, or it can be formalized by means of a check list or other type of instrument. For specific check lists, the interested reader might study those presented by Grambs et al.[3] Faunce and Bossing,[4] and Alexander and Halverson.[5] These check lists tend to jog the pupil to think about his progress in specific areas of growth—for example, in taking part in class discussions, assuming responsibility, cooperating with others, using time wisely, and developing wholesome attitudes.

The merits of self-evaluation we do not question; about the merit of the check-list approach we have a few reservations. Too often the check list is artificially superimposed on a pupil out of the true context of the learning situation—this despite a recognition that the best time for a trait to be evaluated is in a situation where it is being emphasized or demonstrated. Furthermore, a check list may be somewhat overpowering to the neophyte who has done little self-evaluating previously. If used at all, it should be introduced to a pupil slowly, part at a time, to enable him to reflect on one phase of self before moving to another. However, the exact method of self-evaluation is less important than the fact that it is included in some way as a part of a total learning and growth experience.

Many teachers successfully inject pupil self-appraisal into the curriculum by asking pupils to evaluate their responses to a unit being studied, how their behavior was modified as a result, and what they felt they needed to work on more specifically. Actually, every time a student consciously realizes an inadequacy and then works toward greater competency, he is engaging in self-evaluation. In the process of helping students toward this outcome, the teacher must provide helpful encouragement, accenting the positive and discouraging the negative when the latter can be overly damaging to personality. The process of insight flowers in

[3] Jean D. Grambs, William J. Iverson, Franklin K. Patterson, *Modern Methods in Secondary Education* (New York: Holt, Rinehart and Winston, 1958), pp. 506–507.

[4] Roland C. Faunce and Nelson Bossing, *Developing the Core Curriculum* (Englewood Cliffs, N.J.: Prentice-Hall, Inc., 1958), pp. 363–364.

[5] William M. Alexander and Paul M. Halverson, *Effective Teaching in Secondary Schools* (New York: Holt, Rinehart and Winston, 1956), p. 403.

an atmosphere of warmth and positivism; it degenerates when surrounded by ill-conceived negativism.

Peer-evaluation

Peer-evaluation, like self-evaluation, is engaged in informally almost constantly in the classroom. This process is as normal as being with others is normal. Pupils "size up" associates every time they get together. The problem for the teacher to decide is how extensively pupils should be encouraged to evaluate other pupils in a straight-from-the-shoulder manner. We have observed this direct approach in action many times in a core class without apparent harm to pupils, but we have also seen it become harmful to human personality in other classes. Our attitude, in general, is that peer-evaluation is of inestimable worth provided a few operating principles are followed.

First, if engaged in at all, it probably should become a routine facet of the curriculum. When it appears only sporadically, it may disturb adolescent emotions unduly. Peer-appraisal, a built-in function of the core curriculum wherever it is found, tends to surprise observers with its apparent casualness, without even drawing a grimace from the object of the criticism. The reason may well be, and probably is, that such calm acceptance is the product of a long-term process that has permeated the curriculum from the adolescent's first exposure to it, a process that soon permeates the adolescent also. Both thus profit from the cumulative effect.

Another principle is that peer-evaluation should be rooted in tenets that have been identified and aired in open discussion. Selected of these follow:

1. Criticism must be backed up by logical or scholarly evidence.
2. The performance, not the individual, is to be evaluated.
3. Evaluation can be frank but also wholesomely pleasant.
4. Evaluation should almost regularly work from the positive to the negative.
5. It should be no respecter of persons, but should be "fitted" to persons.
6. It should be well thought out, organized, and expressed.
7. It should shun dogmatism or absolutism.
8. It should be serious.

A good way for a teacher to start peer-evaluation is to introduce it subtly by asking for written evaluations of committee reports and other pupil-leader situations. Then candid oral discussion can more comfortably ensue at a later time. When gradually introduced, frequently employed, and guided with discernment, it can be an effective means of pupil growth.

SUMMARY

This chapter's concern has been with the process of appraisal apart from testing. The term *evaluation* was defined as the process of making a judgment about a person, place, or episode. As a canopy-like term, it covers both subjectively and objectively based judgments, whereas measurement more narrowly covers only those judgments that are made in terms of identifiable units.

As an important function, evaluation is identified in a general way with the enterprise of education as a whole, and in a more specific way with the teacher and the school administrator, particularly the former. With any of the three, its goal is to determine to what extent of effectiveness the purposes of education at any level have been and are being achieved.

Some principles which underlie evaluation are that it is never exact, only approximate; that it is never more valid than the teacher is perceptive, and that it should be continuous and comprehensive. The integral steps of the process are goal determination, accumulation of information, judgment-making, and a decision on next steps.

The three broad approaches to appraisal were identified as those made by the teacher, the pupil, and peers. Under the first category were treated the methods of informal and formal observation, written projects, oral projects, the academic record, the interview, the health record, home and family questionnaires, the home visit, the log or diary, the autobiography, the sociogram, and the cumulative record.

The final goal of all evaluation was identified as self-evaluation, with peer-appraisal giving it support.

REFERENCES

Ahmann, J. Stanley, and Marvin D. Glock, *Evaluating Pupil Growth.* Boston: Allyn and Bacon, 1958.

Association for Supervision and Curriculum Development, *Guidance in the Curriculum.* Washington, D.C.: National Education Association, 1955.

Grambs, Jean D., William J. Iverson, and Franklin K. Patterson, *Modern Methods in Secondary Education.* New York: Holt, Rinehart and Winston (rev. ed.), 1958. (Chapters 19 and 20)

Kettelkamp, Gilbert C., *Teaching Adolescents.* Boston: D. C. Heath and Co., 1954.

Wrightstone, J. Wayne, Joseph Justman, and Irving Hobbine, *Evaluation in Modern Education.* New York: American Book Co., 1956.

EVALUATING
GROWTH
BY
TESTING

Few movements in any discipline have been more active for the past century than has testing in the fields of education and psychology. When Binet and Simon in 1905 completed the first instrument for measuring intelligence, the modern testing movement was born. This first creation was halting and inadequate by contemporary standards, making only an insignificant contribution in its time, but its legacy to the future was momentous.

The contrast between this lone beginning and the active state of affairs in the testing movement today almost resists description. The current healthy state of testing, as measured in quantitative terms, is revealed by a few statistics from Buros' *Fifth Mental Measurements Yearbook,* 1959. Between 1952 and 1958, 957 tests were submitted for analysis by a reviewing committee of 350 experts. For the same period, the *Yearbook's* section on "Books and Reviews" includes 458 books on measurement or related fields. The testing instruments themselves cover all areas of the school's curriculum, as well as specialized aptitudes, the panorama of personality dynamics, and the many vocations.[1]

[1] Oscar K. Buros (ed.), *The Fifth Mental Measurements Yearbook* (Highland Park, N.J.: The Gryphon Press, 1959), p. xxiii.

The constantly growing interest in testing is a direct correlate of man's almost relentless pursuit of accuracy in the process of appraisal. Or, stated conversely, it reflects an acute dissatisfaction with subjectively based evaluation, laden as the latter is with human error. In this regard, although sharing the concern over man's fumbling attempts at behavioral assessment, and although encouraging scholarly effort to create and refine testing instruments, we are of the opinion that this swing toward testing may have become too one-sided. Thus, it may need to be watched more closely in the future, lest it permit attention to stray too far from those traits and syndromes that resist exact measurement. Testing has a vital position in the configuration of evaluation, but it must not be allowed to become overly dominant.

At its best, appraisal is of ensemble proportions, with each technique selected for what it can do most effectively. In schools particularly is such breadth necessary, since pupil growth must be assayed in terms of the value intangibles as well as the more manifest achievement tangibles. From this "whole man" approach, the typical teacher, if confronted with a forced choice, would more likely give up testing than the benefit of informal observation. Without the former, education could continue; but without the latter, it is likely that it could not. Happily, however, testing and other methods will continue to serve teachers, and it is to a closer analysis of the one technique that this chapter is dedicated.

TESTING TERMINOLOGY

To understand the process of testing, one must have a minimum of familiarity with its technical vocabulary. The first term to be considered is the word "test" itself. Shunning an exact definition, we offer four basic specifications:

1. A test confronts the testee with a series of tasks to be performed.
2. The testee is conscious that he is being tested.
3. The testee responds to the tasks with answers that are right or wrong, even though rightness and wrongness may be elusive.
4. At the end of the process, the test remains as a tangible product of behavior.

These elements characterize the written test, but not the so-called routine tests of life or the oral test and inventories (of interest, personality, and value). Regarding the first step, the student who reads a book is, in a broad sense, undergoing a test, but steps 3 and 4 are not applicable. The laborer who is confronted with a task, unless operating under a "quality-controlled" set of circumstances, cannot be considered to be taking a test, because steps 2, 3, and 4 all would be missing. The oral test is within the province of steps 1, 2, and 3 but outside the province of 4, because no tangible record remains, barring a tape or disk reproduction.

The category of the inventory is distinct in the field of evaluation in that it resembles a test, containing as it does stimulus items and norms, but fails the specification of rightness and wrongness. The personality inventory, which confronts the testee with such an item as, "I have trouble going to sleep," implies a medically correct answer; however, its primary concern is not with correctness but with what the given answer reveals about the human personality that provided it. In the same way, a Kuder-type elicited interest preference for "making a boat" over "reading a book" does not conceive either choice as being more right or more wrong than the optional one. Each merely reveals an interest that is uniquely a part of a personality pattern. Thus, since an absolute standard of correctness in their results is nonexistent, inventories should not be called tests.

Test dichotomies

Within the specific field of testing itself, operational sub-classes exist, paired off in the following selected ways: standardized versus nonstandardized, subjective versus objective, ability versus aptitude, global versus diagnostic, power versus speed, and verbal versus performance. Distinctions between these polar sets are identified in the following listing.

Standardized test. A term descriptive of the process whereby a test: (1) Is administered to a sample group selected because of predetermined characteristics. The sample might be, for example, all high school freshmen in a town, randomly selected freshmen throughout the country, all second-generation emigrants, or all sons of physicians. The intent of the test would decide the kind of sample. (2) Follows established procedures for determining validity and reliability and is administered in the same way by all testers, who give the same instructions in the same way, allot the same amount of time, and adopt the same posture during the testing process. (3) Emerges with norms which can be used for comparative purposes: for example, chronological age, grade levels in school, percentiles, intelligence quotients, or standard scores. With such norms, a student's raw score of 154 on an achievement test could thus be equated to the performance of the sample group. The raw score might place him at the sixteen-year level, at the twelfth-grade level, at the 85th percentile, or at a standard-score position of 1.43, depending on the conversion medium.

Nonstandardized test: A term usually descriptive of the tests which have not undergone these screens. It includes the broad category of teacher-made tests.

Subjective test: Those tests in which a determination of the rightness and wrongness of the answers is strongly dependent on the subjective interpretations of the scorer. The so-called "essay" examinations are obvious illustrations. But even the occasional short-answer item which demands interpretation is also illustrative.

Objective test. Those test items with answers that, according to accepted criteria and without modification, are manifestly all right or all wrong.

Ability test: Those tests which measure what a person can do or could learn to do.

Achievement test: Those tests which measure what an individual has done or has learned to do.

Global test: Any test that, from various dimensional areas, employs items without regard for their diagnostic ability to discriminate by area. An academic-aptitude test where the mathematical items are included with the verbal, and where only a single score is reported, is an example.

Diagnostic test: Any test that reports performance by dimensional areas as a means of revealing specific strengths and weaknesses. The Minnesota Aptitude Test that identifies the spatial component, or the California Aptitude Test that identifies the verbal component discretely, is an example.

Power test: An untimed test, for example, the Ohio Psychological Examination.

Speed test: A rigidly timed test. Most standardized tests fall into this category.

Verbal test: A test that uses verbal symbols; sometimes also descriptive of one that employs mathematical as well as word symbols.

Performance test: A test designed primarily for the uneducated, where responses are made to pictorial stimuli rather than to words or numbers.

Validity and reliability

The most important factor of any test is its validity, that is, the degree to which it evaluates what it is intended to evaluate. Thus, a test in music theory cannot allow music appreciation to become involved, or a test of intelligence to become heavily weighted with achievement items. The concept of validity must also take into account the mental depth of penetration which a test is intended to make. For instance, if a teacher of the social studies desired to probe beneath the surface reasons for Nixon's defeat in 1960, he could scarcely accomplish his mission with a few objective-type items. These would oversimplify, and would fall short of analysis. Nor could the same teacher assume that a pencil-and-paper test about citizenship would actually evaluate the attributes of a given student as a citizen.

Pertinent to the present topic is an episode that allegedly took place in the early days of the academic-aptitude testing movement. As the handed-down story, or maybe legend, goes, a foreign government became so interested in testing that it sent a delegation of experts to the United States to study, and ultimately to pre-empt, a designated test. So appropriated, it was taken back to the mother country, reproduced, and administered to the native population, with the shocking result of a mean I.Q.

score of 78. The reported reaction was one of chagrin and self-defacement. Instead, it should have been one of tolerant amusement at their own naïveté in supposing that test items relevant to an almost exclusively Occidental population would be equally appropriate for one where East and West were intermingled. The error was obviously not in the population but in the low validity of the test.

We shall offer one further illustration of the concept of validity. Let us assume that a teacher wishes to determine how effectively a class can employ the problem-solving method. Accordingly, as one question on an examination, he asks the students to list the essential steps of problem-solving, which have been identified previously. The performance of the class ranges from complete accuracy by some to complete inaccuracy by a few. Would it be plausible for the teacher, therefore, to conclude that the pupils with a perfect score on the question understand the complexities of problem-solving? Obviously not, with such limited evidence! The examination question was valid only in determining to what degree of accuracy pupils could reproduce from memory the designated steps of problem-solving. Not by even a stretch of the imagination could it be interpreted as testing the more complex processes. Starting with the six steps and asking students to apply them to a specific problem situation, or asking them actually to solve a problem of common concern, would come closer to the desired goal.

The issue of English expression always crops up in the present context. Specifically, is validity adversely affected when a teacher "counts off" for errors in grammar and vague expression? The answer is an obvious affirmative unless a fundamental purpose of the test was to evaluate the students' ability to express themselves. Otherwise, unless English usage is so faulty as to be incomprehensible, the substantive knowledge itself can be the only criterion. Validity, in effect, says to the teacher: Decide what you want your test to do, and then make sure that it gets the job done.

Reliability, often confused with its sister term, relates to the consistency with which a test, or comparable tests, evaluate when administered more than once. If Test X, when administered in January, places Tom in a rank-order spot of tenth in the class and Terry in twentieth place, but reverses the order when administered in March, the test is proportionately that much less reliable—unless factors within Tom and Terry could be held accountable for the shift of positions.

In the case of the standardized instrument, the qualities of validity and reliability cannot be empirically assumed; they must be demonstrably evidenced in scientifically defensible ways. With the teacher-constructed instrument, however, face validity or face reliability is usually sufficient, that is, prima facie evidence of these qualities that are the inferred resultants of careful thought and meticulous preparation of the test items. Since time is a precious teacher commodity, only approximations of validity and reliability are possible.

Central tendencies

After tests have been administered and scored, for them to be really meaningful, they need some kind of statistical analysis. Although relinquishing the more detailed picture to such specialized treatments as those by Cronbach, Thorndike and Hagen, and Garrett, listed in the bibliography at the end of the chapter, we shall define and illustrate the more elementary terms of statistics here. The first to be analyzed briefly are the measures of *central tendency,* referred to roughly, at times, as the *statistical averages.* They are three in number: the *mean,* the *median,* and the *mode.*

As a concrete vehicle on which to focus these and other abstract terms, we project the following simple test data. In Situation A, 10 slow learners earned the listed raw scores on an arithmetic examination administered in a general mathematics class. In Situation B, 30 students in a seventh-grade core class received on a monthly test raw scores which, to expedite later arithmetical manipulations, were grouped in intervals of five. Thus, a score of 96, losing its original identity, became one of the two included in the interval 95–99, enumerated under N (number).

SITUATION A		SITUATION B		
				X
				(Interval Mid-
			N	*point multiplied*
		Intervals	*(number)*	*by* N)
98		95–99	2	194
94		90–94	4	368
87		85–89	8	696
87		80–84	6	492
85		75–79	4	308
84		70–74	4	288
79		65–69	1	67
78		60–64	1	62
75			$N = 30$	Sum of X's $= 2475$
60				
$N = 827$				

Mean $= 82.70$		Mean $= 82.50$
Median $= 84.50$		Median $= 83.66$
Mode $= 87.00$		Mode $= 87.00$

One way of determining the relative performance of any single student is, thus, to compare it with one or more of the three aforementioned measures of central tendency. Each will be briefly treated, first at the theoretical level and then reduced to the concrete by application to Situations A and B.

The *mean* is the arithmetical average of all scores on a given test, being derived by dividing the sum of all the scores by the number of individuals who took the test. As the most extensively employed and serviceable of the three measures, its essential value is as a statistic on which other statistical processes are based. The median and mode have central-tendency implications only; the mean, these and many others. The greatest limitation of the mean is in a distribution which is heavily weighted by a minority of the entries. For instance, if five people in a town drew yearly salaries of \$4,000, \$5,000, \$6,000, \$7,000, and \$48,000, respectively, the mean average salary of \$14,000 $\left(\dfrac{\$70,000}{5}\right)$ would scarcely be representative.

In the illustrative situations, however, with the scores uniformly distributed along a continuum, the mean is a stable statistic. In Situation A, it is derived by dividing the sum of the raw scores (827) by the number of students who earned the scores (10), the result being 82.70.

In Situation B, where the test results are grouped by intervals of 5 (a limit arbitrarily selected following inspection of the 30 original scores), the mid-point of each interval is assumed to be the correct score of all those that fit into the interval. Thus, in the interval 60–64, the one score is inferred to be 62; in the interval 75–79, each of the four scores is inferred to be 77. The column captioned "X" lists the various products of the mid-points of the intervals multiplied by the number of the respective scores in the intervals. The mean is, thus, 2475 divided by 30, or 82.50.

The *median* is the statistic that occurs in the middle of a distribution. In a total of 11 figures rank-ordered from low to high, the median is the 6th figure up or down in the distribution, with 5 figures above it and 5 figures below it. In the distorted spread of the five salaries reported in the previous section, the median salary of \$6,000 would be a better index of "average" than the mean of \$14,000. However, in more normal distributions, the median usually concedes to the mean, which, as was indicated, is foundational to more advanced processes.

In Situation A, with 10 students providing no mid-point score, a contrived mid-point must be identified halfway between the 5th score up of 84, and the 5th score down of 85. The contrived median thus becomes 84.5.

In Situation B, the process is slightly more complicated. Since 30 students also fail to provide an actual mid score, a contrived one halfway between the 15th score up and the 15th score down must be discovered. This, by inspection, falls in the interval 80–84. Since six scores are contained in the interval and 10 below it, the hypothetical median score of 15 will rest ⅚ of the way into this interval. And the interval itself, as arbitrarily conceded in statistics books, extends really from 79.5 to 84.5, instead of from 80 to 84. Thus, we need to go either ⅚ of the way up from 79.5, or ⅙ of the way down from 84.5.

The two respective formulas, either of which can be pursued in search of the contrived median, along with the arithmetical implementations, are submitted here. One can serve as a check on the other.

(1) Low point of the interval $+ \left(\dfrac{\text{No. of cases needed in the interval}}{\text{Total cases in the interval}} \right) \times$
(Score points in the interval) $= 79.5 + (\%)5 =$
$79.5 + 4.16 = \underline{83.66}$ (median)

(2) High point of the interval $- \left(\dfrac{\text{No. of cases needed in the interval}}{\text{Total cases in the interval}} \right) \times$
(Score points in the interval) $= 84.5 - (\%)5 =$
$84.5 - .834 = \underline{83.66}$ (median)

The third central tendency is the *mode,* or the score earned by the greatest number of students who took the examination. In Situation A, it is 87 because 2 students earned it, whereas only 1 earned any other score. In the intervaled distribution, 8 students earned scores that fell into the interval 85–89; therefore, a contrived modal score of 87 would have to be reported.

Variability

The central-tendency measures provide indices of average-type performance but reveal nothing about the extensity of the spread of scores. For instance, a mean of 60 could be the arithmetical average of 5 scores distributed in each of the following three ways, with none giving any clue about the type of distribution: 58, 60, 60, 60, 62; or 40, 50, 60, 60, 90; or 10, 20, 90, 90, 90. These all have means of 60 but are vastly different in variability.

The simplest measure of variability is the *range,* or the arithmetical distance between the lowest score and the highest score. In the three instances above, the respective ranges would be 4 (58–62), 50 (40–90), and 80 (10–90). Another measure is the *quartile,* which is the range of scores in any one-quarter of a group; also the *inter-quartile,* which is the range of scores from the 25th percentile to the 75th percentile. Either of these is determined in a way comparable to that employed in discovering the median. But the most common measure of variability is the *standard deviation,* or *Sigma,* as it is sometimes called. Mathematically, this is the square root of the arithmetical average of the squared distances from the mean. The logical question is, Why the square root and the squares? Why not keep life simple? The answer lies in the plus and minus values of unsquared distances, based on the range alone, which cancel out when totaled. For instance, the mean of 5 scores of 50, 60, 70, 80, and 90 is 70. The first two scores are -20 and -10 away from the mean, respectively; and the last two, $+10$ and $+20$ away, respectively. These cancel out when added, as any set of scores always do when related to the mean— with the obvious implication that unsquared distances are of little help in providing insight to the average deviations of the various scores of a set.

The standard deviation, or S.D., using squared variables, thereby negates the influence of the minus signs and thus provides a better statistic of average variability. The simple arithmetical illustration of a few lines back, extended into the S.D., should clarify what presently may be mildly confusing.

Raw Scores	Distance from Mean	Squares of Deviations
90	+20	400
80	+10	100
70	—	—
60	−10	100
50	−20	400
	Sum of Squared Deviations	= 1,000

$$\text{S.D.} = \sqrt{\frac{\text{Sum of Squared Deviations}}{\text{Number of cases}}} = \sqrt{\frac{1000}{5}} = \sqrt{200} = 14.14$$

The S.D. of the earlier 10 scores (Situation A) is computed as follows:

SITUATION A

Raw Scores	Deviation from Mean	Squares of Deviations
98	+15.3	234.09
94	+11.3	127.69
87	+ 4.3	18.49
87	+ 4.3	18.49
85	+ 2.3	5.29
84	+ 1.3	1.69
79	− 3.7	13.69
78	− 4.7	22.09
75	− 7.7	59.29
60	−22.7	515.29
$N = \overline{827}$		1016.10

Mean = 82.7

$$\text{S.D.} = \sqrt{\frac{1016.10}{10}} = \sqrt{101.61} = 10.08$$

The question is always raised as to what a large or a small standard deviation is, with no really satisfactory answer ever being possible. Two basic principles should be retained, however, despite this lack of specificity: (1) a large standard deviation means greater variability and a small one, less variability; and (2) with a hypothetical normal distribution of any range of scores, the standard deviation is an exact index of relative standing in a group.

Assuming a *Gaussian* or bell-shaped curve such as on p. 286, there is certainty that the measured trait was a commonly possessed one, that the population to which it was applied was representative and therefore probably of considerable size, and that predictability of percentages of individuals who deviated from the mean by given distances was thus assured. It

Gaussian Curve

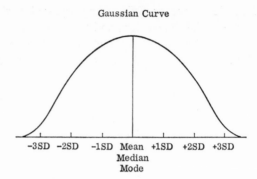

-3SD -2SD   -1SD Mean +1SD   +2SD +3SD
                  Median
                  Mode

is important for the teacher to keep in mind that the Gaussian curve is an outcome, not a goal. Since class groups of students are atypical because of size and natural selection, most teachers go through life never having had a normal distribution result from a test or any other source of scores.

Assuming a representative population, the S.D. enables one to predict the percentage spread of individuals along the horizontal abscissa of the curve. The expected distribution would be as follows:

Standard Deviation Value	*Per Cent of Scores Above*
+3.0	Infinitesimal
+2.5	0.6
+2.0	2.3
+1.5	6.7
+1.0	15.9
+0.5	30.8
0.0	50.0
−0.5	69.1
−1.0	84.1
−1.5	93.3
−2.0	97.7
−2.5	99.4
−3.0	Almost 100 per cent

The value of the above percentage data to the classroom teacher rests primarily in its meaningfulness to him in interpreting standardized-test data. The College Board Examinations appear in a new light if he knows, for instance, that:

1. The mean score is always 500.

2. The score moves from 200 at the −3 S.D. level in successive intervals of 100 per each increase of 1 S.D. unit, until it reaches a score of 800 at the +3 S.D. point on the abscissa.

3. Per the prior S.D. column listing, 68.2 per cent of the students who take the CEEB earn scores of from 400 to 600.

These and other valuable insights accrue to the teacher who makes elementary statistical terms a part of his vocabulary. At the practical level, he will use the mean and median frequently as a reflector of average performance. The range will serve most of the day-to-day demands of variability. The standard deviation will enable him to relate to test results and testing literature with more understanding and sophistication. Regardless of specific uses, since the symbolism of teaching is partially statistical, teachers should respond to its implications at a defensible level of insight.

STANDARDIZED INSTRUMENTS

Between the above discussion of the terminology of testing and the ensuing treatment of the chapter's major topic of teacher-made testing, we interpolate a few brief comments about standardized tests and inventories. Because these constitute a sizable part of the evaluative programs of most secondary school systems, an orientation to their purposes and functions is necessary for the future teacher. Their advantages over teacher-constructed instruments are three-dimensional: (1) they meet higher standards of construction, (2) they reflect and insure more care in administration, and (3) they provide a sample for comparative purposes.

Prepared and published either by private industry or by universities (a few by the government), standardized tests, almost wherever found, are the product of skilled technicians and are supported by considerable monetary output. This progress toward greater quality is as much a result of the growing sophistication of the various consumers—psychology, education, and personnel management—as of the competitiveness within the movement itself. The school or industry with a competent psychologist on its staff is less likely to be gulled with false claims than was the less informed status person in a similar position several decades ago. Also, as the demand for tests is increasing, the financial posture of companies shows steady improvement. The net result of added money and more qualified personnel is greater test quality. Matched against these factors, the teacher-made test is made either to look bad by comparison or to counter with its own unique strengths.

In the specific matters of preparation and administration, standardized tests excel in their greater concern for high validity and reliability, their greater clarity of instructions, and their greater concern with time refinements. These are ideals of the classroom test which may actually be realized by the standardized type because more time and expert effort are expended.

A third advantage of standardized tests is the comparison sample group that a standardized test provides. The teacher-made test at infrequent times can serve as a comparative base for four or five classes taught by the same teacher, but most often a determination of relativity is possible only within the confines of a single class group. In contrast, a standardized test enables a teacher to compare the scores earned by a specific group of students or by an individual with announced norms. Thus, a raw score of a student might place him at the 75th percentile in his class but only at the median, or 50th percentile, in the sample group. This second statistic permits inter-group as well as intra-group comparison.

Along with the obvious advantages of standardized tests go several just as obvious limitations. One is the ever-present danger that their content will only approximate the needs of a single classroom situation. In an English class if verbals are included in a standardized test for tenth-graders who have not been exposed to their complexities, both the subject matter and the norms become less meaningful as a result. A second disadvantage is the danger that a teacher will aim a curriculum *at* a test, once he knows that the test will be administered. This places evaluation in the queer position of formulating, not assessing, the goals of education. A third disadvantage, although not inherent, is teacher-rating by an administrator based on student performance on standardized tests. Unfortunately, while theory relentlessly attacks this practice as inexcusable, more than a few principals continue to employ it, despite the narrowness of its scope and its possible unrelatedness to the unique given class of adolescents.

Whatever the specific advantages and disadvantages, evidence supports the greater positive weighting of standardized instruments. Thus, it behooves the teacher candidate to get acquainted with the types of standardized tests with which he is likely to come into contact. For the candidate who desires to pursue the topic in detail, we recommend the following sources: (1) *Guidance Testing,* by Froehlich and Hoyt, 1959. This treats of tests relating to academic and special aptitudes, achievement, interest, and personality, following chapter-length discussions of the individual topics. (2) *Mental Measurement Yearbooks,* edited by Oscar K. Buros, 1938, 1941, 1949, 1953, and 1959. Each lists and annotates those tests that were published prior to the *Yearbook's* date; that is, a test published in 1950 would appear only in the 1953 edition. (3) *Personnel and Guidance Journal, Journal of Counseling Psychology,* and *Journal of Consulting Psychology.* These contain the new tests of the months prior to the specific publishing date of each journal and treats them in considerable detail.

The instruments themselves fall primarily into the following categories: academic aptitude, special aptitude, achievement, interest, and personality, with a small sixth category of values. All of these are too specialized for a general text such as this; therefore, we shall comment only briefly about each of the first five, encouraging the reader to consult one of the aforementioned specialized sources for additional information.

Academic-aptitude tests

The term "academic aptitude" has come to parallel "intelligence" in recent years as descriptive of those testing instruments which purport to measure how well an individual can do or can learn to do. For more than half a century now, psychology and education have been struggling with these basic questions: What is intelligence? Is it a single factor or a multi-factor? Can tests be constructed to measure whatever it is? And, if so, how accurate will they be? Regarding the first two, obviously only approximate answers have been forthcoming, the fundamental dilemma being the extent to which intelligence should have social and creative outward manifestations. Existing tests, to date, have consistently ignored these factors, although scholarly criticism of the academic testing movement has not.

In analyzing intelligence quotients, a teacher should realize that the higher scores indicate a greater and the lower scores a lesser ability to work with abstract ideas, including both verbal and mathematical symbols. Accordingly, a curriculum of the academic subjects of English, social studies, science, the foreign languages, and mathematics will have to be fitted to the slow, inasmuch as the latter cannot fit themselves to a classical level of learning. Yet, because I.Q. scores are fallible as prognosticators, they should never be relied on completely apart from teacher observation and other evidences of pupil performance. In the fields of the social, creative, mechanical, artistic, and musical, the I.Q. scores are even less reliable.

Skepticism over the accuracy of academic-aptitude test scores should particularly be exercised when the following variables are operative: (1) a low reading score accompanies a low I.Q., (2) emotional disturbance is manifest, or (3) the cultural background is considerably different from that of the group. These, along with the inaccuracies of the test itself, are sufficient to justify cautious interpretation.

Specialized aptitude tests

In addition to aptitude tests in the area of the abstract are those in the areas of the mechanical, spatial, musical, artistic, clerical, manipulative, and special academic. Many vocational and educational activities demand certain specific aptitudes which can be measured and the results used for guidance purposes. If a draftsman, for instance, needs more spatial perception than the average; if an accountant needs more numerical skill; or if a farmer needs more mechanical skill, an early determination of the degree of an interested student's adequacy in the necessary component would have untold prognostic value. However, aptitude tests are primarily of a specialized nature, and the classroom teacher customarily defers to the guidance department for selection and administration.

Achievement tests

Tests of achievement evaluate how well an individual has performed or is performing. Almost universal throughout secondary education are achievement test batteries in the major content areas of the curriculum, standardized most often on nation-wide sample groups. Thus, when such tests are employed in a given school, they provide age, grade, or percentile norms which facilitate comparisons along an extensive continuum. Their purposes usually constitute one of the following—all but the last being legitimately conceived: (1) to plan a future program for class groups, (2) to diagnose specific weaknesses in individuals as a step toward guidance, (3) to channel students into the proper classes when homogeneous grouping is practiced, (4) to identify curriculum areas in need of further emphases, and (5) teacher evaluation.

Selected batteries with a high incidence of usage are the *Sequential Steps of Educational Progress* (STEP), Cooperative Testing Service, 1958; *Metropolitan Achievement Tests,* World Book Company, 1959; *Iowa Tests of Educational Development* (ITED), Science Research Associates, 1952; and *California Achievement Tests,* California Test Bureau, 1957. The classroom teacher in the smaller school may be called on to administer one or more of these periodically, whereas in the larger schools the task will be performed by a more specialized counselor. Regardless of who does the job, the mechanical process itself is relatively simple. More complex, however, is the after-the-fact interpretation, which must be approached thoughtfully and professionally. The quick leap to the conclusion that a teacher is inadequate or superior, or that a class is motivated or apathetic, must be resisted until supplementary evidence is provided. Achievement tests should serve to reinforce, affirm, and challenge, but never to convince independently.

Interest inventories

The inventory, as may be recalled, differs from a test in that a right or wrong answer is nonexistent. An answer to any inventory item serves only to reflect a trait or preference of the person making the response. One of the several types of inventories is the *vocational interest inventory,* which presents an individual with a series of broadly conceived vocational activities from which he is asked to select according to his interest preference. From his many selections is woven a profile of generalized or specialized interests in designated vocational outcomes. In the Kuder inventory, for instance, a three-pronged stimulus like the following is typical, with a choice being demanded for one of the three actions: sitting with a sick friend, repairing a household gadget, or reading a good book. Selection of the first might indicate a predilection for nursing; of the second, a leaning toward mechanical endeavor; of the third, an attachment to literary activity.

In all such inventories, the interpreter of the resulting profiles should never forget that verbally expressed preferences of whatever kind may be more the result of a family or cultural inclination than the real heart-felt desire of the person himself. Many sons of professional men have spent most of their early years verbalizing preferences for their fathers' professions, only to realize sooner or later that enculturation only was operating. Another admonition to the interpreter is that he not assume the existence of ability from a verbally expressed interest. John may express symbolic interests in medicine but discover later that science is beyond him and that blood is repulsive to him.

Despite their manifest limitations, interest inventories such as those by Strong, Cleeton, and Kuder make a worthwhile contribution to pupils, teachers, and counselors alike. In a single class period, they secure information about the vocational preferences of students that might take months to secure through the more laborious methods of observation and the interview. It is important, however, that they always be regarded only for what they are—just verbal expressions of interests.

Personality inventories

Like their interest counterparts, personality inventories also are pencil-and-paper media, relying on forced verbal choices to indicate personality structure. Instruments, such as the Bell, California, and Kuder inventories, commonly used in secondary schools, or one of a more sophisticated nature, such as the Minnesota Multiphasic Personality Inventory or Humm Wadsworth Personality Inventory, contain items similar to the following: Do you believe in third-degree methods? Do you have continued guilt feelings? Are you as popular with the other sex as you think you should be? Do you feel depressed often? These and similar types of stimuli are presumed to elicit responses that will reveal differential gradations on such personality dichotomies as introversion-extroversion, masculinity-femininity, manic-depressive reactions, schizoid cycloid manifestations, and tolerance-intolerance levels.

The first impression of the less informed is that anyone who wishes "to beat" the inventory can do so by giving the "socially approved" answer. This reaction is only partially valid in view of the number of items with shaded nuances of meaning included in any one syndrome area. A more acceptable attitude, we feel, is one of modified confidence which rejects unfounded skepticism. In this way, personality inventories, like other clinical instruments that fall equally short of perfection, can be employed as another supporting document in the cumulative record. When students are educated to face them honestly and positively as a method of enhancing self-discovery, insight does accrue; and with a similar posture, teachers will take the reported findings of a personality inventory seriously but not without relating them to other available information.

TEACHER-MADE TESTS

From the foregoing treatment we turn to the basic teacher-constructed instrument, which is the real heart of classroom testing. The standardized models may meet higher criteria of validity, reliability, versatility, and comparability, but they can only supplement without ever replacing the teacher-prepared counterparts. The former are like the "experts" in business or industry who, although appearing periodically to check up on the operation, leave the major responsibility for its success or failure with the on-the-job supervisory personnel. Classroom testing thus is a routine, but yet very necessary, part of teaching.

This section will be directed first toward the principles that should undergird any effective school testing situation, then toward the specific types of teacher-made tests, and finally toward a few selected administrative considerations.

Selected principles of classroom testing

First priority goes to those principles which are fundamental to the success of the entire testing process, with a convincing testimony to their importance coming resoundingly, although obliquely, from those teachers who ignore them. The more operationally basic of these principles will be enumerated and discussed briefly for clarification, serving thereby as a list against which tests may be compared and thus partially validated.

1. *The effective classroom test grows out of the curriculum context, drawing the great body of its items from the more important areas of content before tailing off toward the more obscure.* The real message here is that subject matter which is worthy of emphasis in class demands commensurate evaluative coverage; otherwise, the time originally spent could well be questioned. In contrast, a number of teachers, too preoccupied with the range and discriminatory powers of a test, ignore the test's primary purpose, namely, to extend the curriculum into appraisal. The fear of some that testing the truly consequential will result in students' performing too well is both illusory and a trifle morbid. First of all, empirical evidence relating to individual differences indicates such an outcome to be highly unlikely; second, the fear that students will do too well should be replaced by the eternal hope that all students will reach unforeseen heights of accomplishment.

2. *A test should be a member of an evaluative ensemble.* As commented on several times previously, testing is, and in the classroom always should be, just one of many methods of assessment. It should be called on only when its unique properties can best serve. It supplements, without replacing, such allies as the discussion, recitation, written composition, and social groups.

3. *Test selection is related to the type of response desired.* This might be recognition or recall, short or long answer, surface or depth of penetration. A presumptive determination within each of these as well as within comparable dichotomies leads to a closer approximation of the tester's purposes.

4. *Ideally, tests should be commonplace in the classroom situation.* Evaluation is always shadowed by the specter of marks, so that fear can never be eliminated, although it can be controlled. One way is for teachers to attempt to secure casualness in testing, destroying the threat. Greater comfortableness is attained thus when testing makes a more habitual appearance—in between six-weeks marking periods as well as at these specific times of crisis.

Whether in secondary school or in college, a contrasting and highly questionable practice is the disproportionate weighting of a single test situation, with all or most of the final mark dependent on its outcome. From both the mental-health and the learning vantage points, such an approach is almost universally less defensible than evaluative weighting more equitably spaced. Testing cannot be so frequent as to steal from learning, but neither can it be so infrequent as to invalidate sampling and create undue tension.

5. *Tests need to be kept current.* With learning content ever in a state of dynamic metamorphosis, the test as a mirror of the curriculum cannot afford the luxury of fixity. Both must change in near unison. Counter to this plain admonition, we recently heard a teacher with 25 years' experience boast that he finally had a testing instrument that was valid and reliable, for, said he, "I revised it fifteen years in a row, and for the last five years it has worked perfectly." Although delighted that revisions were made for 15 years, we wonder how a test could be up to date if unchanged for five years.

The psychologist-testing technician and the teacher often take opposing sides on this issue. The psychological purist stresses perfection of the instrument by item analysis and other approaches, sometimes at the expense of contemporaneousness, whereas the teacher-practitioner stresses the up-to-dateness of the items. A progressive reappraisal of items over a period of years might sift the chaff from the wheat; but if the wheat when sifted is too old to be useful, testing has won a hollow victory. A backlog of examinations may serve as a core for key questions, but the professional teacher must ever re-vitalize evaluative material with cognizance of current conditions, not just evaluate an assumed *status quo.*

6. *Results are to be kept confidential.* Appraisal is in a broad sense therapeutic; therefore, the results, unless divulged by the student himself, should be the possession only of pupil, parents, and professional school personnel. This principle, accordingly, condemns the too-common practices of posting names and grades on bulletin boards, reading grades aloud in class, returning papers in rank order from high to low, and placing

papers face up on students' desks. A sound mental-health orientation to this issue begs for teacher respect of pupils' right to privacy.

7. *Instructions must be unmistakably clear.* A fundamental of test validity is the clarity of instructions preceding the various sections. Instructions should be worded concisely and illustrated meaningfully. Such preliminaries will pay response dividends at the time of the test's administration. The following is illustrative:

INSTRUCTIONS. The next ten items are True-False. On the blank line before the item, please write in the word *True* or *False,* as appropriate. Items marked in any other way will be counted as incorrect. *Do not use such symbols as T, F, + or −.*

Note the following example:

<u>True</u>   The binomial theorem may be used to determine chance probability.

8. *Most often, tests should be announced in advance of administering them.* The issue here is the surprise versus the scheduled examination. As an occasional motivator, the teacher may condone the unannounced test; but if he is interested in such outcomes as pupil good will, the classroom as a lifelike situation, and the containment of apprehension, he customarily should forewarn. Too many surprises make for unnaturalness in both teacher and pupil posture.

9. *The type should usually be announced in advance also.* This practice removes some of the fear of the unknown and enables pupils to adjust their study habits to the anticipated type of instrument, that is, subjective or objective. Since examinations, in actuality, are a kind of homework, secretiveness should be shunned.

10. *Preparation of test items should be spaced.* Ideally, test construction for the classroom teacher is a continuous process that never terminates. After a day's or a week's activity, or after a unit, he words questions that later lead to an appraisal of what has transpired. So oriented, the questions tend to be more natural and relevant. Conceived in this way, they likewise lend themselves to the process of screening and sifting, with resulting greater fidelity. This system obviates the last-minute scurrying by the teacher for questions the night before the examination—an unprofessional pattern, at best, with negative results for both teacher and adolescents.

11. *Clarity of expression is paramount.* Short of the meat of the item itself, nothing is more shattering to validity and reliability than faulty English usage. First of all, the vocabulary needs to be simple. In the present context, the statement: "Verbosity obfuscates import," would be more subject to misunderstanding than: "Wordiness obscures meaning." Ambiguity also is to be avoided; for example: "Sociograms are most helpful in a large-group situation." Expression, furthermore, should shun the double

negative; for example: "Not joining a national army in wartime does not necessarily reveal one as unpatriotic." And such absolute modifiers as *always, all,* and *none* should be employed sparingly; for example: "misrepresenting truth is *always* sinful." Finally, bookishness should be replaced by naturalness. That items are to be grammatical is taken for granted.

12. *Quality is more important than length.* When in doubt, the teacher should reject the element of length if necessary to preserve the integrity of the examination. One of the more meaningless practices in education is the tendency of classroom leaders to add a few last questions so that totals will be an even 20, 50, or 100. Personally we see little wrong with a total of 17, 31, or 73, even if the teacher has only a moderate flair for arithmetic. The reverse practice leads to the inclusion of a few ill-conceived test items appended merely for arithmetical proportioning, which is not that important in the first place.

13. *Subjective and objective items should both be employed.* Although strongly recommending the presence of either essay or objective items on any one examination, we recommend the employment of both, with their many shadings, throughout the course of a year. The curriculum extends from the basic level of fact to the highest level of understanding and generalization; therefore, test items should extend in similar manner along a wide continuum. Because each testing type stimulates a different kind of response pattern, a greater variety appropriately allows for the interplay of individual and subject matter differences. Within this multiple framework, however, we advocate a far more frequent use of the essay examination whenever analytical thinking is the desired outcome.

14. *Tests should be evaluated, returned, and discussed.* While allowing for occasional pupil-scoring and self-scoring of test instruments, we more strongly recommend teacher-scoring, with the tests then being returned to the students for discussion. If appraisal leads to growth, and if a knowledge of progress is conducive to this outcome, there is little justification for an opposite point of view, save for the issue of time. Growth measured should be growth understood.

15. *Items should be arranged from easy to difficult.* This last principle, although more applicable to the longer objective than the shorter essay examination, is pertinent even to the latter. The graduation of item difficulty relaxes all at the beginning by discouraging none, and then permits each learner to move up the ladder to the point of his individual ceiling.

These are the principles on which a legitimate program of testing should operate. They will apply in different degrees of emphasis from situation to situation, but throughout they will stand as evaluative bulwarks. An examination validated against them should lose much dead wood in the process. Next, we shall analyze the types of testing instruments themselves.

The various testing instruments

Despite the various polarities that exist between and among testing types, fundamentally there are only two classes: subjective and objective types. Both confront the testee with a problem, make him conscious of being examined, pose questions that have hypothetically correct answers, and leave a product of behavior. But with subjective instruments, the determination of rightness and wrongness in the answer, although theoretically attainable, is practically an impossibility. The objective instrument, in contrast, is less plagued by this limitation.

In the remainder of this section, the several kinds of tests under these two broad categories will be identified and analyzed from the standpoint of advantages, limitations, suggestions to the teacher, and grading.

The Essay Test. Although regarded often as discrete, the essay category in itself runs a broad gamut from simple to complex. For example, Walter Monroe and Ralph Carter as early as 1923 recognized 20 subtypes.[2] Although a few of the groups overlap, and some others would be considered today as objective types, the range of possible divisions is still extensive, including: comparison, decision for or against, cause and effect, explanation, summary, analysis, relationship, illustration "in your own words," selection of errors in items, application of generalizations, discussion, identification of purpose, criticism, and outlining.

A few examples follow.

Essay Question 1. (Comparison): Compare the motives of the American revolutionists of 1775 with those of the Algerians in 1962. Identify the primary similarities and differences between the two groups, commenting briefly at each point of comparison.

Essay Question 2. (Explanation): Explain the manner in which the properties of a dry-cell battery combine to produce an electrical current.

Essay Question 3. (Analysis and Application): Clarence Darrow once said: "I am an agnostic; I do not pretend to know what many ignorant men are sure of." Analyze the meaning of this statement and then relate it to the current social scene.

Essay Question 4. (Discussion): The textbook identifies the causes of the Civil War as economic, political, and social. Discuss these in detail, extending each into the life of the pre-Civil War times.

These are four selected examples of essay questions which may now be evaluated against the following listed advantages and disadvantages.

(A) *Advantages:* Essay tests are relatively easy to prepare, although not so easy that the task should be performed "the night before." They

---

[2] Walter S. Monroe and Ralph E. Carter, "The Use of Different Types of Thought Questions in Secondary Schools and Their Relative Difficulty for Students," *Bureau of Educational Research Bulletin No. 14* (Urbana, Ill.: University of Illinois, 1923), pp. 1–26.

permit the interplay of the higher cognitive processes in achieving such outcomes as the organization of ideas, application of principles to specific situations, transfer of concepts from one situation to another, and other challenging aspects of reflective thinking. Furthermore, they make for study habits that channel the thinking of the pupil toward these higher intellectual outcomes.

(B) *Disadvantages:* Essay tests are difficult to grade accurately because many factors stand in the way of objectivity, for example: handwriting, ability of the pupil to express his ideas clearly enough to prevent misinterpretation, the mood of the teacher, halo—or prejudicial effect of the pupil on the teacher, and the time the paper is graded—before or after a well- or poorly written paper. It also can sample only a small part of a course, thus affecting validity adversely. In the event of pupil absences and the need of a second examination, preparing one that is comparable in difficulty to the original one is uncertain of accomplishment.

(C) *Suggestions to the teacher.*

1. Hold the number of questions to a reasonable minimum so that a pupil is given ample opportunity to organize his ideas and present them thoughtfully. Essay examinations normally should not be geared to speed, lest their purpose of evoking thought be lost in the rapid pace of answering.

2. Prepare questions early and revise them often before finally including them in the test.

3. Make questions specific. Whenever possible, refrain from such instructions as: "Write for twenty minutes on _____"; or "Tell all you know about _____"; or "What is your opinion on _____?" Specificity not only gives direction to pupils but aids the teacher in the process of grading.

4. Have the questions either mimeographed or written on the board before the class begins. Do not dictate them. The latter process may inadvertently invite questions and counter explanations that will detract from the testing atmosphere. If the examiner's handwriting is only mildly legible, the examination should definitely be mimeographed.

5. When warranted, give pupils a choice of two out of three or three out of four questions, so that their fear of "drawing a blank" on any one question will be eliminated. Losing out completely on a half or third of an examination is a real disaster to pupils who may have studied earnestly but neglected in some way to focus on a certain content area. Permitting pupils to make a choice of questions is not always recommended, however, particularly when a common coverage of important content is desired or when a test covers easy material that all should know.

6. Instruct pupils in the process of writing essay examinations as you would for performance in any other phase of the curriculum.

(D) *Grading the essay test.* Grading is the largest single obstacle to the effectiveness of essay testing, and unusual care needs to be exercised in the process. Here are some suggestions for the teacher who wishes to reduce grading errors to a minimum and yet grade on a relative basis, that is, on a basis whereby the performance of one pupil is compared with that of others.

1. Scan-read the answers given to one question by approximately a third of the pupils in class. The purpose is to give the teacher a "feel" of relative performance.

2. Read carefully the answers (of all the pupils) to the one question, placing the answers in three to five piles, depending on whether three, four, or five grading categories are desired.

3. Next, sample two or three from each pile to determine whether the quality of answers is comparable.

4. Then place a symbol mark on the question (A, B, C, D, F or excellent, average, poor, and so forth).

5. Repeat the process for each of the other questions.

The teacher who grades with an absolute answer in mind has a simpler job: he evaluates each answer against the "master answer sheet" prepared beforehand. If it calls for six points and the pupil includes only four, he places a 4 in the margin, or a minus 2, or some other symbol which will lead him eventually to the assigning of a final score. The initial grading against an absolute standard, however, does not lead necessarily to an absolute marking system. The top pupil, for example, who scores 70 out of a possible 100 might be given an A on a relative basis despite the initial employment of an absolute standard.

Throughout the marking process, the names of pupils should be concealed in spite of the fact that by the end of the first month of a semester, the handwriting of each pupil, in reality, will be his signature. But, to maintain the proper pose of anonymity, the teacher should ask that names be written on the reverse side of papers that are handed in.

The Completion Test. One of the oldest of the so-called objective tests is the completion type. It is based on the process of recall, giving the pupil no recognition help whatsoever, as do the true-false, multiple-choice, and matching tests. First of all, we offer a definition: *a completion test is a sequence of sentences or questions from which significant parts have been omitted for testing purposes, which, when restored, complete the initial meaning once more.* A few examples should make for clearer understanding.

Instructions. Please fill in the missing parts of the following sentences or quotations. Only the exact words will suffice.

1. "The Assyrian came down like a ＿＿＿＿＿＿ on the fold,
   And his ＿＿＿＿＿＿ were gleaming with purple and gold."
2. To the painter, the primary colors are: ＿＿, ＿＿ and ＿＿.

Instructions. In the spaces provided at the beginning of each statement, write in the appropriate missing word or words.

_____ 1. Whose name is most often associated with the concept of evolution?

¿Qué_____ ? 2. Complete the translation into Spanish of the question: "What time is it?"

Instructions. At the end of each sentence, in the space provided, write in the correct counterpart of the incorrect grammatical element.

1. Due to his fall, he was unable to play. _____.
2. The lady objected to him fighting. _____.

(A) *Advantages of the completion test.* The primary advantage of the completion-type test is its usefulness in a testing situation where specificity is in order. It is apropos when, for instance, the exact word, phrase, number, or arithmetical symbol is sought. It is particularly applicable to the scientific and mathematical areas. It it also fairly simple to construct.

(B) *Disadvantages of the completion test.* The primary disadvantage is its restriction to learning outcomes which demand specificity of response. Thus, in any situation, where the formulation of ideas and other reflective-thinking outcomes are of the essence, other media of testing must be substituted. That it tests rote memory may or may not be a disadvantage, depending on the purpose of the test.

(C) *Suggestions to the teacher.*

1. Make certain that the statement in which the blank occurs gives the pupil sufficient insight to the answer desired. In this regard, in the following, a. is preferable to b. because of its greater delimitation.

a. Shakespeare had his greatest success in the literary medium of the _____ (drama) _____ .
b. Shakespeare had his greatest success in _____ ?? _____ .

2. Don't test for trivia. In example a. below, unimportant words (*own* and *even*) from Tom Paine's statement have been omitted; in b., the omission is properly of more vital substance (*liberty* and *enemy*).

(1)_____ a. He that would make his (1) liberty secure
(2)_____   must guard (2) his enemy from oppression.
(1)_____ b. He that would make his own (1) secure, must
(2)_____   guard even his (2) from oppression.

3. Make all the blank lines of equal length, lest you provide an unnecessary clue.

4. Insist on *the* answer, not an answer just as good. When the teacher begins to compromise with exactness in a completion item, he should use another type.

5. Do not have so many words omitted in a passage that the meaning is obscured. For instance, if only the first few words of Voltaire's aphorism, "I may disapprove of what you say but," were followed by

blank lines for fill-in insertions, few would be able to add "will defend to the death your right to say it."

(D) *Grading the completion test.* If blank lines are placed at the right or left of the page, the scorer can use a key to greater advantage than if the blanks are placed in the middle of sentences. Normally each response should receive equal numerical value. Again, we suggest that answers which only approximate correctness be marked wrong. Looseness in marking makes the instrument less than objective.

The True-False Test. The common term *true-false test* will be used to describe the instrument which is also often referred to as an *alternate-response, same-opposite,* and *right-wrong test.* Probably, next to the completion type, it is the most popular with teachers. Selected illustrations follow:

Instructions. Before each of the following statements, write in the word *False* or *True* (No other symbols will be accepted). Please do not write any comments in the margin to modify your responses.

———— 1. John Henry is a folksong character.
———— 2. The Federal government is the basic political unit of education.
———— 3. Common law has its roots in the Napoleonic Code.

(A) *Advantages of the true-false test.* This testing medium provides relative ease of preparation, permits extensive sampling of a wide range of subject matter material, and can be scored rapidly and objectively.

(B) *Disadvantages of the true-false test.* This medium is more inclined to test superficial than the more complex types of mental responses. Furthermore, it forces the testee to make a categoric response without giving him the added opportunity to qualify. This situation is particularly oppressive to the bright student who in other learning situations rarely looks for or finds an answer that is absolutely correct or incorrect. His inclination usually is to answer only after some qualification. That it invites guessing may or may not be a fault; if it is, the length of the test can correct it.

(C) *Suggestions to the teacher.*

1. Observe English usage carefully. An awkward expression, an unfamiliar polysyllabic word, or an ambiguous phrase can obscure the meaning. The reader would be confused, for instance, over the following true-false item on testing: "Be careful of statements that are partly true or partly false." What does the ambiguous imperative, "Be careful," mean in this instance?

2. Avoid long, highly modified, and involved statements. They tend to be true more often than false.

3. Avoid negatives which obscure meaning, as, for instance, in the following confusing statement: "In a lifetime, it is unlikely that a normal person will not be mentally ill at some time."

4. Do not "lift" statements verbatim from a textbook.

5. If a statement that is only partially true is to be marked wrong, the reader should be so informed in the instructions. The advisability of the practice, however, is questionable.

6. Avoid containing two or more ideas in one statement.

7. Avoid trick questions, lest they cheapen evaluation. The following is an example: *Mainstreet* was written by Sinclaire Lewis.

8. Realize that the ease of preparation of true-false tests is more apparent than real; in fact, preparing them is a time-consuming task. Items should be accumulated over an extended period of time, should be read and reread, and should be tried out occasionally, before employment, on willing colleagues.

9. Usually avoid such absolutes as *all* and *never*. Substitute, in lieu thereof, *some* and *usually*.

10. Balance numerically the number of true and false statements. A flip of a coin to determine whether a true or false item will be inserted is a simple and defensible practice.

11. Use many true-false questions over a period of a semester or year if greater reliability and validity are desired. Chance is controlled in this way.

(D) *Grading the true-false test.* A primary issue here is whether to penalize more heavily for an answer that is wrong, presumably as a result of guessing, than for one that is left blank. When such a differential approach is employed, a double penalty is normally assessed for incorrect items, and a single one for those items not answered. By this method, then, a pupil who answered 20 answers incorrectly out of 100 would receive a score of 60, reflecting the double-penalty philosophy; another who answered 10 incorrectly and left 10 additional blank would be given a score of 70.

The propriety of this grading method rests, first of all, on the inferred heinousness of guessing; second, assuming such heinousness, on the demonstrated value of the arithmetical manipulations. We reject either justification as valid: the former from a personal orientation; the latter, from a skepticism toward the actual changes in grading thereby effected. In this connection, if a relative approach is employed wherein the grades of students are rank-ordered according to test scores, the place of rank is little different when the double or the single penalty is the criterion. And if absolute scores are the criteria of marks, dare a teacher justify the lower grades that the double penalty usually brings? In the last analysis, the extra manipulation involved is probably not worth the effort. A simpler and better way to control chance in any testing instrument is to solicit greater length as an ally. Any coin-flipping situation attests to the validity of this statement.

The Matching Test. The matching test is another approach to measurement which is based on recognition. It usually consists of a column of stimulus items on one side of an examination and a related column of answers on the other. The pupil's task is to match the two. Early in the testing movement, it was customary for the two columns to contain the same number of items; more recently, practice has supported the insertion of a larger number of answers than of stimuli. An example of the uneven-column approach is contained in the following:

Instructions: In this matching test, there are two columns of items. The column on the left contains ten stimulus items, unnumbered, pertaining to the cell, with a blank line in front of each. The column on the right contains 13 descriptive terms, only 10 of which are associated with the statements. Your job is to place *the number* of the descriptive term in the blank line before the appropriate stimulus item. Remember that at the end of the test, you will *not* have used three of the descriptive terms.

Example

————— Red coloring matter in certain cells.
————— One of the three main parts of a cell.
————— Substance that is non-living.
————— All cells of any one kind that do the same kind of work.
————— A message-conducting structural component.
————— Green bodies in a plant cell.
————— The only known living substance.
————— The basic living unit.
————— A covering surface for inner and outer parts of the body.
————— An organized group of tissues.

1. epithelium
2. organ
3. chlorophyll
4. hemoglobin
5. cytoplasm
6. chloroplasts
7. body system
8. blood
9. nerve tissue
10. any of the types of tissue
11. cellulose
12. cell
13. protoplasm

(A) *Advantages of the matching test.* The matching test has some value in situations where associated learning is considered desirable. It does particularly well in associating terms and their descriptive counterparts, people with places and happenings, and dates with events.

(B) *Disadvantages of the matching test.* That the section on advantages was kept so brief is an indication that, although not seriously disapproving of the particular testing device, we give it somewhat faint praise. Its limitations are that it emphasizes memory outcomes more than the higher processes of understanding, organization, and application; is more time-consuming to construct than other types of objective tests that could do the same job equally well; and is likely to provide inadvertent clues to the correct response. In general, the matching examination has some merit in that it breaks the monotony of testing, but too much time is usually spent in preparation for the good that it accomplishes. In the ten-item test presented, would not a completion test have accomplished the same purpose in a more economical and effective way? The only difference is that recall would have been substituted for recognition. If only this minor change, would the outcome compensate for the extra effort?

(C) *Suggestions to the teacher.* To improve the effectiveness of the matching test, the teacher should:

1. Provide more answers than stimuli in order to control the factor of guessing.
2. Include responses that are in discrete categories, for example, dates or people or processes, but not a combination.
3. Include in the test a substantial number of items.
4. Include all of the test on a single page.
5. Arrange the column of choices alphabetically or in some other random way.

(D) *Grading the matching test.* The grading of matching tests is too mechanical for further comment to be necessary.

The Multiple-Choice Test. Regarded by the author as probably the best type of objective test is the multiple-choice test. Each item consists of an introductory stem and usually four or more choices of answer. All but one of the choices are referred to as distractors. The exception is the correct answer. Some sample questions follow:

Example 1. I give a true-false test of 100 items to a science class. I furnish a key to five scorers, all of whom turn in the same results. All of my colleagues tell me that the test is excellent. The pupils report that it is very fair. I can therefore conclude that it was: (A) reliable, (B) objective, (C) valid, (D) standardized, (E) discriminating.

Example 2. The following expansion of the binomial theorem contains two errors. Place the numbers of the two errors in the appropriate parenthetical spaces to the right of the answers. $(A + B)^4 =$:
(1) A^4+ (2) $4A^3B+$ (3) $8A^2B^2+$ (4) $4AB^4+$ (5) B^4 (　) (　)

Example 3. One major difference between communism, as theorized by Marx, and capitalism, as practiced in the United States, is that capitalism places much greater stress on: (1) democracy, (2) the interests of the nation, (3) a minimum standard of living, (4) the freedom of the individual, (5) industrial expansion.

(A) *Advantages of the multiple-choice test.* Properly conceived, multiple-choice tests come closer than any other objective-type to the goal of soliciting the highest intellectual responses of understanding and reasoning. For instance, Examples 1 and 3 above stimulate the reader to analyze all of the five listed choices before accepting the appropriate one as the correct answer. This process involves analytical thinking. This type of test is also easy to administer and score.

(B) *Disadvantages of the multiple-choice test.* The primary disadvantage is that it is difficult and time-consuming to construct. In preparing a 50-item multiple-choice test for any course, it would not be unusual for a teacher to spend 15 to 20 hours in item selection and refinement. Initial preparation, sifting, trying-out, and final selection are all time-consuming.

Another disadvantage, more in implementation than inherent, is the tendency of teachers to employ multiple-choice items for trivial purposes which could be achieved better by completion or true-false questions. In the following two examples, because of the specificity of the material and the un-seductiveness of the distractors, a completion item would accomplish the test's mission more simply and thus more justifiably.

Example 1. President Kennedy's first Secretary of State was: (A) Stevenson, (B) Rusk, (C) Dulles, (D) Herter, (E) Dillon.

Example 2. Columbus discovered America in: (A) 1492, (B) 1522, (C) 1592, (D) 1692, (E) 1392

(C) *Suggestions to the teacher.*

1. Make certain that the listed responses are plausible enough to stimulate thought. When, as in the following, four of the choices are too far removed from the right answer to be credible, they become filler items only. Unless distractors approximate the right answer, they are meaningless.

Example: An effective teacher consistently: (A) allows a class to direct itself, (B) consistently follows a predetermined day-to-day schedule, (C) bows to the wishes of the class, (D) motivates self-direction, (E) minimizes skills and emphasizes social development.

2. Include as much in the stem as you can so that the choices stand out clearly and simply. In the first example which follows, the stem is too stark and the choices, too verbose. In the second example, the improvement in the stem leads to the resultant of choices that are more succinct and meaningful.

Example 1. In the area of individual differences:
(1) bright students excel the slow on motor skills,
(2) slow students excel the bright on emotional adjustment,
(3) slow students are more social than the bright,
(4) bright students think better reflectively than the slow.
Example 2. In relative contrast to the slow-learning student, the bright excels most demonstrably in the area of: (A) motor skills, (B) emotional adjustment, (C) social adjustment, (D) reflective thinking.

3. Avoid ambiguity to enhance validity and reliability. The following example fails this criterion because of its vagueness of wording.

Example. When a class shows apathy, the first concern of a teacher should be for: (A) himself, (B) the curriculum, (C) the students, (D) the principal.

4. Make all responses of approximately equal length.

5. Provide four or five choices so as to minimize the element of chance.

6. Indicate in the instructions how an item is to be marked, for example, whether the correct response is to be underlined, the appropriate letter placed in the margin, and so forth. The examples that the author presented in the past several pages would be responded to in many different ways because instructions were not included in some instances.

7. Avoid the frequent usage of the responses: "All of these," and "None of these." Often their inclusion is for filler purposes, as in the following:

Example. A test which measures what it purports to measure is said to have: (A) objectivity, (B) reliability, (C) validity, (D) all of these, (E) none of these.

(D) *Grading the multiple-choice test.* For ease of hand-grading, it is suggested that a half-inch line be placed at the beginning of each item so that the identifying symbol of the proper response can be written in. A vertical key can then be placed alongside the examination sheet and scoring greatly facilitated. However, the use of an answer sheet for machine scoring is recommended whenever the examination is long and the school has the proper facilities.

Making an item analysis

After an objective-type test has been administered and the papers collected, the dedicated teacher is interested in the quality of the items. Did they accomplish their anticipated purposes? It is not enough for the teacher to know that the test as a whole discriminated; he should also know how each item performed. A simple procedure for determining the quality of the items is as follows:

1. While scoring each test, the teacher keeps a record of the specific items that were missed. At the end of the process, he will then know that Question 1, for example, was missed by 10 out of 30 pupils; question 11, by 16 out of 30; and question 15, by 5 out of 30.

2. Next, he will select from the class two groups, for example, the highest five and the lowest five on the test; or the upper third and the lowest third determined by the test or by a broader criterion. In analyzing the performance of these two groups, he will need to determine whether the test items discriminated properly between the upper and lower class divisions. For instance, if 10 missed Question 16, and 9 of the 10 who missed it were in the lower third and only 1 in the upper third of the class, the question should probably be regarded favorably as discriminatory. However, if 5 in each of the upper and lower thirds of the class missed the question, the teacher might well desire to discount it in the immediate testing situation and revise it before using it again.

After making the item analysis, the teacher will have accomplished two major purposes: he will thus be enabled to use his findings when leading a discussion of the test with pupils; and he will have validated, in part, the various items of the test.

Administering a test

While a test is being taken by pupils, the teacher should proctor it actively rather than sit at his desk in the front of the room. When he moves quietly around the room every few minutes, answers the questions that seem to be an inevitable part of any testing situation, and, in general, makes his presence felt, he becomes a positive influence on behavior in general and the testing situation in particular.

Effective proctoring is also one way to control cheating. With young people frequently overstimulated by the fierce competition for grades, a teacher's moralizing after the fact of cheating is not enough. Prevention is what is needed. And one easy as well as commendable method is for the teacher during the test to relate closely to pupils. This does not mean that he should smother pupils with attention, unnaturally looking over their shoulders to see what they are writing. Proctoring, rather than interfering with the pupils' sovereignty or privacy, when performed properly will serve to establish a professional atmosphere.

SUMMARY

This chapter has treated of the indescribably rapid growth of the testing movement in the United States during the past half-century, a phenomenon to be commended unless tending to replace or dull interest in the broader psychological growth of individuals.

An early distinction was made between standardized and nonstandardized, subjective and objective, ability and achievement, global and diagnostic, power and speed, and verbal and performance tests. Other terms of testing were also defined and clarified: *validity, reliability, central tendencies,* and *variability.*

Next, standardized instruments were discussed by type and service rendered. Their purpose was identified as strictly supplemental to teacher-made tests, without ever being conceived as replacements for the latter. The last sections of the chapter treated of the basic principles of teacher-made tests and the specific types, organized according to advantages, disadvantages, suggestions to the teacher, and hints for grading.

The over-all view was that tests, important as they are, will never replace other methods of evaluation; but as supplements, they are invaluable. Strongly implied throughout was that tests can attain their maximum potential only when teachers approach them with craftsmanlike skill and professional insight.

REFERENCES

Cronbach, Lee J., *Essentials of Psychological Testing.* New York: Harper & Row, 1961.

Froehlich, Clifford P., and Kenneth B. Hoyt, *Guidance Testing*. Englewood Cliffs, N.J.: Prentice-Hall, Inc., 1959.

Furst, E. J., *Constructing Evaluation Instruments*. New York: Longmans, Green and Co. (5th ed.), 1958.

Garrett, Henry E., *Elementary Statistics*. New York: Longmans, Green and Co., 1956.

Greene, Harry A., Albert N. Jorgensen, and J. Raymond Gerberich, *Measurement and Evaluation in the Secondary School*. New York: Longmans, Green and Co., 1954.

Guilford, J. P., *Fundamental Statistics in Psychology and Education*. New York: McGraw-Hill Book Co., 1956.

Kettelkamp, Gilbert C., *Teaching Adolescents*. Boston: D. C. Heath and Co., 1954.

Ross, C. C., *Measurement in Today's Schools*. Englewood Cliffs, N.J.: Prentice-Hall, Inc., 1953.

Thorndike, Robert L., and Elizabeth P. Hagen, *Measurement and Evaluation in Psychology and Education*. New York: John Wiley and Sons, Inc., 1961.

DETERMINING
AND
REPORTING
MARKS

Once a teacher has engaged in and completed the function of value-judging, he faces the additional burden of having to report his findings. Society demands that the school inform the pupil and his parents of its observations. Unfortunately, the dictum is not accompanied by the monetary support to make the reporting process scientifically defensible. Smaller classes are needed for this outcome to be feasible. Accordingly, the schools face the dilemma of being expected to report pupil progress with justifiable accuracy although they are not endowed with the requisites for the task. The compromise has been the controversial single-symbol grade, which, while it has characterized secondary school education for generations, has consistently bedeviled evaluation by its oversimplification.

A paradox exists between the grandiose goals of education, on one hand, and the childlike narrowness of the single mark, on the other. The school initially accepts responsibility for the mental, social, physical, and emotional growth of students—a sweeping dedication, to say the least; but, when marking time comes, progress within the framework of this impressive commission is forced into the ludicrous constriction of a single response. For this fundamental reason, then, the topic of marks and marking is usually associated with emotionalism: resulting in parent and pupil euphoria when high grades are received; in despondency when low grades are received; and in teacher frustration following all grades, of whatever dimension. This frustration of teachers emanates from their being expected to do what they know they cannot do well: namely, to evaluate human growth in a word, a number, or some other single symbol. The solitary mark is more comprehensible as a vestige of the past than as a feature of the present. At a time when the curriculum was basically essentialist in character, concerned primarily with the uncomplicated elements of arithmetic, grammar, and reading, a conventional mark probably had considerable relevance. But when in face, for instance, of the sophistication of reflective thinking and problem-solving, the relevance begins to dim.

Nevertheless, despite the validity of the theoretical case against traditional marks, school personnel are not yet ready at the practical level to make a frontal assault on existing practices. But neither are they any more ready to defend the *status quo*. Thus, the teacher candidate, just a psychological step from the classroom, realistically can expect administrative vagueness in this important curriculum function. In fact, the typical principal or superintendent, in most instances, would gladly evade the direct question from the neophyte incumbent: "What is the school's policy on grading?" If compelled to make a reply, his would be a recommendation of moderation, resting comfortably only when not veering toward "too many" D's and F's, or A's and B's.

On this structure of practice that is ambivalent and theory that is well ahead of its time, we build our case for marks and marking. Unable to escape completely from the present, the treatment will identify the more legitimate practices employed in the better schools while rejecting the spurious. Intermingled with this realism will be a frequent look at the brighter reflections of theory.

PURPOSES OF REPORTING

The reporting of pupil progress, like all other aspects of a school's curriculum, can have only one fundamental purpose: the maximum development of the pupil. This must be the lodestar which irresistibly guides in the direction of growth. In the process, it needs to shun the attempts at adulteration by such antagonists as expediency, the foolish hobgoblins of tradition, and the seduction of half-truths. By brushing these aside with courage, it preserves its legitimacy. Properly conceived, school marks or grades (terms which will be used interchangeably) constitute means of keeping pupils, parents, and professional personnel informed of the progress that students are making.

Specifically, how efficiently do school marks serve as motivators of improved performance? And a related question: If school marks were removed from the classroom scene, would performance show an appreciable decline? Unfortunately, research findings in these areas are too limited to support either a pro or a con stand. In one of the few matched-group studies at the elementary level, Cook reported only minor differences between schools where retardation was common and other sample schools where failure was rare or nonexistent. His conclusion was that the threat of low grades did not work against failure.[1]

The greatest weight of evidence concerning the effect of grade reports on students rests on logic, however, with the following constituting a fairly accurate status picture. In a tradition conditioned to the assumed importance of marks, their removal would undoubtedly have an initial depressing effect on performance, although probably of somewhat limited dimensions. Affected most adversely would be the achievement of those students who had responded to high marks as symbols of prestige value. This depressant would be more noticeable in the suburbs than in the subcultures of large cities. Following the initial removal of grades, just what would happen over a projected subsequent period is anyone's guess. Ours is that, with psychic energy basically positive, young people would soon perform just as effectively as they had previously, maybe more so. The influence of a well-conceived curriculum and mature teacher behavior is undoubtedly a more significant motivator than marks at their best.

However, even though marks fail to motivate as much as many would like, the significance of keeping pupils informed of progress should not be underestimated. The field of reading, in this regard, testifies convincingly that the student who knows where he stands in terms of reading speed and comprehension is thereby accelerated toward greater accomplishment. Thus, while being skeptical of the one-symbol report as motivational, teachers should employ other reporting methods to convey a status picture. These might be written comments in the margins of English themes, corrections of foreign-language translations, the underlining of incorrect processes or answers in a mathematics course, and oral comments pertaining to demonstrated performance in any course. The day-to-day classroom exchanges between pupil and teacher are probably the most natural and therefore most meaningful ways of communicating impressions about behavior. They far outdistance the single symbol in significance.

The report to the home also demands justification. Its manifest intent, of course, is to acquaint parents with the performance of their children, but its success is only as extensive as the language of communication is properly descriptive. In the teacher-pupil relationship, even when a single symbol is reported, other media of evaluation can serve as supplements. In the teacher-parent relationship, however, barring the occasional conference or home letter, the portrayal of pupil behavior normally

---

[1] Walter W. Cook, *Grouping and Promotion in the Elementary School* (Minneapolis: University of Minnesota Press, 1941).

rests tenuously on the infrequent and overly compressed mark. When an F, its meaning is moderately clear; but in the graduated shadings above F, the message becomes more blurred. In the latter instance, the parent and child each reads into the symbol of "80," or "C+," or "Fair" his own interpretation, and attacks the issue from that vantage point. The over-all purpose is unquestionably laden with the positive; but the language of communication is fuzzy, and meaning often fades into distortion.

Also, as was pointed out by Smith and Tyler in the Wilford Aiken study, parents so often get lost in the success symbols of marks that they lose sight of the development of the child.[2] A goal of the future thus must be the continuation of reporting student progress to parents, but in a manner that is more extensive and revealing.

The third purpose of reporting pertains to its services to teachers and administrators. In this function, evaluation is reduced by the economy of symbolism to serve the causes of grade placement, graduation, college attendance, and future employment. The more ulterior services to honor societies and rank-in-class outcomes, we mention only in passing. Whatever the purposes of grade reports are, the process itself should be conceived as evaluation compressed narrowly into the abstract and made to pay the price of such constriction by resulting inaccuracies of interpretation. The greater the constriction, the less reliable is the final remaining element as a condensed capsule.

LIMITATIONS

What has already been written in this section should make any illusions about marking being scientific vanish, encumbered, as we have seen it to be, with subjectivity. We shall now take a detailed look at the many individual factors which cast an unfavorable academic light on marking.

Grading creates barriers between teacher and pupil

One of the more regrettable evils of grading is that it inevitably leads to the blockage of communication between teacher and pupils. In one situation, the teacher plays the role of righteous judge (sensitively, he hopes) as he evaluates the performance of young people, sentencing some to F's and D's. Then, in the next moment, he is placed in a personal relationship with a failing student in which warmth, objectivity, and empathic understanding are demanded of him. Clinically speaking, the latter is not only a *non sequitur* of the former, but an impossible situation to contend with, shadowed as it is with the emotionalism that hovers over the F grade.

[2] Eugene R. Smith and Ralph Tyler, *Appraising and Recording Student Progress* (New York: Harper & Row, 1942), p. 489.

Even at the level of human relationships, marks germinate suspicion and distrust between teacher and pupil. Nearly every teacher has at some time impugned the motives of a sincere adolescent who seemed to be playing an out-of-part role of ultra-friendliness. That the teacher saw chicanery where none existed may be attributable to the lurking presence of grading fears. No less unfortunate is the reverse twist of events, where the teacher gives the benefit of the doubt to a student, only to realize later that the student's innocence was a pre-grading veneer. In either event, two human beings were forced into artificial roles.

The conflicting personal and grading demands of the classroom will come as quite a surprise to the new teacher. He will never wish to conceal his basic warmth for young people, nor should he. But, with his evaluative responsibility, neither can he be "just a friend." Out of innate niceness, he will slant grades, although maybe unconsciously, toward the adolescent who needs the extra symbol of help; but if he slants too much, he will become an easy touch. At the other extreme, when he is too impervious to student differences and consistently grades severely, he will get the reputation of being "hard."

Within this current of conflicting pressures, the teacher needs the maturity that will keep him a human being while helping him retain that minimum of detachment from the group that he can never afford to lose. In this framework, then, he strikes an evaluative posture of fairness and lives with the consequences. In the process, he takes a realistic view toward the significance of grades, never treating them as ends. His primary emphasis is always on learning by itself, relegating grades to a place of secondary importance. If he cannot eliminate barriers, he can at least lessen them.

Grading creates barriers among pupils

An obstacle as great as that between teacher and pupils is the one that rises between and among the pupils themselves when competition for marks is intense. An accepted maxim in any school is that young people should cooperate with one another; yet, contradicting it, adolescents are forced into the competitive stresses of the academic prize ring to vie for school recognition and marks. To stay within even the reasonable bounds of sound mental-health practices, the school of the future will have to place less emphasis on high grades as an index of distinction.

When competition is permitted to operate without firm control, the tendency of pupils is, either to plunge headlong into the race to do better than someone else, in hopes of winning a "prize," or to withdraw from the race. Which is more unwholesome from the mental-health point of view is difficult to say—the latter probably. The retreat from the rivalry of academic accomplishment is, in part, symptomatic of the personality dynamics of those who withdraw, as well as due to the situation. The many who definitely are unable to hold their own have no other choice. In the fringe-level group immediately below any marking gradient, some stay in the contest hoping that over-achievement, so-called, will compensate for their marginal limitations; others in this group fall back to the lower level of competition. However, permeating the entire function of marking are also the peer influences, which frequently correlate high achievement and prestige negatively. Regardless of specific conditions, the teacher needs to be forewarned of the divisive influences that grades have on students. So informed, he can plan ways to reduce tensions. Needless to say, he should never heighten tensions by using grades primarily to motivate.

The weak compete inequitably with the strong

Related to the preceding problem is another obvious one: that students at all levels of ability are forced into the same academic contest, despite the advance knowledge that only some will be able to make the higher grades. The remainder of the class—almost by design—are made to feel the depression associated with defeat, partial or total—most often, through no fault of their own. The grade of A is just as unattainable to pupils at the low end of the I.Q. continuum as cognitive perspicacity is within reach of the emotionally disturbed. To give the rigid neurotic a grade of D and the psychotic an F is only slightly less ludicrous than to give these grades to slow learners.

Those who defend competitive grading in school as inherently proper take the stand that, since life is competitive, schools unapologetically can be equally competitive in grading. This argument has enough logic to pass muster in a society that is admittedly materialistic. Even so, we question, as did Thorndike almost half a century ago, whether a process will transfer from one situation to another when the two are dissimilar. Will competition in school, with its attendant allocating of differential marks, get young people ready for the commercial competition of Main Street or the cultural competition of upper Elmtown, assuming the legitimacy of this goal in the first place? Might it not just as likely get them less ready as a result of a too early and too forceful reminder of their inadequacies? How can brutal frankness in school be condoned when indirection and gentility of understatement are advocated as proper in other aspects of social living!

Grades tend to become ends

Grades not only force the weak to compete with the strong, but they tend to become ends in themselves. In every walk of life, the symbol often supersedes what it originally symbolized. Production initially was recognized as a means to better living; now it is worshipped as a discrete entity— it is the end, no longer the means. Idolatry exists whenever the symbol assumes autonomy over the primary entity itself. In school, the grade all too often likewise becomes the "end all and be all" of accomplishment. The magic A or B keeps the parent content for six weeks, the teacher happy with the pupil who earned it, and the pupil conscious that he is doing better than some other pupils. But neither it nor any other grade can be defended as spurring the pupil on to truly creative heights. Regardless of the grading symbol and the community's attitude toward it, the values of knowledge for its own sake, of reflective thinking, and of a pupil's working up to capacity become obscured when they relinquish first priority to a shadowy substitute.

Grades are undiagnostic

By the very nature of the process of compressing so much into so little, a grade is always more or less undiagnostic. A medical examination culminating in a B would tell nothing about any specific bodily organ or system. A teacher who received a C for his first year's performance would know little specifically about how he had done. Nor does a mark in a classroom situation tell much more, particularly when it is employed as a condensation at the end of a protracted marking period. For instance, when a youngster brings home a grade of 85 or B in sophomore English, just what does it mean in descriptive terms? To what extent can he write with organization and clarity, or interpret a novel's characters, their emotions, and their feelings? Has his interest in creative writing increased? Does he read more widely and selectively? Can he spell, punctuate, and capitalize accurately? These and other similar questions are left unanswered by the percentage score or the grade of B because the one symbol is too condensed to get into the vitals of true meaning.

Accuracy is distorted by extraneous factors

As if grading as a method did not have enough trouble with the manifest variables within the school situation, it also has to meet the opposition of sex differences and socioeconomic factors. Most studies on the subject agree that marks favor girls in a significant way. Schinnerer, for instance, drawing on his study of 340,000 final marks of pupils in the Cleveland School System, revealed a failure ratio between the sexes of 2 boys to 1 girl.[3] In one school, the ratio was even as high as 6 to 1. Walker,[4] too, reported that girls fail less frequently than boys; and Swenson,[5] that girls "pack" the honor societies, despite a comparability of intelligence quo-

---

[3] Mark Schinnerer, "Failure Ratio: 2 Boys to 1 Girl," *Clearing House* (January, 1944), pp. 264–270.

[4] Margaret M. Walker, *A Study of High-School Failures* (Scottsdale, Penna.: Mennonite Press, 1935), p. 96.

[5] Clifford Swenson, "Packing the Honor Society," *Clearing House* (May, 1942), pp. 521–524.

tients between the sexes. Hansen[6] states without equivocation that boys are undoubtedly discriminated against.

Reasons for the sex difference in grading is by no means as clear as the fact of its existence. Some suggested possibilities are that: (1) boys at this age are more interested relatively in physical than in mental activity; (2) boys mature more slowly and thus suffer because of accompanying social and emotional retardation; (3) boys are less verbal and therefore lose out in the battle of communication; (4) boys are more aggressive and thus bear the brunt of teacher retaliation. If the last is at all valid, the teacher with a prior understanding of adolescent male truculence should make appropriate concessions for it.

Like the sex factor, socioeconomic class status is also a determinant of grades. *Elmtown's Youth,*[7] already alluded to or discussed several times, indicated that the higher grades go to the children of the "better" homes, and that fewer of these children fail. Likewise, such children have higher I.Q.'s than the children who come from families of lower socioeconomic status. However, Hollingshead stated that the grades of the upper groups are much higher than would have been predicted from their intelligence quotients. His explanation for the differential in grades was that the pupils from the lower two of the five categories into which he divided his sample have not been trained to respond as well to competitive situations in school as have the more aggressive pupils in Classes I, II, and III, whose egos drive them more compulsively toward success. In inverse manner, the Class V pupils, said Hollingshead, have not been imbued with a compulsive need for social advancement or impressed with the fact that good grades are a necessity for success. Apart from these observations was the direct implication that, because pupils in Classes I, II, and III are expected to do well, the teachers' mind-sets have already decided the outcome. Even more disturbing was the finding that the typical Elmtown teacher helped upper-class adolescents meet the higher levels of anticipated expectation out of fear of trouble with the parents, or from a desire for their upper-class support.

Standards differ among teachers

Another limitation of grades is that, among the great body of teachers, standards of accomplishment as a determining factor differ so widely as to stagger the imagination. A pupil, for instance, expands the binomial theorem to the fifth power with the following resultant:

$$(A + B)^5 = A^5 + 5A^4B + 10A^3B^2 + 10A^2B^4 + 5AB^4 + B^5$$

[6] Kenneth Hansen, *High School Teaching* (Englewood Cliffs, N.J.: Prentice-Hall, Inc., 1957), p. 256.
[7] August de Belmont Hollingshead, *Elmtown's Youth* (New York: John Wiley and Sons, 1949), pp. 172–176.

We have underlined the one element of the process where he erred. He either mistakenly or accidentally wrote into the expansion the exponent 4 instead of 3. What grade should be given him? Remember that mathematics is an "exact science," and precision of grading in it should be easy of accomplishment.

And what mark should be assigned to evaluate the performance of the seventh-grade pupil who wrote the following paragraph?

Jack London is not like the other writers that we have read. He is real interesting. Take his "Call of the Wild". That is a book that everyone should say was tops. As for as I am concerned, it is the best book that I have read yet, period. He takes a fellow into the North Woods, lets him see nature in the raw, and gives it to him strait. Yes, London is the best.

If the reader asked 100 experts in the respective fields of mathematics and English to evaluate these efforts of two pupils, how much uniformity could he expect in their grading? If the many studies that have been made on similar situations are typical, grades would vary widely.

The transfer value of grades is limited

Whatever the limitations of specific marking symbols, a logical question relates to the part that they play once adolescents have left high school. An obvious value is their instrumentality in helping youth to get themselves enrolled in college. As of the moment, many institutions of higher learning, mostly the state-supported, initially accept all secondary school graduates for, at least, a first-semester attempt, placing those immediately on probation who are in the lower quarter or third of their graduating classes. Practices vary from this standard to the practice of certain institutions which consider applications from only the upper 5 or 10 per cent of the senior class. However, colleges and universities are turning more and more to the College Board scores, either in lieu of or as supplements to high-school grades, with the result that secondary school marks are losing some of their importance as symbolic images of a student's ability to perform. As statistical predictors, they correlate on the order of .50 with college grades; the academic aptitude test does even a little better.

The value of high school marks when the adolescent applies for a job in business or industry is quite limited. Some employers send for a transcript, but the majority are willing to settle for references. A truism is that marks in one academic situation predict results more accurately in another academic situation than they do in an environment that is non-academically oriented. An evaluation broadly conceived in terms of study habits, personality, ability, and achievement might carry over somewhat to a job situation, but normally the transfer value is limited.

Marks are often used punitively

This final section on marking limitations is more functionally related to existing practices than directly pertinent to the process itself. We speak of the mark used punitively. Not uncommon in many classrooms are such remarks as: "If you don't change your attitude, you will get a low mark in this course." "You seem to be doing your best to get an F in here." Or, "You would have gotten a higher mark, but your behavior is so poor." These and like comments unnecessarily emphasize the horrendous nature of the low grade while diverting attention from the performance itself. When the teacher uses a grade to punish, he removes professionalism from the whole process of evaluation—and from himself. A grade, if justified at all, must be regarded as an academic and clinical aid, not a vindictive weapon.

Marks should not be employed to conceal unrelated inadequacies

At times, a grade is also employed, although perhaps unconsciously, to conceal a curriculum inadequacy or teacher incompetency. When seventh-graders, for instance, are unable to understand noun clauses, the grades of D and F are poor substitutes for the time wasted on such content. And when a low grade distracts the teacher from a well-needed look, for example, at his low level of tolerance, values are out of joint. Better an analysis of the real causes of classroom dislocations than a blameworthy employment of grades to conceal them!

THREE MARKING STANDARDS

Even though aware of the many limitations in marking just discussed, the typical teacher nonetheless has to determine and report selected symbols to the home and the school. And since railing against the unfairness of existing practices will avail him little, he searches next for an approach to marking which, when proceduralized, will contain more of the positive than of the negative. His first obligation, in this regard, is to weigh the relative merits of the absolute, relative, and clinical orientations.

The absolute standard of the teacher

When employing an absolute standard of grading, a teacher, before meeting with adolescents, makes a predetermination of performance expectancy and then applies it to the later accomplishments of students. If, for instance, a teacher of the social studies has drilled students on the names of the ten cabinet members, highlighting overlearning to such an extent that no student, he thinks, should get fewer than two wrong, a score of seven is converted to an automatic F. What grades he would assign to pupils who got none, one, or two wrong, respectively, also would have been predetermined. Other examples of this kind of absolutism are the familiar F for a comma or period fault in a senior English theme; an all-or-none evaluation of a problem in trigonometry; and a weighting, before the fact, of the relative importance of selected evaluative components in any course.

With the absolute standard, the teacher, independent of pupils individually or as a group, constructs a measuring rod with appropriate gradations and then applies it to behavior. If, in the process, the performance of all falls short, all fail! If their performance is superior, all commensurately get A's. Such a positive approach assumes that the evaluator is highly accurate in his prior judgments, that he can live with the absolute consequences of the resulting grades, and that the differences of students will not be ignored unduly.

The first of these assumptions is tenuous, at best: namely, that a fixed standard can be constructed before the overt act of evaluation and maintained without change throughout. That all teachers daily superimpose some kinds of fixed standards on a classroom, we do not doubt or even question; but when the practice attains such rigidity that the door to change is locked, a suspicion of the Messiah complex is not unwarranted.

A common approach of teachers is an unquestioning obedience to an absolute standard up to a certain point, followed by a conversion to a relative standard as events unfold. For example, on the basis of teacher absolutism, the ten best adolescents in class, at the end of a six-week rating period, might conceivably have "earned" the raw-score averages of 76, 69, 69, 68, 66, 65, 65, 62, 50, and 50. Although absolute up to this point, the typical teacher is almost forced to "go relative," as will be observed next.

Being unable to justify the assigning of a grade of C to the top pupil in the class, and grades of D and F to nine of the top ten pupils, he conceivably would interpret the absolute numerical grades in relative terms. That is, he would allocate a grade of A or B, rather than C, to the student with the top grade of 76, and also comparably higher grades to the other students, depending on the rank-order listing of their scores. In similar manner, many teachers operate on an absolute basis up to the time of reporting grades to the school office or home. During the conventional six-weeks marking period, they assign raw scores in terms of how well, percentage-wise, students have measured up to a predetermined standard of performance. At the end of the marking period, however, when grades have to be sent to the administration or home, these teachers make adjustments in grades based on relativity. Failing to make such adjustments, they would incur the indignation or wrath of both the administration and parents. A few in the community might respect their alleged defense of maintaining high standards, but most would not.

A third restriction of the absolute standard is that it ignores the individual differences of adolescents, as did the classically oriented secondary curriculum of the 1800's. The design of the latter was simple: students were made to measure up to pedagogical expectancies or drop out. But the students then were the intellectual cream, the upper 5 to 10 per cent. With almost all youth today in the lower secondary grades and over half that number in the upper, such unvarnished rigidity is misplaced. The curriculum anchorage of a century ago to the dictum of "You come to me," must be exchanged today for a substitute one of: "We shall discover where you are and fit a curriculum to you." If laws are passed to keep children in school, professional policy must be adopted to make their stay profitable, and such policy could not entertain for long a grading system that regularly suppresses even the bright into its more lowly recesses.

The relative standard

In contrast to the absolute standard anchored in teacher expectancy is the relative standard based on comparative class or school performance. This second approach rests its case on competition, allocating grades according to the relative standings of pupils in relationship to one another. All such other factors as teacher expectancy, pupil ability, and effort are subjugated to the process of comparison.

Like any rank-order method, this method of grading stands or falls on the inherent justice of rewarding individuals for doing better than others and punishing those who do worse than others. That this practice has possible merit when the field of competition is somewhat homogeneous cannot be denied. Identifying those who do better when all can do equally well is understandable; but rewarding those who do better than others when the latter are not even in the competition is less defensible. This is the predicament of the school that employs the relative standard—and most do in some way. It places a premium on such terms as "better than" and "in the higher category of" without regard for the more important qualifier of "doing his best." Being only better than another, even though given an A grade, may be a far cry from the mental-health index of measuring up to the optimum of ability and potential. And being identified as the lowest in a class, with the rank-order position reinforced by an F or D, may constitute a misconceived social indictment when a student is doing the best that he knows how.

Another shortcoming of the method is that, when employed indiscriminately, it disregards the ability level of any single group. Rank-order placement and corresponding grading in a class of less ability is of different dimensions from that in a class of greater ability. For the lower 5 per cent of a seventh-grade class to receive F grades is at least slightly more logical than for the lower 5 per cent of a doctoral-level seminar to receive the same failing grade. As natural selection operates over a long period, the resultant population inevitably becomes so narrowed that the previously mentioned terms "better than" and "worse than," or "first" and "last," become ludicrous, whatever the philosophical orientation. Regardless, we can say without fear of contradiction that a predetermined relative system of grading freshmen cannot with fairness be regarded in the same light when applied to seniors.

Within the framework of relative grading, the time inevitably comes when raw-score totals have to be converted into grading symbols. One method is by an arbitrary projection of fixed percentage ratios on a class or larger school group; a second is by a hit-or-miss plan whereby breaks in a list of evaluative scores determine the final groupings.

The most widely advertised system falsely operates under the label of the so-called "normal curve," but in the process it does disservice to the cause of probability. The Gaussian curve cannot be used for this purpose for two reasons: first, it is the *end result* of a spread of scores, not *a means* of determining new statistical phenomena; second, it presupposes a normal population, which most high school teachers probably will never have. And even if employed to divide a distribution into classes, some identified technique of determining the size of differential grade groups would be needed. If, as covered in the last chapter, the standard-deviation distance were selected, approximate percentage divisions of 2, 14, 68, 14, and 2 would result, which, when applied to a class of 30, would culminate in 1 A, 4 B's, 20 C's, 4 D's, and 1 F. If, on the other hand, the binomial theorem were arbitrarily employed and expanded to the fourth power, as recommended by Nelson Bossing, the resultant percentage categories would be 6, 25, 38, 25, and 6. Regardless of the conversion method selected, it would have to be regarded as purely arbitrary and not necessarily applicable to any given group. Probability percentages do not apply to a situation in which the outcomes are known beforehand to be improbable of occurring.

A second approach is one wherein the breaks in a distribution are noted and used as grade-category limits. For illustrative purposes, the following 30 raw scores are submitted for analysis to the end of separating them into five categories. Somewhat sizable breaks will be observed be-

93	85	80	76	73
92	85	79	76	72
92	85	78	74	68
91	81	77	74	67
88	81	77	74	61
87	80	76	73	49

tween 91 and 88, between 85 and 81, between 72 and 68, between 67 and 61, and between 61 and 49, respectively. Using this "look-see" method, a teacher would probably convert the scores into 4 A's, 5 B's, 17 C's, 2 or 3 D's, and 1 or 2 F's. That this procedure is pure manipulation and thus scientifically indefensible we cannot deny, but it is as defensible as the curve and the binomial theorem. Thus, in addition to the philosophical shortcomings of relative grading, a moderately logical means of dividing a group four, five, or more ways is impossible to concoct.

The clinical standard

In contrast to a system whereby a grade is determined by fixed teacher standards or by competition among pupils, the clinical approach begins and ends with pupil uniqueness. With its emphasis on standards within, not apart from, the individual pupil, each pupil is expected to make the most of his abilities and aptitudes. As in mental health, the goal is optimum development. So conceived, an adolescent is never just a fraction or a degree of an arithmetical stereotype, or a measurable distance from an ideal; rather, he is a dynamic person expected to work with what he has and develop it as much as circumstances permit. By this standard, the teacher's commission is to respect the worth of each student, understand him as best he can, discerningly help him develop, and evaluate him separately from all others.

Aligned in corroboration of the clinical is an interesting array of value systems: Judaism, Christianity, and humanism, to name but three. These and any other systems that place the individual man on a level higher than mankind *en masse* and competitive factors could give no other than complete philosophical support to the tenets of the last paragraph. If as meritorious as described, then the question logically follows: Why aren't they practiced more? The contradiction may be explained in three ways: by the lag between theory and practice, by the impossible time demands thus imposed on teachers in a confused educational setting, and by the inadequacy of clinical instruments and methods.

Hiatus is known to be an operating phenomenon, and the lag between what even highly convicted people profess to believe and what they then proceed to do is significant. Practically speaking, society in general, and the majority of teachers in particular, are as yet not ready to receive the full impact of the clinical point of view. They feel comfortable when verbalizing clichés such as "You can do only your best"; but when contemplating the next step of conferring as much commendation to a loser as to a winner, they feel less comfortable. Thus, rewards still go to the genetically and environmentally favored, with the less fortunate being thereby accorded second-class standing. Against these distorted values, the school, even though dedicated to the clinical, would have difficulty penetrating the perversity of the *status quo*. Unquestionably, the world's fastest human being receives more credit for performing to his capacity than the world's slowest does for achieving his optimum. Firstness and betterness are difficult opponents to overcome.

Also, assuming a proper orientation, the teacher, who must work with the many, can scarcely be as clinically analytical as if he were allowed to work with the few. Society and an administration being willing, he might desire above all else to study each pupil closely and assign a grade that would reflect the growth of the individual in the light of his potential or his needs, but the problem of numbers would stand in the way. The self-contained classroom of the elementary school provides a laboratory where the clinical process may operate moderately effectively, but the greater personnel demands of secondary education are almost insurmountable. Necessity thus demands that he settle for less than the ideal.

Even if teachers at the secondary level were able to transcend the obstacle of numbers, there would still remain the inadequacy of instrumentation and methods of diagnosis. To insist theoretically that an adolescent work up to his potential is easier than to determine the potential. As of the present, education and psychology are operating with close approximations in the area of the mental and with even less accurate estimates in the personal. At first glance, this vagueness might appear to condemn the clinical as impossible of implementation; however, intelligent guesses are not uncommon in other disciplines which have the public's respect—medicine, for one, which operates most often in the absence of absolute answers.

Thus, despite handicaps and limitations, teachers can, and many do, perform on a modified clinical basis. And those who reject this standard as too idealistic only negate a basic educational premise, that teachers can understand and help individual children. With tests, social grouping, conferences, written projects, oral methods, and observation at the classroom leader's disposal, clinical understandings may be more accessible, and even more accurate, than most are ready to admit. When these are properly utilized, a curriculum emerges that relates more intimately to adolescents, who are recognized as having unique abilities, unique potentials, and unique needs. In such a setting, rewarding the fast or deprecating the slow is counterindicated. In the clinical process, the teacher asks the individual to compete only with himself, removed as far as possible from teacher absolutism and peer relativism. And the inaccuracies that permeate grading will probably be no greater than those that pervade other academic endeavor.

WHAT GOES INTO MARK

Whatever approach to grading is adopted by a school or teacher, sooner or later a decision must be reached on the specific elements to be incorporated in the final composite. The ones most often considered are achievement, relative growth, effort, and citizenship intangibles. Of the four, the only one on which even a semblance of agreement has been reached is achievement, and even it partitions on the issue of absolute versus relative performance. None the less, whenever a one-symbol mark is given, a fundamental ingredient is bound to be achievement, determined in some way.

Less consensus exists, however, on the criteria of evaluating accomplishment, that is, on whether the basis should be the amount and quality of the output itself, or the substantive related to the ability of the individual pupil to perform. The absolutists and relativists move directionally toward the first, although in different ways; but both agree that dimensional considerations of performance are vital. The more clinically oriented would find their members extending between two extremes. At one pole would be a few advocates of the highest possible mark for any student who was working and achieving at his optimum, regardless of his level of ability. At the other pole would be liberal absolutists and relativists, under different labels, advocating growth and progress as lesser basic elements within the framework of raw achievement. These latter, for instance, might elevate a D+ to a C in concession to growth, in spite of limited ability and measured outcome. The element of effort would undergo essentially the same scrutiny and final treatment.

The most controversial of all the components of a mark are the factors of attitudes, ethical considerations, and social behavior. If achievement is the "end all," these should have no bearing. But in practice, might they not enter into even the "purists'" grading, even though unconsciously? What part might they play in the following situations?

1. Jack Manders has an I.Q. of 75, is always at the foot of the class, but is one of the most courteous and considerate boys in the school.

2. Jane Mercier has an I.Q. of 155, near the highest in the school, does well on all exams, but is lackadaisical in turning in assignments and is inclined toward sloppy work.

3. Jeff Maroni is a bright youngster who always does well but is insolent to the teacher and a veritable social boor, antagonizing everyone.

4. Tom Muldoon is a bright "A" student who is caught plagiarizing on a term paper.

5. Whenever the teacher inquires about time spent on homework, Mary Malloy insists that she works "hours" every night. In a parent conference, the teacher discovers that Mary rarely "cracks a book." This knowledge comes when the teacher is trying to decide between a lower grade and the next higher grade symbol.

6. In a social studies class, Larry Hines does well on all cognitive tasks relating to democracy but openly verbalizes hatred of certain races and religions of his classmates, becoming obnoxious with his attitudes.

This issue of one versus the several elements that might enter into a grade has no answer apart from school policy, teacher philosophy, and validity. Statisticians, for instance, advocate the exclusion of "extraneous" factors lest the grade be misunderstood and made thereby less discrete.

The counter argument is simply that a grade can be employed to evaluate any dimensions of performance so long as they are properly identified, defensible, and announced in advance. The validity of the grade thus resides in its attempts to do what a school or teacher has decided in advance that it should do.

Confronted with the argument that a one-symbol mark when extended into many evaluative channels appraises none of them well, we are forced to agree. But obliquely, we would have to add that a one-symbol grade in the area of achievement alone is already so overextended, and accuracy thereby already so seriously affected, that the insertion of a few factors in addition to achievement would do little harm. And at the practical level, if such elements as relative growth, effort, ethics, and attitudes are going to enter unconsciously, why not be intellectually honest and thus face them consciously? The desirable statistical property of discreteness begs for the narrower marking base, whereas educational purposes broadly conceived support a wider base. In the last analysis, a given teacher has to decide; but the decision, whatever it is, should be communicated to those affected.

THE LANGUAGE OF REPORTING

The process of reporting reaches its culmination when such selected information that the school has about the pupil is conveyed to parents and pupils who do not have it. Requisite to its effectiveness is the wise selection of a language that will convey desired meanings. In this section will be discussed the more widely employed practices of the past and present.

The percentage method

The oldest organized method of reporting pupil progress is by percentages or numbers, with a theoretical zero the lowest possible grade and 100 the highest. In practice, however, when this system is used, the range more often extends from a level not lower than 50 or 60 to a maximum of 100. This method has logical roots in the field of mathematics, where fractionated and percentage components can be assessed in relation to a perfect outcome. So conceived, a resultant of three problems incorrect out of ten conveniently lends itself to a score of 70, but less conveniently to an analysis of the subtler implications of work habits and mental processes. This system, which was nearing its zenith in the 1920's, began to decline because of its propensity for overrefinement. Knowledgeable practitioners, always aware of the vast range of human error, became more and more restive when forced to distinguish between a 94 and 95 for a B-and-A cleavage, or between a 97.65 and 97.67 for a valedictory selection.

The alphabetical method

The percentage method, which pretended to have far greater evaluative delicacy than it actually possessed, has conceded in the past three or four decades to one which employs alphabetical symbols. The reporting instrument incorporating the alphabetical method normally carries the information that an A is from 95 to 100; a B, from 85 to 94; a C, from 75 to 84; a D, from 65 to 74; and an F, from 0 to 64. The five-symbol approach actually retains the percentage basis but compresses the units of measurement into five arithmetical compartments.

Ironically, the very reason why high schools deserted the percentage plan for a broader one, namely, the need to avoid refined exactness in reporting, has given rise to complaints by teachers that the five-symbol approach is too unspecific. In compensation, some schools have adopted the plus-minus system, thereby making for a 13-unit plan, assuming that the grade of F is not modified in any way. The teachers who prefer more than five symbol gradients contend that giving a grade of B to two pupils who have raw scores of 85 and 94, respectively, is more unfair than to give the corresponding grades of B− and B+ (or A−).

Pass versus failure

A system more unrefined statistically than the five-symbol plan is the *pass-fail* system. It has been tried by a number of high schools and even a few colleges, only to be dropped by most after a short period of experimentation. Society apparently is not yet ready for such an abrupt departure from tradition. This system is opposed on the grounds that a grade which does not identify pupils as somewhat, or much, better or worse than others in a given area of the curriculum is unfair and therefore categorically inadequate. Once more the mental-health proponents have lost a battle to the worshipers of hierarchical gradations, who, in the traditions of Al Capp, seem to be most comfortable when firstness, in particular, and other rank-order positions can be identified unmistakably. Since the pass-fail dichotomy denies this insight into place identification, it usually has been short-lived whenever tried. Its opponents customarily have been parents of the bright, who thereby lost prestige identification; teachers, who lost the power that goes with rewards; and colleges, which became petulant when forced to rely almost solely on College Board scores and other standardized instrumentation for purposes of selection.

A symbol mark supplemented by description

Because of a desire by many teachers and administrators to tell more than one symbol can possibly be expected to tell, many schools provide a "remarks" column on the report card for descriptive comments to supplement the mark itself. The comments of teachers vary from laconic utterances to more meaningful but brief descriptions of pupil behavior. Usually, however, lack of space prevents any genuine depth of descriptive analysis. Too frequently the teacher reaches into a repertoire of stereotyped expressions ("educanese") for descriptive words and phrases that at times are actually meaningless. They include such safe clichés as: *organizes well, evidences improvement, adjusts to course easily but needs to work harder, should study more thoroughly, needs to develop more accuracy, neatness and order characterize, participates actively, commands respect from the group,* and *is well liked.* Or single adjectives such as the following are employed: *alert, earnest, orderly, pleasant, motivated, dependable, disinterested, unpredictable,* and *unimaginative.* Although conscious of the undesirability of stereotyped expressions, we feel that any comment which rings with even a semblance of sincerity will get a longer look and more thoughtful response from a student or parent than a symbol with no comment at all.

A letter to the home

A more abrupt departure from tradition than a few remarks added to a report card is the periodical letter to the home, in which the many aspects of the behavior of the adolescent are described. A typical report might be similar to the following:

John is doing acceptable work in Algebra 1, almost regularly revealing a mastery of the arithmetical skills. Mechanical errors are rare.

To date, he has made reasonable progress in understanding and working with the abstractions of algebra—the unknown quantity and minus values. He also is adept at manipulating parts of equations and arriving at book answers.

Despite his mechanical understandings, he is having some trouble grasping the real meanings of algebra; but this is a phase, I feel. When I try to move him faster than an average pace, he resists. Maybe he isn't ready. But maybe also he prefers the easy way. I favor the latter point of view because of a few indications that he does not do more than enough to meet minimum standards.

John is well liked by associates at all levels, although maybe he should lead more and follow less. He tends to slouch, make ready quips, and in other ways convey an occasional impression of indifference to the seriousness of learning.

Let me work with him for a month or so longer to see if I can motivate him more. Maybe a word or two from you about the importance of his doing his best might also be helpful. If there is no change by the end of a month, I'll get in touch with you. I really enjoy John in class. Rest assured that his problems are probably those not uncommon to adolescence. Yet if I can help him reach his considerable potential, I wish to do so.

Please feel free to communicate with me if I can be of further assistance.

This letter is fairly brief as a description of one youngster's performance and personality in an algebra class. Its comprehensiveness, supported by examples, its reference to attitudes as well as performance, and its discussion of total growth all help create a more complete picture—one that parent and child can study and profit by. However, the time spent by the teacher in preparation is a factor to be reckoned with. A classroom leader would spend from 15 minutes to half an hour in writing one such evaluation, which, when multiplied by 125 or 150, would have an enervating effect. Such a burden cannot be superimposed on teachers unless their loads are otherwise lightened proportionately. That the letter method tells more than the one-symbol mark is too obvious almost to be questioned. But that its use is surrounded by many obstacles is equally obvious.

Parent conferences

Inherent in parent conferences is the same time problem as in the letter approach. Most are regarded as adequate only when half an hour can be devoted to each one. Furthermore, the school's schedule is rigid, and conferences are convenient for the teacher only after 3:30 in the afternoon. Already the reader can understand why the interview technique operates primarily as an emergency expedient. A compromise with the ideal is made by some high schools which invite parents to the school for very brief conferences with teachers on one or more so-called "teacher-parent nights." Reactions to these are always mixed. Some teachers feel that five minutes gives so little opportunity to communicate with a parent that the result may be more harmful than helpful. Nor are parents any more enthusiastic, at times. On the positive side, however, such conferences, if sensitively handled, can develop improved school-community relations by leading to subsequent relationships less circumscribed by time limitations.

A check-list approach to trait evaluation

As a feature of many reporting systems, supplemental to the letter or percentage grade on a report card is a list of selected personal and professional traits to be evaluated by the check-list method. Not untypical is the checklist shown on the next page.

Since the school is dedicated to the intangibles of development as well as cognitive growth, a defensible reporting system should mirror this greater breadth. One method is to compress it into a one-symbol grade; another is to give it independent status in a checklist; and a third might be to employ it in both. Whatever the plan, the ethical, social, and personality intangibles have sufficient stature to demand identification and communication in a manner that best meets the philosophy of the school and the teacher.

Growth As a Person and Citizen

We consider the traits listed below as important factors in the total development of your son or daughter and solicit your help in areas where inadequacy is indicated. A check ($\checkmark$) in Column 1 indicates maturity of growth; one in Column 2, satisfactory growth; one in Column 3, less-than-adequate growth.

PERSONALITY CHECKLIST

INDIVIDUAL TRAITS	1	2	3
1. Effort			
2. Work habits			
3. Paying attention in class			
4. Assuming responsibility			
5. Enthusiasm for the subject			
6. Profiting from criticism			
7. Poise and confidence			
8. Self-understanding			
9. Personal appearance			
GROUP RESPONSIBILITIES			
10. Courtesy toward others			
11. Respecting opinions of others			
12. Working with others in groups			

FAILURE AND HONORS

The processes of evaluation and reporting inevitably have the issues of failure and honors following in their wake. These reach to the heart of an educational philosophy, challenging school personnel to re-evaluate such practices as compulsory attendance to a given age, the value of a student's repeating a course, the sequential relationships between and among courses, and the criteria for bestowing honors. The emotionally laden concept of failure will be examined first.

Failure

All teachers, regardless of their orientations and philosophies, come face to face a few or many times during their careers with the prospect of failure. The absolute and relative avenues lead almost inevitably to this consideration; the clinical, less often. No teacher worthy of being one treats the prospect lightly, involved as it is with the egos and future plans of young people. By the conscientious teacher, final decisions are reached only after painstaking thought and investigation.

The formal disciplinarians throughout the centuries have failed students in order to "toughen them up for life." Those teachers who envision the six-year high school curriculum as carefully graded from step to step fail students to get them more ready for the next rung. The proponents of the doctrine that the school is a social institution dedicated to the establishing of a cross section of life are more hesitant to employ failure, regarding it as an emergency expedient only. Other reasons that have underwritten failure, for better or worse, are: to make adolescents understand the importance of standards, to teach them that indifference has consequences, to punish them for disorderliness, and to let them know that cheating and plagiarism are "immoral."

Would the reader feel justified in failing any of the following?

1. Pete Markham, a Negro migrant from Louisiana, has an I.Q. of 78, is 15 years old, and is consistently last on the classroom projects required of a general science class. He seems to be doing his best.

2. Lou Palmer, with an I.Q. of 110 and blonde hair, is more interested in the boys than in Algebra. Her performance is never up to ability, and usually she ranks twentieth, or thereabouts, out of 25 students. She intends to go to college.

3. George Hanna has a low I.Q. and regularly irritates with his inattentive ways and social childishness. His performance always hovers around last in the class. His father is a leading physician in town, doing a lot of charity work.

4. Sally Proctor is a bright student who has been getting A's and B's in a problems-of-democracy class. Needing a final grade of A to get a promised convertible, she is caught "red-handed" in the act of cheating on the final examination.

Like all cases of prospective failure, none of these four examples leads neatly to an easy decision. Each has its own dynamics peculiarly unique to the single individual. In facing these and other related cases, every teacher at some time in his life would have weighed the following valid or spurious assumptions in search of the proper decision.

1. *A standard of pass and fail can be readily justified.* This statement entices with its inviting simplicity but fails to take into account the subjectivity of the teacher and the inaccuracy of measuring instruments. In this regard, studies in evaluation attest to the fact that, when a number of experts appraise a common academic specimen of student performance, for example, an English composition or a mathematical problem, the grades they assign often vary as widely as from D or F to A or B. The thoughtful teacher, therefore, while not convinced that standards of pass and fail are completely elusive, will never regard them as easily identifiable.

2. *Repeating a course is profitable.* Assuming a sequential curriculum pattern where one course leads to the next, an issue of failure is always tied to the anticipated gains the second time around. Research points to only a slight improvement, if any, when a student is made to repeat a course.[8]

3. *The pupil was capable of passing the course in the first place.* Denying credit to an adolescent who is unable to meet the course standards should give pause. Unless the curriculum is within reach of a child, the act of failing him may approach the unjustifiable.

4. *Failure in school will help the pupil face failure in life.* With the two psychological areas so dissimilar in a multitude of ways, failure in academic pursuits must be rejected as a defensible means of getting an adolescent ready for possible later failure on the job, in matrimony, in physical health, or in the self-estimate. Each instance of failure is associated with a set of circumstances unique to that one situation; at best, there are too few overlapping emotional components to make for any assurance of successful transfer to the indefinite unknown. In essence, such an expectancy smacks of formal discipline, a doctrine which psychology has declared outmoded. And, even more fundamental, secondary education should be so preoccupied with positive learning values as a means of preparing the adolescent for life that it has little time for this type of wasteful negativism.

5. *Failure is necessary to motivate others.* This often employed justification for failure has a surface appearance of validity without offering any real proof of its soundness. Research on this proposition is nebulous, and the postulate therefore should be rejected on the grounds of humaneness. In a good society, teachers cannot be permitted to sacrifice one or more students on the weakly grounded assumption that others will thereby be frightened into goodness.

6. *The mental-health trauma can be kept in bounds.* This sixth checklist principle is tantamount to a demand that the teacher work out a type of balance sheet in which the anticipated academic gains will be weighed against the possible injuries to the psyche. Assuming a mental-health orientation to education by the teacher, the psychic effects cannot be ignored.

These six jogs to the teacher are reminders that the process of failure is multi-faceted. They likewise serve as mandates for him to consider every case on its own merits. Failure is never in general; it is always very much in particular, with each adolescent bringing a composite pattern of variables never seen before or to be seen again. Similarities between cases exist, but never identicalness.

[8] Carleton M. Saunders, *Promotion or Failure* (Columbia University: Teachers College, Bureau of Publications, 1941), pp. 27–29.

After heeding the six warning signals, any teacher might fail a student with justification emanating from one or more of the following:

A. The student did not measure up to his achievable potential and needed to be so informed by the act of failure.

B. If the course in which failure is contemplated is in a sequence, repetition may be mandatory. For example, if a student is determined to attend a girl's college in the East which requires two years of Latin, she may have to repeat Latin I if she is to be able to compete in Latin II.

C. The teacher worked earnestly throughout to understand the pupil, to relate the curriculum to him, and thus tried to prevent failure.

D. In general, after an exhaustive study of all aspects of the case, the teacher decided that failing the student would be more helpful than passing him.

This professionally thorough approach to failure is in deference not only to a basic humanistic orientation, but in recognition of the complexity of behavioral causality. Failure cannot be regarded lightly, since its causes are many-patterned. As indicated by Burton,[9] the causes might be in the person of the adolescent, involving physical or mental shortcomings; in the social order, involving socioeconomic status of parents or subcultures; or in the school itself. Regardless of reasons, failing a student can be justified only when accompanied by a highly ethical seriousness of purpose.

Honors and honor societies

As controversial and emotionally toned as failure is the other marking polarity of *honors*. These latter manifest themselves when the magic rectangular area on the blackboard contains the names of the chosen few who got all A's and B's for the six-weeks marking period; when, in a setting of subdued lighting, the favored are initiated into the National Honor Society to the accompaniment of soft music; when final rank-in-class recognition is taken of the top few per cent of their class; or when the valedictorian is announced at a graduation exercise. The avowed purposes of these and related testimonials are to reward excellence and motivate others to its attainment.

The purpose of rewarding excellence we accept with reservation, provided, as stressed many times before, honors are bestowed in a climate that is earmarked by maturity. In such a climate, quality is identified as significant, but the one possessing it not commensurately credited with creating it. However, even in such a setting, honors are an adulteration, being conferred almost always on the "haves," as determined by absolute

[9] William H. Burton, *The Guidance of Learning Activities* (New York: Appleton-Century-Crofts, 1952), pp. 633–638.

or relative standards, and rarely or never on the "have nots," who by clinical standards might be equally worthy.

Regarding the second justification, namely, that honors encourage many outside the select circle to work hard enough to get in, our skepticism enters an objection. It is granted that a few borderline cases from time to time do make the grade; even that an infrequent C student does likewise; but motivation is definitely limited to a select population—more circumscribed, probably, than the honors group itself. Rather than motivating a sizable number of outsiders into the fold, honors probably lead as much in the direction of regression as a result of pupil discouragement.

The following example illustrates the latter point. The male reader is asked to study List A below, identifying himself with "the other gladiators" who are being considered for the honor society of boxing. The winner of each of the pairs receives this distinction. The female reader is correspondingly asked to study List B, identifying herself with the "other famous actresses" who are being considered for the honor society of histrionics.

LIST A	LIST B
Floyd Patterson	Ingrid Bergman
Ingemar Johannsen	Gwen Verdon
Sonny Liston	Carole Channing
Archie Moore	Jayne Mansfield
Dick Tiger	Elizabeth Taylor
Male Reader	Female Reader

In the above competition for final honors, it is academic only to ask how well either reader would fare. And for him who yells, "Foul," or tears a passion, protesting that the analogy is forced, we point out the following ingredients common to the academic and the illustrative situations: in both, the inadequate are made to compete with the adequate, and prestige is associated with those who have greater natural endowments. We enlist additional support by asking whether the distance between two I.Q.'s of 75 and 150 is any less than between the reader and one of the listed celebrities.

Getting away from this controversial analogy, the reader should try to predetermine the reaction of a youngster with an I.Q. of 75, who sees four honor-roll students being recognized while knowing full well that he will *never* be in a similar group; or of the adolescent with an above-average I.Q. who because of fear of testing situations can never make the grade. Our attitude candidly is that honor rolls and honor societies of whatever kind—academic, athletic, or forensic—serve only to perpetuate the immaturity of a culture, removing performance from a status of intrinsic worth for its own sake to one of artificial symbols and false values. The limelight is on relativism rather than excellence determined by individual ability and potential. Even if honors and honor societies motivate the "haves," they commensurately discourage and irritate the "cannots" and the "have nots."

Grades as prerequisite to leadership in the co-curriculum

Removed from the area of failure and the atmosphere of honors, grades will now be analyzed briefly in their relationship to the co-curriculum. The issue here fundamentally is whether a designated level of academic achievement should be a requisite for co-curricular participation. Should the musically talented student who fails solid geometry be denied the senior play's leading role? Or should a student be excluded from the student council because he has less than a "C" average? The dimensions of the academic curriculum are often different from those of the co-curriculum, and administrators and teachers should refrain from applying inviolable rules for membership in the latter. A known phenomenon is that members of the upper socioeconomic classes participate, whereas the members of the lower ones rarely do. If co-curricular activities are worthwhile in themselves—and if they are not, they should be eliminated—the right of participation should be determined on clinical grounds, not by an inflexible dictum applied to all circumstances and all students in disregard of individuals and their needs.

IMPROVING MARKING PRACTICES

Since the academic world is raising more questions about marking than it can answer, and since it is more enamored of existing practice than desirous of change, improvements will be slow, though not impossible of attainment. Basic to this process is the need for schools to temporize with the best of the existing state—of the absolute and relative methods—while incorporating into it parts of the clinical method. This is definitely not a refusal by the author to face up to possible conflict on the road to marking revisions; rather, he regards it a realistic recognition of tradition's resistance to change, which will need to be countered gradually with convincing substitutions for older ineffective practices.

The first step, however, is for any given teacher to search carefully for a philosophy of grading that he can feel comfortable about and defend. In this search, he will inevitably be forced to take a stand on the underlying principles of evaluation. Is it the basic purpose to compare people favorably or invidiously against an external standard, or to determine how well an individual has responded to his own inner dynamics? If the latter, the instructional leader is committed thereby to the employment of some kind of clinical approach.

A fundamental next step will be the securing of pertinent data about individuals, either from the personnel records of a centralized guidance office or through independent means that the teacher may have to initiate. All teachers should have I.Q. scores and past performance records of students in the teachers' own specialized curriculum fields. Other data on reading abilities and personal behavior should also be accessible for use as needed. So equipped, even though a five-class teaching load will prevent the dedicated teacher from consulting these records routinely, he will have them at his disposal when the occasion dictates their employment.

If this plan is followed, when at marking time the teacher notes significant differences between ability and performance, or between present and past achievement, he can take steps to investigate causality as a means of validating future action. It is important that he know within definable operating limits whether a pupil has worked up to a reasonable optimum. Against this approximate knowledge, he then evaluates and grades against certain absolutes of his own, pays only as much heed to relativism as a school demands, and proceeds to make grading adjustments in the light of his composite insights.

Even in a school where traditionalism defies major grading change, a teacher has certain approved methods at his disposal to soften the effect of absolutism and relativism. One of these is the employment of descriptive comments on projects in lieu of one-symbol marks. Annotations, for instance, on English themes, science homework, art projects, or home economics dress designs often can have more vital import because the grading symbol is not present to emotionalize the situation. A few students will continue to pester for the percentage or alphabetical mark, but most will respond in good grace to its occasional or frequent omission.

Another escape from the tyranny of the single symbol is a divided mark which differentiates diagnostically. If the desired elements of a biology drawing are neatness and fidelity of reproduction, the two might be evaluated with a split grade of, for example, B/C; or if an English composition is directed at the goals of originality, organization of ideas, and the mechanics of expression, a three-pronged grade of B/C/B could be given.

When confronted by the issues of grading, because teachers bring different philosophies to bear on the problem, they can be forgiven for possessing contradictory attitudes. But they cannot be forgiven if they stop short of a defensible point of view on the subject. A minimum essential thus is a credo that faithfully represents what a teacher believes to be right and that accordingly rests on a foundation of careful thought. If pressed, the author would offer the ensuing tenets as basic to his credo. They are a compromise between a conviction that grades are fundamentally wrong and a recognition that, right or wrong, if they are an operational component of education, they should rest on the soundest operational principles obtainable.

1. A school mark of any kind is only a rough estimate of performance.

2. Yet, despite its known fallibility, a teacher should make it as accurate as possible within the framework of his own and other standards that he has to live with.

3. A grade should be for the good of the pupil as much as, if not more than, for the good of the school.

4. A high school grade should not be dictated by the demands of higher education; that is, high schools should work out their own standards of practice in the light of what is good for high school pupils, not of what will serve college registrars well.

5. The basal ingredient of a grade should be achievement.

6. Other important ingredients, however, should be performance as measured against capacity, effort, growth, and citizenship factors.

7. Regardless of relative performance, the higher symbols should not be given unless a student reasonably approximates capacity performance.

8. Neither should a failing grade be given a student who is doing his best, unless a sequential curriculum arrangement so indicates.

9. Within the framework of a one-symbol system, a grade should be conveniently manipulated one gradient up or down in recognition of such factors as effort, persistence, and citizenship. On occasion, when the outcomes seem to support such action, the grade might be adjusted as much as two gradients, but this action would be unusual.

10. A grade should never be used punitively or regarded as a token either of respectability or unrespectability; neither should it be a fixed criterion for leadership in school activities or for membership in clubs.

11. A grade should not be revealed by the teacher to any pupil other than the one who earned it. It rightfully should be the personalized possession only of the school, the designated pupil, and his parents.

12. The grading policies of the teacher should be explained to pupils, impartially and objectively.

13. Each teacher, within the limits permitted by a school system, is obligated to formulate his own grading standards, never introjecting those of another.

The above statement of conviction about grading, whether the reader agrees with it or not, represents the best thinking of an individual who, having searched himself for a point of view, arrived at a number of tenets that could be announced to a high school class. They are specific enough to let a class know in advance the governing standards. Later, if a student ranked at the top of his class in performance despite less than adequate effort, a grade of B would come as no surprise. And by the same logic, a grade of C for the slow learner, despite his low absolute level of performance, would not be necessarily suspect. The conditioning of adolescents to a grading scheme, prior to the act of grading itself, will go far in achieving a climate of acceptance.

A goal of the educational future should be to eliminate comparative marks of any kind. But until a competitive society gets its values more into line with humanistic aspirations, the classroom teacher will continue to face a task that defies propriety of execution. Thus confronted with the impossible, he can only make the best of a bad situation by holding personality injury to a minimum. Movement toward the clinical methods is the one defensible direction for grading to take.

SUMMARY

Grading has been presented as an extension of evaluation into the quantitative, with the heavy hand of tradition strongly in control. Contemporary educational theory is opposed to the preoccupation of schools with the inadequate single-symbol mark which at times is so undiagnostic and oversimplified as to be rendered meaningless. Its simplicity was not so out of harmony in an essentialist curriculum of the past as it is today when projected against a broader mental health-oriented curriculum.

The purposes of reporting were identified as the conveying of information to pupils, parents, and the school's administrative personnel. The limitations are that grades establish barriers between teacher and students, establish barriers also among students, force the weak to compete unfairly with the strong, become ends in themselves, are undiagnostic, are easily distorted by trivia, have little transfer significance, and lend themselves to loose employment for punitive purposes.

The three broad approaches to marking were presented as the absolute, relative, and clinical, with the first two governing educational practice and the last permeating theory. The clinical approach advocates the taking of a student where he is and helping him to work up to an optimum of ability. The possible ingredients of a grade were identified as achievement measured against an external or internal standard, growth, and citizenship traits.

The methods of reporting were treated sequentially as follows: percentage, alphabetical, pass-fail, a single symbol with comments, the home letter, the parent conference, and the check-list of traits.

Next it was stated that failure should be approached as a guidance worker would approach any serious problem; also, that the continued existence of honors should be questioned. Finally, a grading credo was announced as an example of recommended practice for the classroom teacher. Informing students of expected standards is a basic step in gaining acceptance for a formulated credo.

REFERENCES

Alcorn, Marvin D., Richard A. Houseman, and Jim R. Schunert, *Better Teaching in Secondary Schools.* New York: Holt, Rinehart and Winston, 1954. (Chapter 22)

Burton, William R., *The Guidance of Learning Activities.* New York: Appleton-Century-Crofts, Inc., 1952. (Chapter 21)

Department of Classroom Teachers and Research Division, *School Marks and Promotions.* Washington, D.C.: N.E.A., Pamphlet No. 9, 1950.

Educational Policies Commission, *Learning the Ways of Democracy.* N.E.A., Washington, D.C., 1940.

Rivlin, Harry, *Teaching Adolescents in Secondary Schools.* New York: Appleton-Century-Crofts, Inc., 1961. (Chapter 11)

Rothney, John W. M., *Evaluating and Reporting Pupil Progress.* N.E.A. Department of Classroom Teachers, Washington, D.C., 1955.

Strong, Ruth, *How to Report Pupil Progress.* Chicago: Science Research Associates, 1955.

Walker, Margaret M., *A Study of High School Failures.* Scottsdale, Pa.: Mennonite Press, 1935.

Wrinkle, William L., *Improving Marking and Reporting Practices.* New York: Holt, Rinehart and Winston, 1947.

DISCIPLINE:
CONCEPTS
AND
INFRACTIONS

Unless razed recently, a rustic one-room country schoolhouse still stands in Cave Springs, Missouri, known as the Reed's Defeat School. It received its name at the turn of the century when the schoolmaster, named Reed, was manhandled by the overgrown male members of the class and forcibly propelled through one of the four windows. The defeat of Mr. Reed was followed by the advent of a schoolmistress, Miss Kathryn Scott, who, from all reports, kept the pupils under excellent control until she left voluntarily several years later.

Members of that little Missouri community reacted to the schoolmaster's undignified treatment with such remarks as: "He just didn't know how to discipline the kids." Or, "Those children were an undisciplined group who needed the wrath to descend." Like many others who have used the controversial term "discipline," they were vague about its basic meaning, some regarding it as a process of bringing about a desired outcome; others, as a condition resulting from governing influences.

In this chapter, "discipline" will be employed as descriptive of *the state of organization or control within an individual or group which propels toward positive goal achievement.* This orientation places the primary accent on inner dynamics, not on pressures applied to persons or situations from without. So envisioned, it becomes a state of mind characterized by orderliness and self-control. By the same logic, those actions which have as their intent the disruption of discipline will be identified by the term *infractions.* Third, when individuals guilty of such anti-disciplinary actions are made to pay the penalties for them, the term *punishment* will be employed. Surface attempts at preventing infractions without necessarily changing personality will be labeled *managerial manipulation,* whereas attempts at personality change will be covered by the term *corrective therapy.*

The history of society's attitude toward discipline and punishment of offenders against it has been an interesting one. Bossing[1] and Burton[2] trace it sequentially through the categories of the vindictive, retributive, deterrent, remedial, and, finally, the preventive or prophylactic. Significantly, if not surprisingly, the attitude of schools toward discipline has roughly paralleled that of the law toward civil and criminal offenses and that of the church toward sin. In all three, the progression fortunately has been from the negative to the positive in terms of humaneness toward the individual. However, the advance has been irregular and tortuous, with only the enlightened making satisfactory progress toward the higher goal.

In all three areas, the most primitive approach to offenders has always been the retaliatory one where the defender of "righteousness" vindictively vents his passions on the student, legal culprit, or sinner, as the case may be, with no regard for motives. Of greater justification, at least from the position of logic although not of result, is the retributive, inherent in which is the implication that punishment in kind must balance out infraction. Here we have the Old Testament speaking: "An eye for an eye and a tooth for a tooth." The minion of the law sits in a chair of judgment, weighs the magnitude of offenses, and metes out penalties. His primary interest is in the offense, not the offender.

The deterrent is a mild advance toward human values but is conceived more as a protective process than a corrective for the offender. From the standpoint of hard, practical logic, the deterrent motive still has a legitimate place in the greater social scene, including the classroom, whenever a transgressor must be discouraged from repeating an act harmful to others or to himself. But it falls short of corrective therapy when ignoring psychic motivation and causality.

The remedial approach includes the one very important element that the other three do not: a major preoccupation with the offender and a desire to help him become a better citizen and person. Remediation permeates the thinking of truly professional teachers and of hygienists and psychia-

---

[1] Nelson Bossing, *Teaching in Secondary Schools* (Boston: Houghton Mifflin Company, 1952), pp. 476–482.
[2] William H. Burton, *The Guidance of Learning Activities* (New York: Appleton-Century-Crofts, 1952), pp. 709–712.

trists who are thrown into contact with both minor and major offenders of social mores. Removed from the thinking of these therapists are such negative undertones as the vengeance of a wrathful God, the innate depravity of man, and the self-righteousness of those who want the offender to rejoin the ranks of "good people." In their place are the overtones of helpfulness and identification aimed at aiding another to solve his problem. So oriented, the teacher would take the un-judgmental approach of: "You broke a school rule. Let's face it realistically and then decide what we shall do."

In contrast to the remedial approach, which operates only after an offense has been committed, the prophylactic is concerned with prevention. Its goal is for authority figures to so structure the environment that offenses will be headed off before they can take place. In civic affairs, boys' clubs and park programs are in this category. In the school, an interesting curriculum and an empathic teacher are the bulwarks. Such a teacher who knows students well and is thus sensitive to the classroom climate at any time diverts negativism by crowding a program with positivism.

The ideal classroom leader, therefore, without abstaining from deterrents as a commonsense measure and remediation as a justifiably practical antidote to transgression, is irresistibly lured by the magnetism of prevention. In its pursuit, he makes choices between contrasting values: expression rather than repression, respect rather than fear, flexibility rather than rigidity, industriousness rather than silence, understanding rather than conformance, and causal influences rather than symptomatic manifestations.

BASAL CONCEPTS OF DISCIPLINE

Discipline's lofty goal of inner orderliness immediately transports it from the commonplace to the abstruse, demanding that issues which reach to the deeper recesses of human nature be examined. Because discipline is concerned with psychic forces as well as with their external manifestations, theory which undergirds it accordingly is rooted in the many behavioral sciences. Sociology, education, and psychology have been the most contributive, implanted as they all are in humanistic settings. From the investigations in these fields, a number of principles have emerged which logically should precede other considerations pertinent to the topic.

Discipline is a means to ends

Although the outcome of the orderly mind is in itself a value, it should never be endowed with independent status and thus be separated from the greater purposes that it is designed to serve. The old adage, "all dressed up and no place to go," is analogous to the well-disciplined individual or group that has no genuine goal. In such a vacuous setting, orderliness soon vanishes. Like the paired terms of *interest* and *effort, discipline* and *goal achievement* mutually reinforce one another. Discipline leads to greater commitment and accomplishment, which, in turn, sharpen the fine edge of discipline.

In a classroom setting, then, silence or other manifestations of mechanical conformity can never be regarded highly unless they are associated intimately with the desired ends of education. But when the disciplined mind or the disciplined group is provided the leadership that goal direction can bring, learning is so much more the victor. The mental, social, emotional, and physical soon become categories with little form or substance when not conceived in an environment of purpose and design.

Discipline exists first in the individual, then in the group

Although living in a group-oriented generation characterized satirically by gray flannel suits, organization men, and many other extensions of conformity, the teacher must not forget that discipline is first the lengthened shadow of a person, and second a collective entity only as a result of the contributions of specific individuals. Within the group, there is no substitute for personal worth and competence; without these, real cohesion is impossible. A teacher's attention, accordingly, can never be diverted for too long a time from any single student without the possibility of doing harm to the entire class as well as to the student himself. The adolescent is, by definition, an ego-centered organism eager for recognition, and the cost of ignoring him may run high.

A second personnel responsibility of the teacher is to amalgamate individuals into a harmonious relationship so that they can function in concert. Although a group is incapable of responding to stimuli exactly as single organisms do, any group has definable characteristics which make responses somewhat predictable. More than a mere sum of human atoms, it possesses that "extra something" that makes the whole more than the combined total of its parts. The positive intangibles might be any of the following: pride in collective accomplishment, tolerance of the frailties of selected individuals, pleasure in identification with those who perform best in given situations, a genuine delight in working together, and a willing rotation of leadership opportunities. Some negative intangibles could well be the reverse of these five, as well as others, such as apathy, divisiveness, and antagonism toward leadership.

In this connection, Newton's law of gravity applied to human dynamics has an interesting connotation. At the physical level, every particle of matter is known to have a relationship to every other particle in a mathematically predictable way, with nothing physical existing independently and all things physical attracted or repelled by mutual stresses. The same law applied to the psychological might emerge somewhat as follows: every person in a group influences every other person in it in relation to what he is intra-personally and inter-personally and in relation to what the group is as a collective entity.

Students as individuals thus can be units of positive or negative influence. However, operating in the psychological mass, their influence can be multiplied, dulled, or negated by their inter-personal relations and the collective impact of the group on them. Discipline in a class ebbs and wanes as individuals and issues change, but the range of variation is rarely beyond prediction. Invariably, however, every class contains a few ringleaders, usually not more than two or three in number, whose influence psychologically is in disproportion to their numerical importance. In working with these adolescents, if the teacher can establish rapport with them without unduly losing rapport with the remainder of the class, sounder discipline will usually be the reward. Whatever the exact characteristics of any collective body of high school youth, the teacher's task is manifestly clear: to help individualism flower while at the same time paradoxically helping it to consolidate into a psychological mass.

Discipline changes with situations

Since individuals are strongly instrumental in making a group what it is, and since they react in varying ways to differing stimulus conditions, discipline in the classroom may be envisioned as never existing merely "in general" but always existing in terms of a group's reaction to specific conditions. Thus, expectancy for behavior in the chemistry laboratory may be out of line with what is expected in the school assembly. Discipline is also related to method, as pupil reactions are expected in advance to differ, depending on the specific type of procedure employed. The greater silence demanded by the lecture could not equally be expected for committee planning. And the initial presentation of a new medium in an art class would be received in a significantly different way from that of the subsequent laboratory assignment in clay modeling.

This phenomenon of discipline's responding to situational dynamics can be related, for purposes of clarification, to a series of events in the teacher candidate's college life. In a student-teacher seminar, for instance, informality usually reigns. In a large lecture class, silence is almost mandatory. In a fraternity touch-football practice, emotions are permitted spontaneous expression. The situations thus can be seen to demand different student responses because of the factors uniquely inherent in each.

The mature teacher, regarding discipline as a function of the many operating elements in and out of the classroom, changes with the shifting demands of the learning environment. His is a posture of expectancy and flexibility. The inexperienced teacher, in contrast, may be prone to create a stereotype, implement it, and then strait-jacket youth into it regardless of changed conditions. This lure of easy consistency must be resisted, lest it alienate learners by distorting the learning process. Discipline emerges in many legitimate forms, depending on the specific needs of the moment.

Discipline is not always possible

Discipline is a function not only of the curriculum content or of the activity of the moment, but also of the maturity levels of individuals and that of the group itself. Some pupils bring inner organization and stability to the school; others attain it during their period of enrollment; some never attain it. This vast range of difference is not surprising, since the degrees of emotional adjustment of pupils extend across a broad mental-health continuum. The social statistic which says that one person in ten is destined to receive some form of depth therapy before his death is seen in a new light when viewed from the position of the teacher, who may have this one person in his class.

In recognition of group variability, the sensitive teacher thus never sets a standard of group action at so high a level that only the exceptional class is able to measure up. Absolutism in discipline is just as impractical as absolutism in grading, especially when it is carried to extremes; it then leads to continual conflict between teacher and class members, with the teacher expecting too much and the class resisting the unreasonable demands. The compromise that is necessary is inevitably a mixture of realism and expediency. It demands, first, that any teacher worthy of the title set those behavioral limits that are requisite for the group process to know success, at least at the minimum level. The more highly unified classes he expects to reach a higher plane; but for the less integrated, he holds forth a lesser standard. Under no circumstances, however, except in crises, will he condone behavior that sinks below a minimum level of operating efficiency. This is his response to realism, which insists that, when more than one person is involved, all must defer to standards outside themselves.

The teacher's use of expediency occurs when the behavior of a group nears the critical point. At this juncture, the adult authority figure has no choice but to impose controls from without, inasmuch as those from within are not operating. He forces order on the class with some regret, but realizes its necessity. Nor does he necessarily in the process condemn himself as a failure any more than does a clinical psychologist who is unable to effect desired gains in therapy. Each operates in recognition of the extreme variability of human nature, optimistically anticipating satisfactory progress toward self-development in some but no gain at all in a few.

Neither is artless enough to assume that in the space of a few months he can succeed dramatically where other longer-term influences have been less effective.

With his efforts affected by the demands of the immediate moment, the teacher moves throughout toward the ideal of the integrated person and the integrated class. He keeps the academic house in order as a caretaker while at the same time playing the more difficult role of developmental engineer. The latter part impels him toward the evasive gleam of sound student adjustment, demanding at times that he permit adolescents to work together in social groups even though they might not be quite ready, or to embark on cognitive learnings of a precocious nature in the hope that the challenge of maturity will win the day. Development thus is seen to arrive unevenly, achieving gains of commendable proportions in certain individuals and groups but inching forward with discouraging slowness in others.

Leadership needs to be shared with the group

Regardless of the developmental progress that any group makes toward the goal of self-discipline, growth is related to the opportunities of its members to exercise independence of thought and action. The moral lecture loses its message apart from an opportunity for the listeners to put the precepts into practice. The verbalized admonitions about discipline in like manner become blunted when given in an operational vacuum. Before they can penetrate the vitals of individual students and classes, the known tenets of group living must be conceived in part by the students themselves, tried out and evaluated by them in a framework of reality, and incorporated by them in the daily routines of classroom living.

This admittedly ambitious scheme relies on the psychic energy of a group to provide positive student leadership in at least sufficient quantity to counteract existing negativism. When a teacher discovers this latent force in the group, he must give it constant nurture in the school environment to encourage its exercise. This point of view is tangibly implemented when a teacher:

1. Searches in his students for evidences of a positive personality orientation on which leadership can rest solidly.

2. Then studies the group for obstacles that might block the positive exercise of these discovered components.

3. Proceeds to nourish the positive while counteracting the negative.

4. Creates situations in the classroom environment where student decision-making can be exercised.

5. Resists, whenever possible, making decisions about students without engaging them in the deliberation process.

6. Increases the opportunities for student leadership and self-discipline to flower as readiness flashes its cues.

7. Retains the legal and administrative functions which cannot be delegated, explaining their categorical exclusiveness, without apology.

8. Leads the minority negative element toward the positive, sealing it off, when necessary, to permit the majority to grow.

In such a setting, the *power with* principle of leadership, with its emphasis on cooperation, operates to support the goals of discipline. Freedom is highlighted as a virtue of great value, but its price is revealed as not being accessible to those who regard it lightly. The teacher in this setting, without abdicating his rights and duties, invites pupils to work together with him toward the personality goals of self-control, altruism, and wisely conceived independence for all.

Infractions may be indicators of maladjustment

For those students who pit themselves against the directional radar of the class or teacher, normal adolescent rebellion must be entirely ruled out as a cause before a diagnosis of maladjustment is made. When so screened, the more serious infractions remain as indicators of abnormal behavior. This conclusion is consistent with the thread that runs throughout this text, namely, that psychic energy when normal operates constructively; that when pathological, it spends its energies, as the late psychiatrist, Karen Horney, would say, moving against others. In either event, behavior in the classroom must be scrutinized apart from the outmoded framework of goodness and badness, convenient as these descriptive labels are. The price of these convenient labels is misunderstanding and oversimplification.

Abnormal behavior may be distinguished from adolescent rebellion generally by its compulsiveness, repetitiveness, age inappropriateness, and contextual misplacement. The normal high school youth may "act out" on occasions, but the performance is not inspired by irresistible inner forces. Furthermore, his behavior is in reasonable harmony with the age of the "actor" and the classroom context. In contrast, the pathological performer seems to be motivated by an uncontrollable inner compulsiveness that triggers off action unrelated to time or place.

In such situations, the teacher's obligation is many-featured. First, he must be un-judgmental and objective if he is to retain his usefulness. Second, as long as the abnormally behaving student remains in the classroom, the teacher, while taking appropriate corrective action, strives to be to the student a respected and admired adult figure with whom the younger associate can identify and on whom he can rely. Adopting Aichhorn's point of view, we contend that a growing organism always needs adult figures to identify with and to secure succor from.[3] The effective teacher thus many times, as a parent surrogate, serves as a transference figure for those adolescents who may have been denied identification opportunities in the home.

Deviate tendencies are often complex and deeply rooted, and the group with one or more seriously disturbed individuals might never reach a state of satisfactory control. Under such circumstances, the teacher might have to settle for the minimum goal of order imposed from without. Yet even then, he continues to strive for those necessary changes in the few individuals that will make inner control of the entire group a possibility.

CAUSES OF INFRACTIONS

From these principles to which discipline is moored, we turn to the causes of infractions against school rules and regulations. These causes are recognized as residing in the person of the individual himself or in the home, the community from whence he comes, the school's curriculum to which he is exposed, and the person of the teacher.

The individual pupil and home

As was indicated in the closing paragraph of the previous section, at least a few students from time to time resist the efforts of the school to assist them toward a state of inner orderliness. From a Freudian orientation, the school's failure might be attributed to an inadequate super-ego structure reflecting value inadequacies in the home. These youth might well be regarded as emulating parents who, mostly at the unconscious level, were absolving their own guilt and dissatisfactions by transferring them to their offspring.

Whatever the exact nature of the causes of anti-social behavior in the school, a reasonable hypothesis is that limits have not been set in the home—or, if set, have been unreasonably severe, lenient, or vacillating. Any of these three outcomes makes for an abrupt adjustment when the young person is confronted with sharply different school standards. Adelaide Johnson's excellent chapter in the *Handbook of American Psychiatry* is recommended reading for anyone wanting an insight into inner dynamics deeper than this section can provide.[4] Even at a less profound level, the adolescent's plight can be envisioned as unenviable when he is

---

[3] August Aichhorn, *Wayward Youth* (New York: Viking Press, Inc., 1935).
[4] Adelaide Johnson, "Juvenile Delinquency," in *Handbook of American Psychiatry*, Silvano Arieti, ed. (New York: Basic Books, Inc., 1959), pp. 840–856.

forced to make a transfer from one of the three home situations described to a classroom where nominal order is expected to prevail.

1. Lee Heintz has a swashbuckling father who demands unlimited obedience in the home, but who conveys a feeling of sly satisfaction when Lee, just short of getting into serious trouble, antagonizes neighbors and "throws his weight" with other youngsters. Mrs. Heintz is a "mousy" little woman who is seen and not heard. Mr. Heintz in a teacher-parent conference dominates the conversation by boasting of his boyhood episodes which allegedly were of an offbeat variety.

2. Candy Sands has the run of the home, going when she wishes and returning home at any hour. The parents, rather than being concerned, assume a façade of pious condemnation as a cover for their disinterest. They insist, however, that Candy stay out of "real trouble."

3. John Engle has a widowed mother who blows hot and cold on behavioral standards, insisting on rigid adherence to adult rules one moment and condoning flagrant violations the next. She alternates between moods of cold detachment and maudlin sentimentality.

All three of these adolescents—Lee, Candy, and John—would have difficulty in adjusting to the school's standards of social living, accustomed as they all would be to differing ones. Each of them probably could be forced to conform, but true discipline would be impossible until all became able to forge a set of values more in harmony with those of the school.

If psychological factors are injurious to systematic classroom order, the physical ones are no less so. Adolescents with glandular, organic, or neurological disorders delay the cause of adjustment until at least a semblance of cure is effected. And others characterized by unsightly physical defects or physical deprivation make discipline that much more elusive.

Invariably, the psychological and the physical are inextricably woven into a psychosomatic pattern. A dramatic illustration of such entwining, not uncommon in therapy, occurred several years ago in a large Midwest university where an adult student for several years regularly came to the university in a wheel chair, was carried up a flight of stairs by helpful fellow students and faculty, and wheeled into classrooms in dramatic style. The student wore braces on both lower limbs and one arm, and purportedly had an incurable case of dystrophy. Personally, he was opinionated, often belligerent, sometimes pouty, manifestly bright, and regularly ego-centered. He was finally forced to drop out of school for health reasons, being hospitalized thereafter for almost a year. He ultimately made his appearance "sans" braces, having been cured of conversion hysteria. In reacting to this incident, the reader should not conclude that the student had had nothing physically wrong with him; for the phenomenon of psychological causality made the physical symptoms no less severe.

The community as a cause

A second major cause of deviant behavior in school is sociological, with antecedents in the mores and expectancies of a subculture. The cultural transmission theory postulates that adolescents who live in a community with one set of standards and attend a school with conflicting standards are bound to clash with the new standards. Customarily, their loyalty is to the subculture, which may, on rare occasions, even approve stealing, aggression, and bodily harm to people, so long as these affronts are to members of an out group. As Albert Cohen points out, these individuals become so confused by cultural diversity that "right" and "wrong" emerge as amorphous terms with little moral significance.[5]

More often than not, the issue is one of the "have nots" rebelling against the "haves," with a Robin Hood type of logic permeating the actions of the subgroup members. The teacher confronted with this type of deeply rooted cultural orientation can only insist on the minimum level of order necessary for group functioning while striving for rapprochement between the two disparate outlooks on life. What the pupil is as a person is often the scale-tipping element, despite the deeper implications of the confused intercultural schism. However, when the rift is too great, a school system needs the cooperation of the greater culture itself so that governmental, community agency, and school personnel can combine as a unit to attack the problem.

The school curriculum as a cause

When the adolescent is absolved of neurotic tendencies and the community of undue diversity, the school should next look at its program and those responsible for it to detect possible internal aggravators of discipline. One commentator facetiously notes that many a tenth-grader is more suited to portray Caliban than to read *The Tempest*.[6] Although a curriculum is not expected to be symphonically sensitized to every fluctuating need and interest of every adolescent, it cannot depart so far from the students' frame of reference as to exist in an adult vacuum only.

The greater educational world has agreed, with few opposing, that approximately half of the secondary school curriculum should be in general education, wherein the basic learnings needed by all youth will be engendered. But it has agreed less closely on the exact nature of the content, with the result that some schools are still academically oriented, others

[5] Albert K. Cohen, *Delinquent Boys: the Culture of the Gang* (Glencoe, Illinois: The Free Press, 1955).

[6] Norma E. Cutts and Nicholas Moseley, *Teaching the Disorderly Pupil in Elementary and Secondary School* (New York: Longmans, Green and Co., 1957), p. 4.

almost completely utilitarian, and the remainder a combination of the two. For educators to reach consensus on the essentials of reading, arithmetic, listening, and other basic skills is less of a task than for them to decide whether, for instance, certain geometrical processes are more a vestige of the past than a need of the present; or whether algebra is more important for its general-education content than as a tool of logical reasoning. Whatever the curriculum ultimately should become, it is important that it not be permitted today to drive youth out of school or work against the cause of discipline. The adolescent, parent, or community may at times be only the scapegoat for a school program that is not fitted to the needs of youth.

The teacher as a cause

While the school studies its course offerings, the individual faculty member can, with profit, engage in the rewarding process of self-appraisal to determine whether he is performing a disservice to the cause of discipline. The probe might uncover shortcomings either in the field of teaching method or in the more basic fundamentals of personality dynamics, or both. Apropos of the first, he might discover that he dominates too much and includes the group too little, that he selects methods that are inappropriate to the learning situation, or that he over-indulges one approach to the exclusion of others more relevant.

The search into his own personality might also reveal blocks to classroom discipline: the frequent sarcastic remark, a hard-to-control temper, the occasional fit of moodiness, a chronic detachment from the group, phlegmatism, or a consistent gravitation toward ego involvement—all of which would be considered harmful when projected on a class. Thus, the underlying reasons why certain classes fail to reach a desired state of inner control may be no further away than the instructional leader himself.

PREVENTION OF INFRACTIONS

Contemporary thinking about discipline rests firmly on the concept of prophylaxis before infraction, instead of treatment afterward; therefore, attention is next directed at certain specific ways of circumvention. We begin by canalizing the components of the curriculum and the teacher in a positive direction, in contrast to their reverse direction considered in the last section.

The curriculum

If an ill-conceived curriculum has adverse effects on class members, a well-conceived one can perform magic, not only on their minds but also on their emotions. First of all, the content must be relevant and vital, attuned closely to the needs and interests of young people while not sacrificing in the process the more significant goals of the greater society. When the adolescent's and society's demands are consonant, learning progresses smoothly; but when the two are not harmonious, only the finesse of a skillful teacher can heal the schism. In such a situation, the teacher makes as palatable as he can the curriculum content which all youth—regardless of background—need, but rewards them later with latitude in other content areas where student choice can be exercised. The curriculum thus defers to the uniqueness of students without ignoring societal expectancies.

A curriculum designed to have a prophylactic effect on disciplinary infractions must also be characterized by teaching methods that appeal. These need to engulf students in active learning processes, conform to the content of the moment, and demonstrate variety in order to fend off boredom. The creatively active class is invariably too busy to generate any mood other than positivism, for the premeditation requisite to misbehavior is difficult to come by when the adolescent is actively engaged in learning's meaningful outcomes.

The teacher

Along with the curriculum, the teacher as a person stands out as a major deterrent to infringements against classroom order. The instructional guide who has resolved the more pressing of his own personal problems is that much more effective in helping others to attack theirs. Without such victory over self, ego involvement might well stand in the way of understanding.

Psychology would describe the effective teacher personality in a number of ways, with the following points of view expressed by one or more individuals.

1. He should see reality for what it is, be undefensive, have few guilt feelings, shun the role of poseur, enjoy privacy, have profound interpersonal relations and shun enculturation. (Maslow)[7]

2. He should have "social feeling" in the sense of establishing a singleness of purpose with all associates. (Adler)[8]

3. He should know his real self in a world of people, moving toward them, not away from or against them. (Horney)[9]

---

[7] A. H. Maslow, *Motivation and Personality* (New York: Harper & Row, 1954), Ch. 12.

[8] Alfred Adler, *Understanding Human Nature* (New York: Permabooks, 1949), pp. 30–32.

[9] Karen Horney, *Neurosis and Human Growth* (New York: W. W. Norton, Inc., 1950).

4. He should be able to see others with a keenness of psychological vision removed from invidious associations with other similar or like people of the past. He would see others as they really are. (Sullivan)[10]

5. The students would describe the wholesome teacher personality in such understandable terms as *cooperative, kindly, patient, diversified in interests, fair, flexible,* and *consistent.* (Witty)[11]

In the composite of these verbal sketches, the model teacher is seen as one who makes ready identification with others, sees situations realistically for what they are, and projects the more wholesome personality traits on the unfolding scene of the moment. Having himself made such satisfactory progress toward maturity, he thereby serves as the best prophylactic agent possible. In his well-run classroom, behavioral deviations will be few, and when they do occur, they will be handled with a marked absence of emotionalism. He and students will be so involved in creative endeavor that prevention will replace correction. This picture of teacher personality is projected as a goal toward which young teachers should strive. Personality is not all, but without it, classroom decorum is the loser.

An edge of scholarship

Because the classroom is a people-centered environment, an integrated teacher personality is paramount; because it is also a learning environment, teacher scholarliness is likewise necessary. The basic purpose of a scholarly attitude is to foster cognitive growth, but its secondary service to the outcome of discipline cannot be overlooked. The scholarly classroom leader is one who possesses a wealth of knowledge about his chosen instructional field or fields. In addition, having plumbed the deeper insights of general education, he is able to relate the more technical to the general in life, and the past to the present. Then, as observation and experiment become increasingly contributive, he progresses toward that rare combination of the abstract and concrete which have characterized the true scholar throughout the centuries.

This is the type of teacher who, although manifestly planning and organizing curriculum outcomes, unconsciously communicates an inner spontaneity. He leavens the methodical with the urgent and the conditional with the imperative. More than just prepared for the known, he is also ready for the unknown. His is the scholarship that sets off a chain reaction. It announces to students that learning is a valuable commodity inestimably worthy of emulation. Because such scholarliness endows him with somewhat more than his share of organization, poise, and control of self, these

[10] Harry Stack Sullivan, *Conceptions of Modern Psychiatry* (Washington, D.C.: William Alanson Whyte Psychiatric Foundation, 1947), pp. 102–106.
[11] Paul Witty, "Some Characteristics of the Effective Teacher," *Educational Administration and Supervision* (April, 1950).

latter tend to bend outward toward students as inevitably as motivation gravitates toward favorable learning outcomes. Scholarship breeds scholarship, and maturity breeds maturity. Thus, the intellectually capable and informed teacher mirrors on students his positive qualities. In so doing, discipline becomes an accepted classroom attribute with infractions rare or nonexistent with reasonably normal students.

We wish to emphasize at this point that the term *scholar* is in no way being associated here with the long-existing stereotype of the detached, feckless individual who, although steeped in knowledge of a narrow field, is restricted by inflexible time, place, and cognitive horizons. Neither is he being associated with the poor imitation who affectedly assumes a role. On him the front of scholarship fits awkwardly and artificially, showing up obviously as a façade of pseudo-intellectualism. Such pedantry brings out the sham in students, defeating, not fostering, the goals of discipline.

From firmness to freedom

Notwithstanding a curriculum that is challenging and a teacher whose personality is integrated and whose scholarship is keen, progress from authority to freedom in the secondary school classroom still cannot be rushed. The ideal would be for adolescents to respond in kind to friendliness and sincerity and quickly accept the responsibilities of freedom as well as its privileges. But human nature is complex, the roots of behavior go in many directions, and maturity is a developmental process; therefore, the beginning teacher is wise to keep the reins taut early in a school term and to relax them only when readiness flashes the cue.

This recommendation is supported by tenets of adolescent growth and by the concept of limits that psychology postulates. From the point of view of growth, pre-adolescents and post-adolescents, although approaching adulthood physically, are removed many years from it as seventh-graders, and even a few years from it as seniors. And psychologically, the disparity is as great or greater. Yet welling in most adolescents is the urge for emancipation from adults, and its excesses must be controlled from without when they do not succumb to controls from within.

The doctrine of limits is also interesting in this regard. Adelaide Johnson, for instance, attributes a sizeable incidence of juvenile delinquency to the inability or refusal of adult authority figures to establish clear limits for youth to operate within.[12] When these limits are clearly understood and accepted, young people feel secure in the knowledge that life has been defined for them. Such limits are needed by all, in differing degrees depending on maturity levels; for the insecure teenager at loose ends with life, they are mandatory. In a world of conflicting values, interests, and

[12] Adelaide Johnson, *op. cit.*, p. 846.

behavior, firmness within reason provides stability until a more relaxed society characterized by greater freedom can take its place.

Unfortunately, no teacher can tell exactly when a group is ready for freedom. Even the experienced teacher is perplexed by at least a certain amount of unpredictability in groups and is often disgruntled over the trial-and-error behavior that he has to engage in as a means of detecting readiness. Of one thing a teacher can be certain, though: he will never discover readiness unless he permits freedom. Thus, teachers must forego some of their rigid insistence on absolute controls in order that pupils may grow. And at times they must tolerate awkward first efforts in the process.

Order before opening

Freedom, however, does not encompass the following, which is typical in certain schools. Pupils file into the classroom from the noisy hallways. A few shuffle about the room until the class bell rings; then they proceed to their respective seats, where they continue to converse, even though at a slower tempo. Some teachers break through the sound barrier, although with difficulty, with a staccato: "Quiet!" or "Give me your attention!" Others less vocally equipped use the same exclamatory methods but are unable to break through. These may resort to a soliloquy until the audience finally tunes itself off, before they attempt to tune in. Many teachers, however, quite properly refuse to open a class until they have the attention of pupils.

Granting all that has been said about adolescents pulling away from adults and being individualistic, they should be required to respect time and place. The class bell is a signal to young people to be in their seats and ready to respond to the learning demands of the curriculum. A well-disciplined class automatically gets into an attentive mood shortly after the bell rings; but moving down the scale of adjustment is the class that insists on being quieted by the teacher, and finally, the extreme instance, where the class resists completely. Thus, it is a wise young teacher who "demands" attention from the start and takes whatever action is required in order to get it. The obviously self-evident insistence that learning is to begin when the bell rings can do more for a group than a reprimand after the fact of infraction. This organized type of classroom climate if initiated in September will, with occasional reinforcement, carry through the year. And most adolescents in search of limits will prefer this regimen to license.

Sustaining the feeling of urgency

When the well-disciplined class has responded in an adult way to the warning bell, its members justifiably expect the 40-, 50-, or 60-minute period to start with vigor, be pursued with a businesslike seriousness of purpose, and terminate on a high note of interest. The first few minutes can well initiate a climate of success or failure, depending on how well a teacher employs them. Therefore, when the class bell rings, the instructional leader should immediately go into his role of teacher guide, thereby demonstrating to pupils by his manner that, since he believes education to be a significant part of their lives, he will not condone a less serious posture on their part.

Of equal importance are the closing moments of a period, when pupils, with just a minimum of provocation, tend to look at the clock, close books with audible reverberations, and fidget, as only adolescents can, during the last minute or two of a class. The late Shirley Hamrin, well known in guidance circles, used to advise teachers to save their best punch lines for the concluding moments in order to give needed conclusion to the period. In the interim between the beginning and end, the purposeful classroom authority figure strives to make learning vital and interesting, realizing that, if he sells it short by word or demeanor, his younger associates will buy it at the value he places on it. Nor is this businesslike person an automaton substituting detachment for empathy, compulsiveness for humaneness, or mechanical efficiency for flexibility. Rather, he taps the powers of organization as a medium for expressing and demonstrating the ultimate importance of learning. In the process, discipline becomes a bonus byproduct of a class too gainfully occupied to offend against decorum.

In contrast to this picture of a teacher with a mission and a curriculum component with a purpose is the "ho hum" type of class environment which drags endlessly through the torpor of tedium and listlessness. If lassitude and personality disorganization are the unenviable possessions of a teacher, they too, like their positive counterparts, soon become the legacy of pupils. At least in that situation, pupils feel exonerated when mirroring these attitudes back to their source. In the process, discipline becomes more elusive as indifference multiplies.

Involve the students

Another investment in prevention is the involvement by the teacher of adolescents in the activities of learning. Theory says that such involvement should be continuous and multi-dimensional, on the supposition that an active participator in an enterprise supports it more energetically than does a spectator. We do not propose to shunt the lecture and the other less physically active methods to the sidelines any more than to insist on activity for activity's sake. Rather, we remind the teacher that the important functions of the classroom are to be built around the individuals for whom learning is designed.

The informal lecture interspersed with questions, supervised study actively participated in by all, the daydreamer aroused with a quip, teacher demonstration followed by pupil engagement, or any other phase of classroom activity accompanied by anticipation and participation—these are illustrations of prophylactic involvement. With the adolescent organism active, the curriculum interesting, and the teacher sensitive to learning's possibilities, the student will become so immersed in the affairs of the classroom that negativism will offer less competition.

Pupils need to be personalized

A second goal of extensive student involvement is a more personalized kinship between teacher and pupils. Such a relation will have overtones both for learning and for preventive discipline. In respect to either, adolescents, because of their ego preoccupations, desire even more than adults to be known and accepted as human beings in their own right. In the university, professor-student acquaintanceships are more incidental than typical, and being the third person in the seventh row is not degrading to a student. But in the secondary school, the adolescent almost demands recognition. Students respond much better to the teacher who "first names" them, knows of their interests and out-of-school activities, and in other more or less subtle ways identifies them as unique and important people.

Thus, the teacher who prefers prevention to treatment as a goal of discipline dedicates himself to a personalized relationship with his younger associates. Although never just "one of the boys," as a high-type legal parent he recognizes the tremendous value of the human equation. He speaks to his student friends in the halls, greets them when they enter the class, inquires about their health after they have returned from an illness, and always avoids the cold, detached role of authority figure. In the process, he accomplishes two purposes: he measures up to a high standard of professional expectancy, and he thwarts behavior that might retard progress toward discipline. Not always, but significantly often, pupils who view the teacher as a warm and empathic human being respond affirmatively to the many values to which he subscribes.

The merit of eye contact

To put into effect the concept of personalization, a teacher must maintain eye contact with his class. In deference to it, the admonition to teachers to "ride your eye around the room" has become almost a cliché. Throughout the course of a single period, the teacher needs to make visual touch with all members of the class, not once, but many times. Through this device, he witnesses that learning is for them, that they are expected to respond to it, and that their deviations from it will not be lightly ignored. Accordingly, if lecturing, even though needing contact with his notes, he addresses himself primarily to the listening audience. When pupil committees are reporting, he maintains a visual relationship with all members of the larger group while concentrating more particularly on the committee.

The teacher who isolates himself visually or otherwise from a class creates a schism in the learning pattern by depriving it of the needed personal element. The price is inevitably student withdrawal with its many manifestations: disinterest, inattention, the dime novel being read furtively, careless posture, social interchanges, and the nodding head. These can be prevented in most adolescents if the teacher knows what is going on in the room. One such method is as simple as the look itself.

Infractions necessitate action

This discussion of preventive measures ends with the suggestion that appropriate action at the time of an infraction works wonders in preventing a future one. In contrast, off-beat behavior, when permitted to repeat itself, snowballs inevitably into something more serious. The typical teacher understandably resists punishment as an unpleasant task and one that outwardly appears harmful to personality. But the choice is not between punishing and not punishing; it is rather between acting fast but reasonably at the time an offense occurs in preference to applying more severe measures later.

A FINAL WORD

These measures have been identified and discussed as possible means of heading off rule violations before they occur. As such, they fit into a humane setting that sees validity in the old "ounce of prevention." Admittedly, they are not a cure-all. In fact, teachers could well follow all of them religiously and still have occasional individuals and groups in need of corrective action. Misbehavior is often deep-seated, and the approaches which are designed to appeal to the more normal student cannot be expected to eliminate all offenses. As preventive media of merit, however, next steps should never be taken without these being considered first.

At this point, we lead into correction and change, which are the central motifs of the next chapter.

SUMMARY

Discipline in this chapter has been approached first from the principles on which it rests, then from the causes, and finally from the preventive methods designed to ward off infractions against rules. Throughout, the term *discipline* has been employed as descriptive of inner organization and orderliness of an individual or group. Violations of such orderliness have been referred to by the term *infractions,* with punishment reserved as the complement of the infractionary cause.

The basic concepts on which any sound program of discipline should rest were presented as the following: discipline is a means to an end; it exists first in the individual and then collectively in the group; it is a variable of situations; it is not always a possible resultant; leadership needs to be shared; and infractions are indicators of maladjustment.

The causes of value infractions were observed to rest in the individual, the home, the community, the curriculum, and the person of the teacher.

Prevention was identified as emanating from a valid curriculum, a well-adjusted teacher personality, a teacher's edge of scholarship, a teacher's acting firmly with a group by setting limits, a teacher's making learning urgent by being businesslike, the involvement of students actively in learning activities, the personalization of learning, and the need of immediate action to prevent future violations.

The motif of this chapter has been discipline and its prevention; that of the next will be punishment and change.

REFERENCES

Aichhorn, August, *Wayward Youth.* New York: Viking Press, Inc., 1935.

American Orthopsychiatric Association, *American Journal of Orthopsychiatry.* 1790 Broadway, New York. (Any issue)

Baruch, Dorothy, *New Ways in Discipline.* New York: McGraw-Hill Book Company, 1949.

Burton, William H., *The Guidance of Learning Activities.* New York: Appleton-Century-Crofts, Inc., (2nd ed.) 1952. (Chapter 22)

Cutts, Norma, and Nicholas Moseley, *Teaching the Disorderly Pupil in Elementary and Secondary School.* New York: Longmans, Green and Co., 1957.

Eissler, E. R., *Searchlights on Delinquency.* New York: International Universities Press, 1949.

Hymes, James L., Jr., *Behavior and Misbehavior, A Teacher's Guide to Action.* Englewood Cliffs, N.J.: Prentice-Hall, Inc., 1955.

————, *Discipline.* New York: Columbia University, Teachers College, Bureau of Publications, 1949.

Jersild, Arthur T., *In Search of Self.* New York: Columbia University. Teachers College. Bureau of Publications, 1952.

Kettelkamp, Gilbert C., *Teaching Adolescents.* Boston: D. C. Heath and Co., 1954. (Chapter 8)

National Education Association, *Teacher Opinion on Pupil Behavior.* Washington, D.C.: *Research Bulletin,* Vol. XXXIV, No. 2, April, 1956.

Ritholz, Sophie, *Misbehavior? How Do You Evaluate It?* New York: Bookman Associates, Inc., 1960.

Sheviakov, George V., and Fritz Ridl, "Discipline for Today's Children and Youth," *Association for Supervision and Curriculum Development.* Washington, D.C.: N.E.A., 1944.

Wickman, E. K., *Children's Behavior and Teachers' Attitudes.* New York: Commonwealth Fund, Inc., 1928.

DISCIPLINE:
PUNISHMENT
AND
CURRICULUM CHANGE

The ideal of every law-enforcing figure is to work himself out of a job by preventing violations of authority. This goal allures with its patent simplicity: establish the proper climate, lead associates to maturity, and then delight in the absence of imposed controls. Unfortunately, however, this position is more tenable at the theoretical than the practical level because of the inability of all but a few to attain its lofty goal. As with any long-range crusade for change, the present cannot be ignored while the future is being planned. In the case of discipline, the academic world, while striving for the ideal of inner control, must ever be ready to deal with the current offenders against classroom rules. Until unsocial acts can be eliminated, then, they will continue to require antidotes selected and administered for their benefit to the larger social group as well as for their possible remedial value to the single offender.

In the last chapter, the groundwork was laid for a better understanding of discipline and the causes of infractions against it, with special attention being given to prevention. In this chapter, the starker realities of the infractions themselves will undergo scrutiny, with punishment and correction as the focal centers. In the final section, we shall treat of curriculum change aimed, once more, at prevention.

PRINCIPLES OF PUNISHMENT

At the beginning of this discussion, we take note of the seriousness of the act of one individual punishing another. Involved in the act are these factors: a given person has offended against accepted order, an observer notes and assays the offense, then an authority figure metes out appropriate punishment. All of these actions, reaching as they do into the intimacies of personality and human relationships, are potentially divisive and harmful. Accordingly, punishment must be approached thoughtfully to hold personality harm to a minimum.

Undergirding the use of punishment regularly should be a philosophical base to provide needed validity. In this connection, each of the five stages of punishment previously discussed—vindictive, retributive, deterrent, remedial, and preventive—has or had a theoretical base for support. In the vindictive stage, the one sinned against—that is, the law or the individual—had the right to vent his spleen against the offender. This assumed a rigid point of view regarding justice, the emotions, and catharsis. In the retributive stage, the offender was expected to get as much as he gave. This point-counter-point relationship also was premised on certain theoretical underpinnings. In the deterrent stage, punishment was (and is) expected to be only of sufficient magnitude to prevent the rule violator and other possible identification figures from repeating the act. This, too, is based on assumptions, as are the remedial and the preventive stages. In like manner, the teacher should look to a body of theory to support whatever punishment he administers during a professional lifetime. Included in it might well be some of the following points of view.

The offender, not the offense

A moot question which gets at the root of penology itself is whether punishment is a function of the offender or of the offense. Is it wise to determine punishments for infractions prior to the time of their being committed? An affirmative answer may be based on the belief that the individual warned in advance that a certain misdemeanor will result in a previously determined penalty will be deterred from the act. Another basis for agreeing is the feeling that, with the same punishment meted out for all offenders, fair play will be assured. A major reason for a negative answer is that punishment tends to become a mechanical process when set apart from the individuality of the offender.

Despite the logic of like punishment for all who commit the same offense, categorical support for it disregards the importance of individual differences and the relatedness of cause-and-effect factors. For these reasons, we unequivocally advocate that punishment should fit the offender, not the offense. Only in this way can it be defended as remedial. A reprimand in class to the shy person, for instance, might be severe punishment; to the frustrated exhibitionist, very possibly a reward. Sending one child to the principal might offer him a welcome escape from a class which he despises, whereas identical treatment administered to another might be a serious trauma.

The punish-the-offender principle is defended despite possibilities of misunderstanding. If Peter is punished more severely than John for the same offense, Peter could be somewhat justified in accusing the teacher of unfairness. The logic of such an argument would have to be respected despite its oversimplification. In actuality, the issue poses a philosophical choice between the best interests of an individual on one side and measures to prevent group misunderstanding on the other. Our compromise is for the teacher to punish in the light of the uniqueness of the offender, but only after initially engaging a class in a thoroughgoing discussion of the major issues of discipline. This would include an overview of the ultimate goal of the orderly mind, the need for a relinquishing of some personal liberty when two or more individuals are associated, the necessity of humane punishment when rules are violated, and, finally, the case in point: that class members occasionally might be punished differently for the same offense. Such an airing of discipline's tenets would minimize hurt feelings and promote understanding. Adolescents are reasonably sensitive to the feelings of their fellow students, and the justice of differential punishment for the same act would ultimately permeate the thinking of most of them. The care exercised in implementing the concept would go far toward giving it success. But, apart from the possible group outcomes, if punishment is to be remedial, under no circumstances can the individual be shunted to a place of secondary importance.

Punishment related to means and ends

Consideration must be given to the level of punishment that might be appropriate for a given situation, and the final selection can be only in terms of the ends which it will serve. This principle is illustrated by the following episode, with three approaches to punishment differing according to the ends they are designed to serve.

The episode. Bill Lee is a volatile youngster, aged 14, who explodes emotionally, often with little provocation; a snide remark from a peer or a mild reprimand by the teacher is usually sufficient to set him off. When he loses his temper, he is prone to make or threaten physical contact with the instigator; however, to date he has confined this action to fellow stu-

362 Chapter 16

dents. The teacher, manifestly concerned about Bill's inappropriate expression of his emotions, contemplates each of the following three counter measures in view of the possible ends that they would serve.

1. In order to stop Bill from threatening others with physical contact, the teacher debates the advisability of a severe penalty. After consulting with the principal, he notifies the boy that another threatening gesture made toward any person in the classroom will carry with it an automatic suspension from school for one week, with readmittance possible only if Bill, his parents, and selected school personnel can reach agreement on next steps. The goal here is to deter, but by neglect or deliberate omission it has no preconceived design to make Bill a better-adjusted boy.

2. In order to protect others from Bill's aggression, the teacher provides him with a seat a short distance from the teacher's own in front of the room. The adolescent is informed of the reason for the environmental change. The goal here is admittedly an expedient, aimed not at all at the dynamics of the problem—only at the protecting of others.

3. Realizing that Bill's aggressive tendencies are possibly indicative of a deep-rooted personality syndrome, the teacher, while adopting the second approach just discussed, also arranges an interview for Bill with the school psychologist. Following several preliminary sessions, the psychologist reports a tentative finding of: "Aggression probably due to the neglect of parents, who are physically abusive to him." The goal finally decided on by the psychologist and the teacher is personality change, with the expectation of limited gains only in deference to realism. Although the class members, it is agreed, must be protected from Bill's aggressive tendencies, the boy's need of adjustment is viewed as too important to be ignored. A tentative plan of corrective action is worked out by the psychologist and the teacher, calling for the following: (a) a relationship between the teacher and Bill to be characterized by warmth, respect, and firmness by the teacher; (b) the confinement of Bill to his front seat until he demonstrates enough control to return to his former seat; (c) when required, the administering of fair and reasonable punishment in a kindly way; and (d) bi-weekly interviews to be held between Bill and the psychologist, with the acknowledged purpose of helping Bill understand himself more clearly.

The foregoing choices recognize that effective punishment needs goal reference. Never an independent entity or end in itself, punishment is always a means to a predetermined outcome. Thus, punishment assessed to achieve an individual purpose may be vastly different from that administered for a group outcome. And in a one-to-one clinical relationship, the therapist of whatever orientation has a primary dedication to the client, with outside loyalties only tangentially significant. In the classroom, the teacher, in contrast, has a twofold relationship, being endowed with some of the clinical obligations of his therapist counterpart while also being held responsible for the welfare of the larger group. This dual confrontation is discussed by Sheviakov and Redl under the "law of marginal antisepsis."[1] By this term they mean that, when working with an individual, a teacher's relationship with a group should usually be positive, and never worse than neutral; and when working with a group, the teacher's relationship with any individual likewise should usually be positive, and never worse than neutral.

Arriving at a happy compromise between these two almost conflicting demands is no easy assignment for the teacher. We strongly suspect that the two cannot consistently receive comparable attention; however, in responding to their respective demands, the teacher cannot afford the luxury of a distorted one-sidedness without courting failure. If satisfying the demands of both may require the wisdom of a Solomon and the ubiquity of a spirit, ignoring either for too long a time will lead to personality or academic regression. The answer for the teacher, unlike that for the clinician, is always in compromise. But in the ageless means-ends battle, the teacher needs to define his intentions at all times. Whether he punishes an individual for clinical reasons or to save the group, he must always analyze motives as a first preliminary step.

The need for objectivity

Once a violation has been appraised against a background of the offender, and also against the behavioral ends to be achieved, the punishment decided upon should be administered objectively. This qualification dictates the subordination of the emotions of the authority figure. Throughout the entire process of analyzing classroom behavior, the teacher who does the best clinical job is invariably the one who can remove himself far enough away from the emotional biases of self and the situation to appraise realistically.

An obstacle to desired objectivity customarily resides in the conflict between the values of the teacher and those of the student. The teacher, for instance, who is strongly oriented in religious orthodoxy may be unable to resist attaching stigma to certain unsocial acts, thus adulterating the major purposes of correction. Or the teacher of one subculture may be so unable to divest himself of its influences that dealing objectively with a person of another subculture becomes an impossibility.

Illustrative of the relation of behavioral observations to background is the Wickman study of 1928, often quoted in educational literature.[2] In it,

---

[1] George V. Sheviakov and Fritz Redl, *Discipline for Today's Children and Youth* (Washington, D.C.: National Education Association, 1949), p. 25.
[2] E. K. Wickman, *Children's Behavior and Teacher's Attitudes* (New York: The Commonwealth Fund, Division of Publications, 1928), pp. 124–126.

over 500 classroom teachers and 30 clinical psychologists observed student behavior and then rank-ordered specific manifestations in terms of seriousness. The teachers included in their top ten ratings the patterns that revolved around sex interests and aggressive acts. Such unsocial reactions as shyness, sensitiveness, and tattling were placed in the lower ten ratings. Quite inversely, the psychologists rated the unsocial patterns as more serious, and the more extrovert, aggressive ones as less serious. Although the dual responsibility of the teachers for the group as well as for the individual may be one explanation for the difference in results, another equally plausible interpretation is that the value differences between the teachers and psychologists were responsible. Mildly supporting the latter hypothesis is Mitchell's comparable study, where the observations by the same two categories of professionals were more nearly alike in 1943 than they had been in 1928.[3]

Regardless of any teacher's philosophical or religious orientation, if punishment is to meet the test of being remedial, it must be devoid of color connotations that prevent objective understanding and clearly conceived purpose. When a satisfactory theoretical base has been established, objectivity in the administering of punishment is more of a natural *sequitur*.

The pupil should know why he is punished

A presupposition of the remedial approach to corrective action is that the adolescent who is being punished will know why. This requirement obligates the teacher to think through the series of events that led to the act of correction, and then to provide a logical explanation to the offender. The purposes of making the explanation are to acquaint him with the knowledge that limits exist, that certain acts in life have consequences, that other people have rights, and that corrective action is designed to help him adjust better to the problems of his environment. Thus, if a pupil is removed from class because of talking with a friend during a study period, the teacher owes him the explanation that the punishment is necessary to stop the disturbance at that time and to prevent a similar occurrence in the future. Or, in a more severe case of suspension from school, the punishment demands explanation in relation to the specific offense itself as well as its antecedents and future next steps.

This interrelating of remedial action to the many precipitating circumstances once more places the process of reformation in the proper perspective of helping the offender by having him face reasonable consequences. It also helps the group by neutralizing the violation. The traditionally sweeping accusation of, "You are bad and have to be punished,"

---

[3] J. C. Mitchell, "A Study of Teachers' and Mental Hygienists' Ratings of Certain Behavior Problems of Children," *Journal of Educational Research* (36, 1943), pp. 292–307.

would fail the criteria of soundness on two counts: first, it would conceal the exact offense by glossing it over with the hazy, innocuous term "bad"; second, it would place the entire event in an emotionally loaded setting of sin, guilt, and retribution. An uncalled-for feeling of badness, when unqualified, can well lead to an undesirable self-image, which, in turn, can easily result in aggressiveness or withdrawal. In contrast, a sensitively conceived explanation of the "why" of punishment places it in mature perspective by relegating the phony and false to the background.

Punishment needs to be firm but not harsh

After a specific corrective has been elected, it should be applied promptly and firmly, but never harshly. Punishment seems to achieve the best results when, despite possible unpleasantness, it is administered in a convincing but courteous manner; is definite, not indecisive; and is severe enough to get into the consciousness without being harsh enough to defeat the cause of attitude change. Interestingly in this regard, the military as early as 1861 abolished bodily contact in dispensing punishment and since then has insisted that manifestations of harshness, violence, or even impatience be dissociated with it.[4] And if the authoritative military has seen fit to ameliorate its beliefs about behavior, education cannot appraise its values any less carefully.

An example may be useful. In spite of receiving punishment previously for the same infraction, Louise Levin is caught reading a pulp magazine during a class discussion. Although Louise is known to be merely serving time in school pending the age of permissible dropout, the teacher feels that her disdain for authority should be resisted and countered. Thus, the teacher advises Louise that she is to report to the homeroom the next day, from 3:30 until 4:20, to make up the work lost. The student fails to come, later giving the excuse that she had a job that conflicted. The teacher next doubles the penalty to two days: one to be spent by Louise in making up the curriculum time lost, and the second for a discussion by Louise and the teacher of her behavior. In the process, the teacher firmly but kindly lets Louise know that all steps necessary will be taken to consummate the punishment. He stays calm, answers the sensible questions while deftly bypassing the irrational, and generally treats the situation no differently from the way he would any other learning episode. He also plans subsequent action involving the parents in the event Louise continues to resist. Having decided that she must conform to limits, he pursues his course calmly but firmly.

In contrast to this consistent pattern are punitive actions stamped by vacillation and indecision. The type of inane remark heard so often: "Mary, I just don't know what to do with you," makes the student the victor and

[4] George Sheviakov and Fritz Redl, *op. cit.*, p. 11.

the teacher the vanquished. Equally ambivalent is the not untypical remark: "Let's see, Tom; I have engagements this afternoon and tomorrow; why don't you come to see me after school Wednesday or Thursday?" Indefensible also is the punishment that rewards: for example, permitting the exhibitionist to sit in the hall where he can demonstrate his talents more admirably. Corrective action, to be meaningful, needs to be severe enough to convince the recipient that his misdemeanor was so serious as to bear consequences. Although far from a martinet or avenging angel, the teacher must be decisive if corrective action is to produce the desired results.

A closed case should remain closed

After appropriate action has been taken, the mature teacher can forget that the offense occurred. Once a case has been closed, the seal should rarely be broken. This approach is more humane than the one taken by a judgmental teacher who never seems to let a child forget that he has erred. Legal parents cannot afford to act so unlike adults. Denying the adolescent the opportunity to obliterate past errors can easily lead to deep-seated enmity toward the teacher and a generalized resentment toward the entire school setting—outcomes which are scarcely consonant with discipline's goals of prevention and inner change. As with learning itself, the teacher cannot without harm permit the past to serve as a deterrent to the present. Since the authority figure himself insists that society make concessions to parts of his own past, he can scarcely do less for his younger associate.

Referral may be demanded

Notwithstanding his conscientious efforts, the capable and well-meaning teacher will occasionally discover that his actions, if not exactly in vain, have resulted in few positive outcomes. With his own resources depleted, he next logically considers the wisdom of referral. The avenues differ from school to school, but in the composite include the following.

1. *The principal.* In the small school system, the principal may be the only school figure to whom the teacher can turn. Although not a therapist, he can contribute better to the solution when he shares the problem. Referral to the principal, however, should follow other attempts at solution.

2. *The school nurse.* The physical is closely related to the psychological; thus physical causation of disturbance may be suspect at times. In this event, the school nurse or visiting physician should share in the problem. After passing this screening, psychological causation can be pursued with greater confidence.

3. *Other specialized guidance personnel.* In urban and suburban schools, the existence of various categories of guidance specialists is not

unusual. These may include family counselors, school psychologists, or people by other titles who can assist the teacher in need of help with a so-called disciplinary problem.

4. *The parents.* If a pupil problem persists or becomes acute, the parent should be called to the school for consultation. When the exceptional parent refuses consistently to appear despite a letter to the home and a phone call at his place of employment, the issue should be turned over to the legal authorities.

5. *Outside agencies.* In urban and suburban communities where they exist, institutions such as family agencies, child welfare groups, and juvenile authorities should be the last resorts. These are usually consulted when direct school efforts have proved unsuccessful.

Common errors to be avoided

Corrective action, whether implemented by a classroom instructor or by a referral specialist, should be devoid of threats, scoldings, unnecessary warnings, thoughtless admonitions, requests for apologies, sarcasm, and anger. These are to be avoided, first, because they are not remedial, but even more important, because often they are so harmful as to defeat the cause of discipline.

Threats. Most classroom observers have frequently heard such remarks as: "If you do that one more time, James, I'll make you leave class and never let you back in." Or "Bill, if you don't move when I ask you, I'll see that you do." These and like threats are objectionable for two reasons: being often made in anger, they may be ill-conceived; furthermore, they consistently require follow-through. The one doing the threatening could well ask himself first whether he would take the indicated action if his "hand were called"—and if he would feel right about taking it. Unless these are answered in the affirmative, the ground on which he treads is shaky, at best. Not to follow through on a threat makes the teacher lose face; to follow through merely because the threat was made and not because the action is proper is even worse.

Emotionalism invariably is the motivator of the threat. With this unpredictive component in control, primitive forces tend to dominate while reason recedes. In such circumstances, the teacher responds to whimsy, whereas society expects him to respond to reason. Just as harmful as the emotionally charged behavior itself is its residual influence on the teacher. A violent display of temper or other retreat from emotional control is not infrequently followed by a feeling of regret or embarrassment, either of which makes for a distortion in pupil-teacher relationships. How much more sensible for the teacher to escape these consequences by avoiding threats which might initiate them. The quick counter of action removes the need of the threat.

Scoldings. Although probably not so harmful to teacher-pupil relationships as threats, scoldings also set up barriers. When a class needs a reprimand, unquestionably the teacher is obligated by expediency, if for no other reason, to take firm and decisive action. But he can deliver the needed reprimand in normal voice, with a minimum of emotion and in a non-judgmental way. The relationship that he establishes in this manner is certainly superior to the one created by a tiresome berating of pupils which may result in a resistance to future teacher efforts. A called-for reprimand should not be avoided, but it need not be vituperative to be effective. When the rebuke is acrimonious, it is more often remembered by pupils for the emotional reflection of the teacher than for the effects of the reprimand itself.

Frequent warnings. Punishment that is clear-cut is inharmonious with the purposeless warnings that many individuals employ before taking action. In the spirit of fairness, a first warning might be encouraged, or at least condoned. Subsequent delays, however, tend to reveal that the teacher has little desire to cope with the problem. The invidious product of this practice of delay is that pupils capitalize on the license thus delegated. They misbehave while the teacher warns.

Ludicrous corrections. Associated with not one but many types of punishment is the tendency of teachers to ask for the impossible. A prime example is the suggestion that a recalcitrant pupil go into the hall and not return until his attitude has changed. With attitudes requiring months or years—some requiring even lifetimes—to change, naïve is the teacher who expects miracles in minutes. Another familiar order is that the student go and not return until he is ready to apologize. If these words were accepted at their face value, the occasional student would possess the right never to return to the classroom. An apology given sincerely and without coercion probably has therapeutic value because it reflects a generosity of spirit and a desire to correct a wrong. But an apology brought about by coercion breeds resentment, rebellion against authority, and hatred. And in reality, its only purpose is to place the teacher back on his rather shaky seat of authority. Admitting that pupil apologies reinforce the superiority image of the person who can coerce them into being, adulthood can certainly discover more wholesome ways of solving problems.

Sarcasm. Decidedly within the framework of destructiveness to human personality is the use of sarcasm by the teacher. Illustrative are such expressions as: "You would be surprised at what a little study will do." Or, "Nice going, John, you're sharp today." Or, "If you used your eyes, you'd be amazed at how many things you could see." The dividing line between sarcasm and humor admittedly is not always easy to find. The mildly barbed remarks of a teacher who has rapport with a class can be relatively harmless, whereas the identical remarks by another with a less desirable relationship can be destructive. Any disciplinary approach, however, which makes a child feel foolish by placing him in the position of

deliberate subservience is inherently wrong. Even though sarcasm admittedly is a function of time, person, and place, a studied avoidance of
the very appearance of it in the classroom is a safer approach.

Anger. Last in the treatment of negative characteristics to be avoided
in the meting out of punishment is anger. In its more severe expression,
the manifestation of this emotion indicates that the human organism is out
of the control of the higher and more civilized brain centers, and is correspondingly under the influence of those primitive forces over which an
individual has little or no control. Punishment administered in anger, thus,
cannot be more rational than the teacher is at the time that he administers
it. Once more we emphasize that, if corrective action is for the purpose of
rehabilitating the individual, as well as for protecting the group, it must be
endowed with the dignity that only one in command of himself can bring
to it.

METHODS OF CORRECTION

Having approached a number of classes
with the unconscious hope that true discipline will be achievable—only to
be later disillusioned by reality—the realistic teacher soon faces the conclusion openly that certain students must be made to respond to controls
imposed from without. At any such point of disenchantment, he takes inventory of the methods at his disposal to help students respond better to
learning's broad demands. These resources may be purely manipulative or
manifestly punitive, immediate or long-range, expedient or rehabilitative.
Regardless of their exact position in these dichotomies, a number of the
more common methods will be identified and discussed approximately in
the order from the less to the more obviously severe.

The appeal

The most common method of correction employed by teachers daily
is the verbal appeal issued either to the individual or to the class. In the
former, it customarily takes the form of the friendly request for the pupil
to desist from disturbing those around him; for example: "Ann, your talking distracts; will you please follow the discussion?" Or, "Ellen, you are
separating Linda as well as yourself from the rest of the class." Under
normal circumstances, the thoughtless action can be curbed by such a
mild admonition. When the action is more blatant, the request might have
to carry more authority: "Fred, I have to insist that you pay attention."

The verbal request for an entire class to conform to existing standards
is also commonplace. It may occur directly at the time that a class is becoming restive, or more subtly and appropriately in a contemplative atmos-

phere following the time that school or class regulations have been violated. In the latter circumstance, the group process is brought into play, with the teacher and class sharing ideas on the behavior in question, why it occurred, and preventive next steps. The practicality of this approach is always a function of readiness, with some groups able to drop their defenses sufficiently to study their actions with clarity, and with others too unaccustomed to the procedure, or too ego-involved, to reward it with other than preliminary success.

Standing in the vicinity of the offender

Another mild—in fact, almost matter-of-fact—gesture by a teacher faced with a rule infraction is a movement in the direction of the offender. The desirability of this procedure is that the learning routine is scarcely interfered with at all, and the student who has affronted is not singled out in any negative way. From the vantage point of parsimony—the least punishment necessary being always the best—this unobtrusive employment of teacher presence has real merit. If the directional move fails in its purpose, the teacher can always supplement it without fanfare by a quietly uttered verbal appeal. Although the more seriously disturbed adolescent will resist these corrective subtleties, most students will respond to them in a satisfying way.

Changing the student's seat

A second environmental approach to neutralizing disturbance is the change of a pupil's seat. The teacher takes this admittedly expedient action to protect a segment of a class from one or more erring individuals, or the individual from his own temptations. It is employed most frequently to break up a clique that has placed the interests of a small in-group above those of the other class members. The danger in the procedure is that the source of trouble may merely be transferred from one room location to another, in which event the affected student may need to be seated close to the teacher. More often than not, however, the student whose seat has been changed, although perhaps tending to act up for a day or so to save face by temporarily defying authority, will soon settle down in the new location. And even if the result is unsatisfactory, at least the teacher will have experimented with a less offensive approach before adopting a severer one.

After-school reporting

The time-honored, possibly timeworn, practice of requiring students to report to the classroom for after-school activities still has merit if employed for the proper purposes and if kept within reasonable bounds. Its best implementation is with the individual or small group, and only rarely with the entire class. One of two outcomes customarily sought is either the making up of academic work by the student or the treating of his misbehavior. For the latter purpose, the after-school teacher-pupil discussion of standards and conduct potentially has real merit, providing both individuals with the interview atmosphere that would be inaccessible if the other class members were present.

Too prevalently, however, the practice of detention becomes completely unrelated to the misdemeanor which caused it. Children are made to do busy work under the surveillance of the classroom teacher himself, or, worse, are herded together in a large study room under the auspices of a member of the faculty who happens to be there only as a result of a teacher-rotation policy. In neither eventuality can idleness or pointless activity be regarded as remedial, and only with certain of the students can it be a deterrent. Without completely negating the merit of occasional after-school incarceration, we plead against its overuse. Detention for detention's sake at best can be regarded only as an expedient.

Depriving of after-class privileges

As a corrective measure, the school may make inroads not only into a student's free after-school time, but into his "belongingness" privileges as well. Selected of these might be: playing on an athletic team, participating in a club, being a member of a student governing body, or having "honor" rights to a student lounge. A fundamental objection to punishments of this kind is that, like retention after school, they also may have little relationship to the offense itself. Removing one student from an honor study hall and his excessive talking in class, or pre-empting another student's part in a senior play and his bullying tactics in the halls, may have little affinity. Correction may be the outcome of the punitive acts, but it is far from being assured.

Another fundamental issue here is whether certain privileges withdrawn from students may not be vital to their all-around growth. Notwithstanding the significance of English, mathematics, science, social studies, and the foreign languages, not to mention the fine and practical arts, can the school dismiss lightly the social and personality benefits of the co-curriculum? If not, it had better debate before employing deprivation as a punitive procedure. If the formal subjects are the queen of a curriculum, and the less formal activities only maidservants, pupil exclusion from the latter, with design to punish, has some justification—if it works. But if the activities have real merit in themselves, they should no more be withheld as an incentive for good behavior than the formal subjects themselves.

Dismissal from the classroom

In the ranks of corrective measures, just as controversial as deprivation is the practice of dismissing a pupil from the classroom. Fundamental to such practice is the issue of where the pupil is to go when dismissed. If to the hallway, he not only may be unsupervised, but he becomes a public spectacle; if to a guidance office, the function of rehabilitation becomes confused with the act of punishment; if to the principal or his representative (a dean of men or women), the factor of timing and communication loom important. Regardless of the place to which the student is removed, the tug of war always goes on between those who regard sending a pupil from the room as a sign of weakness, and their opposites who consider it a legitimate practical measure. Our point of view is that the practice is legitimate if other less severe methods have been tried without success.

Supporting this point of view is the conviction that the cause of learning must never be endangered by the notorious "bad actors" in any school. Individual rights undeniably are a cherished product, but they cannot be allowed to rule supreme. Neither can a teacher be allowed to diffuse so much of his psychic energy negatively that positive goals become sidetracked. In emergency situations, the teacher not only should be permitted, but should even be encouraged, to transfer a troubled youngster to the office of a designated administrative official. In this event, a note of explanation should precede the arrival of the student, and in it the official should be informed of the reason for the referral. Following the referral deliberations, the three individuals should have an early meeting of the minds regarding what transpired and the next steps to be taken. Under no circumstances should the two professionally involved adults allow themselves to work at cross purposes. When one is unaware of what the other is thinking or doing, the student, having divided and thus conquered, escapes the inherent benefits of corrective therapy.

The student council as a court

Somewhat distinctive from the other methods already discussed, but yet a rather prevalent practice in a number of schools, is the student court which sits in judgment on a fellow student and assesses penalties. The proffered merit of such a judicial student agency is that it educates in the ways of democracy. While in favor of the laudable outcome, we question the means. Our reason is categorical: if discipline is as elusive as society knows it to be, and violations against it are as complex as they unquestionably are, then only the best-informed should have the right to deliberate or judge the actions of another. Adolescents, with their own major emotional problems as yet unresolved, and without formal training or experience in the area of human dynamics, are unlikely candidates for such status positions. Even when a teacher or administrative adult possesses veto power, a student judiciary should not be condoned. The school's aim is to unify the student body, not divide it; also, adolescents should be cooperative, not formally judgmental. Therefore, student infractions must be assessed by authority figures attuned to their complexities. The "reasonable man" cannot settle for less.

Corporal punishment

Exceeding in volatility any method of attempted correction yet discussed is corporal punishment. The practice, although primarily a vestige in many places, is still prevalent on the European continent, in England, and in a number of privately owned school systems in the United States. A few states still legalize it for the public schools, whereas a few others, by ignoring it in the school code, give tacit approval to its employment, provided that a local community endorses the practice.

Basic to any further consideration of the topic is an understanding of exactly what constitutes corporal punishment. The most obvious manifestation is the spanking. A more common manifestation is the employment by the teacher of a ruler or back of the hand in striking a student. A less obvious method, but one also intended to harm the person of the pupil, is that by which the teacher exerts unnecessary pressure on the arm or shoulder of a young culprit while escorting him from one place in the school to another. The common feature of all of these is that contact with the body of another is made with the intent to inflict some degree of physical harm or pain.

More important, however, than the definitive qualities of corporal punishment are the psychological intangibles that surround it. Even if the method deters—a questionable assumption, at best—what adverse effects might it have on student attitudes and personalities? And if the method deters, does it act remedially? And if it acts remedially, aren't there more desirable methods? These fundamental questions demand clear-cut answers based on unequivocal evidence before corporal punishment in schools can be encouraged. With such answers not forthcoming, we go on record as opposed to the practice. Corporal punishment involves possible legal dangers and the establishing of barriers between teachers and pupils. These are too important to be ignored by the employment of a method that is of only doubtful value, if it is a value at all.

For the teacher, however, who sees some merit in corporal punishment and decides on its employment, the following procedural steps should be followed: (1) consult the principal to assure his support; (2) ask the principal to notify the parents regarding the contemplated action; (3) whenever possible, have a central authority figure administer the punishment; (4) have a witness present; (5) ascertain that the one who administers the punishment is of the same sex as the offender; and (6) keep the case in strict privacy from beginning to end. And after these criteria have been adhered to, it is quite possible that such premeditation will result ultimately in the selection of a substitute form of punishment.

Probation, suspension, and expulsion

The last corrective devices to be considered in this section are the most serious ones: probation, by which a pupil is told that he will be suspended if he offends again; suspension, by which a pupil is banned from school for a few days or weeks until parents and the school authorities can decide on a plan of action; and expulsion, the most climactically severe of all punishments, because it usually places the pupil under the care of juvenile authorities. The first of the three measures, probation, informs the student that, because of the previous offenses against good order, he will be suspended in the event of another violation. This method has doubtful value because it constitutes an unnecessary threat and also keeps him dangling in a state of apprehension.

Suspension, although extreme, is called for when other efforts have failed. Occasionally an adolescent needs reminding in a determined way that rules are not made to be broken. However, when suspension is practiced merely to save a teacher or principal from being bothered, or before less stringent means have been exhausted, it lacks validity. The period of suspension, depending on the misdemeanor, varies from a half-day in certain instances to a week or longer in others. Usually a teacher-parent-pupil conference culminates the suspension and leads to an agreement on future action to be taken after the pupil has been reinstated.

Expulsion, contrary to the other two media, must be seen by teachers in its stark reality. The legal age for school attendance has been set by statute, and the pupil who has not attained it and is expelled must continue his schooling as a ward of the state. If he is near the age of legal dropout, in a few states he can work part-time and attend a public school part-time. This is one of the more fortunate outcomes. More sordid, as well as frequent, is the alternative practice: the expelled pupil is forced into the custody of juvenile authorities. The sequence is usually as follows: a serious offense is committed by a student; expulsion is the penalty decided on by the school after all other alternatives have been ruled out; the pupil is made to inhabit an administrator's office until the school and juvenile authorities have agreed on procedure; expulsion follows; then comes the tedium of conferences between juvenile authorities and the youth (including his parents); and, finally, the youth is incarcerated in a state-operated school, which is routinely overcrowded and usually inadequately staffed.

Prior to entering the state-run school, the expelled pupil may fall into the hands of the occasional case worker, who is more of a political appointee than a professionally trained person, in which instance threats and ignominy are heaped on his head, making him feel indeed like a criminal. After entering the state-run school, he may be subjected more to punitive action than to a continuance of an interrupted education. States are moving in the direction of professionalism for those who work with the young misfits, but many have a long way to go. Inadequate salaries rarely attract highly competent people, and the facilities are usually too minimal and inappropriate to permit high-type learning experiences for adolescent inmates.

Because expulsion is so often associated with subsequent mishandling and resultant psychological scars, caution before its final employment is urged. If all other attempts at remedial accomplishments have been tried and found wanting, we accord the practice grudging support. Until these other measures have failed, however, individuals in authority should hesitate a long time before taking the final step. Teachers admittedly are not expected to suffer torment from delinquents, but neither should they precipitate action of this seriousness without weighing all the consequences. The student offender conceivably is psychologically ill, and the psychologist and sociologist should pass judgment first before the radical step becomes irreversible.

TOWARD PERMANENT CHANGE

The more this treatment of discipline and its many components has dwelt on the negative aspects of the topic, the more apparent becomes the requirement that the school, in pursuit of change in the student, investigate its total program. The need is for so much positivism in education that the unsavory opposite will be overcome by default. In the last chapter, the importance of prevention was underscored, but more in relationship to infractions of rules and regulation than to the major curriculum and personality factors. In this final section of the present chapter, the discussion will revolve around some of the major changes that the school might initiate to effect long-term permanent alterations in the personalities of young people. Certain significant possibilities in this regard are: (1) the injection into the program of a curriculum element dealing specifically with human behavior, (2) a better utilization of the existing curriculum, and (3) employment of more teachers who are interested in personality as well as mental dynamics.

A curriculum component relating directly to human behavior

Almost from the inception of understandings about mental health, conjectures have been made about the feasibility of a curriculum approach to the topic. Simply put, can education make a direct contribution to sound human adjustment by teaching about it at the cognitive level? The fundamental issue, in reality, is, will intellectual understandings about behavior ultimately lead to emotional transformation? First to defend the affirmative is the entire enterprise of education, dedicated to the postulate that, if people can respond to the cognitive, they will make many necessary transfers to the broader and more complex areas of life. A qualitative extension of this general point of view has been made at the college level, and in a few high schools likewise, in the form of courses in psychology designed ostensibly to make for change in student behavior, as well as to "teach about" a growing body of curriculum content. However, these courses are too often geared to the history of psychology, the mechanical processes of the human organism, and animal experiments. Thus, their value in making for significant behavioral change is commensurately reduced.

Concerning the practicality of teaching about mental-health concepts to effect personality change, a recent study by the author may cast some needed light on the topic. In 1960, the opinions of psychiatrists and clinical psychologists were solicited on this issue, with 48 of 81 replying in the positive, 23 in the negative, and 10 ambivalent about its possible success.[5] The 60 per cent who were optimistic suggested that the following dynamic concepts could be introduced with profit, some as early as the first grade and all by the tenth grade. The parenthetical figure indicates the number of therapists who proposed the concept, or some phase of it, as eligible for inclusion in a school's curriculum.

1. Defense mechanisms (36).
2. Emotions, desires, attitudes, and drives (30).
3. Symptomatic reactions (27):
   Rivalry.
   Aggressivity.
   Narcissism.
   Acting out, as hostility, etc.
4. Interpersonal relationships (22).
5. Self concept (21).
6. Sex and its normal manifestations (20).
7. Conscious and unconscious mind (14).
8. Id, ego, superego (12).
9. Mental health and mental illness (11).

With the gratifying progress being made by the psychological disciplines in bringing about self-discovery, the secondary schools of the future will be remiss if they ignore the curriculum possibilities of this newly found content. Whether it should be incorporated into courses already in existence, such as social studies and biology, or made to stand as an independent academic subject is immaterial. Regardless of the instrumental

---

[5] Gail M. Inlow, "Can the School Curriculum Make a Frontal Approach to Mental Health?", *Journal of Educational Research*, LVI (April, 1963), pp. 395-402.

means, human personality as a substantive curriculum ingredient should get into the program of education at the proper levels. Its content, rephrased from the previously listed nine divisions, might consist of the following, along with others:

Appropriate behavior for the different ages.
Inappropriate behavior for the different ages.
The specific categories of adjustment: solid contact with reality, engagement in the defense mechanisms, neurotic symptoms and behavior, psychotic symptoms and behavior, and psychopathy.
The mental, emotional, and physical extensions of the various levels of adjustment.
The sex function as one of these extensions.
Family relationships as another function: marriage, love, resentment of parents, sibling rivalry, etc.
Social relationships and altruism.

This proposed addition to the curriculum would thus be anchored in human behavior, dealing forthrightly with the understanding of self and others, to the avowed end of behavioral change. For the earlier seventh grade, it would be more simple and straightforward; for the later secondary years, more sophisticated. And it would be designed to culminate in the vitals of selected understandings, for example: that behavior is caused; that forces shape personality; that people differ, but none are "queer"; that certain are compulsive; that races vary but all have nobility; that individuals can be retarded without being less worthy—these and other necessary understandings would be sought. The final outcome would be a hoped-for change in self and human relationships, which reaches to the highest goal of learning.

Yet the path to this outcome is laden with obstacles. A major one is the scarcity of teachers qualified for such a program. A second is the resistance of traditionally oriented parents and teachers who might sabotage the new curriculum with direct opposition or faint support. A third is the issue of what old content would give way to the new. Despite these and other blocks, however, if the understanding of self and others is vital, and if a planned curriculum can contribute to it directly, the academic world will soon find the way. This curriculum innovation is not only significant for its own sake, but it carries the additional bonus of being fundamental to other learnings. With these attributes, education in search of the disciplined mind cannot persist in turning away from such innovations.

A re-direction of the existing curriculum

Before going too far afield to uncover a new tenant for the high school curriculum, an investigation might first be made of the possibilities for the dynamic approach in the present one. A reasonable conclusion, in this regard, is that many more opportunities exist than the typical teacher realizes or avails himself of. Since the tide of human behavior never flows in a vacuum, it is quite possible that the humanities and social sciences have already provided teachers with more springboards for psychological interpretation than they can conveniently utilize. If this is a justifiable assumption, then the issue is more one of teacher readiness, insight, and desire than search for opportunity. The following are illustrative of dynamic possibilities available for the taking:

Civics: Social attitudes of subcultures with conflict resulting from differences; corruption in politics as a reflection of id and ego drives; the electorate as too self-centered to be interested in social welfare; and election campaign tactics as illustrations of doubtful morality.

United States History: The case of the dispossessed Indian; the Puritans escaping religious discrimination only to discriminate; the dynamics of selected key individualists of history: Benjamin Franklin, Andrew Jackson, Robert E. Lee, Theodore Roosevelt, or Woodrow Wilson; the social and personality implications of loyalty oaths, congressional witch hunts, and extreme nationalism; and reasons for man's inability to prevent war.

Literature: Motives of goodness and badness in a Hester Prynne; psychological derangement in a Lady Macbeth, with evidences of guilt, hallucinations, and other manifestations of possible schizophrenia; psychotic ambivalence in an Edgar Allan Poe; emotional displacement in an Othello; or a wide gamut of personality types in a Geoffrey Chaucer.

The range of possibilities for self- and social analysis in a typical program of studies is tremendous. Nor, contrary to practice, does the content of a curriculum have to exist outside the frame of reference of the youthful individuals who interact with it; in fact, such psychological distance works against meaning. In contrast, theory that plays on the keys of student personalities and activities becomes therapeutic as well as cognitively significant, because the heart of the process is located in the emotions of the students themselves. While not proposing a reinterpretation of the current curriculum as a substitute for direct approaches to human dynamics, we recommend that the two become mutually supportive.

Permanent change through the teacher

Whatever the ultimate design of the secondary school curriculum in terms of the mental-health goal of inner orderliness, the classroom teacher must be the catalyst. He stands with learning stimuli on one side and the student on the other, and only to the extent that he unifies them will he have accomplished his mission. If these stimuli get into the emotional as well as the intellectual bloodstreams of students, permanent personality change will be the resultant. As an identification object, the teacher stands as a unit of critical importance in the growth progression of adolescents.

If his basic needs have been at least moderately satisfied, he can help others satisfy theirs. When he responds objectively to an emotionally loaded situation, he has served as a unit of positive influence. His job is to recognize conflicting forces without entering the conflict, to judge without being judgmental, and to set an example without mounting a pedestal. When these intangibles are characteristic, permanent change in students is not only eminently possible but gratifyingly probable.

SUMMARY

The principles on which the case for punishment should rest were identified and briefly discussed in the first part of the chapter. These were as follows: the offender, not the offense, should be punished; punishment should always be regarded as a means to a greater end; punishment must be administered objectively to accomplish its desired purposes; the pupil should know the reason for the applied corrective action; punishment is defensible if firm but not if harsh; closed cases should remain closed; referral should not be avoided; and such emotional incongruities as anger, threats, and warnings should be banished to the background.

The methods of correction most practical for the teacher to employ were then discussed, appearing in approximately an ascending order of seriousness: the verbal appeal, standing close to an offender, changing the seat of the offender, using after-school time for conferences, depriving students of extra-class privileges, removing bad actors from the classroom, the student court, corporal punishment, probation, suspension, and expulsion.

Finally, as a preventive measure, three approaches to permanent change were considered: a new curriculum element to deal with personality dynamics, the better relating of the present curriculum content to the individual, and the schools' greater reliance on teachers who not only can teach cognitive learnings but who can engender personality growth as well.

REFERENCES

Aichhorn, August, *Wayward Youth*. New York: Viking Press, Inc., 1935.

American Orthopsychiatric Association, *American Journal of Orthopsychiatry*. 1790 Broadway, New York. (Any issue)

Baruch, Dorothy, *New Ways in Discipline*. New York: McGraw-Hill Book Co., 1949.

Burton, William H., *The Guidance of Learning Activities*. New York: Appleton-Century-Crofts, Inc. (2nd ed.), 1952. (Chapter 22)

Cutts, Norma, and Nicholas Moseley, *Teaching the Disorderly Pupil in Elementary and Secondary School*. New York: Longmans, Green and Co., 1957.

Eissler, E. R., *Searchlights on Delinquency*. New York: International Universities Press, 1949.

Hymes, James L., Jr., *Behavior and Misbehavior, A Teacher's Guide to Action*. Englewood Cliffs, N.J.: Prentice-Hall, Inc., 1955.

————, *Discipline*. New York: Columbia University, Teachers College, Bureau of Publications, 1949.

Jersild, Arthur T., *In Search of Self*. New York: Columbia University, Teachers College, Bureau of Publications, 1952.

Kettelkamp, Gilbert C., *Teaching Adolescents*. Boston: D. C. Heath and Co., 1954. (Chapter 8)

National Education Association, *Teacher Opinion on Pupil Behavior*. Washington, D.C.: *Research Bulletin,* Vol. XXXIV, No. 2, April, 1956.

Ritholz, Sophie, *Misbehavior? How Do You Evaluate It?* New York: Bookman Associates, Inc., 1960.

Sheviakov, George V., and Fritz Ridl, "Discipline for Today's Children and Youth," *Association for Supervision and Curriculum Development*. Washington, D.C.: N.E.A., 1944.

Wickman, E. K., *Children's Behavior and Teachers' Attitudes*. New York: The Commonwealth Fund, 1928.

A CHAPTER
OF CASES

Up to this point, our analysis of teaching method has been based on theory, supported by anecdotes and other illustrations. For theory respecting teaching method to be meaningful and lucid, students should have early and extensive contacts with youth, and should engage in curriculum experiences which approximate those of a high school. Short of this extension into reality, the next best substitute is for students to analyze selected case problems taken from "real life."

This chapter thus is designed to provide the extra dimension of case studies, each of which has situational parallels in a school setting. Some of the studies are taken almost verbatim from primary sources; a few have undergone minor change in deference to the personal character of the material. Several are mildly prosaic. One or two are definitely unusual but not melodramatic, unless the unexpected in life is also so regarded. Whatever the individual reader's orientation, the studies should serve as practical extensions of the theoretical concepts already presented. In responding to the substance of the various cases, the reader should employ an emerging philosophy that will give all his responses a reasonable and consistent point of view.

The Bright, Underachiever

Name: Penny Porter   Class Structure: Heterogeneous
Age: 15   I.Q.: 125 (Otis)
Grade Level: 10th   Reading Rate: 425 w.p.m.
Subject: English   Class Grade: C−

1. *Past academic performance:* Penny had a composite average of C during the past three years; a combined average of C in English; a highest average of B− in Spanish; and a lowest average of D in mathematics.

2. *Home conditions:* The father is a department manager at a local clothing store and the mother is a homemaker. There are no brothers or sisters. The parents are only mildly interested in Penny's school work, but think that she probably should go to college for a year or two. The family is of secure middle-class status.

3. *Personal-social factors:* Penny seems to be a happy person, rarely moody, who takes life pretty much as it comes. When chided about her below-average academic achievement, she usually responds with a plausible-sounding reason for it, without appearing really convincing.

Socially, she is a "belonger" in the co-curriculum, being a member of a dramatic group, an officer of the Spanish Club, and a homeroom representative to the Student Council. Her informal peer relationships are warm and outgoing.

4. *Future plans:* Penny tentatively plans on going away to college, "provided I don't get married first."

5. *Discussion:* The crux of the case of Penny Porter is that she is a bright young lady who has never worked up to capacity. The I.Q. of 125 projects her well into the upper quartile of the sophomore class, in contrast to her performance, which is average at best. She moves through the curriculum, never doing rock-bottom work but also never catching on fire. Both she and her parents, although not completely satisfied with her response to the curriculum, are not acutely unhappy about it. Here is a distinct case of underachievement with lack of motivation apparently being the reason.

6. *Questions for the reader:*

A. Since Penny is earning a passing mark and, within reason, seems to be conforming to self and family expectancies, should the school interfere with the *status quo?* What philosophical tenets underwrite your point of view?

B. If the school feels obligated to help Penny do better work, what methods should it employ, and how far should it go in accomplishing this purpose? Do you think that:

(1) Teachers should encourage her verbally?
(2) They should require her to re-do work that falls below her ability level?

(3) If necessary, they should keep her after school to accomplish this end?

(4) They should fail her when she works considerably below capacity, even though she does average work on a comparative basis?

(5) The school should refer her to a consulting psychologist?

C. Can Penny get into a few or many colleges and universities with her record?

D. Should her parents be counseled with by school personnel? If so, when and by whom?

E. Should she be forced to drop out of her activities in the co-curriculum?

CASE NO. 2

The Slow Learner—Low Achiever

Name: Amy Steuber	Class Structure: Homogeneous
Age: 18	I.Q.: 74 (California)
Grade Level: 11th	Reading Rate: 90 w.p.m.
Subject: U.S. History	Class Grade: F

1. *Past academic performance:* Amy had an over-all average of D throughout grades 7 through 10, with about 20 per cent F's, 75 per cent D's, and 5 per cent C's; a combined average of D in the social studies; a poorest average in the sciences; and a best average in home economics. In the elementary school, she was "held back" to repeat the second grade; in her two-plus years in high school, she has received four F's, but two sessions of summer school enrollment have compensated for all of them.

2. *Home conditions:* Amy's father is a factory worker, her mother is a part-time employee in domestic service, and her two younger sisters are in the elementary school. The parents are of European ancestry one generation removed. The elder Steubers want Amy to graduate from high school—as a symbol of Americanism and social advancement. The family lives on a slightly below-average income.

3. *Personal-social factors:* Amy appears to be placid, but when ruffled becomes stubborn and, at times, rigid. She has a good friend, Elsie, with whom she associates almost constantly to the exclusion of other possible friends. As the oldest person in her class, Amy is referred to by her classmates as "Mom," which she responds to without rancor—at least, on the surface. Once, however, when between classes a student associate confronted her directly with the issue of her age, Amy lost her temper and made a threatening physical gesture toward the female tormentor. She is meticulously clean, dresses plainly, and is fairly reliable in following through on commitments within her ability range.

4. *The academic situation:* The high school employs homogeneous groupings as a curriculum practice and has placed Amy in the lowest of five

groups in her academic subjects of English and history. In most competitive academic situations, she is at or close to the bottom of the class, on a relative basis. Yet she seems to be working at or near capacity, as best the school can determine. In addition to English and history, she is enrolled in ungrouped classes in textiles and typing. She has enrolled in, or plans on enrolling in, only the required academic classes: four years of English, two of social studies, and one each of science and mathematics.

5. *Future plans:* Amy wishes to be graduated the subsequent year, at the age of 19, but knows that, if this goal is to be reached, she may have to attend summer school once more, or twice more, if she fails more than two additional subjects. After graduation, she hopes to marry a current associate, a widower of 28, whom she has been dating now for almost a year.

6. *Discussion:* The key issue here is the high school's attitude toward standards of graduation. Are they (should they be) fixed or relative? With no ungraded rooms, Amy has been placed in the lowest academic class levels possible and still ranks last or close to last, in the class. Yet she seems to be doing her best.

7. *Questions for the reader:*

A. Should the high school have both quantitative and qualitative standards that all should be required to meet before being considered eligible for graduation?

B. Should a different type of diploma be conferred on Amy from that on one who enrolls in almost all academic subjects?

C. Is Amy better off in a slow-learning homogeneous group than she would be in a heterogeneous group? Give your reasons.

D. If Amy is doing her best, should each of her current and subsequent teachers give her at least a passing grade of D? Why, or why not?

E. Would it be unrealistic for one or more of the teachers to give her a grade of C or B so that she might feel an occasional glow of success as a result of symbolic recognition?

F. Since Amy can drop out of school legally at any time, should she avail herself of this opportunity, or stay in school until being graduated? What are the possible gains and losses?

G. Is it better for her to elect more than half her courses in the practical and fine arts than to be in such courses as science, social studies, and foreign languages geared to her level—assuming that these are available?

CASE NO. 3

The Overachiever

Name: Lloyd Scott   Class Structure: Heterogeneous
Age: 14   I.Q.: 101-Jr. Scholastic Apt.
Grade Level: 8th   Reading Rate: 275 w.p.m.
Subject: Unified Studies   Class Grade: A

1. *Past academic performance:* Throughout the elementary grades, Lloyd has done unusually well in all phases of the curriculum, ranking at or near the top of his class most of the time. His highest-level performance occurs when he can mull over a problem for a protracted period before submitting an answer. His least satisfactory work occurs when he is confronted with a question or problem that needs quick, on-the-spot solution.

2. *Home conditions:* Mr. Scott is a city employee, performing bookkeeping functions in the courthouse as a local civil-service appointee. His childhood was spent on a farm and, because of farm duties, his education terminated with the second year of high school—except for night courses, taken as an adult in a business college. His income is very modest but adequate. Mrs. Scott was orphaned at three and knew real hardship in growing up, living with various relatives from period to period in her childhood and youth. She is a driving person who wants her family to get ahead, by sheer perseverance and long hours, if in no other way. Since Mr. Scott seems to be dead-ended vocationally because of limited educational background, both he and Mrs. Scott look to their younger son, Bob, a fifth-grader, and Lloyd to realize the success that neither parent had or probably will have. Thus, consciously or unconsciously, the goal of "never give up, always do better, don't let anyone get ahead of you" is always lurking in the background or manifestly present in the foreground.

3. *Personal-social factors:* The Scott's social life is limited to a few relatives, one or two close family groups of friends, and church associates in the local Protestant church. The boys are active physically but have little time for the lighter pleasures, with their school, family, and church activities dominating. On the Bell Adjustment Inventory, the results on Lloyd were as follows: Home Adjustment, below average; Health Adjustment, above average; Social Adjustment, retiring; Emotional Adjustment, below average; Total Adjustment, unsatisfactory. In class, Lloyd is a cooperative boy who wishes to be friendly but doesn't seem to know how. His social overtures are halting and awkward; yet he doesn't antagonize. He is neither accepted nor ostracized.

4. *Future plans:* Lloyd's future plans have long since been decided, at least in a broadly general way: "He is to be a professional man—probably a doctor," Mrs. Scott has indicated many times. The entire family have accepted this goal as inviolate.

5. *Questions for the reader:*

A. Do you regard the case material as primarily academic, or might you face similar situations a number of times when you become a teacher?

B. Lloyd gets "A" grades by overachieving. Is he paying too great a price for them? If so, how would you change the picture if you could redesign it?

C. Will it be possible for Lloyd to do well enough in high school and college for him to be accepted in a medical school? What will the requirements likely be, in general terms?

D. Does the school have a responsibility to present to the Scotts a contrary point of view about Lloyd, if the view significantly differs?

E. Since Lloyd is obviously retarded socially and emotionally, would you as a teacher have a responsibility to do something about these personality deficiencies? Does your current philosophy of education embrace these added responsibilities? What specific steps might you take?

F. Assuming that the Scotts come for a conference and refuse to respond to the school's suggestion for a better balance of activities for Lloyd, should, or can, you as a teacher go contrary to the parents' desires both in terms of the program you design for him and the counseling aid you give him?

CASE NO. 4

The Bright But Emotionally Blocked

Name: Ken McLean
Age: 17
Grade Level: 11th
Subject: Chemistry

Class Structure: Selectively homo-
geneous
I.Q.: 138
Reading Rate: 490 w.p.m.
Class Grade: F

1. *Past academic performance:* Throughout the seventh and eighth grades, Ken was a B or B+ student working somewhat under capacity yet doing acceptably. His mind was quick, revealing its true acuteness best in response to the unexpected. In the ninth grade, his work declined to a "C" level; then in the tenth grade, to a D— level.

2. *Home conditions:* Mrs. McLean was widowed when Ken was three. At first, she responded violently to her husband's death; then reacted dully and apathetically for a year or so, being mildly detached from reality, although not psychotic. She and Ken moved in with her husband's family, inasmuch as she had no parents to turn to.

After recovering sufficiently from the death trauma, Mrs. McLean went to work in a nearby suburban paint store: she kept the books, made out invoices and tax forms, and occasionally waited on customers. This job she kept until the time of this anecdote. Leaving at 8:15 in the morning and arriving home at 5:15 in the evening had the effect of giving Ken three parents, all of whom had somewhat conflicting ideas about child-rearing. Mr. McLean, the boy's paternal grandfather, was a rigid task-master of the old school, believing in the "one order" and "the one immediate response to it—or else." Mrs. McLean, the grandmother, was a shy, motherly person who rarely took a stand on anything, but showered food, love, and attention on all around her. They could do no wrong, thus deserved the best. The younger Mrs. McLean realized the danger of conflicting standards when she moved in with her "in-laws," but thought that she could reconcile them. Her approach turned out to be a counter one to Mr. McLean's: she was soft when he was hard so as to offset his "unreasonableness." Ken consequently lived in a scene of clashing standards; the worst feature was that he could always turn to his grandmother or mother when his grandfather demanded a conformance to limits.

3. *Personal-social-citizenship factors:* Ken was fairly normal, until puberty, despite the home conditions. The "little boy" role seemed the best one to play with the adults around him, antagonizing the fewest and accomplishing the most. When adolescence arrived, however, the role of compliance lost much of its appeal, giving way to a muscle-flexing aggressiveness with his grandfather which led to scene after scene in the home, both between the two males and between the mother and father-in-law.

Escaping conflict as much as possible in the home, Ken entered into a series of attachments with fellow adolescents, some of whom were also feeling the gnawing of growing pains. The final outcome was a young teen-age gang of middle-class or fringe middle-class youngsters who turned against society's standards. They operated secretively for a two-year period, engaging in petty thievery, drinking heavily on occasions, "hot-rodding" and "tag racing," and finally shooting 22-calibre shots into a vacant store late at night. This last act brought the local police into the picture.

The ten or twelve boys were shortly thereafter apprehended, with about half of the more mature and aggressive receiving jail sentences, the other half either receiving suspended sentences and being placed on probation, or receiving suspended sentences including the demand that they undergo psychiatric analysis. Ken was in the last of the three categories.

4. *The school response:* During Ken's freshman and sophomore year, even though a gifted boy intellectually, he received, at first, average and then failing or boderline grades. The counseling department had Mrs. McLean in for two conferences during this time, with no tangible recommendations forthcoming. After the boys had gotten into legal trouble and had undergone the court trials, those who received suspended jail sentences, in effect, were expelled from the school—not directly, but through the medium of threatened retaliation if the boys were not withdrawn "voluntarily." All but one, being 16 or over, dropped out of school. Ken, the one, was finally admitted to a private school.

5. *Questions for the reader:*

A. Was the school remiss in not probing more aggressively into the reasons for Ken's sub-mediocre performance in the light of his considerable aptitude? Or is it the school's role mostly to make learning accessible without concerning itself with the dynamics of the students' responses to it?

B. If the school should have helped Ken more than it did, how far should it have gone? Should it have: Had more conferences with Mrs. McLean? Kept Ken after school until he measured up? Provided him with psychological services as a preventive measure? Or what?

C. Was the disparity between Ken's ability and achievement of sufficient import to warrant by the high school a suspicion of serious dis-

turbance? Or do young people, on occasions, just stop studying for protracted periods without thereby reflecting emotional abnormality?

D. Conceivably, might a male teacher have become a strong enough
father-identification figure to have prevented Ken's social and emotional
downfall?

E. Should the school have encouraged the boys on probation to return to their interrupted academic programs?

F. Finally, and fundamentally, what really was the major problem:
Ken's grades or the reasons for them? If your philosophy would involve
you with these reasons, how far do you envision your guidance role to
extend?

CASE NO. 5

The Brilliant But Driving

Name: Beatrice Karl	Class Structure: Immaterial
Age: 17	I.Q.: 141 (P.M.A.)
Grade Level: 12th	Reading Rate: 420 w.p.m.
Subject: Any one	Over-all Grade: A

1. *Past academic performance:* Beatrice consistently has been one of the
top performers in school from the time of her first enrollment in kindergarten. On occasions, she has earned a grade of B, but the A has been
more typical. Her strengths in the curriculum are spread uniformly across
the many offerings.

2. *Home conditions:* Mr. Karl, as vice president in charge of sales of a
large industrial concern, is regarded as a successful businessman by those
who know him. He has come a long way from the poverty of his childhood and is openly resolved to work his way to the top, "even if I have to
sweep a few people aside who are in my way." Mrs. Karl enters into her
husband's scheme of things well, wanting nothing but the best for the
family, including Beatrice's older sister, who is now married to a young
"up-and-coming" lawyer. Mrs. Karl entertains her husband's affluent customers graciously, patronizes his subordinates, helps Beatrice select socially influential friends, and always plans in a somewhat calculating manner
the lives of the entire family in terms of external prestige symbols.

Within this familial framework, Beatrice feels the pressure of never
letting herself or her parents down, because the good name of Karl "stands
for something really significant." Thus, when she takes vocal lessons, she
must do her best; when she is hostess to her parents' guests, she must never
let the Karls down. In school, she must be valedictorian, if she can, because her mother and father would want it that way.

3. *Personal-social factors:* Being in an upper middle-class social-status
group, Beatrice, although pleasant most of the time, acts aloof to her less
fortunate associates. Within the framework of "the haves," she is accepted,
but not popular. Her driving, compulsive desire to get ahead by doing the

right things with and for the right people ostracizes some of her age group. She also conveys the impression that being first is more necessary to her than being friendly.

4. *School factors:* Beatrice is one of three students vying for the valedictory award. While regarding teachers as status personnel in terms of her ego needs, she none the less regards them as social inferiors; yet she conceals this attitude as best she can lest it sidetrack the valedictory. She is considered by teachers to be a bright, methodical, conscientious young lady who can always be counted on to do her best "or better." A few of the more knowledgeable see through some of her façade, recognizing the drive of insecurity, projected into prestige symbols, as the chief motivator in her pursuance of school success, but none of these feels that he could do other than harm in an attempt to help. Their composite regret is that learning for its own sake has made little dent in Beatrice's protective armor; in fact, she adopts from the school program principally what she and her family approve. Ideas and attitudes as emancipators from biases and falseness have no place in her plan of life because she unconsciously fears their distracting influences.

5. *Questions for the reader:*

A. Does the school have an obligation to face the issue of values, frontally, if necessary, with Beatrice and maybe her parents?

B. What might you do as a teacher in a given classroom to break through the attitudinal blockage?

C. If academic honors are to be conferred, should the achievement factor be primary? If Beatrice finished with a 95.63 rating and Joan, an outgoing altruistic girl, with a 95.59, who should get the top award?

D. If grades had been completely removed from the school's thinking, might Beatrice have had a better chance of finding a more defensible value system?

CASE NO. 6

No Outward Problem

Name: Pat Johnson	Class Structure: Heterogeneous
Age: 13	I.Q.: 115 (California)
Grade Level: 8th	Reading Rate: 310 w.p.m.
Subject: English	Class Grade: B

1. *Past academic performance:* Pat has maintained a better-than-average academic record since her first enrollment in school.

2. *Home conditions:* Her father is an electronics engineer, regarded by associates as a brilliant man of near-genius proportions. Mr. Johnson lives in an almost exclusive intellectual world, with his profession comprising his first interest, his secondary concern being his friendships with a small group of professional individuals who get together informally weekends for mutual cognitive stimulation and "relaxation." A number of these male

intellectuals, without consciously recognizing the fact, have become detached from the less gifted of their associates, including members of their own respective families. Mr. Johnson is in this category, going through the motions of being a father and husband without actually living the roles. Thus, although he is pleasant to Mrs. Johnson, Pat, and her younger brother, Les, his attentions are more perfunctory than warmly sincere.

Mrs. Johnson, after Pat's birth, lived for almost a year in a state of withdrawal from her husband and the new baby. At first, the emotional reaction was regarded by her physician as not unusual; but when the period of coldness extended itself, schizoid complications of some kind were suspected. During this first year of Pat's life, she was under the constant attention of a nurse who moved in with the Johnsons as a full-time professional attendant. By Pat's first birthday, however, Mrs. Johnson seemed to be improving sufficiently so that, with the encouragement of the physician, she was willing to take over all the duties of the household with only part-time help provided when needed. After a traumatic start involving one minor emergency after another, she moved toward an ultimately achieved status of mechanical competency in the home. Complete recovery was not to be, however; for, after the birth of a second child two years later, she and Mr. Johnson became increasingly disinterested and detached. And her relationship with Pat and the new infant, although affectively adequate for emotional survival, was less than was needed for sound mental health.

3. *Personal-social:* In this home environment of emotional deprivation, Pat and her younger brother were reared. Their earlier years they spent making overtures for affection, only to be unconsciously rebuffed or turned aside. Once the realization dawned that denial was to be their lot, they began to withdraw from personal contacts, living more and more in a world of autism or fantasy. This latter, however, remained within bounds of reality, never approximating the psychotic. Neither of the siblings had any close friends among children their age or among adults. Each sought the company of younger children because these never appeared threatening.

4. *The school situation:* Pat earned good grades in Mrs. Brown's English class, almost always doing the assigned work and performing generally in a highly commendable manner. The class was a bit on the active, exuberant side, and Mrs. Brown was quietly thankful to have Pat and a few other docile eighth-graders around to act as a counter influence. She was free with such remarks as: "Pat, I wish I had thirty others like you." Yet despite her appreciation of Pat's "soothing influence," as she called it, she unconsciously realized her inability to get close to Pat. Their relationship was more one of externals than of real closeness. But this never disturbed Mrs. Brown unduly in view of the outward appearance of well being.

5. *Questions for the reader:*

A. In terms of what you know about the behavior of adolescents, how would you compare Pat's reactions to people and events against normative expectancy? Specifically, do you regard docility for itself as a goal to be regarded highly? Why or why not?

B. Should a teacher automatically suspect maladjustment when young people are quiet and reserved? What characterizes the difference between a healthy but recessive type of personality and one typical of the chronically withdrawn type of person?

C. Assuming that Mrs. Brown suspected some of Pat's behavior to be emotionally unhealthy, what, if anything, might she have done to alleviate the condition?

D. Should a depth therapist of some kind have been called in for consultation or direct treatment? If so, would such a specialist be readily available to most school personnel? And readily accepted by most families?

CASE NO. 7

A Subcultural Standard Clashes with the School's Standard

Name: Don Haines   Class Structure: Immaterial
Age: 16   I.Q.: 104
Grade Level: 10th   Class Grade: C
Subject: Immaterial

Don Haines is a member of a subcultural group living in a fringe area on the outskirts of the school district. His father is a job drifter, deliberately managing to be employed not over half the time. As a heavy drinker, he is belligerent when intoxicated. Mrs. Haines, while outwardly defensive of her husband, unconsciously lets Don know in subtle ways that he is to aspire to a higher status in life than that achieved by his father. However, despite her aspirations for Don, she is not above joining Mr. Haines on occasion in "making a night of it." Such sprees on her part are usually followed by a period of remorse characterized by acetic-like avoidance of even ordinary pleasures.

In this ambivalent home atmosphere, Don learns to regard drinking as an escape from worry and responsibility, but also as a creator of trouble with the law when carried to excess. Work, to him, is something to be evaded when temptation allures, but yet a necessity "if one," to use his mother's words, "is to get ahead." And morality is more the evasion of behavioral consequences than a conscious adherence to a value system.

Don's approach to the school's demands is unpredictable, varying from a middle-class level of conformity at one time to an almost callous disregard of standards the next. He seems to be testing authority much of the time, seeing how far he can go in circumventing conventions of dress, attendance regulations, and class time schedules. Yet he is never insolent to teachers or a real trouble-maker. He seems more to follow his father's pattern of unreliability and inconsistency.

One morning, however, Don appears in school an hour late and obviously intoxicated. He makes it a distinct point to let his student associates and homeroom teacher know that he is "tight." The teacher, thus, has no choice but to turn Don over to the principal. Later, when Don has sobered sufficiently to react clearly to the incident, he states quite frankly that he got drunk because he wasn't doing too well in school and dreaded facing the consequences. His exact statement was: "Like my old man, I just got lost in drink, I guess, when I couldn't face the fiddler." When admonished about the evils of liquor, he shows some irritation, informing the principal that his father and mother aren't "awful people just because they take a drop now and then." His chief regret seems to be that he was detected in a "stupid" act, not that he was intoxicated.

Questions for the reader:

A. Since Don is accustomed to a value system obviously different from the school's, should he be judged completely according to the school's system? Why, or why not?

B. Would Don's episode be adjudged in the same light if it involved: the offspring of a physician, a local minister, or a bar attendant?

C. Should the school have a fixed penalty for drinking that applies to all in the same way? Why, or why not?

D. If the penalty is dependent on the background of the people involved, would this differential approach be unfair to those judged more severely?

E. If the school "absolutely knew" that Don would never err this seriously again, would it be justified in readmitting him following a designated punishment, then graduating him at the proper time?

F. Do you regard the drinking episode as more or less serious than a student's (1) being deliberately insolent to a teacher, (2) writing an excuse for an illicit absence and signing his mother's name, (3) intercepting a grade report from the mail box before his parents get it, or (4) chronically lying regarding homework done?

G. If Don were expelled, how should the school justify the act: as therapy for the boy, as a deterrent to others, or as retaliation? Do you regard the reason(s) as defensible?

CASE NO. 8

Competition from the Co-Curriculum

Name: Dave Boyer	Class Structure: Immaterial
Age: 17	I.Q.: 122 (P.M.A.)
Grade Level: 11th	Reading Rate: 325 w.p.m.
Subject: Immaterial	School Grades: C average

1. *Past academic performance:* Although at the 75th percentile in ability, Dave had a "straight" C average in his freshman year, one D and three C's in his second year, and 2 D's and 2 C's at the end of the first six-weeks marking period in the junior year. He realizes that his grades aren't

what they should be, but confesses with some perplexity and irritation: "I'm just too busy to do everything I want to do."

2. *Home conditions:* Mr. Boyer is a lawyer of considerable stature in the Cleveland Heights suburb, active in community affairs and well liked. Mrs. Boyer is both a complement to her husband's career role and a vital person in her own right, leading a number of local movements for civic uplift. Dave has an older sister attending a college in Iowa. The Boyers seem to be able to do financially most of the things that many upper-middle-class families like to do—live in a comfortable home, drive two cars, take summer trips, and go to Florida over the Christmas holidays.

3. *Personal-social-co-curricular:* Dave is one of the most active, well-liked boys in Cleveland High School. In athletics, he made the varsity football team in his freshman year and was one of the outstanding ends as a sophomore; in addition, he is on the swimming team. Always interested in drama, he "tried out" for the one big dramatic extravaganza in the winter of his sophomore year and was awarded a lead part. Furthermore, he is his homeroom's representative on the student council, an officer of the career law club, and student liaison between the athletic department and the Dads' Club. He dates several of the more eligible girls in the student body.

4. *Future plans:* Both Dave and his parents are planning for a future Boyer and Boyer law firm after Dave graduates from the University of Michigan's Law School.

5. *Discussion:* On the Primary Mental Abilities Test, Intermediate, Dave scores at the 90th percentile in Verbal Meaning, 60th in Space, 92nd in Reasoning, 72nd in Number, 94th in Word Fluency, and 90th in Age. On the Kuder Vocational Preference Inventory he scores at the 99th percentile on Persuasive, 97th on Literary, 96th on Outdoor, 80th on Social Service, and in rapidly descending order on Computational, Science, Mechanical, Clerical, Art, and Music, down to a low of 10 on the last.

All clinical information possessed by the school prognosticates success for Dave in the career of law—with the one exception of his high school grades. The issue is unmistakably this: can Dave get into the university of his choice with a C− average in high school—an average that seems to be inching downward each semester?

6. *Questions for the reader:*

A. Should Dave be required to drop a number of his co-curricular activities until he shows signs of working up to capacity? Or should he be faced squarely with the facts and possible consequences of his behavior, to the end of making him decide personally on first priorities?

B. If participation in the co-curriculum is to be dependent on academic performance, should eligibility be on the basis of an absolute grade average or on the extent of relationship between ability and achievement? In the latter event, Dave with a C average might be ineligible whereas John with an I.Q. of 78 and one F might be eligible. Do you regard this as equitable?

C. Should every school have a point system which controls the number of co-curricular activities in which a student can participate? If the answer is an affirmative, should it be applied without qualification for all, or only for those who prove unable to live with extensive freedom? Give your reasons.

D. Assuming no central counseling service, would you as a teacher of a subject in which Dave was getting a D feel it your responsibility to talk to the senior Boyers about Dave's problem? Think through the dynamics of such a conference, and then try some role-playing with a fellow student: you as the teacher, he as one of the parents.

CASE NO. 9

He Plans To Be a Physician

Name: Bill Winters   Class Structure. Heterogeneous
Age: 17   grouping
Grade Level: 11th   I.Q.: 116 (Otis)
Subject: Chemistry   Reading Rate: 240 w.p.m.
                                     Class Grade: D

1. *Past academic performance:* Bill has an over-all average of B in his two and a half years of high school work, with his best grades coming in biology and mathematics and his lowest in the course under discussion, chemistry. Chemistry is the only course in which he has fallen below C.
2. *Home conditions:* Mr. Winters is a researcher in a local pharmaceutical laboratory, with a specialized background in biology and chemistry. His salary is somewhat above the national average, but modest in relation to the incomes of his suburban neighbors. Mrs. Winters is a pleasant, well-adjusted person who contributes her share of stability to the household. Bill has a younger brother 15 and a sister 13.
3. *Personal-social factors:* Bill is a conscientious, well-liked young man who fits comfortably into high school life. Although not a belonger, he participates in one varsity sport, wrestling, and belongs to the biology club. He is accepted by the vast majority of his associates as a "nice, regular guy." His primary personality deficiency is "to fold" a bit when under pressure. He seems to succeed best when surrounded with serenity and when removed from "people who push me too hard."
4. *Future plans:* Spurred by his father's interest in science, and lured by the enticements of cultural status, Dave early developed an interest in medicine. This goal jelled when he was in the eighth grade, and since then it has been unconsciously accepted as final by Bill and his family. Clinical data, although not convincing in all instances, mostly support his goal aspirations. The I.Q. of 116 is a little lower than desirable for a future medic, but it still is respectable. His two A's in biology were good prog-

nosticators. Also, his high scores on the Kuder in Science, Social Service, and Mechanical interests are certainly positively oriented toward his goal of physician-surgeon.

5. *Discussion:* Bill's crucial problem is his ineffectual performance in Miss Kaufman's chemistry class, where he is barely doing passing work. By the teacher's own testimony, he seems to study enough, does his homework satisfactorily, and meets all demands but the most significant one: he doesn't do well on the examinations. He explains, or maybe rationalizes, the situation by stating that: "Miss Kaufman is probably all right, but when we take tests, you could cut the atmosphere with a knife." However, he admits that in chemistry he got somewhat lost halfway through the semester and never seemed to regain his academic posture. He scored fifth from the bottom in the class of 30 students and, according to Miss Kaufman's standards, was "very low on an absolute basis."

6. *Questions for the reader:*

A. Since Bill's goal is definitely medicine, if you were in the position of Miss Kaufman or a guidance counselor, would you advise him to accept his D in the course and drop chemistry at the end of the year, or to repeat the first semester's work during the summer term or the following fall?

B. If the latter, would the major intent be to have him learn to respond to pressure by living under it again, or to gain more knowledge of the content of chemistry? Assuming that Bill is very apprehensive about his modified failure in chemistry, what would be the fallacies of recommending a repeat performance? If he decided to repeat anyway, what counseling insights might you try to help him acquire?

C. Would a D in high school chemistry be a "kiss of death" when he applied for medical school acceptance at the end of his junior year at the university? In general, what are the requirements likely to be?

D. Might you suspect Miss Kaufman as the villainess of the play? If so, what other factors would have to be considered regarding Bill's apparent difficulty in responding to pressure?

E. Should Bill be at least mildly encouraged to change his vocational goal? Give your reasons.

CASE NO. 10

Recovering from a Physical Handicap

Name: Art Gorman   Class Structure: Immaterial
Age: 15   I.Q.: 106
Grade: 9th   Class Grade: F (or higher?)
Subject: Immaterial

The hub of this case is a long history of physical disability and corrective therapy. When Art was an infant, his right leg broke below the hip, revealing a bone deficiency. This triggered off a long series of skeletal disorders demanding medical care—sometimes orthopedic surgery and almost regularly a brace on the leg, back, or both. As recently as Art's twelfth year, he underwent surgery on the spine which hospitalized him for three months and kept him out of school the entire school year.

Art is the third of three children, with Bob an older brother of 20, in college, and Kathy, 18, a senior in high school. As the youngest in the family, Art has been the focal center of the entire household, ruling most of the family rather firmly as a diminutive tyrant, dominating more by petulance and helplessness than by orders, realizing full well the greater effectiveness of the first method. Secure in his invalidism and, later, in its residual effects, he is only unconsciously cognizant that acts have consequences; thus, he speaks his mind frankly about his sister's appearance, his mother's over-protective ways, and his friends' inattention. Following the hospital siege and subsequent convalescence during his twelfth year, he embarked on a period of physical well-being for the first time in his life, featured by gains in muscle tone, ultimately almost complete freedom of movement, and a generally increased physical and social horizon. His renascence, however, brought him more problems than he was able to solve, most of them revolving around the blockages that his ego-involved personality projected into his social environment. He soon learned that careless remarks and indifference to others were more readily excused when softened by appearances of invalidism than when standing out harshly and blatantly without dilution. Consequently, his social life was characterized by changing friendships, with none being anchored other than shallowly in the roots of mutual respect and altruism.

When 15, Art and his problems arrived in the high school. Being the oldest in his class was an added handicap for him when he was with individuals who had not known him before. His teachers always seemed to express surprise that "a fifteen-year-old would act so childishly." To make matters more immediately difficult, Art's family, Mrs. Gorman excepted, were gaining insight into the adverse effects of their too-great solicitousness, leading them to compensating behavior that was hard for Art to take, particularly at first. His freshman year, thus, was an unhappy one, to say the least, for him and for most of those with whom he was associated. His teachers, only vaguely familiar with his background, resented his flippancy and impertinence, and let him know how they reacted. In turn, he became more and more resentful, often refusing to work and withdrawing for protracted periods into a protective shell. The composite picture was one of a miserable young man who seemingly had done nothing well and who was only partially accepted by his fellow human beings. And, ironically, he and his associates were neither clearly at fault nor yet innocent of blame.

At the end of the first semester, each of Art's teachers faced the inevitable debate over the D and the F, with none in his most optimistic moments even considering a higher grade. The more important issue of

Art's total adjustment was rarely more than in the background. The school was small and thus without a specialized counselor who otherwise might have shared with the teachers some of the burden of decision-making.
Issues for the reader:

A. First of all, identify the problem clearly, and then define responsibilities for key individuals in Art's life.

B. In your judgment, what mistakes of omission or commission were made by the family and the school?

C. Do you believe that Art's case in the high school could be handled by the authority figures around him, provided that they, themselves, were mature enough to take action dictated by common sense reason? Or does Art need some type of professional therapy? Give your reasons.

D. Which grade would you recommend: F, or D, or a higher grade? Justify it.

E. The axis of the case may be Art's lack of success. How would you help him achieve it, either as one of his teachers or as one of his parents?

F. Despite his minimal success in academic endeavor, might the co-curriculum provide a few answers? Or should he be denied participation because of his low grades?

A FEW GENERAL COMMENTS

Each of the previously discussed cases projects teaching, and decisions that are a part of it, into a framework of complexity. Also, the instructional figures themselves find themselves in a state of perplexity and, we are certain, humility regarding rightness and wrongness. Each case tantalizes with its narrow shading between action that might be appropriate or inappropriate, depending on a minor change in circumstances. The cases run a rather wide gamut of personality types, home backgrounds, vocational plans, ability levels, cultural differences, motivational factors, and developmental disparities. Only after gaining insights into the many aspects of any one of the ten problems highlighted could school personnel of whatever status take defensible action. With Bill Winters, for instance, who wanted to be a physician but did poorly in chemistry, repeating the course might be clinically indicated to get him more ready for a chosen career. However, with Amy of the second case, a series of additional F's, which would reinforce her inadequacy, might be disastrous to her entire personality structure. By the same logic, "firming up" the behavioral limits for Penny Porter could be defended, whereas like action with Lloyd Scott might be the worst possible step.

Thus teaching, like other human-relations endeavor, must never be allowed to rigidify into a series of repetitive responses or patterns which disregard the fluctuating personality and curriculum dynamics of any given situation. When the teacher is in doubt, action should conform to the standard of what is best for the individual—this as a fundamental consideration that cannot ever be ignored. Although rules are not made to be broken, neither are they customarily so inviolate that application can be mechanical. The best solutions to problems are conceived in a philosophy which endorses the human element as of supreme worth. To this the guidance-minded teacher should moor his decisions.

SUMMARY

This chapter was devoted to a presentation and discussion of ten problems, most of which were relatively commonplace, a few of which were more unusual. The central themes were as follows:

1. The Bright Underachiever
2. The Slow Learner—Low Achiever
3. The Overachiever
4. The Bright But Blocked
5. The Brilliant But Driving
6. No Outward Problem
7. A Subcultural Clash
8. Competition from the Co-Curriculum
9. He Plans To Be a Physician
10. Recovering from a Physical Handicap

The purpose of describing the cases was to highlight the fact that problems are many and varied and that they demand sensitive solution dependent on the circumstances of the moment. Never should action be allowed to become rigid or narrowly prescriptive.

REFERENCES

Loughary, John W., *Counseling in Secondary Schools*. New York: Harper & Row, 1961.

Maslow, A. H., *Motivation and Personality*. New York: Harper & Row, 1954.

Miller, Carroll H., *Foundations of Guidance*. New York: Harper & Row, 1961.

Miller, Frank W., *Guidance Principles and Services*. Columbus, Ohio: Charles E. Merrill Books, Inc., 1961.

Ritholz, Sophie, *Misbehavior? How Do You Evaluate It?* New York: Bookman Associates, Inc., 1960.

Rothney, John, *The High School Student, A Book of Cases*. New York: Holt, Rinehart and Winston, 1953.

White, Mary Alice, and Myron W. Harris, *School Psychology*. New York: Harper & Row, 1961.

STUDENT
TEACHING

Although we have utilized the case study method as a stimulant of thought and as a near-reproduction of reality, it is none the less a step away from the classroom itself. This last step is taken when student teaching begins. Of all the experiences that the teacher candidate has in the period of professional preparation, this one stands out as the most unadulterated approximation of "the real thing." Up to the beginning of student teaching, general education, with its broadening influences, has been operating; the teaching major and minor are usually in an adequate state of completion; and, in many instances, work in community agencies or observations in high school classrooms have provided insights into the behavioral patterns of adolescents. All of the elements are present; they just need to be fitted into place and tried out.

Student teaching brings with it a series of diverse impressions and judgments. After participating, students almost consistently look back to it as the most rewarding single curriculum experience in college. But in its early stages, they report being both enamored with it, yet threatened by it; happy to be weaned from theory, but apprehensive about their ability to apply it; stimulated by high school pupils and teachers, but somewhat appalled by their demands; eager to teach sizable units of learning, but fatigued at their completion; in general, both delighted with, yet more than a little concerned over, the situation.

Customarily, however, as the days pass, the negative feelings give way to the positive, with new experiences bringing new successes and other rewards that make all expenditures of thought, time, and effort seem worthwhile. Because student teaching is of such inestimable value, we urge candidates not to succumb to the lure of easy certification in those states which permit the bypassing of the student teaching requirement. Shunning such an escape, most states, in contrast, have been moving in the direction of more student teaching because of its recognized value. The underlying assumption is that a college student with a background of theory needs the opportunity to observe, work cooperatively with, and receive help from an experienced teacher who has been carefully selected for this special role of supervision. Until this assumption is proved false, students thus should tend to enroll for more, not less, student teaching, when given the option.

PURPOSES OF STUDENT TEACHING

As in the beginning practice of any profession, student teaching postulates the need for a controlled laboratory experience to bridge the gap between the province of the conceptual and the world of application. The slow learner in the classroom is quite different from his abstract counterpart in the educational text. And method which works smoothly when incorporated into a narrated case study may fall short of such effectiveness when the teacher candidate employs it in a tangible situation. Actual classroom experiences introduce shades and subtleties of behavioral phenomena which transport teaching from the mechanical to the professionally unpredictable as well as the predictable. Broadly conceived, student teaching is a testing ground for both the individual and the program of teacher education, the strengths and limitations of which are brought into the open when theory is applied in a classroom learning laboratory.

Student teaching evaluates the entire program of teacher education

When professional candidates engage in the experiences of the classroom, the total program of preparation undergoes scrutiny. Student teaching thus becomes a test of its quality. If the majority of the students evaluated fail to meet desired standards, the mirror reflects the inadequacies directly back to the college or university; and, just as consistently, when most individuals realize success, the same mirroring process operates positively. The occasional student exception is forgiven even many shortcomings, but his numbers cannot greatly multiply without the collegiate institution being assessed adversely. In this practical part of its program, then, the teacher-preparatory institution has a chance to look at itself and adjust to what it sees.

The student's personality is revealed

If student teaching evaluates a total program of teacher education, it just as certainly appraises the student himself, who is forced to play an admittedly varied and, therefore, sometimes difficult role. On many occasions, he is manifestly subordinated to the classroom teacher; on other occasions, he must assert himself as a professional person in his own right. He thus alternately follows and leads, withdraws and projects. And, unlike the teacher himself, who has the status of a recognized authority figure, the student, who is denied such status, may have to draw more heavily on his personality resources to realize comparable success.

Trying though the demands of the new role may be, the student with vision gets a careful look at himself, both short- and long-range, in a context of professional adults and adolescents. From the experience usually emerges a refinement of insight into the following selected traits or sensitivities.

Personal appearance	Tolerance of stress
Poise and confidence	Empathy for pupils
Enthusiasm	Attitude toward criticism
Sense of humor	Absence of dogmatism
Dependability	Respect for the opinions of others
Imagination	Respect for the rights of others
Creativity	Persistence
Adaptability	Ability to evaluate self

The student analyzes his subject matter competency

When the invitation for student teaching is extended, both the college and the secondary school assume that the individual invited to participate has at least a minimum of subject matter competency. The pupils, in particular, expect commendable scholarship from their teachers. Accordingly, it behooves the teacher candidate to take a searching look at the adequacy of his subject matter preparation in the teaching specialties, the broad area of general education, and English usage. Few experiences in life are more shattering to aplomb than that of an authority figure humbled when faced by adolescents with his shortcomings. At these times, even the most phlegmatic of personalities regret that more time and effort had not been devoted to the exposed areas of weakness.

Content deficiencies frequently exist because of the too great emphasis placed by colleges and state departments of public instruction on courses taken and number of credit hours earned. Although quantitative standards are needed to protect the teaching profession from grossly unqualified individuals, such standards are harmful when equated automatically with adequacy of preparation and personal competency. This additive approach to teacher preparation or to any other professional goal is one of the evils of an academic culture which subordinates quality to quantity.

To escape such tyranny, teacher candidates should press toward outcomes that will satisfy a built-in set of defensible standards. These will serve as a guide when the legalistic formula falters. The teacher who becomes an artist and not a mechanic at the job early identifies desired outcomes of teaching and moves professionally toward their accomplishment. Realistically, he meets the goals of the college, state, or other accrediting agency; but transcending this conformity to legality are the higher motivational standards that he has established for himself. From their stimulation he becomes more interested, for instance, in acquiring a comprehensive background in ancient world cultures than in earning 15 semester-hours of course work in ancient history; more concerned about the extent of his knowledge and understanding of a foreign language than in the fact of his having completed a 32-semester-hour major.

Decidedly, student teaching is the testing ground for demonstrating competency in the content fields. If his knowledge and understanding prove inadequate, the student usually can take subsequent steps to compensate for the revealed shortcomings. Ideally, such inadequacies should not exist; but, since they often do, it is better if they are uncovered prior to the time that the student undertakes the responsibilities of his first teaching position.

The student tries out teaching method

Along with the assessment of subject matter scholarship, student teaching also provides the candidate with the opportunity to try out method in the many activities of learning: classroom management, planning, preparation of materials, presentation of information, problem-solving, discussion, evaluation, and others.[1] Normal progression is from the lesson or lesson fragment to the more comprehensive unit, and from close supervision to greater independence and individualism.

In the process of application, theory about method can be validated in the learning laboratory of the classroom. It is important that the reader remember, however, that final judgments about the efficacy of certain methods will have to await a long-term period of testing. The approach

---

[1] We recommend the following as informative on the present topic: The Association for Student Teaching, *Thirty-Eighth Yearbook* (Dubuque: Wm. Brown Co., 1959).

that may fail dismally when the teacher is apprehensive and inexperienced may succeed beyond fond hopes when it is attempted at a later time. And method that works in one situation may not work equally well in another. But regardless of limitations, the internship opportunity gives the student a much-needed chance to try out techniques of his, as well as the teacher's, choosing.

The student studies youth

Sharing the center of attention with subject matter and teaching method are the adolescents themselves, who learn best when understood. Thus, another noteworthy purpose of student teaching is to extend the textbook on child development or adolescent growth into the concrete, especially for the candidate who previously has worked little with youth; or to provide yet another base of insight for the contrasting candidate who has worked with young people in other settings. In the process, both will discover, or rediscover, that the periods of pre- and post-puberty are characterized by certain developmental behavior patterns which need to be understood and adjusted to if learning is to be effective. The candidate ideally should study youth in two ways: informally, by day-to-day observation of routine actions and performance; and formally, by the brief clinical case study or anecdote.

Assistance is provided by supervisors

A final purpose of student teaching, which reaches to the heart of the organizational design itself, is to project the student into a laboratory environment where he will receive needed assistance from supervisory personnel: from the cooperating teacher, on a day-to-day basis; from the college supervisor, at more widely spaced intervals. In such a setting, the candidate is introduced sequentially first to the elementary, then to the more advanced, demands of learning—but consistently only when one or more professional associates are available for consultation. These latter participants provide assistance, as required, at all levels of teaching: planning, implementation, and evaluation. Thus, when apprehension becomes disruptive, assurance can be provided; when subject matter deficiencies are noted, the vacuum can be filled; and when the emergency baffles, help will not be too far away. In this way, the candidate is rewarded with the major benefits of a learning laboratory without bearing the full responsibility for its success or failure.

In the experience of the practicum, the possibility always exists that an individual will change his mind about teaching—whether from inadequacy or from disinterest is immaterial. In either event, the counselors who have been in contact with the situation will be familiar with the dynamics of the case and thus able to render valid professional opinions regarding the advisability of the proposed action. So informed, they can distinguish between temporary discouragement and chronic insecurity, between diffi- culties in handling young people and a lack of interest or understanding, and between content deficiency gaps and an over-all lack of preparation. Thus, a final decision can ultimately be made by colleagues thinking in concert rather than by one discouraged individual deliberating in isolation.

In brief, the period of student teaching is a vital phase of teacher edu- cation in which the student studies himself and is studied by professional associates in an ongoing pupil-centered laboratory. From the experience, insights into personality attributes, into his status of content knowledge, and into pupils undergo refinement. When acceptable standards are met, all partners of the enterprise feel more secure in encouraging the candidate's continuance. When standards are too loosely approximated, final decisions may rest on the hard rock of the practical as well as the theoretical.

SELECTED CONCEPTS

The candidate who knows the intended purposes of student teaching immediately can take a more analytical look at himself as a person and scholar who is soon to be projected into an academic setting of students and professional adults. The attributes of his personality and the quality of his preparation thus revealed will be the basis of his success in the program. However, these broad understandings should be accompanied also by an insight into the constituent features of student teaching itself, that is, into some of the inherent fundamentals of all professional programs, wherever they might be found. Selected ones of these principles will be discussed in the present section.

Student teaching should be a logical extension of youth experiences

Ideally, the major internship experience should be a natural exten- sion of youth participation started several years earlier. In this way, the transition is comfortable and unspectacular, leading from one situation to a similar one, although the latter conceivably will be of a different type and with different people. A number of teacher education institutions have this sequence built into their programs. In the far greater number which do not, we strongly urge students to contact a nearby community agency so that, with a minimum of delay, they can embark on what really will be the beginning of their student teaching. In the process, they will discover more vividly what young people are like and, more important, what they themselves are like in working with young people.

To bring this concept down to a state of functional reality, we direct attention to the experiences that five university students had during the school year 1957–1958 at a home for boys whose own homes were less than desirable. The lives of these male youngsters had been traumatized by one or more influences in the home like the ensuing: poverty, occasional insanity, robbery, divorce, prostitution, rejection, common-law marriage, and penal incarceration. These boys, because of such home conditions, had been sent to the Smith Home (as it shall be referred to here), which had a limited professional staff of four people to supervise 200 boys. That they welcomed the assistance of the college students is an understatement. And that the college students profited is an even greater understatement. The experience had such an impact on the college students that identification with their young associates became almost an obsession. It was not unusual for the students to bring their problems to the author late at night or early in the morning.

When the Home felt the need of a procedural guide for new counselors, the five college students were asked to prepare it. An excerpted version of the guide follows. The wording is that of the students.

OBJECTIVES:

A. To provide the most benefit for the boys emotionally:
   1. Should be able to discuss personal problems with the boys.
   2. Should have more than a parent-teacher relationship (should be a friend, or a guide, but not "parentish" or completely "teacherish").
B. To provide the most benefit for the boys scholastically:
   1. Should provide help in specific problems.
   2. Should provide motivation for higher-quality work.
   3. Should facilitate working singly or in groups with a minimum of outside help.
C. To provide the most benefit for the (college) students:
   1. Must drop the "poor little boy" attitude and adopt "this-is-life" attitude. Be realistic. Empathy, not sympathy, is needed.
   2. Should realize that counselors will face comparable problems in the future either in teaching or club work.
   3. Should get a background for student teaching.
   4. Should learn to transfer some of the problems of the Smith Home to problems in related situations.

SUGGESTED WORK AREAS:

A. Library
B. Lounge
C. Dining room
D. Dorms
E. Study halls

SKELETAL PROGRAM BY AGE LEVELS:

A. Two youngest dorm groups: one person to work with them for a half hour in each dorm: school work when necessary, story-telling or quiet bed-time games if school work is not pressing.
B. Grade-school age group; one-half to one hour per evening. Children could be grouped by grades, for practice in reading and arithmetic or other homework. Individual help is necessary also.

C. Junior-high-school age group: one hour per evening. Children should be taught to work in groups, but homework should be done singly. Specific questions should be answered, directions explained, practice problems and individual help given as needed. "Bull sessions" should come *after* school work.

D. Senior-high-school age group: one hour per evening, or more, as needed or desired. Children should be grouped as to subjects, but homework should be done individually. Specific questions should be answered, directions explained, practice problems and individual help given as needed. Bull sessions should come *after* school work.

TO STUDENT COUNSELORS:

A. All should meet from time to time to discuss the program.

B. The relationship with the boys should be informal, but never too personal.

C. Counselors must not only show an interest; they must *have* an interest.

D. They should have an initial orientation to the Home: what it is, how it works.

E. Much of the work will be in groups, in which all should be treated alike, but some will be individualized also.

F. You will be temporary; so the children must be taught to help themselves.

G. You are to show the children *how* to do it, but not do the work for them.

H. If you feel the tasks are too much for you to handle, you can discuss your problems with any of the leaders of the program, Mr. Smith, or Dr. Inlow. You can do more harm than good if you are unsure of yourself.

I. You should call if unable to get to the Home at the appointed time.

J. Get down to work quickly; after study hall, you can talk informally.

TO SMITH HOME ADMINISTRATORS:

A. An initial orientation session should be held with prospective student counselors to discuss policies and procedures.

B. An occasional in-service orientation session should be held, as required, with all student counselors present.

C. Records should be made available to the leaders so that problems which may develop may be more easily handled.

Each of the five students averaged three hours or more weekly at the Smith Home. They staggered their hours so as to be of greatest help to the boys. All worked in a tutorial capacity, as group leaders of activities, and as individual counselors. They learned a number of important concepts from their experiences, the most important of which they reported as:

(1) Children differ in abilities, interests, and temperaments.

(2) Learning is more a function of the learner than of the teacher.

(3) The way the less privileged live is often not pleasant; but neither can it be ignored by closing one's eyes to it.

(4) The college student who identifies with children actively learns more about them than when just reading about them.

Students enrolled in colleges and universities which are located in urban centers might have an easier time associating themselves with a young people's group than will their counterparts in small towns. Yet even the latter afford many possibilities, some of which may be in the following listing:

Young Men's Christian Associations	Sunday-school classes
Young Women's Christian Associations	Young people's church societies
	Orphans' homes
Jewish-community centers	Future Teachers of America Clubs
Recreational centers	4-H clubs
Boy Scout troops	Summer camps or day camps
Girl Scout troops	Hospital wards

Students who work with young people throughout all or a part of the period of college residence will unquestionably find the experiences rewarding, leading to greater poise and assurance, a discovery of leadership strengths and weaknesses, a keener social sensitivity, and theory made more vivid by actual experiences. The student thus motivated can take early steps to affiliate himself with a youth-oriented organization. We can almost guarantee that the satisfactions will amply repay the student for the time spent.

The student teacher must fit into the school situation

A natural transition for the teacher candidate is from youth in community agencies to youth in school, a change that normally is accompanied by closer supervision. Characteristic of the new environment is the constant association between student teacher and co-worker, the classroom teacher. The tone of the relationship is habitually congenial, with the new arrival being welcomed cordially and encouraged to be creative without being allowed to deviate too far from existing standards and practices. It is to be remembered that public and private schools have as their major reason for being the education of pupils, and, although willing to work with student teachers, they cannot, nor should they, subordinate their primary function. Accordingly, within the framework of this basic pupil dedication, the schools will adjust to the reasonable demands of a student-teaching program, but not at the sacrifice of those whom they are legally and professionally obligated to serve.

Requiring students to integrate with an existing school pattern of policy, organization, and procedures, although ostensibly arbitrary on the surface, is fundamentally logical. First of all, the school invariably will have been selected because of its higher-than-average academic standards. Furthermore, the teachers invited to serve in a supervisory capacity most often will be the more capable instructional leaders in the system. Thus, when inexperienced initiates are asked to conform to this level of *status quo,* the only harm that can result is when rigidity replaces reason—which is scarcely likely to happen in an otherwise well-screened situation. Within this framework of considerable flexibility, creativity and originality will not only be condoned but will be encouraged, provided they stay within justifiable bounds.

In helping the student fit into an ongoing situation, we propose the following imperatives:

1. Be punctual. Arrive at the school not later than the opening of class, and usually a few minutes earlier. If the classroom teacher has special reasons for wishing you to be there sooner, conform to this reasonable demand.

2. Observe accepted standards of attire by following the lead of your more experienced co-workers. If the male faculty members wear suit coats, the student should not appear in shirt sleeves. If the women faculty members wear sweaters, such attire is not inappropriate for the student.

3. Be dependable. When you agree to accept a responsibility—a lesson, a unit, papers to grade, or materials to prepare—regard it as a mandate to follow through. Yours is a professional obligation.

4. Plan early and carefully. In this way, you can first discuss the plan with the cooperating teacher and then make changes, as required, before implementing it.

5. Integrate but do not imitate. Although you need to fit into a context, remain an individual in the process.

6. Learn school regulations and observe them. The visitor should be extra careful to conform to existing codes of behavior lest he lose some of his usefulness in the classroom by going counter to standards.

7. Refrain from hypercritical comments or loose talk about students within or outside the school. Remember that, like any other professional person—physician, lawyer, or clergyman—you can be held liable for revealing information of a strictly personal nature about an individual with whom you are associated in a service capacity.

8. Be ethical in your relations to and remarks about teachers and administrators, realizing the harmfulness of degrading personality by word or action.

9. Do not become a self-appointed agent commissioned to improve the school or classroom. Improvement will usually be the result of your efforts, but let others solicit this type of help from you; don't volunteer it freely.

10. Be flexible enough to respond comfortably to the unexpected.

When in violation of one or more of the above ten precepts, students can be units of negative influence in a school system. The author, as director of student teaching in a large university for a number of years, can recall a few graphic examples of such individuals. One student teacher, for instance, arose in a department meeting to: "give you the benefit of my observations about your program." Another kept tab of the instances of teacher behavior which, he felt, were in contradiction to what he had learned in a methods course; and, to make matters worse, he made this information available to his teacher colleague. A number of student teachers were Monday-morning hypochondriacs for whom reliability was only an academic term. And a sizable group, over the years, were not beyond accepting assignments for a future date, only to appear at the designated time bright and cheerful but totally unprepared. These and others like them are not eligible to don their professional robes, needing some or much preliminary readying for this step. In contrast to such practices, the candidate's responsibility is to fit maturely into the role which awaits him; and it will be expansive enough to provide a place for individualism. But exercise of the latter should have as forerunners careful observation of teacher practices, acquaintance with school policies, and insights into pupil behavior. The student's major task, none the less, is to learn—not crusade; to test himself in a learning laboratory without striving to make major changes in the laboratory.

The candidate identifies with his fellow teachers

As he moves directionally toward the learning goal just described, it is necessary for the student to identify his status, which, perhaps to his distress, will stand revealed as not yet teacher but, likewise, no longer student. Notwithstanding the uncertainty of his position, his choice can be none other than to gravitate toward the authority position of teacher without denying students warmth and friendliness in the process. In subtle ways, his responsibility is to adopt the posture of a professional figure, which will set him apart, but not too far apart, from students. Having made this role determination, he will already have answered in the negative such questions as the following: May I date one of the secondary school pupils? Should I let the pupils call me by my first name? Should I attend all-pupil social functions? While maintaining an atmosphere of congeniality, the student candidate, not unlike the cooperating teacher, must construct the image of himself as a mature adult in a status role which he recognizes and is proud to assume. Student teaching is a transition from the state of dependence within a college framework to independence in a profession, and immaturity should not be permitted to obstruct the transition. When the student over-identifies with pupils, he is, in effect, refusing to become the legal parent that society demands him to be; and in refusing the new role, he is being not only unfair to pupils but also an obstruction to the classroom teacher whose job is thereby made more difficult.

Student teaching is primarily not a learning but a laboratory experience

In making this transition from the college to the practical world of learning, the student has an obligation to bring to the latter a scholarly competency that will simplify the task of status achievement. Although he will gain more valuable knowledge about children and subject matter than he ever dreamed of in anticipating the event, student teaching is not intended fundamentally to teach him new concepts. Instead, it is conceived as a laboratory situation where he can try out the ideas and teaching methods which he has already learned. In the process of putting into practice what he knows, the extra understandings and insights will be bonuses and, thus, secondary to the primary purpose of the experience.

Consistent with this point of view, then, the student with a major in art, for example, cannot hope to learn about copper enameling by facing this medium for the first time in student teaching; nor the teacher of general science by being exposed to physics, maybe for the first time since his own high school days; nor the teacher of English by learning grammar while he is teaching it. While conceding that even knowledgeable instructional leaders from time to time have to address themselves to new content, the fact is that they try to delay such an eventuality until achieving adequacy in the areas of the known. In contrast, the candidate who enters a classroom in a state of unpreparedness sacrifices some of his much-needed stature by asking student teaching to be what it is not.

The experience should be broad

In order to make maximum use of the student's richness of background, the scope of practice teaching should be broad. Although a college or university determines the pattern of a student-teaching program, students need not always be limited by it. For instance, if an individual is required by a college to spend only two periods a day in a high school and can spend a third period or more, he should take advantage of the extra opportunity. Or, if he is not required to work in a co-curriculum and has the chance to assume leadership in a club activity, he should willingly assume this extra responsibility. The benefits of fuller, more active participation and observation are of distinct help to the teacher-to-be, whose aim should be the richest, most meaningful experience possible.

Ideally, student teaching should be on the basis of an entire day at a time, during which the participant engages in almost all the professional activities of the teacher. These might include teaching in the minor as well as the major field; supervising a study hall; exercising leadership in a co-curriculum activity; attending P.T.A. meetings, Dads' nights, homeroom and all-school meetings; working on a teacher-committee; preparing an occasional case study; and entering into the many other important functions of teaching.

Such a rich experience is readily available for students of institutions which have off-campus student-teaching programs inherent in which is the requirement that students live in the community and become a vital part of the school. Other institutions which send students to near-by schools on an all-day basis, while permitting them to live at or in the vicinity of the college, also provide an across-the-board student-teaching experience of great breadth. But the enrollees of those institutions which cannot or do not provide such extensive student-teaching opportunities should, when practical, take extra steps to gain the needed breadth. The greater variety of activities will make them better teachers by providing a more realistic overview of the many functions of American secondary education.

Student teaching normally flows from little to much responsibility

Student teaching usually begins more passively and ends more actively, starts with much student observation and terminates with the student being observed, and generally moves from less responsibility along a progression toward greater responsibility. Because the process of gradualness normally operates, the apprehensive student can feel assured that he probably will not be made to run until he has walked, or required to teach a unit until he has taught a lesson, or asked to teach a lesson until he has had a chance to plan, or even expected to plan a lesson until he has had an opportunity to get acquainted with the class. On occasion, the exception may be tossed into his lap before he is ready, but that happening is in contrast to the general rule. For the most part, the classroom teacher with whom the college student is associated is just as attuned to the need for student-teacher readiness as he is for pupil readiness.

The unexpected may happen

Within this logical and expected pattern, however, the unexpected eventualities at times have a way of breaking through the planned progression. Nor are they always deterrents to progress. In fact, when they are not totally unreasonable and their appearance not too frequent, they may contribute to the growth of the candidate by providing greater breadth to the student-teaching experience. A few such out-of-the-ordinary contingencies might well be as follows:

1. The co-operating teacher becomes unexpectedly ill, a substitute is not immediately available, and the student teacher, even though in the early stages of the program, is asked to "hold the fort" until further help arrives.

2. A teacher of a subject other than the student's major or minor becomes ill, and the student is asked to serve temporarily as a substitute teacher. It can be a nonplussing but challenging experience, for instance, for a major in Spanish to be put in charge of a class in physics.

3. The co-operating teacher is unexpectedly called out of the room

early in the student's tenure as a student teacher, and the latter is left to decide what role he should play: one of authority figure in charge or of a visitor waiting for the teacher to return.

4. The several co-operating teachers forget that the student works with others, and all converge on him with papers to be graded by a given deadline.

5. Or, under the same circumstances as in 4 above, all assign lessons or parts of units for him to teach on the same day or in the same week, thereby over-involving him in an otherwise desirable active role. This possibility is particularly likely for the full-day student teacher.

6. Pupils ask questions that the student teacher cannot answer.

7. The co-operating teacher insists on the use of methods which the student prefers not to employ.

8. The student teacher runs out of ideas 10 or 15 minutes before the class bell rings.

In student teaching, as in any phase of academic existence where human beings are interacting, normalcy is sometimes asked to concede to the unforeseen. To both the inexperienced and the rigid, such concessions may be mildly threatening and, occasionally, disruptive; to the more seasoned and adaptable, however, they come to be regarded as parts of the many-sided composite of teaching. Expecting the unexpected conditions the teacher for the latter's advent. Today a college enrollee, tomorrow a student teacher, and then a teacher! In any of these roles, flexibility is a protective cushion for the unpredictable.

STAGES OF PROGRESSION

The topic of student teaching, when projected beyond the scope of purpose and supporting concepts, soon gets into the program itself. Not too many decades ago, a gloomy picture of program sequence would have had to be reported, with most colleges and schools playing by ear. Today, in contrast, a concerted move is under way to "phase" a program to include the following components in the order listed: the period of college preparation, orientation to the classroom and school, the period of active teaching, and finally, evaluation.

The period of preparation

Many students, having decided on teaching as a career early in their period of college enrollment, move inexorably toward the goal with a minimum of backtracking. Others make the decision at the beginning or toward the midpoint of the college sequence. And a few, whose numbers seem to be increasing, are individuals in their thirties or forties who, having graduated a number of years previously, now wish to prepare for teaching. Ideally, plans for teaching should be formulated by not later than the freshman year in college, thereby giving guidance a maximum opportunity to extend its helpful services. Yet because secondary school teaching leans so heavily on general education, which is also foundational to the baccalaureate degree, a decision made late in, or at the end of, the degree period may be early enough to enable the occasional individual to complete the requirements after one or two additional years of college work.

Regardless of when people announce their intent to enter teaching, they need to face realistically a number of issues. These divide into three academic areas, whether related to the requirements of an institution of higher learning or to those of a state department of public instruction: (1) general education, (2) the teaching major and minor, and (3) professional education. Because colleges and universities vary in their graduation requirements, and because each in its own way makes guidance services available to interested students, nothing more will be said about institutional requirements. However, a few comments will be made on state requirements. In this regard, the teacher candidate should recall, if he has forgotten, that education is a basic function of the state, not of the federal government. Although operational authority is regularly delegated to local communities, each of the 50 states establishes and maintains standards for certification. Accordingly, it behooves the student to consult early with an advisor, or by correspondence with a member of a state department of public instruction, to discover what the unique requirements of any single state are.

Regardless of whether the goal of any teacher candidate is graduation from a college or university or meeting certification requirements of a specific state, or both, the problem of readiness for student teaching should be primary. And, as was stated earlier in the chapter under a different context, the factor of readiness should operate as a variable independent of legality and organizational demands. For the most part, state and institutional standards are set at minimum levels, more to discourage the individual who wants a *carte blanche* than to serve as a rigid guide for the dedicated candidate. Thus, the obligation of the student during the period of preparation is to anticipate the demands of the classroom and greater school role, to set his standards high enough to satisfy these demands, and then to measure up to his own prescription. He will be "legislated at" by the state and guided by representatives of a college or university, but, in the last analysis, the professional task of effective preparation will be essentially his.

Orientation to the classroom and school

At some distinctive point in the program of teacher preparation, a decision will be reached by the institution and the individual that student teaching is to begin on a certain date. Depending on college policy and curriculum, it may be a full-day or a one-period program; it may extend for six weeks or the greater part of a year; it may be in a college laboratory school or in an off-campus public or private school; it may require the student to live at or away from the college; it may include work in only one or in as many as three subjects; it may be in a junior or a senior high school; and it may be supervised carefully or only superficially by college representatives. As may be inferred from the above diverse possibilities, student-teaching programs vary enormously throughout the country. But all begin in some way with orientation experiences, which will be discussed under the following subtopic headings: (1) the orientation visit, (2) getting acquainted with the teacher, (3) getting acquainted with classroom policy and procedures, (4) getting acquainted with the pupils, (5) getting acquainted with school policy and procedures, and (6) becoming a member of the school staff.

The orientation visit. When the assignment to a specific public or private school has been made early enough to warrant such action, the student should visit the school as soon as possible before student teaching begins. In this way he will be able to meet the teaching and administrative personnel with whom he will later be associated. Whenever visits to classrooms are made, they serve as a favorable transition to the student's new role: by relieving tension, initiating positive expectation, and enabling the teacher to establish a receptive climate for the arrival of the student teacher.

Getting acquainted with the teacher. After the orientation visit has been completed and a few days or weeks have elapsed, the student arrives at the school to assume the responsibilities of his new role. Whether he has been assigned to a single teacher or to two or three, one of his important functions is to study each teacher associate carefully in order to integrate more effectively in the classroom situation. And the study should be reciprocal. The closer the understanding that exists, the better the two co-workers will be able to unify and direct their combined efforts in what is now a common enterprise.

While working with the teacher co-worker, the student teacher should realize that, although his adult associate has been carefully selected by the college, teachers, like students, are fallible. Therefore, he should not place his professional counterpart on a pedestal, lest he topple later. A more wholesome relationship exists when, without questioning the admitted professional competence of his associate, the student envisions him basically as a human being susceptible to occasional failures as well as capable of successes. With this type of realistic appraisal, the student can intensify his search for the affirmative qualities in each teacher, first evaluating and then introjecting, not being surprised at the occasional shortcoming. Such a relationship is sought by the majority of cooperating teachers, who thereby escape the burden of living up to an overexalted image.

Getting acquainted with classroom policy and procedures. In addition to analyzing some of the personality characteristics of the teacher co-worker, the student should become familiar with classroom policy and procedures. The student needs to understand in advance the position taken by teachers on the following functions or issues:

1. The aims of education, as the teacher envisions them.
2. The limits of freedom to be maintained.
3. Corrective measures to be employed and avoided.
4. Policies regarding parent conferences.
5. Policies regarding work missed by students, including examinations.
6. Policies and procedures on illnesses, absences, and tardinesses.
7. Procedures for roll-taking.
8. Approximate amount of homework to be assigned.
9. The place of homework in the total program.
10. How supplies are to be requisitioned.
11. Policies on marking and reporting.
12. Teaching methods preferred and disliked.
13. Classroom policies regarding an honor system.
14. And others.

Most of the college student's information will be gained by the process of observation and mental note-taking, although occasionally he will wish to ask specific questions of the teacher or even of pupils. This direct approach can be encouraged just so long as it does not get bogged in minutiae. A good rule of thumb is: ask whenever the needed information is important, but don't become a walking expert on rules at the sacrifice of a more professional posture. It is vital to the student teacher that he know his individual place in the class situation. For instance, when the teacher steps out of the room, what role should the student teacher play? When pupils ask him questions, does he answer them or refer them to the teacher? When a pupil needs desk help, does he take initiative or not? If these and similar issues are not resolved early, the student needs to draw on his close relationship with the cooperating teacher so that doubts may be resolved comfortably and expeditiously as they arise.

Getting acquainted with the pupils. A further and most imperative requirement is that the student teacher become acquainted with the pupils. When he first arrives in the classroom, he should begin to learn pupils' names, either incidentally or, if needing a prop, from a prepared roster. Such information will be invaluable in helping him personalize his many relationships with class members. Rarely should a student teach the whole group until he is able to call all pupils by name. This beginning step of simple identification, followed later by the more personalized allusion, brings the curriculum and the learner together in an atmosphere of warmth.

Once the names are mastered, the major functions of learning and guidance are made easier.

Getting acquainted with school policy and procedures. The orientation responsibilities of the student teacher do not stop in the classroom, but extend to the entire school. When the latter in good faith invites a student teacher to become a part of it, inseparable from the invitation is the responsibility of helping him to become acquainted with the school policies that will apply to him. But by the same logic, the student tacitly agrees to live by school policy. His source of information, on occasion, may be a handbook; more often, it will be a word-of-mouth discussion with the teacher, department head, or principal; and it may even, at times, be an unplanned, incidental, catch-as-catch-can approach. The student teacher can always hope for one of the first two, but he should not be surprised when the third operates by default.

Whatever the source of information, the student teacher needs to become familiar with school policy related to areas such as are contained in the following listing. Those enumerated previously in connection with the classroom have been omitted here.

1. Traffic flow in the hallways and stairways.
2. Legitimate reasons for pupils leaving classrooms, homerooms, and study halls.
3. Parking regulations.
4. Places which are off limits to students.
5. Library regulations and procedures.
6. Steps to be taken by teachers when absent or late.
7. Recommended practice regarding written teaching plans.
8. Recommended practice regarding attendance at P.T.A. meetings, athletic events, and other important extra-school functions.
9. Recommended practice regarding times of arrival at and departure from the school, and regarding signing in and signing out.
10. Places in the school, if any, where teacher-smoking is approved.

Some student teachers, and understandably so, in small part, tend to feel that school rules and regulations work against their professionalism. A more wholesome and practical attitude is to realize that, when a number of people have to live together, harmony can result only when limits exist and are respected. Administrative fiat viewed in this light is merely an expedient to facilitate group aims, and, so conceived, it should be honored by all partners to it, including student teachers.

The student begins to teach

Following the period of early orientation and initial adjustment to the problems, people, and issues of the classroom and school, the student teacher begins to move in the long-dreamed-of direction of actual teaching. The transition is rapid for some students, slow for others. Rapidity and slowness are functions both of student readiness and of teacher philosophy. Regarding the first, many students are ready for full-group teaching at the end of a week or two of observing, whereas others need a longer period of orientation and preparation. Regarding the second, a few teachers literally propel the student, whereas most move him gradually, into the act of teaching. Ideally, student teaching should progress from the more specific responsibilities such as taking the roll, grading papers, and tutoring an individual, to the more broadly dimensioned responsibilities of planning, teaching a lesson, and ultimately presenting a unit.

Planning. In preparing for a learning situation for high school pupils, the student teacher is obligated to plan early and carefully. First, the plan should be in writing to insure retention of ideas. A lesson or a unit plan, or both, may be absolute requirements, depending on the magnitude of the segment of learning. However, we have in mind a plan that is not a textbook stereotype, but one that presents coherently and meaningfully for the student the goals of a lesson or unit, desired activities, a method of evaluation, and a transition to future learning.

In preparing the written plan, particularly for a daily lesson, the student is advised to prepare for a period longer than the expected 40 minutes. Many student teachers in their early attempts at teaching become disorganized because of an unplanned-for vacuum during the final ten or more minutes of the period. A new teacher sometimes tends to "recite" the lesson plan—a process by which the lesson is completed in shorter time than when active learning is elicited from the group. A preferable approach, of course, is for the student to utilize the curriculum materials and class members so effectively that time and content will fit into a natural and meaningful context. Developmental methods move in these directions. When unable to achieve such outcomes by these natural means, however, the student should take the logical step of extending his lesson plan beyond its anticipated class-length limits so as to be ready with material to fill the time block that might unexpectedly be unfilled.

Utilizing the services of the supervising teacher. Student teaching is, by definition, a cooperative relationship, and the less experienced associate in the shared enterprise should regularly draw on the good services of the more experienced. This statement applies to all phases of the mutual endeavor: planning, actual teaching, and evaluating. Its logic is obvious. First of all, the teacher is the legal authority figure responsible for the classroom; therefore, he cannot be expected to abdicate, except for training purposes, to his interning counterpart. Second, he undoubtedly is a resource person of stature who can be looked to and consulted for insights to content, students, materials, and teaching methods. Finally, the teacher's role automatically makes him a guide to his less experienced and usually younger co-worker. For these and other reasons, the student teacher should never press so aggressively toward independence that he dilutes the benefits available in the nearby person of the cooperating teacher.

The two individuals reap the greatest rewards when working in concert, with neither regarding the other as a threat, in any sense. Yet in this relationship, the senior partner must set the guidelines for the junior partner to work within. These should establish the curriculum sequence in broad terms, but should not constrict unduly. They should encourage creativity in planning without condoning radical departures from the *status quo*. They likewise should permit freedom in evaluating the results of teaching, but in the framework of established limits. In effect, the student should never lose sight of the fact that his efforts are best expended when they supplement those of the teacher and become woven into the classroom mosaic as he finds it. Certainly he should be permitted the right to be original and creative. But these qualities must be tempered to conform generally to the academic pattern that existed at the time of his arrival. The student thus becomes a part of the existing teacher-class-course relationship.

The student teacher is evaluated

Throughout the period of teaching practice, the student teacher makes evaluations, but he is also evaluated. The process of student-teacher appraisal can take place in five ways: as a developmental part of the day-to-day classroom contact between the student and the supervising teacher, in conference with the college supervisor, as a process of pupil analysis, as a final rating by the school or college, and as an emerging outcome of self-analysis.

Day-to-day classroom observation. Probably the most satisfying method of student-teacher assessment is that employed by the cooperating teacher in working informally on a day-to-day basis with his student associate. Evaluation of growth does not have to be spectacular to be effective; in fact, it operates best when it is a natural part of any cooperative relationship. Accordingly, the effective teacher deliberately attempts to utilize the many little but important opportunities that arise daily to help the student gain more effective insight into himself and his teaching efforts. When the student plans and submits his plans for appraisal, the teacher has an opportunity to evaluate. When the student works with pupils in small groups or as individuals, the teacher by observation receives impressions that he can translate into evaluation casually but none the less meaningfully. From his vantage point, he can perceive and pass judgment on such necessary qualities or traits as depth of scholarship, interest in young people, flexibility, dependability, enthusiasm, self-assurance, and creativeness. These cross his mirror of perception when he sits back and observes the student at work with individuals or with the entire class group, when he informally visits or plans with his counterpart, and when both of them are engaged in a shared teaching process. Evaluation thus accomplished at the many incidental points of contact ultimately culminates in tangible dimensions after a period of time. These, in turn, provide a defensible foundation for the more formal attempts at evaluation which may or may not be deemed necessary at some future date.

The conference with the college supervisor. Supplementing the appraisal efforts of the cooperating teacher, which are an integral part of his daily responsibilities, are those of the college supervisor, who, depending on local institutional practice, visits the student teacher intermittently throughout the extent of the program. He may visit as infrequently as once or twice, or as often as eight to ten times, during a quarter or semester; but after each visit, common practice is for the candidate and the college representative to meet informally to share observations and experiences. Rarely does, or should, the supervisor sit in a chair of exalted authority to pass down "superior" knowledge to the "lesser" member of the conference twosome. In contrast, the situation more frequently is one in which a wholesome give-and-take discussion takes place between two mutually interested people.

To help clarify what may transpire when a college supervisor and student teacher confer, we present an anecdote written by a designated university supervisor of student teachers following one classroom observation. Following it is an account of the first few minutes of the conference that transpired two days later. The hypothetical names of "Smith" for the university supervisor and "Dave" for the student teacher are employed.

Notes of Mr. Smith covering one visit. On November 14, I visited Dave, who had been left to teach Mr. X's combined eighth-grade English-social studies class. He had charge of the class for 50 minutes, during which he reviewed with the group a number of redundancies ("the man, he"; "with whom did you go with?" "he, himself went"; etc.) which had been covered in a workbook grammar lesson. This review lasted for 20 minutes, after which Dave proposed that each member of the group write a paragraph illustrating three concepts: (1) the topic sentence, (2) one idea to a paragraph, and (3) the transitional sentence. During the written work, Dave moved around the classroom for 5 minutes and sat at his desk for 25.

Dave was well prepared. Not once did he reach for an idea and fail to find it. He also was poised and comfortable, with the seeming result that the class was relaxed, although not too much so. A feeling of mutual respect appeared to reign. His sense of timing was good. He moved naturally from idea to idea, pupil to pupil, and method to method.

Next follows a near word-for-word reproduction of the first part of the conference that took place in Mr. Smith's office a few days following his visit to the classroom where Dave was a student teacher.

Mr. Smith: "Hello, Dave. Glad you were able to make it this late in the afternoon. All-day student teaching and a five o'clock conference make a full day."

Dave: "I'll be a pushover for whatever you say tonight; I'm too tired to talk back. But seriously, I'm having fun at H. School, even though I'm working all day long and carrying my problems home at night. I'm curious about your reactions to the last visit. Frankly, I was a bit petrified when you walked in, but it soon wore off."

Mr. Smith: "I enjoyed my visit, Dave, and if you were frightened, you certainly didn't show it. You performed like an old pro. By the way, how often have you been teaching?"

Dave: "Well, I've been there a month. As you remember, the first week I did very little. During the second week, I was put to work doing a lot of little things. But beginning last week he threw me into the fray. I took over one complete double period, and a single period on each of two other days. This week I have done even more. As far as I am concerned, I like to keep active. This is for me."

Mr. Smith: "You did a fine job discussing redundancies, Dave. You acted as if you had done it all your life. Have you thought of any other approach you might have taken?"

Dave: "Exactly what do you mean?"

Mr. Smith: "Well, you stuck pretty closely to the grammar book, although there is certainly nothing wrong with that approach. But how else might you have covered the subject?"

Dave: "You mean, for instance, using their own written work?"

Mr. Smith: "Possibly, although admitting that there is no pat answer, Dave. How do you feel about it?"

Dave: "Well, that would have been more work, but I guess that it might have been better. He does it the other way, though."

Mr. Smith: "Think about the merit of the two approaches. Maybe both should be used. When we talk the next time, I'll see if you have come to any conclusions," etc.

From the foregoing excerpt, and it is typical, we may infer that a conference situation with the college supervisor is usually earmarked by informality, a helpful exchange of ideas, and mutual stimulation. It varies, naturally, from person to person and from situation to situation; but rarely does it disintegrate into a telling-listening situation. With proper rapport between the two individuals, the conference proceeds along developmental lines with a minimum of structure and a maximum of student participation.

Pupil evaluation of student teachers. Supplementary to the evaluative efforts of the classroom teacher and college supervisor are often those of the pupils with whom the student is associated. Since these young people undoubtedly have received impressions from their observations, a logical *sequitur* is to elicit these reactions from them in some formalized way. A natural skepticism exists in the minds of some regarding the validity of the opinions of young and inexperienced youth. For this reason, their appraisals, while significantly a part of the total composite, should be considered against a background of recognized inexperience and emotional bias. Such factors limit without obliterating the merit of this not-often employed medium.

Pupil opinions, however, should never be solicited at the behest of the teacher or college supervisor, but only when the student teacher himself has the desire for such information. Although the admitted outcome will be the tapping of this source by the more capable and secure candidates, such an approach is more legitimate than forcing negative reactions on student teachers who are unable and unready to face them. The effects of the latter could be harmful to the respective students' egos. Unfortunately, in this regard, the emotionally mature students who could tolerate negative criticism are normally those, who, because of their over-all competency, receive very little of it. And the less mature, whose tolerance level for it is usually much too low, are prone to receive more than their prorated share.

For students who at some future time might wish to engage pupils in

---

Date _____

PUPIL EVALUATION
Of the Student Teacher

Name of Student Teacher: _____

Subject: _____

	*1	2	3	4	5
A. With Respect to Knowledge of Subject Matter, How Well Did He					
1. Demonstrate competency?					
2. Improve during student teaching?					
B. With Respect to Teaching Ability, How Well Did He					
3. Explain his ideas?					
4. Adapt his ideas to the group's level of understanding?					
5. Organize his ideas in sequence?					
6. Emphasize the more important ideas?					
7. Encourage wide pupil participation?					
8. Work with the class in developing the subject?					
9. Use illustrations and examples?					
10. Lead discussions?					
11. Use audio-visual aids effectively?					
a. Blackboard?					
b. Others?					
12. Begin and end the class with vigor and promptness?					
C. With Respect to Classroom Management, How Well Did He					
13. Maintain discipline?					
14. Regulate lighting in the room?					
15. Streamline the passing and collecting of materials?					
16. Take the roll with a minimum of confusion?					
D. With Respect to Personal-Professional Qualities, How Well Did He					
17. Use the English language?					
18. Use his voice in terms of					
a. Projection?					
b. Modulation and change of pace?					
E. With Respect to Personal Qualities, How Well Did He					
19. Demonstrate a sense of humor?					
20. Demonstrate tidiness and grooming?					
21. Handle difficult classroom situations?					
22. Demonstrate poise?					
23. Seem to enjoy working with the class?					
24. Follow through on commitments such as conferences, paper grading, etc. ?					

*1 - Outstanding   3 - Good
2 - Excellent   4 - Less than satisfactory
     5 - Unsatisfactory

the evaluative process, the form given on page 421 can be administered intact or modified, depending on local circumstances.

The final evaluation. Although evaluation will have been a persistent part of the entire experience, at the end of the period of student teaching a so-called final rating is usually prepared by the supervising teacher and/or the college supervisor. The appraisal may be of a check-sheet variety or a descriptive statement. Regardless of the medium, it is customarily anti-climactical. Most of the traits and qualities which are covered in the evaluation instrument usually will have been discussed with the student previously. To acquaint the reader with some of the qualities analyzed by at least one institution, a check-list type of rating instrument employed by a large midwestern university is here presented. Studying it prior to the experience of student teaching should highlight some of the expected competencies.

SCHOOL OF EDUCATION
NORTHWESTERN UNIVERSITY

Secondary

SUPERVISOR'S EVALUATION OF STUDENT TEACHER

The School of Education would appreciate your help in evaluating personal characteristics and professional competencies exhibited by the student teacher with whom you have worked this current quarter. We encourage you to discuss this form with your student teacher. In instances where you do not have enough information to give a rating, please leave the item blank. Feel free to utilize the space on the last page for additional comments you wish to make. We thank you for time and concern you have given to this prospective teacher.

Name ——————— Critic teacher ——————— Date ————

Subject taught ——————— Grade level ——— Ability level ———

How frequently did the student teach this class? ———————

PROFESSIONAL COMPETENCIES

1. Knowledge of Subject Matter and/or Teaching Areas:

    ———1. Inadequate, has a very weak background.
    ———2. Effective only with prepared material.
    ———3. Has an adequate but not extensive background.
    ———4. Is competent; deficiencies are rare.
    ———5. Has an exceptional background.

2. Preparation for Classroom Activities:

    ———1. Is a poor planner; trusts to luck; rationalizes.
    ———2. Amount and quality of preparation are unpredictable from day to day.
    ———3. Prepares adequately; quality is average.
    ———4. Plans and organizes well; quality shows some variation.
    ———5. Prepares carefully; quality is excellent.

3. Directing Discussion Groups:

_____1. Is very ineffective as a discussion leader.
_____2. Tends to dominate or to be dominated; needs much improvement.
_____3. Shows average skill, but needs to improve.
_____4. Is effective and rarely over or under-aggressive.
_____5. Is a skillful leader of group discussions.

4. Directing Other Learning Activities:

_____1. Is inept; shows little interest or versatility.
_____2. Tries hard; is interested but lacks skill and/or versatility.
_____3. Does an adequate job but doesn't scintillate.
_____4. Is interested and quite successful.
_____5. Directs activities naturally and effectively with maximum results.

5. Establishing and Utilizing Classroom Routines:

_____1. Ignores the values of routines as a tool of learning.
_____2. Utilizes routines in a hit-or-miss manner; profits little from them.
_____3. Profits from routines but needs to streamline procedures.
_____4. Organizes and utilizes routines effectively.
_____5. Utilizes the techniques of classroom management to the maximum.

6. Organizing for Discipline:

_____1. Is unable to maintain effective discipline; class is rowdy or cowed.
_____2. Maintains discipline at the cost of wholesome relationships; or class is often rowdy.
_____3. Maintains acceptable discipline.
_____4. Has few disciplinary problems; creates an atmosphere of mutual respect.
_____5. Creates enough interest so that discipline is no problem.

7. Understanding the Individual:

_____1. Almost always fails to recognize individual differences and needs; or over-individualizes at the expense of the group.
_____2. Administers only to obvious individual differences and needs.
_____3. Administers to individual and group needs in an acceptable way but still needs to improve.
_____4. Is frequently successful in meeting individual and group needs.
_____5. Is usually successful in meeting the needs of the individual and the group.

8. Attitude Toward Pupils:

_____1. Dominates and stifles the independence of pupils, antagonizes, or is consistently much too friendly.
_____2. Is the boss but occasionally permits freedom of action; or often is too friendly.
_____3. Strikes a fair balance between domination and familiarity; but needs to improve.
_____4. Encourages independence of action in most instances; occasionally needs greater finesse.

———5. Directs his efforts, by example and precept, toward situations which encourage independent thought and action.

9. Reaction to Criticism:

   ———1. Resents criticism; reacts negatively and childishly.
   ———2. Accepts criticism but not too gracefully; profits from it occasionally.
   ———3. Accepts criticism and profits from it often.
   ———4. Accepts criticism gracefully and often asks for it; usually profits from it.
   ———5. Considers criticism as part of professional growth.

10. Word Usage:

   ———1. Vocabulary is small; diction and grammar are bad.
   ———2. Gets by, but considerable improvement is needed.
   ———3. Vocabulary, diction, and grammar are average.
   ———4. Vocabulary, diction, and grammar are above average.
   ———5. Vocabulary, diction, and grammar are excellent.

11. Ability To Communicate in the Classroom:

   ———1. Consistently talks "down to" or "over the heads" of pupils.
   ———2. Often talks "down to" or "over the heads" of pupils.
   ———3. Can communicate successfully; but errs on occasions.
   ———4. Communicates successfully except in rare instances.
   ———5. Is unusually successful in communication skills.

12. Professional Ethics:

   ———1. Self-centered; injures personality and relationships by malicious gossip, betrayal of confidential information, etc.
   ———2. Tends to engage in idle gossip and related unprofessional behavior.
   ———3. Usually is ethical but occasionally gossips or encourages thoughtless unprofessional behavior.
   ———4. Ethics are above average.
   ———5. Is personally and professionally highly ethical.

PERSONAL TRAITS AND QUALITIES

13. Relationship with the Supervising Teacher:

   ———1. Makes himself obnoxious and is quite insensitive to cues; or withdraws from unnecessary contact.
   ———2. Tries to make a good adjustment but doesn't seem to know how.
   ———3. Has acceptable rapport but makes little effort to improve it; or is unable to do so.
   ———4. Has better than average rapport and tries to improve it continually.
   ———5. Always has the highest type of personal and professional relationship with the supervising teacher.

14. Personal Appearance:

   ———1. Is unkempt, careless and poorly groomed; or often overdresses.
   ———2. Appearance is barely acceptable; much improvement is needed.
   ———3. Appearance is average.
   ———4. Is neat and well groomed most of the time.
   ———5. Is regularly well groomed.

15. Poise and Confidence:

    ———1. Is ill at ease, shy or fearful; or compensates by being over-aggressive.
    ———2. Is poised only in familiar situations.
    ———3. Occasionally lacks confidence but no more so than the average.
    ———4. Has more poise and self-confidence than the average.
    ———5. Poise and self-confidence are unusual for his age.

16. Voice:

    ———1. Speaks inaudibly, in a monotone, or distracts in some other way.
    ———2. Voice is a distractor but he gets by.
    ———3. Voice is acceptable.
    ———4. Voice is good, pleasant.
    ———5. Voice is unusually resonant, well modulated.

17. Enthusiasm:

    ———1. Is apathetic and listless, or very nervously excitable.
    ———2. Lacks sparkle, or shows frequent signs of excitability.
    ———3. Is interested and enthusiastic but may lack discrimination as to time and place.
    ———4. Usually is enthusiastic and inspiring on appropriate occasions.
    ———5. Has a rare degree of enthusiasm, appropriately directed.

18. Sense of Humor:

    ———1. Lacks a sense of humor and distracts because of the deficiency.
    ———2. Has only a fair sense of humor.
    ———3. Has a good sense of humor when things are going right.
    ———4. Has a sense of humor that is average.
    ———5. Has a good sense of humor that is appropriate to the occasion.

19. Opinionation:

    ———1. Is dogmatic and inconsiderate of the ideas of others.
    ———2. Tends toward opinionation and dogmatism but is not unduly offensive.
    ———3. Is opinionated at times but not more so than the average.
    ———4. Is quite interested in and considerate of the opinions of others.
    ———5. Regularly tries to understand the other man's point of view.

20. Dependability (reliability, punctuality, etc.):

    ———1. Is undependable and cannot be relied on.
    ———2. Can be depended on when impressed with the importance of occasions.
    ———3. Can usually be depended on.
    ———4. Dependability is well above average.
    ———5. Is an unusually dependable person.

21. Adaptability:

    ———1. Is at a loss when unexpected situations arise.
    ———2. Adjusts slowly or poorly to the unexpected.
    ———3. Adjusts fairly well to the unexpected.
    ———4. Adjusts well to the unexpected.
    ———5. Is equal to almost any occasion.

22. Initiative:

———1. Sits back and waits to be told; or takes entirely too much initiative.

———2. Shows somewhat too little or too much initiative.

———3. Shows initiative often although not consistently.

———4. Is a self-starter in most instances.

———5. Reveals an unusual balance of initiative and common sense.

23. Ability To Evaluate Self:

———1. Rarely if ever sees self in proper perspective.

———2. Self-evaluation is sound in certain areas, but mostly unrealistic.

———3. Understands self fairly well and often profits from this knowledge.

———4. Usually makes responses as a result of self-understanding.

———5. Has a keen insight into self and guides actions accordingly.

FINAL RATING: In the light of your over-all evaluation, how do you rate this student as a prospective teacher:

———1. Totally unacceptable.

———2. A doubtful prospect.

———3. An average prospect.

———4. A good prospect.

———5. An unusually good prospect.

May we discuss this evaluation with the student teacher?———

Student teaching done full time for a quarter carries 16 credits. The grades are given in 2 eight-hour sections. This is purely mechanical to provide for the student who does half-time practice teaching. It enables us to give, for example, 8 hours of "B" and 8 hours of "A," which is comparable to 16 hours of an "A minus" or "B plus." Due to our present IBM system, plus and minus grades are not now possible in regular NU courses.

If you could take time to complete the following check list, we would appreciate it very much. It would be of help in determining grades.

EVALUATION

This candidate is rated in comparison with other students who have worked toward teacher certification at Northwestern.

EVALUATION

	OUT-STANDING	THOROUGHLY SATISFACTORY	AVERAGE	BELOW AVERAGE	UNSATIS-FACTORY
	90th %ile	75th to 89th %ile	50th to 74th %ile	26th to 49th %ile	1st to 25th %ile
Emotional stability					
Vitality					
Appearance and grooming . .					
Dependability					
Cooperation and helpfulness .					
Knowledge of subject matter .					
Classroom management . . .					
Effective teaching methods . .					
Understanding of pupils . . .					
Promise of professional growth .					

Additional Comments:

_____
Critic Teacher

The extensive inclusion of professional and personal traits reveals an institutional philosophy toward teaching, namely, that it is many-sided and demanding of breadth from the incumbent. En route to the classroom, the candidate might profitably use the 23 traits listed as a reminder of what may be expected from him when he makes the transition from theory to the practical. The most interesting feature of the appraisal form is that the personal qualities seem to be inextricably interlocked with the professional—once more a flashback to our insistence that, without the necessary personality competencies, content and method may be relatively unproductive.

Self-evaluation. The ultimate in evaluation which transcends all other methods is that which operates within the individual himself. It is the process of self-analysis which mirrors the event back to the perceptualizing person, who thereby is expected to make value judgments pertaining to what he sees. Regardless of what the cooperating teacher or college supervisor may think or say, or what the actual classroom performance may have been, such elements exist without substance or meaning unless the individual himself reacts to them and assesses their worth. Thus, the acid test of appraisal is whether the person is able to appraise himself with accuracy on the progress that he has made toward developmental standards of growth. Life once more apparently admonishes: Know yourself so that events and individuals outside yourself will be observed as they actually are.

Whatever the method or methods of evaluation used in student teaching, their purpose is to help the student achieve personal and professional growth. Through the new insights gained, it is hypothesized by the college and cooperating-school personnel that the student will correct a few or many of his shortcomings. These might be in the areas of personal qualities, understanding of young people, the major or minor field, teaching method, or general education. Whatever the specific weaknesses, the recognition of their existence should motivate realistic action.

That action should follow cannot be emphasized enough. It might take the form of more self-analysis, to the end of personality improvement; more work with young people, so that adolescents and their problems are more clearly understood; more courses at the undergraduate or graduate levels in the content teaching fields; or additional experiences of diversified kinds in general education. It is imperative, though, that evaluation lead to some type of action. To be aware of a problem in a specific area and then ignore it is escape. But to face up to a weakness and do something constructive to eliminate it is reality.

SUMMARY

Student teaching has been presented in this chapter as one of the most important milestones in teacher education for any student. We acknowledged the fact that it differs from institution to institution. Some programs are on an all-day, others on a one-hour per-day, basis; some extend over a period of only six weeks and others for a semester or longer; in some the student teacher is assigned only one subject, while in others as many as three.

Selected purposes of student teaching are (1) to provide the teacher-training institution with a means of evaluating its effectiveness and that of any single student or group of students, and (2) to enable the student to evaluate his adequacies in terms of personal adjustment, knowledge of subject matter, ability to employ teaching method appropriately and effectively, and knowledge of young people.

The various stages of a typical program of student teaching were next described: the orientation visit, the early orientation phases, the period of assuming considerable teaching responsibilities, and the evaluative phase.

The avowed general purpose of the chapter was to help the reader to anchor theory to a simulated classroom situation.

REFERENCES

Association for Student Teaching, *The Evaluation of Student Teaching, Twenty-Eighth Yearbook*. Lock Haven, Pa., 1949.

Association for Student Teaching, *Four Went To Teach, Thirty-Fifth Yearbook*. Lock Haven, Pa., 1956.

Adams, H. P., and F. G. Dickey, *Basic Principles of Student Teaching*. New York: American Book Co., 1956.

Brown, Thomas J., *Student Teaching in a Secondary School*. New York: Harper & Row, 1960.

Grim, Paul, and John Michaelis, *The Student Teacher in the Secondary School*. Englewood Cliffs, N.J.: Prentice-Hall, Inc., 1953.

Schorling, Raleigh, *Student Teaching*. New York: McGraw-Hill Book Co., (2nd ed.) 1949.

————, and Howard T. Bachelder, *Student Teaching in Secondary Schools.* New York: McGraw-Hill Book Co., Inc., 1956.

The Sub-Committee of the Standards and Surveys Committee of the American Association of Teachers Colleges, John G. Flowers, Allen D. Patterson, Florence B. Stratemeyer, and Margaret Lindsey, *School and Community Laboratory Experiences in Teacher Education.* American Association of Teachers Colleges, Oneonta, New York, 1948.

Woellner, Robert C., and M. Aurilla Wood, *Requirements for Certification.* University of Chicago Press, Chicago, 1962–1963 (and subsequent annual editions).

FUTURE NEEDS
IN
SECONDARY
EDUCATION

As society takes a critical look at education in the past and present, it inevitably begins to raise thought-provoking questions about education in the future. Many of these questions relate directly to the awesome issue of survival—world as well as personal, psychological as well as biological—and society and education are newly discovering an inseparable bond of common purpose. They are aware as never before that education can never be set apart from national and world destiny, and also that society can never be set apart from a system of life values.

The growing kinship between society and education allures for a number of reasons. First of all, despite their present close unification around the cause of escape from destruction—a negative value, admittedly—the unity none the less serves to make both more sensitive to world conditions, thus operating as a motivator and potential harbinger of change. A satisfied culture, in contrast, resists alteration by the very smugness of its narcissism. Second, the alliance involves society so intimately with education that the former is encouraged to give increasing support to newer practices in education that pass the test of plausibility.

During the early decades of the present century, the most notable educational activity took place in the secondary schools of the country, at a time when the high school population was experiencing a transmutation from the most gifted upper 10 per cent of the total number eligible to what later became a more diffuse 85 per cent. In the shift, the curriculum made many concessions to the newly arriving masses of students, as secondary education *in toto* engaged in a search for a more defensible philosophy and program. With the adoption of the Seven Cardinal Principles in 1917, a liberal expression of belief, the high school embarked on a course which for 30 to 40 years led more to refinement than to redefinition.

During this period, important reaffirmations of belief were announced by such agencies as the Educational Policies Commission, the Youth Commission, or the Commission on Re-organization; but, generally speaking, experimentation in education gravitated toward the elementary field. However, in the early part of the 1950 decade, secondary education once more began to shake itself, losing its lethargy so completely in the latter part of the decade that a real resurgence of experimental activity began to take place. Curriculum breakthroughs are now occurring in the big city suburbs and will soon reach into the less economically favored school districts. Because of our concern that they be anchored to justifiable educational moorings, we devote the remainder of this final chapter to a description of the specifications that should underwrite them.

A PHILOSOPHICAL BASE IS A PRIMARY NEED

The most pivotal of all the elements which go into an educational program is the philosophy which holds it up, and, unfortunately for the cause of the high school today, the supporting creedal beliefs are far from being universal in character or acceptance. These basic questions are being answered indistinctly or discordantly by the greater culture:

1. Should secondary education be concerned primarily with the academic man, or with the emotional, social, physical, and ethical man as well?

2. Is the ultimate goal of secondary education to help young people grow toward values that have already been predetermined, or to help them to change values through greater knowledge and insight?

3. To what extent does man have control over his will and, consequently, over his choices and actions?

The academic versus the whole man

The issue of the mental versus the many-sided man is theological as well as philosophical and educational. Philosophical idealists with certain religious orientations defend the school's dedication to mind training on the grounds that, since God is pure mind, only the monistic element of mind has supreme worth. By the same logic, the student with more of this mental quality is therefore correspondingly more worthy of the school's and society's attention and respect than those not so richly gifted. Other components, such as the personal-emotional, personal-physical, or social, are regarded by the idealists (idea-ists) as of purely secondary importance and existing only to serve the cause of the one enduring element of mind.

Aligned with this tradition, although on a non-theological basis, are the secular idealists or literary humanists, such as Mark Van Doren, Abraham Flexner, Robert Maynard Hutchins, and Mortimer Adler. These classically oriented scholars are enamored of the man of reason, who, they say, by "dint of hard discipline" and aided by a liberal arts education, can be counted among the intellectually chosen few.[1] Theirs is a dedication to the genetically favored élite who can read the so-called classics with interest and understanding; who can reach into the Occidental past for the "great ideas" and apply them to the present; and who look to philosophy, not science, to lead man out of the land of the Philistines.

Hutchins and Adler, in particular, are opposed to so-called "trades training" or any specialized, vocational approach to education in high school or college. If the door to a liberal education is opened by the academic subjects, the nonacademic, they feel, have little or no place. By the same logic, they are opposed to so-called "life adjustment" programs because they lead, they say, to an overemphasis on the current scene and therefore the nourishing of the *status quo*. They object to educators who allegedly are so preoccupied with the immediate needs of youth that their attention is diverted from the past and future.[2] By inference, then, they have little interest in a frontal approach to character development, preferring to let the liberal-arts, great-books approach operate indirectly to bring about needed personal and social adjustment and character change.

Arrayed against these protagonists of mind as the supreme essence are spokesmen from assorted orientations and disciplines who, like their opposites, also respect the mental and encourage development along cognitive lines, but who resist the simplicity of the "mind only" point of view. They take issue with this stand almost immediately on the grounds that the mind is a nonlocalized and diffused component which cannot be separated from the emotional, biological, value, and social constituents and which, if inseparable, therefore is untrainable as a discrete entity. To them, mind is the brain and central nervous system, but more. It is also the peripheral and autonomic nervous systems, but more. It consists of

[1] R. Freeman Butts and Lawrence A. Cremin, *A History of Education in American Culture* (New York: Holt, Rinehart and Winston, 1953), p. 495.
[2] Robert Maynard Hutchins, *The Conflict in Education* (New York: Harper & Row, 1953), pp. 26–47.

these biological correlates but also man's relationships with others, and his attitudes, feelings, and values. It is process as well as substance; in effect, it is man acting as a whole organism in a dynamic world of people. With mind so conceived, then, if students are to be educated, attention must be paid to their emotional, social, physical, and ethical, as well as to their academic growth by itself.

The curriculum implications of these almost polar extremes are tremendous, leading to divisions of opinion and action such as the following:

The Mind Proponents	*The Mental-Health Proponents*
1. Mind training is the "be all and end all" of the curriculum.	1. The whole man and his development are the "end all and be all."
2. The academic subjects of English, social studies, science, mathematics, and foreign languages are the fundamental province of the high school.	2. The province of the high school is any subject matter that leads to the accomplishment of the goal stated in 1. above.
3. The world of the abstract is the key to growth.	3. The abstract and concrete are reinforcing, even in the world of the cognitive.
4. The high school's responsibility for such intangibles as citizenship and the social graces is an indirect one only, emanating as an outcome of cognitive learnings.	4. The high school must make a frontal approach to citizenship and the social graces by giving pupils the opportunity to develop these desired outcomes in the life of the school.
5. The high school's responsibility for the emotional well-being of students is also conceived as an indirect outcome of cognitive learnings.	5. The high school's responsibility for the emotional well-being of students is one to be faced frontally, as well as indirectly, through mental-health practices and services.
6. The gifted should be uniquely challenged with mental stimulation.	6. All must be uniquely challenged mentally, but each according to his needs.
7. The high school must develop the man of reason, worrying little about the specific outcomes of the future, particularly as related to the vocational.	7. The high school must get youth ready for life in a broad sense, including the vocational, but to change life as well as to fit students into a *status quo*.

To the philosophical idealists, the high school should be cognitively oriented to rigorous classical material, with the gifted being able to respond and the less gifted, when soon convinced of their inability to respond, channeled into some other field of endeavor dealing mostly with trades activities. To the mental-health exponents, the academic content of the curriculum should not be either rigorously challenging or nonexistent, but graded according to the ability and interest levels of students. Under the

latter circumstances, the unfounded practice of assuming mechanical aptitude for those with limited academic aptitude would terminate.

Instead of this separation along artificial lines, both the academic
and the practical subjects would exist to serve both the gifted and the
slow, depending on need. Thus, if a general-education program for all were
conceived as embracing skills in the media of wood, metals, and basic
electronic material and equipment, such experiences would be provided
regardless of labels of the courses or their degree of social respectability.
The college-bound and the terminal students both would be enrolled, to
the end of graduating "a man of many parts." Consistent with this line of
reason, the slow learner would not continue to be rejected consistently by
the academic curriculum with the rationalized justification that he could
not "keep up." Instead, the academic curriculum would be made flexible
enough to reach to his level.

In this connection, it is distressing to note how many academic
courses in the typical high school program are soon terminal for the
student with an I.Q. within the approximate range of 75 to 89. Algebra
immediately gives way to general mathematics. Foreign language is almost
universally denied. In the sciences, general science is usually the only offering within his reach, with biology occasionally a sequel. In chemistry and
physics, natural selection always operates to exclude. Only in the academic
fields of English—with three years customarily demanded and a fourth
permitted—and social studies—with two years approved, one each in
civics and United States history—does a slow learner have even a fighting
chance of receiving a reasonably adequate general academic education.
More often than not, losing the struggle against the formidable obstacles
of academic custom and tradition, he either accepts the inevitable sentence
of the practical and esthetic arts or drops out of school.

Our contention is that, if slow learners in Spain can learn Spanish,
their counterparts in North America can learn it as a second language.
Neither group will become as fluent as their more gifted opposites, but this
outcome should not be a deterrent. Likewise, why should the less privileged
not be permitted to enjoy chemistry, physics, and geometery at their own
level—to name just a few courses heretofore denied them? Isn't this a
more defensible solution than to bring about the prevalent dropout at the
minimum legal age or an automatic transfer to the curriculum of the
manipulative? We give wholehearted support to the manual and fine
arts when employed as general education for all and specialized education
for the interested, but we take definite issue when they become a dumping
ground for the waste academic products. Not intended for this purpose,
they should not be used for this purpose.

Other curriculum implications of the "mind-only" versus the "mind-
plus" issue involve the guidance point of view and social learnings. To the
cognitively oriented, mental health is a hoped-for outcome of intellectual

experiences, with the more direct approaches to therapy incidental to or, at most, supportive of the cognitive. To the mental-health proponents, however, emotional and social well-being are ends in themselves, not means to greater academic ends. The goals of self-esteem and altruism are defended as justifiable in their own right apart from any supportive associations with the so-called discretely mental. Likewise, social learnings which emanate from classroom as well as co-curricular experiences are defended as laudable apart from any further excuse for being.

Although the secondary school is more nearly allied with the mental-health than with the mind-only point of view, the issue is far from being finally resolved. Evidences of regression appear when the talented receive national and local recognition disproportionate to their numerical importance; when the academic subjects continue to be endowed with disproportionate prestige; when teachers of the slow are apologetic about their "lowly" roles; and when the culture hides behind national emergencies to defend an unconscious desire for intellectual fascism. The junior, regular, and senior high schools, we contend, must take a more forthright stand on the whole-man concept of education, victim though it is of opposition and laden with difficulties of implementation. For better than its contrasted counterpart, it fits into a developmental frame of reference bolstered by the findings of educational and psychological research.

Should youth be educated to fit into or to change
society and its values?

The issue of education for adjustment or for change, like the issue just discussed, also reaches into theology and philosophy as well as educational practice. The controversy, in reality, rages more around the shadings of the issue than around the extremes. For instance, no organized group, to our knowledge, believes education's job to be purely one of helping youth fit narrowly into what is. Nor does any group at the other pole support change merely for the sake of change. The enjoinment is more along the lines of the permanence of values, with change being recommended or not, depending on the value system subscribed to.

In defense of a greater stability of values are religious fundamentalists —Protestant, Catholic, and Jew—who envision education's role as helping youth get ready for the changeless theological demands of a God figure. The task thus is one of conforming to preconceived standards which are immutable. At the secular level are the classical perennialists, most of whom are also philosophical idealists, who see values, if not absolutely, at least, firmly, anchored to the great ideas and minds of the past. From these orientations, the task of the secondary school is to discover the values already existent.

Somewhat, or often very, antithetical to this point of view is a contrasting camp, which houses an assorted range of philosophical orientations: logical positivism, with scientific empiricism its chief ally; pragmatism, with relativism its bulwark: and reconstructionism, with a planned future its goal. All of these, in different ways, reject absolutism: the first, by adopting agnosticism when scientific proof is unattainable; the second, by accepting the best evidence of *what is* at any given time while hypothesizing that circumstances tomorrow might, and probably will, alter it; the third, by planning change deliberately and then moving toward it—a perpetual process, which thereby enables it to avoid absolutism.

The essentials of a curriculum constitute no problem to any of these orientations, even though they may differ widely on other curriculum issues. All agree that the skills and a basic body of knowledge about the world, past and present, are fundamental. However, when a departure is made from the basic essentials of a curriculum, differences between and among the various orientations sharpen. Some demand, as the next step, an adjustment to what is; others insist on change.

Such indecision casts doubt on the existence of cultural unanimity. Does society want other-directedness or individualism; the comfortableness of unquestioned absolutism, or the motivating effects of doubt and indecision; a constant perpetuation of an unchanging image, or change? The democratic traditions of the nation and the dynamic qualities of education itself both speak in stentorian tones for individualism, modified skepticism, and change. But for the secondary school to pursue these aims, it must be possessed of courage to face the protests of the reactionaries and conservatives, and of a will to combat the seduction of changelessness. And once more we call on the dynamics of adjustment and the services of scholarship to make this outcome possible.

History is a mute witness that life cannot stay the same or go back. Its vast sweep has been one of progress toward the better life. Therefore, the secondary school can afford only a philosophy that is forward-looking, courting, not condemning, the cause of change. This, however, is not to suggest a specific packet or to write a blueprint for the future—a task that only the best combined minds from all the disciplines should accept, and then with trepidation. It is rather to educate youth toward the methods of questioning and honest doubt which through the quality of inquisitiveness, will effect change. And when sacred taboos are toppled in the process, they probably were long ripe for the fall.

The limits of will

While we are in the intriguing field of theology and philosophy, we ask the secondary school of the future to continue to examine the issues of "will" and "determinism" analytically in its progress toward a more complete personnel point of view which will harmonize with action. As of the moment, theory in these areas is far in advance of conviction and practice. For instance, despite the convincing sound of the words, how many teachers actually believe that failure to learn is caused? Or that a consistent pattern of law breakage, either in school or the greater society, reflects a kind of illness? Most would subscribe with caution to both, but only after modifying them almost out of existence first.

The felt need for caution is understandable, however, for the terms "free will" and "determinism" are emotionally loaded with religious and philosophical overtones. The issue is just as clear as the questions: Are all individuals able to measure up to high standards of excellence despite genetic and environmental limitations? Or are they victims of, or at least inhibited by, such limitations? Can people become masters of their destinies, or is this an impractical goal? In the classroom, to what extent can students meet standards imposed from without? Many teachers act as if students can "will" themselves into the near-impossible of achievement despite genetic, psychic, and environmental circumstances apparently to the contrary.

Support for the idea of greater, or even an unlimited, power of will comes from fundamentally-oriented religions which place the responsibility for behavioral performance, in or out of school, almost completely on the person. Operational support for this stand, without philosophical buttress, comes from thoughtless teachers so involved in the absolute rightness of their standards that the student is regularly blamed when failing to measure up to outside expectancy. At the other extreme, determinism, in contrast, places responsibility for behavior and final life outcomes on preconceived circumstances and decisions removed in time and place from the person.

A compromise between these categorical opposites almost inevitably has to be made by teachers and other workers in the behavioral sciences. Assuming that adolescents, or others, are in complete control of their behavioral destinies is too potent a tonic for most. Also aciduous, however, is the equally unpalatable proposition that adolescents have no responsibility for their acts, all of which have been predetermined for them. When it comes to operational practice, a necessary settlement places responsibility for performance on the individual himself in great part, but on forces outside him as well. In this way, students, while not regarded as completely accountable, are made to share accountability for their actions. In similar manner, teachers and other professional individuals, although desirous that all students reach peaks of excellence, take into consideration the counter influences of personal and environmental limitations which might work against such an outcome.

Thus, the teacher's role emerges as one which demands the study of the adolescent and his background, to the end of helping the younger person reach his optimum of growth. In the process, the teacher becomes involved with the adolescent at three points of contact: these three are the causes of behavior, the external symptoms of behavior, and the limits of growth. The causes are considered important because they motivate action. The symptoms are important because they are cues to causality. And limits are important because they confine growth expectancy to the boundaries of reason.

In all of these, learning's outcomes and individual growth loom as relative. Through the power of will, which is tied in strangely with motivation, a student, when circumstances are propitious, will always improve. On the other hand, when he fails to improve, it cannot be assumed that he "willed" this outcome deliberately as a result of unfettered choice. Rather, he must be regarded as a partial product of forces and circumstances which restrict or accelerate, but which also leave him some measure of election. Thus, he is never in supreme control of his actions, but neither is he usually a helpless victim of forces over which he has absolutely no control.

LEARNING THEORY NEEDS
TO BE APPLIED

With a philosophical base postured around the whole-man concept of learning, around values that, in great part, are dynamic, and around behavior conceived in causality yet susceptible to some conscious control, the secondary school has a solid structure on which to superimpose an educational program. But somewhere in between is needed a body of learning theory that can make the transition from an educational psychology textbook to the classroom. The specialized concern of this section accordingly will be with those learning principles which have immediate and lasting relevance for a teacher as he and his adolescent associates move toward the accomplishment of the philosophical goals just mentioned. The emphasis will be less on any formal tenet of learning than on the broader classroom base of the tenet, with its many implications. Only six of these principles have been selected for development.

The well-being of the student affects learning

If the mind is accepted as nonlocalized in the body organism, the *sequitur* is that any serious deficiency in the organism, physical or emotional, will serve as an obstacle to mental functioning. Thus, the teacher, without any loss of scholarly dedication, is presented with an added obligation to assure that the interacting student is biologically and psychologically ready to react maturely to the learning content of the curriculum. The obvious implication of this commission reverts once more to the whole-man concept, which premises that students are totalities, not additive sums of many parts.

The specific message to the teacher here is that he cannot ignore the interlocking relationship among the physical, emotional, social, and mental components. Although each can be isolated for formal study purposes, not one, nor even part of one, can function without the others feeling the effect. For instance, the student who is tired or undernourished usually has a low emotional tolerance and may respond sluggishly to learning stimuli. The adolescent with a low basal metabolism may be lured at the 8:30 morning hour more invitingly by Morpheus than by Agamemnon and Helen.

The emotions are no less interrelated. When one of them becomes dominant—fear, anger, or grief, for instance—conscious control of action concedes not unexpectedly to the more primitive autonomic, with behavior characterized by a minimum of cognitive regulation. The rapid heart beat, dilation of eyes, and the act of "freezing" are just a few of the physiological correlates. And closely allied to the emotional is the social, with each vitally affecting the other and both affecting learning.

Thus, although the classroom teacher is not expected to be a physician, psychological therapist, and specialized counselor for the social outcast, when the well-being of the student can be enhanced, he plays parts of all of these roles, as would a sensitively informed parent. The purpose is two-faceted: first of all, the happiness of students needs no other excuse for being, grounded as it is in mental-health overtones; and second, a student's feeling of being in tune with self and others leads to possibilities in learning otherwise undreamed of. Since this outcome becomes possible only when the entire organism is able to focus its energies directionally, the teacher cannot afford to neglect any part.

Every student needs success

If adolescents are to achieve a feeling of well-being within themselves and toward their respective worlds, each must realize recurring successes in the curriculum and in relationships with others. A positive self-image eventuates when positivism in the environment is absorbed by an individual. And this assimilative process becomes operative when the individual is accepted for doing his best, no matter how lowly that best may be. The first response has to come from the teacher, whose professional insight has convinced him of the significance of this therapeutic approach. It may be an encouraging remark, a friendly smile, a comment in the margin of a paper, or a pat of recognition. Each in its own way says to the student: You have performed up to expectancy and your efforts are being recognized. And each is customarily mirrored by students in their attitudes toward the one in question as well as toward others. Teacher-acceptance goes far in generating a high tolerance level of acceptance within the ranks of youth. Approval from both teacher and pupil associates soon becomes part of the growing sinew of a self-image.

The frequently expressed danger of creating an unrealistic self-image by approving low-level performance when it is the best that can be done has to us no basis of fact. If the teacher is modest with his praise and selective of time and place, the humaneness of the approach is equalled by its reasonableness. Why, in contrast, should teachers who themselves crave recognition from colleagues and administrators, withhold it from their younger associates who should need it more! A minimum knowledge of developmental needs should dictate otherwise.

Learning is reinforced by purpose

Students who, as well-integrated organisms, press for success in the learning process inevitably search for purpose and meaning in the curriculum. The purpose may be immediate: learning how to write a letter, the improvement of speech habits to increase the possibilities of winning an inter-school debate, understanding a piece of social legislation that has relevance to the community, or grasping the intricacies of probability for transfer to a game of chance. Purpose may also be futuristic: developing skills and accumulating knowledge that life requires adults to have for employment in the world of work and adjustment to the greater society.

Purpose translated into the immediacy of home life has a graphic extension in a group of nine- or ten-year-old Cub Scouts trudging miles, brushing off mosquitoes, suffering but not complaining, and later boasting of their virility. Their older counterparts, the Boy Scouts, go one step further in giving up the comforts of innerspring mattresses and other conveniences for a so-called night's sleep (an ironic misnomer) on the ground. These youngsters have a feeling of purpose which makes sacrifices of comfort seem trivial.

At the level of campus life, the concept is comparably applicable. Certain "dedicated" college students spend almost countless hours on such nonacademic activities as those related to student government, service groups, athletics, dormitory affairs, publications, and honoraries. These students, without protest, except for the sake of getting attention, work almost the clock around: the campus politician in his feverish search for votes, the editor of the annual in his uncertain march toward a deadline, or the campus group caught in the emotional grip of a worthwhile philanthropic cause. This fervor is invariably the envy of the academic scholars, who look for the same magic key without often finding it.

The teacher in the secondary school classroom, even more than his college counterpart, needs to identify and uncover purpose in the affairs of the curriculum. In so doing, his discoveries will inevitably be conveyed to students. Some specific reflections of purpose are described in the following:

(1) The teacher is a salesman of purpose when he lives it in the classroom. The students, in turn, evaluate the worth of the academic commodity by the intangible cues which the instructor flashes: whether he approaches the course with verve or boredom, keeps it dynamic or unconcernedly allows it to stultify, prepares carefully or lackadaisically, is scholarly or only pseudointellectual.

(2) The curriculum should be justified by a balance of present and future outcomes. The lure of the immediate should never go unattended, but neither should the long-term goals be ignored because of their mildly depressing influence on enthusiasm.

(3) The curriculum should have justification along a broad base. Its worthwhileness, when practicable, should be evaluated from a multiple approach: vocational, cultural-social, physical-emotional, and intellectual. Courses traditionally have been justified primarily on the basis of their intellectual appeal. This narrowness fails to recognize the vocational implications of, for instance, a course in French for a student who plans to work in the import-export field; the cultural-social advantages which accrue from a mastery of the English fundamentals; or the emotional growth to be had from pupil leadership in a classroom activity.

(4) Purpose should grow out of classroom situations naturally and subtly, unsupported by belabored and tired clichés. Examples of such trite maxims are these: "Without grammar, you can't compete in the adult world." "Latin is the best way to train the mind." "Four years of science and mathematics will assure us victory in the cold war." Justification of course content must be on sounder bases than these.

Interest supports learning

Not unrelated to the factor of purpose in motivating a curriculum is interest. When interest is manifested adequately, the inhibiting influences of the limited background and ability of pupils are reduced to manageable proportions; when interest is present in insufficient quantity, even richness of background and brightness may not be sufficient to compensate for its delimitations. Not at all a simple and uncomplicated dimension, interest is a complex of the complete human organism and the many factors that make it what it is. Here are a few selected guide lines that may make the classroom leader more successful in eliciting interest.

(1) Interest can be a correlate only of a curriculum that is at the specific comprehension level of any given pupil. When beyond that level, it expects the impossible; even worse, may lead to guilt feelings and an

inadequate self-image on the part of a student who fails to pass the test of improperly conceived adult standards. As indicated in the chapter on individual differences, fitting a curriculum to an individual is a difficult task but none the less one that a teacher cannot evade, at least, in approximation. Expecting a slow learner to understand the intricacies of electromagnetism, or a fast learner to dwell too long on elementary drill, is, in either situation, an invitation to disinterest.

(2) Interest almost universally is a function of involvement. The exact nature of the latter—whether via listening, discussing, writing, or researching—is less important than the fact of its existence. And it is significant to note in this connection that the more intense the involvement, the more rewarding the learning outcome. More active pupil participation in a curriculum is facilitated as classroom learning moves from teacher absoluteness toward student-oriented situations, and from teacher-direction to pupil-leadership.

The lecture gives pupils little opportunity for active participation in the affairs of the learning situation except as somewhat passive recipients of knowledge. The discussion makes them more outwardly active. A committee report increases the extent of their involvement. Giving them an occasional opportunity to help plan the curriculum, or part of it, goes even further. Allowing a student to teach the group, the class to set up projects for research, committees to organize learning content and discuss it with the class—these are definite leads to adolescent interest. The young teacher who, in disregard of them, assumes the absolute leadership role too long, possibly for fear of losing rapport with the group, should realize that disinterest, restiveness, and ineffective learning might well result. It is imperative, then, that a teacher who wishes to utilize the dynamic effects of interest as a motivator must structure the classroom environment so as to bring that outcome about. One very positive means is for him to include the pupil in as many affairs of the classroom as he possibly can. The chain reaction that will be set off as a result will come as no surprise to the experienced teacher.

A basic curriculum issue is whether involvement follows or creates interest. Actually, the two variables are mutually interrelated, despite the fact that more has been written about the effect of interest on effort or involvement than the reverse.[3] Yet experience has provided most teachers with convincing evidence that students often get involved in activities that they initially dread only to discover later that they have a keen interest in them.

(3) Teacher-interest should serve as a catalyst for pupil-interest. Such precipitators as careful planning, enthusiasm, and empathy have a real

[3] Kenneth Hansen's comments on this issue are interesting. See his *High School Teaching* (Englewood Cliffs, N.J.: Prentice-Hall, Inc., 1957), pp. 129–130.

contagion all their own. When associated with a well-designed curriculum that involves students actively, teacher-interest provides an added spark.

Learning increases when multi-dimensioned

Mentally healthy students who have been allowed to experience learning successes and who are consistently exposed to a curriculum characterized by the attributes of purpose and interest next need teaching method that is multi-sensory and varied. Theory has demonstrated in a number of ways that individuals learn better when the several senses operate as reinforcing agents and when a variety of approaches to learning are taken. This is a phenomenon with which new teachers and some not-so-new teachers have to become acquainted. The typical teacher on his first job has spent the preceding 16 years in school, specializing a considerable part of that time in the field of his major. When he teaches pupils for the first time, he sometimes assumes that they can learn almost momentarily what he has spent years in learning. The resulting approach may be the overpowering of adolescents with complex verbalisms, the almost grudging entertainment of a question or two, and unfeigned amazement when the outcomes of the learning situation prove unsatisfactory.

Fortunately for most newcomers to the profession, the period of expecting miracles in learning is short-lived. Before very long, the potentially capable teacher begins to realize that at least one reason why pupils do not learn as well as they might is in his own improper embracement of method. Once this light dawns, the conscientious teacher becomes more intelligently aware of the pupils' place in the learning structure. He approaches them henceforth with more sensitivity and variety, working with pupils individually or as a group, but only when such methods pass a standard of appropriateness. At certain times he may lead them to probe depth-wise into knowledge by confronting them with penetrating questions; at other times he may get them to challenge accepted points of view; and occasionally he may have them engage in research or participate in other problem-solving situations. Moving in a multi-sensory direction, he may use audio-visual methods to prove a point: a film, a filmstrip, a map, a recording, realia, or a blackboard illustration. When warranted, he may "turn pupils loose" in the library for individual study. In brief, he builds his case for learning on a multiple, not a single, foundation; but his choices of method are sensitively attuned to the demands of the learning environment.

With a heterogeneous class, the teacher particularly should feel the need to approach the learning situation with diversity. With a wide range of intelligence quotients, interest patterns, attention spans, special abilities, and social and cultural differences, he can scarcely presume to take a one-shot method approach and make 30 hits. With this many diverse pupils in class, seven or eight may be slow readers; these assuredly will not respond to a regular diet of: "Open your books and read for the rest of the period." If they read at a pace of 175 words per minute and the top ten readers exceed that number by 300 words or more, a vast range of learning outcomes, as well as of overt classroom responses, will be the result.

The range might be narrowed if the slow readers were given ample opportunity to share the ideas of others in a group-reading situation. Some students might learn more effectively in a give-and-take discussion; others, when asked to organize their ideas in writing or when making an oral report to the class. Certain pupils learn much from each other; a few profit less from the give-and-take. Regardless, the teacher must not conceive a single approach as the primary impetus for pupil growth! Rather let him meet student differences with a variety of teaching methods.

Learning should result in action

A final concept of this section is that learning, when significant, should lead to action; when static, it dies by reason of sterility. Scarcely no one is more inadequate than the individual who, although steeped in the knowledge of the world about him, refuses to apply what he knows to the end of bringing about positive change in the environment. Satisfaction with the *status quo,* though comfortable, cannot be condoned in the maturing learner because it eventuates in a do-nothing approach to life. Knowledge should be more energizing and vital than this. It must draw on the past and let filter through the mistakes and successes. These, in turn, need to be focused on the present as a mandate to pupil action. Only learning of a primitive order tolerates fragmented knowledge and disconnected understandings. As knowledge integrates, it weaves fragments into relationships. The process of generalization then follows, with the final goal application.

The reader is now requested to relate the various levels of learning to the subject of protective tariff as viewed progressively by a student. The student probably has heard the term many times, without seriously thinking about it until faced with it in a textbook definition: "A protective tariff is a tax imposed by one country on the exports from another as a means of protecting internal production." As he extends the abstraction, he sees home production always favored over foreign, with nationalism invariably the victor. Sooner or later, he associates its implications with his avowed humanistic interest in all the people, realizing that in a world revolution between the "haves" and the "have not's," protective tariff may work against the needy. Now the issue is ethical as well as economic.

Ultimately, after all the ideas have been mustered, organized, and examined, the student will arrive at a point of view about protective tariff which properly should serve as a basis for future action. The latter might be only quiet reflection at first; later it might be conversationally verbal;

and ultimately it might become political or social in nature in the pursuit of change, assuming enough personal conviction. Whatever the specific type of action, however, the important outcome is that the person has acted on belief—not as a crusader, but as a thinker.

Learning that is other than academic, teachers should encourage to be extended into the arena of performance. This view alone is consistent with a previously expressed related one, namely, that the purpose of education is change. If individuals who know do not act, society some day may be at the mercy of those who act but do not know. The implementation of learning, thus, should be the climax of all educational endeavor.

WHO RUNS THE SCHOOLS

The latitude of implementation, however, is in large part dependent on the academic freedom possessed by teachers, an assessment of which can be made only within the authority structure of the school itself. To the extent that this structure is malleable, any given teacher can take reasonable steps to terminate learning with action; to the extent that it is rigid, his power of freedom is accordingly delimited. The crux of the issue is contained in the terse question: "Who runs the schools?" The oversimplified answer is that the entire issue has been settled constitutionally, and therefore no problem exists: the state runs the schools per authority of the elastic clause of the Constitution. And on legal grounds, this answer is valid, because the state has the right to pass school legislation of many and diverse kinds so long as it does not interfere radically with the general welfare of people. Practically, however, the state has delegated many of its educational responsibilities to the local community, so that the issue operationally should be restated: "To what extent can the lay people of a local community run the schools as they see fit?"

The authority of a local community for its schools

Despite the fact that, except for the details of management, an individual state *could* operate the schools from a central office in the state capitol, each state regularly has refused to do so. In practice, states have instead passed broad school legislation, maintained customarily a small central staff to implement the legislation, and delegated much authority for operational implementation to the local communities. Because of this delegation, the elected school board at the local level is a power body within the American culture. It normally consists of from five to nine members who hold office from two to six years. In its membership ranks are usually one or more professional men: lawyers, physicians, dentists, or engineers; several upper- or middle-echelon business executives; and perhaps a store owner, a housewife, or a local banker. Rarely, however, does just ordinary John Q. Citizen make the grade.

From the point of view of the local community having extensive operational authority for its schools, we submit a few hypothetical situations that the reader is asked to analyze in terms of how high school teachers might be affected by them.

Situation 1. Dadeville in Wisconsin is a dyed-in-the-wool isolationist, America-First, white community which barely tolerates foreigners, suspecting them of being anti-American or pro-communistic until they can remove all doubt. This town has elected a school board, the members of which represent its basic philosophy. To make certain that the high school does not get out of line, the board members regularly insist on reading textbooks in the fields of the social studies and literature prior to approving them for adoption. Occasionally, they interrogate selected pupils and teachers as another means of assuring adherence to the town's philosophy. At times, they personally have been known to make visits to the classrooms of the school, or, in lieu thereof, to approve the visits of selected townspeople as insurance against nonconformity. They also interview teachers carefully before hiring them lest "false doctrines" be brought from the outside into the community.

Situation 2. Stanley, Illinois, has had for ten years a high school superintendent who has performed his administrative duties in a reasonably capable way. During his tenure, he has hired a full-time speech correctionist, three full-time guidance workers, and a reading specialist—these to supplement the teaching staff of 110 for a community high school of 2,000 enrollment.

Three board candidates at election time run on an economy platform of: "Let's get the frills out of the high school and save money." Despite the fact that the tax rate is already slightly lower than that of comparable surrounding communities, the economy ticket wins. Because one of the four hold-over board incumbents is also in favor of greater economy, the conservative group has a majority of one on the new high school board.

After several deliberative sessions controlled by the four-man majority, the board informs the superintendent that he must get rid of the guidance specialists, only one of whom has tenure; also, that he should increase class size by an average of three to effect a greater saving. The superintendent, after consulting with the teachers, is so reluctant to take these steps that he delays action. Shortly thereafter he is told that his services are to be terminated immediately but that he will be reimbursed for the remaining period of his contract.

In analyzing the situations in Dadeville and Stanley, the reader may ask, first, if the school boards could take the actions that were described. The answer is a decided affirmative, although the National Educational

Association, by an investigation or threatened investigation, might make a community think twice before taking action that would condemn it in a court of public opinion. Also, the guidance specialist with tenure could undoubtedly retain a position in the system. Regardless, a local community with a solid front can go so far as to get textbooks banned, teachers without tenure fired, and administrators removed when the philosophy or practices of the school are in contrast to that of the greater community or a sizable part of it. Even when the philosophy and practices are in harmony with national ideals, such local action is possible.

A countering influence can be exerted in two ways: by means of greater centralized controls exercised by the state, or by means of steps taken by the professional teacher group to prevent local excesses from gaining dominance. Because the United States is dedicated to as much decentralization of authority as possible in almost every organizational walk of life, and because this concept of decentralized control is in harmony with sound organizational practice, we reject the first alternative while supporting the second.

The teaching profession needs to become professional

For teachers and administrators of secondary and elementary schools, however, to be able to uphold reasonable standards even to the point of defending them against a community with distorted biases they and all their colleagues throughout the country must become a profession—not just in name only, but in terms of the real vitals. The requirements of professionalism are essentially as follows:

1. Agreement on a credo or philosophy.
2. Establishing and maintaining high standards of membership.
3. Implementing the credo and membership standards with an efficient organizational structure.

A credo. Fundamental to any profession is a credo to which all members can subscribe; in fact, such a statement of belief is basic to any subsequent progress. Although educators may not be completely unified around common purposes, they have considerable unanimity of opinion on many of the more important educational issues. That they have reached consensus within a broad frame of reference on the Seven Cardinal Principles of Education and the objectives as announced by the Educational Policies Commission indicates that bonds do exist. For example, they generally agree that education is dedicated to helping children and youth press toward competency in the interrelated phases of mental health. Furthermore, they agree that education, because it is not exclusively essentialist in nature, should allow teachers to lead students into problem-solving avenues. The extent of this freedom may not as yet have been defined, but it could be. And, again, they agree that school boards should not make direct forays on teachers and curricula. These convictions, and others like them, could soon become a hard core of a credo.

Once the body of beliefs had been agreed on, special note would have to be made of those beliefs regarded as sufficiently sacred to be defended with courage. The philosophy might well state forthrightly that the profession would resist attempts by misguided lay boards of education or extremist members of a community to censor textbooks, supervise teachers in the classroom, or assume other executive functions of school administrators. It would further have to clarify the term "academic freedom" so as to let the world know thereby that teachers have certain inalienable rights that no community can invade with impunity.

In the creed would be included also a code of accepted practices for in-service members: for example, ethics of job application, what action to take when improper community pressures are exerted, broadly conceived standards of community living, and recommended means of in-service growth. The creed would do all this and much more, but its greatest contribution would be the announcement to society that education is a profession with beliefs that it is willing to defend against the more flagrant abuses.

Standards of membership. In addition to a creed, teachers and administrators would also be compelled to formulate standards of professional membership. Although for the most part complementing some of the existing state and regional standards of certification, the new standards would insist on three features: reasonable uniformity among the states, a requirement of personal as well as academic competencies, and the sealing off of "cheap" certification loopholes. Membership in any profession must be more than a reflection of social and economic expediency. Such factors as supply and demand, pressures of local power groups, political chicanery of elected public officials, and general indifference cannot be other than incidental to the avowed function of service.

A needed organization. Assuming a credo and high standards of membership, teachers and administrators would next need a formal organization of some kind to set and keep in operation the credo and standards of admission. It would have to be a combined legislative, executive, and judicial body; such would give the profession structure. The formulation of an unwieldy, highly centralized, and authoritarian body is far from our thinking here; rather, one strong enough and efficient enough to do away with such injustices as existed in the hypothetical towns of Dadeville, Wisconsin and Stanley, Illinois is needed.

To the suggestion that the National Education Association already exists to perform the functions herein described, most educators would counter that its status is not at all synonymous with that of the hypothetical organization being advocated here. The former has exerted dynamic leadership throughout its existence, even to the extent at times of taking aggressive action against community abuses, but basically its function is and has been advisory, not executive.

To the original question, Who runs the schools? we answer that the state does, in a broad, general way; the local community does, in a more operationally detailed way; and members of the profession do, to the extent that they are willing enough and courageous enough to defend high standards. A number of educational writers have oversimplified the conflict between certain local communities and teachers by stating that the people determine *the what;* teachers, *the how.* To this we reply: "Why do we need professionally trained teachers if untrained laymen can tell them exactly what to teach?" Also, "Why relegate teachers to the level of manipulators by making them responsible only for the *how?*" Professionalism must be made of such stern stuff that at the national level it soon will arrive at a point of announcing to everyone: "This I believe. This is a line over which uninformed, even if well-meaning, individuals, groups and communities can cross only at their own risk." Teaching must become truly professional if it is to lead the way to maturity. Intelligence and common sense speak out in despair when the blind are permitted to lead those who can see. But if teachers are identified as those who can see, they must be well trained for their positions and well adjusted personally. Then they can unite to give to education the leadership that society deserves.

THE FUTURE SECONDARY
SCHOOL CURRICULUM

In this the final section, the irresistible impulse to divine the future will be partially indulged. Restraints will be imposed, however, in recognition of the potential deviousness of any man with a crystal ball. The likelihood of hallucination, illusion, and other excesses will be curbed by narrowing prediction to those curriculum trends which already have become rooted somewhere in practice—usually in one or a number of suburban communities.

The most carefully organized and professional job of secondary school curriculum divination has been performed during the past few years by the Ford Foundation. In 1956, The Fund for the Advancement of Education commissioned Alexander Stoddard to study methods of circumventing the teacher shortage in large cities, with the result that in 1957 the booklet, *Schools For Tomorrow,* carried educational speculation into the curriculum supplements of teachers' aids and television.[4] During the next four years, under the same Ford Foundation auspices, the National Association of Secondary School Principals, with J. Lloyd Trump, Dorsey Bayn-

[4] Alexander J. Stoddard, *Schools For Tomorrow: An Educator's Blueprint* (New York: The Fund for the Advancement of Education, 1957).

ham, Lloyd Michael, Matthew Gaffney, and others exercising leadership, conducted further curriculum experimentation which also culminated in written presages based on growing experimental practices.[5]

The efforts of the National Association of Secondary School Principals have been commendable and their experimentation has been highly contributive to educational thought. In fact, the recent shift of experimental attention from the elementary school to the secondary school has been largely due to the labors of this organization. However, with no attempt at deprecation, we note that the concern of the organization seems to be more with quantitative and mechanical extensions of method than with objectives or an underlying philosophy. Since each is fundamental and necessary to the growth of its opposite, we hope that secondary education will continue a search for refined objectives as vigorously as it is now pursuing a search for new or refined methods.

Personal growth will be emphasized more in the future

Following the present preoccupation with such mass academic media of instruction as television and team teaching, and such individualized academic media as the language laboratory and teaching machines, we predict that secondary education will give increasing attention in the future to the emotional development of the individual pupil. Emphasis on the individual and his personality has been a trend for almost a half-century, with regression occurring at times but never for long. The statistic that one person in ten will receive some form of organized depth therapy before his death and that over half of the nation's hospital beds are filled by mentally ill persons is too staggering to be ignored or treated lightly by the schools.

The implications of this prediction for teacher education and the field of psychology are tremendous. In a publication of the American Psychological Association, it was estimated that schools in the future may need one clinical psychologist for every 1,000 to 3,000 students, or a total of approximately 15,000 in all.[6] Regardless of the number of specialists needed, the demand will be filled if society comes to believe firmly enough in the merit of the cause. Our prediction is that the growing incidence of mental illness and juvenile delinquency will force society's hand and that of the school's to take action not only in the area of prevention but even, to a degree, in the province of therapy as a public responsibility.

[5] J. Lloyd Trump, *The Images of the Future* (New York: The Fund for the Advancement of Education, 1959).

J. Lloyd Trump and Dorsey Baynham, *Guide to Better Schools* (New York: The Fund for the Advancement of Education, 1961).

[6] Norma Cutts, ed., *School Psychologists at Mid-Century* (Washington, D.C.: American Psychological Association, 1955), p. 4.

Ethics will be emphasized more in the curriculum

A second conjecture about the secondary school curriculum of the future is that it will become more concerned with ethical considerations than it has in the past. Society is currently witnessing a decline both of religious orthodoxy and its built-in features of sin and hell. As these latter have become less a deterrent to unsocial behavior, the vacuum created by their growing de-emphasis craves to be filled. The result, we predict, will be a growing dedication of the secondary school to ethical values implemented in two ways: by emphasizing better ethical living in the school itself and by relating the theory and study of values to the content of the curriculum. The former, in a sense, was ushered in by John Dewey, in his concern for the school as a place in which pupils should live as well as learn. The latter is still spotty in implementation, with teachers almost universally more concerned with *what was* and *what is* than with the ethical propriety of either. Plato's defense of slavery can be explained historically but not written off ethically. And international "truth-stretching" is still unsavory even when excused on the grounds that "We have to fight fire with fire." One reason for the increasing delinquency rate may be this double standard of private and public behavior.

Problem-solving will be emphasized

Along with the re-emphasis on the person and on ethical considerations will be a more faithful dedication to problem-solving. Even at present, this is an avowed goal of most schools, but too often only lip service is paid to it. In the future, this shallow loyalty will be replaced by such sincere expressions as seminars in science where adolescents will identify and actually solve problems, classes in history which will relate more to the dynamics of events than to the substantive fact of the events themselves, and classes in mathematics which will leave the page of theory and truly get into application. The goal of problem-solving is now centuries old, but a true implementation of it in the school will be refreshingly new. Secondary education cannot with impunity continue to let the welling spirit of inquiry go unattended.

The school's organization will change

Mirroring the curriculum image of the future will be a restructured school organization, the first step toward which will involve a determination by researchers of the best methods of achieving the major goals that secondary education has adopted for itself. Assuming that these are the mental-health outcomes, the next step will be a reassessment of large-group, small-group, and individual methods of instruction to discover which ones will most competently serve the mental, personal-emotional, social, ethical, and personal-physical needs of students. The greatest research demand is probably in the field of the mental, with much too little known today about what learnings can be accomplished just as efficiently with an audience of a thousand as with one of thirty.

Like Trump and Baynham, we envision the secondary school of tomorrow built around large groups, some of which may consist of one hundred or several hundred; others as sizable, for instance, as all ninth-graders in a school system or county; many small groups of ten to fifteen; and as many single-person situations as there are students.[7] The purpose of the large-group situation will be to introduce, clarify, demonstrate, synthesize, evaluate, and develop learnings that lend themselves to this larger methods medium. The criteria of selection will always be thoroughness of learning first and economy second. When both are served, unwise indeed will be any school which clings to the less efficient methods of the past.

The smaller groups of seminar size will be built purposefully around social and personal, as well as cognitive, development, with student- and teacher-led methods aimed frontally at such outcomes as self-understanding, group therapy, increased tolerances, and cognitive understandings of a more intensive kind than could be expected from the large-group situation.

Supplementing learning in the aggregate will be learning by the individual, implemented in two ways: in the process of independent study, and in the give-and-take of the counseling interview. Regarding the former, a missing ingredient of most educational programs today is the provision for students to perform academic tasks not structured by an adult authority figure in the school. Homework is too often a response to pages to be read, mathematical problems to be solved, or other specific assignments to be completed, at the end of which the student feels that his job is finished. The school of tomorrow, in contrast, will expect adolescents to select independently certain issues to be resolved and not to be satisfied until they have extended themselves to an optimum. This step will place learning on a level of maturity elevated beyond the adult-child relationship pattern, where conformance is naïvely associated with progress and growth.

The second medium for individual learning will be in the counseling interview, expanded in scope to accommodate the increasingly recognized importance of personal-emotional growth. And with large-group instruction possibly making for an economy in teacher utilization, the saving, if any, can be redirected toward the outcome of more one-to-one relationships between students and specialized adults. Personality formulation is a function of many influences, both direct and indirect; but at times only the direct approach of the therapeutic interview will suffice. In such instances,

---

[7] J. Lloyd Trump and Dorsey Baynham, *op. cit.,* pp. 24–31.

then, the secondary school of the future with the mental-health point of view will provide the necessary organization for this direct outcome to take place routinely.

The existing scheme of time and period blocks will need to undergo change to keep up with the curriculum innovations. The Carnegie Unit, in particular, will have to lose some of its rigidity if it is expected to serve the needs of the revised program. An eight-period day, a four-subject class schedule, or a 180-day school year will be of less significance than the qualitative features of the program itself. Time blocks of several hours for independent study will often be required and blocks of lesser duration for the lecture sessions. Thus, greater time flexibility will have to characterize the school of tomorrow.

Finally, teachers will need to respond to the demands of the developing program and organization, with teacher education falling in line. To the dimensions of today's teacher, the following will be added or, at least, will receive greater emphasis:

1. The personality of the teacher will be regarded as crucial, with mature development considered as much a need as scholarship. The task of understanding and helping others along the road to adjustment will be entrusted only to those who have already made satisfactory progress along that road.

2. More preparatory theory and practical experiences in the areas of psychology, sociology, and guidance will be demanded because of the growing humanistic interests of the schools.

3. More work in value theory will be expected.

4. An increasing sophistication in the area of group dynamics will be required.

5. Greater sensitivity to the demands of the large-group lecture role will be required, with such qualities as the following emerging as important: commendable voice quality and projection, poise before a large group, ability to plan and organize effectively, and familiarity with the many audio-visual media.

6. A longer period of preparation will be increasingly demanded— up to five and conceivably six to seven years—with the newly conceived role of teacher projected in more faithful perspective.

A FINAL WORD

The teacher of tomorrow will need to keep pace with—in fact, to lead—the innovations of tomorrow. Admittedly, the expectancies for teacher competency are increasing, but is the pattern any different in the other professions? We think not. A society develops or deteriorates to the degree that its people progress or regress.

And with education a major contributor to man's development, teachers must learn to regard society's more rigorous demands as a wise investment in their own as well as society's future.

SUMMARY

The emphasis of this final chapter has been on the future in secondary education, determined, in part, by cues taken from existing minority practices in selected secondary schools. The first projected look was toward a philosophical base that would embrace a firmer conviction about the importance of the whole man. To date, the cognitive man has crowded the man of emotions too much into the background. Within the framework of this philosophical base, it was hypothesized that the schools should shape, as well as fit into, *status quo* values, recognizing man as ever-emergent and in partial command of his destinies.

Next it was expressed that the secondary schools of the future will integrate their programs more closely with learning theory, with the following tenets considered highly significant: the student's well-being affects learning, all students need success, learning needs to be reinforced by purpose, interest needs to be enlisted to support learning, learning needs to be consistently multi-dimensional, and learning must inevitably end in action.

In regard to the question: Who runs the schools? the point of view was taken that the state does legally and the local community does operationally, but that the profession plays too weak a hand in the operation. A plea was made for the latter to grow into greater professional stature.

Finally, secondary education of the future was predicted as becoming more concerned than is today's counterpart with human personality, ethics, and problem-solving situations. The organization of tomorrow's schools was logically portrayed as mirroring the many curriculum changes, with large-group, small-group, and individual instructional approaches being complementary. The teacher of tomorrow's schools was described as keeping pace with curriculum progress—in fact, being in the vanguard of it.

REFERENCES

American Association of School Administrators, *The High School in a Changing World, 36th Yearbook*. Washington, D.C.: National Education Association, 1958.

Association for Supervision and Curriculum Development, *Forces Affecting American Education*. Washington, D.C.: National Education Association, 1953.

Committee on Orientation, *Issues of Secondary Education, Bulletin No. 59.* Department of Secondary School Principals, National Education Association, Washington, D.C., 1936.

Educational Policies Commission, *Education for All American Youth,* National Education Association, Washington, D.C. (Ninth Printing), 1952.

Gross, Neal, *Who Runs Our Schools?* New York: John Wiley and Sons, 1958.

Harvard Committee, *General Education in a Free Society.* Cambridge: Harvard University Press, 1945.

Hollingshead, A. B., *Elmtown's Youth.* New York: John Wiley and Sons, 1949.

Hutchins, Robert Maynard, *Education and the Social Order.* Los Angeles: The Modern Forum, 1936.

————, *The Conflict In Education.* New York: Harper & Row, 1953.

National Association of Secondary School Principals, *Planning for American Youth.* Washington, D.C.: National Education Association (rev. ed.), 1951.

National Education Association, *Report of the Committee of Ten.* New York: American Book Co., 1894.

National Education Association, Commission on the Reorganization of Secondary Education, *The Cardinal Principles of Secondary Education.* United States Office of Education, Bulletin 35, 1918.

Spears, Harold, *The High School for Today.* New York: American Book Co., 1950.

Stoddard, Alexander J., *Schools for Tomorrow.* New York: The Ford Foundation, 1957.

Tompkins, Ellsworth, and Walter H. Gaumnitz, *The Carnegie Unit—Its Origin, Status, and Trends, Bulletin No. 7.* Washington, D.C.: U.S. Department of Health, Education, and Welfare, 1954.

Trump, J. Lloyd, *Images of the Future.* Washington, D.C.: Library of Congress, 1959.

————, and Dorsey Baynham, *Guide to Better Schools, Focus on Change.* Chicago: Rand McNally and Co., 1961.

INDEX

A

Ability (*see also* Gifted student; Slow learner):
  grading and, 319, 323
  grouping by, 235–243
  method related to, 56–58
Abstinence:
  alcoholic, 44, 45
  sexual, 205
Academic content (*see* Curriculum; Subject matter)
Achievement tests, 289-290 (*see also* Tests)
Adjustment, as educational goal, 435–436
Adler, Alfred:
  on behavioral extremes, 59
  on effective teacher, 350
  on power complex, 10–11
Adler, Mortimer, 432
Administration:
  delegating responsibility for, 75–76
  democratic, 32–34
  evaluation for, 255
  professional attitudes of, 447–449
  teacher's role in, 31–35
Adolescence:
  age range in, 208–209
  basic needs of, 213–214
  challenges in, 203–204
  conformity in, 201–202, 225
  counseling, 56
  defined, 200
  differences between sexes in, 206–208
  differences in, 206–219
  intelligence range in, 209–211
  interest range in, 214–215
  lecturing to, 135
  mass identification in, 199

Adolescence (*Cont.*)
  maturation in, 55
  need for success in, 439–440
  periodicals dealing with, 80 (*list*)
  reading ability in, 211–212
  rebellion in, 205–206, 345
  setting limits for, 352–353
  sexual interests in, 204–205
  socioeconomic differences and, 216
  student-teacher knowledge of, 403
  truth in, 14
  understanding of, 24
Advisor (*see* Counseling; Guidance)
Age range, 78, 208–209
Agnosticism, 154
Aggression, effect on method, 59–60 (*see also* Infractions)
Aichhorn, August, 345
Alexander, William M., 248–249, 274
American Federation of Teachers, 39
Analysis, of self, 5–6
Analytical positivism, 154
Anderson, Robert H., 234 *n.*
Anecdotal record:
  evaluation through, 262–263
  on student teacher, 419–420
Anger, of teacher, 369
Apologies, value of, 368
Appraisal (*see* Evaluation)
Aptitude tests (*see* Tests)
Aristotle, 154, 177
Assignment (*see also* Homework):
  differentiated, 246–247
  justification of, 173
  long-term, 162
  as teaching method, 161–163
Association for Supervision and Curriculum Development, 37
Athletics, 36, 69 (*see also* Co-curriculum)